LIST OF SYMBOLS "cont."

Symbols		Page Reference
LSD	Fisher's Least Significant Difference test; protected t test	283
LL	lower limit of an interval	28
μ	population mean	49
$\mu_{\bar{x}}$	mean of a sampling distribution of means	132
μ_{alt}	mean of the alternative ("treated") population	251
μ_0	population mean when null hypothesis is true	251
MS	mean square	264
MS_A	mean square for Factor A	312
$MS_{A \times B}$	mean square for A x B interaction	312
MS_B	mean square for Factor B	312
MS_{BG}	mean square between group	265
MS_w	mean square within group	264
MS_{error}	mean square error	356
N	number of scores in a population	49
n	number of scores in a sample	50
n_k	number of scores in the last group	263
n_p	number of pairs of scores	372
P	a person in a repeated-measures ANOVA; probability	344
$p(A)$	probability of event A	493
$p(B)$	probability of event B	494
$p(A\,|\,B)$	probability of event A given event B	498
Q_1	first quartile	71
Q_3	third quartile	71
r	Pearson product moment correlation coefficient for a sample	462
ρ	rho	362
r_{pb}	point-biserial correlation coefficient	466
R	standardized residual	449
r_s	Spearman rank correlation coefficient	459
Σ	sigma (summation)	49
s	sample standard deviation	82
s^2	sample variance	75
s_D	standard deviation of difference scores	203
$s_{\bar{D}}$	standard error of the difference for dependent samples	203

To My Parents

LaMarr and Margaret Grimm

STATISTICAL APPLICATIONS
FOR THE BEHAVIORAL SCIENCES

STATISTICAL APPLICATIONS FOR THE BEHAVIORAL SCIENCES

Laurence G. Grimm

University of Illinois at Chicago

John Wiley & Sons, Inc.

New York Chichester Brisbane Toronto Singapore

Acquisitions Editor	Karen Dubno
Marketing Manager	Carolyn Henderson
Production Supervisor	Micheline Frederick
Designer	Lynn Rogan
Manufacturing Manager	Andrea Price
Copy Editing Supervisor	Elizabeth Swain
Illustration	Edward T. Starr

This book was set in Garamond Light and printed and bound by R.R. DONNELLEY, CRAWFORDSVILLE. The cover was printed by PHOENIX COLOR.

Library of Congress Cataloging-in-Publication Data:

Grimm, Laurence G.
    Statistical applications for the behavioral sciences / Laurence G.
Grimm.
      p.   cm.
    Includes bibliographical references and index.
    ISBN 0-471-50982-5 (cloth)
    1. Social sciences—Statistical methods. I. Title.
HA29.G7735 1992
300'.1'5195—dc20   92-26015
                                          CIP

Printed in the United States of America

10 9 8 7 6 5 4 3 2 1

Preface

This textbook is an outgrowth of my 14-year experience teaching introductory statistics, an experience that has impressed me with the dread students face when entering the course, and the frustration they voice in trying to understand statistics. The dread is a result of the unimaginative manner in which mathematics is taught in the American school system. There is nothing a statistics instructor can do about that. The frustration that students experience during a statistics course *is* something an instructor can (and must) take some responsibility for. To be sure, most students may not find a statistics course as engaging as a course in abnormal psychology or child development, but it need not rival the torture of an enforced labor camp.

This book has been written with the typical student in mind—one who not only dislikes math, but who has no confidence in his or her ability to "deal with numbers." Consequently, even the unlikely student with no background in algebra will be able to understand the computational flow of the formulas. A knowledge of algebraic derivations and proofs is unnecessary for mastering the material in this text.

GOALS OF THE TEXT

The primary goal of this book is to teach students the conceptual foundations of statistical analyses, particularly inferential statistics. Where applicable, the conceptual foundation of statistical tests is explained in the context of z scores. Throughout the chapters on hypothesis testing, the surface mechanics of computing a test statistic are always related to the underlying sampling distribution of relevance. Students thus learn why the formula for a test statistic looks as it does, and they gain an appreciation of the *statistical* meaning of each analysis.

Emphasis on the conceptual underpinnings of hypothesis testing distinguishes this textbook from those that offer a "cookbook" approach. In addition, this text places heavy emphasis on the research context of the statistical analysis under discussion. Thus, students will feel "connected" to the research activities of behavioral scientists and come to view formulas as tools to answer questions about human behavior.

Nonetheless, the arithmetic operations involved in arriving at problem solutions are not sacrificed. Indeed, another goal of this book is to teach students how to "work the formulas." Learning to "crunch the numbers" is accomplished by presenting definable, clearly specified steps in working through statistical problems. Despite the existence of numerous statistical software packages that can quickly and accurately arrive at the solution to problems, I believe that an emphasis on hand calculations provides the student with a deeper understanding of the inner workings of statistical formulas.

ORGANIZATION AND FLEXIBILITY

The text has 18 chapters, organized into three sections: Basic Concepts of Research and Descriptive Statistics; Inferential Statistics: Parametric Tests; and Inferential Statistics: Nonparametric Tests. The breadth of coverage of topic areas makes this book suitable for a semester course, a two-quarter course, or a one-quarter course. If students have had exposure to research design, Chapter 1 may be skipped or used as a brief summary of research concepts.

Because earlier chapters build the conceptual foundation for later chapters, there is not a great deal of leeway in assigning chapters out of sequence. Nonetheless, the chapters covering chi-square and other nonparametric tests may be assigned before the chapter on one-way ANOVA. The chapters covering two-way and repeated-measures ANOVA can be omitted without hampering the students' understanding of subsequent chapters. The chapters covering linear correlation and regression treat these data-analytic procedures in the context of inferential statistics. Consequently, it is not recommended that they be presented immediately after the section on descriptive statistics. Finally, the chapter on power may be omitted without sacrificing the students' understanding of hypothesis testing. The concept of power is defined simply whenever it is mentioned in chapters covering hypothesis testing.

Finally, Appendix A addresses some basic concepts of probability theory (e.g., the addition and multiplication rules). This material is *not* presented in the context of hypothesis testing. Throughout the chapters on inferential statistics, fundamental concepts of probability are integrated with hypothesis testing.

STUDENT AIDS IN THE TEXT

Because most students approach statistics with considerable foreboding, I have included several pedagogical features in the text to enhance learning and maintain motivation.

1. The application of formulas is illustrated in step-by-step computational procedures so that students can master the sequential process of arriving at the correct answer to sample problems.
2. Boxes that highlight the topic under discussion using published and

unpublished research are presented in each chapter. The material is selected for its interest value to students.

3. Spotlights present biographical sketches of some of the luminaries in the field of statistics. Interesting aspects of the person and their times are provided to personalize the material.

4. A freestanding insert with all the formulas is included with the text for easy reference. This insert can also be used for closed-book exams where the instructor wants to allow students access to formulas.

5. Each chapter ends with an extended summary of the chapter, a presentation of the key formulas, and numerous work problems. Many of the work problems are based on published research findings of high interest to students, so that students not only receive practice in data analyses, but increase their knowledge of the content of psychology as well.

6. A glossary of terms is provided at the end of the text.

7. A list of symbols with the page number each symbol first appears is provided on the end papers.

It is my experience that students overwhelmingly prefer that *all* the answers to work problems be provided, and so they are, in Appendix C. In addition, for computation problems, the answers are provided along with interim steps, thus allowing students to locate the source of potential errors in the use of formulas. Most of the chapters also include short data sets that can be used with any statistical software program. The answers to these problems are provided in Appendix C (without computer print-out to allow the instructor a choice of software).

ANCILLARY MATERIALS

The text is accompanied by an Instructor's Resource Guide and Test Bank available in both printed and computerized format, transparencies, and a student workbook. The workbook includes data sets that can be used with any statistical software package. However, the workbook provides computer print-outs based on MYSTAT (ver 2.1), SPSS-PC Studentware Plus (ver 1.0), and SAS (mainframe). Instructions for data entry, requisite commands, and computer print-outs for all three packages are provided in tutorials. The question format in the workbook includes fill-in and open-answer items. The Test Bank includes conceptual and computational questions with answers in multiple-choice form.

SOFTWARE

Although we do not attempt to teach computer skills in the text, for those instructors who like the convenience of a text with computational software, we offer two options: (1) a special packaging of the text with MYSTAT (in IBM 3.5 and 5.25 and Mac formats), the student version of the professional computing package SYSTAT, a product of SYSTAT, Inc.; and (2) a special packaging of the text with *Statistics Tutor: Tutorial and Computational Software for the Behavior Sciences*, by Joseph D. Allen and David J. Pittenger, a menu-driven package with interactive graphic capabilities that gives students a working knowledge of statistics through detailed tutorials and the ability to enter their own data sets from an experiment

for quick analysis with parametric or nonparametric statistical procedures. *Statistics Tutor* (ISBN: 0-471-50279-0) is stand-alone software and thus is also available separately from John Wiley & Sons for use with any statistics text. Contact your local sales representative for further information about these packages.

ACKNOWLEDGMENTS

Many people at John Wiley & Sons have contributed to this textbook. Deborah Moore was the Psychology Editor at the inception of this book. However, Karen Dubno, the present Psychology Editor, guided the text throughout most of its development. Her efforts are greatly appreciated, as are the many productive meetings we had over gourmet meals. Elizabeth Swain, Senior Copyeditor, supervised the entire editing process, including the editing performed by Suzanne Magida. Andrea Bryant was responsible for aiding the development of the ancillary material, Micheline Frederick served as Production Supervisor; I was blessed to have her on the project.

Finally, several people provided the needed sustenance required for such a long journey, among them, Lisa Congelton, Loretta DeKoster, Barbara Cooper, Sue Miller, and Ok Ro Hong. Kathryn Engel, Gus Samios, Richard Wimmer and C.R. Tsaygaye-Spates have been treasured friends throughout. F.H. Kanfer continues as my mentor.

I am grateful to the Literary Executor of the late Sir Ronald A. Fisher, F. R. S., to Dr. Frank Yates, F. R. S., and to Longman Group Ltd., London, for permission to reprint Tables III, IV, and VII from their book *Statistical Tables for Biological, Agricultural and Medical Research* (6th edition, 1974).

My largest debt of gratitude goes to the reviewers of the manuscript. For three years they remained anonymous, yet I came to know many through their styles of criticism, their preferences for how to teach statistics, and their thoroughness. Some went beyond the call of duty in the amount of time spent on the manuscript—to each of you, a special thanks.

Judy Britt performed an accuracy check on the entire manuscript, worked all of the statistics problems, arranged the index, and continually amazed me with her "eagle eye". Her diligence is appreciated beyond words.

To the student, as well as the instructor, please send any suggestions or comments that you think I ought to consider for the next edition to: University of Illinois at Chicago, Department of Psychology, m/c 285, Chicago, Ill. 60680.

REVIEWERS

Tony Albiniak, Coastal Carolina College
Robert W. Allan, Lafayette College
Frank M. Bagrash, California State University-Fullerton
Wendy J. Beller, Quincy College
Stephen S. Cooper, Glendale Community College
Ernest C. Davenport, Jr., University of Minnesota-Twin Cities
Janis W. Driscoll, University of Colorado at Denver
Nicholas J. Esposito, State University College at Cortland
Howard Flock, York University
Rick M. Gardner, University of Colorado at Denver
Linda Heath, Loyola University-Chicago

G. William Hill IV, Kennesaw College
Elizabeth Lynn, San Diego State University
Kevin R. Murphy, Colorado State University
Margaret G. Ruddy, Trenton State College
Robert J. Schneider, Metropolitan State College
Kirk Howard Smith, Bowling Green State University
Jim Staszewski, University of South Carolina
Thomas J. Thieman, The College of St. Catherine
Katherine Van Giffen, California State University-Long Beach
Benjamin Wallace, Cleveland State University

Contents

STATISTICAL APPLICATIONS
FOR THE BEHAVIORAL SCIENCES

BASIC CONCEPTS OF RESEARCH AND DESCRIPTIVE STATISTICS

Basic Concepts in Research

1.1 Why Study Research Design in Conjunction with Statistics
1.2 An Overview of the Research Process
1.3 Basic Concepts in the Conduct of Research

1.1 WHY STUDY RESEARCH DESIGN IN CONJUNCTION WITH STATISTICS

This is a textbook about statistics. Simply defined, statistics are the tools that are used to analyze and interpret data after a study has been conducted. If you have had little or no exposure to research design, it can be difficult to place statistical analyses in their proper context. Although each statistics chapter addresses specific research occasions for the analysis under discussion, it is important that you understand why you should study research design in conjunction with statistics and that you become familiar with basic research concepts. The purpose of this chapter is to acquaint you with many of the terms that are used in the research setting.

3

I recently discussed the divorce of a mutual friend with a student who had just graduated from our university, had successfully completed the premed program, had majored in psychology, and had taken courses in research design and statistics. The student's sole explanation for the breakup of the marriage was the couple's incompatible astrological signs. At first I thought (hoped) that she was kidding. She wasn't. When I tactfully reminded her of all the science courses she had taken, including research design and statistics, she responded, "You have to go to the right astrologer—one who takes all the data into consideration. Let me give you my astrologer's phone number." I remember thinking, "Someone has failed here, and I am not so sure that it is the student."

This student is not unique. Consider the results of a study by Snyder (1974). Snyder wanted to know if the amount of information people offer about themselves affects how much they agree with astrological readings provided to them. Agreement ratings from subjects could range from 1 (very poor) to 5 (excellent). Each subject provided birth date information to the experimenter, and was then given what he or she believed was a personalized astrological reading. In fact, all subjects received the same personality description. In one group, the subjects provided only their year of birth, yet their scores averaged 3.24. The students in a second group provided their birth year and month and averaged a rating of 3.76. The third group of subjects provided the most information about themselves: day, month, and year of birth. These subjects had an average agreement rating of 4.38.

It appears, then, that many people have a great deal of faith in astrological personality profiles, and their faith is stronger as they provide more information about themselves. Indeed, a 1984 Gallup poll showed that 55 percent of American teenagers between the ages of 13 and 18 believe that astrology works (Kurtz and Fraknoi, 1985). In fact, many people base their personal decisions on astrological predictions. Perhaps the most noteworthy example of this is the fact that, when in office, President and Mrs. Reagan scheduled official visits based on consultations with an astrologer (Frazier, Kurtz, and Bob, 1988).

Clearly our culture is currently witnessing "The New Age." You need only browse through a bookstore to confirm the enormous interest in ESP, channeling spirits, the power of crystals, and astrology. The fact that every book written by Shirley MacLaine is a bestseller is, in part, due to the fascination (and belief?) in paranormal experiences. Such unscientific thinking can also be observed in other aspects of everyday life.

Many states now have a weekly lottery in which a single winner can win virtually millions of dollars for choosing the correct six numbers. Despite the astronomical odds against winning, people spend over $1 billion annually playing the lottery. Almost everyone agrees that not only are the odds of winning incredibly small (in some states, 1 in 26 million), but that it is just a matter of luck who wins. However, the way in which many of us select lottery numbers belies our belief that only luck is operating. We select numbers that correspond to birthdays, anniversaries, addresses, telephone numbers, lucky numbers, or the number we dreamed about last night. One woman in Iowa numbers marshmallows and bets on the numbers her dog eats first (*Chicago Tribune,* 1989).

Indeed, there is an entire industry that feeds on the gullibility of lottery players. Books, magazines, newsletters, and the ultimate in scientific credibility, computer programs, are sold to millions of people to give them an edge on the odds. Most of these systems are based on the theory of the "hot numbers"; that is, the theory that those numbers that have not occurred recently are due to come up next. This theory is pure nonsense because weekly drawing is independent of all previous drawings. However, in 1988, a lottery club with ten members, playing the Nevin System, based on hot numbers, split $13 million. When confronted with the statistical fact that no one can predict which lottery numbers will come up in a given week, David Nevin asserted, "They can say what they want, but we deliberately went in playing a system and we won with that system" (*Chicago Tribune*, 1989).

So what is the point? The foregoing anecdotes make an important point: People who believe in astrology, ESP, or hot numbers are not stupid, but they have adopted their beliefs without any apparent evidence of critical thinking. The ability to think critically is largely a learned set of skills, and people differ in how well they have learned these skills and how often they apply them.

It's fun to suspend disbelief when watching a magician. It's entertaining to read our daily horoscopes. And who among us can honestly say they have *never* read the *National Enquirer?* Our lives would probably be very boring if we always used our critical faculties to their fullest. However, when you *need* to be skeptical, are you? When you need to evaluate the evidence for some claim, even a scientific claim, do you know how to think analytically? And if you want to persuade others, do you know what information you need and how to present it?

So why introduce a chapter on research design in a course on statistics? Both fields of study increase critical thinking and promote a healthy skepticism. Courses in statistics or research design do not so much emphasize *what* to think, but rather *how* to think. These are skills that have broad applicability to your everyday life.

We are constantly bombarded with scientific claims, counterclaims, figures, tables, and proven facts. A scientific approach to answering questions emphasizes the importance of objectivity, logic, and gathering information. The field of research design increases our understanding of *how* information should be obtained in order to make certain kinds of conclusions. The field of statistics teaches us how to analyze information (data) so that we can make intelligent statements about the information that has been obtained.

Research design and statistics are intimately linked in the process of research. Without a general understanding of the research process, you will have difficulty appreciating the context within which statistics are used. We turn now to a brief summary of the research process.

1.2   AN OVERVIEW OF THE RESEARCH PROCESS

The research process involves a series of steps taken to answer one or more questions.

Step 1.   All research begins with a question. The question might take the form of, "I wonder what would happen if I did *X*?" Or the question might take the form of a formal research hypothesis. A **research hypothesis,** also called a **scientific hypothesis,** is a statement about the expected outcome of a study—for example—"People who are physiologically aroused are more likely to act aggressively than people who are not physiologically aroused." In other words, the research hypothesis is a prediction made prior to the actual study.

Step 2.   After a research question is posed, the investigator will review theories and learn what information already exists that applies to the research question. Steps 1 and 2 are intertwined. A researcher often arrives at a question based on the theorizing and research findings of others, and then conducts a thorough review of the literature to learn more about the phenomenon (and to make sure no one else has already conducted the study).

Step 3.   The study is designed. This is where one's knowledge of research design enters. The investigator must decide *how* the data will be collected. There are numerous research designs from which to choose. The nature of the research question will, in part, influence the specific study design. Other considerations are the cost of one design compared to another, the availability of subjects, and the amount of time required (available) to conduct the study. It is at this point that the investigator will decide what data will be obtained and what measurement techniques will be used.

Step 4.   The study is conducted. During this step the data are collected. Unless unforeseen circumstances alter the research process (e.g., equipment breakdowns or the sudden unavailability of subjects), no new decisions need to be made during the conduct of the study.

Step 5.   The data are analyzed. Now the investigator uses statistics. The data are summarized, described, and analyzed in various ways to answer the question that prompted the entire research process.

Step 6.   The results of the study are interpreted. Not only is the investigator interested in answering the specific research question at hand, but also he or she will determine the implications of the results—that is—what is the theoretical and/or practical significance of the results of the study?

These steps in the research process have been intentionally oversimplified. In actuality, the conduct of a study is a dynamic interplay among all the steps. Conducting research is both intellectual *and* emotional. The research process can be tedious and frustrating, but it can also be exhilarating. Conducting research is a very personal endeavor. It is *your* research question, *your* design, *your* data, and *your* explanation of the results of the study. To engage in the process of research, you first have to master basic research design and statistics skills. The material is dry, and the personal rewards are delayed. However, once you learn the basic concepts of research design and the fundamentals of data analyses, a whole new set of experiences is open to you.

This chapter will acquaint you with some of the fundamental concepts of research design. No attempt is made to describe various design strategies. In subsequent chapters, the research context within which the statistical analysis under discussion is used will be briefly presented.

1.3   BASIC CONCEPTS IN THE CONDUCT OF RESEARCH

Types of Variables

Researchers make distinctions among different types of variables. In a general sense, a variable is anything that can assume different values. However, as you will learn, this definition is, at times, used very loosely. How one type of variable is distinguished from another type of variable depends on the role it plays in the study. A variable can be used to assess its influence on behavior (an independent variable). Another type of variable is the behavior of the subject (a dependent variable). An uncontrolled source of influence in a study is yet another variable (a confounding or extraneous variable). Enduring characteristics of people are variables (subject variables). These important variables are discussed in the following sections. By the end of this chapter, you will be able to define different types of variables, and identify them when reading a description of a study.

Independent and Dependent Variables

When designing an experiment the researcher attempts to examine how one variable influences another variable. Generally speaking, a **dependent variable** is a variable that is observed and measured in response to another variable. In psychology, one observed variable is frequently the behavior of the subject. The subject's behavior may *depend* on the experimental situation. In this instance, the behavior of the subject is the dependent variable. It is not the general behavior of the subject, but rather a *specific,* clearly defined behavioral response that is observed, measured, and usually quantified.

For example, suppose a psychologist is interested in teaching people self-control techniques to improve pain tolerance. First, pain tolerance is operationally defined. An **operational definition** is the concrete measurement of a concept. Here, pain tolerance is operationally defined as the duration of time the subjects keep their hands in ice water. Pain tolerance is observed and measured as a response to another variable—self-control techniques. As such, pain tolerance serves as the dependent variable in the experiment. While the subjects maintain their hands in the water, an array of other behavioral responses are also occurring, such as anxiety, memories of past experiences with cold water, looking around the room, and so on. Are these other behaviors dependent variables? No, because the researcher does not systematically observe and measure these responses.

An **independent variable** is selected and manipulated by the experimenter to observe its effect on the dependent variable. The manipulation of the independent variable is accomplished by using quantitative or qualitative *levels* of the independent variable. A **quantitative independent variable** means that subjects are exposed to different *amounts* of the independent variable. Suppose a researcher hypothesizes that the amount of time it takes rats to learn a maze depends on the magnitude of reward provided at the end of the maze. Three groups of rats are used, with each group receiving increased amounts of reward—5 food pellets, 10 food pellets, and 15 food pellets. In this example, the three levels of the independent variable are defined along a quantitative dimension.

A **qualitative independent variable** establishes levels by the presence or absence of a treatment procedure, or by contrasting different kinds of treatments. Using the pain tolerance example, one group of subjects received self-control training (level 1) and the other did not (level 2). The groups do not differ in the *amount* of the independent variable, but rather by the presence or absence of a treatment condition. "Treatment" is another generic term used in research design, which refers to any procedure that *might* have an effect on behavior. In the pain tolerance example, the independent variable (or treatment) is manipulated by providing training to one group of subjects and no training to a second group of subjects.

■   QUESTION   *A psychologist is interested in determining which of two sales techniques is more effective in influencing subjects' impressions of a product. In the "Positive condition," subjects are told about the many positive attributes of a particular model of car. In the "Negative condition," another group of subjects is told about all the undesirable attributes of a competing model. In a third condition, subjects listen to a lecture on the economic state of the automobile industry. After the lecture, each subject is asked to state which of the two cars he or she would most likely purchase. Identify the independent and dependent variables.*

SOLUTION   To determine the dependent variable, ask yourself "What is the behavior of the subjects that is being measured?" The dependent variable is specified at the end of the example: "each subject is asked to state which of the two cars he or she would most likely purchase." The independent variable is the conditions that are being contrasted. There are three groups (conditions) in this study. Together they define *one* independent variable. In naming the independent variable, you could use the generic term treatment, or use a more specific designation, such as sales technique.   ■

The purpose of an experiment is to identify a causal relation between the independent variable and the dependent variable. Manipulating an independent variable and measuring its effect on a dependent variable is one defining feature of an experiment.[1] However, to identify a causal relation among variables, it is essential that the causal variable of interest is isolated during the experiment.

Isolating Variables

Isolating Variables by Holding Conditions Constant

The only way a cause-effect relationship between the independent and dependent variables can be discovered is if all factors are held constant *except* the levels of the independent variable. This means that every group of subjects in the study is treated exactly the same, but each group is exposed to a different level of the

---

[1] Sometimes experiments occur in the natural environment. For example, in some parts of the country the speed limit has been changed from 70 mph to 55 mph, and then back to 70 mph. The change in speed limit is thus a manipulated variable and can be examined for its effect on some other variable (e.g., traffic fatalities).

independent variable. The different responses among the groups of subjects can be attributed to the independent variable. Holding everything constant while allowing *only* the levels of the independent variable to vary across the groups is an ideal experiment.

When conditions are not held constant, there is the possibility that some variable other than the independent variable is responsible for the different responses among the groups of subjects. This other variable foils the investigator's attempt to isolate the independent variable. Any variable other than the independent variable that could account for the subjects' behavior is called a **confounding** (or **extraneous**) **variable.**

A distinction is made between a *potentially* confounding variable and a confounding variable. Consider the previous research example in which different sales techniques were compared. One factor that influences people's decisions to purchase a car is the cost of the car. Cost is a potentially confounding variable in our example. What if the car described in the Positive condition were less expensive than the car described in the Negative condition. If it were discovered that the Positive technique led to a greater preference for buying the car, the cost of the car would be confounded with treatment effects because the difference in cost could plausibly account for the difference between the experimental conditions on buying preference. The potential confound would become a true confound. However, if the cars described in each condition were all the same price, cost would not be confounded with treatment. Before an experiment is conducted, the researcher will try to think of all the potential confounds and then design the study in such a way that the independent variable is isolated.

Consider another example of a confounding variable (see Table 1.1). A simple psychotherapy study is aimed at contrasting two therapy approaches to depression. One group of depressed subjects receives psychoanalysis conducted by an experienced psychoanalyst, and a second group of depressed subjects receives behavioral therapy from an equally experienced behavioral therapist (Diagram A,

TABLE 1.1   Diagram A Depicts "Therapist" Confounded with "Treatment." Diagram B Depicts a Redesign in which Therapist Effects are Spread Equally across Treatment Conditions

DIAGRAM A	
Behavioral Therapy	*Psychoanalysis*
Therapist 1 30 Depressed clients	*Therapist 2* 30 Depressed clients

DIAGRAM B			
Behavioral Therapy		*Psychoanalysis*	
Therapist 1 15 Depressed clients	*Therapist 2* 15 Depressed clients	*Therapist 1* 15 Depressed clients	*Therapist 2* 15 Depressed clients

Table 1.1). At the end of the study the subjects who received behavioral therapy were, on the average, less depressed than the subjects who were treated by psychoanalysis.

What is the most obvious confound? It is possible that the behavioral therapist had some personality characteristics (e.g., warmth, understanding) that were responsible for the results. Had the behavioral therapist conducted psychoanalysis instead of behavioral therapy, perhaps the psychoanalytic approach would have appeared superior. In this example, "therapist" is confounded with "treatment." Thus, an interpretive dilemma arises when attempting to account for why one group of subjects improved more than the other group of subjects. How could you control this extraneous variable? The simplest solution is to hold it constant across the two types of treatment. This would entail having each therapist conduct behavioral therapy *and* psychoanalysis (Diagram B, Table 1.1). The effect of therapist would now be equally represented in the two treatment conditions, thus removing any bias toward one form of therapy.[2] Since each therapist's personality would affect treatment outcome equally in both forms of therapy, any differences in the improvement of depression could now be attributed to the treatment rather than the personal characteristics of the therapist.

The importance of identifying confounding variables in an experiment cannot be overemphasized. When potential confounding variables are controlled, the researcher is able to isolate the independent variable to determine if it has a causal effect on the dependent variable. In the planning phase of an experiment, the investigator will imagine the expected results of the experiment and then attempt to account for the results by some variable other than the independent variable. If an alternative interpretation is plausible, it means some variable is not properly controlled, and the design of the experiment is altered. If a manuscript based on the study is submitted for publication, then the journal review panel will try to find an alternative explanation for the outcome of the study. If a serious confound is discovered, the manuscript is likely to be rejected. If the study looks "clean" and is published, then the researchers reading the article will attempt to discover extraneous variables that could account for the results. There are journals that only publish methodological review articles on various areas of research. Review articles invariably raise questions about potentially important variables that have not been controlled across many studies that address a common topic. The extraordinary amount of attention devoted to identifying potential confounds represents a healthy conservatism in the scientific community. Scientists are cautious in accepting conclusions about causal relationships. The attention to confounds also reflects scientists' understanding that it is not an easy task to identify all the important variables that need to be controlled.

How does a researcher know what should be controlled in an experiment? There is no formula you can use. There isn't even a set of questions you can ask about a study that guarantees the identification of extraneous variables. A thorough knowledge of other research in the same area is perhaps the most important

---

[2] It would be important to insure that each therapist was equally proficient in conducting behavioral therapy and psychoanalysis, an admittedly difficult task.

safeguard against falling prey to confounding variables. Investigators rely on methodological review articles addressing the phenomenon under investigation. They constantly ask themselves, "What else is systematically varying in the experiment besides the independent variable?"

This section has emphasized the importance of holding conditions constant so as to isolate the effects of the independent variable. The next section discusses the use of control groups or control conditions to isolate the causal variable in a study.

Isolating Variables by Using Control Groups

So far you have learned that an experiment requires an independent variable to be manipulated, which is accomplished by establishing levels of the independent variable. These levels might differ quantitatively or qualitatively. In either case, an effect due to treatment is determined by comparing the levels of the independent variable with respect to differences in the dependent variable. The **experimental group** or groups receive the treatment that is of interest to the investigator. Many studies include a control group, which is treated in an identical manner to the experimental group, but it does not receive the treatment of interest. A control group serves as a baseline or anchor point for purposes of comparison with the experimental group.

An example of how a control group can be used as an anchor point is taken from a study by Shelton and Mahoney (1978) on the effects of "psyching-up" strategies among competitive weight lifters.

▶ **EXAMPLE 1** Many competitive athletes insist that their athletic performances are enhanced through the use of various cognitive strategies employed prior to an event. Whether these strategies actually are helpful is open to question in the absence of controlled research. The researchers conducted a simple experiment that compared an experimental group with a control group. The dependent variable was how much hand pressure was exerted on a device called a dynamometer. Just prior to squeezing the dynamometer, experimental subjects were told to use their customary cognitive, psyching-up techniques. Members of the control group were told to count backward by sixes, which prevented them from using psyching-up strategies. The results showed that the experimental subjects were able to exert a significantly greater amount of hand pressure than were the control subjects.

The control group in this study served as a baseline of comparison with the experimental group. The researchers treated the subjects similarly; the only difference was the use of psyching-up strategies by the experimental subjects. As a consequence, the difference between the groups on the dependent variable could be attributed to the experimental treatment. ◀

When holding conditions constant, the researcher spreads the effects of potentially confounding variables across all conditions (i.e., levels) of the independent variable. Control groups are used to make comparisons with the experimental groups. Control conditions are established so that an experimental variable can be isolated and a causal relation, if any, between the independent variable and dependent variable can be determined.

There is some inconsistency in the literature on research design as to whether or not control groups are part of the independent variable. The confusion arises because most texts count each control group as a level of the independent variable, yet also consider control groups as a way to isolate the independent variable. In this textbook, a control group is viewed as a *level* of the independent variable, which is consistent with Jaccard and Becker (1990) and Sprinthall (1990). However, the *function* of this level of the independent variable is to isolate the effect of the treatment administered to the experimental group(s).

Isolating Variables Through Randomization

Another basic concept in experimentation that allows an investigator to isolate the effects of the independent variable is the manner in which subjects are assigned to experimental and control conditions. Random assignment is one method of allocating subjects to groups in order to isolate the effects of the independent variable.

Subject Variables Can Create Problems

 Subject variables are characteristics of the subject that are fixed before the subject enters the experiment. Fixed does not, however, mean that subject variables cannot be altered, although some clearly cannot. Categories of subject variables are physical attributes, demographics, intellectual traits, and psychological traits. Table 1.2 lists many common subject variables.

Subject variables can present problems in an experiment when they are confounded with an independent variable. Subject variables become confounding variables when they are unequally represented across groups, *and* when they influence the dependent variable. The following examples will clarify how subject variables can serve as confounding variables.

▶   EXAMPLE 2   An educational psychologist is interested in evaluating the effects of a psychological technique that is expected to help college students become more efficient in completing a series of arithmetic problems. Efficiency, the dependent variable, is defined as the time it takes students to complete one

TABLE   1.2   **Some Common Subject Variables**

Physical Attributes	*Demographics*	*IQ/Personality*
Height	Income	IQ
Weight	Family size	Need for approval
Handedness	Ethnicity	Type A personality
Running speed	Occupation	Trait anxiety
Strength	Education	Introversion
Sex	Religion	Dominance

page of simple arithmetic problems. The technique, or independent variable, is a provision of statements that motivate the students, which they can repeat should they become distracted from the arithmetic problems. The experimental group is trained to repeat self-motivating statements, whereas the control group is not.

The experiment is conducted in a usual, 50-minute class setting. To save time, the experimenter assigns the first 20 students who arrive for class to the experimental group. All late arriving students are asked to wait in the hall until the training has been completed. These students are assigned to the control group. Let's assume that the results of the study show that the training procedure was effective: the experimental group worked twice as fast as the control group.

It is impossible to know, yet it is certainly plausible, that a subject variable (e.g., some personality trait) was responsible for the obtained difference in performance. For instance, Type A people (the coronary-prone personality) tend to be more punctual and work faster than Type B people. The personality trait is a subject variable since it is a trait that exists prior to the study. It is also an extraneous or confounding variable because it too can account for the results of the study. Since subjects were not measured along this personality dimension, there is no way to know if it intruded into the study. Nonetheless, to threaten the validity of an experiment, one need only offer a reasonable alternative explanation for the results. In this instance, the reasonable alternative explanation is that the results are not due to the independent variable, but rather because the experimental group contained more Type A people than the control group contained.   ◄

The following example of confounded results is more complex; it is based on a well-known study in the area of psychosomatic medicine.

► **EXAMPLE 3**   One of the earliest experimental demonstrations of the development of ulcers was conducted by Brady and his associates (Brady, 1958; Porter et al., 1958). Pairs of monkeys were exposed to electric shocks, which could only be avoided if one of the monkeys pressed a lever. The same monkey was always responsible for controlling the lever, and was labeled the executive monkey. If the executive monkey failed to respond in time, not only he, but also the control monkey would receive the electric shock (the aversive stimulus). Thus, while the number of shocks received by the executive and control monkey was the same, the executive monkey was responsible for controlling the onset of the electric shock. Within two months all the executive monkeys had either died or had become too incapacitated to continue in the study. Autopsies performed on the executives showed extensive gastric lesions. In contrast, the monkeys who were not allowed control over shock delivery were discovered to be free of any significant lesioning. Apparently the stress associated with having responsibility and control led to the development of fatal ulcers in the executive monkeys.

Other researchers had difficulty replicating these findings. Ultimately it was discovered that a subject variable was responsible for the ease with which Brady's executive monkeys developed ulcers.

When deciding which of two monkeys would be assigned the executive role, Brady selected the monkey who learned how to press a lever to avoid shock the fastest. Subsequent research has shown that animals can be selectively bred who are susceptible to the development of ulcers (Sines, 1959). One characteristic of ulcer-susceptible animals is that they are more emotional and, as a result, learn avoidance responses quickly (Sines, Cleeland, and Adkins, 1963). Therefore, Brady had inadvertently assigned the more emotional monkey to the executive position, thus confounding a subject variable with the treatment condition.   ◀

In the previous two research examples, the investigators could have controlled the subject variables and eliminated them as extraneous variables. If the subjects had been randomly assigned to the experimental and control conditions, subject variables would have likely been eliminated as confounding variables.

Randomization

 Randomization is a strategy for controlling subject variables based on the statistical notion of the law of averages. **Randomization** means that each subject has an equal probability of being assigned to any treatment condition. The problem encountered in the preceding section is that some subject variable can be over-represented in one of the groups and, if capable of having an effect on the dependent variable, can become a confounding variable. If an important subject variable is spread equally across experimental and control conditions, then it cannot create a bias. Through the random assignment of subjects to conditions, it is *assumed* that the effect of the subject variable is held constant. However, randomization can still fail to equally distribute subject variables. This frustrating situation most often occurs when a small number of subjects is used in an experiment. However, probability is a notion that is based on large numbers. The fact that you would be more surprised by obtaining ten heads in a row when flipping a coin, as opposed to two heads on your first two tosses, reflects your intuitive understanding that the law of averages works. This is why a casino operator is not worried if you hit the jackpot on a slot machine, *as long as you continue to play.*[3] Eventually, you are *very* likely to lose money. The point is the same for randomly assigning subjects to groups. To use an extreme example, if you were to assign 500 subjects to each of four groups, it would be highly unlikely to find a difference among the groups on several important subject variables. However, if you were to assign ten subjects to each group, it is more likely that relevant subject variables would be unevenly distributed. For instance, group 1 may, by chance, include more intelligent people, and thus have an average IQ higher than the other groups. If IQ is related to the dependent variable, as is often the case in experiments on learning, then a confound occurs.

Since random assignment tends to spread subject variables equally across conditions, the researcher has a better chance of eliminating subject variables as

---

[3] I noticed a Las Vegas promotional advertisement in the newspaper. A casino was offering free airfare and a room for one night. When I called for details, I was told that I would be required to play blackjack for eight hours, with a minimum bet of $5 a hand! Knowing something about statistics and nothing about blackjack, I decided it would be cheaper to pay my own way.

an alternative explanation of the findings. Thus randomization helps to isolate the independent variable as a cause of changes in the dependent variable.

Internal Validity

Much of this chapter has focused on the importance of and the means by which definitive conclusions can be made regarding the effect of the independent variable on the dependent variable. In practice there is no such thing as a perfect experiment; there is no way to control *every* potential extraneous variable. Nonetheless, researchers try very hard to control potential confounds by holding constant those factors that can most obviously offer a competing explanation of the results of the experiment. The **internal validity** of an experiment is the degree to which the outcomes of a study result from the variables that are manipulated, measured, or selected in the experiment rather than from other variables not systematically manipulated (Shavelson, 1988). The goal of an investigator is to rule out *plausible* alternative hypotheses, which could account for the findings of the study. Yet the plausibility of competing hypotheses can range in number as well as persuasiveness. As the number and credibility of alternative explanations *increases,* the internal validity of the experiment *decreases.* Since there is no ideal experiment, the internal validity of any one experiment lies on a continuum of plausibility. The extraneous variables most in need of control are determined by the topic of the study. For this reason it is impossible to generate a list of specific factors that should be held constant in every experiment.

Indeed, what may be an extraneous variable in one experiment can be used as an independent variable in a different study. For example, consider the variable anxiety. A researcher is interested in examining the effects of mental imagery on pain tolerance. Evidence from past research suggests that highly anxious people tolerate pain poorly (Barber and Hahn, 1962). Since anxiety and pain tolerance are related, and mental imagery, and *not* anxiety, is the focus of the study, anxiety level needs to be held constant across the treatment groups (e.g., through random assignment of subjects to conditions). If the potentially confounding effect of anxiety is not controlled for, the internal validity of the experiment suffers. Another experimenter may be interested in establishing a cause-effect relationship between anxiety and pain tolerance. Here anxiety is the independent variable, which will be varied across groups to show that changes in pain tolerance are caused by different anxiety levels. This researcher may even decide to control for mental imagery in order to exclude imagery as an alternative explanation of the experimental findings. In fact, anxiety could easily be used as a dependent variable. For instance, the investigator could vary the amount of exposure to the aversive stimulus and assess its effect on anxiety.

A tightly controlled study will rank high on internal validity. The advantage of conducting a well-controlled experiment is that a strong case can be made for a causal relationship among variables. Box 1.1 presents a published study in which a confounding variable provides a plausible explanation of the results of the study.

BOX 1.1

Feeling Good and Helping Others: A Study With a Confound

The topic of generosity and helpfulness has been a popular topic in psychology. Discovering the circumstances that encourage and discourage helpfulness increases our understanding of this behavioral phenomenon, and may suggest ways in which we can facilitate prosocial behavior for the betterment of society (Kanfer, 1980). A number of factors that influence helpfulness include the observation of a charitable model (Rosenhan and White, 1967), the relationship between the helper and the recipient (Goranson and Berkowitz, 1966), and past help received by the would-be helper (Berkowitz and Daniels, 1964). Based on an intuitive formulation (i.e., a hunch) Isen (1970) predicted that the positive feelings one experiences after success (the warm glow of success) would promote generosity. Subjects were randomly assigned to experimental conditions in which half of them received success feedback after completing perceptual-motor tasks; the other half were told that they had failed at the tasks. After the experimental manipulation (success or failure feedback), a confederate entered the room and casually placed a canister on a nearby table for donations toward a school project. (A confederate is someone who unbeknown to the subject, is really part of the experiment.) The dependent variable was the amount of money subjects donated. Consistent with the hypothesis, those subjects experiencing the positive feelings of success donated almost twice the amount of money as did those who had been told they had failed at the task. What is the confound?

The researcher asserted a causal connection between a positive emotional state and generosity. The question to ask yourself is: "Did the experimental manipulation (success/failure feedback) *solely* alter emotional states?" The answer is no. Subjects' self-perceptions of competence were also altered. Success subjects were not only in a better mood than failure subjects, but also saw themselves as more competent than those who failed. Was it the subjects' perceptions of competence that determined generosity, or was it their emotional state? *Competence* and *emotional state* were confounded, which created an interpretive problem. In a subsequent experiment, the researcher was able to induce a positive mood in subjects through an experimental procedure that did not affect self-perceptions of competence, hence isolating mood as a causal variable. A positive affective state was found to enhance helpfulness (Isen and Levin, 1972).

External Validity

 A researcher must also be concerned with the extent to which the findings of the experiment can be generalized beyond the experimental situation. "**External validity** asks the question of generalizability: To what populations, settings, treatment variables, and measurement variables can this effect be generalized" (Campbell and Stanley, 1963, p. 5). The external validity of a study is often very difficult to judge. Strictly speaking, there is no way to determine whether the results of a research study would hold if the experiment were conducted with subjects from a different population, in a different location, or using another means of manipulating the independent variable and measuring the dependent variable. However, one's confidence in generalizing to others *not* in the study can be increased by a method of sampling subjects. **Random sampling** is choosing subjects at random from a defined population. The researcher assumes that the subject characteristics of the population are represented in the sample. (Note that this is different from random assignment. Randomization is used to assign research participants to experimental conditions and affects the *internal validity* of the study.) Even with random sampling, researchers are never certain about the extent to which they can generalize the findings of the study. Caution is always required when making general statements about the results of a study.

A study by Kanfer and Grimm (1978) serves as a good illustration of the sorts of questions about external validity that can arise when a laboratory study is used as an analogue of an entirely different situation. As you read the following example, put aside the notion of internal validity, instead, focus on the issue of generalizability. How similar is the independent variable to the type of treatment in which the investigators are *really* interested? Is the dependent variable representative of the sorts of behaviors about which the investigators would like to generalize? Are the subjects in this study similar to the types of subjects in which the researchers are most interested?

▶ **EXAMPLE 4**   Kanfer and Grimm were interested in the general area of self-management therapy. A self-management approach relies heavily on the collaboration of the client and therapist in deciding what personal problems should be the focus of therapy, how these problems can be resolved, and how the client can learn to become his or her own therapist (Kanfer and Grimm, 1980). Kanfer and Grimm hypothesized that self-management therapy is an effective approach because clients are provided with a sense of control over the course of the therapeutic process. To test the influence of perceived choice on behavioral change, the following study was conducted. To simplify matters, only a portion of the experiment will be discussed.

Subjects were told that the purpose of the study was to evaluate the effectiveness of three techniques used to enhance speed reading. In the Free-choice condition, subjects heard a brief description of the three techniques, and were asked to choose which of the three they would like to learn. In the Denied-choice condition, the same three techniques were offered, but when the subject chose one, the experimenter had to reject the choice "due to equipment failure." The subject was offered one of the remaining techniques. Subjects in the No-choice condition were assigned a technique. In fact, all groups received the same technique. Reading speed was assessed before and after the treatment. The dependent variable was change in reading speed. The independent variable was the method used to establish the perception of control the subjects held regarding the selection of the learning approach. In support of the hypothesis, subjects in the Free-choice condition showed greater increases in reading rate, when compared to subjects in the Denied-choice and No-choice conditions.

The use of suitable controls for extraneous variables in this study maximized internal validity. But what about external validity? All the subjects were college students. Would the same results have been found with children, middle-aged adults, or people in therapy? The behavior chosen as the dependent variable was reading speed, yet the researchers were actually interested in testing their hypothesis that self-management therapy is effective. Do the findings of this study bear directly on psychological problems? And what about the independent variable? Although different therapies vary in how much perceived control or input the client has in the selection of treatment techniques, the procedure used by the investigators to create the perception of choice was certainly not representative of the way therapists operate.

So why didn't the researchers conduct the study with actual clients, using different forms of therapy as the independent variable? There is often a trade-off between internal and external validity. High internal validity requires isolating a treatment variable by holding conditions constant. An investigator is able to achieve this only by exerting a high degree of control over the phenomenon under study. As one approaches settings in which the phenomenon occurs naturally, for example, the therapist's office, a measure of control over important variables is sacrificed, and with it, internal validity. Every study, no matter how externally valid, will be limited by the characteristics of the subjects in the study, as well as the time period and cultural setting of the experiment.   ◀

The external validity of a particular research finding is best judged by examining a body of research to see if the findings have been replicated with subjects from different populations (e.g., age, sex, race), with different experimental procedures (e.g., various ways of manipulating aggression or different types of positive imagery), and different measures of the dependent variable (e.g., various measures of pain tolerance or different measures of aggression). Findings that hold up under a wide range of circumstances are termed *robust*. Scientists will often conduct a series of studies and systematically alter what are believed to be nonessential aspects of a research paradigm in order to establish the robustness of an experimental result.

Causality and Correlation

Behavioral scientists define cause as *conditions that are necessary and sufficient*. Consider the statement, if X occurs, then it is followed by Y, and Y is never observed without being preceded by X. Since Y is never observed without X, X is a necessary condition for Y. And since X reliably produces Y, X is sufficient to produce Y. If two events are related in this fashion there is no doubt as to their causal relationship. However, if the necessary and sufficient rule for causality were required, only a few, if any, events would be established as causally related. Imagine you wanted to identify a causal connection between pushing a light switch down and the bulb it is wired to turning off. As you flip the switch up and down the light goes on and off in perfect order. Clearly, depressing the switch is *sufficient* for turning the light off. But is it necessary? What reasons can you think of that would cause the light to turn off when you are nowhere near the switch? An electrical storm could violate the *necessary* aspect of the rule. Since independent events can cause the same thing to happen, the necessary and sufficient rule is overly stringent and, in fact, unworkable. In the social sciences, researchers are confined to demonstrating that X can be *a* cause of Y, but not necessarily that X is *the* cause of Y.

The term cause is used in the behavioral sciences, but other more modest phrases are also employed to designate the causal influence of one variable on another. For example, a functional relationship is established when one event is made more likely to occur by the manipulation of another. In other words, manipulating X increases the probability that Y will occur. Thus, behavioral scientists do not employ the strict *necessary and sufficient* definition of causality. Instead, cause-effect statements maintain that one or more manipulated variables increase the likelihood that a given event will occur. Scientists value the identification of causal relations because they advance the goals of science. However, a causal relationship is not the only way in which variables can be related. If two variables occur together they *covary* with one another. Variables that covary are *correlated* variables. Height and weight are correlated because taller people are usually heavier. Causally related events are correlated because they occur together. They have a special correlated relation, however, because one happens first and makes the other one occur. When data are gathered without variables being systematically manipulated, two variables can be observed to covary, but it is unknown if there is a causal relation between them.

Literature on clinical depression exemplifies how variables can be found to covary without knowing the causal relation between them. Depression has many characteristics, and the reasons why people become depressed are not fully understood. One view maintains that people feel depressed because of negative thinking. They are pessimistic, self-critical, and do not praise themselves when they do something well. This theory strongly implies that these cognitions have some causative role in depression (Beck, Rush, Shaw, & Emery, 1979). However, it is quite possible that when people become depressed they are more likely to think in a negative fashion. In Figure 1.1, the question marks above the arrows, which are drawn between negative thinking and depression, reflect this interpretive problem.

Although negative thinking and depression are correlated, there is not necessarily a causal relation between these two variables. These variables may occur together because a third variable, loss of control, causes both negative thinking *and* depression. In Figure 1.1, the arrows pointing from loss of control to negative thinking and depression reflect this possibility.

When one event is known to cause another, the two events are correlated in the sense that they are associated and covary. That is, a change in one event

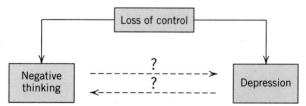

Figure 1.1   Negative thinking and depression are correlated, but does one cause the other? It is possible that a third variable, loss of control, causes both negative thinking and the symptoms of depression.

produces a change in the other event. However, two events may be correlated but may not be causally related—or at least the causal connection is unclear. Thus, *correlation does not imply causation.* If X and Y are correlated it may be because X causes Y, Y causes X, or some third variable causes both X and Y. The manner in which the data are collected will determine the type of interpretation allowable. Causal relations can be established when variables are *manipulated* and observed to influence other variables.

SUMMARY

The research process involves six interwoven steps: posing the research question, reviewing the relevant research literature, designing the study, conducting the study, analyzing the data, and interpreting the findings. A research hypothesis is a statement of the expected outcome of a study.

This chapter presented the basic concepts necessary to discuss behavioral research. A dependent variable is the measured variable in an experiment. The dependent variable is frequently the behavior of the subject. Dependent variables are operationally defined to concretely represent some concept. The independent variable is a systematically manipulated variable, which is examined to observe its effect on a dependent variable. When an independent variable is systematically manipulated, there is the potential to make a cause-effect statement.

Experimentation requires that conditions be held constant so that extraneous or confounding variables cannot offer alternative explanations of the findings. Using control groups and randomly assigning subjects to treatment conditions are ways researchers reduce the possibility of confounds. Subject variables are characteristics of a person that are fixed at the time of the study. If subject variables are not distributed equally across experimental conditions, they can become confounded with treatment.

The internal validity of an experiment is the degree to which a cause-effect relation can be established among variables. External validity refers to the extent to which research findings can be generalized to other populations, settings, treatment variables, and measurement variables. Random sampling increases external validity because the subjects participating in the study are representative of a larger group of people (the population). However, there is a trade-off between internal and external validity. As internal validity increases, external validity may decrease.

When an independent variable is systematically manipulated, it may be possible to draw a conclusion about the causal relation among variables. However, two variables may be discovered to covary (i.e., are correlated), but if variables are not systematically controlled, it may be impossible to determine a causal relation.

WORK PROBLEMS

1. Identify the independent and dependent variables in the following four studies.
   a. A sports psychologist is interested in the effects of vitamin E on physical endurance. One group of subjects receives 20 units of vitamin E, another

receives 60 units, and a third group receives a placebo. Endurance is assessed by the length of time subjects are able to ride a stationary bicycle. (Also, how many levels are there of the independent variable?)

dep ⟵

b. A teacher evaluates the effectiveness of different educational programs on reading speed and comprehension. *dep*

def

c. A social psychologist hypothesizes that attitude change will be greatest when people *voluntarily* do something contrary to their attitudes, as opposed to being *forced* to act contrary to their attitudes.

et manipulable

d. An industrial psychologist hypothesizes that the amount of natural light in the work setting will increase productivity. For 15 days of a month, the blinds are drawn and indoor lighting is the only source of light. For the other 15 days of the month, the shades are left open. Productivity is measured by the number of widgets made. *dep*

2. What is the most obvious confound affecting internal validity in the following four studies? (Hint: Some studies may not have a confound.)

a. An independent marketing company has been hired to assess people's preference for Coors versus Old Style beer. To prevent bias, all of the test cans are covered with paper, revealing only the letter *M* on the Coors cans and *Z* on the cans of Old Style. Half of the subjects taste the Coors first, then taste the Old Style; the order is reversed for the remaining half of the subjects. The results show that the subjects prefer Coors over Old Style by a 2 to 1 margin.

b. An experimental psychologist claims to have discovered an important cause of bizarre behavior. Laboratory mice are taught to discriminate between two geometric designs. The mouse is required to jump from a ledge through a trap door, which has one of the designs painted on it. If the mouse leaps through the door with the correct design, it lands on a table with food. If the wrong door is chosen, the mouse falls 3 feet onto a net. (Falling 3 feet onto a net may be fun for kids, but rather unnerving for a mouse.) Eventually all the mice in the study pick the door that has the correct design painted on it. A discrimination has been formed. To test the intelligence of each mouse, the researcher changes some aspects of the geometric designs so that they look much more alike than they did originally. Now the mice hesitate and many refuse to jump. To observe which door the mice will choose, the psychologist forces them to jump by blasting a loud noise. Faced with such a difficult discrimination, the mice begin to exhibit unusual behavior. They run in circles, jump up and down, and fall into a catatonic state. It is concluded that the stress produced by having to make a choice between two very similar stimuli when the consequences of the choice are extremely important leads to abnormal behavior. What do you think?

c. A particular stretch of highway is noted for an excessive number of traffic fatalities. The city council decides to reduce the allowable speed limit, since the evidence from national statistics clearly shows that traffic fatalities are correlated with speed limits. To make sure that the proper speed limit is observed, radar units are positioned every 5 miles along the highway. Not only did accidents significantly decrease, but because of the increased surveillance, more motorists were following the speed limit. Obviously changing the speed limit had led to a decrease in accidents.

d. Evidence exists that shows that our reactions to pain are, in part, due to psychological factors. A dentist offers earphones with the patient's choice of music to listen to during drilling. Since some patients may prefer the novocaine, that option is also made available. Patients are not allowed to listen to music *and* use the anesthetic, therefore it will be possible to evaluate the independent effects of the two methods. Patients are free to choose which method they want. At the end of the study, the dentist finds that those patients using the earphones reported less anxiety and less pain than those patients who opted for the novocaine. Recognizing a potential confound, the dentist reviewed the records and was able to substantiate that the type of dental problem and the dental procedures were, on the average, similar between the two groups. Since an anesthetic can have side effects, the dentist decides to only offer earphones to his patients. Is everything OK?

3. A popular theory of emotion asserts that we label our emotional states based on the perception of our own physiological arousal and the situation within which we find ourselves. However, one could question whether the presence of physiological arousal is really necessary. Maybe all that is required is the *belief* that we are aroused. A study is conducted with male undergraduates in which 20 slides of naked women are sequentially presented for 30 seconds each. The subject wears earphones and hears what he *thinks* is his heart rate. In fact, the heart rate is a recording. The subject hears an increase in heart rate for some slides, and hears a decrease in heart rate for other slides. The dependent variable is the subjects' ratings of attractiveness made after each slide. The psychologist finds that the naked women observed when the tape-recorded heart rate was high were perceived as more attractive than the women viewed during decreased heart rates. It appears that the belief in arousal determines emotion. Does this experiment have a threat to internal validity?

4. Professors exhibit a good deal of subjectivity when grading papers. They prefer typewritten papers. Do typed papers receive higher grades? Suppose you conduct a study in which you obtain the grades for a paper submitted by everyone in class. Since this professor allows the option to handwrite the paper, you are able to find a number of papers that are typed and about the same number that are handwritten. Your results show that the average grade for typed papers is higher than for papers not typed. Should you conclude that your professor is swayed by the appearance of the paper? What other interpretation of the results can you make?

5. For each of the following research questions, design a study that addresses the question with a controlled experiment. Redesign the study using a correlational methodology. (Hint: It is possible that one or more questions cannot be investigated by controlled experimentation.)

a. Is there a relation between pain and anxiety? (For the experimental design, pain is the independent variable.)

b. Is there a relation between how often a person exercises and resting heart rate?

c. Is there a relation between need for achievement and how many hours a week people work?

d. Do children who attend preschool day care show better social skills in first grade?

Scales of Measurement and Data Display

2.1 Measurement and Its Scales
2.2 Discrete Variables, Continuous Variables, and the Real Limits of Numbers
2.3 Using Tables to Organize Data
2.4 Using Graphs to Display Data
2.5 The Shape of Things to Come

2.1 MEASUREMENT AND ITS SCALES

 Most studies in the behavioral sciences collect data that are in the form of numbers. It is not the actual numbers that are of interest; it is *what the numbers represent.* **Measurement** is the assignment of numbers to objects or events according to predetermined rules. Since there are different rules for assigning numbers, the same number can have a different meaning, depending on the rules used to assign the number. There are, in fact, three different ways in which numbers are used:

1. Numbers are used to name things (*nominal* numbers).

24

2. Numbers are used to rank things (*ordinal* numbers).

3. Numbers are used to represent quantity (*cardinal* numbers).

The first part of this chapter addresses the aspect of the research process that requires the assignment of numbers to the units of a variable. The second section of this chapter focuses on summarizing data with frequency distributions. The third section presents some common ways that data are graphically displayed.

Nominal Scales

The assignment of numbers using a **nominal scale** is a labeling activity. The numbers on football jerseys, designating females 1 and males 2 in a data set and social security numbers are examples of the use of a nominal scale. In these cases one could just as easily use letters instead of numbers. When using a nominal scale, you cannot interpret the numbers as anything other than names of things. For example, it makes no sense to take the average of all the numbers of football jerseys. Moreover, if males are assigned the number 2 and females are assigned the number 1, it does not mean that males are twice as much as females. There is no quantity reflected in nominal numbers; instead, numbers are assigned based on the kind of objects or events. Variables that are measured on a nominal scale are *qualitative variables.*

Ordinal Scales

Similar to nominal measures, ordinal measures categorize things; however ordinal numbers have a particular relation to one another. Larger ordinal numbers represent a greater quantity of something than smaller ordinal numbers. When you think of an ordinal scale, think of rankings. Common examples in which ordinal scales apply are:

1. Jim is more successful than Pam.

2. Laurie is more popular than Jennifer.

3. Corey Everson is ranked higher as a bodybuilder than Rachel McLish.

An **ordinal scale** is used to identify the relative position of an individual in relation to other individuals. Even though ordinal scales are quantitative, there is only a limited sense in which quantity is implied. Rankings reflect more or less of something, but not *how much* more or less of something. The difference between the winner and runner-up may not be the same amount of difference than there is between the fourth- and fifth-place designates. In other words, the intervals between adjacent ranks are not constant over the entire range of ranks.

Interval Scales

A third level of measurement is the interval scale. An **interval scale** possesses the qualities of the nominal scale in that different numbers represent different things. The interval scale is also like the ordinal scale in that different numbers reflect more or less of something. In addition, however, the interval scale has the property that numerically equal distances on the scale represent equal distances on the dimension underlying the scale. The Fahrenheit scale is an interval scale. The difference between a temperature of 80 and 85 degrees is the same amount of heat (measured in units of mercury) as the difference between 90 and 95 degrees.

The distinction between an ordinal and interval scale is not as straightforward as it may appear, especially in the behavioral sciences. For instance, is the interval between an IQ of 100 and 105 the same as the interval between an IQ of 45 and 50? The numerical distance between the scores is the same, but it is not the numerical distance between numbers that defines the difference between ordinal and interval scales. It is the underlying dimension that the scale is tapping which is important. Is the difference in *amount of intelligence* between an IQ score of 100 and 105 the same as the difference in the amount of intelligence between IQ scores of 45 and 50? Using another example, if the highest score possible on a measure of depression is 30, is the amount of depression between scores of 20 and 30 the same as the amount of depression between scores of 5 and 15? Many statistical tests require that the data represent an underlying dimension of equal intervals. Although it is open to question whether or not a variable can be scaled as equal intervals, behavioral scientists are willing to assume that most of their measures are interval scales.

Ratio Scales

 A **ratio scale** possesses all of the properties of an interval scale, with the addition of an absolute zero point. The Fahrenheit scale is not a ratio scale because 0 is not the complete absence of heat. A measure of length is a ratio scale because there is an absolute zero point (i.e., a point of no length). With an absolute zero point, any number on a ratio scale can be used to establish its standing relative to any other number on the scale; in addition, a given number also represents an absolute amount of something. Could intelligence be measured on a ratio scale? No, because an IQ of 0 is meaningless. As a consequence, someone with an IQ of 100 is not twice as smart as someone with an IQ of 50. On the other hand, because the underlying dimension of height has an absolute zero point, a person whose height is 80 inches is twice as tall as someone whose height is 40 inches. Time is another variable that has an absolute zero point. Therefore, one subject's reaction time of 2 seconds is twice as slow as another subject's reaction time of 1 second.

In the behavioral sciences, the kinds of variables that lend themselves to ratio scales are not as common as variables in which an interval scale is most appropriate. No measures of achievement, aptitude, personality traits, or psychopathology have a meaningful absolute zero point. Without an absolute zero point to serve as an anchor point, two different scores can only be interpreted relatively; a score that is twice the size of another score does not represent twice the amount of the thing being measured. On the other hand, studies that measure learning often use a ratio scale—the number (or percentage) of correct answers, the number (or percentage) of errors, the amount of time to complete a task, and the number of trials taken to master a task are all variables that lend themselves to a ratio scale with a meaningful absolute zero point.

2.2 DISCRETE VARIABLES, CONTINUOUS VARIABLES, AND THE REAL LIMITS OF NUMBERS

Discrete Variables (or Can One Be a Little Bit Pregnant?)

We have all seen averages of some variable that don't seem to make much sense. The average number of children of American couples should be 2.11; the average resting pulse rate of marathon runners is 56.4 beats per minute; the average number of farms per county is 35.9; the average number of pregnancies among unwed mothers per year is .13 are examples of averages that seem odd because in each case the underlying dimension of interest is discontinuous. A **discontinuous** (or **discrete**) **variable** is one that typically increments from one whole number to another whole number. Discrete variables are characterized by gaps between numbers that cannot be filled by any number. There is an all-or-none property to discrete numbers: there either is a heart beat or not; there is a person or there isn't; one is either pregnant or not pregnant. It is permissible to use averages with discrete numbers, even though the underlying dimension of interest is discontinuous. You just need to keep in mind the correct interpretation of the average. For instance, what does it *really* mean to say that the population of the United States can be held constant if each couple has 2.11 children? It means that 211 children are allowed for every 100 couples. It should be clear that, provided the counting procedure is accurate, discrete (discontinuous) measures are always exact. There is no underlying dimension that could be more accurately measured with a more precise measuring instrument.

Continuous Variables

A **continuous variable** can theoretically have an infinite number of points between any two numbers. Unlike discrete variables, continuous variables do not have gaps between adjacent numbers. Although 7 inches and 8 inches may be given as adjacent numbers, there is an infinite number of values between them. Even if the scale of inches is marked to the second decimal place, there is still an infinite number of values between 7.34 and 7.35. When the underlying dimension of a scale is continuous, any number on the scale is an approximation. Even though you could measure someone's height to a thousandth of an inch, this measurement could still be refined with a more precise instrument—one that measures to the 100 thousandths of an inch, for instance. Therefore, with more refined measuring instruments, you could increase the precision of measurements of continuous variables. This is not the case when measuring discrete variables. Greater measurement precision will not alter the fact that, for instance, children exist as whole numbers—as do the number of pregnancies among unwed teenagers, and the number of yearly divorces in America.

Returning to the height example, if you report heights only as whole numbers, it may appear that you are measuring a discrete variable, but the underlying dimension is clearly continuous. The same point can be made with respect to psychological measures. Suppose a psychologist administers an anxiety questionnaire in which scores can range from 16 to 30. Although it is impossible for an individual to receive a score that is not a whole number, the interval scale is tapping an underlying, continuous variable.

Real Limits of a Number

 If a variable is continuous, any number along the dimension of the variable is an approximation. When someone weighs 195 lb, it does not mean that the person is exactly that weight since a more precise measurement is always possible. If the desired level of precision leads us to use a unit of measure of 1 lb, then a weight of 195.3 lb would be reported as 195 lb and a weight of 194.6 lb would likewise be reported as 195 lb. The number 195 lb is thus located at the midpoint of an interval. The upper and lower boundaries of the interval are the **real limits** of the interval. The upper real limit of the number is one-half the unit of measurement above the number; the lower real limit of a number is one-half the unit of measurement below the number. If the unit of measurement is 1 lb, the real limits for the number 195 lb. are 195.5 lb. and 194.5 lb. If the unit of measurement is tenths, then the real limits of the number 195.0 lb. are 194.95 lb. and 195.05 lb. Figure 2.1 graphically illustrates the concept of upper and lower limits for numbers with different units of measurement.

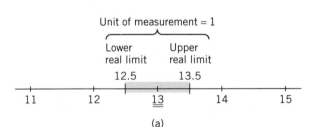

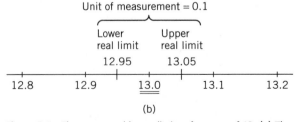

Figure 2.1   The upper and lower limits of a score of 13. (*a*) The unit of measurement is 1. The real limits are $13 + .5 = 13.5$ and $13 - .5 = 12.5$. (*b*) The unit of measurement is .1. The real limits are $13 + .05 = 13.05$ and $13 - .05 = 12.95$.

■   QUESTION   *The following data set contains the average temperature and amount of rainfall of several cities for the month of March. For each number, specify the upper and lower real limit.*

Place	Temperature	Rainfall
Acapulco	88°F	0.1 in.
Chicago	43°F	2.6 in.
Honolulu	77°F	3.1 in.
Orlando	76°F	3.4 in.

SOLUTION   The unit of measurement for temperature is 1 degree. The unit of measurement for rainfall is 1/10 of an inch. Since the upper and lower boundary of a number is one-half the unit of measurement, the upper and lower real limits of 1 degree are .5 degrees above and below the number used to report temperature. Thus, the upper and lower real limits for the temperature in Chicago are 43.5 and 42.5.

Since the unit of measurement for rainfall is 1/10, the upper and lower real limits are specified as 1/20 of an inch (or, similarly, 5/100 of an inch).[1] When establishing the upper and lower real limits, it helps to just think of the decimal place that is one notch greater in precision. If the scale uses whole numbers, the

TABLE   2.1   **The Midpoint, Upper, and Lower Real Limits for Average Temperatures and Amount of Rainfall for Several Cities in the Month of March**

ACAPULCO

Temperature			Rainfall		
Lower Limit	Midpoint	Upper Limit	Lower Limit	Midpoint	Upper Limit
87.5	**88**	88.5	0.05	**0.1**	0.15

CHICAGO

Temperature			Rainfall		
Lower Limit	Midpoint	Upper Limit	Lower Limit	Midpoint	Upper Limit
42.5	**43**	43.5	2.55	**2.6**	2.65

HONOLULU

Temperature			Rainfall		
Lower Limit	Midpoint	Upper Limit	Lower Limit	Midpoint	Upper Limit
76.5	**77**	77.5	3.05	**3.1**	3.15

ORLANDO

Temperature			Rainfall		
Lower Limit	Midpoint	Upper Limit	Lower Limit	Midpoint	Upper Limit
75.5	**76**	76.5	3.35	**3.4**	3.45

[1] A brief calculation shows why: .1 × .5 = .05, or 5/100 of an in., which is 1/20 of an in.

limits will be stated using the tenth decimal place. If the scale of measurement uses one decimal place (e.g., rainfall), the upper and lower limits will be reported using the second decimal place. For example, the upper and lower real limits for the March monthly rainfall of Honolulu are 3.15 and 3.05. The number 3.1 is the midpoint between 3.05 and 3.15. Table 2.1 presents the upper and lower real limits for the temperature and rainfall data of this problem.   ■

 In most research situations, the investigator will use at least an interval scale of measurement, and sometimes a ratio scale of measurement. In either case, a list (distribution) of numbers, called **raw** (or **original**) **scores,** will be obtained. When conducting an experiment, the raw scores will be subjects' measures on the dependent variable. This mass of unorganized data is not in a form that can be usefully displayed to others. Without analyzing the data, the distribution of raw scores can be summarized in a table or on a graph. Using tables and graphs to organize data allows you (and others) to view a summary of the raw scores of the study. The use of tables and graphs is not confined to summarizing experimental data. For instance, the tabulations of the Census Bureau can be summarized and presented in tables.

The remainder of the chapter presents numerous ways in which data can be presented in tables and on graphs. Box 2.1 discusses some notable achievements in the history of statistics.

2.3   USING TABLES TO ORGANIZE DATA

Simple Frequency Distributions

Table 2.2 presents scores from 90 subjects who completed a questionnaire measuring need for achievement. A quick glance at this table reveals relatively little. Indeed, even a longer glance at this table reveals little information about the distribution of scores. At the very least, one would wonder how many subjects received each of the scores. A simple frequency distribution answers this question.

TABLE   2.2   **Unorganized Raw Data**[a]

15	8	20	16	12	18	14	22	17	5
19	15	18	29	6	13	16	19	10	24
15	3	26	30	13	17	7	16	23	25
1	15	18	14	5	27	16	20	14	6
24	14	20	25	21	15	17	8	23	21
17	14	10	13	18	16	21	9	11	22
15	12	9	16	20	11	13	22	17	13
9	22	16	12	19	17	14	10	19	18
11	16	12	18	13	17	15	14	15	28

[a] Each number is a score from a need for achievement questionnaire.

A simple frequency distribution lists all the *possible* scores and the frequency with which each score appears. Table 2.3 is a simple frequency distribution of the unorganized scores in Table 2.2. Note that all possible scores are listed under the heading X. Even if no one obtained a score that was possible, that possible score is still included in the frequency distribution under X. The number of subjects that received each score is placed under the heading f (frequency). Adding all the scores under f will tell you the total number of subjects in the study. Constructing

BOX 2.1

Some Notes on the History of Statistics

The earliest use of statistics involved the tabulation and summary of data by means of tables and charts (descriptive statistics). The ancient Egyptians and Chinese used statistics to keep track of tax collections and government expenditures. They also maintained statistics on the availability of soldiers.

The study of statistics began with the Englishman John Graunt (1620–1674). Graunt tabulated information on deaths and noted that the frequency of certain diseases, suicide, and accidents occurred with remarkable regularity from year to year. His work led to the establishment of insurance companies. Graunt also found that there were more male than female births. But due to the greater mortality rate among men (occupational accidents and wars), by the marriageable age, the number of men and women was about equal. Graunt believed that this arrangement was nature's way of assuring monogamy.

The earliest use of statistics was to describe data. The next advance in statistics occurred in the seventeenth century, which sprung from mathematicians' interest in the "laws of chance" as they apply to gambling. The mathematician Blaise Pascal (1623–1662) was asked the following question by Chevalier de Méré, a mathematician and a professional gambler: "In what proportion should two players of equal skill divide the stakes remaining on the gambling table if they are forced to stop playing the game?" Pascal and Pierre Fermat (1602–1665), a French mathematician, arrived at the same answer, although they offered different proofs. It was their correspondences in the year 1654 that established modern probability theory.

The work of Pascal and Fermat was anticipated a century earlier by the Italian mathematician and gambler, Girolomo Cardan (1501–1576). His volume, *The Book on Games of Chance,* contains many tips on how to cheat when gambling, and established some of the origins of probability theory. Cardan also believed in astrology. Indeed, by using astrological charts he was able to predict the exact date of his death. To make sure that his prediction was accurate, he committed suicide on that day!

The third advance in the field of statistics occurred in the nineteenth and early twentieth centuries. Many of the chapters of this, and every other statistics text, are based on the statistical advances of the period between 1850 and 1930. Sir Francis Galton (1822–1911) formalized a method for making predictions of one variable with knowledge of a second, related variable (regression analysis). Samual Gossett (1876–1936) ushered in the era of modern experimental statistics by developing analyses that could allow a researcher to make generalizations based on only a small number of observations (the t test). Sir Ronald Fisher (1890–1962) made extensive contributions to the field of research design and developed statistical analyses that can be used to compare the relative influence of several different treatment variables on a dependent variable (the F test).

Contemporary statisticians are continuing to make advances in statistics, which allow researchers to ask increasingly complex questions to unravel the mysteries of human behavior.

TABLE 2.3   The Simple Frequency Distribution Constructed from the Unorganized Data of Table 2.2

X	f	X	f
30	1	14	7
29	1	13	6
28	1	12	4
27	1	11	3
26	1	10	3
25	2	9	3
24	2	8	2
23	2	7	1
22	4	6	2
21	3	5	2
20	4	4	0
19	4	3	1
18	6	2	0
17	7	1	1
16	8	0	0
15	8		

TABLE 2.4   A Grouped Frequency Distribution Based on the Raw Data from

Class Interval	Midpoint	f
30–32	31	1
27–29	28	3
24–26	25	5
21–23	22	9
18–20	19	14
15–17	16	23
12–14	13	17
9–11	10	9
6–8	7	5
3–5	4	3
0–2	1	1
		90

a frequency distribution is easy. Simply list the X values in descending order and indicate the number of observed instances of each score under f. Simple frequency distributions have the advantage of displaying all the data from the study. Further, each X score is the midpoint of an interval. For example, the number 5 in Table 2.3 is the midpoint of the interval 4.5 to 5.5. However, researchers often collapse the simple frequency distribution by grouping scores in equal intervals.

Grouped Frequency Distributions

 A **grouped frequency distribution** indicates the number of scores that fall in each of several ranges of scores. When using a grouped frequency distribution to organize data, there is some loss of information. As you look at a grouped frequency distribution, it is impossible to know how many subjects obtained a given score (see Table 2.4). Instead, you will only be able to observe how many subjects obtained scores within a class interval of scores. **Class intervals** are intervals of equal-sized ranges. Formal presentations of raw data almost always use grouped frequency distributions when the number of possible raw-score values exceeds 10.

Real Limits and Grouped Frequency Distributions
Class intervals have midpoints, lower, and upper limits. You will recall that when using an interval or ratio scale, a single number is the midpoint of an interval. The number 7 lies midway between 6.5 and 7.5. An interval of 22–24 has a lower limit of 21.5 and an upper limit of 24.5. The midpoint of the interval is 23. Table 2.4 illustrates a grouped frequency distribution using the need for achievement data.

The midpoints of each interval are represented in the second column. When presenting data in a grouped frequency distribution, the midpoint of each interval is usually not displayed.

Conventional Rules for Establishing Class Intervals

When data are presented in an unorganized fashion, it is difficult to see how the numbers are distributed. When using a simple frequency distribution, one can easily see the relative frequency of occurrence of each score. A grouped frequency distribution sacrifices information by collapsing numbers, but it is assumed that the loss of information is inconsequential. Being able to examine the pattern of scores over the range of potential scores is often more useful than knowing the frequency of occurrence for each individual score. Although an investigator is willing to give up some information when organizing data, it is important that the grouped frequency distribution does not lose one essential feature: the table should allow the observer to gain a good idea of how the numbers are patterned (distributed).

Table 2.4 uses eleven intervals. As you view the frequency column of the table, you can easily see that just a few people received scores in the extreme ends of the distribution. Most of the scores are in the middle of the distribution, with the greatest number of scores in the interval 15–17. If too few intervals are used, or alternatively, if too many intervals are used, it is difficult to see the way numbers are concentrated. The use of 10 to 20 class intervals is the customary rule for selecting the number of class intervals. However, it is not uncommon to see grouped frequency distributions with fewer than ten class intervals. When the span of numbers in the distribution is small and/or the total number of scores is small, you might want to use fewer than ten intervals. The researcher will select the number of intervals that illustrates most clearly the way in which the numbers are concentrated, or patterned.

The width of the class intervals (i) is related to the number of intervals: the fewer intervals used, the larger the intervals. Common intervals are $i = 3$, $i = 5$, $i = 10$, or $i =$ some multiple of 10. There are no hard-and-fast rules for constructing a grouped frequency distribution. However, the following guidelines should prove helpful.

1. Use somewhere between 10 to 20 class intervals to group the data, which will usually preserve a useful picture of the trends in the data.
2. Select an interval size that is convenient. Any interval size that leads to 10 to 20 class intervals is appropriate. One consideration in selecting class intervals is the midpoint of the interval. Any graph of a continuous measure requires the use of the midpoint of an interval. A midpoint that is a whole number makes a graph easier to read. Try to combine the interval width and the number of intervals in such a way that the midpoint is a whole number. Using an i that is an odd number will have a whole number as the midpoint. In Table 2.4, the midpoint of each interval is a whole number. For example, the midpoint of the first interval, 0–2, is 1. The midpoint of the next interval, 3–5, is 4. (Technically, the interval 3–5 includes the lower and upper real limits: 2.5–5.5.)

3. The first number of the interval should be a multiple of i. If the interval width is 5, then the first number of the interval should be a multiple of 5. If the interval width is 2, then the first number of the interval should be a multiple of 2. This rule is sometimes violated when the interval width is 5. For instance, instead of using an interval of 25–29, with a midpoint of 27, you may decide to use an interval of 23–27 so that the *midpoint* is a multiple of 5. The midpoint of the interval 23–27 is 25.

Cumulative Frequency Distributions

 A **cumulative frequency distribution** has a column in which each class and frequency represents cumulative data up to and including that class.[2] Table 2.5 presents the grouped frequency distribution in Table 2.4. The third column of Table 2.5 lists the cumulative frequencies, abbreviated cum f. Determining the cumulative frequencies is easy. The arrows in the table show you the additive procedure that is used to specify the cumulative frequency of scores at each interval. It is customary to start at the bottom of the frequency distribution. For the first interval, cum f is the same as the number of scores for that interval. The cum f for the next interval is the number of scores in that interval, *plus* the total number of scores for all the lower intervals. Follow the arrows in Table 2.5 to be sure that you know how to build the cum f column. Note that the total number of scores in the distribution is the top number of the cum f column.

TABLE 2.5 A Cumulative Frequency Distribution Based on the Grouped Frequency Distribution in Table 2.4

Class Interval	f	Cum f
30–32	1	90
27–29	3	89
24–26	5	86
21–23	9	81
18–20	14	72
15–17	23	58
12–14	17	35
9–11	9	18
6–8	5	9
3–5	3	4
0–2	1	1
	90	

[2] Chapter 3 discusses the importance of cumulative frequency distributions. Statistics will be computed from data represented in frequency tables.

2.4   USING GRAPHS TO DISPLAY DATA

One of the best ways to display data trends is to summarize data in the form of a graphic. In this section, you will learn about some common graphic displays used in the behavioral sciences, as well as how to construct graphic representations of data. You will also learn how to view graphs with healthy skepticism. You may have heard the saying, "There are lies, damn lies, and statistics." Well, one way to present a misleading impression of data trends is by graphing data in a technically correct manner, yet one that is entirely misleading.

The Axes of a Graph

 The typical graph has two axes. The horizontal axis is called the X axis, or **abscissa.** The vertical axis is called the Y axis, or **ordinate.** Larger numbers are to the right on the abscissa and upward on the ordinate. Smaller numbers and negative numbers, if any, progress to the left on the X axis and downward on the Y axis. Figure 2.2(a) shows the X and Y axes of a graph with no negative numbers. Figure 2.2(b) illustrates the axes of a graph with negative numbers.

The Frequency Polygon

 A **frequency polygon** plots the number of scores in each of the intervals of a frequency distribution. The interval width may be 1, as is often the case with a simple frequency distribution, or greater than 1, as is the case with a grouped

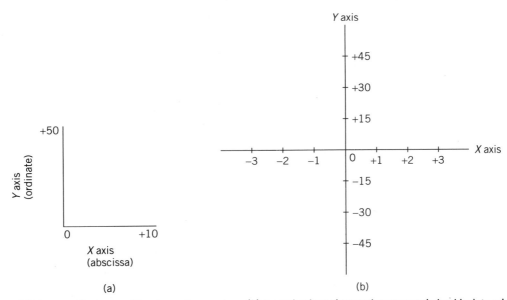

Figure 2.2   (*a*) The axes of a group without negative numbers. (*b*) A graph where the axes intersect at their midpoints, which allows for the inclusion of negative numbers on each axis.

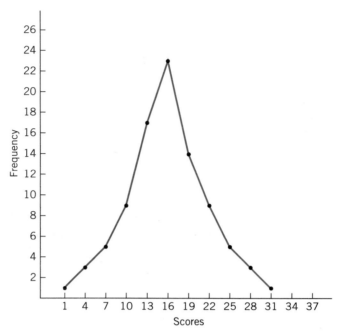

Figure 2.3   A frequency polygon of the data in Table 2.4. Points are plotted above each interval's midpoint.

frequency distribution. Figure 2.3 is a frequency polygon drawn from the grouped frequency distribution in Table 2.4. You will note that in Figure 2.3 (as well as Figure 2.4) the first and last points of the graph do not meet the horizontal axis. Whether or not to draw the graph so that the endpoints meet the X axis is a matter of personal preference. If you want to indicate that there are no observations associated with the first and last score of the distribution, then draw the graph so that the endpoints meet the horizontal axis.

As you view Figure 2.3, note that the X axis has the midpoints of the class intervals on it. The Y axis is labeled frequency and presents equally spaced numbers that specify the frequency of scores. A *single* point on the graph indicates the midpoint of an interval represented on the X axis, and the number of scores found in the interval is indicated on the Y axis.

The intersection of the X and Y axes usually represents the 0 point for each of the variables. However, sometimes the first number of a class interval is some distance from 0, or the first frequency count of an interval is quite a distance from 0. Should this situation arise, the X and/or Y axes are truncated with broken lines. Figure 2.4 shows a frequency polygon in which the first midpoint of the lowest class interval is 20 and the first frequency count is 100.

The frequency polygon is a useful graphic for depicting the overall concentration of numbers. It is easy to construct and it is possible to compare two or more distributions on the same graph. However, frequencies are easier to read when using a histogram.

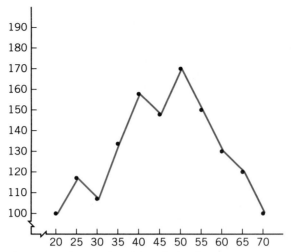

Figure 2.4 The *X* and *Y* axes are broken between 0 and the lowest scores of each axis.

The Histogram

 The histogram in Figure 2.5 is based on the frequency distribution in Table 2.4. There are two points to keep in mind when constructing a **histogram.** First, the width of the bar spans the width of the class interval. Second, there is no space between the bars. The frequency polygon and the histogram are related. If you were to place a point at the midpoint of the top of each bar of the histogram, erase the bars, and connect the data points, you would have a frequency polygon. A frequency polygon has been superimposed on the histogram depicted in Figure 2.5 so that you can directly compare these two graphical displays.

The Bar Graph

 A **bar graph** is used to represent the frequency of scores associated with categories. A bar graph looks like a histogram except that the bars do not share a common border. The reason there are no shared borders in a bar graph is because the categories represented on the *X* axis are discrete in nature. For example, in Figure 2.6, the scale used on the *X* axis is nominal. Psychology, history, and so on, are names of different majors. Figure 2.6 shows hypothetical data on the number of undergraduate majors in each of several programs.

Graphs Can Be Misleading

Suppose a researcher compares two different methods for enhancing learning. As it turns out, Method B produces a relative gain of three points, whereas Method A does not have any effect on learning. However, let's suppose that the difference

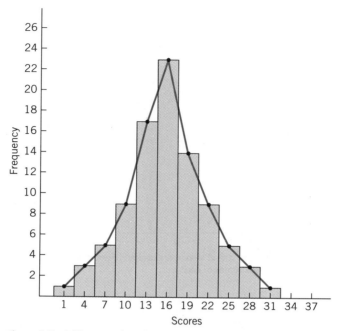

Figure 2.5 A histogram based on the data in Table 2.4.

between no change and a three-point change is actually a trivial finding. Figure 2.7 labels pretest and post-test on the *X* axis. The data points above the pretest indicate the number of correct responses for each method *before* the subjects are administered any training. The data points above the post-test represent the number of correct responses for each method after training. Note that the line for Method A

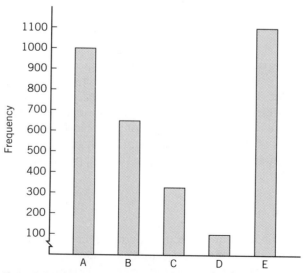

Figure 2.6 The number of undergraduates majoring in psychology (A), sociology (B), history (C), biology (D), and business (E).

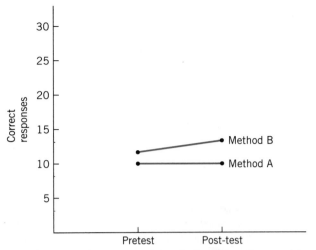

Figure 2.7   A graph that shows the relative effects of two training methods on performance. The lines on the graph indicate that there is little difference between the two methods.

is parallel with the *X* axis, which indicates no change in performance as a result of training. The line for Method B rises *slightly,* indicating the small increase in performance. Since the lines show little divergence, it appears that the two methods are very similar in their effects on performance.

Now examine Figure 2.8. The same data are graphed, but now it looks like Method B is vastly superior to Method A. Why? Notice the *Y* axis. The scale of

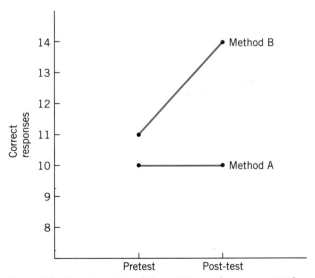

Figure 2.8   The data points of Figure 2.7 are redrawn to create the impression of a vast difference between the two training methods. Altering the numbers on the *Y* axis can give a misleading picture of the results of the study.

BOX 2.2

Using a Graph To Provide a Visual Display of Data

For the past 25 years, social scientists have been asking Americans how much confidence they have in specific public institutions. Some interesting trends have been noted. Some of the results of these surveys are summarized in the following table (*Science Indicators*, 1985).

The following table is a useful summary of the percentage of people who have a great deal of confidence in three public institutions. However, to determine if there is a change in confidence over the years for any one institution requires careful examination of each row of the table. To compare differences in the degree of confidence among the three institutions expressed by Americans requires looking back and forth between the columns. Nonetheless, one can see that the public has much more confidence in medicine and education than in Congress, and that people express more confidence in our medical institutions compared to our educational institutions. Representing these findings on a graph provides a visual display that allows one to quickly observe important differences among categories and trends over time.

As you view the graph provided, keep these points in mind. First, the abscissa presents the years. This variable is discrete. The numbers 1973, 1974, and so forth, represent categories. When data are graphed using categories on the *X* axis, a bar graph can be drawn. In fact, with some thought and creativity, the per-

Percent of the Public Expressing a Great Deal of Confidence in Three Public Institutions: Medicine, Education, and Congress

	1973	1974	1975	1976	1977	1978	1980	1982	1984
Medicine	54	60	50	54	51	46	52	46	52
Education	37	49	31	37	41	28	30	33	29
Congress	23	17	13	14	19	13	9	13	13

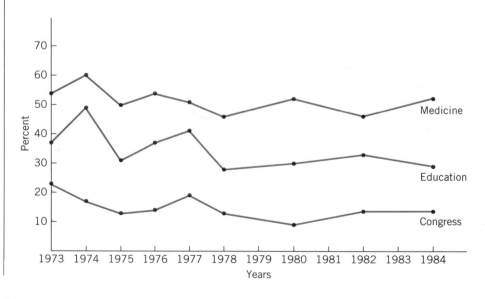

centages for each institution, across years, could be presented with bars on the same graph. However, by using the line graphs for each institution, trends in the data can be observed. Each point above a year represents the percentage of people who reported a great deal of confidence in each of the institutions. These points are *not* midpoints. Why? Because only numbers representing a continuous variable have midpoints and real limits. The *X* axis represents *categories*. There are no midpoints for categories.

Examine the relative heights of the lines to compare the differences among institutions in terms of the percentage of people expressing confidence. Finally, do not forget to examine the span of percentages along the *Y* axis. In this case, the relative heights of the lines reveal meaningful differences among the three institutions. However, if there were very small, trivial differences in percentages, it would be possible to adjust the scale on the *Y* axis and arrive at a graph that looks identical to the one provided.

measurement has been altered so that an increase of two points spans a much greater distance along the *Y* axis. The two graphs are both *technically* accurate. However, the second graph is very misleading. When viewing graphs, there is a natural tendency to focus on the lines drawn on the graph. You must *always* pay attention to the way in which the axes, especially the *Y* axis, are constructed.

Box 2.2 illustrates the use of a graph to display data. Note how the graph allows you to make a quick comparison of trends between medicine, education, and Congress.

2.5 THE SHAPE OF THINGS TO COME

Thus far the depiction of data in the form of tables and graphs has been illustrated. A graph is a drawing of the relative frequency of scores. A pictorial representation of data is one way to describe the form or shape of a distribution of scores. Another way to describe the shape of a distribution is verbally. Statisticians have coined terms for important features of the shapes of distributions. This section addresses some of these terms.

Bell-Shaped Distributions

Bell-shaped distributions are aptly named because they look like bells. These distributions are symmetrical; one half of the curve describing the distribution is a mirror image of the other half of the curve. Figure 2.9 is one type of bell-shaped distribution, which is called a **normal distribution** (or **normal curve**). You will learn much more about normal curves in later chapters. For now, note that the normal curve is symmetrical. Moreover, most of the scores group in the middle of the distribution.

Skewed Distributions

When most of the scores are found near one end of a distribution, it is referred to as a **skewed distribution.** Figure 2.10 shows a positively skewed distribution and Figure 2.11 depicts a negatively skewed distribution. When most of the scores

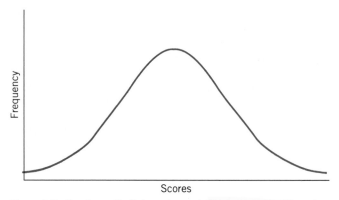

Figure 2.9   One type of bell-shaped curve is the normal curve. Note that it is symmetrical, and most of the scores are found in the middle of the distribution.

Figure 2.10   A positively skewed distribution. Here, most of the scores are found in the lower end of the distribution.

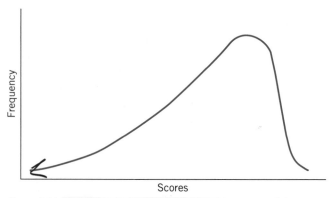

Figure 2.11   A negatively skewed distribution. Here, most of the scores are found in the upper end of the distribution.

group at the lower end of the distribution, the distribution is positively skewed. When most of the scores group at the upper end of the distribution, the distribution is negatively skewed.

There is an easy way to remember these terms. With a number line, positive scores lie to the right and negative scores lie to the left. Examine Figures 2.10 and 2.11. In each figure, imagine an arrow at the end of the long tail of the distribution. In the *positively* skewed distribution in Figure 2.10, the arrow is pointing to the right, toward what would be *positive* numbers on a number line. In a *negatively* skewed distribution (Figure 2.11), the arrow points toward what would be *negative* numbers on a number line.

Kurtosis

Kurtosis refers to the quality of peakedness or flatness of a curve. Knowing how flat or peaked a curve is reflects the relative concentration of scores on the scale of measurement. In Figure 2.12, most of the scores are concentrated very close to the middle of the distribution. When the shape of the curve is relatively narrow, the distribution is called **leptokurtic.** In Figure 2.13, the curve is relatively broad, indicating that the scores are widely dispersed. This curve is referred to as **platykurtic.** Refer to Figure 2.9. This curve illustrates a peak that is intermediate between leptokurtic and platykurtic, and is called **mesokurtic** (from the Greek work Meso, meaning intermediate).

The curves drawn to illustrate the concepts of skewness and kurtosis in no way exhaust the myriad ways in which scores can be patterned. A distribution can be shaped like a *J*, a rectangle, or an inverted *U*; in fact, distributions can theoretically assume practically any shape.

Chapters 3 and 4 discuss numerous statistical indices used to describe data. You will learn that the shape of a distribution will influence the value of various descriptive statistics. How to choose indices to use to summarize a distribution of scores will also be addressed.

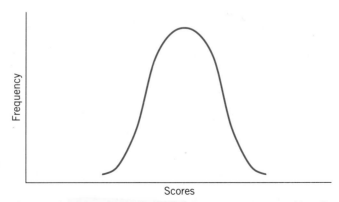

Figure 2.12 A leptokurtic distribution. Scores are concentrated heavily around the middle of the distribution, with little dispersion among the scores.

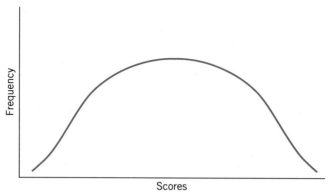

Figure 2.13   A platykurtic distribution. Scores are dispersed widely, and the shape of the curve is relatively broad.

SUMMARY

The assignment of numbers using a nominal scale is a labeling activity. There is no quantity reflected in nominal numbers; instead, numbers are assigned based on the type, or kind of objects or events being numbered. Variables that are measured on a nominal scale are qualitative variables.

Similar to nominal measures, ordinal measures categorize things, but they have a particular relation to one another. An ordinal scale is used to identify the relative position of an individual in relation to other individuals. Variables that are measured using an ordinal scale are quantitative because one can interpret a difference between ranks as more or less of something. Even though ordinal scales are quantitative, there is only a limited sense in which quantity is implied. Rankings reflect more or less of something but not how much more or less of something.

The interval scale is like the ordinal scale in that different numbers reflect more or less of something. In addition, however, the interval scale has the property that numerically equal distances on the scale represent equal distances on the dimension underlying the scale.

A ratio scale possesses all of the properties of an interval scale, with the addition of an absolute zero point. The importance of an absolute zero point is that any number on a ratio scale can be used to establish its standing relative to any other number on the scale; in addition, a number also represents an absolute amount of something.

A discontinuous or discrete variable is one that typically increments from one whole number to another whole number. Discrete variables are characterized by gaps between numbers that cannot be filled by any number. A continuous variable does not have gaps between adjacent numbers. Numbers that are used to represent an underlying continuous measure are approximate. The upper and lower boundaries of the interval are called the real limits of the interval. The upper real limit of the number is one-half the unit of measurement above the number and the lower real limit of a number is one-half the unit of measurement below the number. In most research situations, the investigator will use at least an interval scale of measurement, sometimes a ratio scale of measurement.

Using tables and graphs to organize data allows you to view a summary of the raw scores of the study. A simple frequency distribution lists all the possible scores and the frequency with which each score appears. A grouped frequency distribution indicates the number of scores that fall in each of several intervals. Class intervals are intervals of equal-sized ranges used to organize data in a grouped frequency distribution. A cumulative frequency distribution includes a column that shows the accumulation of the number of scores for a given interval, plus all the intervals below a given interval.

The typical graph has two axes. The horizontal axis is called the X axis or the abscissa. The vertical axis is called the Y axis or ordinate. Larger numbers are to the right on the abscissa, and upward on the ordinate.

A frequency polygon plots the number of scores in each of the intervals of a frequency distribution. A histogram represents the frequency of scores for a class interval by using bars that span the interval and share common borders. A bar graph is used to represent the frequency of scores associated with categories. A bar graph looks like a histogram except that the bars do not share a common border.

Statisticians use terms to describe important features of the shape of distributions. A bell-shaped curve is symmetrical; it pictorially indicates that most of the scores center around the middle of the distribution. The normal curve is an example of a bell-shaped curve. A distribution that has scores that bunch at one end of the distribution is skewed. A positively skewed distribution has scores that bunch at the lower end of the distribution. A negatively skewed distribution has scores that group around the upper end of the distribution. Kurtosis is a term that refers to the amount of dispersion of scores in the distribution. A leptokurtic distribution has a relatively high concentration of scores at the middle of the distribution. A platykurtic distribution has scores that are widely dispersed around the middle of the distribution.

WORK PROBLEMS

1. Indicate whether each of the following scales of measurement is nominal, ordinal, interval, or ratio.
   a. Amount of change in attitudes.
   b. Attitudes toward nuclear disarmament (for/against).
   c. Ratings of popularity.
   d. Amount of time tolerating a painful stimulus.
   e. Heart rate under stress.
   f. A measure of need for approval.
   g. Amount of weight lifted.
   h. Numbers assigned based on political affiliation.
   i. Numbers assigned to diagnostic categories.

  j. Thought disorder versus no thought disorder.
  k. A listing of tennis players from best to worst.
2. For each of the following class intervals, specify the width of the class, the real limits, and the midpoint.
   a. 1–3
   b. 5–10
   c. −4−−8
   d. −2−+2
   e. 1.50–3.50
   f. 25–50
3. The data in the following table are from a midterm examination. Set up frequency distributions with:
   a. $i = 1$ (simple frequency distribution)
   b. $i = 3$
   c. $i = 10$
   d. $i = 20$
   e. include columns for cum f (b.–d.)

Midterm Examination Scores

40	98	63	90	70	60	45	43	78
67	56	54	78	87	43	90	81	81
77	80	79	80	81	66	75	88	84
49	63	78	79	80	92	89	84	77

4. For each of the frequency distributions in Problem 3, specify the real limits of each class interval.
5. Construct histograms for each of the frequency distributions of Problem 3.
6. Based on the histograms of Problem 5, draw frequency polygons.

Work Problems for the Computer

7. Use your software package to establish simple, grouped and cumulative frequency distributions for the following numbers. Also, generate a graphic of the following numbers. If your program allows for various graphics, represent the data in each graphic form (e.g., polygon, histogram, etc.).

15	12	13	14	10	15	30	12	17	15	15	30
16	17	28	19	22	25	10	19	32	11	22	32
14	43	32	20	25	29	19	18	29	10	18	39
30	35	19	29	47	25	25	45	16	75	60	25
74	55	18	70	50	20	40	50	45	60	40	62
62	89	61	72	90	65	85	80	60	45	22	49
35	18	49	25	30	59	50	78	35	60	75	39
60	70	25	53	74	74	43	74	72	70	90	75
75	99	77	75	89	60	67	80	80	64	77	82
68	85	80	63	82	75	48	34	16	17	22	25

Measures of Central Tendency

3.1 DESCRIBING A DISTRIBUTION OF SCORES

When behavioral scientists collect data, they usually obtain scores that are arranged as a distribution (i.e., arranged in order of size). The scores may represent such measures as heart rate, anxiety, marital satisfaction, family income, number of problems solved, or performance on a midterm exam. Viewing a list of scores is rather uninformative. For example, if you have recorded the number of hours spent studying each day during an 8-week period, and you are asked how productive you have been, you could simply recite 56 numbers, each number representing the amount of time spent studying on a given day. Although a lot of information is communicated, it is not in a form that is very useful to the listener. In Chapter 2 you learned ways in which a distribution of scores could be *visually* displayed.

 Descriptive statistics are statistical indices that summarize and communicate basic characteristics of a distribution. They are used to *verbally* communicate features of a distribution.

What are the most relevant aspects of a distribution to communicate? Usually the scores of a distribution tend to bunch or center on a particular segment of the distribution. **Measures of central tendency** are indices designed to communicate where scores center in the distribution. However, measures of central tendency only communicate part of the distribution, albeit a very important part. Other statistics are needed, which reflect the degree to which the scores are spread out. **Measures of variability** (or **dispersion**) are statistical indices that communicate the degree to which scores are spread out in a distribution. (See Chapter 4 for a further discussion.)

3.2   POPULATIONS AND SAMPLES

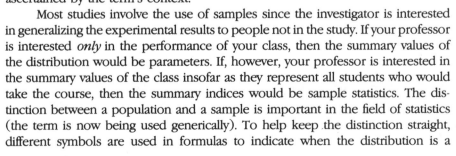 A **population** and a **sample** differ depending on the investigator's primary interest. If the investigator is only concerned about the group of people from which the scores are obtained, then those scores define a population. **Parameters** are statistical values that describe the distribution characteristics of a population. Summarizing students' test scores on an examination is a common example of the use of population parameters. However, if the investigator's interest in a group of scores goes beyond those persons providing the scores, then the distribution is a sample. A sample is used to generalize the results to a larger group of persons. **Statistics** are those numbers used to describe the characteristics of a sample distribution. This may seem a bit confusing because the term statistics can refer to the field of statistics, a number ("Bob got divorced and is now just another statistic"), or to a value that summarizes some aspect of a sample of scores. Whether the term is used generically or to represent sample summary values can easily be ascertained by the term's context.

Most studies involve the use of samples since the investigator is interested in generalizing the experimental results to people not in the study. If your professor is interested *only* in the performance of your class, then the summary values of the distribution would be parameters. If, however, your professor is interested in the summary values of the class insofar as they represent all students who would take the course, then the summary indices would be sample statistics. The distinction between a population and a sample is important in the field of statistics (the term is now being used generically). To help keep the distinction straight, different symbols are used in formulas to indicate when the distribution is a population or a sample of scores. Moreover, some formulas, such as those used for measures of variability, are slightly different, depending on whether the distribution is a sample of scores or a population. Before discussing three measures of central tendency—mean, median, and mode—a brief digression is in order.

3.3 THE ROUNDING RULE —3 places

Since this is the first of many chapters in which you will be performing calculations, we should reach some agreement on how numbers will be rounded. Because this book is *about* research and not the actual conduct of a study, it is unnecessary to use the level of quantitative precision that is mandatory during actual data analysis. As such, the rounding rule used in this text is to *round to two places.* This entails completing your computations to the *third* place to the right of the decimal point, and then rounding the value to *two* places to the right of the decimal place. Thus, 27.534 would be rounded to 27.53. If the third decimal place is a 5, always round up. Hence, 34.785 becomes 34.79. Throughout the text, multistep computations are illustrated and interim values are rounded to two places. If your answers to work problems are slightly different than the answers provided, it is likely that the difference is due to rounding errors. These minor discrepancies should not alter your conclusions about the outcome of your calculations, nor should they compromise your understanding of the material presented in the text.

3.4 THE MEAN

 The **mean** is the most frequently used measure of **central tendency.** It can be used as a descriptive index of central tendency; in addition, it is often used in formulas designed to test experimental hypotheses. As a descriptive index, the mean has advantages and disadvantages, which will be discussed later. You have been calculating means for years, calling them averages. The mean of a population is given in the following formula.

Population Mean

$$\mu = \frac{\Sigma X}{N}$$

(Formula 3.1a)

where,

μ = (pronounced "*mu*") the symbol for the mean of a population

X = a score in the distribution

N = the total number of scores

Σ = (pronounced "sigma") a notation that indicates an operation to be performed on a set of numbers. It directs you to sum a set of scores. Thus, $\Sigma X = X_1 + X_2 + X_3 \cdots X_n$

The formula for the mean of a *sample* of scores is identical to the population formula, with the exception of two different symbols, so as to remind you that a sample, rather than a population, is being considered.

Sample Mean

$$\overline{X} = \frac{\Sigma X}{n}$$

(Formula 3.1b)

where,

$\overline{X}$ = (pronounced "X bar") the symbol for the mean of a sample

n = the total number of scores

■ QUESTION *What is the mean of this population of scores?*

5, 8, 10, 11, 12

SOLUTION $\mu = \dfrac{46}{5} = 9.20$ ■

There are three measures of central tendency discussed in this chapter—the mean, median, and mode. Each measure is designed to communicate where scores tend to center or group in the distribution. However, each measure approaches the concept of centrality differently. In what way does the mean reflect the center of a distribution?

 Except for the case in which a particular subject's score is the same as the mean, each score is some distance from the mean. Stated differently, each score deviates from the mean by some amount. The degree to which a score deviates from the mean is simply $X - \overline{X}$. A **deviation score** (or **error score**) is the distance a score is from the mean, which is symbolized as x (pronounced "little x"). Therefore, $x = X - \overline{X}$.

In Table 3.1, the deviation score for each raw score is listed in the fourth column. Note that a raw score has a negative deviation score when it falls below the mean, and a positive deviation score when it falls above the mean. *The sum*

TABLE 3.1 Deviation Scores Always Sum to Zero

	Distribution A				Distribution B		
Subject	*Score*	$\overline{X}$	$X - \overline{X}(x)$	*Subject*	*Score*	$\overline{X}$	$X - \overline{X}(x)$
S_1	2	6	-4	S_1	2	10	-8
S_2	4	6	-2	S_2	4	10	-6
S_3	6	6	0	S_3	6	10	-4
S_4	8	6	$+2$	S_4	8	10	-2
S_5	10	6	$+4$	S_5	30	10	$+20$
			$\Sigma x = 0$				$\Sigma x = 0$

of all the deviation scores equals 0. Hence, $\Sigma(X - \overline{X}) = \Sigma x = 0$. In Table 3.1, both distributions have identical scores except for Subject 5. A score of 30, instead of 10, is obtained by Subject 5 in Distribution B. As a consequence, the $\overline{X}$ of Distribution B (10) is greater than the $\overline{X}$ of Distribution A (6). However, the deviation scores still sum to 0. In a manner of speaking, the mean has adjusted itself so that the Σx is still 0. It is in precisely this sense that the mean is the center of a distribution. For every distribution, no matter what its shape, no matter the value of the mean, no matter how many raw scores, *the sum of the deviation scores always equals 0.*

The Weighted Mean

Imagine that the mean SAT scores from three high schools in one school district are 425, 470, and 410. If you wanted to find the mean SAT score for the district, would you be justified in taking the mean of the three high school means? Think of it this way. If you had each student's score, irrespective of the school, you would sum all the scores and divide by the total number of students who took the exam. Since it is unlikely that each school has the same number of students, some schools would be contributing more scores than others. If you are working from raw scores, this would not be a problem. However, when presented with just the means from the schools, you need to take into account the number of students that contributed to each mean. When calculating the overall mean, you must weight each mean by its respective n. Only when the n is the same for each mean can you simply take the mean of the means [i.e., $(425 + 470 + 410)/3 = 435$]. Formula 3.2 is used to calculate the **weighted mean** (or **grand mean**).

Weighted Mean

$$\overline{X} = \frac{n_1(\overline{X_1}) + n_2(\overline{X_2}) \cdots + \cdots n_n(\overline{X_n})}{n_1 + n_2 \cdots + \cdots n_n}$$

(Formula 3.2)

where,

n_1, n_2 = the number of scores in the first group, the second group, and so forth

n_n = the number of scores in the last group

$\overline{X_1}, \overline{X_2}$ = the mean of the first group, the second group, and so forth

$\overline{X_n}$ = the mean of the last group

■ QUESTION *What would be the weighted mean, assuming the following values?*

School 1	School 2	School 3
$n_1 = 220$	$n_2 = 178$	$n_3 = 192$
$\overline{X_1} = 425$	$\overline{X_2} = 470$	$\overline{X_3} = 410$

SOLUTION

$$\overline{X} = \frac{220(425) + 178(470) + 192(410)}{220 + 178 + 192}$$

$$= \frac{255,880}{590}$$

$$\overline{X} = \textbf{433.69}$$

■ QUESTION *The mean blood pressure for three age groups has been recorded. What is the overall mean blood pressure?*

	Age		
	20–39	*40–59*	*60+*
systolic	118	128	145
diastolic	70	78	82
n	13	12	16

SOLUTION $\overline{X}$ systolic = 131 and $\overline{X}$ diastolic = 77 ■

The Mean of a Frequency Distribution

Chapter 2 showed how a distribution of scores can be displayed in a table, which allows you to ascertain the frequency with which each score occurs. It is an easy matter to calculate the mean of a distribution displayed in such a fashion. Simply use the following formula.

Mean of a Frequency Distribution

$$\mu \text{ or } \overline{X} = \frac{\Sigma Xf}{\Sigma f}$$ *(Formula 3.3)*

where,

f = frequency with which a score appears

Table 3.2 includes a column of raw scores, a column that indicates the frequency with which each score occurs, and a column of cross products, *Xf*. Follow the steps of the problem to see how the mean can be calculated from a frequency distribution.

A Note of Caution About the Mean

In Table 3.1, replacing a raw score of 10 with one having the value of 30 shifted the mean from 6 to 10. The inclusion of just one extreme score can have a profound

TABLE   3.2   **Calculating the Mean from a Frequency Distribution**

X	f	Xf
7	1	7
6	3	18
5	2	10
4	5	20
3	4	12
2	1	2
1	1	1
	$n = \Sigma f = 17$	$\Sigma Xf = 70$

$$\overline{X} = \frac{\Sigma Xf = 70}{\Sigma f = 17} = 4.12$$

effect on the mean. The more extreme the score, the greater its effect on the mean; in other words, the mean has to make a bigger adjustment in order to satisfy $\Sigma x = 0$. The fact that the mean "behaves" in this way can be a problem or a blessing, depending on what effect you would like to have on your audience. It can provide the perfect opportunity to commit a lie while technically remaining truthful.

Suppose Congressman Mackey is elected on the promise that he will bring prosperity to his district. During the next election he would like to convince his constituents that he has made good on his promise. His definition of prosperity is the mean income of families living in his district. When the congressman was first elected, the mean income in his district was $20,000. Two years later, one couple moved into the district with a yearly income of $150,000. Everyone else's income remained the same. Look what happens to the average family income when the mean is used as the measure of central tendency.

Family Income (1990)	Family Income (1994)
$14,000	$ 14,000
$18,000	$ 18,000
$20,000	$ 20,000
$22,000	$ 22,000
$26,000	$ 26,000
$\mu = \$20,000$	$150,000
	$\mu = \$41,667$

Congressman Mackey could honestly report that the average income per family had more than doubled during his term in office. Because extreme scores can "throw off" the mean, it is necessary to have an index of central tendency that is not so sensitive to extreme scores. If you are interested in accurately communicating where scores of a distribution are bunched, and the existence of extreme scores would lead to a misleading impression, then the median is a better measure of central tendency. Thus, skewed distributions lend themselves to the use of the median as the most important measure of central tendency.

3.5   THE MEDIAN

You have learned that the mean is the center of a distribution in the sense that $\Sigma x = 0$. The **median** is the center of the distribution in that 50 percent of the scores fall above and 50 percent of the scores fall below the median. In other words, the median divides the distribution based on the *frequency* or *number* of scores above and below the median. In some instances a formula is not required when locating the median.

Finding the Median When Given an Odd Number of Scores

■   QUESTION   *What is the median of this distribution?*

1, 4, 6, 8, 40, 50, 58, 60, 62

SOLUTION   40

The median is 40 because the same number of scores (four) fall above 40 as fall below 40. Note that the values of the scores surrounding the median are irrelevant. The median is based on the ranking of scores. To find the median, you need to position the scores in ascending (or descending) order and then identify the midpoint of the distribution. Since the actual value of the scores has no effect on the median, one could say that the median is "rank sensitive." In contrast, the mean is "value sensitive" since it is influenced, sometimes greatly, by the value of extreme scores. A few illustrative problems will emphasize this point.   ■

■   QUESTION   *What is the mean and median of this sample distribution?*

2, 4, 7, 9, 12, 15, 17

SOLUTION $\overline{X} = 9.43$ Median = 9   ■

■   QUESTION   *What is the mean and median of this sample distribution?*

2, 4, 7, 9, 12, 15, 17, 46, 54

SOLUTION $\overline{X} = 18.44$ Median = 12   ■

Look closely at the foregoing two distributions. The inclusion of two extreme scores to the right (or top end of the second distribution) has greatly influenced the mean, in fact doubling it—whereas the median was only shifted to the next score to the right.

Finding the Median When Given an Even Number of Scores

In the examples provided thus far it was easy to identify the median because there were an odd number of scores in the distribution. But what do you do in these situations?

$$4, 6, 9, 10, 11, 12$$

$$4, 6, 8, 8, 8, 9, 11, 12$$

The median will fall between two scores anytime there is an even number of scores; it will typically be a value that does not occur in the distribution. The median may even be a number that does not seem to make much sense in terms of what is being measured. For example, the median number of daily high dives at the local swimming pool may be 37.5. What is the meaning of one-half of a dive? This also can arise when using the mean. Suppose the mean number of children per family is 2.4. What do those 0.4 children look like? Nonetheless, the following will show you how to calculate the median when there is an even number of scores in the distribution.

■   QUESTION   *What is the median of this distribution?*

$$3, 9, 15, 16, 19, 22$$
$$\uparrow$$
Median

SOLUTION   15.50

The median of a distribution having an even number of values is the mean of the middle two numbers.   ■

Finding the Median When There Are Identical Scores in the Middle of the Distribution

■   QUESTION   *What is the median of the following distribution?*

$$7, 7, 7, 8, 8, 8, 9, 9, 10, 10$$
$$\uparrow$$
Median

SOLUTION   8.17

It is not immediately obvious why 8.17 should be the median. Recall from Chapter 2 that every number of a distribution is considered to be the midpoint of an interval. In fact, this notion was used to draw histograms. In this case, 8 is the midpoint of the interval 7.5 to 8.5. You will need to come up a certain distance from 7.5. If you choose a spot between the second and third 8, you will have five numbers on either side of that spot. In doing so you have put two-thirds of the total number of 8s below the chosen spot. So you simply add 2/3 to 7.5 (7.5 + 0.67) to arrive at 8.17.   ■

■   QUESTION   *What is the median of this distribution?*

$$7, 7, 7, 8, 8, 8, 8, 8, 9, 9, 10, 10$$
$$\uparrow$$
Median

SOLUTION   8.10

By choosing a spot between the third and fourth 8, you will have six numbers on each side. Three of the five 8s are below that spot (three-fifths of the 8s): 7.5 + 3/5 = (7.5 + 0.60) = 8.10.   ■

Calculating the Median from a Frequency Distribution

One can also calculate the median from a frequency distribution, although it is more complex. However, complexity does not necessarily mean more difficult to understand. In this instance it just requires more steps. Table 3.3 contains a cumulative frequency distribution with grouped data. The cumulative frequency column will make the task of finding the median easier. The following steps help to determine the median of data organized in a cumulative frequency distribution.

Step 1.   Look at the highest number in the Cumulative Frequency (cum f) column and divide that number by 2: 76/2 = 38. The 38th score is the median.

Step 2.   Find the class interval that contains the 38th score. The class interval 15–19 contains the 14th to 39th score. The 38th score is in this interval, in fact, near the top of the interval. (It is assumed that the 26 scores in this interval are evenly distributed among the values within the interval.)

TABLE   3.3   **Finding the Median of a Cumulative Frequency Distribution**

Class Interval	Frequency	Cum f
45–49	1	76
40–44	2	75
35–39	3	73
30–34	6	70
25–29	8	64
20–24	17	56
15–19	**26**	**39**
10–14	11	13
5–9	2	2
0–4	0	0

Step 3.   Now you zero in on that 38th score of the distribution. Count from the *bottom* of the Frequency column (not the cum f column). The first three intervals contain 13 scores ($0 + 2 + 11$). You now have 13 scores, but to reach 38 scores, you need to dip into the next interval, the critical interval. How many scores do you need from that interval? You already have 13 scores. To reach 38 scores, you need another 25 scores. The critical interval has 26 scores. You thus need 25 of the 26 scores. Divide 25 by 26 and convert to a decimal: $25/26 = .96$.

Step 4.   Find the width of the critical class interval by determining the exact lower and upper limits of the critical class interval. The lower limit is 14.50, the upper limit is 19.50. Therefore, the interval width is 5.

Step 5.   Multiply the value computed in Step 4, .96, times the interval width: $.96 \times 5 = 4.80$.

Step 6.   Add 4.80 to the lower limit of the critical class interval: $4.80 + 14.50 = $ **19.30.** You now have the median!

It should be mentioned, however, that since it is assumed that the scores of the critical interval are evenly distributed, determining the median from a frequency distribution gives an approximation of the median.

This method of finding the median has been presented to emphasize that the median is the *exact* middle of the distribution, or at least an approximation of the exact middle of the distribution. Moreover, this method bears some resemblance to how the median is found with ungrouped data. In practice, however, Formula 3.4, which follows, is a more expedient method for finding the median of a frequency distribution.

Median of a Frequency Distribution

$$\text{Median} = L + \left[\frac{(N/2) - F}{f_m} \cdot b \right]$$

(Formula 3.4)

where,

$L = $ the exact lower limit of the critical interval
$F = $ the sum of all frequencies below L
$f_m = $ the number of scores in the critical interval
$N = $ the total number of scores in the distribution
$b = $ the width of the interval

Determining the Median of a Cumulative Frequency Distribution by Formula

Using the data in Table 3.3, the steps involved in using Formula 3.4 are provided in the following list.

Step 1.   Look at the highest number in the Cumulative Frequency (cum f)

column and divide that number by 2: $76/2 = 38$. The 38th score is the median.

Step 2.   Find the class interval that contains the 38th score. The class interval 15–19 has the 14th to 39th score. The 38th score is in this interval, in fact near the top of the interval. (It is assumed that the 26 scores in this interval are evenly distributed among the values within the interval.)

Step 3.   Determine L, the exact lower limit of the critical interval: 14.50.

Step 4.   Determine F, the total number of scores below the critical interval. Look at the number in the Cumulative Frequency (cum f) column that is just below the critical interval: 13.

Step 5.   Find f_m, the number of scores in the critical interval. Look in the Frequency column (not the cum f column). The number of scores in the critical interval is 26.

Step 6.   Determine N, the total number of scores. Simply look at the top number of the cum f column: 76. You already used this number in Step 1 to locate the 38th score of the distribution.

Step 7.   Identify b, the interval width, by subtracting the exact lower limit of the critical interval from the upper limit of the interval: $19.50 - 14.50 = 5$.

Step 8.   You now have all the values you need to work the formula. Just do the arithmetic.

$L = 14.50$, $F = 13$, $f_m = 26$, $N = 76$, and $b = 5$. You then have:

$$\text{Median} = L + \left[\frac{(N/2 - F)}{f_m} \cdot b \right]$$

$$\text{Median} = 14.50 + \left[\frac{38 - 13}{26} \cdot 5 \right]$$

$$= 14.50 + .96(5)$$

$$= 14.50 + 4.80 = \mathbf{19.30}$$

Note that the formula method gives us the same median as was found using the longer method.

We turn now to a third measure of central tendency—the mode.

3.6   THE MODE

Determining the mode is the easiest of all the measures of central tendency. Since no computations are required, it might be more accurate to say you *identify* rather than compute the mode. The mean is an index of central tendency in that the numbers to the right of the mean balance the numbers to the left of the mean,

TABLE 3.4   **A Distribution with Two Modes: 40 and 34**

X	f
43	1
42	4
40	6
39	3
37	2
34	6
30	1

so that $\Sigma(X - \overline{X})$ (or Σx) = 0. The median is a measure of central tendency in that half of the scores of the distribution fall above the median and half fall below the median. The **mode** is a measure of central tendency in that it identifies the most typical score. That is, the mode is the score in the distribution that occurs most often. A distribution can have more than one mode if there is more than one score that occurs most often.

■   QUESTION   *What is the mode of this distribution?*

100, 101, 105, 105, 107, 108

SOLUTION   105   ■

A distribution may have two scores that occur the same number of times, and with the greatest frequency in comparison to all other scores. Consider the frequency distribution in Table 3.4. Here, the distribution has two modes: 40 and 34. This is known as **bimodal distribution** ("bi" meaning two). A distribution with a single mode is **unimodal** ("uni" meaning one). The mode is used to convey the score that most people received. The graph of a bimodal distribution has two distinct humps. The humps do not have to be the exact same height to be a bimodal distribution. Consequently, two modes can be reported, even though the number of observations associated with each modal score is not identical. In the rare case in which all scores occur with the same frequency, there is no mode.

3.7 HOW THE SHAPE OF DISTRIBUTIONS AFFECTS MEASURES OF CENTRAL TENDENCY

Chapter 2 introduced you to the notion that distributions can assume different shapes. A distribution can take any shape, and there are names for some of them (platykurtic, leptokurtic, mesokurtic, skewed, normal, etc.). The particular shape of the distribution has implications for the relative position of the mean, median, and mode. If the distribution is symmetrical, then all three measures of central tendency will be identical. Figure 3.1 depicts this fact. Note that symmetry is what is important here, not kurtosis (peakedness).

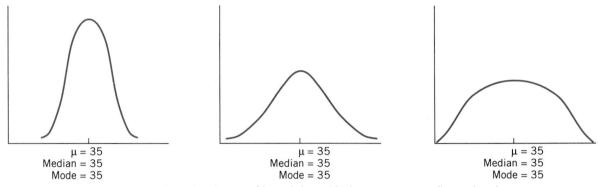

Figure 3.1 Three distributions with varying degrees of kurtosis but with the same mean, median, and mode.

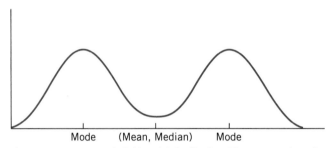

Figure 3.2 A symmetrical, bimodal distribution. The mean and median are the same.

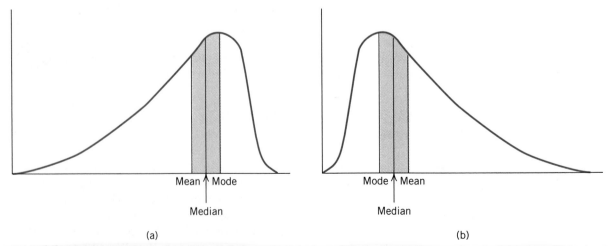

Figure 3.3 (*a*) The mean is to the left of the median in a negatively skewed distribution. (*b*) The mean is to the right of the median in a positively skewed distribution.

Can you think of an exception to this rule—that is—a symmetrical distribution in which the mean and median are the same, but the mode is different? One exception occurs with a symmetrical, bimodal distribution, as shown in Figure 3.2. Also, note that the use of the mean and median as measures of central tendency can be quite misleading with a bimodal distribution. In Figure 3.2, the mean and median lie at a point where relatively few scores are found. In this instance, the mean and median do not reflect where scores bunch.

If a distribution is skewed, then the mean, median, and mode will all be different. Figure 3.3 shows two distributions, (*a*) negatively skewed and (*b*) positively skewed. In a positively skewed distribution, the mean is to the right of the median. In a negatively skewed distribution, the mean is to the left of the median. This is because the mean is sensitive to extreme scores and is pulled in the direction of the long tail of the distribution.

3.8 WHEN TO USE THE MEAN, MEDIAN, AND MODE

Advantages of the Mean

Using the mean as an index of central tendency has several advantages. First, the mean takes into account all the scores in a distribution. For this reason, the mean usually offers a good representation of the central tendency of a distribution. Second, the mean is a stable measure of central tendency when you repeatedly sample from the same population. This feature of the mean is important when the investigator wants to use the mean of a sample to infer the mean of a population. Third, because of the preceding two reasons, the mean is used in many statistical formulas. Nonetheless, when deciding which measure of central tendency to use descriptively, there are certain circumstances in which the mean is not the most desirable measure.

Advantages of the Median

Since the mean is sensitive to extreme scores, it is not a particularly good measure of central tendency when the distribution is skewed. Another problematic situation for the mean is when a distribution is truncated. For example, suppose a researcher is interested in teaching a self-control technique for tolerating pain induced by immersing a subject's hand in freezing water. Since some subjects might keep their hands in the water a very long time, the experimenter establishes a cutoff time of 300 seconds. The exact scores of the subjects who kept their hands immersed in the water for the full 300 seconds cannot be known. Therefore, the mean, as a descriptive index, is influenced by the arbitrary cutoff time. In a similar vein, the median is usually the measure of choice for a distribution of annual incomes because no one's annual income can be less than $0.00. On the high side, there is practically no limit to annual income. Therefore, a distribution of incomes is truncated at 0 and positively skewed. Beware the article that reports "mean annual income" instead of "median annual income." Since the median is not influenced by the value of extreme scores it should be used when the distribution is skewed, truncated, or has inexact upper or lower cutoff scores. The median is almost always confined to descriptive statistics.

Advantages of the Mode

The mode is the least useful measure of central tendency. The mode of a sample is never used to infer the mode of a population. In addition, the mode ignores all the numbers in a distribution except the one score that occurs most often. The mode does have its place, however. The mode is used when one wants to convey the most typical score such as when students want to know what score on an exam was received by the most people.

There is one instance in which only the mode can be used. Recall from Chapter 2 that a nominal scale is simply, and only, a naming operation. Suppose you ask students at your university to name their favorite leisure activity. You report that 12 percent state dancing, 50 percent report television, and 38 percent claim that sports is their favorite pastime. These three activities are categories on a nominal scale. There is no way to compute a mean or median. But the mode can be declared as television. Whenever the data are in the form of *how many* (i.e., a nominal scale) rather than *how much* (i.e., an interval or ratio scale), the mode is the only appropriate measure of central tendency.

It should now be clear that each measure of central tendency has advantages and disadvantages. Bear in mind that when using descriptive statistics, the goal is to communicate the features of a distribution in as accurate a manner as possible. Further, there is no rule that says you cannot report two, or even all three measures of central tendency.

3.9   EXPERIMENTAL RESEARCH AND THE MEAN: A GLIMPSE OF THINGS TO COME

In Chapter 1, several fundamental concepts of experimentation were presented. At the most basic level, experimental designs compare the performance of groups of subjects. The means of the groups are the ultimate statistics by which research groups' performances are compared to determine objectively whether the independent variable has affected the dependent variable. Some examples of studies in which group means are compared to reach a conclusion about the effect of the independent variable on the dependent variable are presented in the following.

▶   **EXAMPLE 1**   An educational psychologist is interested in comparing the effectiveness of two teaching techniques. One group of students is exposed to educational material via a computerized teaching machine. A second group of subjects listens to lectures on the same material. The dependent variable is the amount of material learned. The mean of the amount of material learned is computed for each group. Through the use of statistical analyses (presented in later chapters), the means of the groups are compared to decide which teaching method is superior. ◀

▶ EXAMPLE 2   A social psychologist is interested in how mood states affect the amount of money people are willing to donate to a charity. In one condition, it is arranged that subjects experience a pleasant interaction with the experimenter. In another condition, subjects are treated in a cold, rude manner by the experimenter. Soon after leaving the laboratory, a person approaches the subject and asks for a donation for the homeless. The dependent variable is the amount of money donated. The means are computed for each group and compared to see if mood state influences generosity. ◀

▶ EXAMPLE 3   A child psychologist would like to evaluate two treatment techniques for helping children overcome their fear of the dark. Subjects in one group are taught to imagine themselves as a superhero on a mission during the night. Subjects in a second group are told to repeat over and over, "I'm a big boy/ girl." The dependent variable is the amount of time the child is willing to stay in a dark room. A mean is calculated for each group; the group means are compared to assess which method is more effective in helping children tolerate the dark. ◀

This chapter has presented several factors that should guide you in deciding which measure of central tendency to use when describing a distribution of scores. As you continue reading this text, you will discover that, when conducting an experiment, the mean is the statistic that serves as the vehicle for determining the influence of one variable on another.

Box 3.1 presents a study that teaches subjects how to control their heart rate. Means are computed for groups of subjects at two points in the study. Statistical techniques discussed in later chapters would use the means to compare the two groups of subjects and interpret the results.

BOX 3.1

Learning to Control Your Heart Rate

Biofeedback has become a popular treatment modality for many stress-related physical ailments. Biofeedback entails the provision of external feedback in the form of a visual display or varying auditory stimulus, which changes as some physiological response changes. Biofeedback therapy has been useful to patients who suffer from tension headaches; they learn how to control the muscle tension in their shoulders and necks. As well, hypertensive people have learned to lower their blood pressure through biofeedback. Thousands of people have learned how to relax with biofeedback training; there is little doubt that most people can achieve an impressive degree of control over their physiological responses, at least while they are attached to the biofeedback equipment. But therein lies the problem. What good is it to learn how to relax if you can only experience that state when you're hooked up to a machine? Posed as a research question, you might ask, "When subjects learn how to control one of their physiological responses, will they be able to transfer learning to control that response during their everyday activities"? It was this question that led Gloria Balague-Dahlberg (1986) to conduct the following study.

STUDY METHOD

Eighteen subjects who scored high on an anxiety questionnaire participated in the experiment. To assess the subjects' heart rate throughout the day, they were asked to wear a Holter Monitor (a device that continuously records heart rate). The participants were asked to try to keep their heart rate low while going about their usual daily routine.

Half of the subjects were seen individually for five biofeedback sessions, during which time they tried to lower their heart rate as much as possible. Although biofeedback is always conducted in a relaxed, comfortable atmosphere, Balague-Dahlberg reasoned that the transfer of learning to the natural environment would be augmented if subjects initially learned to control their heart rate in a setting filled with distractions. So with each successive session, subjects attempted to lower their heart rate amid increasing distractions. This was procedurally accomplished by having subjects sit in a hard chair while performing a series of mental tasks. As the sessions progressed, a tape of distracting noises was played: people talking, phones ringing, machines typing, and other "office noises."

Since the purpose of the study was to evaluate the carryover effects of biofeedback training, it would not be very impressive to discover that subjects who were simply told to try to lower their heart rates without biofeedback training did as well as those who received the training. Therefore, a control group was included—a group that received the same instructions but did not have experience with the biofeedback equipment. After the training phase of the experiment, all subjects' heart rates were once again monitored for a 24-hour period.

RESULTS

The data from this study are presented in the following tables. The baseline score (also called a pretest score) is the mean heart rate for the 24-hour period before training; the post-test score is the mean heart rate during the final 24-hour recording period. A graph is presented so that you can easily see the difference between the groups at each phase of the study.

The biofeedback and control groups have similar mean heart rates during baseline. This was to be expected because subjects were randomly assigned to conditions and had not yet received the different

Biofeedback Group

Subject	Baseline	Post-test
1	92	92
2	64	70
3	93	86
4	70	71
5	67	69
6	93	74
7	63	62
8	86	93
9	84	79
	$\overline{X}_{pre} = 79.11$	$\overline{X}_{post} = 77.33$

Control Group

Subject	Baseline	Post-test
10	90	95
11	92	99
12	79	82
13	85	86
14	75	73
15	82	84
16	78	73
17	80	83
18	61	63
	$\overline{X}_{pre} = 80.22$	$\overline{X}_{post} = 82.00$

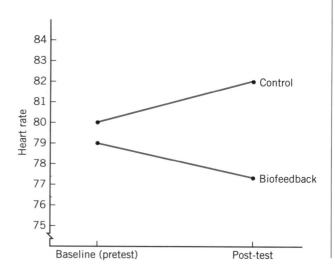

treatments. It is evident from the 24-hour post-testing data that the biofeedback subjects appear to have learned from the training and were able to keep their heart rate at a level lower than the control subjects. However, one would not want to conclude anything by visually comparing the means. At this point, the experimenter would conduct the appropriate statistical tests that would determine if these differences are unlikely to occur by chance. If these differences are unlikely to occur by chance, then conclusions could be made about the superior effects of biofeedback during training and follow-up assessment.

SUMMARY

Descriptive statistics are statistical indices that summarize and communicate basic characteristics of a distribution. Values that communicate where scores center in the distribution are called measures of central tendency. Measures that communicate the degree to which scores are spread out in a distribution are called measures of dispersion or measures of variability. Statistical values that describe the distribution characteristics of a population are called parameters; they are called statistics when the distribution is comprised of a sample of scores.

The mean is the most important measure of central tendency. Not only can it be used as a descriptive index of central tendency, but the mean is frequently used in formulas designed to test experimental hypotheses. The degree to which a score deviates from the mean is $X - \overline{X}$. A deviation score, also called an error score, is the distance a score is from the mean, symbolized as x. Therefore, $x = X - \overline{X}$. The sum of all the deviation scores equals 0. Hence,

$$\Sigma(X - \overline{X}) = \Sigma x = 0.$$

The particular shape of the distribution has implications for the relative position of the mean, median, and mode. If the distribution is symmetrical, then all three measures of central tendency will be identical. In a positively skewed distribution, the mean is to the right of the median. In a negatively skewed distribution, the mean is to the left of the median. The mean is sensitive to extreme scores and is thus pulled in the direction of the long tail of the distribution.

The mean has several advantages. First, it takes into account all the scores in a distribution. Second, it is used in many statistical formulas. Third, the mean is a stable measure of central tendency. A sample mean is usually a good estimation of the mean of a population. However, since the mean is sensitive to extreme scores, it is not a good measure of central tendency when the distribution is skewed. Using the mean as a measure of central tendency can also present a problem when the distribution is truncated—that is—when one or both ends of the distribution have inexact scores.

The median is that point in the distribution above and below which 50 percent of the scores fall. Since the median is not affected by the value of extreme scores, it should be used when the distribution is skewed or has inexact upper or lower cutoff scores. The median is almost always confined to descriptive statistics.

The mode is the least useful measure of central tendency. It is never used to estimate a population mode. In addition, the mode ignores all the numbers in a distribution except the one score that occurs most often. On the other hand, the mode is the only measure of central tendency that has any meaning when the scale of measurement is nominal.

KEY FORMULAS FOR CHAPTER 3

Population Mean

$$\mu = \frac{\Sigma X}{N}$$

(Formula 3.1a)

Sample Mean

$$\overline{X} = \frac{\Sigma X}{n}$$

(Formula 3.1b)

Weighted Mean

$$\overline{X} = \frac{n_1(\overline{X_1}) + n_2(\overline{X_2}) \cdots + \cdots n_n(\overline{X_n})}{n_1 + n_2 \cdots + \cdots n_n}$$

(Formula 3.2)

Mean of a Frequency Distribution

$$\mu \text{ or } \overline{X} = \frac{\Sigma Xf}{\Sigma f}$$

(Formula 3.3)

Median of a Frequency Distribution

$$\text{Median} = L + \left[\frac{(N/2 - F)}{f_m} \cdot b \right]$$

(Formula 3.4)

WORK PROBLEMS

1. Given a distribution in which $\overline{X}$ = median, what must be true about the shape of the distribution?

2. Identify the mean, median, and mode of these four distributions.
   a. 3,3,4,5,6,8,8,8,9   d. 1,1,3,4,4,5,9
   b. 2,4,4,4,6,7,7   e. 1,4,6,7,8,8
   c. 7,7,8,9,10,10,10

3. For distributions a and b of the previous problem, identify
   a. $\Sigma(X - \overline{X})$.   b. $\Sigma(X - \text{Median})$.   c. $\Sigma(X - \text{Mode})$.

4. What is the (a) mean and (b) mode of this frequency distribution?

X	f
12	3
10	4
9	6
7	5
4	2

5. What is the (a) mean and (b) mode of this frequency distribution?

X	f
23	1
19	3
16	4
15	4
12	2

6. What is the median of this distribution?

$$4, 5, 7, 7, 7, 7, 9, 10$$

7. What is the median of this cumulative frequency distribution?

X	f	cum f
16–20	5	30
11–15	10	25
6–10	11	15
1–5	4	4

8. What is the median of this cumulative frequency distribution?

X	f	cum f
28–30	2	16
25–27	4	14
22–24	6	10
19–21	3	4
16–18	1	1

9. What would you say about the shape of each of these distributions?
   a. mean = 24; median = 16; mode = 12
   b. mean = 123; median = 143; mode = 150
   c. mean = 6; median = 6; mode = 6
   d. mean = 19; median = 19; mode = 9 and 29
   e. mean = 56; median = 66; mode = 70
   f. mean = 48; median = 36; mode = 32

10. A national team of researchers is studying depression among women. Several samples are taken across the country and the mean score on a depression

inventory is computed for each sample. The data are summarized in the following table. What is the mean depression score for all women?

	East	Midwest	West
$\overline{X}$	12	19	14
n	46	29	32

11. A school psychologist obtains the following sample of IQ scores from a local high school. What is (a) the mean and (b) the median?

98 111 101 100 99

99 123 100 134 101

96 102 102 101 105

Work Problems for the Computer

12. The distribution in the following list is a hypothetical sample of IQ scores from the incoming freshman class at a university. From the data set, plot a histogram and compute the mean, median, and mode. In what way does the shape of this distribution influence the relative values of the three measures of central tendency?

100	100	102	135	143	94	120	114	111	87	95
109	82	94	142	100	97	100	100	101	99	98
167	176	154	100	85	88	124	180	90	96	92
149	103	102	101	104	92	103	103	105	99	92

13. The following hypothetical data set is all the scores obtained by a statistics class on a final exam. Construct a histogram, compute all the measures of central tendency, and comment on the relative values of the mean, median, and mode in the context of the shape of this population distribution.

35	35	36	50	23	16	22	23	35	35	42	43	47
13	20	9	11	2	42	23	35	40	42	47	22	19
11	8	22	19	4	8	14	28	29	32	41	40	44
2	10	38	33	9	16	22	31	30	35	35	5	20
19	23	35	44	48	34	34	29	33	36	37	37	39
12	35	33	32	33	30	30	29	35	28	39	40	4
11	49	50	35	37	37	38	33	34	35	32	30	28
13	16	17	11	19	18	15	10	35	17	40	41	42

Measures of Variability

4.1 THE IMPORTANCE OF MEASURES OF VARIABILITY

Chapter 3 discussed the three measures of central tendency: the mean, median, and mode. Although conveying central tendency is crucial to the description of a distribution, it is only part of the picture. Measures of central tendency do not provide information about the degree to which scores are spread out in a distribution. If you were asked to imagine two distributions, each with a mean of 100, it would be a mistake to automatically form a mental image of two identically shaped distributions. For instance, a platykurtic (mound-shaped) and a leptokurtic

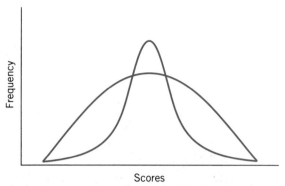

Figure 4.1   Two distributions with different degrees of variability but with the same mean, median, and mode.

(narrow-shaped) distribution may each have the same mean, but their distributions are very dissimilar. Figure 4.1 shows two very differently shaped distributions, which nonetheless have the same mean, median, and mode.

   An index, or set of indices, would be helpful in conveying something about the degree to which scores differ from one another. Measures that reflect the amount of variation in the scores of a distribution are called **measures of variability** (or **dispersion**). Several measures of variability along with their advantages and disadvantages will be discussed in this chapter.

4.2 RANGE

   The range is the simplest measure of variability to calculate. The **range** simply reflects the range of scores by defining the overall span of the scores. The range is calculated by subtracting the lowest score of the distribution from the highest score.

Range

$$\text{Range} = X_H - X_L \qquad \textit{(Formula 4.1)}$$

where,

X_H = highest score in the distribution
X_L = lowest score in the distribution

■   QUESTION   *What is the range of this distribution?*

17, 23, 42, 44, 50

SOLUTION $50 - 17 = 33$ ■

The next worked problem illustrates one of the main problems that can arise when using the range as a measure of variability.

◼ QUESTION *What is the range of this distribution?*

2, 4, 5, 7, 34

SOLUTION 32

Do you see how the range can give a misleading impression of dispersion? Most of the numbers are fairly close together, but there is one extreme score (34), which creates the impression that the distribution of scores is really spread out when the score is used to calculate the range. If you are going to use an index of dispersion that reflects the span of scores, then you need to use a measure that is less affected by just one extreme score. In other words, you should use a measure of variability that is not influenced by extreme scores at either end of the distribution. ◼

The Interquartile Range and Semi-Interquartile Range

 Every distribution can be divided into four equal sections or quartiles. A **quartile** is one-fourth of a distribution of scores. The bottom 25 percent of the distribution is the first quartile. The second quartile marks the next 25 percent of the distribution. The *total* percentage of scores below the second quartile is 50 percent. The median, in fact, is the second quartile of a distribution. The third quartile marks the point below which falls 75 percent of the distribution. The upper 25 percent of the distribution defines the fourth quartile.

 A **percentile** is a point in the distribution below which falls a certain percentage of scores. Thus, the first quartile is the 25th percentile, the second quartile is the 50th percentile, and so on.

 The **interquartile range (IQR)** is the span of scores between the first and third quartile of the distribution. Stated in terms of percentiles, the interquartile range is the span of scores between the 25th percentile and the 75th percentile. The interquartile range effectively lops off the upper 25 percent and lower 25 percent of the distribution. The two numbers that define the interquartile range bracket the middle 50 percent of the distribution (see Figure 4.2). As a consequence, the interquartile range circumvents the problem of one extreme score creating the impression of vast dispersion because one extreme score has no effect on the interquartile range.

Interquartile Range

Interquartile Range = $Q_3 - Q_1$ (Formula 4.2)

where,

Q_3 = the third quartile (75th percentile)
Q_1 = the first quartile (25th percentile)

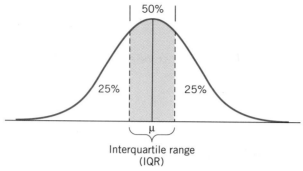

Figure 4.2 The interquartile range (IQR) marks the upper and lower 25 percent of the distribution.

The **semi-interquartile range (SIQR)** is the interquartile range, divided by 2.

> **Semi-Interquartile Range**
>
> $$\text{Semi-Interquartile Range} = \frac{Q_3 - Q_1}{2} \quad \textit{(Formula 4.3)}$$

Like the IQR, the SIQR is more stable than the simple range because it is unaffected by an extreme score. The SIQR has an important quality: The median, plus and minus the SIQR, identifies the *exact* middle 50 percent of the distribution. However, this statement only holds for a bell-shaped, normal distribution. If the distribution is skewed, the median, plus and minus the SIQR *approximates* the middle 50

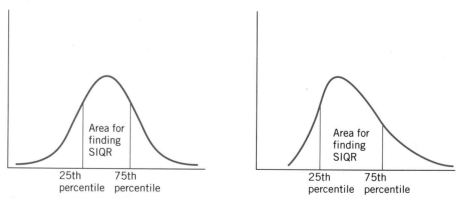

Figure 4.3 A normal distribution and a positively skewed distribution with the areas that are used to determine the SIQR indicated.

percent of the distribution. Figure 4.3 depicts the area of a normal and skewed distribution that is used for determining the SIQR. Note that the area used to determine the SIQR is slightly larger when the distribution is skewed. Although neither the IQR or SIQR are affected by a single extreme score, they are influenced by whether or not the distribution has many extreme scores. A skewed distribution has many extreme scores.

■   QUESTION   *The hypothetical "Livonia Community College Aptitude Test" has a median of 100. The score that is the 75th percentile is 130 and the score that is the 25th percentile is 70. What are the IQR and SIQR?*

SOLUTION

$$IQR = Q_3 - Q_1 = 130 - 70 = \mathbf{60}$$

$$SIQR = \frac{Q_3 - Q_1}{2} = \frac{60}{2} = \mathbf{30}$$

Assuming the scores of the aptitude test are normally distributed, the middle 50 percent of the distribution is between: $100 + 30 = \mathbf{130}$ and $100 - 30 = \mathbf{70}$. ■

The IQR and SIQR are commonly presented, along with other descriptive statistics, when conveying the distribution characteristics of standardized psychological or intellectual tests (e.g., the Wechsler Adult Intelligence Scale). The range can be a misleading measure of variability because just one extreme score can create a misleading impression of tremendous dispersion. The interquartile range obviates this problem, but in the process, sacrifices half the distribution (the top 25 percent and the bottom 25 percent). The IQR and SIQR do not provide a complete picture of the variability of a distribution. A useful measure of variability would be one that takes into consideration the magnitude of every score. These are the measures of variability that have become most valuable to researchers.

4.3   MEAN DEVIATION

Each raw score in a distribution stands some distance from the mean. This distance is called a deviation, or error ($X - \mu$ or x). The degree to which scores deviate from the mean is a direct reflection of the variability of a distribution. Consider these two distributions:

Distribution A: 11, 12, 13, 14, 15, 16, 17 $\mu = 14$
Distribution B: 5, 8, 11, 14, 17, 20, 23 $\mu = 14$

The mean of each distribution is 14. However, Distribution B shows more variation than Distribution A. In other words, in relation to the mean, there is an overall greater amount of deviation among the scores with respect to the mean. But how can you arrive at an index that reflects overall deviation? You cannot simply sum the deviation scores of each distribution because Σx always equals 0. This is because the negative deviation scores from below the mean *balance* the positive deviation scores from above the mean. Taking the absolute value of each deviation score will remove negative signs and free you from this problem. Taking the average of the absolute values of all deviation scores will give you a measure of the degree to which the raw scores of a distribution deviate from the mean. This arithmetic manipulation is called the **mean deviation.**

✓

Class :
$$MD = \frac{\Sigma \, |X - \overline{X}|}{N}$$

.

Mean Deviation

$$MD = \frac{\Sigma |X - \mu|}{N} \qquad \textit{(Formula 4.4)}$$

■   QUESTION   *What are the mean deviations for these two distributions?*

	Distribution A				Distribution B		
Scores	μ	$(X - \mu)$	$|X - \mu|$	*Scores*	μ	$X - \mu$	$|X - \mu|$
11	14	-3	3	5	14	-9	9
12	14	-2	2	8	14	-6	6
13	14	-1	1	11	14	-3	3
14	14	0	0	14	14	0	0
15	14	1	1	17	14	3	3
16	14	2	2	20	14	6	6
17	14	3	3	23	14	9	9
$N = 7$			$\Sigma|X - \mu| = 12$	$N = 7$			$\Sigma|X - \mu| = 36$

SOLUTION

$$MD = \frac{\Sigma|X - \mu|}{N} = \frac{12}{7} = 1.71 \qquad MD = \frac{\Sigma|X - \mu|}{N} = \frac{36}{7} = 5.14$$ ■

The mean deviation accurately represents the degree of dispersion of a distribution. Any formula that uses deviation scores as a measure of variability has the advantage of using *all* the scores of the distribution, unlike the various measures of range. Also, one extreme score will not have a large effect on the mean deviation. However, the mean deviation has some undesirable properties, due to the use of absolute values, which preclude it from being used in formulas that will be discussed in subsequent chapters.[1] What is needed is a formula such as the variable, which

---

[1] When interpreting scores in a distribution, there is no mathematically precise relation between the location of the scores and the mean deviation. Another problem with the mean deviation has to do with estimating the variability of a population from a sample of scores. The mean deviation of a sample does not bear a consistent relation to the mean deviation of the population from which the sample was drawn. Since much of the field of statistics involves using samples to infer the characteristics of populations, the mean deviation is not used.

capitalizes on the conceptual basis of deviation scores as a measure of variability, but does not have the disadvantages that arise when using absolute values.

4.4 THE VARIANCE

One way to remove the negative signs of deviation scores is to take the absolute value which is done in the mean deviation. Another method to remove negative signs, is to square each deviation score, since a negative number multiplied by another negative number yields a positive number. This rather minor change defines the difference between the average deviation and what is called the variance of a distribution. The **variance** of a distribution is the average of the squared deviations. The formula for the variance of a *population* is slightly different than the formula for a *sample* variance.

Population Variance

$$\sigma^2 = \frac{\Sigma(X - \mu)^2}{N}$$

(Formula 4.5)

where,

σ^2 (pronounced "sigma squared;" σ is the
    Greek lower case of Σ) = the symbol for the population variance
    X = a raw score
    μ = the population mean
    N = the number of scores in the population

Sample Variance

$$s^2 = \frac{\Sigma(X - \overline{X})^2}{n - 1}$$

(Formula 4.6)

where,

    s^2 = symbol for sample variance
    $\overline{X}$ = the sample mean
    n = the number of scores in the distribution

The Sample Variance as an Unbiased Estimate of the Population Variance

A sample is a subset of scores from a population distribution. Researchers are always interested in the characteristics of a population; they use a sample to make inferences about a population. Suppose you want to know the mean of a population but a sample of scores from the population is all that is available. The best estimate of the mean of the population is the mean of the sample. Usually your estimate will be off; rarely is the sample mean identical to the population mean. Sometimes the estimate will be larger than the population mean and sometimes the estimate will be smaller. However, the formula for the sample mean, $\overline{X} = \Sigma X/n$, provides an unbiased estimate of the population mean. To understand the notion of a biased versus an unbiased estimate of a population parameter, consider the following exercise.

Suppose you take 100 samples from a large population and compute the mean of each sample. Let's assume that you actually know the population mean to be 75. Some of the sample means will be 75, but most of the sample means will be either larger or smaller than 75. If the formula for the sample mean were a *biased* estimate of the population mean, you would find that most of the sample means would be either larger or smaller than the population mean, depending on the direction of the bias. The fact that the sample means do not tend to be consistently larger or smaller than the population mean indicates that the mean of a single sample is an *unbiased* estimate of the population mean.[2]

In comparing the formulas for the variance of a population and a sample, note that the denominator of the sample variance is $n - 1$, instead of N.

<table>
<tr><th>Population Variance</th><th>Sample Variance</th></tr>
<tr><td>$$\sigma^2 = \frac{\Sigma(X - \mu)^2}{N}$$</td><td>$$s^2 = \frac{\Sigma(X - \overline{X})^2}{n - 1}$$</td></tr>
</table>

Suppose that you conduct the same exercise with variances that was conducted with means. Take 100 samples and compute the variance of each sample using the formula for the *population variance* (Formula 4.5). Note: you would normally use the sample formula. Assume that you know the true population variance. What you would discover is that, of the 100 computed variances, most would be smaller than the true population variance. If you were to apply the *population* formula for variance to a single *sample* of scores, and then use that value as an estimate of the population variance, you would most likely *underestimate* the size of the population variance. Dividing by $n - 1$ provides a correction so that the formula for the variance of a sample is an unbiased estimate of the population variance.

Figure 4.4 explains why the $n - 1$ correction factor is necessary when estimating the variance of a population. In this figure, the scores of the population

---

[2] Technically speaking, the concepts of *biased* and *unbiased* estimates of a population parameter apply to "the long run," which refers to infinity, not, as in this example, to 100, or any other specific number of samples. The importance of the concept of infinite sampling will be developed in subsequent chapters.

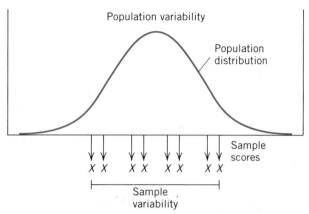

Figure 4.4   The variability of a sample of scores will tend to be less than the variability of the population from which the scores are taken. So that the variance of a sample is an unbiased estimate of the population variance, a correction factor ($n - 1$) is used in the denominator of the formula for the variance of a sample.

assume a normal distribution. Since most of the population scores are found in the middle of the population, a random sample of, for instance, eight scores, would likely come from the middle of the population distribution. Thus, the spread of sample scores is not as spread out (variable) as the spread of population scores. For this reason, the variance of a sample will tend to underestimate the variance of a population. Placing $n - 1$ in the denominator of the sample variance formula effectively increases the value of the sample variance and provides an unbiased estimate of the population variance.

■   QUESTION   *What is the variance of this sample of scores?*

$$3, 4, 6, 8, 9$$

SOLUTION

X	$\overline{X}$	$X - \overline{X}$	$(X - \overline{X})^2$
3	6	-3	9
4	6	-2	4
6	6	0	0
8	6	2	4
9	6	3	9
30			26

$$s^2 = \frac{\Sigma(X - \overline{X})^2}{n - 1} = \frac{26}{4} = \mathbf{6.50}$$

■

Equivalent Formulas for the Variance

If you were to take a random sample of introductory-level statistics textbooks, and turn to the chapters covering measures of variability, you would be surprised, and maybe confused, by the many different formulas that can be used to compute the variance of a distribution. All of the formulas will give you the same answer (provided you note the distinction between a population and sample of scores). Several formulas will be offered for the variance for two reasons. First, one formula may be easier to use when performing hand calculations with raw data and a different formula may be helpful in reminding you of the conceptual basis of variance. Second, by presenting a few formulas for the variance, you will be able to easily make the transition to other textbooks. Formulas 4.5 and 4.6 (page 75) are the basic formulas for the variances of the population and sample. They are called definitional formulas. In Chapter 3, you learned that a single score minus the mean, $X - \mu$, can be expressed as x, a deviation score. Therefore, Formulas 4.5 and 4.6 can be written as Formulas 4.7 and 4.8, respectively. These formulas are called deviation score formulas.

The Deviation Score Formulas

Population Variance   *Sample Variance*

$$\sigma^2 = \frac{\Sigma x^2}{N} \qquad\qquad s^2 = \frac{\Sigma x^2}{n - 1}$$

(Formula 4.7)   *(Formula 4.8)*

The numerators of both sets of variance formulas direct you to sum all the squared deviation scores. For this reason, the numerator of a variance formula is referred to as the **sum of squares** (or **SS**). Hence, $SS = \Sigma(X - \mu)^2$ or $\Sigma(X - \overline{X})^2 = \Sigma x^2$. Substituting SS in the numerator of the population and sample formulas for the variance defines the sum of squares manner of expression.

The Sum of Squares Formulas

Population Variance   *Sample Variance*

$$\sigma^2 = \frac{SS}{N} \qquad\qquad s^2 = \frac{SS}{n - 1}$$

(Formula 4.9)   *(Formula 4.10)*

When working with raw scores, a **computational** (or **raw score**) **formula** eases the task. Formulas 4.11 and 4.12 are used to compute the population and sample variances, respectively. When using a computational formula, pay close attention to the difference between ΣX^2 and $(\Sigma X)^2$! The ΣX^2 is found by first squaring each raw score and then summing all squared values. The quantity $(\Sigma X)^2$ requires that you first sum the raw scores and then square the final total.

> **The Computational Formulas**
>
> *Population Variance*
>
> $$\sigma^2 = \frac{\Sigma X^2 - [(\Sigma X)^2/N]}{N}$$ (Formula 4.11)
>
> *Sample Variance*
>
> $$s^2 = \frac{\Sigma X^2 - [(\Sigma X)^2/n]}{n - 1}$$ (Formula 4.12)

Keep in mind that all of the sample formulas will lead to the same answer, with any discrepancies accounted for by rounding errors. And, of course, all of the population formulas will yield the same answer. Table 4.1 presents all of the formulas for the variance.

TABLE 4.1 **Several Equivalent Expressions of the Population and Sample Variances**

VARIANCE FORMULAS	
Population Variance	*Sample Variance*
Definitional Formulas	
$\sigma^2 = \dfrac{\Sigma(X - \mu)^2}{N}$	$s^2 = \dfrac{\Sigma(X - \overline{X})^2}{n - 1}$
(Formula 4.5)	(Formula 4.6)
Deviation Score Formulas	
$\sigma^2 = \dfrac{\Sigma x^2}{N}$	$s^2 = \dfrac{\Sigma x^2}{n - 1}$
(Formula 4.7)	(Formula 4.8)
Sum of Squares Formulas	
$\sigma^2 = \dfrac{SS}{N}$	$s^2 = \dfrac{SS}{n - 1}$
(Formula 4.9)	(Formula 4.10)
Computational Formulas[a]	
$\sigma^2 = \dfrac{\Sigma X^2 - [(\Sigma X)^2/N]}{N}$	$s^2 = \dfrac{\Sigma X^2 - [(\Sigma X)^2/n]}{n - 1}$
(Formula 4.11)	(Formula 4.12)

[a] Use these two formulas when working from raw data.

■ **QUESTION** *Use the computational formulas to determine the variance of this distribution when it is a sample of scores and when it is a population of scores.*

X	X²
2	4
4	16
5	25
7	49
9	81
$\Sigma X = 27$	$X^2 = 175$

SOLUTION

Sample Formula

$$s^2 = \frac{\Sigma X^2 - [(\Sigma X)^2/n]}{n-1}$$

$$s^2 = \frac{175 - [(27)^2/5]}{5-1}$$

$$= \frac{175 - (729/5)}{5-1}$$

$$= \frac{175 - 145.80}{4}$$

$$= \frac{29.20}{4}$$

$$s^2 = \mathbf{7.30}$$

If the distribution were a sample of scores, the variance would be 7.30. If the scores were a population, you would use the following formula.

Population Formula

$$\sigma^2 = \frac{\Sigma X^2 - [(\Sigma X)^2/N]}{N}$$

$$\sigma^2 = \frac{175 - (729/5)}{5}$$

$$= \frac{175 - 145.80}{5}$$

$$= \frac{29.20}{5}$$

$$\sigma^2 = \mathbf{5.84}$$

Viewing the scores as a population, the variance is 5.84.   ■

BOX
4.1

The Substantive Importance of the Variance

Measures of variation are essential indices for describing the degree of dispersion among scores of a distribution. Variance, and its square root, standard deviation, can both be used as descriptive indices of dispersion; however, standard deviation is the more useful index because it is stated in the original units of the measured variable. Yet variance is still used in many statistical formulas designed to answer research questions.

In experimental research, comparisons are typically made between the means of the experimental and control groups. Evaluating two methods for improving communication skills would entail a comparison between the group *means* of some measure of communication. Discovering ways to help children overcome their shyness would involve comparing *mean ratings* of shyness after different treatments. In other words, in the experimental context, investigators examine group means to determine the effect of the independent

variable on the dependent variable. However, sometimes between-group differences in *variability* can reveal an important facet of the phenomenon under investigation. An example in which variability has substantive importance comes from the literature on aging. Chronological age is intrinsically a poor predictor of almost any measure of psychological functioning (Woods and Rusin, 1988). However, as an investigator compares different age groups, he or she would find that the within-group variability—on a number of measures—increases with age (Krauss, 1980). In other words, older individuals are more unlike each other than are younger individuals. When conducting research with older people, careful attention must be paid to individual differences. A treatment that is ineffective for some older people may prove highly beneficial to other older people.

Sometimes an investigator will learn something important about a phenomenon when the dispersion of scores is examined. Box 4.1 presents findings in which the variability of scores reflects an interesting aspect of aging.

4.5 THE STANDARD DEVIATION

The variance measure of dispersion is especially important because it is used in many statistical formulas. However, it is not the best measure when you want to communicate the variability of a distribution. This is because the variance is a squared value; it is *not* stated in the original units of the measured variable. For example, if someone told you that a sample mean IQ was found to be 100 and the *sample* variance was 225, you would wonder if there was a small, medium, or large amount of variation among the scores. The **standard deviation** is the square root of the variance. The definitional, deviation score, sum of squares, and computational formulas for the standard deviation are identical to the formulas for the variance, *except the formulas for the standard deviation are under square*

TABLE 4.2   Several Equivalent Expressions of the
Population and Sample Standard Deviations

STANDARD DEVIATION FORMULAS

Population Standard Deviation	Sample Standard Deviation
Definitional Formulas	
$\sigma = \sqrt{\dfrac{\Sigma(X - \mu)^2}{N}}$	$s = \sqrt{\dfrac{\Sigma(X - \overline{X})^2}{n - 1}}$
Deviation Score Formulas	
$\sigma = \sqrt{\dfrac{\Sigma x^2}{N}}$	$s = \sqrt{\dfrac{\Sigma x^2}{n - 1}}$
Sum of Squares Formulas	
$\sigma = \sqrt{\dfrac{SS}{N}}$	$s = \sqrt{\dfrac{SS}{n - 1}}$
Computational Formulas	
$\sigma = \sqrt{\dfrac{\Sigma X^2 - [(\Sigma X)^2/N]}{N}}$	$s = \sqrt{\dfrac{\Sigma X^2 - [(\Sigma X)^2/n]}{n - 1}}$

root signs. To solve the standard deviation, simply calculate the variance and take its square root. The symbols for the population and sample standard deviation are σ and s, respectively. Therefore, using the distribution in the preceding worked example, the sample and population standard deviations would be

$$s = \sqrt{7.30} = \textbf{2.70} \quad \text{and} \quad \sigma = \sqrt{5.84} = \textbf{2.42}$$

Table 4.2 presents the same formulas found in Table 4.1. Now, however, each formula is under a square root sign, thus defining them as standard deviation formulas.

The Standard Deviation and the Normal Curve

In Chapter 5, much more will be said about the characteristics and importance of the normal distribution. For now, recall that one distribution that has a symmetrical, bell-shaped form is referred to as a normal distribution. When depicted on a graph, a normal distribution is called a normal curve. The standard deviation has a very attractive property when the scores of the distribution are normally distributed. This property is one reason the standard deviation is so useful in describing the variability of a distribution. In a **normal distribution** (or **normal curve**) approximately 68 percent of the total number of scores lie between one standard deviation below and one standard deviation above the mean. If a distribution of IQ scores has a mean of 100 and a standard deviation of 15, then one standard deviation equals 15 IQ points. Therefore, 68 percent of the scores fall between

BOX 4.2

The Origins of the Standard Deviation

Karl Pearson proposed the standard deviation as a measure of dispersion in 1894. Before Pearson, statisticians used a closely related index of variability: the *probable error* (pe). Approximately 68 percent of the scores of a distribution fall between plus and minus one standard deviation of the mean. The formula for the probable error is:

$$pe = .6745 \sqrt{\frac{\Sigma(X - \mu)^2}{N}}$$

The mean, plus and minus one probable error, includes 50 percent of the scores of the distribution. Pearson believed that multiplying by .6745 was an unnecessary step in the calculation. Moreover, as a measure of variability, there was no compelling advantage to the probable error; both the standard deviation and the probable error reflect the degree to which a distribution of scores is spread out. Pearson dropped the multiplier, named the new index of variability *standard deviation*, and symbolized it as σ. The probable error is still used, although seldomly. Remember that in a normal distribution, the mean and median are the same. The semi-interquartile range is the index of variability that marks the middle 50 percent of the distribution when it is added to and subtracted from the median.

115 (100 + 15) and 85 (100 − 15). Remember that the standard deviation is stated in the original units of the scale. In this case, one standard deviation is 15 IQ points. Also, the standard deviation, and for that matter, any measure of variability, can never be a negative number. Variation is always based on distance, whether it is the span of scores or the average distance scores are from the mean; there is no such thing as a negative distance.

Box 4.2 presents the origins of the use of the standard deviation as a measure of variability.

4.6 SIMPLE TRANSFORMATIONS AND THEIR EFFECT ON THE MEAN AND VARIANCE

As recently as 25 years ago, researchers analyzed data by hand. A single, advanced statistical analysis could literally take an entire week to complete. That same analysis is now performed in a few seconds with a desktop computer. Sometimes the scores of a distribution are very small—for instance—.026 or .001, or very large, 10,054, 11,123, and so forth. To make the numbers easier to work with, researchers transform the numbers; for example the number .026 might be transformed to 26 or the number 10,054 might be transformed to 54. Performing simple arithmetic operations on a distribution of numbers has predictable effects on the mean and

TABLE   4.3   The Effect on the Mean and Variance when the Scores of the Distribution are Transformed by the Four Basic Arithmetic Operations

Original Scores		+ 100	− 100	× 100	÷ 100
μ	105.5	205.50	5.50	10,550	1.055
σ^2	9.67	9.67	9.67	96,700	.000967

variance:

1. Adding a constant to every number of a distribution will increase the mean of the distribution by the value of the constant. For example, if the mean is .01, adding 10 to every score changes the mean to 10.01.
2. Subtracting a constant from every number of the distribution reduces the mean by the value of the constant. If the mean is 1003, subtracting 1000 from every score will change the mean to 3.
3. Adding or subtracting a constant will *not* have an effect on the variance. This is because adding or subtracting a constant does not alter the relative positions among the numbers. The variance is based on the relation each number has to the mean of the distribution. That relation is not altered when adding or subtracting a constant.
4. When each number of a distribution is multiplied or divided by a constant, the mean will change by the value of the constant.
5. Multiplying or dividing each number by a constant *will* change the variance. This is because multiplication and division will change the relative spacing among the numbers. For example, multiplying every number by 10 will increase the variance by 10^2 (100). (Remember that the variance is in squared units of the original scale.) Dividing each number of the distribution by 10 will reduce the variance by whatever the original variance is, divided by 10^2.

Table 4.3 shows the effect on the means and variances when each score of a distribution is transformed by the four basic arithmetic operations.

4.7   DECIDING WHICH MEASURE OF VARIABILITY TO USE

Descriptive statistics are used to communicate important characteristics of a distribution of scores. The two most important features of a distribution are the place in the distribution that scores tend to center and the extent to which the scores are dispersed. The following principle guides the selection of which descriptive statistic to report: The statistic should provide an easily understandable and accurate depiction of the distribution. Some of the features of a distribution that should influence your decision about which measure of variability to report follow.

Extreme Scores

Just one or two extreme scores in a distribution can greatly affect most of the measures of variability. As a consequence, any measure of variability that is influenced by extreme scores will convey a misleading impression of the overall degree of dispersion among the scores of the distribution. The range is the statistic most sensitive to extreme scores. Since only the highest and lowest scores of a distribution are used to compute the range, one odd score can lead to an inaccurate view of dispersion.

The interquartile and semi-interquartile range (IQR and SIQR) are not influenced by a *small* number of extreme scores, and thus offer a more reasonable statement of variability when extreme scores occur in the distribution. The variance and standard deviation are also affected by extreme scores. Since both measures use squared deviations, an extreme score that is, by definition, a great distance from the mean, will have a disproportionate effect on the variance. You must exercise caution when using the variance and standard deviation as measures of variability when there are extreme scores. It is a shame that one extreme score can throw off the measures of variability. Researchers have adopted the attitude that one extreme score is probably a fluke; therefore, they will consider discarding that score so that the range, variance, and standard deviation can all provide accurate indices of variability. But what if there are several extreme scores? There is no justification for discarding several scores. If there are many extreme scores, which is true in skewed distributions, the variability of a distribution is best described by the interquartile or semi-interquartile range statistic.

An Arbitrary End Point to the Distribution

Consider a study about self-control and pain tolerance (Grimm and Kanfer, 1976). Subjects were asked to place their hands in ice water and were told that they could remove them whenever they wanted. The number of seconds that the subjects kept their hands in the water was the dependent variable. The researchers found that some of the subjects did not remove their hands from the water, and would have continued to keep their hands in it indefinitely. The researchers decided to terminate the task at 300 seconds, which was an arbitrary end point for the high side of the distribution.

Another example of an arbitrary end point to a distribution occurs when subjects are asked to complete a problem-solving task. What score should be assigned to subjects who can't figure out the answer? At some point the researcher has to stop them and assign a score, which is supposedly the time it took them to complete the problem-solving task. These situations present a problem when you would like to describe the variability of the distribution. Since, in these two examples, the highest score is arbitrary, any measure of variability that relies on these scores is also arbitrary. The IQR and SIQR are relatively impervious to arbitrary cutoffs at the tail end of a distribution, provided there are not too many arbitrary scores.

Common Practice

Every author of an introductory-level textbook on statistics is obligated to discuss the pros and cons of various measures of variability. This time-honored tradition is adhered to here. It is instructive for you to learn about the type of discussions that routinely occur among researchers when they talk about data. These discussions occur in dissertation meetings, between research assistants and their advisors, and in research seminars, to name just a few occasions. The following comments will be confined to the aspect of discussions that have to do with describing the variability of data.

It is extremely rare to hear someone report the IQR or SIQR when describing a distribution. The main reason is that researchers, at least in psychology, do not have an "intuitive feel" for these measures. Telling a research colleague that the SIQR of your data is 6 will likely produce a blank stare. The range, despite all its vulnerabilities, is often stated because it tells the listener the span of obtained scores. However, in most instances, the range is communicated by stating the highest and lowest scores in the distribution, *not* the actual range between the scores. The variance, despite its essential role in statistical formulas, is never stated among researchers because there is no "intuitive feel" to the variance since this value is in squared units.

The most commonly reported measure of variability is the standard deviation, which is the square root of the variance, and is stated in the original units of the measured variable. Therefore, if someone says, "The mean was 50," you can bet that the first question asked is, "What was the standard deviation?" Moreover, articles in scientific journals often include a table of means and standard deviations. You will rarely see a table of means and variances.

Although the standard deviation is the most popular measure of variability, do not ignore all the other measures of variability. Indeed, researchers may err in relying too much on the standard deviation as *the* measure of dispersion when describing a distribution. It is the responsibility of the researcher who has the most knowledge of the characteristics of the data to choose the best measures of variability to convey an accurate picture of the degree to which a distribution varies. Nowhere is it written that you can only report one measure of variability. In general, you should feel free to communicate the overall characteristics of a distribution by reporting more than one measure of central tendency and more than one measure of variability.

SUMMARY

Measures that reflect the amount of variation in the scores of a distribution are called measures of dispersion or measures of variability. The range defines the overall span of scores. It is calculated by subtracting the lowest score of the distribution from the highest score. The interquartile range (IQR) avoids the problem of one extreme score creating the impression of vast dispersion—a problem that can occur when using the range. The interquartile range is the span of scores between the first and third quartile (the 25th and 75th percentile). The semi-interquartile range (SIQR) is the interquartile range divided by 2. In a normal distribution, the median, plus and minus the SIQR, will exactly define the middle 50 percent of the distribution. If the distribution is skewed, the SIQR approximates the middle 50 percent of the distribution.

Taking the average of the absolute values of all deviation scores will provide a measure of the degree to which the raw scores of a distribution deviate from the mean. This is called the mean deviation. The variance of a distribution is the average of the squared deviations. The population variance formula is used when the scores represent a population. If your intent is to infer the variance of a population, based on a sample of scores, then the formula for sample variance is used. The sample variance provides an unbiased estimate of the population variance.

The variance measure of dispersion is important because it takes into consideration all the scores of a distribution, and is used in many statistical formulas. It is not, however, the best descriptive index of variability. This is because the variance is a squared value; it is not stated in the original units of the measured variable. The standard deviation is the square root of the variance. As a descriptive index, the standard deviation improves on the variance by converting the variance to the original units of the measured variable. The standard deviation has a very useful function when the scores of the distribution are normally distributed. In a normal distribution, approximately 68 percent of the total number of scores lie between one standard deviation below and one standard deviation above the mean.

Transforming the original scores of a distribution by the four basic arithmetic operations will have a predictable effect on the mean and variance. Transforming original scores will exactly alter the mean by the constant and the arithmetic operation used to transform the scores. Adding a constant to and subtracting a constant from each score will have no effect on the variance since the relative position of scores to the mean of the distribution is unaffected. Multiplication and division alter the variance by the square of the constant and the arithmetic operation performed.

Deciding the most appropriate measure of variability to use depends on various features of the distribution. Factors such as extreme scores, sample size, common practices, arbitrary endpoints of a distribution, and the importance of a stable estimate of the population variability will influence a researcher's decision as to which measure of variability is most desirable.

In experimental research, the statistic of primary interest is the mean; comparisons are made between the means of the experimental and control groups. Sometimes, however, between-group differences in *variability* can reveal an important aspect of the phenomenon under investigation.

KEY FORMULAS FOR CHAPTER 4

Range

$$\text{Range} = X_H - X_L \qquad \textit{(Formula 4.1)}$$

Interquartile Range

$$\text{Interquartile Range} = Q_3 - Q_1 \qquad \textit{(Formula 4.2)}$$

Semi-Interquartile Range

$$\text{Semi-Interquartile Range} = \frac{Q_3 - Q_1}{2}$$

(Formula 4.3)

Mean Deviation

$$MD = \frac{\Sigma |X - \bar{X}|}{N}$$

$$MD = \frac{\Sigma |X - \mu|}{N}$$

(Formula 4.4)

Definitional Formulas

Population Variance   *Sample Variance*

$$\sigma^2 = \frac{\Sigma(X - \mu)^2}{N}$$ *(Formula 4.5)*

$$s^2 = \frac{\Sigma(X - \bar{X})^2}{n - 1}$$ *(Formula 4.6)*

Deviation Score Formulas

Population Variance   *Sample Variance*

$$\sigma^2 = \frac{\Sigma x^2}{N}$$ *(Formula 4.7)*

$$s^2 = \frac{\Sigma x^2}{n - 1}$$ *(Formula 4.8)*

The Sum of Squares Formulas

Population Variance   *Sample Variance*

$$\sigma^2 = \frac{SS}{N}$$ *(Formula 4.9)*

$$s^2 = \frac{SS}{n - 1}$$ *(Formula 4.10)*

Computational Formulas

Population Variance

$$\sigma^2 = \frac{\Sigma X^2 - [(\Sigma X)^2/N]}{N}$$

(Formula 4.11)

Sample Variance

$$s^2 = \frac{\Sigma X^2 - [(\Sigma X)^2/n]}{n - 1}$$

(Formula 4.12)

Any formula for the standard deviation is the square root of the variance formula.

WORK PROBLEMS

1. Given two samples, one in which $n = 36$, the other where $n = 60$, which distribution would have the larger variance? Which sample is likely to have the larger range?

2. Assume two samples: $\overline{X}_1 = 78$ and $\overline{X}_2 = 155$. Which sample would have the larger variance?

3. A school psychologist wants to inform a teacher about the mean and standard deviation of the students' IQ scores. Calculate the mean and standard deviation of the scores. Assume scores are a sample.

    IQ scores: 98, 111, 102, 100, 101, 109

4. Calculate the range, variance, and standard deviation of this sample of scores.

    2, 4, 7, 4, 8, 5, 1, 4, 4, 5

5. A researcher who uses heart rate as the dependent variable finds that the distribution of heart rate scores is positively skewed. The 75th percentile is found to be a heart rate of 111 and the 25th percentile is found to be 81. The second quartile is 101.
    a. Compute the IQR.
    b. Compute the SIQR.

6. For each situation, specify whether you should use s or σ.

    a. A coach is interested in the variability of his basketball team's scores over the season. σ
    b. A clinician is evaluating a new treatment for sexual dysfunctions. s
    c. A teacher is interested in providing feedback to students about the class' performance on the midterm exam.
    d. A manufacturer takes a sample of light bulbs to estimate the variability of their life.

7. Calculate the variance and standard deviation of these scores. Assume that they are *not* to be used to infer the degree of variability in the population.

    22, 32, 21, 20, 19, 15, 23

8. Which distribution of <u>sample</u> scores has the larger variance?

    Distribution A: 2, 4, 5, 1, 1, 2, 3, 9
    Distribution B: 34, 39, 34, 35, 33, 32

9. A distribution has a mean of 500 and a standard deviation of 100. Assume that the distribution is negatively skewed. Given what you have learned in this chapter, can you determine the percentage of scores that fall between 400 and 600? If so, what is it?

10. What is the main disadvantage in using the range as a measure of dispersion?

11. As a descriptive statistic, is the variance or the standard deviation a better index of variability? Why?

12. What is the standard deviation of this population of scores?

    9, 7, 10, 14, 12, 9, 16, 13, 11

13. If a distribution has a $\overline{X} = 4.5$ and $s^2 = 1.6$, what would be the $\overline{X}$ and s^2 if all the raw scores have 10 added to them?

14. Refer to Chapter 3, Box 3.1. Compute the standard deviations of the experimental and control groups, for each phase of the study.
    a. Baseline
    b. Post-testing

15. An experiment is conducted to evaluate the effectiveness of two different attitude change techniques. The dependent variable is attitudes toward immigrants. In the following table, higher numbers reflect more positive attitudes.

Technique A		Technique B	
Pretest	*Post-test*	*Pretest*	*Post-test*
3	7	2	4
4	4	3	2
5	6	4	5
2	5	3	3

Technique A

Calculate:
a. Pretest $\overline{X}$ b. Pretest s^2 c. Pretest s
d. Post-test $\overline{X}$ e. Post-test s^2 f. Post-test s

Technique B

Calculate:
a. Pretest $\overline{X}$ b. Pretest s^2 c. Pretest s
d. Post-test $\overline{X}$ e. Post-test s^2 f. Post-test s

16. Complete the following table. $\mu = 50$ and $\sigma = 5$. The constants specified are used to transform the scores of the distribution.

$X + 10$	$X - 10$	$X \cdot 10$	$X \div 10$
$\mu = ?$	$\mu = ?$	$\mu = ?$	$\mu = ?$
$\sigma^2 = ?$	$\sigma^2 = ?$	$\sigma^2 = ?$	$\sigma^2 = ?$

Work Problems for the Computer

Determine the mean, variance, standard deviation, and range for each of the following sample distributions.

17. Scores:

3	5	3	7	9	10	2	12	15
1	8	9	6	4	11	1	11	10
1	4	5	5	3	10	9	13	14

18. Scores:

102	100	99	81	75	113	100
106	114	82	79	88	111	104
100	106	85	99	82	101	100

19. Scores:

1020	1000	990	810	750	1130	1000
1060	1140	820	790	880	1110	1040
1000	1060	850	990	820	1010	1000

The Normal Curve and Transformations: Percentiles, z Scores, and T Scores

5.1   PERCENTILE RANK

How did you do on your last exam? This simple question raises the issue of how best to convey a person's level of performance. Stating that you received a score of 35 is not helpful because it fails to provide the context of the score. Stating that your 35 was a B is better because it provides a rough indication of how you did with respect to some absolute standard, or how you did relative to the rest of the class. Stating the mean of the distribution, and perhaps the lowest and highest scores of the distribution, would be helpful in defining the context of the number 35. However, providing the letter grade or descriptive statistics will not *specifically* locate a single score in the distribution. Locating the score based on its *relation*

the Score

o the other scores* of the distribution is the best way to communicate the meaning of a grade of 35.

One method used to specify the location a score has in a distribution involves transforming a score to a percentile rank. The **percentile rank** of a particular score states the percentage of scores below that score. For instance, if 54 percent of the scores of the distribution fall below the number 35, the percentile rank is 54 percent. When a score is identified by its percentile rank, that score is referred to as a *percentile*. Thus, the number 35 is the 54th percentile. Percentile rank is stated in terms of percentages; the percentile refers to the score.

There are two types of questions that you will learn to answer. Generally stated, the first question is, "What is the percentile rank of X?" The second question is, "What score is at a given percentile?" Each of these questions is answered in the following section.

Computing the Percentile Rank of a Score

The formula for transforming a score to its percentile rank is very easy to use.

Formula for Finding the Percentile Rank of X

$$\text{Percentile rank of } X = \left(\frac{B + 1/2\,E}{N}\right) \cdot 100 \qquad \textit{(Formula 5.1)}$$

where,

B = the number of scores *below* the given score X
E = the number of scores *exactly* the same as X; if there is only one X score, then $E = 1$
N = the total number of scores in the distribution

QUESTION *For the following distribution, what is the percentile rank of a score of 16?*

$$12, 13, 13, 14, 16, 18, 22$$

SOLUTION $N = 7$, $B = 4$, $E = 1$. Using Formula 5.1, you find that:

$$\text{Percentile rank of } 16 = \left(\frac{4 + 1/2(1)}{7}\right) \cdot 100$$

$$= \left(\frac{4 + .50}{7}\right) \cdot 100$$

$$= (.64)100$$

$$\text{Percentile rank of } 16 = \mathbf{64\%}$$

Hence, 64 percent of the scores of this distribution fall below a score of 16. The score 16 is the 64th percentile.

Computing the Percentile Rank of a Score from a Grouped Frequency Distribution

Formula 5.1 can be used to specify the percentile rank of a score when data are presented in a grouped frequency distribution. The following worked example will be used to illustrate how to solve for a percentile rank when a particular score is placed in the context of a grouped frequency distribution.

■   QUESTION   *What is the percentile rank of a score of 70?*

Class Interval	Frequency
80–84	8
75–79	12
70–74	**14**
65–69	13
60–64	11
55–59	8
50–54	7

SOLUTION

Step 1. Locate the critical interval within which lies the score to be transformed to a percentile rank. A score of 70 lies within the interval 70–74.

Step 2. Determine B. B is the number of scores below the critical interval: $B = 7 + 8 + 11 + 13 = 39$.

Step 3. Determine E. E is the number of scores in the critical interval. $E = 14$. It is assumed that the scores in the critical interval are evenly distributed.

Step 4. Determine N. The total number of scores in the distribution is found by summing all the numbers in the Frequency column. $N = 73$.

Step 5. Place the preceding values into Formula 5.1:

$$\text{Percentile rank of 70} = \left(\frac{39 + 1/2(14)}{73}\right) \cdot 100$$

$$= \left(\frac{39 + 7}{73}\right) \cdot 100$$

$$= (.63)100$$

Percentile rank of 70 = **63%**

The percentile rank of a score of 70 is 63 percent; 63 percent of the scores fall below a score of 70. Seventy is the 63rd percentile.   ■

Finding a Score Value Given the Percentile Rank

Suppose you administer an achievement test to a group of students. Formula 5.1 can be used to transform each student's score to a percentile rank, thus allowing you to determine how any one student scored on the test with respect to the group. The question of interest now is, "What score is at a given percentile rank?" Instead of using a score to find a percentile rank, you use a percentile rank to find a score. Formula 5.2 is used to identify the score that is a given percentile rank.

Formula for Finding *X* Given a Percentile Rank

$$X_P = L + \left(\frac{(N)(P) - F}{f} \right) \cdot h \qquad \textit{(Formula 5.2)}$$

where,

X_P = the score at a given percentile
N = the total number of scores in the distribution
P = the desired percentile, expressed as a proportion
L = the exact lower limit of the class interval
F = the sum of all frequencies below L
f = the number of scores in the critical interval
h = the width of the critical interval

Although Formula 5.2 requires you to determine six values to find the score at a given percentile rank, determining these values is really quite easy. The computational steps of Formula 5.2 are specified in the context of the next worked example.

■   QUESTION   *Two hundred twenty-four students are administered an achievement test. The grouped frequency distribution of the obtained scores is presented in the following table. What score is at the 85th percentile?*

Class Interval	Frequency	Cum f
450–499	15	224
400–449	**29**	**209**
350–399	46	180
300–349	65	134
250–299	32	69
200–249	20	37
150–199	9	17
100–149	8	8

SOLUTION

Step 1.   Determine N. The highest number in the cum f column is the total number of scores in the distribution. $N = 224$.

Step 2.   Identify the critical interval within which lies the score at the 85th percentile. You want to find the score below which falls 85 percent of the total number of scores. Eighty-five percent of 224 = (.85)(224) = 190.40, or rounded, 190. The interval 400–449 contains the 181st through the 209th scores. The 190th score is somewhere in this interval.

Step 3.   Determine L. The exact lower limit of the critical interval is 399.5.

Step 4.   Determine F. F is the sum of the scores below the critical interval. Simply look at the cumulative frequency just below the critical interval: $F = 180$.

Step 5.   Determine f. The number of scores in the critical interval is 29. It is assumed that the scores within the interval are evenly distributed.

Step 6.   Determine h. The real limits of the critical interval are 399.5 to 449.5. The interval width, h, is $449.5 - 399.5 = 50$.

Step 7.   Determine P. P is the desired percentile rank, stated as a proportion. $P = .85$.

Step 8.   Plug the preceding values into Formula 5.2.

$$X_P = L + \left(\frac{(N)(P) - F}{f} \right) \cdot h$$

$$X_{85} = 399.50 + \left(\frac{(224)(.85) - 180}{29} \right) \cdot 50$$

$$= 399.50 + \left(\frac{190.40 - 180}{29} \right) \cdot 50$$

$$= 399.50 + [(.36)(50)]$$

$$= 399.50 + 18$$

$$X_{85} = 417.50 \text{ or } \mathbf{418}$$

The score that is at the 85th percentile is 418. Alternatively, 85 percent of the achievement scores fall below a score of 418.   ■

You may have noticed that Formula 5.2 bears a striking resemblance to Formula 3.4 (p. 57)—the formula for calculating the median. This should come as no surprise since the median is the 50th percentile. If you wanted to find the median of the foregoing distribution, you would begin by multiplying 224 by .50 instead of .85. Whenever you find the percentile rank from a grouped frequency distribution, the percentile rank is an approximation. This is because you have to assume that the scores in the critical interval are evenly distributed—a reasonable assumption that might be incorrect.

Some Characteristics of Percentile Ranks

Consider the following worked example.

■   QUESTION   *LaMarr and Margaret are in different statistics classes. They each scored 42 on the midterm. Who did better?*

LaMarr's Class

50, 49, 49, 47, 44, 42, 42, 42, 42, 41, 39, 37, 37, 36

Margaret's Class

44, 44, 43, 42, 41, 40, 40, 39, 39, 35, 32, 30

SOLUTION   Using Formula 5.1,

$$\text{Percentile rank of } X = \left(\frac{B + 1/2\ E}{N} \right) \cdot 100$$

$$\text{LaMarr's Percentile Rank} = \left(\frac{5 + 1/2(4)}{14} \right) \cdot 100 = \mathbf{50\%}$$

$$\text{Margaret's Percentile Rank} = \left(\frac{8 + 1/2(1)}{12} \right) \cdot 100 = \mathbf{71\%}$$

Even though both students received identical scores, Margaret's performance was superior since her percentile rank was higher. However, what if you were told that they took the same exam? Since they took the same exam, and received the same score, their performances were identical. Margaret's score only looked better because she was in a class that did not do as well. It is quite likely she would finish the course with a grade higher than LaMarr's, even though she might not know more about statistics than LaMarr. This problem always arises when you transform a raw score by using data from one distribution and then try to compare that score to one from a different distribution. The second score has been transformed based on the characteristics of the distribution to which it belongs.   ■

Suppose you had the task of admitting students to your university. It would be a mistake to base your decision for admittance on only students' percentile ranks taken from grade point averages. To state it rather bluntly, the smartest student from a school filled with unintelligent kids probably is not going to do as well at your university in comparison to the student who graduated in the middle of a very bright class of students. This is the reason why undergraduate admission committees consider the quality of the applicant's high school, and especially scores on nationally standardized tests [e.g., the Scholastic Aptitude Test (SAT)]. The SAT is standardized on a very large national sample; therefore the problem of interpreting some measure of achievement that is based on local standards is circumvented. By using SAT scores, a student from Irvine, California, can be compared to a student from Kalamazoo, Michigan. However, caution must be exercised when the percentile ranks of scores, based on different populations, are compared.

The percentile rank is used to locate where a score lies with respect to other scores of a distribution. However, the manner in which the percentile rank locates scores has an important weakness. Percentile ranks are based solely on the rank ordering of scores. Similar to the median, a percentile rank is determined by the *number* of scores below it. The way that the scores are spaced is disregarded. The fact that this can present difficulties is illustrated in the next worked example.

■   QUESTION   *What are the percentile ranks of the score 80 for Distributions A and B?*

SOLUTION

Distribution A	Distribution B
82	90
81	89
81	87
81	82
80	**80**
60	79
60	79
59	79
58	77
56	76
40	76

$$\text{Distribution A:} \quad \text{PR} = \left(\frac{6 + 1/2(1)}{11}\right) \cdot 100 = \mathbf{59\%}$$

$$\text{Distribution B:} \quad \text{PR} = \left(\frac{6 + 1/2(1)}{11}\right) \cdot 100 = \mathbf{59\%}$$

The problem is that even though the percentile rank is the same, there is a big gap just below 80 in Distribution A. In addition, notice all the low scores below the gap. Furthermore, 80 is very close to the highest score in Distribution A. In Distribution B, a score of 80 looks more like it is in the middle of the distribution. Also, a few scores are quite a bit higher than 80 (87, 89, 90), and many scores are just barely below 80. Yet a percentile rank of 59 percent is assigned to both 80s. This example illustrates the fact that percentiles are sensitive only to the *number* of scores below the percentile.   ■

One advantage of percentile ranks is that they are versatile; they can be used with any distribution, no matter the shape of the distribution. But this advantage is mitigated by the caution that must be exercised when using percentile ranks. A percentile rank can tell you that one score is more or less than another score, but not *how much* more or less than another score. A distribution of percentiles is a distribution of ranks—in other words—an ordinal scale. As such, percentile ranks cannot be meaningfully subjected to arithmetic operations. Moreover, there is a certain insensitivity associated with percentiles; they do not take into consideration all the scores of the distribution and the manner in which all the scores are spaced. A useful statistic for exactly locating a score in a distribution would be one that avoids the shortcomings of percentile ranks.

5.2 THE NORMAL DISTRIBUTIONS

Chapters 2–4 introduced you to the notion of a normal distribution (curve). In this section, a normal distribution is discussed in greater detail. Throughout the remainder of this textbook, the normal curve will be used extensively. In the context of the discussion of transformations, you will learn that some transformations gain their greatest benefit when used with data that take the form of a normal distribution.

The Importance of Normal Distributions

Normal distributions are of fundamental importance in the field of statistics for two reasons. First, measurements of many naturally occurring phenomena in the behavioral sciences are normally distributed. Tests that assess intellectual ability and tests that tap various personality dimensions often approximate a normal distribution. Furthermore, the performance of a large number of subjects on an experimental task is usually normally distributed. Second, if you were to take a sample of scores from a population, calculate $\overline{X}$, take another sample, calculate $\overline{X}$, and so on until you had a large number of sample means, those *means* would be normally distributed. This latter fact establishes the basis for most statistical methods used to analyze research data. This point will be developed extensively in later chapters.

Characteristics of Normal Distributions

For a distribution to be called normal, it must conform to a certain mathematical model:

$$y = \frac{1}{\sqrt{2\pi\sigma^2}}\, e^{-(X-\mu)^2/2\sigma^2}$$

where,
y = the ordinate on the graph; that is, the height of the curve for a given X
X = any given score
μ = population mean
σ^2 = population variance
π = the value of pi: 3.1416 (rounded)
e = 2.718 (rounded); the base of the system of natural logarithms

Don't experience "formula shock"; you will never use this equation. However, this formula can be used to make some valid points about normal distributions. The formula for a normal curve is a general formula; it is not tied to a specific set of scores. All the values in the equation are fixed, except for X, μ, and σ^2, which will vary from distribution to distribution. To draw any curve, you need to know, for each X, how far up on the graph to go to plot a point. This distance along the ordinate (y) reflects the relative frequency of scores for the given X. The distance along the ordinate is different for every combination of μ and σ^2. The mean locates the center of the distribution on the abscissa and the variance indicates the degree of dispersion among the scores. Once μ and σ^2 are specified, as X scores inserted into the equation increasingly deviate from μ, y becomes smaller. What this means is that scores *close to* the mean occur more frequently (higher on the ordinate) and scores *far away from* the mean occur with less frequency (lower on the ordinate). It follows that there are an infinite number of normal distributions since μ and σ^2 can take any value. Hence, one refers to a *family of normal distributions.* Nonetheless, all the normal distributions in the family share five characteristics.

1. A normal distribution is *unimodal,* meaning it has one hump.
2. A normal distribution is *symmetric.* This means that the right half of the curve is a mirror image of the left half. If you were to fold the curve at the midpoint, the two sides of the distribution would coincide.
3. A normal distribution has the same value for the *mean, median,* and *mode.* This follows from the fact that a normal distribution is unimodal and symmetric.
4. A normal distribution is *asymptotic;* the tails of the distribution never touch the abscissa. This is dictated by the mathematical model. Thus, a normal curve will always have some relative frequency associated with every value of X—even those remote from the mean. However, just because you can place any X value in the equation does not mean that the X score will have any rational correspondence with the variable being measured. For instance, you are not going to find anyone with a height of 20 feet, but theoretically there is a relative frequency that would correspond to that X value.
5. In a normal curve, approximately 68 percent of the scores of the distribution lie between $\mu \pm \sigma$.

There may be other distributions that have some of the characteristics of the preceding list, but only the family of normal distributions will share all five characteristics. It is easy to forget that there is a family of normal distributions because all statistics books use very similar drawings to depict a normal curve. Moreover, a normal curve is often referred to as *the* normal curve, as if there is just one. Keep in mind that any curve that possesses all of the foregoing five characteristics is a normal curve. Figure 5.1 illustrates three normal distributions.

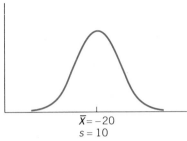
$\bar{X} = -20$
$s = 10$

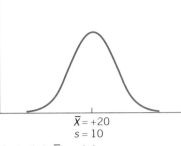
$\bar{X} = +20$
$s = 10$

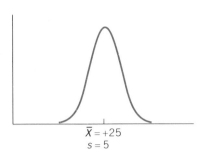
$\bar{X} = +25$
$s = 5$

Figure 5.1   Three normal distributions that differ in their $\bar{X}$'s and s's.

The concept of the normal curve has broad application. Behavioral scientists base many of their statistical analyses on the normal curve, yet the discovery of the normal distribution emanates from a mathematician's interest in gambling. Spotlight Box 5.1 traces some notable historical advances in the use of the normal curve.

Area Under the Normal Curve

You will recall from Chapter 2 that a simple frequency distribution can be depicted as a histogram or a frequency polygon. The frequency of every X score is represented on the graph. Accordingly, you can say that all of the scores of a distribution fall in the area under the curve, which goes hand in hand with the concept of probability. In general terms, the probability of an event occurring is simply the likelihood of that event occurring. Statistically speaking, probability values can range anywhere from 0 to 1. A probability of 0 means that an event cannot occur, while a probability

SPOTLIGHT
5.1

Abraham De Moivre

The discovery of the normal curve is attributed to Abraham De Moivre (1667–1754) and can be traced to a publication of his in 1733 (De Moivre, 1738; English Translation). He was a friend of Halley (of Halley's comet fame) and Sir Isaac Newton. De Moivre was held in high esteem. Apparently Newton occasionally replied to questions, "Ask Mr. De Moivre, he knows all that better than I do" (Walker, 1934, p. 322). De Moivre's discovery grew out of his interest in the probability of chance occurrences, in which an event could take on one of two values. Imagine you wanted to know the probability of getting between 500 and 600 heads after tossing a coin 1000 times. Given repeated tosses, if the number of tails is plotted on the horizontal axis and the probability of obtaining any number of tails is plotted on the vertical axis, the graph looks like a normal curve. As the number of tosses increases, the distribution becomes more and more like a normal curve. How De

Moivre arrived at the formula for the normal curve is unclear, since it was the writing style of the day to publish results and conceal methods. It would be interesting to know De Moivre's thought process because he used two constants from areas not associated with statistics: π, the ratio of the circumference of a circle to its diameter, and *e*, a constant that is used in calculating financial growth rates, exemplified by interest-bearing accounts.

Although the context of De Moivre's discovery had to do with binomial events (i.e., two possible outcomes) and gambling procedures, the curve has extensive application to errors of measurement, a fact that has made it useful in observations of planets and stars. In addition, the curve approximates measurements that are not errors, such as heights of human beings, IQ, some personality variables, and even the widths of foreheads of crabs. It was De Moivre who worked out the area under the curve for distances up to three standard deviations. Because he worked out the formula for the normal curve and the areas under the curve, De Moivre is duly credited with the normal curve's discovery. However, other mathematicians deserve credit for popularizing the normal curve.

The first person to extend the normal curve to continuous measures was the English mathematician, Thomas Simpson. Suppose you are interested in determining the position of a star. Each independent observation will yield a slightly different number. The amount of variation among the numbers would be a function of the reliability of your instrument. But which observation should you trust? It seems obvious today that the best way to handle this problem would be to take the mean of the observations. However, this was not the practice of the time. In a statement that could easily be found in any modern day statistics text, Simpson concluded a paper by saying:

> Upon the whole of which it appears, that the taking of the Mean of a number of observations, greatly diminishes the chances for all the smaller errors, and cuts off almost all possibility of any great ones; which last consideration alone, seems sufficient to recommend the use of the method, not only to astronomers, but to all others concerned in making of experiments of any kind (to which the above reasoning is equally applicable). And the more observations or experiments there are made, the less will the conclusion be liable to err, provided they admit of being repeated under the same circumstances (1755, pp. 92–93).

The idea of the normal distribution was extended even further when the French mathematician, Pierre LaPlace (1749–1827), proved the Central Limit Theorem. This theorem is the single most important theorem in statistics. It allows for the use of sampling distributions in hypothesis testing. You will learn about the central role of this theorem in later chapters. In essence, the Central Limit Theorem states that the means of many samples from a population will be normally distributed. This allows you to use the normal distribution to figure the probability of obtaining a mean by chance. The beauty of the Central Limit Theorem is that it specifies a normal distribution of sampled means, even when the population is not normally distributed.

The normal distribution was also popularized by the German mathematician, Carl Gauss (1777–1855). In fact, the normal distribution is also called the Gaussian distribution. Gauss was one of the greatest mathematicians who ever lived. At the age of 3 he discovered an error in his father's calculations of employee wages! Later in Gauss' life, when working at the University of Gottingen, Napoleon's armies were advancing on the city. LaPlace is reported to have contacted Napoleon, his longtime friend, asking him to spare Gottingen because "the foremost mathematician of his time lives there" (Dunnington, 1955, p. 251). Gauss' most lasting contribution was the use of statistics to relocate an asteroid. With only a few observations with which to work, Gauss predicted exactly where the asteroid, Ceres, would reappear. He was using the *method of least squares* to predict the location of Ceres, a method that he had invented, which eventually found its way into modern statistics.

There are many mathematical curves today that serve as statistical models. However, De Moivre's normal curve serves as the cornerstone of descriptive and inferential statistics. There are several versions of De Moivre's death. One version says that he predicted the day of his death. When ill, at the end of his life, De Moivre noticed that he began sleeping 15 minutes longer each night. Using progressions, he predicted that he would die the day after he slept 23 hours and 45 minutes. The day after he slept 24 hours, he died. Another story says that with advancing years, De Moivre was forced to make a living solving "brainteasers" in coffeehouses. In despair he simply went to sleep and died. Although these stories are most likely apocryphal, it is true that De Moivre died at the age of 87, after spending 8 days in bed, sleeping 20 hours a day.

of 1 means an event is certain to occur. A probability of .50 means that there is a 50:50 chance of an event occurring. Since the area under the curve defines 100 percent of the scores of a distribution, the probability that a score from the distribution will be found under the curve is 1. Furthermore, since a normal curve is symmetrical, what is the probability that a score taken at random will be greater than the mean? Because half of a normal distribution lies above the mean, the probability is .50. By segmenting portions of the normal curve, you can determine the percentage of scores falling within any area under the curve.

Throughout this chapter reference will be made to the percentage of scores and the probability of a score occurring. Although these phrases represent two concepts, any point made about a percentage is true for probability. Saying that fifty percent of scores fall above the mean is the same as saying the probability is .50 of randomly selecting a score above the mean.

With the basic concepts of a normal curve in place, transformation methods that allow you to locate exactly the position of a score in a distribution can be presented.

5.3   STANDARD SCORES: z SCORES AND T SCORES

z Scores

 A **z score** is a measure of how many standard deviations a raw score is from the mean of the distribution.[1] Given a normal distribution, suppose the mean is 20 and the standard deviation is 4. A score of 24 is one standard deviation above the mean. As a consequence, a score of 24 would be 1 z score above the mean ($z = +1$). What z score would be assigned to a score of 16? Since 16 is one standard deviation below the mean ($20 - 4$), a score of 16 would transform to a z score of -1.

 A z score is also called a standard unit or **standard score.** When all the raw scores of a *normal distribution* have been transformed to z scores, the resulting distribution is called the **standard normal distribution.** The standard normal distribution has a mean of 0 and a standard deviation of 1.

Two z-score formulas are provided; one is used to transform the scores of a population while the other is used to transform the scores of a sample.

---

[1] Before we go any further in our discussion of z scores, I'd like to offer a motivating remark. While percentile ranks have their place in statistics, they are nowhere near as important as z scores. The concept of z scores is ubiquitous in the field of statistics. They can be used to calculate correlations, they are fundamental to the understanding of sampling distributions, and they are an integral part of hypothesis testing. This may not have much meaning to you now, but the extent to which you understand much of the rest of the textbook will depend on how well you master the intricacies of z scores and the standard normal distribution.

Formulas for Transforming an *X* Score to *z*

Population	Sample

$$z = \frac{X - \mu}{\sigma} \qquad z = \frac{X - \overline{X}}{s}$$

(Formula 5.3a)	*(Formula 5.3b)*

where,

X = the raw score to be transformed
$\overline{X}$ = the mean of the sample
s = the sample standard deviation
μ = the mean of the population
σ = the standard deviation of the population

■   QUESTION   *For a distribution with μ = 4.80 and σ = 2.14, what is the z score of a raw score of 6?*

SOLUTION

$$z = \frac{X - \mu}{\sigma}$$

$$z = \frac{6 - 4.8}{2.14} = \textbf{+.56}$$

Given the characteristics of this distribution, a score of 6 is .56 standard deviations above the mean.   ■

The following table lists several characteristics of *z* scores and the standard unit normal curve.

Important Facts About *z* Scores

---

1. A *z*-score distribution is established by transforming every raw score to a *z* score.
2. A *z*-score distribution always has a mean of 0 and a standard deviation of 1.
3. All raw scores that fall below the mean have some *z* value that is negative; all raw scores that fall above the mean have positive *z* scores.
4. A raw score that is one standard deviation from the mean has a *z* score of either ± 1, depending on whether it is above or below the mean.
5. A raw score that is the same as the mean has a *z* value of 0.
6. The *z*-score distribution will have the same shape as the raw-score distribution.

Area Under the Curve and *z* Scores

All the scores of a distribution are contained in the area under the curve. When the distribution is normal, half the scores are above the mean and half the scores are below the mean. In Chapter 4, you learned that approximately 68 percent of the scores fall between plus and minus one standard deviation of the mean. In a distribution of *z* values, approximately 68 percent of the *z* scores will fall between a *z* score of $\pm 1^2$ (see Figure 5.2). Statements of percentages can be translated to probability statements. For instance, the probability that a score selected at random will have a positive *z* score is .50. The probability that a randomly selected score will be between ± 1 *z* score is approximately .68.

It is mathematically possible to specify the probability that a given score will be drawn from any area of the curve. However, you have been mercifully spared the arduous task of calculating the probability that a score drawn at random will come from some particular area under the curve. Probabilities can be obtained through the use of the *z* table (Table Appendix B.1). With the aid of this table, you can answer such questions as: "What percentage of scores fall below a given *X* score?" or "What is the probability that a score taken at random will fall between any two scores?" However, the *z* table can only be used when working with a normal distribution.

Using the *z* Table

The following is a portion of the *z* table found in Appendix B.1.

(A)	(B) Area Between Mean and z	(C) Area Beyond z
z		
⋮	⋮	⋮
1.00	.3413	.1587
1.01	.3438	.1562
1.02	.3461	.1539
1.03	.3485	.1515
1.04	.3508	.1492
⋮	⋮	⋮

Column A lists *z* scores. Column B provides the probability that a single score will fall between the mean of the distribution and the *z* value in column A. By moving the decimal point two places to the right, the numbers in column B would

---

[2] For the remainder of this chapter, unless otherwise noted, a normal distribution is assumed.

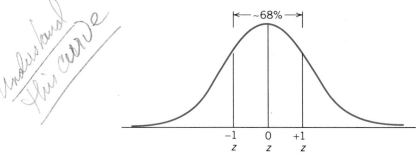

Figure 5.2   Two-thirds of the scores of a normal distribution fall between *z* scores of ±1.

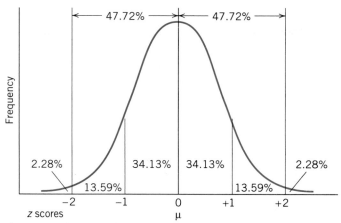

Figure 5.3   The percentage of scores that lie between various points of a normal distribution.

represent the percentage of scores falling between the mean and a given *z* score. Column C specifies the probability that a score will fall beyond a particular *z* score. Beyond means to the *right* of a *positive z* score and to the *left* of a *negative z* score. The *z* table has no negative *z* scores. This is because a normal distribution is symmetrical and, therefore, the area between the mean and a *z* score of, say, +1 is the same as the area between the mean and a *z* score of −1. Figure 5.3 shows the percentage of scores falling between various points of a normal distribution. Several worked examples are now provided in order to familiarize you with the use of the *z* table.

■   QUESTION   *What is the probability that a randomly selected score will fall between the mean and a z score of .39 (Figure 5.4)?*

.39 – Column A

SOLUTION   **.1517**   ■

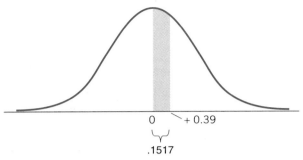

Figure 5.4   The probability that a randomly selected score will fall in the shaded area is .1517.

■   QUESTION   *What percentage of scores fall between the mean and a z score of 1 (Figure 5.5)?*   *1.00 - Column B*

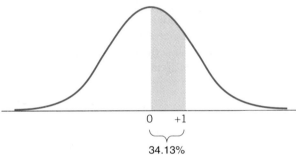

Figure 5.5   The shaded area includes 34.13 percent of the scores.   *— Column B*

SOLUTION   **34.13%**   ■

■   QUESTION   *What percentage of scores fall between ± 1 z score (Figure 5.6)?*

34.13 × 2

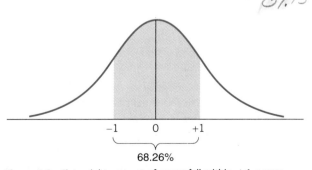

Figure 5.6   Sixty-eight percent of scores fall within ± 1 *z* score.

SOLUTION   34.13% + 34.13% = **68.26%**   ■

■   QUESTION   *What is the percentage of scores that fall between a z score of +.25 and +1.20 (Figure 5.7)?*

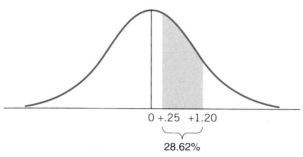

0 +.25 +1.20

28.62%

Figure 5.7   The shaded area contains 28.62 percent of the scores.

SOLUTION   The percentage of scores between the mean and a z of $+1.20$ is 38.49. This also includes the unwanted area between the mean and the z of $+.25$. Subtracting the percentage of scores falling between the mean and $+.25$ from the percentage of scores found between the mean and a z value of $+1.20$ will isolate the proper area:

$$38.49\% - 9.87\% = \mathbf{28.62\%}$$ ■

■   QUESTION   *What is the total percentage of scores that fall above a z score of +1.96 and below −1.96 (Figure 5.8)?*

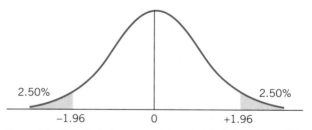

2.50%   2.50%

−1.96   0   +1.96

Figure 5.8   The shaded areas contain a total of 5 percent of the scores.

SOLUTION   Use the third column of the table when looking up 1.96. There is 2.50 percent of scores in each tail of the distribution beyond a z of 1.96. Therefore, the total percentage of scores is 5 percent. Stated differently, the probability that a score drawn at random will fall *beyond* ±1.96 is .05. Moreover, 95 percent of all scores fall within the boundaries of ±1.96 z scores.   ■

■   QUESTION   *Find the z-score cutoffs within which fall 90 percent of the scores of a distribution (Figure 5.9).*

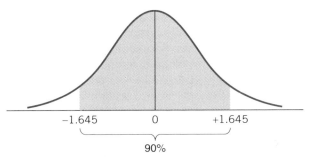

Figure 5.9 Ninety percent of the scores fall between *z* scores of ±1.645.

SOLUTION   First enter the second column of the table. Next find the *z* score in column A that comes closest to the probability value of .4500. Both 1.64 and 1.65 are equally close to .4500. Taking the midpoint between 1.64 and 1.65, the precise values within which fall 90 percent of the scores are ±1.645. ◼

Using the *z*-Score Formula

◼ QUESTION   *Given a distribution in which* $\overline{X}$ = 25 *and s* = 5, *what percentage of scores fall between 25 and 32?*

SOLUTION   To use the *z* table, the raw scores of 25 and 32 must be transformed to *z* scores. Using Formula 5.3b (the symbols $\overline{X}$ and *s* should tip you off that the scores are from a sample) you find:

$$z = \frac{X - \overline{X}}{s} = \frac{25 - 25}{5} = 0$$

$$z = \frac{32 - 25}{5} = \frac{7}{5} = 1.40$$

Now that you have converted the raw scores to *z* scores the question can be rephrased as: What percentage of scores fall between a *z* score of 0 (the mean) and 1.40? The answer is 41.92 percent of the scores fall between the raw scores of 25 and 32. (Next to a *z* score of 1.40, see the value in column B.) ◼

◼ QUESTION   *Given* $\overline{X}$ = 100 *and s* = 25, *what percentage of scores fall between 75 and 125?*

SOLUTION   Don't you dare use the *z* table! Look at the values. The standard deviation is 25 units of whatever is being measured. The score 125 is one standard deviation above the mean while 75 is one standard deviation below the mean. By now you should know that approximately 68 percent of the scores fall within plus and minus one standard deviation of the mean (68.26%, to be exact). ◼

So far you have been using z scores to find the percentage of scores falling within a given area of the normal curve, or the probability that a score will fall within an area. Moreover, Formulas 5.3a and b show how to transform a raw score to a z score. Some problems that require a z score to be converted to a raw score will now be presented. Formulas 5.4a and b are the formulas used with populations and samples, which are used to accomplish this conversion.

Formulas for Transforming z to an X Score

Population Formula	Sample Formula
$X = \mu + z\sigma$	$X = \overline{X} + zs$
(Formula 5.4a)	*(Formula 5.4b)*

■ QUESTION   *A teacher administers a placement test in order to assign each student to one of three classrooms: an accelerated, a remedial, and a regular class. The regular class will have those students who obtained scores falling within the middle 60 percent of the distribution. All students scoring in the upper 20 percent of the distribution will be assigned to the accelerated class, and those receiving scores in the lower 20 percent of the distribution will be assigned to the remedial class. The mean of the class distribution is 75 with a standard deviation of 7. What raw score cutoffs should be used to make the assignments (Figure 5.10)?*

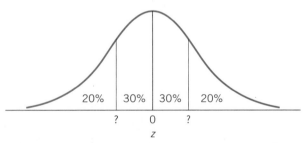

Figure 5.10   What are the cutoffs that bracket the middle 60 percent of scores in the distribution?

SOLUTION   This is the kind of problem that at first glance seems over-whelming. If you represent the problem visually, you will simplify matters. Your illustration should look like Figure 5.10. Since you want the middle 60 percent of the distribution, you need a z score that has 30 percent of the scores between it and the mean. Since it is assumed that the distribution of placement test scores is normal, the same percentage of scores that fall between the relevant positive z score and the mean will fall between the *same* negative z score and the mean. Instead of using the first column of the z table—the column of z scores—use the second column to find the percentage closest to 30. The percentage 29.95 is close enough. The *z* score that corresponds to 29.95 is +.84. Thus, approximately 30 percent of the scores fall between the mean and a *z* of +.84. Since the distribution is symmetrical, another 30 percent of the scores fall between the mean and a *z* score of −.84. Therefore, the middle 60 percent of the distribution falls between *z* scores of ±.84.

You are now in a position to convert the *z* scores to raw scores. Since you are looking for the raw score cutoffs that correspond to a positive *and* negative *z* score, two separate calculations that use Formula 5.4a are required. The use of Formula 5.4a assumes that the teacher is only interested in that one group of students.

$$\text{Upper Cutoff} = 75 + (+.84)(7)$$
$$= 75 + 5.88$$
$$= \mathbf{80.88}$$
$$\text{Lower Cutoff} = 75 + (-.84)(7)$$
$$= 75 - 5.88$$
$$= \mathbf{69.12}$$

Those students with scores above 81 are assigned to the accelerated class; those students with scores below 69 will be assigned to the remedial class; all students with scores from 69–81 will participate in the regular class.   ■

Using *z* scores to Calculate Percentile Rank

The percentage of scores falling below a given score is the percentile rank of that score. Any score can be transformed to a *z* score; using the *z* table that identifies the percentage of scores within various areas under the curve will enable you to easily calculate percentile ranks via *z* scores. Bear in mind that percentile ranks can be used with distributions not normally distributed. However, to compute percentile ranks with the *z* table requires that the scores be normally distributed.

■   QUESTION   *What is the percentile rank of the score 15, when $\overline{X} = 18$ and s = 4?*

SOLUTION   The *z* score of 15 is:

$$z = \frac{15 - 18}{4} = \frac{-3}{4} = -.75$$

Again, use the third column of the *z* table, which allows you to determine the percentage of scores *above* a *positive z* score or *below* a *negative z* score. Figure 5.11 depicts the shaded area that you are going to identify in the third column.

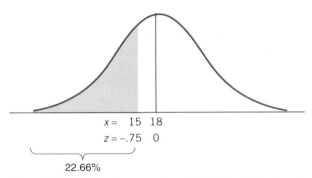

Figure 5.11   In finding the percentile rank of 15, the shaded area is the percentage of scores that fall below a raw score of 15.

The *z* score that corresponds to the raw score of 15 is −.75. The percentage of scores that fall below a *z* of −.75 is 22.66. Hence, the percentile rank of 15 is 22.66 percent. ■

■   **QUESTION**   *What is the percentile rank of 30, when $\overline{X} = 27$ and s = 2?*

SOLUTION   The *z* score associated with a raw score of 30 is:

$$z = \frac{30 - 27}{2} = \frac{3}{2} = +1.5$$

The percentage of scores between the mean and a *z* of 1.50 is 43.32. However, the percentile rank includes *all* the scores below *X*, so you need to add the lower half of the distribution to 43.32. Thus, the percentile rank of 30 is 43.32 + 50 = 93.32 percent. You can calculate percentile ranks using either the second or third column of the *z* table. If you draw a picture of the normal curve, shade the appropriate area, and understand what the second and third columns are giving you, the arithmetic operations will be obvious. ■

Identifying the Interquartile Range

You will recall from Chapter 4 that the interquartile range marks the middle 50 percent of the distribution. It is a descriptive measure of variability that is unaffected by extreme scores. The way in which you go about finding the interquartile range is similar to the way you solved the problem of assigning students to advanced, regular, and remedial classes.

■   **QUESTION**   *A distribution has μ = 80 and σ = 5. What is the interquartile range?*

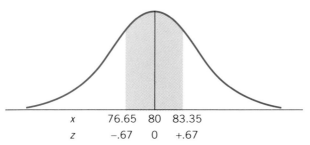

| x | 76.65 | 80 | 83.35 |
| z | −.67 | 0 | +.67 |

Figure 5.12   The shaded area defines the interquartile range.

SOLUTION   Figure 5.12 shows the middle 50 percent of the distribution. You need to identify the *z* scores that bracket the middle 50 percent. Enter the second column of the *z* table and find the percentage closest to 25 percent. A *z* of .67 is close enough. Since the distribution is symmetrical, 50 percent of the scores fall between *z* scores of ±.67. Now convert the *z* scores to raw scores using Formula 5.4a.

Upper Cutoff	*Lower Cutoff*
$X = 80 + (.67)(5)$	$X = 80 - (.67)(5)$
$= 80 + 3.35$	$= 80 - 3.35$
$= 83.35$	$= 76.65$

The interquartile range is $83.35 - 76.65 = $ **6.70.**   ■

T Scores

A *z* score is a useful transformation because it allows a researcher to identify how many standard deviations a score is from the mean. All the raw scores of a distribution can be transformed to *z* scores, thus yielding a *z* distribution that has a mean of 0 and a standard deviation of 1. When using *z* scores, you are forced to deal with decimals and negative *z* values. There is nothing inherently wrong with this, but at times it can be awkward to deal with decimals and negative numbers. Thus, *z* scores themselves are sometimes transformed. The *T*-score transformation is used to remove the decimal places and negative numbers of *z* scores. Formula 5.5 is used to calculate *T*-scores.

Formula for a *T* Score

$$T = z(10) + 50 \quad \textit{(Formula 5.5)}$$

---

z Scores	T Scores = z(10) + 50
−4.0	10
−3.0	20
−2.0	30
−1.0	40
0	50
+1.0	60
+2.0	70
+3.0	80
+4.0	90

Notice that the *T*-score transformation gets rid of one decimal point. Thus, a *z* score of +1.20 is a *T* score of 62 [1.20(10) + 50]. However, a *z* score of +1.25 would be a *T* score of 62.50. *T* scores are always represented as whole numbers, so you would round up or down. If you are going to use the *T*-score transformation, you should be willing to give up a little precision. If you aren't willing to do so, then you could multiply by 100 or 1000. When using 10 as the multiplier and 50 as the additive constant, the *T*-score distribution has a mean of 50 and a standard deviation of 10. The numbers stand in the same relation to one another as they do in the raw-score and *z*-score distributions. *T* scores are usually used in tests of ability, personality, or psychopathology. It is rare for a researcher to transform the data of an experiment to *T* scores and then perform statistical analyses on the *T* scores.

One popular psychological test that reports findings in terms of *T* scores is the Minnesota Multiphasic Personality Inventory (MMPI). Test scores are standardized with a mean of 50 and a standard deviation of 10. With the MMPI, a score 1.50 standard deviations above the mean (i.e., 65) is considered a sign of abnormality.

Figure 5.13 shows the relation between raw scores, *z* scores, and *T* scores of a normal distribution. The raw scores used in the illustration are arbitrary and would depend on the unit of measure used in the study.

One advantage of using *z* scores is that raw scores from different distributions can be converted to *z* scores and compared. Box 5.1 explains how this is accomplished.

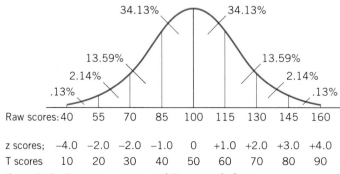

Figure 5.13   Raw score, *z*-score, and *T*-score equivalents.

BOX 5.1

With *z* scores You Can Compare Apples and Oranges

Are you taller than you are heavy? This question, at first glance, seems to be nonsensical. The reason the question appears to be unanswerable is because height and weight are measured in different units. How can you say that 6 ft 2 in. is more or less than 145 lb—or in other words—you can't compare apples and oranges. However, in the world of statistics you *can* compare apples and oranges by using a transformation. The *z*-score transformation will convert original scores, from different scales, to a common unit. The common unit is the *z* score, which is the number of standard deviations a score is from the mean of the distribution. Now if you were told that a man's height transforms to a *z* of +1.3, and his weight to a *z* of −.42, could you answer the question is he taller than he is heavy? You would be justified in saying that he is taller than he is heavy, but it is important to understand exactly what this means. When his height is transformed to a *z* score, the mean and standard deviation of a distribution of heights is used to make the transformation. His weight score is transformed using the mean and standard deviation from a distribution of weights. Thus, to say that he is taller than he is heavy is to say that his transformed height value locates him *higher* on the *z* distribution of heights than his transformed weight score locates him on the *z* distribution of weights.

This way of comparing scores from different scales of measurement is very useful in psychology and education. You can ask, for instance, if a person is more depressed than anxious, more paranoid than manic, or better at math than at reading. There are several psychological tests that assess numerous dimensions of psychopathology and personality [e.g., Minnesota Multiphasic Personality Inventory (MMPI) and California Personality Inventory (CPI), respectively]. Although the scales of a test may be designed to tap various traits, and each scale has its own mean and standard deviation, by standardizing the raw scores with some appropriate transformation (e.g., *T* scores) the examiner can easily make cross-scale comparisons.

SUMMARY

Percentiles, *z* scores, and *T* scores are statistical transformations of original scores. They provide information about where a score stands in relation to other scores in the distribution. The percentile rank of a score is expressed as the percentage of scores in the distribution that fall below that score. The percentile rank of a score is based on the rank order of scores; it does not take the distance between scores into consideration. The *z*-score transformation avoids this problem by using the variability of the distribution in the transformation formula. A *z* score is the number of standard deviations a raw score is from the mean of the distribution. All *z* scores above the mean are positive; those below the mean are negative. A *z*-score distribution has a mean of 0 and a standard deviation of 1. In a normal distribution 68 percent of the scores fall between plus and minus one *z* score. In addition, the *z* distribution will only be normal if the raw-score distribution is normal.

T scores are transformations of *z* scores. They are used when a researcher wants to remove decimals and negative signs from *z* scores.

KEY FORMULAS FOR CHAPTER 5

Formula for Finding the Percentile Rank of X

$$\text{Percentile rank of } X = \left(\frac{B + 1/2 \; E}{N} \right) \cdot 100 \qquad \textit{(Formula 5.1)}$$

Formula for Finding X Given a Percentile Rank

$$X_P = L + \left(\frac{(N)(P) - F}{f} \right) \cdot b \qquad \textit{(Formula 5.2)}$$

Formulas for Transforming X to z

Population	Sample
$z = \dfrac{X - \mu}{\sigma}$	$z = \dfrac{X - \overline{X}}{s}$
(Formula 5.3a)	*(Formula 5.3b)*

Formulas for Transforming z to X

Population	Sample
$X = \mu + z\sigma$	$X = \overline{X} + zs$
(Formula 5.4a)	*(Formula 5.4b)*

Formula for a T Score

$$T = z(10) + 50 \qquad \textit{(Formula 5.5)}$$

WORK PROBLEMS

1. Using the following frequency distribution, what is the percentile rank of a score of:

   a. 56   b. 60   c. 54   d. 49

X	f	cf
62	3	49
60	4	46
58	7	42
56	12	35
54	10	23
49	7	13
44	6	6

2. Transform these scores of a population distribution to *z* scores and *T* scores.

Raw Scores: 4, 5, 7, 9, 10, 11

3. Given $\overline{X} = 14$ and $s^2 = 16$, what is the *z* score of a raw score of 11?
4. In a distribution where $\overline{X} = 25$ and $s = 3$, what raw score corresponds to a *z* score of .36?
5. If a distribution has a mean of 130 and a standard deviation of 13, what is the probability of randomly selecting a score above 140?
6. When $\overline{X} = 34$ and $s = 3$, what percentage of scores are lower than 27?
7. What is the total percentage of scores that lie beyond *z* scores of ± 1.96?
8. What percentage of scores fall between the *z* scores ± 1.645?
9. What is *z* when the probability of selecting a score at random is:
   a. below (to the left of) $z = .4207$ f. above $z = .2946$
   b. below $z = .3821$ g. above $z = .4641$
   c. above (to the right of) $z = .3192$ h. below $z = .4247$
   d. d. above $z = .0694$ i. above $z = .2119$
   e. e. below $z = .1151$
10. What is the probability of randomly drawing a score between the *z* scores $+.56$ and -1.2?
11. In a distribution with $\overline{X} = 78$ and $s = 7$, what is the probability of selecting a score between 72 and 80?
12. In a distribution having a mean of 123 and a variance of 49, what is the total percentage of scores falling above 130 and below 116?
13. If a standardized anxiety questionnaire has a mean of 25 and a standard deviation of 5, what is the probability that an individual selected at random will score between 20 and 30?
14. A standardized test of reasoning ability has a mean of 70 and a standard deviation of 7. The principal of a school would like to identify the best and worst students, as defined by their scores on the test. The best students are those with a percentile rank of 90 and above, and the worst students are those with a percentile rank of 10 and below. What are the raw-score cutoffs the principle should use to identify the two groups of students?
15. Transform the following population of raw scores to *T* scores.

2, 4, 5, 6, 8, 9

16. For a distribution with $\overline{X} = 48$ and $s = 4$, what is the percentile rank of:
   a. 43   b. 57   c. 48   d. 50   e. 47
17. A 100-point final exam is administered in a class where $\mu = 78$ and $\sigma = 7$. What score did these four students receive?
   a. Laurie, with a percentile rank of 95 percent.
   b. Jennifer, if she is in the 80th percentile.
   c. Jim, who scored better than 30 percent of the other students.
   d. Gus, with a percentile rank of 45 percent.

18. For a distribution with $\overline{X} = 35$ and $s = 3$, find the percentage of scores that are:
    a. above $z = +1.20$
    b. above $z = -.36$
    c. below $z = -.56$
    d. below $z = -.79$
    e. below $z = -1.10$
    f. below $z = +.98$
    g. above $z = +.13$

19. Professor Engel gives a final exam to her abnormal psychology class and finds that $\mu = 56$ and $\sigma = 5$.
    a. If the passing score is 38, what percentage of students will fail?
    b. If Professor Engel wants the C category to span the middle 30 percent of the distribution, what would be the cutoffs?
    c. What score would serve as the cutoff for an A if only the top 10 percent of the class is to receive an A?

20. A student receives a score that corresponds to a percentile rank of 80 percent.
    a. What z score corresponds to this rank?
    b. Given the information available here, can you determine the raw score?

21. Using the following grouped frequency distribution, what is the percentile rank of a score of 172?

Class Interval	Frequency
180–184	7
175–179	11
170–174	16
165–169	15
160–164	11
155–159	9
150–154	7

22. For the following grouped frequency distribution, find X_{40}, X_{50}, X_{65}, X_{90}.

Class Interval	Frequency
26–29	17
22–25	13
18–21	23
14–17	27
10–13	25
6–9	12
2–5	9

Work Problems for the Computer

23. For the following data set, determine the scores that are at the 25th, 50th, and 75th percentile. (Save the file for Problems 24 and 25.)

12	15	34	23	32	12	22	21	19	25	14	11	12
11	10	14	15	13	12	16	18	21	29	32	31	30
24	30	29	28	26	21	19	17	16	15	11	10	17
32	30	29	29	28	27	21	14	21	18	16	16	11
20	23	14	15	17	11	21	32	20	20	25	15	17
14	15	23	26	30	24	19	23	22	21	24	17	15

24. For the preceding data set, transform all the raw scores to z scores. What are the mean and standard deviation of the z-score distribution?

25. Specify the following descriptive statistics if the data set is a population: μ, σ^2, σ. What if the data set is a sample of scores?

INFERENTIAL STATISTICS: PARAMETRIC TESTS

Hypothesis Testing and Sampling Distributions

6.1 INFERENTIAL STATISTICS

Inferential statistics originated from gamblers' desire to use mathematics in order to maximize their chances of winning bets. The modern era of inferential statistics began early in this century. Agricultural companies and breweries hired mathematicians to formulate ways to assess the influence of various treatments on crop yields. **Inferential statistics,** based on probability theory and logic, are used to make inferences about the characteristics of a population from the characteristics of a random sample drawn from the population.

What if you wanted to know the level of reading skills among the high school students of a large city? You can proceed by testing every student in the city (a costly and time-consuming effort) or you can test a random sample of all the students and use their scores to infer the reading skills of the entire population. Given ever-present budgetary constraints and the desire to obtain answers to questions as efficiently as possible, inferential statistics is a godsend to behavioral scientists.

In inferential statistics, the key word is random sample. A **random sample** is a sample of scores taken from a population in such a way that each score of the population has an equal chance of being included in the sample. Random sampling maximizes the likelihood that the sample is *representative* of the population.

Inferential statistics requires random sampling, but it is not always easy to achieve. Consider a typical psychology experiment. The sample of subjects is college students, enrolled in an introductory-level psychology course; they have volunteered for the experiment to fulfill a course requirement. What is the population to which you can generalize? Strictly speaking, the population is the type of student who attends that university, takes an introductory-level psychology course, and signs up for that experiment. Because of the large number of studies conducted with college students, you have to wonder to what extent the field of psychology applies only to college undergraduates. The problem here is not one of mathematics, but rather one of logic. You cannot make statements about people who are different (in important ways) from the participants in your study. In inferential statistics, the researcher is bound by the degree to which samples are representative of the populations of interest. Given the uncertain nature of generalizing research findings to others *not* in the study, researchers are aware of the importance of replicating studies with *different* samples of subjects.

6.2   TWO KINDS OF INFERENTIAL PROCEDURES

Estimation

Recall that a parameter is a numerical characteristic of a population (e.g., mean, standard deviation, variance, etc.). A statistic is a numerical characteristic of a sample, which can be used to infer population parameters. Thus, parameter estimation uses data from a sample to infer the value of a population parameter. There are two kinds of estimation: point estimation and interval estimation. Suppose you take a random sample and compute the mean of the sample. If someone asks you what you think the mean of the population is, and your answer is the mean of the sample, you are making a **point estimation.** Any sample statistic can be used to make a point estimation of a population parameter. The other kind of estimation is **interval estimation** (or **confidence interval**). If, instead of inferring a specific value, which you do in point estimation, you state two values between which you think the population parameter falls, you are making an interval estimation. To determine the interval within which you believe the population parameter lies requires the use of a formula.[1]

---

[1] Chapter 10 gives an in-depth discussion of interval estimation.

Hypothesis Testing

  A **scientific** (or **research**) **hypothesis** is a formal statement or expectation about the outcome of a study. Scientific hypotheses are usually stated in terms of independent and dependent variables, and the relation between them. The accumulation of knowledge in the behavioral sciences relies heavily on the process of formulating theories, stating hypotheses, gathering data to test hypotheses, revising theories, making new hypotheses, and conducting more research. **Hypothesis testing** is a set of inferential procedures, which uses data from samples to establish the credibility of a hypothesis about a population. Although hypothesis testing is conducted in many different contexts, all instances of hypothesis testing share common characteristics: the use of samples to represent populations, applying inferential statistics, and the possibility of errors in decision-making.

Common Characteristics of Hypothesis Testing

The Use of Samples to Make Inferences About Populations

If the investigator of a study is interested *only* in making conclusions about the subjects in the study, then hypothesis testing is irrelevant. Confining one's interest to the subjects in the study defines those subjects as the population and no inference is required. One goal of science, however, is to acquire general knowledge about our world. The behavior of your research participants is interesting only insofar as it allows you to make statements about the behavior of people who are *not* in your study. Representative samples of subjects are used to generalize study results to a larger group. Conducting research with samples is not only efficient, it is a virtual necessity, since it is almost always impossible to include entire populations in a study. Hypothesis testing involves the use of formal procedures for making statements about populations based on representative samples.

The Use of Inferential Statistics

In order to use samples to infer the characteristics of populations, mathematical tools to accomplish the task are needed. Because, in a sense, the researcher is forced to work at the level of samples, anything he or she concludes about populations is always clouded in uncertainty. Inferences about population parameters are, therefore, probabilistic in nature. The statistical methods of hypothesis testing allow us to use sample data to make probabilistic statements about the credibility of hypotheses at the level of populations.

Errors Are a Fact of Life in Hypothesis Testing

Hypothesis testing leads to a yes or no answer. Suppose a researcher wants to know if the population mean is a certain value, say 100. A random sample is drawn, the mean is calculated, and with the use of inferential procedures, a decision is made whether or not the population mean is different than 100. Another question you might ask in hypothesis testing is "Do you think the mean of population 1 is different from the mean of population 2?" For example, you might want to know which of two therapy approaches is superior in reducing stress. Your yes/no question becomes: "Is there a difference between the two therapies?"

One implication of a yes/no question is that hypothesis testing is decision-making: Is the answer yes or is it no? Whenever you commit to a yes or no answer, there is a possibility of a mistake. When you are hypothesis testing, you must accept the risk of making errors of inference. There are ways to reduce the likelihood of errors as well as ways to compute the probability of making certain types of errors. Yet the possibility of committing inferential errors remains a fact of life in hypothesis testing.

The Many Faces of Hypothesis Testing

There are many ways that scientific hypotheses can be worded. The research methods that are used to evaluate a hypothesis determine how the hypothesis will be phrased. A distinction is made between a *research hypothesis* and a *statistical hypothesis*. A research hypothesis is a statement about the expected outcome of a study. It prompts a study—or in other words—it is the study's reason for being. A **statistical hypothesis** serves as a vehicle for evaluating the research hypothesis. It is a numerical statement regarding the potential outcome of a study. Some common research approaches and examples of research and statistical hypotheses appropriate to the research context are given in the following sections.

Case I Research

Case I research uses *one* sample to test a hypothesis about the value of a population parameter. Suppose an existing validated stress questionnaire has a mean of 50. In other words, the average person will receive a score of 50. A person under a lot of stress will receive a higher score, and someone experiencing less stress will score below 50. A community psychologist is interested in the emotional effects of natural disasters. Soon after an earthquake, 100 randomly sampled people are asked to complete the stress questionnaire. The research hypothesis may be stated as, "Natural disasters create stress reactions among the victims." Next, the research hypothesis is refined to a statistical hypothesis, which reflects the specific research design and the measures used to assess the credibility of the research hypothesis. Here, the statistical hypothesis can be stated as, "Is the mean stress score of this sample different from a mean of 50?" In keeping with the yes/no aspect of hypothesis testing, the investigator will decide if there is enough evidence to conclude that the mean of the population from which the sample is taken is different from 50. (See Chapter 7 for a discussion of the statistical procedures that are used in Case I research.)

Case II Research

Case II research uses *two* samples to test a hypothesis about the difference between two population means. When two samples are used, the investigator has an opportunity to establish the comparative effectiveness of two treatments. An example of a Case II research hypothesis from medicine is, "Heart patients who receive a beta-blocker will experience fewer cardiac arrhythmias than patients who receive a placebo." Refined to a statistical hypothesis, the researcher asks, "Is there a difference in the mean number of arrhythmias between the "beta-blocker" population and the "placebo" population?"

Keep in mind that hypothesis testing asks questions about *populations,* not samples. The difference between two sample means is used to make an inference about whether it is reasonable to conclude that there is a difference between population means. Imagine that you take all the heart patients in the world, administer the beta-blocking drug to one-half of the patients and the placebo to the other half, and then compute the mean number of arrhythmias for each population. Should you use inferential statistics at this point to test your hypothesis about the relative effectiveness of the two treatments? No, because you have tested everyone; there is no need for inference. Realistically, you cannot include everyone in the study, so you must administer the drug to one sample, and allow these subjects to represent the population of heart patients prescribed beta-blockers. The sample that receives the placebo represents the placebo population. This is the logic behind why statistical hypotheses are phrased as statements (or questions) about *populations,* not the samples from which the data are obtained. (See Chapter 8 for a discussion of the inferential procedures for hypothesis testing in the context of Case II research.)

Beyond Case II Research

Case I research uses a single sample to test a hypothesis about a specified population mean. Case II research uses two samples to test a hypothesis about the *difference* between population means. The majority of experimental research, however, is an extension of Case II research, where more than two samples are used. For example, an experimental psychologist might formulate the research hypothesis: "Does the magnitude of reinforcement influence the number of trials it takes to learn a task?" The psychologist might then examine the influence of five different incentive conditions on learning. In the form of a question, the researcher might ask, "Is there a difference among the populations in the mean number of trials it takes to learn the task?" (See Chapters 12, 13, and 14 for in-depth discussions of experimental designs and statistical tests appropriate in situations where there are more than two samples of subjects.)

Correlational Research

In the behavioral sciences, hypothesis testing does not always take place in an experimental context. The correlational approach is an alternative research method, which differs from experimentation in that it does not attempt to exert an influence on a measured response. Because variables are not controlled, **correlational research** cannot identify causal relations among variables. The correlational approach is aimed at identifying the variables that occur together. An example of a correlational research hypothesis is, "First-time parents who have newborns who cry a lot are more dissatisfied with their marriages than first-time parents who have quiet babies." The investigator would search for an association between the amount of time an infant cries and the parents' reports of marital dissatisfaction. No attempt is made to manipulate some variables and hold other variables constant. (You would not want to randomly assign noisy and quiet babies to parents and observe the hypothesized deterioration of the marital unit.) Another example of a research hypothesis from a correlational design is, "Achievement-oriented men are more domineering toward their wives than nonachievement-oriented men." The researcher would obtain measures of achievement orientation and dominance to see if these two variables are associated.

Although the correlational approach does not manipulate variables, it does *not* alter the fundamental characteristics of hypothesis testing. A sample is used to make an inference about a population, inferential statistics are used, yes/no answers are given to statistical hypotheses, and errors in inference can be made. (See Chapter 15 for a discussion of hypothesis testing in the context of the correlational design.)

More on Statistical Hypotheses: The Null and Alternative Hypotheses

Statistical hypotheses are numerical statements regarding the potential outcomes of an experiment. When conducting a study, statistical hypotheses always come in pairs—a null hypothesis, denoted H_0, and an alternative hypothesis, denoted H_1. In the context of an experiment, the **null hypothesis** states that there is *no* effect of the independent variable on the dependent variable. The **alternative hypothesis** states that there is an experimental effect of the independent variable on the dependent variable. The alternative hypothesis is the logical alternative to the null hypothesis. It is the alternative hypothesis that you hope your research supports since it is the statistical refinement of the research hypothesis.

The null and alternative hypotheses are statistical hypotheses and are therefore numerical expressions. For example, if an educational enrichment program is expected to increase IQ, and you know that the average IQ in the population is 100, the null and alternative hypotheses are stated as:

$$H_0: \quad \mu = 100$$

$$H_1: \quad \mu \neq 100$$

Here, the null hypothesis is a statement that the program has no effect. The alternative hypothesis states that the program has an effect. In this instance, the null hypothesis can be determined as untenable, whether the program increases *or* decreases IQ. To reject the null hypothesis, you need only obtain evidence that it is likely to be false.

Considered together, the null and alternative hypotheses are mutually exclusive in that only one hypothesis can possibly be true. Moreover, statistical hypotheses are collectively exhaustive in that they cover all possible outcomes. Consider the statistical hypothesis that the population mean is 50. The population mean either equals 50 or it does not, symbolically $\mu = 50$ or $\mu \neq 50$. These two hypotheses satisfy the conditions of mutual exclusivity and collective exhaustiveness. They are mutually exclusive in that only one of the hypotheses can be true. They are collectively exhaustive because no other possible outcome can occur.

Truth in Hypothesis Testing

Once the data are analyzed in hypothesis testing, you have to make a decision about whether to believe the null hypothesis or the alternative hypothesis. If the null hypothesis is *not* rejected it does not mean that it is true. In fact, the null hypothesis can *never* be proven true. A poorly designed study with insensitive measurement instruments may fail to detect an experimental effect. Or, using a small number of subjects may make it difficult to accurately infer the true population mean. However, even if the study is performed expertly, with a large number of subjects, there is a possibility that the researcher may fail to reject the null hypothesis just by chance. Therefore, failure to reject the null hypothesis does not necessarily mean that the null hypothesis is true.

On the other hand, if the null hypothesis is rejected it means that the alternative hypothesis is *probably* true. For instance, a sample that is unrepresentative of the population may lead us to reject the null hypothesis, even if the null hypothesis is actually correct. It is not the case that the null and alternative hypotheses do not have an ultimate truth; clearly they do, one or the other must be true. However, the methods of hypothesis testing are probabilistic, and probability, by definition, means that there is some level of uncertainty.

Using the jargon of statistical hypothesis testing, you may decide to retain, accept, or reject the null hypothesis or to accept or retain the alternative hypothesis. Some researchers are uneasy using the phrase "accept the null hypothesis" because it seems to imply that the null hypothesis is true. They prefer a phrase such as, "we failed to reject the null hypothesis." Just keep in mind that, no matter what the terminology, these terms are *probabilistic* and carry no implication for the ultimate truth status of the null and alternative hypotheses. Although this might seem unsettling, you must accept the ambiguity inherent in hypothesis testing. However, you can determine the probability of making errors in accepting or rejecting the null hypothesis. Since you must always operate in the realm of uncertainty, at least you *can* know how uncertain you are.

Statistical hypothesis testing is the topic of interest for the rest of this textbook. The mathematical underpinnings of hypothesis testing will not be stressed. Instead, the conceptual foundation of statistical hypothesis testing and the application of formulas to research data will be emphasized. These two topics are intertwined. Without understanding the conceptual basis of statistical hypothesis testing, there is no way to understand *why* a formula looks as it does and why the formula should be used in a given situation. The most important concept in inferential statistics is the sampling distribution. As you read the remainder of this chapter, be forewarned that the connection between sampling distributions and hypothesis testing may not be immediately obvious. Subsequent chapters will deepen your understanding. For now, understand that if the characteristics of sampling distributions had not been worked through by statisticians, statistical hypothesis testing would be impossible.

6.3 SAMPLING DISTRIBUTIONS

Population and Sample Distributions

You know the difference between a population and a sample, the latter being a portion of the former. Every population of scores can be depicted as a frequency distribution that reflects the frequency of occurrence of every score in the distribution. Frequency distributions are also called probability distributions because the probability of selecting a given score at random depends on the frequency with which that score occurs in the population. Also, if you know the mean and standard deviation of a normal distribution, you can make probability statements about the likelihood of selecting a score from a specified area of the distribution (remember all those z-score problems?)

With a sample, you are rarely interested in the actual sample; the emphasis is on what the sample allows you to infer about the population from which it was taken. Most importantly, when you make inferences from a sample to a population, you do not make inferences about a specific *score*. Instead, you make inferences about a population parameter from a sample statistic. For example, you may infer the mean or the variance of a population based on the mean or variance of your sample. It is meaningless to take a single score from a sample and try to estimate a single score of a population.

In the discussion of z scores in Chapter 5, questions were asked like, "What is the probability of selecting a *score* of less than 20, given that the mean of the population is 26 and the standard deviation is 4?" You were able to answer such questions because you used a standardized normal distribution—the z-score distribution. The z-score distribution is a distribution of transformed raw *scores*. However, in hypothesis testing, you are interested in means (usually), never individual scores. If you want to make a probability statement about a randomly selected *mean* falling within a specified area under the normal curve, you need a *normal distribution of means*, which is addressed in the following section.

A Sampling Distribution of Means

 Generally stated, a **sampling distribution** is a theoretical frequency distribution of a statistic, based on a very large number of repeated samples of size n. With respect to means, a sampling distribution shows the relative frequency of all possible values of sample means. A researcher never actually goes through the process of constructing a sampling distribution. Knowledge of sampling distributions comes from mathematics. Because sampling distributions are based on mathematical models, they are called *theoretical distributions*. The concept of a sampling distribution is easily grasped by walking through the steps that, *theoretically*, would be taken to establish a sampling distribution.

Step 1. Choose a population of scores. It might be a population of IQ scores, heights, weights, or scores from a population of subjects who have taken some personality inventory.

Step 2.   Decide on a sample size, *n.* Your sample size can range from 2–infinity. (Since means are being used, a sample size of 1 has questionable meaning.)

Step 3.   Take a random sample of size *n,* the size of the sample you decided on in Step 2.

Step 4.   Compute the mean and replace the scores back into the population. This is called *random sampling with replacement.*

Step 5.   Repeat Steps 3 and 4 an almost infinite number of times. *Each repeated sample must be the same size.* How do you know when you are finished? At some point it will be impossible for you to randomly select a sample that you have not already selected. This does *not* mean that it is impossible to select a sample with a mean identical to a previously drawn sample; rather, there is no combination of subjects left that you have not already drawn.

Step 6.   Finally, plot the relative frequency distribution of the means. This distribution is the sampling distribution of that population of scores, *for the sample size used in repeated sampling.*

In specifying the steps of constructing a sampling distribution, the statistic of interest was the mean. The steps are the same no matter what statistic you select. If you want a sampling distribution of variances, use the same procedure, except compute and plot variances. You could even take two samples, calculate the means, take the difference between the two means, and establish a sampling distribution of differences. There are, in fact, many occasions in hypothesis testing when the sampling distribution will not be a distribution of means. In this chapter, however, the discussion of sampling distributions will be confined to sampling distributions of means.

Characteristics of Sampling Distributions

The Central Limit Theorem

This section begins with a theorem, which is the most important theorem in the entire field of inferential statistics. It was formulated in 1810 by Pierre LaPlace (1749–1827) and is called the **Central Limit Theorem.**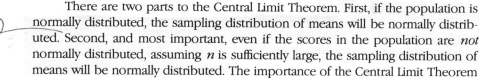

There are two parts to the Central Limit Theorem. First, if the population is normally distributed, the sampling distribution of means will be normally distributed. Second, and most important, even if the scores in the population are *not* normally distributed, assuming *n* is sufficiently large, the sampling distribution of means will be normally distributed. The importance of the Central Limit Theorem will become obvious as the topics of confidence intervals (interval estimation) and hypothesis testing are further presented.

One characteristic of a sampling distribution of means is that it is normally distributed, no matter what the shape of the population from which the sampling distribution is derived. Other characteristics of a sampling distribution have to do with how the mean and standard deviation of the sampling distribution correspond to the mean and standard deviation of the parent population.

The Mean of the Sampling Distribution, $\mu_{\overline{x}}$

How would you compute the mean of a sampling distribution? Theoretically speaking, you would add all the sample means and divide by the number of means. The mean of a sampling distribution is the mean of all the means in the distribution and is symbolized $\mu_{\overline{x}}$ (pronounced *mu-x-bar*). *The mean of the sampling distribution is exactly the same as the mean of the population.* Thus, $\mu = \mu_{\overline{x}}$. The subscript of $\mu_{\overline{x}}$ reminds us that $\mu_{\overline{x}}$ is the mean of a distribution of sample means.

The Standard Deviation of the Sampling Distribution, $\sigma_{\overline{x}}$

How would you compute the standard deviation of a sampling distribution? In Chapter 4 you learned that the formula for computing the standard deviation of a population of *scores* is:

$$\sigma = \sqrt{\frac{\Sigma(X-\mu)^2}{N}}$$

The formula for the standard deviation of a sampling distribution, $\sigma_{\overline{x}}$ (pronounced *sigma-ex-bar*) has the same form as the standard deviation of a population. This formula is a *definitional* formula since it defines the standard deviation of the sampling distribution. Although Formula 6.1 is not used to compute the standard deviation of a sampling distribution, it is presented here to underscore the point that the standard deviation of a sampling distribution has the same mathematical form as the standard deviation of the population.

**Definitional Formula for the Standard Deviation
of a Sampling Distribution**

$$\sigma_{\overline{x}} = \sqrt{\frac{\Sigma(\overline{X}-\mu_{\overline{x}})^2}{N_{\overline{x}}}} \qquad \text{(Formula 6.1)}$$

Since the "scores" of a sampling distribution are means, $\overline{X}$ replaces X. And since the mean of a sampling distribution is $\mu_{\overline{x}}$, $\mu_{\overline{x}}$ replaces μ. The denominator of Formula 6.1 is $N_{\overline{x}}$, which is the number of sample means that comprise the sampling distribution. You would never use Formula 6.1 to calculate the standard deviation of a sampling distribution because $N_{\overline{x}}$ is almost infinite.

The Relation Between σ and $\sigma_{\overline{x}}$

Whereas the mean of the sampling distribution is identical to the mean of the population, $\mu = \mu_{\overline{x}}$, the standard deviation of the sampling distribution is not equal to the standard deviation of the population. The two measures are related, however. Formula 6.2 shows how the standard deviation of the population is related to the standard deviation of the sampling distribution. The standard deviation of the sampling distribution of means is called the standard error of the mean or simply the **standard error.**

Standard Error of the Mean

$$\sigma_{\bar{x}} = \frac{\sigma}{\sqrt{n}} \quad \textit{(Formula 6.2)}$$

Note the denominator of the standard error. The n refers to the sample size used when taking repeated samples. Remember that when constructing a sampling distribution every sample is the same size. Thus, the relation between σ and $\sigma_{\bar{x}}$ depends on the size of the samples. The variability of the sampling distribution is determined by the variability of the population distribution *and* the size of the samples used to theoretically establish the sampling distribution.

There is some potential for confusion when discussing the means that comprise the sampling distribution. You are used to thinking of a distribution of *scores* that has one mean. A sampling distribution is a distribution of means. The mean of the sampling distribution is the mean of all the means, $\mu_{\bar{x}}$. For example, if you move one standard error away from the mean of the sampling distribution, you will land on a mean; but this mean is not *the* mean of the distribution.

How *n* Affects the Standard Error of the Mean

The following discussion first addresses how n influences $\sigma_{\bar{x}}$, and then why n has an effect on $\sigma_{\bar{x}}$. Suppose two different sampling distributions from the same population are established. In the first sampling distribution, the sample size is 4. In the second sampling distribution, the sample size is 25. The standard deviation of the population is 32. Using Formula 6.2,

$$\sigma_{\bar{x}} = \frac{32}{\sqrt{4}} = 16 \quad \text{and} \quad \sigma_{\bar{x}} = \frac{32}{\sqrt{25}} = 6.40$$

The standard error of the mean becomes smaller as the sample size becomes larger. This is not the case with the mean of the sampling distribution; $\mu_{\bar{x}} = \mu$ no matter what the size of n. Step 2, page 131, required you to specify the size of the samples when constructing a sampling distribution. By using the preceding equation, you can see that n influences the variability of the sampling distribution. However, you may be wondering, "What is the real sampling distribution?" or, "What is the best sampling distribution?" First, there is not just one sampling distribution for a single population. Since there are as many sampling distributions for a population as there are sample sizes, statisticians use the term a *family of sampling distributions.* Whenever you refer to a sampling distribution, you are actually referring to a sampling distribution of a particular size n. Keeping in mind that sampling distributions are theoretical, one sampling distribution is just as "real" as the next. Which one is the best? There is no best one. However, *as the sample size increases, the sampling distribution will approach a normal distribution.* How large does the n have to be before the sampling distribution is normal?

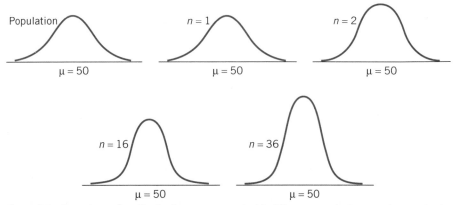

Figure 6.1 Several sampling distributions constructed with different sample sizes. As the sample size increases, the standard error, $\sigma_{\bar{x}}$, reflected in the width of the distribution, correspondingly decreases.

The standard answer is when n is 30. However, if the population is normal, any size n will lead to a normally distributed sampling distribution. If the population is *very* nonnormal an n somewhat larger than 30 may be needed to yield a normally distributed sampling distribution of means.

Given two sampling distributions, why does the one with a smaller n have a larger standard error? As an example, let's contrast a sampling distribution in which $n = 2$ with one in which $n = 20$. Each one of the means of the sampling distributions is comprised of scores. When $n = 2$, there are two scores that are averaged to arrive at the mean for that sample. When $n = 20$, there are 20 scores averaged to arrive at the mean for that sample. Which is more *unlikely,* selecting two extreme scores or selecting 20 extreme scores? Although you do not usually get two extreme scores in a row, it is much more unlikely that you would get 20 extreme scores. In other words, with a small sample, there is no opportunity for the other scores to compensate for extreme scores; in large samples, the other scores *can* compensate for extreme scores. Therefore, a sampling distribution based on $n = 2$ will contain many more extreme means than a sampling distribution in which $n = 20$. As a consequence, there are fewer and fewer means in the tails of a sampling distribution as n becomes progressively larger. Just as fewer extreme scores produce a population or sample distribution with a relatively small standard deviation, fewer extreme means produce a sampling distribution with a relatively small standard error of the mean. Figure 6.1 shows how the shape of a sampling distribution is affected by changes in the size of the samples.

The following list summarizes the main points of sampling distributions of means.

1. A sampling distribution of means is a theoretical distribution derived by computing the means of an almost infinite number of samples of size n.

2. If the scores of a population are normally distributed, irrespective of sample size, the sampling distribution of means will be normally distributed.

3. If the population distribution is not normally distributed, the sampling distribution approximates a standard normal curve as the sample size increases. The more the population distribution deviates from normality, the larger the sample size must be to establish a normally distributed sampling distribution.

4. The mean of the sampling distribution will be exactly the same as the mean of the population, $\mu = \mu_{\bar{x}}$.

5. The standard deviation of the sampling distribution is called the standard error of the mean. The relation between the standard error of the mean and the standard deviation of the population is: $\sigma_{\bar{x}} = \sigma/\sqrt{n}$.

Estimating the Standard Error of the Mean
When σ is Unknown

Only in rare situations will a researcher know the value of population parameters. In most cases, population parameters must be estimated from sample statistics. If σ is known, then $\sigma_{\bar{x}}$ can be computed with certainty. When σ is unknown, σ must be estimated by s. Therefore, $s_{\bar{x}}$ is an estimate of $\sigma_{\bar{x}}$. Formula 6.3 is the standard error of the mean estimated from a single sample.

Estimated Standard Error of the Mean

$$s_{\bar{x}} = \frac{s}{\sqrt{n}}$$ *(Formula 6.3)*

where,

$s_{\bar{x}}$ = the estimated standard error of the mean
s = the sample standard deviation
n = the sample size

Formula 6.3 allows us to estimate the amount of variability of a sampling distribution. As an estimate of $\sigma_{\bar{x}}$, $s_{\bar{x}}$ becomes more reliable as the sample size increases.

Table 6.1 clarifies the various symbols and estimates that are characteristics of sampling distributions.

TABLE 6.1   Important Symbols of Sampling Distributions and Population Estimates

1. $\overline{X}$ is an estimate of μ

2. s is an estimate of σ

3. $\mu_{\bar{x}}$ is the same value as μ; $\mu_{\bar{x}}$ is *not* an estimate of μ

4. $\sigma_{\bar{x}}$ is the standard deviation of a sampling distribution, called the standard error; it is not an estimate of anything

5. $s_{\bar{x}}$ is an estimate of $\sigma_{\bar{x}}$

Sampling Distributions and Sampling Error

The notion of sampling error is fundamental in statistical inference. When discussing the mean in Chapter 3, an error was defined as the distance a score is from the mean of the distribution, $X - \overline{X}$. The term error may have been confusing because error implies a mistake; the fact that a raw score can be different from the mean is hardly a mistake. However, the term error has real meaning in relation to a sampling distribution. Within the sampling distribution of means, the only value that is the same as the mean of the population is $\mu_{\overline{x}}$. Only those sample means that are equal to $\mu_{\overline{x}}$ are perfect estimates of μ. Any sample mean that is different from the mean of the sampling distribution is an error—in the sense that it is an inaccurate estimate of μ. A **sampling error** is the difference between a population parameter and the estimate of that parameter provided by a statistic. Hence, when estimating μ, a sampling error is $\overline{X} - \mu$.

When working with a population distribution of raw scores, σ is the overall measure of error. With a sampling distribution, the overall measure of error is $\sigma_{\overline{x}}$. This makes perfect sense. Figure 6.2 shows two sampling distributions that have the same mean. Figure 6.2(a) has a smaller standard error, and as a result, the distribution is narrower than the sampling distribution in 6.2(b), where there are many more sample means a great distance from $\mu_{\overline{x}}$. Suppose you select a mean at random from each distribution in Figure 6.2. With an error defined as $\overline{X} - \mu_{\overline{x}}$, in which case would you expect the larger error? Since the distribution in 6.2(b) has more means far from $\mu_{\overline{x}}$, you are more likely to select a sample mean farther from the mean of the distribution. In other words, when comparing sampling distributions that have different standard errors, a randomly selected mean from the broader distribution will likely be a poorer estimate of μ than a randomly selected mean from a sampling distribution with a smaller standard error.

At this point there is no way for you to fully appreciate the importance of sampling distributions. However, it is impossible to understand the statistical foundation of hypothesis testing if you don't understand the characteristics and logic of sampling distributions. In large measure, the difference between being a statistical "number cruncher" and *understanding* statistics will be due to your grasp of sampling distributions. If you have understood this chapter's discussion of sampling distributions, you will have a much easier time mastering much of the material presented in subsequent chapters. If you feel confused, you are urged to reread

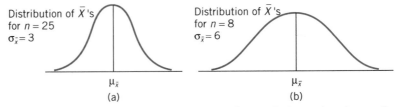

Figure 6.2 (*a*) The sampling distribution has a smaller standard error than the sampling distribution in (*b*). The amount of sampling error is greater as $\sigma_{\overline{x}}$ increases.

those sections of the chapter that were troublesome to you. Throughout the remainder of this text, how the concept of a sampling distribution figures into the topic under discussion will be presented.

SUMMARY

The field of inferential statistics, based on probability theory and logic, is used to make inferences about the characteristics of a population from the characteristics of a random sample drawn from the population. A random sample is a sample of scores taken from a population in such a way that each score of the population has an equal chance of being included in the sample. Researchers use random sampling to obtain samples that are representative of populations. Random sampling forms the basis on which you can generalize from samples to populations.

The field of inferential statistics includes estimation and hypothesis testing. Parameter estimation uses data from a sample to infer the value of a population parameter. There are two kinds of estimation: point estimation and interval estimation or confidence intervals. Point estimation entails estimating a parameter as a single value. Interval estimation establishes a range of values within which the parameter is expected to lie. The second, and most common type of inferential procedure is hypothesis testing.

Several characteristics of hypothesis testing were discussed:

1. A scientific hypothesis is a formal statement or expectation about the outcome of a study. A scientific hypothesis precedes the collection of data.

2. A statistical hypothesis is a numerical statement regarding the outcome of a study.

3. Hypothesis testing uses samples to make inferences about populations. Statistical methods are used to make these inferences.

4. The null hypothesis states that there is no effect of the independent variable on the dependent variable. The alternative hypothesis states that there is an experimental effect. Null and alternative hypotheses are statistical hypotheses and are thus presented as numerical statements.

5. Hypothesis testing is framed as a yes/no question. Since any answer is probabilistic, there is always a risk of committing an error.

Case I research uses one sample to test a hypothesis about the mean of a population. Case II research uses two samples to test a hypothesis about the difference between two population means. When two samples are used, the investigator has an opportunity to establish the comparative effectiveness of two treatments. Many research designs go beyond Case II research in that more than two samples are used to make inferences about populations. The correlational approach is an alternative research method that differs from experimentation in that it does not attempt to exert an influence on a measured response. Because variables are not controlled, the correlational approach cannot identify causal relations among variables. The correlational approach is aimed at identifying the variables that occur together.

A sampling distribution is a distribution of some sample statistic. It is the conceptual and mathematical cornerstone of hypothesis testing. This chapter discussed the sampling distribution of the mean. Five facts about the sampling distribution of means were presented:

1. A sampling distribution of means is a theoretical distribution derived by computing the means of an almost infinite number of samples of size n.
2. If the scores of a population are normally distributed, irrespective of sample size, the sampling distribution of means will be normally distributed.
3. If the population distribution is not normally distributed, the sampling distribution approximates a standard normal curve as the sample size increases. The more the population distribution deviates from normality, the larger the sample size must be to establish a normally distributed sampling distribution. (Points 2 and 3 define the Central Limit Theorem.)
4. The mean of the sampling distribution will be exactly the same as the mean of the population, $\mu = \mu_{\overline{x}}$.
5. The standard deviation of the sampling distribution is called the standard error of the mean. The relation between the standard error of the mean and the standard deviation of the population is: $\sigma_{\overline{x}} = \sigma/\sqrt{n}$.

KEY FORMULAS FOR CHAPTER 6

Definitional Formula for the Standard Deviation of a Sampling Distribution

$$\sigma_{\overline{x}} = \sqrt{\frac{\Sigma(\overline{X} - \mu_{\overline{x}})^2}{N_{\overline{x}}}}$$ *(Formula 6.1)*

Standard Error of the Mean

$$\sigma_{\overline{x}} = \frac{\sigma}{\sqrt{n}}$$ *(Formula 6.2)*

Estimated Standard Error of the Mean

$$s_{\overline{x}} = \frac{s}{\sqrt{n}}$$ *(Formula 6.3)*

WORK PROBLEMS

The first ten questions are all conceptual; no computations are required. Try to answer these questions without referring to the text.

1. How would you go about constructing a theoretical sampling distribution of means?
2. How does the population standard deviation influence the variability of the sampling distribution?

3. What is the difference between point and interval estimation?

4. How does hypothesis testing differ from estimation?

5. How is the variability of a sampling distribution affected by the sample size?

6. What is meant by Case I and II research? How is correlational research different from Case I and II research?

7. What is the difference between a scientific and statistical hypothesis?

8. Define null and alternative hypotheses.

9. Give examples of null and alternative hypotheses for Case I and Case II research.

10. A normally distributed population of scores has $\mu = 100$ and $\sigma = 10$. A sampling distribution is established with $n = 9$. Describe the sampling distribution in terms of $\mu_{\bar{x}}$, its standard error, and shape.

Work Problems for the Computer

11. Consider the following data set as a population of scores. Compute μ and σ. Take a random sample of 5, 10, 15, and 20 scores. Compute the sample means and the standard errors, using σ. Note how the sample size influences the variability of the sampling distribution that would be derived from this population. The overall measure of sampling error is the standard error of the mean. As the sample size becomes larger, sampling error becomes smaller.

A Population of Scores

22	11	7	9	9	8	7	23	45	9
23	21	8	8	5	16	9	22	17	6
12	29	6	5	9	23	7	33	24	5
15	14	9	7	3	17	8	19	15	8
11	10	8	6	1	11	9	25	35	9
10	18	6	5	4	13	8	21	20	9
14	17	5	6	2	34	2	35	35	5
35	36	8	1	3	37	1	32	33	4
33	29	7	7	6	28	9	27	26	9
27	28	5	5	4	27	8	26	25	7

Testing the Significance of a Single Mean: The Single-Sample *z* and *t* Tests

7.1 THE RESEARCH CONTEXT

This chapter addresses the statistical analyses used in Case I research. You will recall that Case I research uses one sample of subjects to make an inference about whether the mean of the population is some specified value. Does the obtained sample come from a population with a specified mean or from a population with a different mean? It is easy to think of research questions that could be answered by using a single sample of subjects; a few examples are presented in the following. The single-sample methodology for testing a hypothesis about a specified population mean has its place in the behavioral sciences. However, it is one of the least used research methods. It is certainly less commonly used than the type of study that compares the relative effects of two or more experimental treatments, or the type of study that attempts to discover the correlation between two or more variables.

This chapter is devoted to Case I research because it is the perfect vehicle for discussing many basic statistical concepts used in hypothesis testing. Once you learn these concepts in the context of the simplest of research designs, you will be able to understand the statistical inner workings of hypothesis testing in more complex designs—designs that are more commonly used in the behavioral sciences.

▶ **EXAMPLE 1**   Assume that the mean weight of newborn babies is 7 lb, with a standard deviation of 1 lb. A study is conducted with the following research question: "Do newborn babies of mothers who drink alcohol during pregnancy weigh less than the average baby?" To answer this question, the investigator would take a single random sample of newborns of mothers who consumed alcohol during pregnancy, compute the mean, and using the methods discussed in this chapter, come to a decision about whether or not the sample came from a population with a mean of 7 lb.   ◀

▶ **EXAMPLE 2**   Suppose a college admissions director wants to know if the college is attracting excellent mathematics students. Assume the national mean of the quantitative section of the Scholastic Aptitude Test (SAT-Q) is 500, with a standard deviation of 100. The admissions director takes a random sample of SAT-Q scores from the incoming freshman class, computes the mean, and learns whether the population of incoming freshmen has a mean SAT-Q that is different from 500.   ◀

▶ **EXAMPLE 3**   The chairperson of a graduate-program in psychology reads that the national average of the time it takes a graduate student to earn the Ph.D. is 6.8 years, with a standard deviation of 1.2 years. She wonders how the students of her program compare. A random sample of 32 recent graduates is examined and found to have a mean of 5.2 years. Can she conclude that her student sample comes from a population that has a mean different from 6.8 years?   ◀

 The statistical test used to decide if a sample mean does or does not come from a specified population, *when the standard deviation of the population is known*, is called a **z test.** Since only one sample of scores is taken, the z test applied in this situation is a single-sample or one-sample statistical test. There are times when a single-sample z test *seems* appropriate to the research context, but if the standard deviation of the population is not known, a single-sample t test is used. The single-sample t test uses the sample standard deviation as an estimate of the population standard deviation. This chapter discusses both tests. You will discover that the arithmetic computations for each test are simple. The most important material of this chapter is the discussion of sampling distributions, the reasons the formulas for the z test and t test are expressed as they are, and the implications of shifting from a z test to a t test. Equally important is the discussion of what is meant when researchers say that a difference between means is statistically significant.

7.2 USING THE SAMPLING DISTRIBUTION OF MEANS FOR THE SINGLE-SAMPLE z TEST

This section begins where Chapter 6 ended: the importance of sampling distributions in hypothesis testing. To recall, the following list highlights the facts about the sampling distribution of means.

1. A sampling distribution of means is a theoretical distribution. It specifies the relative frequency of all possible sample means for a given size n.
2. If the population distribution is normal, then the sampling distribution will be normally distributed. If the scores in the population are not normally distributed, then the sampling distribution will approximate normality with a sufficiently large n (around 30).
3. The mean of the sampling distribution equals the mean of the population $(\mu_{\bar{x}} = \mu)$.
4. The standard error of a sampling distribution is related to the population standard deviation by $\sigma_{\bar{x}} = \sigma/\sqrt{n}$. When σ is unknown, the standard error is estimated by $s_{\bar{x}} = s/\sqrt{n}$.

z Scores and the Sampling Distribution of Means

The z-score formula for transforming a raw score to a z score was given in Chapter 5 as:

$$z = \frac{X - \mu}{\sigma}$$

A z score specifies how many standard deviations the transformed raw score is from the mean of the distribution. If every score of a population that is *normally distributed* is transformed to a z score, the result is the standard normal curve; this curve has a mean of 0 and a standard deviation of 1. The standard normal curve was used in Chapter 5 to solve all the z-score problems. Using the z table in Appendix B.1, it is possible, for example, to make statements about the probability of selecting a score at random from some area under the normal curve. In every one of the z-score problems you worked in Chapter 5, the focus was on *scores.* For example, a typical question was, "Given $\mu = 50$, and $\sigma = 5$, what is the probability of drawing a *score* at random above 60 or below 40?" The strategy you used to answer this type of question involved transforming the numbers 60 and 40 to *z* scores, and then using the *z* table to identify the area of the curve above the *z* score for 60, and below the *z* score for 40.

In inferential statistics, a sample statistic (e.g., the mean) is used to infer a population parameter. It is meaningless to take a *score from a sample* and attempt to *infer a score from the population.* When testing a hypothesis about the value of a population mean, a sample mean is used to decide whether the population has a stated value. The decision is based on the probability of finding a sample mean of a certain value, *given a hypothesized value of the population mean.* The *z*-score formula cannot be used to arrive at a probability statement regarding the likelihood of drawing a *sample mean* of a certain value. This is because the *z*-score formula is applied to *scores,* not *means.* However, with a slight adjustment in the *z*-score formula, and by using the concept of a sampling distribution, you can make probability statements about selecting a sample mean from an area under the curve of a sampling distribution.

The *z* Statistic

The *z*-score formula transforms raw scores into *z* scores. The formula for the *z* statistic transforms the means of the sampling distribution into *z* scores. Formula 7.1 is used for this transformation.

---

z Statistic

$$z_{\text{obt}} = \frac{\overline{X} - \mu}{\sigma_{\overline{x}}}$$

(Formula 7.1)

where,

$\overline{X}$ = the mean of the sample
μ = the hypothesized mean
$\sigma_{\overline{x}}$ = the standard error of the mean

---

z_{obt} is used to indicate that this *z* value is obtained from a mean. The *z* statistic has the same basic form as the *z*-score formula. Table 7.1 contrasts each value of the two formulas. Technically, the population mean of the *z*-score formula is replaced by the mean of the sampling distribution. Since the mean of the sampling distribution, $\mu_{\overline{x}}$, is the same as the population mean from which the sampling distribution is established, the formula for the *z* statistic uses the symbol μ in place of $\mu_{\overline{x}}$. The sample mean, $\overline{X}$, replaces the *X* score. In the denominator of the *z*-score formula the standard deviation of the distribution of population scores is found. In the denominator of the *z* statistic the standard deviation of the sampling distribution is found, which is the standard error, $\sigma_{\overline{x}}$.

TABLE 7.1 A Comparison of the z-Score Formula Used to Transform Raw Scores with the z Statistic Used to Transform a Sampling Distribution of Means

z-Score Formula	z-Statistic Formula
$z = \dfrac{X - \mu}{\sigma}$	$z_{obt} = \dfrac{\overline{X} - \mu}{\sigma_{\overline{x}}}$
X = a single score	$\overline{X}$ = a single mean
μ = the population mean	μ = the hypothesized population mean
σ = population standard deviation	$\sigma_{\overline{x}}$ = standard error of the sampling distribution

If you transform the raw *scores* of a *normally distributed* population to z scores, you have the standard normal distribution. The z table can then be used to identify areas under the curve and to make probability statements. When a sampling distribution of means is *normally distributed,* transforming all the means to z values (using Formula 7.1) produces the same standard normal distribution. You can now use the z table to make probability statements about *means.*

The Logic of the *z* Test

As a vehicle for discussing how a researcher conducts a statistical test with the mean of a population when σ is known, we'll use a hypothetical study. An educational enrichment program is developed to teach math skills. The program entails the use of individual computerized instruction to teach basic algebra skills. A *random sample* of 36 students is selected, given the individual instruction, and tested at the end of the school year. The test has been extensively validated on a large population and is known to have a mean of 100 and a standard deviation of 10. A statistical test, based on a single sample, will be conducted to test the hypothesis that the population mean is 100. Thus,

$$H_0: \quad \mu = 100$$

$$H_1: \quad \mu \neq 100$$

You are *not* testing the hypothesis that the mean of the national exam is 100. You already know that the mean of the test is 100. The population to which you are making an inference is a hypothetical population—the population of all students that *theoretically* could have received the training. Since you cannot include the entire population in the study, a representative sample is used. When the training is completed, you must assume that your sample of subjects is performing the same way as the entire population of students would have, had they all been exposed to the enrichment program. The population of interest is the *hypothetical population of students.* The sample is a subset of all these hypothetical students. You can see why the population is hypothetical since the whole population is not receiving math enrichment instruction.

The null and alternative hypotheses in the example are statements that derive from the question, "Is the mean of the population from which the sample is taken 100?" In essence, you are asking if the treatment has any effect on math skills. If the treatment has an effect, you would expect to obtain a sample mean that is "different enough" from the hypothesized population mean, such that it would be "highly unlikely" that the population mean is 100.

Sampling Error and Hypothesis Testing

Suppose the null hypothesis is true—that is—the math enrichment program has no effect, and the population mean is 100. When you gather the data and compute the sample mean, would you expect it to be *exactly* 100? Even if the null hypothesis were true, it is extremely unlikely that the sample mean would be exactly 100 due to sampling error. Recall that the sampling error of a mean is the distance the mean of a sample is from the mean of the population. Imagine taking repeated samples from a population and calculating the mean for each sample. Each mean is based on scores randomly drawn from different segments of the population. Due to chance, you might, for example, draw many extreme scores from the right tail of the population. The resulting mean, therefore, will be larger than the mean of the population. Even though the null hypothesis is true and there is no treatment effect, the random selection of scores is subject to sampling error.

Returning to the educational enrichment program, you have to decide if there is a treatment effect; that is, you have to make a decision about whether to reject the null hypothesis that $\mu = 100$. Suppose your sample mean is 100.5. Are you willing to conclude that $\mu \neq 100$? Probably not. Suppose the sample mean is 102. Now are you willing to reject the null hypothesis that the population mean is 100? How about a sample mean of 105, 115, or 130? As you answer these questions, you are operating with some intuitive belief about the credibility of sampling error as an explanation of obtaining a sample mean of a given size. You might assume that a sample mean of 102 could easily occur when the population mean is 100, but you may conclude that the population mean is not 100 if the sample mean is found to be 130. The statistical procedures involved in hypothesis testing reduce the guesswork. When you conduct a z test, the sample mean is transformed to a z statistic, and then the z table is used to judge the probability of obtaining that sample mean when the null hypothesis is true. If it is *very unlikely* that sampling error would have yielded the value of the sample mean, you would conclude that the population mean is not what is specified in the null hypothesis, and the null hypothesis is rejected. The term statistically significant means that it is very unlikely that sampling error accounts for the obtained sample mean. Please reread the last three sentences; they are the most important in the entire chapter.

Sampling Distributions When the Null Hypothesis is True or False

Figure 7.1 depicts two sampling distributions of a mathematics enrichment program. The sampling distribution on the left shows the mean of the population as 100. The overlapping sampling distribution on the right is from a population with a

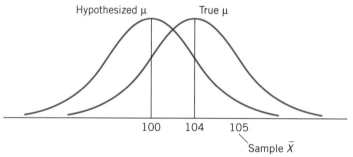

Figure 7.1   The sampling distribution on the left is from a population in which $\mu = 100$. The sampling distribution on the right is from a population in which $\mu = 104$; this represents the *true* state of affairs. A sample mean of 105 falls in the tail of the left distribution, but closer to the middle of the distribution on the right.

mean of 104. As you continue reading, keep the following fact in mind. The goal of hypothesis testing is *not* to infer the value of the population mean. If you want to make an inference of that sort, use a point or interval estimation. The goal of hypothesis testing is to decide whether to reject the null hypothesis. In Figure 7.1, the sampling distribution on the left would be true if the null hypothesis is true ($\mu = 100$). In other words, if the mathematics enrichment program has no effect, you would expect the mean of the sampling distribution to be 100. If the null hypothesis is false, then the mean of the sampling distribution is some number other than 100. In this figure, it is assumed that the true mean of the hypothetical treated population is 104; thus the mean of the sampling distribution must be 104.

Now suppose you take a sample, compute the mean, and find it to be 105. If the true state of affairs is represented by the sampling distribution on the left, $\mu = 100$, then you have sampled from the right tail of the distribution. Since there are few means in the tail of the distribution, it is a statistically rare event to obtain a mean of 105 from a sampling distribution with a mean of 100. However, if the true state of affairs is represented by the sampling distribution on the right, $\mu = 104$, then the sample mean of 105 is not at all unusual. A sampling distribution with a mean of 104 will have many means around the value of 104; obtaining one close to 104 is *not* a statistically rare event.

When hypothesis testing, you don't know the mean of the population, and therefore you don't know the mean of the sampling distribution. Figure 7.1 gives you a glimpse behind the scene—a glimpse that you never have in actual research. With only your sample mean, you need to determine the probability of drawing that sample mean by chance, if the null hypothesis is *true*. If the probability is low, then the null hypothesis is rejected. If you hypothesize $\mu = 100$, obtaining a sample mean of 105 *may* lead you to conclude that μ is probably not 100. The z test and the z table are used to arrive at a decision about whether to reject the null hypothesis.

Using the z Test in Deciding to Reject the Null Hypothesis

Consider again the task of evaluating the effectiveness of the educational enrichment program. When testing the null hypothesis, you proceed *as if* the null hypothesis were true. Since students are tested with an examination known to have a population mean of 100 and a standard deviation of 10, the null and alternative hypotheses are stated as:

$$H_0: \quad \mu = 100$$

$$H_1: \quad \mu \neq 100$$

A sample of 36 students is tested after completion of the program and the sample mean is found to be 105. After the null and alternative hypotheses have been stated, the next step is to transform the sample mean to a z statistic, using Formula 7.1.

$$z_{obt} = \frac{\overline{X} - \mu}{\sigma_{\overline{x}}}$$

$$z_{obt} = \frac{105 - 100}{10/\sqrt{36}}$$

$$= \frac{5}{1.67}$$

$$z_{obt} = \mathbf{2.99}$$

How would you interpret a z_{obt} of 2.99? If you assume that the null hypothesis is true, $\mu = 100$, then your sample mean of 105 is 2.99 standard error units above the mean of the sampling distribution.

Figure 7.2 shows where the sample mean of 105 lies in a sampling distribution, which has a mean of 100 and a standard error of 1.67. Note the z values that correspond to the means in the sampling distribution. Since Formula 7.1 transforms the sampling distribution to a standard normal curve with $\mu = 0$ and $\sigma = 1$, the z value at the mean of the sampling distribution is 0. Since the standard error of

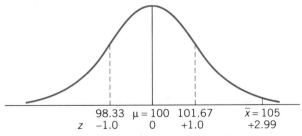

Figure 7.2   In this sampling distribution $\mu = 100$ and $\sigma_{\overline{x}} = 1.67$. A sample mean of 105 is 2.99 standard error units above the mean.

the sampling distribution is 1.67, the means of 101.67 (100 + 1.67) and 98.33 (100 − 1.67) have corresponding z values that are +1 and −1, respectively. The sample mean of 105 is way out in the right tail. If the mean of the sampling distribution is 100, what percentage of means are found at or above a z of 2.99? Refer to the third column in the z table of Appendix B.1. Only .14 percent of the means of the sampling distribution are found at or above a mean of 105 (a z of 2.99).

Now you have a decision to make. You can assume that the mean of the sampling distribution (the mean of the population) is 100, and that you have experienced the highly unlikely event of sampling from the extreme right tail of the sampling distribution. On the other hand, you can reject the assumption that the null hypothesis is true; that is, reject the statement that the mean of the sampling distribution is 100. In this instance, prudence would dictate the latter conclusion and you would reject the null hypothesis.

If it were left up to each individual researcher to decide what is a rare statistical occurrence and when to reject the null hypothesis, hypothesis testing would lead to constant arguments. Individual criteria would be used with no rule as to when the null hypothesis should be rejected. For this reason, behavioral scientists follow a long-standing convention of using a probability value of .05 as the criterion for rejecting the null hypothesis.

The Criterion for Statistical Significance: Acceptance and Rejection Regions

Over the years, statisticians have come to define the criterion of significance to be .05 (for a historical overview see Cowles and Davis, 1982). As applied to the single-sample z test, this means that if the probability of randomly drawing a sample mean of a given value is less than .05, when the population mean is hypothesized to be a specified value, then you reject the hypothesis that the population mean is that specified value. In the z distribution, what are the cutoffs beyond which lie 5 percent of the distribution? Stated differently, what is the probability of selecting a *score* at random that falls in *either* the lower 2.5 percent of the distribution *or* the upper 2.5 percent of the distribution? The z scores of ±1.96 mark the upper and lower 2.5 percent of the distribution. And, of course, the probability of selecting a score at random above or below ±1.96 is .05. When σ is known and $n > 30$, the sampling distribution has the same shape as the z distribution; hence, the probability of selecting a *mean* beyond a z_{obt} of ±1.96 is also .05. Thus, if the z_{obt} shows the mean to be more than 1.96 standard errors from the *assumed* population mean, then reject the null hypothesis.

Alpha Levels and Rejection Regions

 When you use the cutoffs of ±1.96, you are testing the null hypothesis at the 5 percent level of significance. The probability value of .05 is called the **alpha level,** symbolized as $\alpha = .05$. In hypothesis testing, the investigator chooses the alpha level. Other conventional alpha levels are .10 and .01. Before the data are analyzed, the researcher specifies the alpha level at which the null hypothesis is to be tested. In essence, when setting the alpha level, the researcher is defining the criterion for what will be considered a statistically rare event.

As soon as an alpha level is selected, *acceptance* and *rejection* regions are automatically determined. Figure 7.3 shows the acceptance and rejection regions for alpha levels of .10, .05, and .01. The rejection region is in the tails of the sampling distribution. The absolute value of the z scores that define the rejection regions is called the **critical value.** Since 10 percent of the distribution falls above and below z's of ± 1.65, the null hypothesis is rejected at the .10 level of significance if the absolute value of z_{obt} is larger than the critical value of 1.65. If the alpha level is set at .05, the null hypothesis is rejected if the absolute value of z_{obt} is greater than 1.96. And since only 1 percent of the sampling distribution is beyond

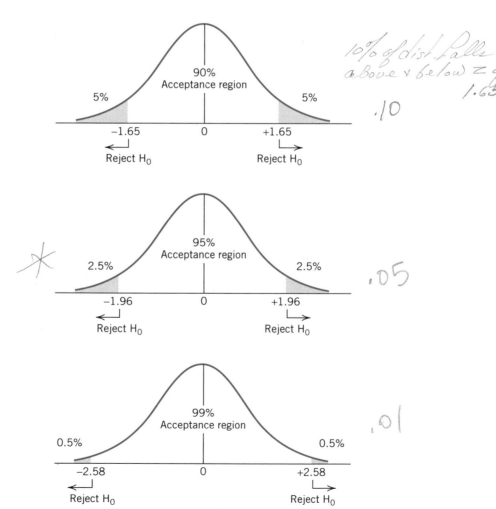

Figure 7.3   The acceptance and rejection regions for alpha levels of .10, .05, and .01.

z's of ± 2.58, the null hypothesis is rejected at an alpha of .01 if the absolute value of z_{obt} is larger than the critical value of 2.58.

If alpha is set at .05, and the null hypothesis is rejected, then you would state $p < .05$, which means that the probability of obtaining a mean beyond the critical value is less than .05 *when the null hypothesis is true*. The critical values of 1.65, 1.96, and 2.58 can be verified by using the z table in Appendix B.1. Use the third column of the z table and look up $\alpha/2$. Note that the rejection region defined by the critical values is in both tails of the distribution. The fact that the rejection region is in both tails reflects the investigator's willingness to reject the null hypothesis if the sample mean is either considerably above or below the hypothesized population mean. This is known as a *nondirectional* hypothesis test or a *two-tailed* hypothesis test. In the educational enrichment program example, the z_{obt} was 2.99. If prior to collecting the data, alpha was set at .01, you would reject the null hypothesis in favor of the alternative hypothesis because 2.99 is larger than 2.58 ($p < .01$). Now that the null hypothesis has been rejected, what does this mean about the educational enrichment program?

7.3 THE IMPLICATIONS OF REJECTING THE NULL HYPOTHESIS

What would you conclude if the null hypothesis is rejected? In an experiment, testing the null hypothesis is the statistical process used to discover if there is a treatment effect. When the null hypothesis is rejected, you would conclude that the difference between the sample mean and the hypothesized population mean is probably not due to sampling error (chance). What caused the difference? The difference between the hypothesized population mean and the sample mean is presumably due to the experimental variable. For example, the mean of the sample of students in the educational enrichment program was determined to most likely come from a population that had a mean that differed from 100. One would like to attribute the difference between means to the educational training that the students received. Generally speaking, in the context of experimentation, any time the null hypothesis is rejected, a researcher would like to conclude that it was because of the manipulation of an independent variable. However, you cannot automatically assume that the independent variable is responsible for the observed difference between means. Sampling error *might* have produced the difference, but because the null hypothesis is tested and rejected at, say, the 5 percent level of significance, sampling error is an unlikely explanation. It is possible, however, that the experimental effect was due to a variable not controlled by the experimenter. Recall from Chapter 1 that an experimental confound presents an interpretive dilemma for the investigator since alternative explanations can be offered for the research findings. Rejecting the null hypothesis has no bearing on what is the best interpretation of an experimental effect. After rejecting the null hypothesis, the most reasonable interpretation of the findings is advanced in the context of a well-controlled study that minimizes the number of alternative hypotheses. A poorly designed study cannot be saved by even the most sophisticated statistical techniques.

7.4 TYPE I AND TYPE II ERRORS

Whenever the null hypothesis is rejected, it is because it is the most reasonable conclusion given the obtained sample mean and the assumed population mean. However, in the field of inferential statistics, there is always a chance of error. The whole inferential enterprise rests on probabilities. By definition, probable does not mean certain. There are two kinds of errors that you can commit when rejecting or retaining the null hypothesis.

Imagine that you are a member of a jury that must decide the guilt or innocence of a defendant. Independent of what you decide, the defendant is either truly guilty or truly innocent. In this situation, there are four possible outcomes. First, if the defendant is guilty and you decide guilty, you are correct. Second, if the defendant is innocent and you decide innocent, you are correct again. Third, if the defendant is guilty and you vote innocent, you have committed an error. Finally, if the person is innocent and you say guilty, another error is committed. Although the legal criterion for deciding guilty is "guilty beyond a reasonable doubt," the criterion you use to define "reasonable doubt" may change depending on the consequences of each kind of error. For example, if you know that the defendant will receive the death penalty if found guilty, you will want to be *very* sure of your decision when you vote guilty. Under this circumstance, you may require more evidence of the defendant's guilt before you are willing to decide guilty. As your cutoff for defining reasonable doubt becomes more stringent, it reflects the fact that you are protecting yourself from making a certain kind of error: the error of calling an innocent person guilty. However, by making your criterion more stringent, you increase the likelihood of the opposite error: calling a guilty person innocent. There is a trade-off between the two types of errors. Two points are important to remember. First, whether it is deciding on the guilt or innocence of a defendant, or the status of the null hypothesis, there are two types of errors. Second, the criterion you use to make a decision is influenced by the relative consequences of committing each type of error.

 Our judicial example is analogous to the situation faced by the investigator when deciding to reject the null hypothesis. Two types of errors are possible. A **Type I error** is committed if a true null hypothesis is rejected. A **Type II error** is committed when a false null hypothesis is retained. Table 7.2 specifies the four possible outcomes when deciding to reject or retain the null hypothesis under the conditions that the null hypothesis is actually true or false. The problem is that

TABLE 7.2   **The Four Outcomes When Deciding Whether to Reject or Retain a True or False Null Hypothesis**

| | | TRUE STATE OF AFFAIRS | |
		H_0 *is True*	H_0 *is False*
Your Decision	*Retain* H_0	Correct	Type II error
	Reject H_0	Type I error	Correct

you never know when you have made an error because you never know the real status of the null hypothesis.

In hypothesis testing, the investigator is in a better position than the juror because the investigator is able to directly control the probability of a Type I error. The alpha level set by the researcher specifies the probability of a Type I error. Suppose alpha is set at .05. *Given a true null hypothesis,* if the study were conducted an infinite number of times, the null hypothesis would be mistakenly rejected 5 percent of the time. Thus, when the null hypothesis is true, the z_{obt} will not exceed the critical value of 1.96 and the null hypothesis will be correctly retained approximately 95 percent of the time. Likewise, if alpha is set at .01, you can expect to sample from the rejection region 1 percent of the time when the null hypothesis is true. When $\alpha = .01$, the probability of a Type I error is less than when alpha is set at .05. An error, however, is still possible.

Wouldn't this suggest that you should make alpha as stringent as possible? Why not set alpha at .0001? Now you will only commit a Type I error 1 out of 10,000 times! But remember the trade-off for the juror: If you're too afraid to convict an innocent person, you'll probably make it easier for a guilty defendant to be set free. If alpha is made more stringent, the probability of a Type I error decreases, but the probability of a Type II error increases. Therefore, as you reduce the risk of rejecting a true null hypothesis, the risk of retaining a false null hypothesis increases. Therefore, there is a trade-off between a Type I and Type II error.

A word of caution: Don't make the mistake of thinking that if the probability of a Type I error is .05, the probability of making a Type II error is .95. Calculating the probability of a Type II error is not so straightforward. The method for determining the probability of a Type II error will be discussed in Chapter 11.

Deciding on Alpha

How do researchers decide on an alpha level? Just like jurors, they weigh the consequences. Suppose a researcher becomes involved in an uncharted research area. There may be something there, no one knows. Failing to reject a null hypothesis is like saying "there is nothing here." It tends to halt further research in the area. In a new research area, the investigator may relax the alpha level and test at the 10 percent level of significance. An alpha level of .10 makes it easier to reject the null hypothesis since the critical value at the 10 percent level of significance is smaller (1.65) than the critical value at the 5 percent level of significance (1.96). Once an experimental effect is identified, subsequent studies of the phenomenon can use the more conservative alpha of .05, or even .01. A more liberal alpha level reflects the investigator's belief that a Type II error (failing to reject a false null hypothesis) is more serious than a Type I error (rejecting a true null hypothesis).

There are instances in which the consequences of making a Type I error are so serious that a researcher would want to set a very stringent alpha level. Consider a study that tests for serious drug side effects. Deciding that the medicine is safe, when, in fact, it produces side effects in a large number of people, is a potentially life-threatening error. If H_0 is cast in such a way that rejecting H_0 means that the drug is medically safe, the researcher might set alpha at .001. This practice reflects the researcher's belief that it is much more serious to conclude that the drug is safe when it is not, than to mistakenly conclude that the drug is not safe when in fact it is.

One final point about making a Type I error. Suppose a researcher conducts a study and fails to reject the null hypothesis. Would the investigator be justified in repeating the exact same study over and over again until the null hypothesis is rejected? No, because eventually a statistically significant finding will occur by chance. That is, eventually the null hypothesis will be rejected when it should not be rejected. This does not mean that researchers should not revise their experimental procedures and run the study again. But conducting the same study repeatedly is not only a waste of time, it is scientifically unacceptable.

7.5   IS A SIGNIFICANT FINDING "SIGNIFICANT"?

The use of the word significant in association with a rejected null hypothesis is unfortunate. In ordinary parlance, significant means important. It is possible to achieve statistical significance even when the research finding is trivial. Consider the educational enrichment program as an example. Instead of using a sample size of 36, suppose you had used a sample of 1000 students. Further, suppose that the sample mean turned out to be 101 instead of 104. Using Formula 7.1,

$$z_{obt} = \frac{\overline{X} - \mu}{\sigma_{\overline{x}}}$$

$$= \frac{101 - 100}{10/\sqrt{1000}}$$

$$= \frac{1}{.32}$$

$$z_{obt} = \mathbf{3.13}$$

Even if you set a conservative alpha level of .01, which has a critical value of 2.58, the null hypothesis is rejected. Do you think all the time, effort, and expense of the program is worth one point on the national exam? In this case, there is a statistically significant improvement that probably has little *practical* significance.

An interesting exercise is to read the clinical treatment literature. Be assured, if the article is published, there is a statistically significant finding, often having to do with the success of some treatment procedure. As you read these studies, ask yourself the question, "But is it *clinically significant?*" Under certain conditions, an inconsequential decrease in distress may produce a statistically significant finding.

The other side of the issue arises when the null hypothesis is not rejected; the statistical test is *nonsignificant.* Note that nonsignificant is not the same as *not significant.* A statistically nonsignificant finding may be important. For example, new treatments are advertised all the time in the back of magazines—treatments for arthritis, obesity, stress, or whatever ails you. If you contrast a no-treatment control group with a group receiving an ineffective treatment, you'll likely end up retaining the null hypothesis. However, since you cannot prove the null hypothesis to be true, you cannot conclude that the treatment is *proved* ineffective. Nonetheless, in the absence of evidence that the treatment *is* effective, there is no reason to use it. The fact that the treatment had a chance to show its effect and failed exemplifies a statistically nonsignificant finding that *is* significant.

Another problem in wording that is ubiquitous in significance testing is the use of phrases such as marginally significant, or highly significant. The phrase marginally significant is often used when the alpha level is set at .05; however, the test of significance would only lead to a rejection of the null hypothesis if the alpha level were set somewhere between .06 and .10. The phrase highly significant is often used when the null hypothesis is rejected at the .01 or .001 level of significance. This phrasing implies that as the p value decreases, a researcher should be more impressed with the strength of the effect produced by the treatment (Bakan, 1966; Cohen, 1990). This is misleading. Again, refer to the enrichment program example where the sample mean was stated as 101 and the n was increased to 1000. The test was significant at $p < .01$—highly significant. However, how much of an effect did the treatment program have on the performance of the students? Not much. The point is to avoid the use of modifiers when referring to p values.[1]

7.6 THE STATISTICAL TEST FOR THE MEAN OF A POPULATION WHEN σ IS UNKNOWN: THE t DISTRIBUTIONS

The t Distributions

We have used the z distribution to establish cutoffs for testing the null hypothesis at a given alpha level. However, when σ is unknown, transforming all the means of a sampling distribution by the z statistic cannot be accomplished. Instead, the sample standard deviation, s, must be used as an estimate of σ. This necessitates a change in the formula, and defines a t statistic.

---

t Statistic

$$t_{obt} = \frac{\overline{X} - \mu}{s_{\bar{x}}} \quad \text{(Formula 7.2)}$$

where,

$$s_{\bar{x}} = \frac{s}{\sqrt{n}}$$

---

[1] There are statistical techniques that can be used to directly reflect the amount of influence one variable has on another. These methods are used to assess effect size or the strength of association between two variables. A few of these analyses are presented in later chapters.

A **t distribution** is theoretically established by transforming every mean of a sampling distribution to a *t* statistic. The transformation is achieved by applying Formula 7.2 to every sample of the distribution, using $\overline{X}$, μ, s, and n. However, the *t* formula will not produce a standardized normal curve identical to the *z* distribution. This means that you can no longer use the critical values of 1.96 and 2.58 to test the null hypothesis at the 5 percent and 1 percent levels of significance. However, when the sample size is sufficiently large, around 25 or 30, the *t* distribution closely approximates the standard normal curve. A *t* distribution can be formed for any sampling distribution comprised of means that are based on an *n* of 2–∞. As the sample size of a sampling distribution gets progressively smaller than 30, the *t* distribution departs more and more from the shape of a standardized normal curve. Specifically, as *n* decreases, the tails of the *t* distribution get higher. Since a different *t* distribution can be established for each sampling distribution of size *n*, there is a *family of t distributions*. Figure 7.4 illustrates four *t* distributions

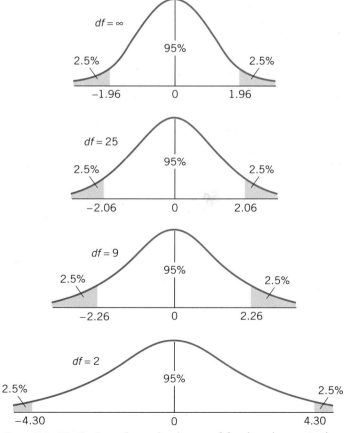

Figure 7.4   Distributions of *t* as the degrees of freedom change. As the sample size decreases, the tails of the distribution become higher. Note that the critical values that define the rejection region become larger as the sample size decreases.

based on sampling distributions of increasingly larger n's. Note how the distributions approximate the standardized normal curve as n increases. The sample size is *roughly* shown by df, the degrees of freedom. The degrees of freedom for the single-sample t test is $n - 1$, which is discussed in the following section.

As you examine Figure 7.4, remember that the t distribution is not a sampling distribution of means. The t distribution is a distribution of t values. Each t statistic is a sample mean transformed by the t formula. The mean of the t distribution is 0. However, unlike the z distribution, the standard deviation of the t distribution is not 1. The standard deviation of the t distribution changes, depending, in part, on the size of the samples used to establish the sampling distribution.

In Figure 7.4, also note that the rejection region for testing the null at the 5 percent level of significance is farther out in the tails as the sample size decreases. For example, the critical value when $df = 2$ is 4.30; when $df = 25$, the critical value is 2.06. The broader t distribution associated with $df = 2$ requires that you move 4.30 standard error units in each direction from the mean, to bracket the middle 95 percent of the distribution. When the $df = 25$, you need only move 2.06 standard error units from the mean to bracket the middle 95 percent of the t distribution. You have to go farther out in the tails to bracket the middle 95 percent of the t distribution as the distribution becomes broader because a broad distribution means that there are more t values in the tails.[2]

Degrees of Freedom

 Whenever a significance test is conducted, an obtained value is computed and compared to a critical value. The critical value is found by referring to a table of critical values appropriate to the particular test statistic. You will get used to finding critical values for various kinds of significance tests by looking up the degrees of freedom to find the critical value for the test statistic. Moreover, **degrees of freedom (df)** are used to compute the obtained values, which are used to compare to the critical values. The reasons *why* mathematicians use degrees of freedom in developing tests of significance are complex and beyond introductory statistics (Walker, 1940). Instead of discussing why df is used, only the concept will be explained.

Suppose you are asked to pick four numbers. Since there is no restriction imposed, you are free to pick any four numbers. All four numbers are free to vary; thus you have four degrees of freedom. Now a restriction is imposed: the four numbers must equal 10. You are free to pick any three numbers, but the fourth number must be selected so that the sum adds up to 10. Since three numbers are free to vary, you have three degrees of freedom. In general, degrees of freedom refer to the number of values that are free to vary under some restriction. The concept of degrees of freedom applies only when making a statistical inference. Recall from Chapter 4 that there is a difference in the denominator when calculating the sample standard deviation as opposed to the population standard deviation. The sample standard deviation is used as an estimate of the population standard deviation.

---

[2] Technically, there are more t values in the tails because $s_{\bar{x}}$ is variable and can take extreme values.

Sample Standard Deviation

$$s = \sqrt{\frac{\Sigma(X - \overline{X})^2}{n - 1}}$$

Population Standard Deviation

$$\sigma = \sqrt{\frac{\Sigma(X - \mu)^2}{N}}$$

The restriction imposed when computing s is $\Sigma(X - \overline{X}) = 0$. All the numbers are free to vary, but the last number must satisfy the restriction that $\Sigma(X - \overline{X}) = 0$. The t test used to test the mean of one sample against a specified population mean (Formula 7.2) uses s in the denominator to compute the standard error of the mean, $s_{\overline{x}} = s/\sqrt{n}$. Thus, the df associated with this formula is $n - 1$. When you use the t table to locate the cirtical value for the t test, the sample size -1 will be used.

Using the t Table to Find Critical Values

Table B.2 in the Appendix is the t table, a portion of which is reproduced below.

Level of Significance for Two-Tailed Test

df	.05	.01
⋮	⋮	⋮
8	2.306	3.355
9	2.262	3.250
10	2.228	3.169
⋮	⋮	⋮
∞	1.960	2.576

The first column of the t table specifies degrees of freedom. Each df corresponds to a t distribution. For *each df*, it would be possible to construct a table just like the z table. You could then answer a question such as, "What percent of t values fall between a t of .34 and a t of 1.2?" However, no one is ever interested in asking this type of question. The t table is used to find cutoffs for different alpha levels used in hypothesis testing. As a consequence, only the t values that correspond to various conventional rejection regions are presented.

The top two rows of the t table in Appendix B.2 state different alpha levels for one-tailed and two-tailed t tests. Only the two-tailed test is discussed in this chapter, and therefore only two alpha levels and their critical values for a two-tailed test are reproduced.[3] Suppose you set alpha at .05 and the sample size is 10. What is the critical value? Find $df = 9$, go across the page to the .05 column. The critical value is 2.262. What is the critical value when $\alpha = 0.01$ and the sample size is 9? The answer is 3.355 (remember that $df = n - 1$).

Now, follow the .05 column to the bottom row, ∞. The critical value is 1.96. When n is very large, the t distribution assumes the shape of the standard normal curve. Thus, the cutoffs for the 5 percent rejection region are the same as if you were to use the z table. As you move from the bottom of the table to the top, the critical values increase. This reflects the fact that the t distribution becomes broader as the sample size decreases.

Now let's use the t formula and the t table to test a hypothesis about the mean of a single population. To reject the null hypothesis, the absolute value of t_{obt} must equal or exceed the critical value.

■   QUESTION   *A local newspaper reports that the average high school student drinks a six-pack of beer a week. The high school principal would like to know if her students are drinking that much beer. With confidentiality assured, 15 students are randomly selected and asked about their drinking habits. The mean number of beers consumed per week is found to be 4.2, and the sample standard deviation is 1.5. Test the hypothesis that the news report is accurate for the students at this high school.*

SOLUTION

Step 1.   Identify the null and alternative hypotheses.

$$H_0: \quad \mu = 6$$

$$H_1: \quad \mu \neq 6$$

Step 2.   Set alpha. Use an alpha of .05.

Step 3.   Compute t_{obt} using Formula 7.2.

$$t_{obt} = \frac{\overline{X} - \mu}{s_{\bar{x}}}$$

$$s_{\bar{x}} = \frac{s}{\sqrt{n}}$$

$$= \frac{4.2 - 6.0}{1.5/(\sqrt{15})}$$

$$= \frac{-1.8}{.39}$$

$$t_{obt} = \mathbf{-4.62}$$

---

[3] The distinction between a one-tailed and two-tailed test is discussed in Chapter 8.

Step 4.   Using the t table, find the critical value for $df = 14$ and $\alpha = .05$. The critical value is 2.145.

Step 5.   Compare the absolute value of the t_{obt} of -4.62 to the critical value of 2.145. Since t_{obt} is larger than t_{crit}, the null hypothesis is rejected, and the alternative hypothesis that $\mu \neq 6$ is retained.

Step 6.   Interpret the findings. The amount of beer consumed per week among this school's students is significantly less than the amount stated in the newspaper.   ◼

◼   QUESTION   *A bank president states that the average amount of money on deposit in savings accounts is $6500. To test the hypothesis that $\mu = \$6500$, a random sample of nine deposits is examined. The mean of the sample is $7500 and the standard deviation is $1500. Is there evidence to reject the president's claim?*

SOLUTION

Step 1.   Identify the null and alternative hypotheses.

$$H_0: \quad \mu = 6500$$

$$H_1: \quad \mu \neq 6500$$

Step 2.   Set alpha. Use an alpha of .05.

Step 3.   Compute t_{obt} using Formula 7.2.

$$t_{obt} = \frac{\overline{X} - \mu}{s_{\overline{x}}}$$

$$= \frac{7500 - 6500}{1500/(\sqrt{9})}$$

$$= \frac{1000}{500}$$

$$t_{obt} = \mathbf{2.00}$$

Step 4.   Find the critical value for $df = 8$ and $\alpha = .05$. The critical value is 2.306.

Step 5.   Compare the t_{obt} of 2.00 to the critical value of 2.306. Since t_{obt} is *smaller* than t_{crit}, the null hypothesis is retained.

Step 6.   Interpret the findings. There is no evidence that the mean of all the savings accounts is *not* $6500. Keep in mind that this interpretation does not mean that $6500 *is* the average amount of money on deposit; that would be proving the null hypothesis. All you can say is that you have failed to obtain evidence leading you to reject the claim stated in the null hypothesis, $\mu = \$6500$.   ◼

BOX 7.1

Visual Illusions and Immaculate Perception

Perceptual illusions reflect the fact that human perceptions are imperfect and are not just copies of images on the retinas. People actively construct sensory information, and in the case of illusions, their perceptions are hardly immaculate.

One visual illusion is called the Morinaga misalignment illusion. First examine the alignment of the angles on the left. You will note that the apex of the middle angle does not appear to perfectly align with the apexes of the top and bottom angles. Now, take a ruler or the edge of a sheet of paper and see if the apexes of the angles fall along a straight line. They do. You experienced a perceptual illusion as you perceived the middle angle to be misaligned.

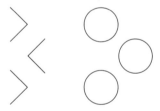

Day and Kasperczyk (1984) wondered if the same illusion is found with the circles on the right. (Notice that the left side of the middle circle does not appear to align with the right sides of the circles above and below.) Twelve subjects were asked to move the middle circle (without the help of a straight edge) so that the left side of the middle circle aligned perfectly with the right sides of the top and bottom circle. Since the circles were already perfectly aligned, any adjustment by the subject defined an error of some magnitude, and reflected the workings of the Morinaga illusion. Errors were measured in millimeters (mm). If the illusion did *not* exist for circles, then there should not have been realignments by the subjects and the errors would equal 0. The null hypothesis is a statement of no perceptual illusion: H_0: $\mu = 0$, with H_1: $\mu \neq 0$. The authors found an average error among the 12 subjects to be 1.44 mm with $s = 2.07$ mm.[4] The question is, how unlikely is a sample mean of 1.44 mm when the population mean is hypothesized to be 0? The question can be answered with a single-sample t test.

$$t_{obt} = \frac{\overline{X} - \mu}{s/(\sqrt{n})}$$

$$t_{obt} = \frac{1.44 - 0}{2.07/(\sqrt{12})}$$

$$= \frac{1.44}{.60}$$

$$t_{obt} = \mathbf{2.40}$$

$$df = n - 1 = 12 - 1 = 11$$

$$\alpha = .05$$

$$t_{crit} = 2.201$$

Since the obtained t of 2.40 exceeds the critical value of 2.201, the null hypothesis is rejected. The evidence suggests that the sample mean of 1.44 mm is unlikely to come from a population with a mean of 0. The findings can be summarized as: The Morinaga illusion is a general perceptual effect that is shown not only with angles, but circles as well, $t(11) = 2.40$, $p < .05$.

---

[4] These values are reported by Kiess (1989, p. 214).

A Note on Notation

The use of t_{obt} refers to the t value obtained from Formula 7.2; t_{crit} refers to the critical value to which t_{obt} is compared. The subscripts remind you which t value is being used. In journal articles, however, t_{obt} is reported as $t(df)$. If $df = 7$, then the obtained t value is written, $t(7)$. To report the results of a significant t test, use the following format to specify t, df, and p: "The difference between means was statistically significant, $t(13) = 2.89; p < .05$."

The critical value of t is not reported when presenting the results of a study. Some computer printouts will indicate the critical value as t_α. Thus, if $\alpha = .05$, and the critical value is 2.56, the correct representation is $t_{05} = 2.56$.

Box 7.1 presents a study in which a single-sample t test is used to test a hypothesis about visual perception.

Assumptions of the *t* Test

Behavioral scientists use an array of research methods to answer questions. Research can be conducted without controlling variables, experiments using different designs can be employed, and various scales of measurement can be used. The appropriate statistical test for significance will depend on the research method and the research question of interest. All statistical tests are based on assumptions. Accurately interpreting the results of a statistical test is based on the degree to which the assumptions are met. Some assumptions can be violated without seriously compromising the interpretation of a statistical test. Other assumptions are critical. The assumptions for the single-sample t test, as well as the z test, are presented in the following.

1. ***Random sampling.***   It is assumed that the subjects comprising the sample have been randomly selected. The goal of inferential statistics is to generalize to a population. If the sample is not representative of the population, it is possible that an untrue statement about the population will be made. The random sample assumption is *not* a mathematical assumption. Random sampling is an assumption of the research method, but, if violated, will compromise the interpretive conclusions that follow from the t test.

2. ***Independent observations.***   This is the most important assumption of the t test. Independent observations mean that each score *within the sample* is independent of all other scores. In most applications, independent observations mean that each subject supplies only one score. However, it is possible to violate the independence assumption even when only one score is obtained per subject. If the behavior of one subject in the study is influenced by the behavior of another subject, then the scores from these two subjects are *not* independent. For instance, earlier in this chapter, a research example was used in which the effects of an educational enrichment program were evaluated. Suppose that two subjects studied

together and, as a result, their performances were influenced by their contact. The scores from these subjects would not be independent of one another.

3. ***Normality.***   The third assumption of the single-sample *t* test is that the scores of the population from which the sample is taken are normally distributed. If the population deviates from normality, the *t* test will still lead to valid conclusions, *provided the sampling distribution is normally distributed.*

SUMMARY

Hypothesis testing involves choosing either the null or the alternative hypothesis. The decision is probabilistic in nature, and the ultimate truth value of the null and alternative hypotheses can never be known. The decision to reject or retain the null hypothesis risks two types of errors. A Type I error is committed when a true null hypothesis is rejected. The probability of making a Type I error is directly controlled by alpha, the criterion of significance. A Type II error is committed when a false null hypothesis is retained. However, as the probability of a Type I error increases, the probability of a Type II error decreases, and vice versa.

The single-sample *z* test is used to decide if a population mean is not a specified value. The z_{obt} transforms a sample mean to a *z* score, which indicates the number of standard error units that the sample mean is from the mean of the sampling distribution. If the z_{obt} equals or exceeds the critical value, then the null hypothesis is rejected.

The *t* statistic is used to test the null hypothesis when σ is unknown. In the *t* formula, *s* is used to estimate σ, and $s/\sqrt{n}$ is used to estimate $\sigma/\sqrt{n}$. The *t* statistic is used to transform a sampling distribution of means to a *t* distribution. The shape of the *t* distribution will approximate the standard normal curve when $n > 30$. The critical value to which t_{obt} is compared is based on $n - 1$ degrees of freedom.

The assumptions for the single-sample *z* and *t* tests are the use of a random sample, independent observations, and population distributions that are normally distributed.

KEY FORMULAS FOR CHAPTER 7

z Statistic

$$z_{obt} = \frac{\overline{X} - \mu}{\sigma_{\overline{x}}}$$ (Formula 7.1)

t Statistic

$$t_{obt} = \frac{\overline{X} - \mu}{s_{\overline{x}}}$$ (Formula 7.2)

WORK PROBLEMS

1. A statistical test aids a researcher in deciding whether an experimental effect is due to chance. What does this mean? Is it possible to know for sure that an effect was not due to chance? Explain your answer.

2. Provide some examples of Case I research. In each instance, provide a research and a statistical hypothesis.

3. For each of the following situations, specify the null and alternative hypotheses.
   a. The average respiration rate per minute is 8. Do smokers have an average rate different from 8?
   b. The average score on the Beck Depression Inventory is 12. Does the average depression score of mothers with young children deviate from the population mean?
   c. The average miles per gallon (mpg) of American cars is 20. Is the observed mpg of a sample of Corvettes different from the average American car?

4. When conducting a test of significance, when should you use the t distribution?

5. On what basis does a researcher decide on a given alpha level?

6. Among trained typists, suppose the average typing speed on an electric typewriter is 60 words per minute (wpm), with a standard deviation of 5 wpm. The manufacturer of a personal computer claims that their PC will improve typing speed. A random sample of 50 typists are tested on the PC and the mean wpm is 65. Test the hypothesis that using this PC affects typing speed. Set alpha at .05.
   a. Should you use the z distribution or t distribution? Why?
   b. State H_0 and H_1.
   c. What is the critical value?
   d. What is the obtained statistic?
   e. Reject the null hypothesis?
   f. Is there sufficient evidence to support the manufacturer's claim?

7. On one standardized measure of IQ, $\mu = 100$ and $\sigma = 15$. Imagine that you want to test the hypothesis that children of parents with college degrees have an average IQ that is greater than the national average. A sample of 100 students who have college-educated parents is randomly selected and the mean is 110 with a standard deviation of 12. Conduct a significance test and set alpha at .05.
   a. Should you use the z distribution or t distribution? Why?
   b. State H_0 and H_1.
   c. What is the critical value?
   d. What is the obtained statistic?
   e. Reject the null hypothesis?
   f. Is there sufficient evidence to support the contention that children of college-educated parents have higher IQs?

8. Suppose the mean weight of adult golden retrievers is 90 lb. A veterinarian claims to be able to double the size of golden retrievers by injecting a hormone

into retriever pups when they are 8 weeks old (why someone would want to produce humongous golden retrievers, who knows; it may have theoretical significance). A sample of 40 pups is injected with the hormone and their average weight at maturity is found to be 110 lb, with a standard deviation of 30 lb. Conduct a significance test with $\alpha = .05$. (Note that the significance test will not be able to address the assertion that the hormone doubles the size of dogs. The statistical test will only be able to help you decide if the hormone has a significant effect on weight, be it an increase or a decrease.)

a. Should you use the z distribution or t distribution? Why?
b. State H_0 and H_1.
c. What is the critical value?
d. What is the obtained statistic?
e. Reject the null hypothesis?
f. Is there sufficient evidence to support the claim that the hormone alters the normal weight of golden retrievers?

9. How would you use the concept of sampling error in discussing hypothesis testing?

10. Your subjective life expectancy is your belief in how long you will live. Robbins (1988) found that a sample of females estimated their life expectancy to be 77.2 years, which is close to the actual life expectancy for women, 79.2 years. Males, on the other hand, tend to overestimate their life expectancy. The actual life expectancy for males is 72.4 years. The following hypothetical data are consistent with Robbins' findings. μ

Subjective Life Expectancy for Males (Years)

$n = 9$

77
74
80
72
82
76
78
75
79

a. Should you use the z distribution or t distribution? Why?
b. State H_0 and H_1.
c. What is the critical value?
d. What is the obtained statistic?
e. Reject the null hypothesis? yes
f. Interpret the findings.

11. An anthropologist hypothesizes that physical stress in childhood increases height (Landauer and Whiting, 1964). The researchers locate a tribe of people in which physical stress is a byproduct of frequent tribal rituals (piercing and molding body parts, exposure to extreme temperatures, etc.). The mean height of the people in the region who do *not* use physically stressful rituals with their young is used as the population mean. The following raw data are for adult men and women of the tribe in question. Conduct a t test for men and

a t test for women. The population mean height for men is 65 in. and 59 in. for women.

Men	Women
67	59
69	63
72	65
70	60
70	59
72	62
64	61
70	66

a. What is t_{obt} for men?
b. What is t_{obt} for women?
c. What is the critical value for each test ($\alpha = .05$)?
d. Compare each t_{obt} with its respective critical value and interpret the findings.

12. The chairperson of a sociology department at a major research institution claims that the mean number of publications by the department's faculty is higher than the mean for other sociology departments at comparable schools across the country. Suppose the mean number of publications in the population is 16. A random sample of eight professors is taken from the sociology department in question. The sample mean is found to be 20, with a standard deviation of 2.8. Is there any evidence to support the chairperson's claim? Set alpha at .05 when conducting the t test.

Work Problems for the Computer

13. A health psychologist is interested in educating high school students about the negative effects of smoking. Fifty students who smoke are randomly selected to participate in the program. To measure the success of the program, the average number of cigarettes smoked per day among the participants is obtained 10 weeks after the end of the program. Assume that previous research had shown that, among all smoking students, the average number of cigarettes smoked in a day was 17. Set alpha at .05 and conduct a t test on the following data. Interpret the findings.

Average Number of Cigarettes Consumed Per Day Among Participants

12	11	7	0	0	6	2	23	45	0
0	1	2	0	3	16	8	22	17	9
12	10.	6	5	9	11	0	33	24	5
11	10	0	0	0	22	4	22	21	0
10	11	0	6	7	11	3	42	38	0

14. An insurance company states that it takes them an average of 15 days to process an auto accident claim. A random sample of 40 claims is drawn from processed claims over the past 6 months. Based on the following data, is there any evidence that the mean number of days to pay claims is not 15? Set $\alpha = .05$.

Number of Days to Process a Claim

22	11	7	9	9	8	7	23	45	9
23	21	8	8	5	16	9	22	17	6
12	29	6	5	9	23	7	33	24	5
15	14	9	7	3	17	8	19	15	8

15. Every day a commuter records the amount of time his train is late. Over a period of 2 months, the mean number of minutes that the train was late is 24.5, with a standard deviation of 6.4 minutes. The train authorities state that the problem has been resolved by the addition of extra trains during rush hour. For the next 30 working days, the commuter records the amount of time that his train is late. Based on the following data, does there seem to be an improvement in service? (If your computer program does not accept a population standard deviation, use the sample standard deviation as an estimate. Therefore, you may be conducting a z test or a t test, depending on which standard deviation is used.)

Number of Minutes the Train is Late

22	11	25	19	9	8	7	23	45	20
23	21	8	1	5	16	3	22	17	24
12	16	22	32	9	10	7	11	10	2

Directional and Nondirectional Testing of the Difference Between Two Means: The Independent-Samples *t* Test

8.1   THE RESEARCH CONTEXT

In Chapter 7 the *t* test was used to contrast a sample mean with a specified population value. Only one sample was drawn to infer the mean of a population; the question was whether the population mean was or was not a given value. The more common and interesting uses of the *t* test arise when two samples are used to infer whether there is a difference between the means of two populations. If the two samples are scores from two sets of subjects, the appropriate *t* test is called an **independent-samples *t* test.** Here are three research examples in which an independent-samples *t* test can be used to analyze the data.

▶   **EXAMPLE 1**   Burke and Greenglass (1989) have concluded that, "It may be lonely at the top but it's less stressful." These authors found a significant difference between teachers and principals on a measure of burnout; teachers exhibited higher levels of stress than principals.   ◀

▶   **EXAMPLE 2**   Zakahi and Duran (1988) hypothesized that people who are very lonely are less physically attractive than people who are not lonely. A loneliness questionnaire was administered. Subjects who scored in the top 25 percent were considered very lonely, whereas subjects who scored in the bottom 25 percent were defined as not lonely. All subjects' photographs were rated by three judges for attractiveness (1—very unattractive to 10—very attractive). Males rated females and females rated males. There was no significant difference in attractiveness ratings between very lonely and not lonely females. However, lonely males were rated as significantly less physically attractive than males who were not lonely.   ◀

▶   **EXAMPLE 3**   In 1972, Buffalo Creek, West Virginia, was the scene of a major flood. The flood was a consequence of corporate negligence. Coal waste that was dumped in a mountain stream created an artificial dam. After several days of rain, the dam gave way and a black wall of water, over 30 ft high, descended on mining hamlets in the valley. In less than 1 hour, 125 people were dead and 5000 people lost their homes. Simpson-Housley and DeMan (1989) found that, 17 years later, the residents of Buffalo Creek scored higher on a measure of trait anxiety in comparison to the residents of Kopperston, a nearby mining town that did not experience the flood.   ◀

The Between-Subjects Design

Between-subjects designs (also called between-groups designs, or independent-samples designs) are defined by the fact that each group of subjects receives a different treatment. Moreover, no subject or group of subjects receives more than one treatment. Shelton and Mahoney (1978) conducted a study with athletes on "psyching-up" strategies. Subjects in the experimental group were asked to employ their customary psyching-up strategies, whereas the control group was told to count backward by sixes. Performance on a strength task served as the dependent variable. The averages of the two groups were then compared to evaluate the effect of using psyching-up strategies. Because each group received a different treatment, this study was a between-groups design.

The independent-samples *t* test can be used whenever a researcher wants to compare the means from two independent samples. The substantive interpretation of the *t* test depends on the method used for collecting data. If subjects are randomly assigned to treatment conditions, it *might* be possible to make a causal statement about the relation between the independent and dependent variables, depending on the presence of confounding variables (see Chapter 1). However, the independent-samples *t* test can be used to compare two means that are obtained from a study in which subjects are not randomly assigned to groups. The three

SPOTLIGHT

8.1

William Gosset

William Gosset (1876–1937) developed the *t* distribution as well as the independent- and dependent-samples *t* tests. After receiving a degree in chemistry and mathematics from Oxford, Gosset was hired by the Guinness brewery in Dublin in 1899. Around the turn of the century, many companies, especially in the agricultural industry, attempted to apply a scientific approach to product development. A typical research question might have been, "Which fertilizer will produce the largest corn yield?" or "What is the best temperature to brew ale so as to maximize its shelf life?" Until Gosset's work, statisticians dealt with very large numbers of observations, in the hundreds and thousands. Traditional wisdom held that you should take a very large sample, compute the mean and standard deviation, and refer to the *z* table to make probability statements. The problem that confronted Gosset was how to make inferences about the difference between population means when sample sizes were small. For example, suppose ten plots of barley are treated with one fertilizer and ten plots are treated with another fertilizer. With such small samples (before Gosset), there was no way to determine if the difference in yield was due to sample fluctuation (chance) or the effect of the brand of fertilizer.

To test the mean of one sample against a specified population value or test the difference between two sample means, the *t* table (instead of the *z* table) is used to find critical values and make probability statements when σ is unknown. In his 1908 seminal article, "The Probable Error of a Mean," Gosset addressed the problem of small samples: "As we decrease the number of experiments, the value of the standard deviation found from the sample of experiments becomes itself subject to an increasing error, until judgments reached in this way become altogether misleading" (Student, 1908; p. 2). He realized that the standard normal curve, on which the *z* table is based, leads to inaccurate judgments about the area under the curve of a sampling distribution when sample sizes are small and σ is unknown. In the following quote, Gosset expressed the purpose of his 1908 paper.[3] "The aim of the present paper is to determine the point at which we may use the tables of the probability integral in judging of the significance of the mean of a series of experiments, and to furnish alternative tables for use when the number of experiments is too few" (p. 2). His use of the term *significance* was prophetic since at this time the concept of significance testing had not been developed. The conventional use of the 5 percent level of significance emerged over the next 25 years.

Gosset's classic 1908 article is one of the most important publications in the history of inferential statistics. "With one stroke, he: (1) discovered a new statistical distribution; (2) invented a statistical test that became the prototype for a whole series of tests, including analysis of variance; and (3) extended statistical analysis to small samples. . . ." (Tankard, 1984, p. 99). Although *t* tests are one of the cornerstones of modern statistics, Gosset's work was not greeted with enthusiasm. Fisher, the originator of the analysis of variance, described the reaction of colleagues as "weighty apathy" (Fisher, 1939, p. 5), and Cochran stated that "the *t* distribution did not spread like wildfire" (Cochran, 1976, p. 13). Even Gosset underestimated the impact that his discoveries would have, as he wrote to Fisher, "I am sending you a copy of Student's Tables as you are the only man that's ever likely to use them!" (Gosset, 1970; Letter 11).

An interesting aspect of Gosset's work is that he used a pseudonym when publishing: Student. Not wanting the competition to know of its scientific work, the Guinness company forbade their scientists from publishing. So Gosset secretly published all his articles under the name of "Student." It is for this reason that the *t* test is known as "Student's *t* test."

Gosset remained with Guinness until his death, assuming the position of head brewer a few months before he died in 1937.

---

[3] His reference to the tables of the probability integral refers to the *z* table, and "alternative tables" refers to the newly developed *t* table.

research examples presented in the foregoing are cases in point. These designs are not included in the category "between-groups designs." Since there was no randomization of subjects, the research method was correlational in nature. Even though a *t* test can be used to compare means, no causal statement can be advanced about the relation between variables. However, since Shelton and Mahoney (1978) randomly assigned subjects to experimental and control conditions, a causal relation between the independent and dependent variables is possible. In general, the interpretation of any statistical test of significance depends on the manner in which the study is designed.

The *t* test was invented by William Gosset. Spotlight Box 8.1 presents the context of his discoveries.

8.2   THE INDEPENDENT-SAMPLES *t* TEST

The independent-samples *t* test is used when two samples of subjects provide scores on a measure. The *t* test compares the means of the two samples. The ultimate goal, however, is not to determine whether the means of the two samples are different, but rather to make an inference about whether the population means from which the samples are taken are different. Figure 8.1 depicts this arrangement.

Suppose you conduct a study and hypothesize a difference between two groups in their reaction to a stressful situation. This difference is expected to occur due to an exercise regimen. The experimental group receives 10 weeks of aerobic training whereas the control group does not receive any aerobic training. After 10 weeks, both groups are asked to solve a series of simple mental arithmetic problems. Subjects are told to work as quickly as possible; however, if they fail to perform adequately, they will receive an electric shock. The measure of stress is the subjects'

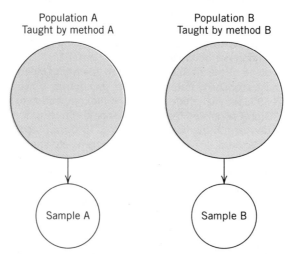

Figure 8.1   An independent-sample *t* test uses two samples. Do the samples come from the same or different populations?

heart rate during the task. The experimental hypothesis is that those subjects who participated in the exercise program will show lower heart rates under stress in comparison to the control subjects.

The two samples represent two hypothetical populations. One hypothetical population is all the subjects who theoretically could have participated in the exercise program; in other words, it is a hypothetical population of treated subjects. Even though the entire population is not participating, the randomly selected sample is assumed to represent the performance of the entire population. The control sample is randomly selected to represent the way in which a hypothetical untreated population would have performed had they all participated in the study.

When performing an independent-samples *t* test, the investigator specifies the null and alternative hypotheses beforehand. In Case I research, the null hypothesis is stated as an equality, μ = some value; the alternative hypothesis is stated as an inequality, $\mu \neq$ the value. Similarly, in Case II research, which is the context for an independent-samples *t* test, the null hypothesis is stated as an equality and the alternative hypothesis is expressed as an inequality.

The Null and Alternative Hypotheses

The null hypothesis is stated as an equivalence between the two populations, which can be stated in two ways.

$$\text{H}_0: \quad \mu_1 = \mu_2 \quad \text{or} \quad \text{H}_0: \quad \mu_1 - \mu_2 = 0$$

Note that these two statements are equivalent. One states that the two means are equal, and the other states that there is no difference between the two means. The alternative hypothesis can also be stated in two ways, depending on how you choose to state the null hypothesis.

$$\text{H}_1: \quad \mu_1 \neq \mu_2 \quad \text{or} \quad \text{H}_1: \quad \mu_1 - \mu_2 \neq 0$$

In the exercise and stress study, the research hypothesis is that exercise will reduce subjects' physiological reactions to a stressor. The statistical hypotheses, reflected in the null and alternative hypotheses, are statements that either the samples are taken from one population (no treatment effect) or come from two populations with different means (a treatment effect).

The Sampling Distribution for an Independent-Samples *t* Test

Theoretically Constructing the Sampling Distribution

The sampling distribution for an independent-samples *t* test is a sampling distribution of the *difference between independent sample means*. In Chapter 7, a sampling distribution was constructed for a single-sample *t* test where one population was used to draw repeated samples. In the present case, two populations are used for sampling.

Returning to the aerobic exercise and stress study, the two hypothetical populations are "treated" and "untreated" subjects. You sample from these two populations in the sense that one of your samples actually receives the exercise treatment and the second sample does not. To theoretically construct the sampling distribution, you would run the study, compute the mean heart rate under stress for each sample, *take the difference between the group means,* and begin to construct a relative frequency distribution. This process would be repeated an infinite number of times. In each instance, the value $\overline{X}_1 - \overline{X}_2$ is computed and included in the frequency distribution. (The subscripts refer to sample 1 and sample 2, respectively.) The result is a sampling distribution that corresponds to the sample sizes used in the study. For a given study, the sample sizes do not have to be the same; n_1 does not have to equal n_2. However, over repeated samples, the number of subjects in both the aerobics group and the control group must stay the same. Changing the sample sizes will yield a different sampling distribution. Therefore, there is a family of sampling distributions; each distribution corresponds to a particular sample size (degrees of freedom).

Characteristics of the Sampling Distribution

Because mathematical statisticians have worked out the characteristics of the sampling distributions of the difference between means, you have been spared the impossible task of constructing these sampling distributions. The following list clarifies the characteristics of sampling distributions, which are theoretically determined by the process described in the preceding section.

1. The mean of the sampling distribution of $\overline{X}_1 - \overline{X}_2$ is equal to the difference between the population means, $\mu_1 - \mu_2$. If the null hypothesis is true—that is, there is no difference between μ_1 and μ_2—then the mean of the sampling distribution of differences between means is 0. If the means of the populations differ by, say 10 units, then the mean of the sampling distribution of differences is 10.

2. The Central Limit Theorem holds for sampling distributions of the difference between means. If the populations are normally distributed, the sampling distribution will likewise be normal. However, if the sample sizes are sufficiently large, the sampling distribution will be normal whether or not the populations are normally distributed.

3. When the two populations have the same variance (**homogeneity of variances**), and it is assumed that they do, then the standard deviation of the sampling distribution is given by Formula 8.1. The standard deviation of the sampling distribution of mean differences is called the **standard error of the difference,** or simply the standard error.

The Standard Error of the Sampling Distribution of $\overline{X}_1 - \overline{X}_2$

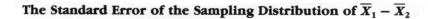

Formula 8.1 is the standard error of the sampling distribution of differences.

Standard Error of the Difference

$$\sigma_{\overline{x}_1 - \overline{x}_2} = \sqrt{\sigma^2 \left(\frac{1}{n_1} + \frac{1}{n_2} \right)}$$ *(Formula 8.6)*

where,

$\sigma_{\overline{x}_1 - \overline{x}_2}$ = the standard error of the difference
n_1, n_2 = the sample sizes of the two samples
σ^2 = the variance of either one of the population distributions. Since it is assumed that $\sigma_1^2 = \sigma_2^2$ (homogeneity of variances), it doesn't matter which variance is used

---

Formula 8.1 describes the relation between the amount of variability in the population and the variability of the sampling distribution of differences between means. Since the population variance is almost never known, sample variances are used to estimate the standard error of the sampling distribution. Recall from Chapter 7 that the denominator of the single-sample *t* test is the estimated standard error of the sampling distribution of means, $t = (\overline{X} - \mu)/s_{\overline{x}}$, where $s_{\overline{x}} = s/\sqrt{n}$.

The Estimated Standard Error of the Difference

The formula for the independent-samples *t* test is presented in this section. The denominator of the independent-samples *t* test is the estimated standard error of the difference, symbolized $s_{\overline{x}_1 - \overline{x}_2}$.

When σ is known, Formula 8.1 is the standard error of the difference. When σ is unknown, which is usually the case, then *s* is used to estimate σ. The estimated standard error of the difference is similar in form to the formula for the standard error when σ is known. In Formula 8.2, a new term is introduced, pooled variance, symbolized s_p^2.

Definitional Formula for the Estimated Standard Error, $s_{\overline{x}_1 - \overline{x}_2}$

$$s_{\overline{x}_1 - \overline{x}_2} = \sqrt{s_p^2 \left(\frac{1}{n_1} + \frac{1}{n_2} \right)}$$ *(Formula 8.2)*

where,

s_p^2 = the pooled variance

Since it is assumed that $\sigma_1^2 = \sigma_2^2$, estimating either variance is like estimating one variance, σ^2. When there are two samples, there are two estimates of σ^2. Which one should be used? The most accurate estimate of σ^2 is a weighted average of the two sample variances. The weighted average of the two sample variances gives the formula for the **pooled variance.**

Pooled Variance

$$s_p^2 = \frac{s_1^2(n_1 - 1) + s_2^2(n_2 - 1)}{n_1 + n_2 - 2}$$ *(Formula 8.3)*

Each variance in Formula 8.3 is multiplied by its degrees of freedom. The variance from the larger sample is multiplied by a larger number than the variance from the smaller sample. This is how the "weighting" of the two samples is accomplished. Substituting the formula for the pooled variance into the formula for the estimated standard error gives Formula 8.4.

Variance Formula for the Estimated Standard Error, $s_{\bar{x}_1 - \bar{x}_2}$

$$s_{\bar{x}_1 - \bar{x}_2} = \sqrt{\frac{s_1^2(n_1 - 1) + s_2^2(n_2 - 1)}{n_1 + n_2 - 2}\left(\frac{1}{n_1} + \frac{1}{n_2}\right)}$$ *(Formula 8.4)*

Formula 8.4 shows that the estimated standard error of the difference combines the variances of both groups (samples) in the study. In addition, since Formula 8.4 is the denominator of the t ratio, it can be used, for instance, to analyze the results of a published study in which s^2 or s is reported in the article. When working from raw data, a computational formula is easier to use. Formula 8.5 is the computational formula for $s_{\bar{x}_1 - \bar{x}_2}$.

Computational Formula for $s_{\bar{x}_1 - \bar{x}_2}$

$$s_{\bar{x}_1 - \bar{x}_2} = \sqrt{\frac{\left(\Sigma X_1^2 - \frac{(\Sigma X_1)^2}{n_1}\right) + \left(\Sigma X_2^2 - \frac{(\Sigma X_2)^2}{n_2}\right)}{n_1 + n_2 - 2}\left(\frac{1}{n_1} + \frac{1}{n_2}\right)}$$

(Formula 8.5)

Hypothesis Testing and the Sampling Distribution of Differences

Hypothesis testing operates statistically at the level of the sampling distribution. The sampling distribution is a theoretical tool that allows researchers to determine if the difference between two means is unlikely due to sampling error, or if indeed there is a treatment effect. The sampling distribution relevant to an independent-samples *t* test is a sampling distribution of differences between means. As the observed difference between the sample means increases, it becomes more and more unlikely that the difference is due only to sampling error; probably the independent variable is causing the difference. The mean of the sampling distribution of differences is the same as the difference between the means of the populations. If there is no treatment effect, the means of the two populations are the same.

Now assume that a sampling distribution of means from *each* population is theoretically established. Furthermore, assume that there is no treatment effect and the population means are the same, both populations have identical standard deviations, and the two sampling distributions are based on repeated samples of the same size. Would there be a difference between the two sampling distributions? No, they would have the same means and standard errors. If you drew them on a graph, they would overlap so that it would look like one sampling distribution.

Now assume that there is a treatment effect and the populations have different means. The sampling distributions would not show a perfect overlap. The mean of each sampling distribution would be the same as the mean of its respective population. As the difference between means becomes greater, the sampling distributions overlap less and less. The sampling distribution of differences is a way of combining the two sampling distributions; basically, this involves taking the difference between the two sampling distributions. The sampling distribution of differences reflects the difference between the means of the two sampling distributions. If there is no treatment effect, the mean of the sampling distribution of differences will be 0. As the size of the treatment effect increases, the mean of the sampling distribution of differences departs from 0. The null hypothesis assumes that there is no treatment effect, and thus the mean of the sampling distribution of differences is assumed to be 0.

Refer to Figure 8.2. In Figure 8.2(*a*) the sampling distributions from identical populations overlap perfectly. The mean of each sampling distribution is the same as the mean of each population—25. The sampling distribution of differences has a mean of 0—the difference between μ_1 and μ_2. In Figure 8.2(*b*), the two sampling distributions are taken from different populations, one with $\mu_1 = 25$ and a second population with $\mu_2 = 27$. The sampling distribution of differences has a mean of 2—the difference between 27 and 25. (The sign of the difference can be ignored since, at this point, the size of the difference between μ_1 and μ_2 is what is important.) In Figure 8.2(*c*) the sampling distributions are generated from populations with $\mu_1 = 25$ and $\mu_2 = 35$. The sampling distribution of differences thus has a mean of 10.

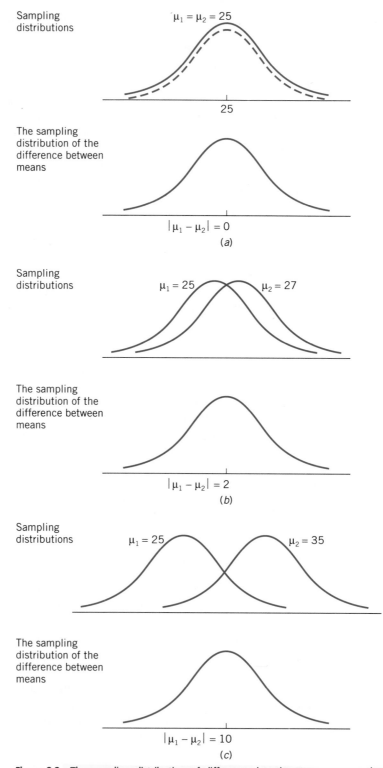

Sampling distributions

$\mu_1 = \mu_2 = 25$

25

The sampling distribution of the difference between means

$|\mu_1 - \mu_2| = 0$

(a)

Sampling distributions

$\mu_1 = 25$ $\mu_2 = 27$

The sampling distribution of the difference between means

$|\mu_1 - \mu_2| = 2$

(b)

Sampling distributions

$\mu_1 = 25$ $\mu_2 = 35$

The sampling distribution of the difference between means

$|\mu_1 - \mu_2| = 10$

(c)

Figure 8.2 The sampling distribution of differences has the same mean as the difference between the means of the sampling distributions of the two populations.

From the Sampling Distribution of Differences to the *t* Distribution for Independent Samples

The sampling distribution of differences is of fundamental importance when using the independent-samples *t* test. However, the sampling distribution is not directly used to conduct the significance test. What the researcher would like to determine is if the difference between sample means places you in the tail of the sampling distribution when the null hypothesis is provisionally assumed to be true. If the obtained difference does place you in one of the tails of the sampling distribution, then question the validity of the null hypothesis. The *t* ratio is a formula that indicates the distance an obtained difference between sample means is from the hypothesized mean of the sampling distribution. The logic of the independent-samples *t* test follows from the discussion of *z* scores and the *z* test.

In Chapter 5, the *z*-score formula was used to indicate the distance a score is from the mean of the raw-score distribution. The *z* score reflects the number of standard deviations that the score is from the mean. In Chapter 7, you learned that the *z* statistic provides a measure of how far a sample mean is from the mean of the sampling distribution. The *z* statistic reflects the number of standard errors a mean is from the mean of the sampling distribution. The *z* statistic requires that you know σ. If σ is unknown, the *t* statistic is used to transform all the scores of the sampling distribution to a *t* distribution. By using the single-sample formula for *t*, you were able to determine how many standard errors a sample mean was from the hypothesized mean of the sampling distribution.

Whether you perform a *z*-test or a single-sample *t* test, a ratio of the difference between two means and the standard error is obtained:

$$z_{obt} = \frac{\overline{X} - \mu}{\sigma_{\overline{x}}}$$

$$t_{obt} = \frac{\overline{X} - \mu}{s_{\overline{x}}}$$

With the standard error in the denominator, the ratio indicates the number of standard error units that the sample mean is from the hypothesized mean. The independent-samples *t* statistic is a ratio that specifies the distance (in standard error units) between the difference between the sample mean and the hypothesized mean of the sampling distribution of differences.

The *t* Ratio

Formula 8.6 is the formula for the independent-samples *t* test.

---

t Statistic for Independent Samples

$$t_{obt} = \frac{(\overline{X}_1 - \overline{X}_2) - (\mu_1 - \mu_2)}{s_{\overline{x}_1 - \overline{x}_2}} \qquad \textit{(Formula 8.6)}$$

First consider the numerator of the *t* ratio in Formula 8.6. To understand why it looks as it does, it is helpful to recall the *t* ratio for a single-sample *t* test. The *t* statistic for a single-sample *t* test was given in Chapter 7 as:

$$t_{obt} = \frac{\overline{X} - \mu}{s_{\overline{x}}}$$

In the numerator of this formula there is an obtained statistic, $\overline{X}$, which is contrasted with a hypothesized parameter, μ. The value of μ is the mean of the sampling distribution of means when the null hypothesis is true. When the null hypothesis is true, the difference $\overline{X} - \mu$ will be close to 0. The formula for an independent-samples *t* test also contrasts a hypothesized population parameter with an obtained statistic. When the null hypothesis is true, the population means are the same. The sampling distribution of differences will then have a mean of 0 since the mean of the sampling distribution is equal to $\mu_1 - \mu_2$. Thus, the hypothesized population parameter is 0, which is the difference between μ_1 and μ_2. The obtained sample statistic is $\overline{X}_1 - \overline{X}_2$. Therefore, you are contrasting an obtained difference with a hypothesized difference. As the obtained difference between sample means departs from the hypothesized difference between population means, you begin to question the hypothesized difference between the population means. In other words, you question the validity of the null hypothesis that $\mu_1 = \mu_2$. Since the hypothesized difference is 0, the expression $\mu_1 - \mu_2$ can be dropped from the numerator of Formula 8.6. The form of the *t* ratio used for an independent-samples *t* test is given in Formula 8.7.

The *t* Ratio

$$t_{obt} = \frac{\overline{X}_1 - \overline{X}_2}{s_{\overline{x}_1 - \overline{x}_2}} \quad \textit{(Formula 8.7)}$$

The *t* Distributions for the Independent-Samples *t* Test and Degrees of Freedom

 A ***t* distribution** is a transformation of a sampling distribution, in this case, a sampling distribution of differences between means.

When the sampling distribution is transformed by the *t* statistic, the true difference between population means does not matter because the mean of the *t* distribution will equal 0. Therefore, the *t* distribution is a standardized distribution, which is symmetric around a mean of 0. The *t* ratio specifies the number of standard errors the obtained difference between sample means is from the difference between population means, which is stated in the null hypothesis.

There is a different sampling distribution for every sample size. In a study with two groups, both groups might have 16 subjects, both groups might have 12 subjects, or one group might have 10 subjects and the other group might have 15 subjects. Each situation yields a different theoretical sampling distribution. Each sampling distribution can be transformed to a *t* distribution. Therefore, there is a family of *t* distributions, each with its own degrees of freedom. For an independent-samples *t* test, the degrees of freedom associated with the *t* distribution is $n - 1$ from the first sample and $n - 1$ from the second sample. The degrees of freedom for an independent-samples *t* test is thus $n_1 + n_2 - 2$.

Table 8.1 summarizes the differences between the formulas for a *z* score, *z* statistic, single-sample *t* statistic, and independent-samples *t* statistic. The purposes of the formulas and the underlying distributions of the formulas are presented. In addition, the degrees of freedom are specified for the *z* test and the *t* tests.

TABLE 8.1   **A Summary Comparison of the Transformation Formulas for a z Score, z Statistic, Single-Sample t Statistic, and Independent-Samples t Statistic**

FORMULA
z Score

$$z = \frac{X - \mu}{\sigma}$$

Purpose

Transforms raw scores to a *z* distribution. A *z* score indicates the number of standard deviations a raw score is from the mean of the raw-score distribution.

Distribution Characteristics

The *z* distribution has a mean of 0 and a standard deviation of 1. It is distributed normally if the population is normally distributed.

FORMULA
z Statistic

$$z_{obt} = \frac{\overline{X} - \mu}{\sigma_{\overline{x}}}$$

Purpose

Transforms a sampling distribution of means to a distribution of *z* values. The z_{obt} indicates the number of standard error units a sample mean is from the hypothesized mean of a sampling distribution.

Distribution Characteristics

If the sampling distribution is normal, and since σ is known, the distribution of *z* statistics will be normally distributed, with a mean of 0 and a standard deviation of 1.

FORMULA
Single-Sample t Statistic

$$t_{obt} = \frac{\overline{X} - \mu}{s_{\overline{x}}}$$

Purpose

Transforms a sampling distribution of means to a *t* distribution. The t_{obt} indicates the number of standard error units a sample mean is from the hypothesized mean of the sampling distribution.

Distribution Characteristics

All *t* distributions are symmetrical with a mean of 0. Each *t* distribution has $n - 1$ degrees of freedom. As the sample size of the sampling distribution increases, the *t* distribution approximates a standard normal curve.

FORMULA
Independent-Samples t Statistic

$$t_{obt} = \frac{(\overline{X}_1 - \overline{X}_2) - (\mu_1 - \mu_2)}{s_{\overline{x}_1 - \overline{x}_2}} \qquad \text{or} \qquad t_{obt} = \frac{\overline{X}_1 - \overline{X}_2}{s_{\overline{x}_1 - \overline{x}_2}}$$

TABLE 8.1   (continued)

Purpose

Transforms a sampling distribution of differences between means to a t distribution. The t_{obt} indicates the number of standard errors the difference between sample means is from the hypothesized difference between population means.

Distribution Characteristics

All t distributions are symmetrical with a mean of 0. Each t distribution is distributed with $n_1 + n_2 - 2$ degrees of freedom. As the sample size of the sampling distribution increases, the t distribution approximates a standard normal curve.

An Example of Hypothesis Testing Using the Independent-Samples t Test

With the logic of the t statistic in place and the requisite formulas provided, you are now ready to work through a problem and decide whether to reject the null hypothesis. Keep in mind that you are making inferences about the means of two populations and attempting to determine if the population means are unequal. In the context of an experiment, deciding that the population means are *not* equal is tantamount to saying that the independent variable has an effect on the dependent variable. Consider once again the study about the effectiveness of aerobic conditioning on subjects' ability to tolerate stress.

Worked Example

Twenty subjects are randomly assigned to an experimental condition ($n_1 = 10$) and a control condition ($n_2 = 10$). The experimental subjects exercise three times a week for 10 weeks. During each workout, they walk a treadmill for 20 minutes while their heart rate is maintained between 160–180 beats per minute. The control subjects do not exercise during the 10-week period. After 10 weeks, all subjects are brought into the lab and asked to solve mental arithmetic problems under the threat of electric shock for poor performance. The measure of stress is the subjects' heart rate during the task. The experimental hypothesis is that, during stress, the aerobic group will have a lower heart rate than the control group. The null hypothesis is that the population means are the same. The data, along with the computation of t_{obt}, are presented in Table 8.2.

The procedural flow for testing the hypothesis is as follows.

Six Steps for Testing the Null Hypothesis Using the Independent-Samples t Test

Step 1.   Define the null and alternative hypotheses:

$$H_0: \quad \mu_1 = \mu_2$$

$$H_1: \quad \mu_1 \neq \mu_2$$

TABLE 8.2 Computing t_{obt} for an Independent-Samples t Test[a]

Aerobic Training	Control
84	88
78	97
67	74
87	80
80	87
78	90
78	90
79	86
82	84
81	78

$\overline{X}_1 = 79.40$	$\overline{X}_2 = 85.40$
$s_1 = 5.25$	$s_2 = 6.69$
$\Sigma X_1 = 794$	$\Sigma X_2 = 854$
$\Sigma X_1^2 = 63292$	$\Sigma X_2^2 = 73334$
$n_1 = 10$	$n_2 = 10$

$$t_{obt} = \cfrac{\overline{X}_1 - \overline{X}_2}{\sqrt{\cfrac{\left(\Sigma X_1^2 - \cfrac{(\Sigma X_1)^2}{n_1}\right) + \left(\Sigma X_2^2 - \cfrac{(\Sigma X_2)^2}{n_2}\right)}{n_1 + n_2 - 2}\left(\cfrac{1}{n_1} + \cfrac{1}{n_2}\right)}}$$

$$= \cfrac{79.40 - 85.40}{\sqrt{\cfrac{\left(63292 - \cfrac{(794)^2}{10}\right) + \left(73334 - \cfrac{(854)^2}{10}\right)}{10 + 10 - 2}\left(\cfrac{1}{10} + \cfrac{1}{10}\right)}}$$

$$= \cfrac{79.40 - 85.40}{\sqrt{\cfrac{(63292 - 63043.60) + (73334 - 72931.60)}{10 + 10 - 2}(.20)}}$$

$$= \cfrac{-6.00}{\sqrt{(650.80/18)\,(.20)}}$$

$$= \cfrac{-6.00}{\sqrt{36.16(.20)}}$$

$$= \cfrac{-6.00}{\sqrt{7.23}} = \cfrac{-6.00}{2.69}$$

$$t_{obt} = \mathbf{-2.23}$$

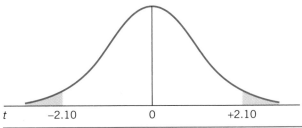

t	−2.10	0	+2.10

[a] Raw scores are heart rates under stress. Since $t_{obt} > t_{crit}$, the null hypothesis is rejected.

Step 2.   Set alpha. Alpha is set at .05.

Step 3.   Compute t_{obt} (see Table 8.2).

Step 4.   Locate the critical t value in Appendix B.2. The degrees of freedom is $n_1 + n_2 - 2$, or in other words, $10 + 10 - 2 = 18$. Enter the left column of the t table and locate the number 18. Now move to the column under alpha of .05 for a two-tailed test. The critical value is 2.10.

Step 5.   Compare the t_{obt} of -2.23 with the critical value of 2.10. Since the absolute value of t_{obt} is greater than the critical value of 2.10, the null hypothesis is rejected in favor of the alternative hypothesis.

Step 6.   Interpret the findings. Aerobic training leads to a reduction in the subjects' physiological reaction to stress, $t(18) = -2.23$, $p < .05$. Additional research would be required to determine if other kinds of stressors can be handled as well after aerobic training.

Assumptions of the Independent-Samples t Test

There are four assumptions that should be met when conducting an independent-samples t test.

1. ***Random sampling.***   It is assumed that the samples are representative of the populations from which they are drawn. Meeting this assumption will allow you to generalize the results of the t test to subjects not in the study.

2. ***The populations from which the samples are taken are normally distributed.***   This assumption assures that the sampling distributions for $\overline{X}_1$ and $\overline{X}_2$ are normally distributed. As a result, the sampling distribution of the differences will be normally distributed. If one of the populations is not normally distributed, the assumption of normality will be violated *unless* the total sample size is sufficiently large (around 30). Recall that sampling distributions approximate the normal curve as the sample size increases. If you suspect that either one of the populations is not normally distributed, be sure to use a sufficient number of subjects in your study.

3. ***Homogeneity of variances.***   The third assumption of the independent-samples t test is that the variances of the populations are equal. A significance test can be conducted on the sample variances to see if the population variances are unequal (see Kirk, 1989). In lieu of this test, you can use a rule of thumb to judge whether the population variances are close in value. Examine the sample variances: if one of them is four times larger than the other, you will probably violate the assumption of homogeneity of variances if you proceed with the t test. The t test is a robust test. This means that it can be appropriately performed even when an underlying assumption is violated, particularly if $n_1 = n_2$. When sample sizes are unequal and the underlying assumptions of the t test are violated, one course of action is to use a significance test that does not make assumptions about the population distributions, called nonparametric tests (see Chapter 18).

4. ***Independent observations.***   This is the most critical assumption of the t test. Independent observations means that the scores *within each sample*

BOX
8.1

Can Epileptic Seizures Be Controlled By Relaxation Training?

In the last 20 years, researchers have begun to discover an association between emotionality and frequency of seizures among those people suffering from epilepsy. For instance, daily hassles, fear, anger, and anxiety have all been found to correlate with seizure activity (Feldman and Paul, 1976; Standage, 1972; Symonds, 1970; Temkin and Davis, 1984). At least one study has shown that symptoms of anxiety are twice as high in an epileptic sample as compared to persons with other kinds of physical problems (Standage and Fenton, 1975).

The standard medical treatment for epileptic seizures is the administration of an antiseizure medication, like Dilantin or phenobarbital. Although the *causal* role of emotionality in producing seizures is debatable (seizures could cause negative emotions), the association between emotions and seizures leads researchers to wonder if perhaps a stress-reduction treatment could reduce the frequency of epileptic seizures.

Puskarich (1988) compared the effects of relaxation training versus a placebo on the frequency of seizures among epileptics. After an 8-week baseline period in which all patients recorded their frequency of seizures, 13 patients received 6 weeks of relaxation training. Eleven placebo-control patients were seen the same number of times as the experimental subjects, but were placed in a room alone and told that sitting quietly would induce relaxation, which would help reduce their seizures. All patients took their usual medications throughout the study. For 8 weeks after treatment concluded, all patients recorded their frequency of seizures. The dependent variable was the change in the number of seizures from baseline to post-treatment.

The raw data are presented in the following table. A negative number means a decrease in seizures; a positive number indicates an increase in seizures. Because this is a relatively new area of research, and because it is important to minimize the probability of failing to reject a false null hypothesis (a Type II error), the investigator set alpha at .10 when conducting the significance test. By not using the traditional alpha of

.05, the investigator doubles the probability of a Type I error.[1] An independent-samples t test is used to compare the means of the relaxation and placebo conditions.

Relaxation	Placebo
$+7$	-1
0	-5
-5	$+16$
-1	-7
-14	$+3$
-5	$+4$
-6	-6
-7	-2
-1	$+2$
-4	-4
-7	-3
-13	
-8	

$$\overline{X}_1 = -4.92 \qquad \overline{X}_2 = -.27$$
$$s_1 = 5.51 \qquad s_2 = 6.51$$
$$n_1 = 13 \qquad n_2 = 11$$

H_0: $\mu_1 = \mu_2$
H_1: $\mu_1 \neq \mu_2$
$\qquad \alpha = .10$
$\qquad df = n_1 + n_2 - 2 = 22$

$$t_{obt} = \frac{\overline{X}_1 - \overline{X}_2}{s_{\overline{x}_1 - \overline{x}_2}}$$

---

[1] If Puskarich submits her article for publication, she will have to make a convincing case for "relaxing" the alpha level. Scientists are a conservative lot. In most cases, they would prefer to miss something that is there (Type II error) rather than think that they have found something that is not there (Type I error). However, the conventional alpha of .05 is not written in stone and, thus, journal editors will entertain an author's argument for setting alpha at .10.

Since the s_1 and s_2 are provided in the summary statistics, Formula 8.4 can be used to compute the standard error.

$$s_{\bar{x}_1 - \bar{x}_2} = \sqrt{\frac{s_1^2(n_1 - 1) + s_2^2(n_2 - 1)}{n_1 + n_2 - 2} \left(\frac{1}{n_1} + \frac{1}{n_2}\right)}$$

$$s_{\bar{x} - \bar{x}} = \sqrt{\frac{(5.51)^2(12) + (6.51)^2(10)}{13 + 11 - 2} \left(\frac{1}{13} + \frac{1}{11}\right)}$$

$$= \sqrt{(35.82)(.17)}$$

$$s_{\bar{x}_1 - \bar{x}_2} = \sqrt{6.09}$$

$$t_{obt} = \frac{(-4.92) - (-.27)}{\sqrt{6.09}} = \frac{-4.65}{2.47}$$

$$t_{obt} = -1.88$$

The critical value for t is: $t_{.10}(22) = 1.72$. Since the absolute value of $t_{obt} > t_{crit}$ (1.88 > 1.72), the null hypothesis is rejected. The author concluded that relaxation training is more effective than a placebo treatment in reducing the frequency of seizures, $t(22) = -1.88$, $p < .10$.

are independent of one another. In most applications, independent observations means that each subject supplies only one score. However, it is possible to violate the independence assumption even when only one score is obtained per subject. If the behavior of one subject in the study is influenced by the behavior of another subject, then the scores from these two subjects are *not* independent.

Box 8.1 presents a study of the effects of relaxation training on the frequency of epileptic seizures. An independent-samples t test is used to determine if the change in the number of seizures of the relaxation group is significantly different from the control group.

8.3 DIRECTIONAL TESTS OF SIGNIFICANCE

So far hypothesis testing has been discussed from a nondirectional perspective, which means that our interest was in detecting a difference between population means, irrespective of whether $\mu_1 < \mu_2$ or $\mu_1 > \mu_2$. The null hypothesis was always stated as an equality (e.g., $\mu_1 = \mu_2$ or $\mu = 100$), and the alternative hypothesis was always stated as an inequality (e.g., $\mu_1 \neq \mu_2$ or $\mu \neq 100$). Research hypotheses (scientific hypotheses) are usually stated as predictions about the expected direction of an experimental effect. For example, persuasion technique A will induce *greater* attitude change than technique B; subjects' perceptions of control over a stressor will *decrease* stress reactions; or higher levels of physiological arousal will create *stronger* emotions. Researchers typically frame their *statistical* hypotheses in a nondirectional form. In other words, even though the research hypothesis makes a prediction about which of two means will be larger, the null and alternative hypotheses allow the investigator to discover if a treatment effect is opposite to the predicted effect. For instance, if a researcher hypothesizes that an advertisement will *increase* the sales of a product, a nondirectional test of this hypothesis allows for the discovery that the advertisement actually *decreases* sales. However, there are times when it is appropriate to use a directional test of the research hypothesis. A directional test is capable of detecting *only* a difference between means in one direction. If a researcher uses a directional test to see if an advertisement increases sales, then it will be impossible to discover if the advertisement decreases sales. As you will soon learn, the decision to adopt a directional versus a nondirectional test has implications for how the statistical hypotheses are stated and how to use the t table. In addition, you will learn why directional tests of hypotheses are controversial.

We will begin the discussion of directional tests of significance by specifying how directional tests affect the way the null and alternative hypotheses are stated; then the implications that a directional test has for the critical value that is used to compare to the test statistic are addressed, and finally when to use a directional test is discussed. As a vehicle for presenting the concepts of directional and nondirectional tests, we will use the research context in which the independent-samples t test is appropriate. A nondirectional test is called a two-tailed test, and a directional test is called a one-tailed test. The reason for the two-tailed/one-tailed terminology will become clear as you read the next section.

One-Tailed and Two-Tailed Tests

The discussion of hypothesis testing thus far has addressed only two-tailed tests. The null and alternative hypotheses for a two-tailed test have been presented as follows:

$$H_0: \quad \mu_1 = \mu_2$$

$$H_1: \quad \mu_1 \neq \mu_2$$

When the null and alternative hypotheses are stated in this fashion, the rejection region is divided equally between both tails of the t distribution. When testing at the 5 percent level of significance, 2.5 percent of the rejection region is in the right tail of the t distribution, and 2.5 percent of the rejection region is in the left tail of the t distribution. With the rejection region in both tails of the distribution, it is possible to detect a difference when $\mu_1 > \mu_2$ *and* when $\mu_1 < \mu_2$. Since a two-tailed test can detect a difference between population means in either direction, it is also called a **two-tailed** (or **nondirectional**) **test of significance.**

Two things change when conducting a **one-tailed** (or **directional**) **test**: the manner in which the null and alternative hypotheses are stated and the placement of the rejection region. (There are no new formulas associated with a one-tailed test.) Consider the following research situation. Suppose a standard drug for treating some illness exists, but this drug has a certain number of side effects. A new, more expensive drug is being tested; despite its cost, if it has fewer side effects, it will become the treatment of choice. Since the new drug is more expensive than the standard drug, the standard drug will remain the treatment of choice if they both have the same number of side effects. The same conclusion would be reached if the new drug had *more* side effects than the standard drug. Thus, whether the new drug has the same or more side effects makes no difference; either way it won't be marketed. The only finding of interest is if the new drug has fewer side effects.

Recall that when setting up the null and alternative hypotheses two related rules must be followed. Together, the null and alternative hypotheses must be mutually exclusive and collectively exhaustive. Defining the sample of subjects receiving the new drug as Population 1, the null and alternative hypotheses for a directional significance test are stated as:

$$H_0: \quad \mu_1 \geq \mu_2$$

$$H_1: \quad \mu_1 < \mu_2$$

How are these hypotheses collectively exhaustive? The null hypothesis, H_0, includes the case in which the population means are the same *and* the case in which the mean of the standard drug, Population 2, is lower. The alternative hypothesis specifies that the mean number of side effects for Population 1 is less than the mean of Population 2. The null and alternative hypotheses cover all of the possible outcomes; therefore, they are collectively exhaustive. They are mutually exclusive because they both cannot be true at the same time.

In this example, note that the difference $\mu_1 > \mu_2$ is embodied in the *null hypothesis*. In this particular directional test, it is impossible to conclude that $\mu_1 > \mu_2$ because the null hypothesis can never be supported. Therefore, even if it is true that $\mu_1 > \mu_2$, there is no way to detect this fact. Researchers conduct a one-tailed test when they are interested only in detecting a difference between the population means in one direction.

Setting up the null and alternative hypotheses as a directional test determines the placement of the rejection region in the t distribution. Since only a difference between means in one direction can be detected, it must be the case that the entire rejection region is in one tail of the distribution. If alpha is set at .05, the entire 5 percent of the rejection region is in one tail. Whether the region is in the left tail or the right tail depends on the direction of the difference in which you are interested. In the drug example, you are only interested in detecting when the new drug has fewer side effects; that is, when the mean of the new drug group is smaller than the mean of the standard drug group, $\mu_1 < \mu_2$. Hence, the rejection region is to the left side of the t distribution. Figure 8.3 uses the t distribution to illustrate the rejection region for a two-tailed and one-tailed test when alpha is .05. It is assumed that the sample sizes are sufficiently large so that the t distribution has the form of a standard normal curve.

The Sign of t_{obt} is Important in a Directional Test

When conducting a nondirectional test, the researcher allows that $\mu_1 > \mu_2$ or $\mu_1 < \mu_2$. Thus, it does not matter if the t_{obt} is positive or negative in value. For this reason you always take the absolute value of t_{obt} when conducting a nondirectional test. The situation is different with a directional test; whether t_{obt} is positive or negative matters. If the alternative hypothesis states that $\mu_1 < \mu_2$, the null hypothesis is only rejected if t_{obt} is a *negative* number that is larger than the critical value. This is because the rejection region is entirely to the left of the mean of the t distribution; all t values to the left of the mean are negative. If your alternative hypothesis is stated as $\mu_1 > \mu_2$, then t_{obt} must be *positive* and greater than the

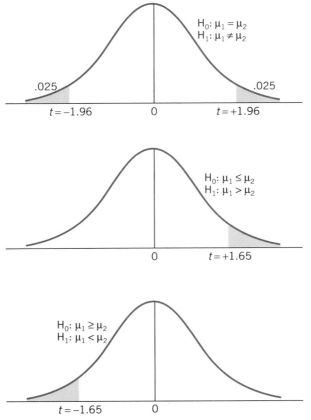

Figure 8.3 The rejection region of a *t* distribution for a one-tailed and two-tailed test, $\alpha = .05$. The critical values reflect the assumption that these *t* distributions are based on sample sizes that are sufficiently large so that the distributions have the form of a standard normal curve.

critical value to reject H_0. When you are conducting a two-tailed test, it does not matter how you arrange the means in the numerator. However, the sign of t_{obt} is important in a one-tailed test, so you must subtract the mean of group 2 from the mean of group 1. How do you know which is group 1 and which is group 2? You already defined them when you stated the null and alternative hypotheses.

For a given level of alpha, the critical value used in a one-tailed test is smaller than the value used in a two-tailed test; therefore, it is easier to reject the null hypothesis when conducting a one-tailed test. This is one reason that the decision to use a one-tailed or a two-tailed test is surrounded with some controversy.

Using the *t* Table for a Directional Test

You already have experience in finding t_{crit} for a two-tailed *t* test: enter the *t* table, find the appropriate *df*, and look under the alpha heading for a two-tailed test. As you view the *t* table in Appendix B.2, you will note that the table has two rows of headings, one for alpha levels for a one-tailed test and one heading for alpha levels used for a two-tailed test.

α Levels for Two-Tailed Test		
df	.10	.05

α Levels for One-Tailed Test		
	.05	.025
⋮	⋮	⋮
6	1.943	2.447
7	**1.895**	2.365
8	1.860	2.306
9	1.833	2.262
⋮	⋮	⋮

■   QUESTION   *Using alpha of .05, what is the critical value for an independent-samples one-tailed t test, if there are four subjects in one group and five subjects in the other group?*

SOLUTION   The *df* for an independent-samples *t* test is $n_1 + n_2 - 2$, or $4 + 5 - 2 = 7$. The critical value is 1.895.   ■

Use Caution in Deciding to Conduct a One-Tailed Test

Research hypotheses are almost always framed as a directional prediction or expectation. Therefore, why not always use a directional *t* test? If you use a one-tailed test, it is impossible to detect a difference between population means in the direction opposite from the experimental hypothesis. Should you not leave yourself open to anomalous findings? A finding contrary to expectations may lead to a revision in theory. When theory testing, performing a one-tailed test is a statement that a finding, contrary to a research prediction, is meaningless. Because the results of a study may not fit current theory does not mean that anomalous findings are meaningless. Failing to reject the null hypothesis tends to halt further research. Unexpected findings should stimulate rather than inhibit additional studies. A researcher never should use a one-tailed test simply because the research hypothesis is stated directionally. The strongest justification for using a one-tailed test is when a new course of action will be taken only if the result of the test is in one direction. Statisticians generally agree that one-tailed tests should be used infrequently (for the debate over directional and nondirectional *t* tests, see Kirk, 1972; Liberman, 1971).

Another point about the use of one-tailed *t* tests is *when* the decision is made to use a directional test. If conducting a one-tailed test is warranted, the decision *must* be made and, of course, justified before the data are analyzed.

Suppose you conduct a two-tailed test and find that the t_{obt} is nonsignificant. However, if you were to use the more liberal critical value associated with a one-tailed test, you note that the t_{obt} would now lead to a rejection of the null hypothesis. Why not ignore the results of the two-tailed test and simply report the statistically significant finding from the one-tailed test? Don't even think about it. This practice inflates the probability of a Type I error. For example, let's say alpha is set at .05. For a two-tailed test, the rejection region is divided equally between both tails. After failing to reject the null hypothesis, you move the entire rejection region to one side of the distribution. Now 5 percent of the distribution is in one tail. You have, in essence, used a 5 percent rejection region in one tail *plus* the 2.5 percent region from the other tail. The alpha is no longer .05, but .075 (.05 + .025).

SUMMARY

The independent-samples t test is used when two samples of subjects provide scores on a measure. The purpose of the t test is to help us decide whether two samples come from the same or different populations. The independent-samples t test is usually used with between-subjects designs with two groups, also called Case II research.

The sampling distribution for an independent-samples t test is a distribution of the difference between independent sample means. Sampling distributions of differences between means have several characteristics. First, the mean of the sampling distribution of $\overline{X}_1 - \overline{X}_2$ is equal to the difference between the population means, $\mu_1 - \mu_2$. Second, the Central Limit Theorem holds for sampling distributions of the difference between means. If the populations are normally distributed, the sampling distributions of differences between means will likewise be normal. However, if the sample sizes are sufficiently large, a sampling distribution of differences will be normal, whether or not the populations are normally distributed. Third, the standard deviation of a sampling distribution of differences is called the standard error of the difference, or the standard error. The t test uses the weighted average of two sample variances (the pooled variance) to estimate the population variance.

The independent-samples t test relies on the t distribution. The t distribution transforms a sampling distribution of differences to a standardized curve by applying the t formula to each mean of the sampling distribution. A different t distribution is established for each sample size. The t distribution, represented in the t table, is used to identify the critical values that t_{obt} must exceed to reject the null hypothesis. The t ratio (t_{obt}) indicates the number of standard errors the difference between sample means is from the hypothesized mean of the sampling distribution of differences. If the null hypothesis is true, then sampling error will occasionally lead to a difference between sample means large enough to reject the null hypothesis. However, the most likely explanation for a significant difference between sample means is that the samples are taken from populations that have different means.

The assumptions of the independent-samples t test are random sampling, normally distributed populations, independent observations, and homogeneity of population variances.

Research hypotheses are usually stated as predictions about the expected direction of an experimental effect. Researchers typically frame their statistical hypotheses such that a difference between means in the direction opposite to their prediction can be detected. However, there are times when it is appropriate to use a directional test of the research hypothesis. When conducting a one-tailed (or directional) test the manner in which the null and alternative hypotheses are stated and the placement of the rejection region both changes. When conducting a one-tailed (directional) test, the entire rejection region of the t distribution is in one tail. As a consequence, for a given level of alpha, the critical value for a one-tailed test is smaller than a two-tailed test, thus making it easier to reject the null hypothesis. Statisticians generally discourage the use of directional tests. The strongest justification for a one-tailed test is when a course of action will be taken only if the results of the study are in one direction.

KEY FORMULAS FOR CHAPTER 8

Standard Error of the Difference

$$\sigma_{\overline{x}_1 - \overline{x}_2} = \sqrt{\sigma^2 \left(\frac{1}{n_1} + \frac{1}{n_2} \right)}$$

(Formula 8.1)

Definitional Formula for the Estimated Standard Error

$$s_{\overline{x}_1 - \overline{x}_2} = \sqrt{s_p^2 \left(\frac{1}{n_1} + \frac{1}{n_2} \right)}$$

(Formula 8.2)

The Pooled Variance

$$s_p^2 = \frac{s_1^2(n_1 - 1) + s_2^2(n_2 - 1)}{n_1 + n_2 - 2}$$

(Formula 8.3)

Variance Formula for the Estimated Standard Error, $s_{\overline{x}_1 - \overline{x}_2}$

$$s_{\overline{x}_1 - \overline{x}_2} = \sqrt{\frac{s_1^2(n_1 - 1) + s_2^2(n_2 - 1)}{n_1 + n_2 - 2} \left(\frac{1}{n_1} + \frac{1}{n_2} \right)}$$

(Formula 8.4)

Computational Formula for $s_{\overline{x}_1 - \overline{x}_2}$

$$s_{\overline{x}_1 - \overline{x}_2} = \sqrt{\frac{\left(\Sigma X_1^2 - \frac{(\Sigma X_1)^2}{n_1} \right) + \left(\Sigma X_2^2 - \frac{(\Sigma X_2)^2}{n_2} \right)}{n_1 + n_2 - 2} \left(\frac{1}{n_1} + \frac{1}{n_2} \right)}$$

(Formula 8.5)

The t statistic for Independent Samples

$$t_{obt} = \frac{(\overline{X}_1 - \overline{X}_2) - (\mu_1 - \mu_2)}{s_{\overline{x}_1 - \overline{x}_2}}$$ (Formula 8.6)

The t Ratio

$$t_{obt} = \frac{\overline{X}_1 - \overline{X}_2}{s_{\overline{x}_1 - \overline{x}_2}}$$ (Formula 8.7)

WORK PROBLEMS

For the following problems, when conducting a t test, assume a two-tailed test unless otherwise specified.

1. A hypothetical study is conducted to evaluate the hypothesis that 2-year-old children with no siblings will show more fear around unfamiliar children than 2-year-old children with one or more siblings. Each child is put in a playroom with an unfamiliar child and fear ratings are obtained through behavioral observations. Fear ratings can range from 1–no fear to 10–a great deal of fear. For the following data:
   a. Specify the null and alternative hypotheses.
   b. Identify t_{crit} for $\alpha = .05$, two-tailed test.
   c. Conduct the t test.
   d. Interpret the findings with respect to the causal influence of being raised as an only child on fear of strange peers.

No Siblings	Siblings
10	7
6	3
8	2
4	4
9	1
7	2

2. A social psychologist is interested in evaluating the hypothesis that anxiety increases males' attraction to females. The scientific hypothesis is that anxiety will increase interpersonal attraction (see Dutton and Aron, 1974). All subjects are told that they are to hear several random bursts of noise in a learning experiment. Half of the subjects are led to expect a loud noise (high anxiety condition) and the other half of the subjects expect to receive a soft noise (low anxiety condition). While waiting for the experiment to begin, subjects are placed in a room with a female confederate. Later, subjects are asked to rate the attractiveness of the female, from 1–unattractive to 5–very attractive. Hypothetical summary statistics are presented in the following tabular list.
   a. Specify the null and alternative hypotheses.
   b. Test the null hypothesis with $\alpha = .05$. What is t_{crit} for $\alpha = .05$, two-tailed test?

    c. Perform the t test.

    d. Interpret the findings.

High Anxiety	Low Anxiety
$\overline{X}_1 = 4.2$	$\overline{X}_2 = 2.2$
$s_1^2 = .5$	$s_2^2 = .7$
$n_1 = 10$	$n_2 = 10$

3. For Problem 25, suppose that the variances of attraction ratings are increased so that: $s_1^2 = 5.2$ and $s_2^2 = 5.4$.

    a. Perform a t test with $\alpha = .05$.

    b. Interpret the findings.

    c. What effect has increasing the variability had on t_{obt} and the final conclusion about the null hypothesis?

4. Using the variance in Problem 3, suppose the number of subjects in each group is increased to 30.

High Anxiety	Low Anxiety
$\overline{X}_1 = 4.2$	$\overline{X}_2 = 2.2$
$s_1^2 = 5.2$	$s_2^2 = 5.4$
$n_1 = 30$	$n_2 = 30$

    a. Perform a t test with $\alpha = .05$.

    b. Interpret the findings.

    c. What effect has the increase in sample sizes had on t_{obt} and your decision to accept or reject the null hypothesis?

5. For an independent-samples t test, to what does the standard error of the difference refer?

6. How does the sample size influence t_{crit} and why?

7. In what way does sample size affect the probability of rejecting the null hypothesis?

8. Biaggio (1989) administered a Personal Incidents Record to male and female college students to assess the frequency of anger reactions. The author found that males reported significantly more anger reactions in comparison to females. The following hypothetical data presented are consistent with Biaggio's findings.

    a. Specify the null and alternative hypotheses.

    b. Test the null hypothesis with $\alpha = .05$. What is t_{crit} for $\alpha = .05$?

    c. Perform the t test.

    d. Interpret the findings.

Frequency of Anger Reactions

Males	Females
16	9
18	10
15	8
20	4
9	14

9. Burke and Greenglass (1989) have concluded that, "It may be lonely at the top but it's less stressful." These authors found a significant difference between teachers and principals on a measure of burnout, with teachers exhibiting higher levels of stress than principals. The following hypothetical data are consistent with their findings.
   a. Specify the null and alternative hypotheses.
   b. Test the null hypothesis with $\alpha = .05$. What is t_{crit} for $\alpha = .05$, two-tailed test?
   c. Perform the t test.
   d. Interpret the findings.

Burnout Scores

Teachers	Principals
42	28
38	35
44	40
33	38
49	30
42	24

10. Zakahi and Duran (1988) hypothesized that people who are very lonely are less physically attractive than people who are not lonely. A loneliness questionnaire was administered. Subjects who scored in the top 25 percent were considered very lonely, while those subjects who scored in the bottom 25 percent were deemed not lonely. All subjects' photographs were rated by three judges for attractiveness (1–very unattractive to 10–very attractive). Males rated females and females rated males. There was no significant difference in attractiveness ratings between very lonely and not lonely females. However, lonely males were rated as significantly less physically attractive than males who were not lonely. The following hypothetical data are in line with the findings of the authors.
    a. Specify the null and alternative hypotheses.
    b. Test the null hypothesis with $\alpha = .05$. What is t_{crit} for $\alpha = .05$?
    c. Perform the t test.
    d. Interpret the findings.

Attractiveness Ratings for Males

Lonely	Not Lonely
3	8
6	9
5	7
4	5
7	8

11. In 1972, Buffalo Creek, West Virginia, was the scene of a major flood. The flood was a consequence of corporate negligence. Coal waste that was dumped in a mountain stream created an artificial dam. After several days of rain, the dam gave way and a black wall of water, over 30 ft high, descended on mining hamlets in the valley. In less than 1 hour, 125 people were dead and 5000 others lost their homes. Simpson-Housley and DeMan (1989) found that, 17

years later, the residents of Buffalo Creek scored higher on a measure of trait anxiety in comparison to the residents of Kopperston, a nearby mining town that did not experience the flood. The following data are hypothetical, but are consistent with the findings of the researchers.

a. Specify the null and alternative hypotheses.
b. Test the null hypothesis with $\alpha = .05$. What is t_{crit} for $\alpha = .05$, two-tailed test?
c. Perform the t test.
d. Interpret the findings.

Anxiety Scores

Buffalo Creek	Kopperston
50	35
45	37
48	36
40	39
42	40
38	38

12. Narcissism is characterized by a feeling of being "special," self-centeredness, and a sense of entitlement. When comparing college students who were first-borns with students who were born later, Jourbert (1989) found that first-borns were more narcissistic than those subjects who were born later in the family. The effect was the same for males and females. Hypothetical summary data are presented, for males and females. Conduct an independent-samples t test between first-borns and later-borns (a) for males and (b) for females. Set alpha at .05.

(a)   **Males**

First-Borns:	$\overline{X}_1$: 23	s_1: 7.84	n_1: 10
Later-Borns:	$\overline{X}_2$: 16	s_2: 6.43	n_2: 15

(b)   **Females**

First-Borns:	$\overline{X}_1$: 17	s_1: 6.52	n_1: 19
Later-Borns:	$\overline{X}_2$: 12	s_2: 6.57	n_2: 28

13. Simon (1989) found that a sample of 54 males and 84 females (mean age of each group = 22 years) reported losing their virginity at the age of 16.1 years and 16.5 years, respectively. Males, however, reported having had sex with 14.6 ($s_1 = 29.2$) different partners, while females reporting having sex with 5.6 ($s_2 = 5.4$) different partners. Conduct an independent-samples t test to determine if there is a significant difference between males and females in the number of past sexual partners. Set alpha at .05.

14. A child psychologist has reason to believe that children who do not spend much time with peers during recess have a problem starting conversations. Sixty children are randomly assigned to two treatment conditions (30 children

per condition). In the Experimental condition, children learn how to begin a conversation. Children in the Control condition are given talks about the importance of having friends. For a 30-day period after treatment, the children are observed during recess. Each child's average amount of time spent with peers is recorded. The mean play time for the Experimental condition is 17.0 minutes; the mean for the Control condition is 13.5 minutes. The standard error of the difference is 2.0.

    a. State the null and alternative hypotheses.

    b. Conduct a t test.

    c. What is t_{crit}?

    d. Interpret the findings.

15. Using the summary data from Problem 14, conduct a one-tailed test that will detect a mean difference only if the Experimental condition produces a higher level of peer interaction.

    a. State the null and alternative hypotheses.

    b. Conduct the t test.

    c. Interpret the findings.

    d. Do you believe that the researcher would be justified in performing a directional test? Support your answer.

16. Think of a study that should be analyzed with a one-tailed t test. Justify your reasoning.

Work Problems for the Computer

17. A social psychologist hypothesizes that when a person believes that he or she has unintentionally harmed someone, the person will be motivated to compensate the victim. However, if compensation is not possible, the "harm doer" will be more likely to act generously to some other person (c.f., Carlsmith & Gross, 1969). Fifty subjects are randomly assigned to two treatment conditions (25 subjects per condition). Participants are told that they will be in a problem-solving study. When a subject arrives, he or she is asked to wait in the hallway while the apparatus is being set up. Soon afterward, two confederates, one carrying a camera, approach the subject and ask if they could have their picture taken together. The camera is handed to the subject and the experimental manipulation begins. In the Compensation condition, the camera is rigged so that it breaks when the subject adjusts the focus. The confederates appear mildly distraught over the mishap, but, if offered, refuse any compensation. In the Control condition, the camera does not break.

      During the problem-solving phase of the study, each subject is asked to write down his or her answers to 75 arithmetic questions. A stack of answer sheets that have been completed by other subjects is next to the subject. At the end of the experiment, the researcher asks if the subject would mind staying and scoring a few of the answer sheets.

      So that the data is in a form appropriate for a t test, let's assume that all subjects agree to help. The dependent variable is how many answer sheets the subject scores before leaving. (If the dependent variable were the percentage of people in each condition who agreed to help, a different statistical analysis would have to be used; see Chapter 17.) The research hypothesis is that subjects in the Compensation condition will score more answer sheets than the subjects in the Control condition. Perform an independent-samples t test on the following data set ($\alpha = .05$) and interpret the findings. Would your conclusion be different if you had performed a one-tailed test at the 5 percent level of significance?

Number of Answer Sheets Scored

Compensation Condition

40	34	48	22	35	16	67	84
33	22	50	54	60	68	59	22
30	29	32	33	19	55	54	49
40							

Control Condition

22	30	40	22	35	16	40	79
13	22	25	40	54	61	59	22
28	24	20	18	19	42	34	40
29							

18. A social psychologist hypothesizes that snake-phobic individuals would be more likely to approach a snake if they believe that they are not experiencing anxiety (see Valins and Ray, 1967). Sixty college students who reported on a "questionnaire of fears" that they were very frightened of snakes served as participants. Upon arriving at the laboratory, all subjects were asked to walk over to a large, nonpoisonous snake and pick it up. Heart rate sensors were attached to subjects, and a speaker on the recording device sounded heartbeats that the subjects believed were accurate recordings of their own heart rate. In the High-Arousal condition, subjects heard a heart rate that was 120 beats per minute. In the Low-Arousal condition, subjects heard a heart rate of 75 beats per minute. In truth, the heart rates were prerecorded and did not reflect the true heart rates of the subjects. The scientific hypothesis was that subjects in the Low-Arousal condition, believing that they were not experiencing anxiety, would walk closer to the snake than subjects who believed that their hearts were beating fast. Subjects were told that they could stop approaching the snake whenever they felt too uncomfortable to continue. Markings on the floor allowed the investigator to determine how close subjects were to the snake when they stopped their approach. Hypothetical data are presented. Lower numbers reflect *greater* approach behavior. Perform an independent-samples t test and interpret the findings. Set alpha at .05.

Approach Behavior (in ft)

Low Arousal

6.0	5.8	3.2	4.5	6.8	8.2
7.4	6.9	4.3	5.5	6.2	7.0
5.2	6.1	5.9	4.4	3.2	1.3
8.7	5.2	4.8	3.2	1.6	4.8
6.6	7.6	8.0	8.5	4.5	7.9

High Arousal

2.0	3.8	2.2	4.5	5.8	6.1
1.2	2.2	2.3	4.5	3.2	4.0
2.2	1.1	5.9	3.4	3.2	1.3
6.7	4.2	8.8	3.2	1.6	4.8
6.6	5.6	4.0	8.5	4.5	7.9

Testing the Difference Between Two Means: The Dependent-Samples *t* Test

9.1 THE RESEARCH CONTEXT

The independent-samples *t* test is used to contrast means computed from two unrelated samples of scores. In *dependent sampling*, each score in one sample is related to another score in a second sample. Pairs of scores are formed either by the way that the treatment conditions are presented or the manner in which the subjects are assigned to treatment conditions. First, a discussion of the case in which pairs of scores are formed by the way in which treatment conditions are presented is addressed. Then the situation in which pairs of scores are formed by the way subjects are assigned to treatment conditions is considered. The *t* test appropriate to the method of dependent sampling is called a **dependent-samples *t* test,** a **paired-observations *t* test,** or a **correlated-samples *t* test.**

Repeated-Measures Designs

 A **repeated-measures design** (or **within-subjects design**) assesses one group of subjects under two or more treatment conditions; however, in this chapter, only the case in which *two* treatment conditions are evaluated is addressed.[1] The following research example is presented as a between-groups design and then as a repeated-measures design.

Suppose a cognitive psychologist is interested in assessing the relative merits of two kinds of memory strategies that are used to remember the names of people. The first strategy involves imagery. A sample of subjects is taught to associate the names of people with a related mental image of the person's face. For instance, when they are presented with a snapshot of Al Rosen, the subjects could picture a tattoo of a rose on his forehead. The next time they see Rosen's picture, these subjects will think of a rose and remember "Rosen." The second method uses repetition and employs a *separate* group of subjects. When viewing snapshots of people, these subjects repeat the person's name three times. Because two separate samples of subjects are used, this is a between-groups design. In this case, an independent-samples *t* test would be used to compare the means of the groups.

This same study might also be conducted using a repeated-measures design. Unlike the between-groups design in which subjects are assigned to *one* of the two experimental conditions (imagery versus repetition); in the within-subjects design, all subjects receive *both* experimental treatments. Each subject supplies a pair of scores, one score for each condition. Thus, the imagery method would be taught and assessed and then the repetition method would be taught and assessed. The means of the two experimental groups are compared with a dependent-samples *t* test. The repeated-measures design is an efficient design because the researcher can use fewer subjects in comparison to the between-groups design. More im-portantly, the repeated-measures design also increases the **power** of the test of the null hypothesis.[2] The power of a statistical test is the probability of correctly rejecting a false null hypothesis. The power of a dependent-samples *t* test is greater than the power of the independent-samples *t* test. Two research examples from the psychological literature are presented in the following sections. A repeated-measures design is used in each instance; the dependent-samples *t* test can be used to analyze the data from these studies.

---

[1] Chapter 14 addresses the analysis of repeated-measures designs in which more than two treatment conditions are used.

[2] See Chapter 11 for a discussion of the concept of power.

▶   **EXAMPLE 1**   Addison (1989) tested the hypothesis that people perceive bearded men differently from nonbearded men. Addison used a repeated-measures design in which one group of subjects rated pictures of bearded (Condition 1) and nonbearded men (Condition 2) on a number of dimensions. The results indicated that, compared to nonbearded men, fellows with beards are rated as more masculine, more aggressive, stronger, and more dominant. They are not, however, viewed as more intelligent.   ◀

▶   **EXAMPLE 2**   Ruth, Mosatche, and Kramer (1989) used a repeated-measures design to test the hypothesis that people would prefer purchasing a liquor product if the product were advertised with sexual symbolism. One group of subjects was shown advertisements with and without sexual symbolism. In each condition, the subjects were asked to indicate their likelihood of purchasing the product. Sexual symbolism was defined psychoanalytically as symbolic depictions of genitalia and the act of sexual intercourse. For example, the authors state, "One symbolic advertisement presented a liquor bottle which was diagonally inserted into a Christmas stocking with the neck of the bottle protruding outward. Another symbolic advertisement presented several skyscrapers with steeples, one of which was positioned under an oval tunnel, and an airplane flying overhead" (p. 1135). An example of a nonsexual advertisement (for most people) was a country scene with grazing cows. A dependent-samples *t* test performed on the data provided support for the psychoanalytic hypothesis that people are more likely to prefer a product when there is symbolic sexual content in the advertisement.   ◀

Another example of a repeated-measures design is when one sample of subjects supplies scores before and after a treatment. This type of repeated-measures design is called a pretest/post-test repeated-measures design. It is useful when a researcher is interested in evaluating behavior change that is caused by the introduction of an independent variable. Studies that examine learning, performance, or therapy effects frequently employ a pretest/post-test design.

Matched-Subjects Design

Another type of design in which the dependent-samples *t* test is used involves two independent but related samples of subjects—the matched-subjects design. A **matched-subjects design** derives its name from the way subjects are assigned to conditions. In this design, subjects are assigned to experimental conditions based on prior information about the subjects. Imagine you are interested in comparing two educational programs designed for a grade school. One program uses behavior modification, emphasizing individually tailored performance goals, positive reinforcement for increasing mastery of material, and the provision of teaching machines. The other program employs the Montessori method in which students are free to learn in an unstructured environment. In this program, the teacher makes learning opportunities available and assumes that students will learn different topics as their interests guide them to new content areas. When comparing the impact of the two programs, the experimenter wants to ensure that the two groups are the same on all variables except for the treatment condition. This can be accomplished through the random assignment of subjects. However, random assignment does not guarantee that two groups of subjects will not differ on an important subject variable. One way to make sure that the groups do not differ on an important variable is by using the matched-subjects design. In the education example, it is important that the two groups of students are, on the average, similar in IQ. If, by chance, one program included children who had higher IQ's than the children in the other program, then the amount of material learned may be due to IQ rather than the educational program.

To contrast these two teaching programs using a matched-subjects design, you would have to obtain the IQ scores for each of the students *before* beginning the programs. Next, rank all the students to be used in the experiment according to IQ. The first two students with the highest IQ's form a pair. One student is randomly assigned to the behavior modification program and the other student is placed in the Montessori program. The next pair of subjects, those ranked third and fourth, are then randomly assigned to the two programs, and so on, until all students are assigned. This assignment procedure almost guarantees that there will be no difference in average IQ between the treatment conditions.

How does the researcher decide which variable to use in matching? One criterion governs this decision. The measure used for matching *must* be related to (i.e., covary with) the dependent variable. If the subject variable is not correlated with the dependent variable, it cannot possibly emerge as an alternative explanation for a between-group difference on the dependent variable. Although the use of one matching variable is most common, researchers sometimes use more than one variable when matching (e.g., age, gender, and IQ).

In this chapter, only the repeated-measures design is used to illustrate the dependent-samples *t* test. However, the formulas and basic concepts of the test are the same for any dependent-sampling design that compares two means.

9.2 THE SAMPLING DISTRIBUTION FOR THE DEPENDENT-SAMPLES *t* TEST

The sampling distribution for the dependent-samples *t* test is based on differences between means of dependent (correlated) samples. Consider a repeated-measures design in which one group of subjects is exposed to two treatment conditions. This one group of subjects supplies two sets of scores; *each set of scores is a sample from a population*. The number of groups in an experiment is the same as the number of samples taken *only* when there is independent sampling that uses one dependent variable. In fact, in a study, each separate measurement defines a sample. Even though there is one group of subjects in a repeated-measures design there are two samples because two measurements are taken. The samples are drawn from hypothetical populations of subjects under Treatment 1 and the same subjects under Treatment 2.

Using Dependent Sampling to Form a Theoretical Sampling Distribution

The sampling distribution formed by dependent sampling is theoretically constructed in the following manner.

Step 1. Take one group of subjects and administer the two experimental treatment conditions, measuring the effects of each treatment. Each subject supplies one pair of scores.

Step 2. For each subject, subtract the second score from the first score. You now have one distribution of *difference scores.*

Step 3. Compute the mean of the distribution of difference scores, symbolized $\overline{D}$.

Step 4. Using the same size samples, repeat Steps 1–3 an infinite number of times.

Step 5. Plot the relative frequencies of $\overline{D}$ to obtain the sampling distribution of differences.

The sampling distribution is a distribution of mean differences. The mean of the sampling distribution, symbolized $\mu_{\overline{D}}$, will be the same as the difference between the means of the two hypothetical populations. If there is a difference of five units between the two populations, then the mean of the sampling distribution will be 5. If there is no difference between the populations, then the mean of the sampling distribution will be 0. The null hypothesis is that the mean of the sampling distribution is 0. This is the same as saying that there is no treatment effect. Under the null hypothesis, $\mu_x - \mu_y = \mu_D = 0$. (The x and y subscripts refer to the first and second set of scores, respectively.) Recall that the mean of a sampling distribution is the same as the mean of the population from which it is taken. Thus, $\mu_{\overline{x}} = \mu_x, \mu_{\overline{y}} = \mu_y,$ and $\mu_{\overline{D}} = \mu_D$. Figure 9.1($a$) shows two populations with different means. Figure 9.1(b) is the sampling distribution of differences derived from the populations. (Ignore Figure 9.1(c) for now.)

The Standard Error of the Sampling Distribution for Dependent Samples

The standard deviation of the sampling distribution is called the standard error of the difference, or standard error. The estimate of the population standard error of the difference is symbolized, $s_{\overline{D}}$. The formula uses the standard deviation of the difference scores, s_D, divided by the square root of the number of pairs of scores. Formula 9.1, the direct-difference method, computes the estimated standard error.

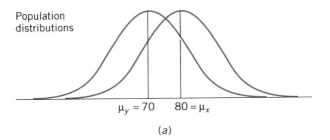

Population distributions

$\mu_y = 70 \qquad 80 = \mu_x$

(*a*)

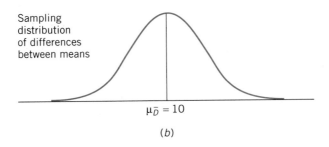

Sampling distribution of differences between means

$\mu_{\bar{D}} = 10$

(*b*)

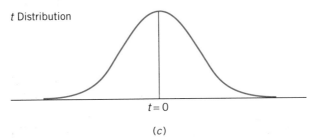

t Distribution

$t = 0$

(*c*)

Figure 9.1   In *a* and *b*, the mean of the sampling distribution of differences, $\mu_{\bar{D}}$, equals the difference between population means, $\mu_x - \mu_y$. In figure *c*, the *t* statistic transforms the sampling distribution to a *t* distribution with a mean of 0.

Stand. Error of Differences

Direct-Difference Method

$$s_{\bar{D}} = \frac{s_D}{\sqrt{n_p}} \qquad \text{(Formula 9.1)}$$

where,
$s_{\bar{D}}$ = the standard error of the sampling distribution of differences
s_D = the standard deviation of the difference scores
n_p = the number of *pairs* of scores

The computational formula for s_D is given in Formula 9.2.

Computational Formula for s_D

$$s_D = \sqrt{\frac{\Sigma D^2 - [(\Sigma D)^2/n_p]}{n_p - 1}}$$ (Formula 9.2)

where,

$D = X - Y$; a subject's score in Treatment 1 minus the same subject's score under Treatment 2

n_p = the number of *pairs* of scores

A word of caution: Remember to calculate the standard error by dividing s_D by the *square root* of n_p.

Before discussing the formula for a dependent-samples t test, let's use raw data to compute $s_{\bar{D}}$. Since $s_{\bar{D}}$ is the standard error of the sampling distribution, it will be placed in the denominator of the t statistic.

■ QUESTION   *What is $s_{\bar{D}}$ for the following data set?*

SOLUTION

		Scores	
X	Y	D	D^2
5	3	2	4
6	4	2	4
7	7	0	0
6	7	−1	1
		$\Sigma D = 3$	$\Sigma D^2 = 9$

Using Formula 9.2 to compute s_D,

$$s_D = \sqrt{\frac{\Sigma D^2 - [(\Sigma D)^2/n_p]}{n_p - 1}}$$

$$s_D = \sqrt{\frac{9 - [(3)^2/4]}{4 - 1}} = \sqrt{\frac{6.75}{3}}$$

$$s_D = \sqrt{2.25} = 1.50$$

The standard deviation of the difference scores is 1.50. Now place 1.50 in the formula for $s_{\bar{D}}$.

$$s_{\bar{D}} = \frac{s_D}{\sqrt{n_p}}$$

$$s_{\bar{D}} = \frac{1.50}{\sqrt{4}}$$

$$s_{\bar{D}} = .75$$

The standard error of the difference is .75. Remember that the standard deviation is a measure of variability with a distribution of *scores;* the standard error is a measure of variability for a distribution of *means* or a distribution of differences between means. In this instance, .75 equals one standard error. ■

9.3 THE *t* DISTRIBUTION FOR DEPENDENT SAMPLES

To test if there is a significant difference between the means of two dependent samples, the sampling distribution must be transformed to a *t* distribution. Here's the logic. You will be testing the difference between two sample means, $\overline{X}$ and $\overline{Y}$. The mean of the sampling distribution will be the same as the difference between the means of the populations, but you do not know what is the true difference between the populations. Without knowing the true difference between the populations, you cannot know the mean of the sampling distribution. If you obtained a difference between your *sample means* of, say, 4, how would you know if that difference is sampled from the middle or a tail of the sampling distribution? There is no way to judge how unlikely it is to obtain a mean difference of, say, 4. By transforming the sampling distribution to a *t* distribution, the sampling distribution is standardized with a mean of 0. Irrespective of the population means, the mean of the *t* distribution will be 0 [refer to Figure 9.1(*c*)]. The formula that is used to transform the values of the sampling distribution to a *t* distribution is always the same formula that is used to conduct the *t* test. The formula for testing the null hypothesis assumes that the null hypothesis is true. Similar to the independent-samples *t* test, the formula for the dependent-samples test statistic acknowledges the contrast between $\overline{X} - \overline{Y}$ and the hypothesized difference between the populations.

Dependent-Samples *t* Statistic

$$t = \frac{(\overline{X} - \overline{Y}) - (\mu_x - \mu_y)}{s_{\overline{D}}} \quad \textit{(Formula 9.3)}$$

However, since $\mu_x - \mu_y$ is typically hypothesized to be 0, the formula for the *t* test omits this term, and appears as Formula 9.4.

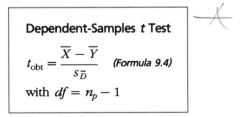

Dependent-Samples *t* Test

$$t_{\text{obt}} = \frac{\overline{X} - \overline{Y}}{s_{\overline{D}}} \quad \textit{(Formula 9.4)}$$

with $df = n_p - 1$

The t value is the number of standard error units the difference between the means is from the mean of the t distribution. Thus, if t equals 1.45, the difference, $\overline{X} - \overline{Y}$, is 1.45 standard error units above the mean of the t distribution.

The degrees of freedom for the dependent-samples t test is $n_p - 1$, the number of *pairs* of scores minus one. There is a different t distribution for every sample size (i.e., every number of pairs of scores). Similar to the independent-samples t test, the number of degrees of freedom is used to find t_{crit} in the t table.

The Null and Alternative Hypotheses for the Dependent-Samples t Test

The null hypothesis states that the population means are the same. The alternative hypothesis states that the means are not the same.

$$H_0: \quad \mu_x = \mu_y \quad \text{or} \quad \mu_D = 0$$
$$H_1: \quad \mu_x \neq \mu_y \quad \text{or} \quad \mu_D \neq 0$$

The requisite formulas are now in place to conduct a correlated-samples t test.

Worked Example

A cognitive psychologist is interested in the effects of alcohol intoxication on learning and recall. A repeated-measures design is used in which one group of subjects is exposed to both an experimental and a control condition. In the experimental condition, subjects consume an amount of alcohol sufficient to raise their blood alcohol level to .10 percent, the legal criterion for intoxication in some states. While subjects are intoxicated, slides of geometric designs and a nonsense word printed below each design (e.g., "geostatic" or "gravoserv") are projected one at a time. After 20 presentations, the slides are presented again, in random order, without the associated nonsense word. The subjects are to provide the word associated with each design. The dependent variable is the number of correct responses.

The control condition is administered 1 week later. Different designs and nonsense words are presented, but now the subjects are given drinks that taste like alcohol but contain no alcohol (placebo). Since improvement in performance between the experimental and control conditions may be because the control condition comes *after* the experimental condition, one-half of the subjects are run through the control condition first, followed 1 week later by the experimental condition. Table 9.1 presents the raw data (number of errors) for each condition, as well as the computation of t.

A dependent-samples t test is used to compare the effects of alcohol on learning and recall. The procedural steps in the analysis and interpretation of the data are presented in the following list.

TABLE 9.1 A Worked Problem Using the Dependent-Samples t Test[a].

Alcohol (X)	Placebo (Y)	D	D^2
8	4	4	16
12	8	4	16
6	2	4	16
4	6	−2	4
11	8	3	9
15	9	6	36
8	5	3	9
7	4	3	9
$\overline{X} = 8.88$	$\overline{Y} = 5.75$	$\Sigma D = 25$	$\Sigma D^2 = 115$

$$t_{obt} = \frac{\overline{X} - \overline{Y}}{s_{\overline{D}}}$$

$$s_{\overline{D}} = \frac{s_D}{\sqrt{n_p}}$$

$$s_D = \sqrt{\frac{\Sigma D^2 - [(\Sigma D)^2/n_p]}{n_p - 1}}$$

$$s_D = \sqrt{\frac{115 - [(25)^2/8]}{8 - 1}}$$

$$= \sqrt{\frac{115 - 78.3}{7}}$$

$$= \sqrt{5.27}$$

$$s_D = 2.30$$

$$s_{\overline{D}} = \frac{2.30}{\sqrt{8}}$$

$$s_{\overline{D}} = .81$$

$$t_{obt} = \frac{8.88 - 5.75}{.81}$$

$$t_{obt} = \mathbf{3.86}$$

$$df = n_p - 1 = 7$$
$$t_{crit} = 2.365$$

Since $3.86 > 2.365$, reject H_0: $\mu_x = \mu_y$; retain H_1: $\mu_x \neq \mu_y$

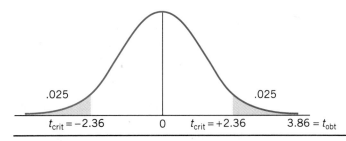

.025   .025

$t_{crit} = -2.36$ 0 $t_{crit} = +2.36$ $3.86 = t_{obt}$

[a] The raw scores are number of errors in recall. Since $t_{obt} > t_{crit}$, the null hypothesis is rejected.

207

Step 1.   Define the null and alternative hypotheses:

$$H_0: \quad \mu_x = \mu_y$$

$$H_1: \quad \mu_x \neq \mu_y$$

Step 2.   Set alpha. Alpha is set at .05.

Step 3.   Compute t_{obt} (see computations in Table 9.1).

Step 4.   Locate the critical t value in Table B.2 in the Appendix. The degrees of freedom is $n_p - 1$, that is, $8 - 1 = 7$. Enter the left column of the t table and locate the number 7. Move to the column under alpha of .05 for a *two-tailed* test. The critical value is 2.365.

Step 5.   Compare the t_{obt} of 3.86 with the critical value of 2.365. Since the t_{obt} is greater than the critical value, the null hypothesis is rejected in favor of the alternative hypothesis.

Step 6.   Interpret the findings. Within the confines of this study, learning and/or recall is negatively affected by the ingestion of an intoxicating amount of alcohol, $t(7) = 3.86$, $p < .05$. Additional research is needed to see if learning other kinds of material is likewise affected. [See Cohen, Schandler, and McArthur (1989) for a study that shows the negative effects of alcohol on·learning.]

9.4   COMPARING THE INDEPENDENT- AND DEPENDENT-SAMPLES t TESTS

The dependent-samples t test is more sensitive in detecting an experimental effect than the independent-samples t test. In other words, the probability of rejecting an incorrect null hypothesis is greater when using the dependent-samples t test in comparison to the independent-samples t test. A good way to demonstrate this point is to imagine that the alcohol and learning study (in the worked example) was conducted using independent samples—that is—two unrelated groups of subjects. Table 9.2 presents the summary statistics of the data in Table 9.1, and the computation of t_{obt} for an independent-samples t test. The obtained t value is 2.06, which just misses the critical value of 2.145. In this case, the difference in designs and type of t test makes the difference between rejecting or retaining the null hypothesis. This is because the use of a repeated-measures design and the correlated-samples t test reduces the variability of the data. If your research question can be answered by either a repeated-measures or between-groups design, choose the repeated-measures design.

The reasons that researchers decide to use one design or the other are beyond the scope of this text. There are many books on the subject of experimental design that adequately cover the topic (Mitchell and Jolley, 1988; Ray and Ravizza, 1988).

TABLE   9.2   **An Independent-Samples *t* Test on the Raw Data of Table 9.1[a].**

	Alcohol	Placebo
	$\overline{X}_1 = 8.88$	$\overline{X}_2 = 5.75$
	$s_1^2 = 12.67$	$s_2^2 = 5.90$
	$n_1 = 8$	$n_2 = 8$

Formula for Independent-Samples t Test

$$t_{obt} = \frac{\overline{X}_1 - \overline{X}_2}{\sqrt{\frac{s_1^2(n_1 - 1) + s_2^2(n_2 - 1)}{n_1 + n_2 - 2}\left(\frac{1}{n_1} + \frac{1}{n_2}\right)}}$$

$$t_{obt} = \frac{8.88 - 5.75}{\sqrt{\frac{12.67(8 - 1) + 5.90(8 - 1)}{8 + 8 - 2}\left(\frac{1}{8} + \frac{1}{8}\right)}}$$

$$= \frac{8.88 - 5.75}{\sqrt{\frac{88.69 + 41.30}{14}(.25)}}$$

$$= \frac{3.13}{\sqrt{9.29(.25)}}$$

$$= \frac{3.13}{\sqrt{2.32}}$$

$$= \frac{3.13}{1.52}$$

$$t_{obt} = \mathbf{2.06}$$

$$df = n_1 + n_2 - 2 = 8 + 8 - 2 = 14$$

$$\alpha = .05$$

$$t_{crit} = 2.145$$

retain H_0: $\mu_1 = \mu_2$

[a] When the scores are treated as unrelated samples, the null hypothesis is not rejected.

9.5   THE ONE-TAILED *t* TEST REVISITED

The difference between a one-tailed and two-tailed *t* test was discussed in Chapter 8. A one-tailed, or directional test places the entire rejection region in one tail of the *t* distribution. As a consequence, for a given alpha level, the critical value to which t_{obt} is compared is smaller when using a one-tailed test. Therefore, it is easier to reject the null hypothesis when using a one-tailed test. However, when using a one-tailed test, it is only possible to detect a difference between means when the difference is in the predicted direction. You have learned that one-tailed tests should be used with caution. Rarely should a directional test be used when

BOX 9.1

An Example of the Questionable Use of a One-Tailed, Dependent-Samples *t* Test

When examinig the use of one-tailed tests in the psychological literature, researchers sometimes wonder if the use of a one-tailed test is reported because the null hypothesis would otherwise not be rejected with the more conservative critical value of a two-tailed *t* test.

Buttery and White (1978) were interested in the relation between affective (feeling) states and biorhythm. According to people who believe in biorhythms, everyone experiences a 28-day emotional cycle. At the peak of the cycle, people are expected to be cheerful and optimistic. At the bottom of the cycle, people are prone to be irritable and negative. This cycle is supposedly initiated by the trauma of birth.

Twenty subjects were asked to provide ratings of 11 emotionally related concepts. Ratings were obtained from subjects at both the high and low points of their emotional biorhythm. Since each subject sup-

plied two scores, a dependent-samples *t* test was conducted. The number of pairs of scores is 20; therefore the *df* is 19. The critical value for a two-tailed test when $df = 19$, is 2.09. The critical value for a one-tailed test, with the same *df*, is 1.73. The authors' t_{obt} was 1.76, which they report as significant since they used a one-tailed test. Even if the authors decided to use a one-tailed *t* test *before* the data were collected, an important issue arises. The authors fail to allow for the possibility that the direction of the effect could have been contrary to their prediction. Perhaps people at the bottom of their cycle are *more* cheerful than when they are at the top of their biorhythm cycle. In an area that does not have strong theoretical or empirical reasons for expecting a directional finding, the use of a one-tailed *t* test is highly questionable.

testing a theory, since findings that oppose a theoretical prediction may be important to detect. The strongest justification for the use of a one-tailed test is when a course of action will only be taken if the mean of a particular group is larger than the mean of the other group. Box 9.1 presents a study in which a one-tailed, dependent-samples *t* test is used. Do you think that the authors were justified in using a one-tailed test?

9.6 ASSUMPTIONS OF THE DEPENDENT-SAMPLES *t* TEST

The underlying assumptions of the dependent-samples *t* test are random sampling and normally distributed populations. Moreover, it is assumed that the scores *within* a treatment condition are independent of one another.

Box 9.2 presents the first application of the *t* test. Gosset was not interested in the topic of the study—indeed, he borrowed published data. Rather, his intent was to provide an example of a research situation for which his *t* table could be used.

BOX 9.2

The First Application of the *t* Test

The first application of a *t* test is found in Gosset's classic 1908 paper, published in the biostatistical journal *Biometrica*. The *t* test was a dependent-samples *t* test, using data from a 1904 study, on the effects of sleep medication (Cushny and Peebles, 1904).

Cushny and Peebles used a repeated-measures design to contrast the effects of Dextrohyoscyamine hydrobromide and Laevohyoscyamine hydrobromide on the duration of sleep among ten patients from the "Michigan Asylum for the Insane at Kalamazoo." The following data are the changes in hours of sleep from a baseline (no drug) period to the period under one or the other drug. A positive score reflects an increase in sleep duration and a negative score reflects a decrease in sleep duration, relative to baseline.

Since the *t* test had not been invented when Cushny and Peebles conducted their study, the authors merely "eyeballed" the raw data and concluded that one compound was more effective than the other. It turned out that they were correct. As you follow the data analysis and the significance test, keep in mind that the convention of using the 5 percent level of significance was not yet standard. The data using Gosset's dependent-samples *t* test is analyzed first, and then a test of the null hypothesis is conducted following modern practices.

Patient	Dextro- X	Laevo- Y	D	D²
1	.7	1.9	-1.2	1.44
2	-1.6	.8	-2.4	5.76
3	$-.2$	1.1	-1.3	1.69
4	-1.2	.1	-1.3	1.69
5	$-.1$	$-.1$	0	0
6	3.4	4.4	-1.0	1
7	3.7	5.5	-1.8	3.24
8	.8	1.6	$-.8$	.64
9	0	4.6	-4.6	21.16
10	2.0	3.4	-1.4	1.96
	$\overline{X} = .75$	$\overline{Y} = 2.33$	$\Sigma D = -15.80$	$\Sigma D^2 = 38.58$

$$t_{obt} = \frac{\overline{X} - \overline{Y}}{s_{\overline{D}}}$$

$$s_{\overline{D}} = \frac{s_D}{\sqrt{n_p}}$$

$$s_D = \sqrt{\frac{\Sigma D^2 - [(\Sigma D)^2/n_p]}{n_p - 1}}$$

$$s_D = \sqrt{\frac{38.58 - [(-15.80)^2/10]}{10 - 1}}$$

$$= \sqrt{\frac{38.58 - 24.96}{9}}$$

$$= \sqrt{1.51}$$

$$s_D = 1.23$$

$$s_{\overline{D}} = \frac{1.23}{\sqrt{10}}$$

$$s_{\overline{D}} = .39$$

$$t_{obt} = \frac{.75 - 2.33}{.39}$$

$$t_{obt} = -4.05$$

$$df = n_p - 1 = 10 - 1 = 9$$

$$t_{crit} = 2.262$$

Since $|4.05| > 2.262$, reject H_0: $\mu_x = \mu_y$; retain H_1: $\mu_x \neq \mu_y$

SUMMARY

In *dependent sampling,* each score in one sample is related to another score in a second sample. Pairs of scores are formed either by matching or by the use of a repeated-measures design. Matching is a method used to assign subjects to groups so that a variable (e.g., IQ) that is related to the dependent variable cannot account for the results of the study. A repeated-measures design presents all levels of the independent variable to the same group of subjects. A dependent-samples t test is performed on pairs of scores. This t test is more powerful than an independent-samples t test because there is a greater likelihood of rejecting a false null hypothesis when using the dependent-samples t test. The sampling distribution for the dependent-samples t test is based on differences between means of correlated samples. The mean of the sampling distribution of differences equals the difference between means of the populations. The null hypothesis for the dependent-samples t test is $\mu_x = \mu_y$ or $\mu_D = 0$. The alternative hypothesis is $\mu_x \neq \mu_y$ or $\mu_D \neq 0$. The assumptions of the dependent-samples t test are random sampling, normally distributed populations, and independent observations.

KEY FORMULAS FOR CHAPTER 9

Standard Error of dist. of differences

Direct-Difference Method –

$$s_{\bar{D}} = \frac{s_D}{\sqrt{n_p}}$$

(Formula 9.1)

Computational Formula for s_D

$$s_D = \sqrt{\frac{\Sigma D^2 - [(\Sigma D)^2/n_p]}{n_p - 1}}$$

(Formula 9.2)

Dependent-Samples t Statistic

$$t = \frac{(\bar{X} - \bar{Y}) - (\mu_x - \mu_y)}{s_{\bar{D}}}$$

(Formula 9.3)

Dependent-Samples t Test

$$t_{\text{obt}} = \frac{\bar{X} - \bar{Y}}{s_{\bar{D}}}$$

(Formula 9.4)

WORK PROBLEMS

For problems that require a statistical test, assume that the test is nondirectional, unless otherwise specified.

1. Addison (1989) found that we perceive bearded men differently from non-bearded men. Compared to nonbearded men, fellows with beards are rated

as more masculine, more aggressive, stronger, and more dominant. They are, however, not viewed as more intelligent. The researcher used a repeated-measures design in which one group of subjects rated pictures of bearded and nonbearded men. The following data are hypothetical, but were generated to reflect Addison's results regarding beardedness and masculinity. A score can range from 1–feminine to 10–masculine.

a. State the null and alternative hypotheses.
b. Specify t_{crit} for $\alpha = .05$, two-tailed test.
c. Perform the t test.
d. Interpret the findings.

	Bearded	Nonbearded	D	D^2
S_1	10	6	4	16
S_2	8	8	0	0
S_3	5	4	1	1
S_4	7	3	4	16
S_5	10	5	5	25
S_6	6	6	0	0
S_7	5	5	0	0
S_8	10	8	2	4
	61	45	16	62

2. Ruth et al. (1989) tested the hypothesis that people would state a preference for purchasing a liquor product if the product were advertised with sexual symbolism. One group of subjects was shown advertisements with and without sexual symbolism. In each condition, the subjects was asked to indicate their likelihood of purchasing the product. Sexual symbolism was defined psychoanalytically as symbolic depictions of genitalia and the act of sexual intercourse. For example, the authors state, "One symbolic advertisement presented a liquor bottle which was diagonally inserted into a Christmas stocking with the neck of the bottle protruding outward. Another symbolic advertisement presented several skyscrapers with steeples, one of which was positioned under an oval tunnel, and an airplane flying overhead" (p. 1135). An example of a nonsexual advertisement was a country scene with grazing cows. The following hypothetical data are generated to yield results consistent with those found by the researchers. Higher scores indicate a greater willingness to purchase the product.

a. State the null and alternative hypotheses.
b. Specify t_{crit} for $\alpha = .05$, two-tailed test.
c. Perform the t test.
d. Interpret the findings.

Subject	Sexual Symbolism	No Sexual Symbolism	D	D^2
S_1	6	3	3	9
S_2	5	5	0	0
S_3	4	2	2	4
S_4	5	3	2	4
S_5	4	1	3	9
S_6	6	3	3	9
	30	17	13	35

3. An industrial psychologist working for a marketing firm wants to know which of two cheeses are preferred by college students. Gouda is tasted first, followed

by Swiss. Taste ratings are obtained after each test and can range from 1–lousy to 7–fantastic. (Bonus Question: How would you redesign this study to remove an obvious experimental confound?)

a. State the null and alternative hypotheses.   c. Perform the t test.
b. What is t_{crit} for $\alpha = .05$, two-tailed test?   d. Interpret the findings.

Subject	Gouda Cheese	Swiss Cheese	D	D^2
S_1	5	3	2	4
S_2	7	6	1	1
S_3	9	4	5	25
S_4	8	7	1	1
S_5	6	8	-2	4
	35	28	7	35

4. What is the advantage of being able to use a dependent-samples t test instead of an independent-samples t test? (Hint: The answer is not that the dependent-samples t test is the easier to compute.)

5. A psychologist tests a new drug for insomnia. The average amount of time (in minutes) it takes subjects to fall asleep is assessed before treatment, over a 1-week period. These data are presented in the Pretest column of the following table. Post-test scores indicate the time to fall asleep during the following week in which the medication is administered. Conduct a directional t test in which the mean of the post-test is expected to be less than the mean of the pretest.

a. State the null and alternative hypotheses.   c. Perform the t test.
b. What is t_{crit} for $\alpha = .05$, one-tailed test?   d. Interpret the findings.

Subject	Pretest	Post-test
S_1	120	30
S_2	60	40
S_3	90	30
S_4	100	80

6. Identify the critical values for the following situations.
   a. Dependent-samples t test, $\alpha = .05$, $df = 19$, one-tailed test
   b. Independent-samples t test, $\alpha = .10$, $df = 16$, two-tailed test
   c. Single-sample z test, $\alpha = .01$, $n = 40$, one-tailed test
   d. Dependent-samples t test, $\alpha = .10$, $df = 7$, two-tailed test
   e. Dependent-samples t test, $\alpha = .01$, $df = 100$, two-tailed test
   f. Single-sample t test, $\alpha = .01$, $df = 8$, one-tailed test
   g. Dependent-samples t test, $\alpha = .05$, $n_p = 5$, one-tailed test
   h. Independent-samples t test, $\alpha = .05$, $n_1 = 6$, $n_2 = 4$, one-tailed test

The next two problems require you to decide which t test is appropriate to the design of the study.

7. A physician is interested in comparing the relative effects of a synthetic anabolic steroid and a recently manufactured natural growth stimulant on weight gain. Sixteen patients in a nursing home are randomly assigned to two treatment conditions. One group (eight patients) receives the steroid for 30 days and a

second group (eight patients) receives the growth stimulant. The dependent variable is the amount of weight gained over 30 days.

a. State the null and alternative hypotheses.　　c. What is t_{crit}?

b. What is t_{obt}?　　d. Interpret the findings.

Weight Gained (lb)

Steroid	Growth Stimulant
6	2
5	5
7	0
2	1
6	2
5	3
4	4
8	7

8. Another researcher asks the same question posed in Problem 7. Four subjects are given the steroid for 30 days, followed by a 30-day period with the growth stimulant. A different four patients receive the two compounds in reverse order. Using the preceding data, conduct the appropriate *t* test.

a. State the null and alternative hypotheses.　　c. What is t_{crit}?

b. What is t_{obt}?　　d. Interpret the findings.

Work Problems for the Computer

9. A study referenced in the *Chronicle of Higher Education* (1990) showed that students write papers of higher quality when they use an IBM-compatible computer instead of a Macintosh computer. One explanation of the findings is that the Macintosh is so user-friendly that students tend to write very casually. The following hypothetical data are based on a repeated-measures design. Each subject writes a paper using an IBM-compatible computer and a Macintosh computer. You will find that the interpretation of the dependent-samples *t* test is consistent with the findings of the original study. Each raw score in the table represents a composite index of the length of the paper and its quality. Higher numbers reflect greater quantity and quality. Set alpha at .05. (Save the file for future use.)

IBM-Compatible	Macintosh	IBM-Compatible	Macintosh
95	80	29	32
88	70	88	66
99	88	42	42
79	54	55	39
80	80	71	65
77	87	97	84
92	75	75	72
55	34	45	65
79	72	84	77
65	70	73	56

10. A manufacturer of sunglasses wants to know if vision is affected by the color of the lens. A test of vision is administered when subjects wear glasses with a blue lens and glasses with a yellow lens. Test the null hypothesis that there is no difference in vision between the two sets of glasses. Higher numbers indicate better vision. Set alpha at .05.

Blue	Yellow
12	15
7	4
22	16
16	12
14	14
10	8
17	17
16	22
14	12
9	15
8	4
21	21
12	14
11	10
11	4
10	19

11. An orthopaedic surgeon is interested in whether the firmness of a mattress influences the amount of back pain experienced by patients. For one week, all subjects sleep on a firm mattress and provide pain ratings each morning. A month later, the same subjects sleep on a soft mattress, again providing pain ratings each morning for a week. In the following table, higher ratings indicate more lower back pain, with each rating an average for the week. Test the null hypothesis that there is no difference in pain ratings between the firm-mattress condition and the soft-mattress condition. Set alpha at .05.

Firm Mattress	Soft Mattress
4	8
2	2
1	7
8	10
6	6
3	6
1	4
5	7
7	9
2	5
4	7
7	10

Confidence Intervals and Hypothesis Testing

10.1 THE RESEARCH CONTEXT

Point and Interval Estimation

Inferential statistics refers to a set of methods used to infer characteristics of a population from a sample. There are two types of inferential methods: estimation and hypothesis testing. Using a sample statistic to estimate a specific population parameter is a **point estimation.** A point estimation can be made for any population parameter, although the parameter that is estimated most often is μ.

A **confidence interval** is the interval between two values; a researcher can have a high degree of confidence that a population parameter lies within a confidence interval. Confidence intervals can be established for the mean, standard deviation, variance, or other statistics. However, only confidence intervals for the mean of a population are presented in this chapter. The following are research examples in which parameter estimation is useful.

▶   **EXAMPLE 1**   The director of the Department of Mental Health has received conflicting reports about the frequency of patient assaults on psychiatric inpatient units. He would like an idea of the mean number of assaults in a 1-month period. A random sample of 50 inpatient units is taken, and the average number of assaults per unit is found to be 24.50. Using the methods for computing a confidence interval, the director is able to state that he is 95 percent confident that the mean number of assaults for *all* inpatient units in the state is between 19.26 and 29.74. ◀

▶   **EXAMPLE 2**   A drug manufacturer is researching a new medication for high blood pressure. Early reports suggest that there are a fair number of side effects to the drug. The question is, what is the average number of side effects? A random sample of 80 patients taking the drug is selected and the mean number of side effects is ascertained. The manufacturer is able to claim that she is 99 percent confident that the mean number of side effects for *all* patients taking this medication is between 3.4 and 8.5. (Of course the manufacturer is not only concerned with the average number of side effects, but also their nature.) ◀

▶   **EXAMPLE 3**   A tire company is interested in knowing the average number of highway miles its tires can tolerate before the treads wear out. A random sample of 60 tires is selected and each is placed on a highway simulator wheel. The mean for the sample is found to be 56,000 miles. The marketing department is able to claim that there is a 90 percent chance that this type of tire has an average life span of between 52,996–59,004 miles. ◀

The Trade-off Between Point and Interval Estimation

Suppose you obtain a sample of scores and find that the sample mean is 50. Your best guess as to the value of the population mean would be 50. By stating a specific value for μ, a point estimation is made. However, the odds are you will be incorrect when making point estimations. Thus, you would not be very confident that your sample mean is the same as the population mean. The sample mean is likely to be close to the population mean, especially if the size of the sample is large, but there is no way to specify a level of certainty with your estimate. Let's assume that the lowest score of the sample is 19 and the highest score is 75. How confident would you be that the population mean falls between 19 and 75? You would be extremely confident. However, the interval is so large that it lacks any degree of specificity. When making a point estimation, there is specificity with little confidence. On the other hand, an interval that spans the range of the sampled scores provides confidence but no specificity. Using a sampling distribution, and the formula for establishing a confidence interval, an interval can be identified that balances specificity and confidence.

The discussion of confidence intervals begins with the 90 percent, 95 percent, and 99 percent confidence intervals. The mathematics to establish confidence intervals are simple. After the confidence interval formulas are presented, the conceptual basis for the formulas is discussed. Finally, using confidence intervals to test hypotheses about population parameters is addressed.

10.2   CONFIDENCE INTERVALS WHEN σ IS KNOWN

Calculating the Upper and Lower Limits of a Confidence Interval

A confidence interval requires the calculation of two values. Since the interval estimation of a population mean is being addressed here, the two values are means. For now, a single, random sample of scores will be used to establish a confidence interval. The lower and upper limits of the interval (called **confidence limits**) are symbolized as *LL* and *UL*, respectively. The following formula is used to establish a 90 percent confidence interval.

The 90 Percent Confidence Interval When σ is Known

$$LL = \overline{X} - 1.65\sigma_{\overline{x}}$$

$$UL = \overline{X} + 1.65\sigma_{\overline{x}} \quad \textbf{\textit{(Formula 10.1)}}$$

■   QUESTION   *A sample of 36 scores is taken in which $\overline{X} = 30$; $\sigma = 8$. What is the 90 percent confidence interval?*

SOLUTION   First compute $\sigma_{\overline{x}}$.

$$\sigma_{\overline{x}} = \frac{\sigma}{\sqrt{n}}$$

$$\sigma_{\overline{x}} = \frac{8}{\sqrt{36}}$$

$$= 1.33$$

Using Formula 10.1,

$$LL = 30 - 1.65(1.33) = \textbf{27.81}$$

$$UL = 30 + 1.65(1.33) = \textbf{32.19}$$

Conclusion: You can be 90 percent confident that the interval 27.81–32.19 contains the mean of the population.   ■

> **The 95 Percent Confidence Interval When σ is Known**
>
> $$LL = \overline{X} - 1.96\sigma_{\overline{x}}$$
>
> $$UL = \overline{X} + 1.96\sigma_{\overline{x}} \quad \text{(Formula 10.2)}$$

■   QUESTION   *Using the same numbers as in the preceding worked problem, what is the 95 percent confidence interval?*

SOLUTION

$$LL = 30 - 1.96(1.33)$$
$$= \mathbf{27.39}$$
$$UL = 30 + 1.96(1.33)$$
$$= \mathbf{32.61}$$

Conclusion: You can be 95 percent confident that the interval 27.39–32.61 contains the mean of the population.   ■

> **The 99 Percent Confidence Interval When σ is Known**
>
> $$LL = \overline{X} - 2.58\sigma_{\overline{x}}$$
>
> $$UL = \overline{X} + 2.58\sigma_{\overline{x}} \quad \text{(Formula 10.3)}$$

■   QUESTION   *Using the same statistics, what is the 99 percent confidence interval?*

SOLUTION

$$LL = 30 - 2.58(1.33)$$
$$= \mathbf{26.57}$$
$$UL = 30 + 2.58(1.33)$$
$$= \mathbf{33.43}$$

Conclusion: You can be 99 percent confident that the interval 26.57–33.43 contains the population mean.   ■

Note how the width of the interval changes as your degree of confidence changes.

90% confidence interval: $32.19 - 27.81 = \mathbf{4.38}$

95% confidence interval: $32.61 - 27.39 = \mathbf{5.22}$

99% confidence interval: $33.43 - 26.57 = \mathbf{6.86}$

The trade-off is clear. When establishing an interval that you believe contains the population mean, an increase in confidence is gained at the expense of the width of the interval. As confidence increases, specificity decreases.

We now turn to a discussion of the statistical basis of confidence intervals.

10.3 SAMPLING DISTRIBUTIONS AND CONFIDENCE INTERVALS

The confidence interval is an inferential method that can be understood in the context of z scores. In Chapter 5, you worked numerous problems that required you to specify two scores between which lie a certain percentage of scores. Those two scores defined an *interval* to which you could attach a probability statement regarding the likelihood of drawing a score at random between the two scores. For example, you were able to state, "The probability is .95 that a score selected at random will fall between 30–35." You construct a confidence interval in essentially the same way. Instead of identifying two scores, you identify two population means; the two population means define an interval that you can be very confident contains the true population mean. Let's begin with a simple z-score problem.

■   QUESTION   *For a given population of scores, $\mu = 90$ and $\sigma = 10$. What are the raw-score cutoffs within which lie 95 percent of the scores?*

SOLUTION   Since the answer is to be stated in raw scores, you will need to use the following formula from Chapter 5:

$$X = \mu + z\sigma$$

The mean, μ, and standard deviation, σ, are given in the question. All you need to do is find z. You will need a positive z score, above which lies 2.5 percent of the distribution and a negative z score, below which lies 2.5 percent of the distribution. Since a normal distribution is assumed, the two z scores are the same. Look up .025 in column C of the z table (Appendix B.1). The z score that corresponds to .025 (2.5 percent) is 1.96. Thus,

$$\text{Lower cutoff} = 90 - 1.96(10)$$
$$= \mathbf{70.40}$$
$$\text{Upper cutoff} = 90 + 1.96(10)$$
$$= \mathbf{109.60}$$

Conclusion: The middle 95 percent of the distribution of raw scores falls between 70.40–109.60.   ■

In solving the foregoing problem, three values were used: μ, 1.96, and σ. Now consider the purpose of each value in the equation. The problem requires you to find cutoffs within which lie the middle 95 percent of the distribution. In a normal distribution, the exact middle of the distribution is μ. Thus, μ serves as an anchor point from which you will go some distance above and some distance below to find the cutoffs. The number 1.96 is the measure of distance, stated in standard deviation units (a z score). To determine the middle 95 percent of the distribution you need to travel 1.96 standard deviations above the mean and 1.96 standard deviations below the mean. The standard deviation, σ, is needed because it is a measure of how spread out the raw-score distribution is and σ will vary from distribution to distribution. In one distribution, traveling 1.96 standard deviations from the mean might require you to move over 15 raw-score points. In another distribution, the point that is 1.96 standard deviations from the mean might be only 5 raw-score units from the mean. Thus, σ needs to be in the formula to indicate the variability of the distribution. In this example, the distribution is comprised of *scores*. The scores that mark the cutoffs of the interval that contains the middle 95 percent of a *population distribution* are found by:

$$\text{Lower score} = \mu - 1.96\sigma$$

$$\text{Upper score} = \mu + 1.96\sigma$$

When establishing an interval of means, it is necessary to use a sampling distribution of means. For the z formula to apply to a sampling distribution, you need to substitute sampling distribution symbols for the mean and standard deviation. When working with a *sampling distribution*, the formulas for identifying the means between which lie 95 percent of the "scores" of the sampling distribution are:[1]

$$\text{Lower score} = \mu_{\overline{x}} - 1.96\sigma_{\overline{x}}$$

$$\text{Upper score} = \mu_{\overline{x}} + 1.96\sigma_{\overline{x}}$$

Because the standard error of a sampling distribution is $\sigma_{\overline{x}}$, $\sigma_{\overline{x}}$ replaces σ in the formula. The mean of the sampling distribution is symbolized $\mu_{\overline{x}}$, and thus replaces μ. If you know $\mu_{\overline{x}}$ and $\sigma_{\overline{x}}$, and the sampling distribution is normally distributed, you can be sure that you have defined the middle 95 percent of the distribution. However, you do not know the mean of the population, so the sample mean is used to infer the population mean. Substituting the sample mean into the formula gives us Formula 10.2, which is used to establish a 95 percent confidence interval.

$$LL = \overline{X} - 1.96\sigma_{\overline{x}}$$

$$UL = \overline{X} + 1.96\sigma_{\overline{x}}$$

As an estimate of the population mean, the sample mean is subject to sampling error. Most of the time $\overline{X}$ is a good estimate of μ, but sometimes it is not a good

---

[1] The word "scores" is in quotation marks because the "scores" of a sampling distribution of means are sample means. Remember that a sampling distribution of means is a frequency distribution of means. There is only one mean to a sampling distribution, the "mean of the means."

estimate. Therefore, any interval that you establish using the sample mean may be accurate in the sense that it contains the true population mean, or inaccurate in the sense that it does not contain the population mean. Confidence intervals are, therefore, probabilistic in nature.

10.4 THE PROBABILISTIC NATURE OF CONFIDENCE INTERVALS

In Figure 10.1, several samples from a population are drawn and a 95 percent confidence interval is computed from each sample. (If you tend to skip over visual representations of concepts, don't do it this time.) Further, assume that you know the values of μ and σ. Of course, in practice, if you knew μ, there would be no need to construct a confidence interval. The values of μ and σ are supplied so that you do not have to estimate $\sigma_{\bar{x}}$ and you can determine which of the computed intervals actually contain μ.

Look carefully at Figure 10.1. The curve is doubling as a z score distribution of the population and a sampling distribution of the population. The sampling distribution has been constructed by repeated samples of $n = 36$.

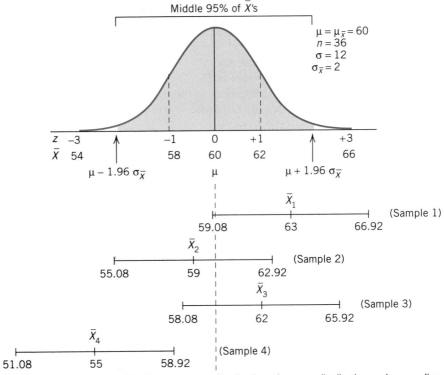

Figure 10.1 The curve is doubling as a normally distributed z-score distribution and a sampling distribution. Both distributions are derived from a population distribution. Each horizontal line is the span of each confidence interval established from the four samples.

Let's first consider the two rows of numbers below the distribution to understand the correspondence between the z scores and the points along the sampling distribution of means. A z-score distribution has a mean of 0 and a standard deviation of 1. A sampling distribution has a mean equal to the mean of the population ($\mu_{\bar{x}} = \mu$) and a standard error of $\sigma/\sqrt{n}$. A normally distributed z distribution will contain 68 percent of the z scores between 0 ± 1 z score. A normally distributed sampling distribution will include 68 percent of the means between $\mu \pm 1\sigma_{\bar{x}}$. In Figure 10.1, the first row of numbers below the curve is z scores. The second row of numbers below the curve is sample means of the sampling distribution. The mean of the sampling distribution is 60. The standard deviation of the *population* is 12, and thus the standard error of the sampling distribution equals 2 (since $n = 36$ and $\sigma = 12$, $\sigma_{\bar{x}} = 12/\sqrt{36} = 2$). Note that the number 62 is directly below a z score of $+1$. Why? Moving one standard error above the mean of a sampling distribution is the same as moving one standard deviation above the mean of a z-score distribution.

Sample 1 has a mean of 63. Using Formula 10.2, the confidence interval is $LL = 59.08$ and $UL = 66.92$. The horizontal line is the span of the interval, bracketed by 59.08 and 66.92. A dotted line is drawn vertically from the mean of the sampling distribution and cuts across the horizontal line, which indicates that the mean of the population (60) falls within the interval. In Sample 2, the sample mean is found to be 59. The 95 percent confidence interval established when $\bar{X} = 59$ is $LL = 55.08$ and $UL = 62.92$. Thus, even though you sampled above μ in Sample 1 and below μ in Sample 2, both confidence intervals contain μ. In Sample 3, a sample mean of 62 is found. The interval is $LL = 58.08$ and $UL = 65.92$. The dotted line crosses this interval, and once again, the interval contains μ. In Sample 4, however, the sample mean is 55. The confidence interval is $LL = 51.08$ and $UL = 58.92$. The dotted line passes to the right of the interval. This time the interval *does not* contain the population mean. You missed, which will occasionally happen. In fact, if we use the formula for the 95 percent confidence interval, take an infinite number of random samples, and establish a confidence interval for each sample, 95 percent of the intervals will contain μ and 5 percent will not.

Finally, bear in mind that the probability of .95 is attached to the interval, not the population mean. The population mean does not vary from sample to sample. The *intervals* vary with each sample. Again, a confidence level of 95 percent means that, *in the long run*, 95 percent of the intervals will contain μ, and thus the probability is .95 that a single *interval* contains μ.

10.5   CONFIDENCE INTERVALS WHEN σ IS UNKNOWN

The formula for the 95 percent confidence interval specifies two means of a sampling distribution within which lie 95 percent of the means. This formula, as well as those for the 90 percent and 99 percent intervals, assumes that σ is known. When you know σ, you can use the z table to find the z scores that serve as cutoffs between which lie a certain percentage of scores. In other words, when σ is known, the sampling distribution of means assumes the shape of the standard normal curve and the z table provides standard scores for the standard normal curve.

However, when σ is unknown, the standard error of the sampling distribution $\sigma_{\bar{x}}$ must be estimated by $s_{\bar{x}}$. In addition, as the sample size becomes progressively smaller, especially under 30, the shape of the sampling distribution becomes broader. Under these circumstances, you can no longer use the z scores of ± 1.65, ± 1.96, and ± 2.58 to help define the cutoffs within which lie 90 percent, 95 percent, and 99 percent of the sampling distribution. Instead, the t table is used to locate cutoffs when σ is unknown.

When using the estimated standard error, $s_{\bar{x}}$, to establish confidence intervals, you will need to use the t table, for $df = n - 1$. Formulas 10.4–10.6 are used to determine the 90 percent, 95 percent, and 99 percent confidence intervals, when σ is unknown.

The 90 Percent Confidence Interval When σ is Unknown

$$LL = \overline{X} - t_{.10}s_{\bar{x}}$$

$$UL = \overline{X} + t_{.10}s_{\bar{x}} \quad \text{(Formula 10.4)}$$

The 95 Percent Confidence Interval When σ is Unknown

$$LL = \overline{X} - t_{.05}s_{\bar{x}}$$

$$UL = \overline{X} + t_{.05}s_{\bar{x}} \quad \text{(Formula 10.5)}$$

The 99 Percent Confidence Interval When σ is Unknown

$$LL = \overline{X} - t_{.01}s_{\bar{x}}$$

$$UL = \overline{X} + t_{.01}s_{\bar{x}} \quad \text{(Formula 10.6)}$$

It should be obvious why the terms $t_{.10}$, $t_{.05}$, and $t_{.01}$ are left unspecified. Each t value will change, depending on the size of the sample. The following worked problem illustrates how to establish confidence intervals when $s_{\bar{x}}$ is used and the t table is consulted.

■   QUESTION   *You are serving as a research consultant to a school system. A gym teacher wants to know what is the average weight lifted in the bench press among 14-year-old males. You take a random sample of ten 14-year-old boys and test them in the bench press with the following results, $\overline{X} = 110$ lb, $s = 20$ lb. What should you tell the teacher about the average strength of the population of 14-year-old boys?*

SOLUTION   The question is phrased as a point estimation, "What is the average weight lifted among 14-year-old males?" Your answer should be a point estimate—110 lb. But suppose the teacher then asks, "How confident are you that the population mean is 110 lb?" You explain that there is no way to attach a degree of confidence to a point estimate of the population mean. However, an interval can be established so you can be 95 percent confident that the interval contains the population mean. What is the 95 percent confidence interval? This problem requires the use of Formula 10.5.

$$LL = \overline{X} - t_{.05}s_{\overline{x}}$$
$$UL = \overline{X} + t_{.05}s_{\overline{x}}$$

Step 1.   Compute the standard error of the mean.

$$s_{\overline{x}} = \frac{s}{\sqrt{n}}$$
$$= \frac{20}{\sqrt{10}}$$
$$= 6.33$$

Step 2.   Find $t_{.05}$ with $n - 1$ degrees of freedom ($10 - 1 = 9$). Enter the t table (Appendix B.2) with 9 df and move to the column for $\alpha = .05$, two-tailed. The t value is 2.262.

Step 3.   You now have all the values for the formula. Compute the interval.

$$LL = 110 - 2.262(6.33)$$
$$= \textbf{95.68}$$
$$UL = 110 + 2.262(6.33)$$
$$= \textbf{124.32}$$

Step 4.   State your conclusion. "I am 95 percent confident that the interval **95.68–124.32** contains the average bench-press weight of 14-year-old males." ■

■   QUESTION   *You have learned that large samples provide more accurate estimates of population parameters. Suppose you establish a 95 percent confidence interval when your sample size is 5. As you look at the interval, why wouldn't you say, "Because my sample size is so small, I can't really be 95 percent confident that the interval contains the population mean?"*

SOLUTION   The formula for the confidence interval takes the sample size into consideration. Therefore, a smaller n will lead to a wider interval. In the preceding problem, the sample size was 10. Using the same data, let's establish a 95 percent confidence interval using a sample size of 5.

Step 1.   Compute the standard error of the mean.

$$s_{\bar{x}} = \frac{s}{\sqrt{n}}$$
$$= \frac{20}{\sqrt{5}}$$
$$= 8.93$$

Step 2.   Find $t_{.05}$ with $n - 1$ degrees of freedom $(5 - 1 = 4)$. Enter the t table (Appendix B.2) with 4 df and move to the column for $\alpha = .05$, two-tailed. The t value is 2.776.

Step 3.   Placing the obtained values into the formula:

$$LL = 110 - 2.776(8.93)$$
$$= \mathbf{85.21}$$
$$UL = 110 + 2.776(8.93)$$
$$= \mathbf{134.79}$$

When the sample size is 10, the span of the interval is **28.64** (124.32–95.68). When the sample size is 5, the span of the interval is much larger: **49.58** (134.79–85.21). No matter what the sample size, you can still be 95 percent confident that the interval contains the population mean. However, as the sample size decreases, you lose specificity because the interval becomes wider. You thus pay the price for a small sample in specificity, not confidence.   ◼

Box 10.1 presents a study on the declining frequency of sexual intercourse among married couples. Ninety-five percent confidence intervals are established to estimate the frequency of sexual intercourse in the population of married couples.

10.6   USING CONFIDENCE INTERVALS FOR HYPOTHESIS TESTING

Hypothesis testing is a decision-making process that entails a yes/no question—that is—you will decide whether to reject the null hypothesis. Interval estimation is not based on a yes/no question. The question involved in interval estimation is an open-ended question: What is the interval within which the population mean is likely to lie? In this section you will learn how to use a confidence interval to decide whether to reject a null hypothesis. When approaching hypothesis testing via confidence intervals, there is no need to perform a t test. Using a confidence interval to test the null hypothesis not only accomplishes the same task as the t test, but has the added benefit of providing an estimation of a population parameter.

BOX
10.1

Where Did the Passion Go?

As a clinical psychologist with a private practice, I frequently become involved in marital counseling and sex therapy. Couples note that they do not make love as often as they used to make love. Therefore, they wonder if their frequency of intercourse is abnormally low, and, in turn, if this change is a reflection of marital problems. Of course, the overriding issue is whether the couple is happy with their sex life, not whether they are living up to some normative standard. Nonetheless, couples find it reassuring (or depressing) to know that the frequency of intercourse naturally decreases with the duration of the marriage.

Although I have never been asked by my clients to provide a confidence interval to estimate the mean frequency of intercourse among married couples, let's use the findings of a study by Greenblat (1983) to make such an estimate.

DATA GATHERING

Greenblat interviewed a random sample of 48 women who had been married between 1 and 6 years. In the context of an extensive interview about the quality of their marriage, they were asked to report the average, monthly frequency of intercourse since they were wed.

RESULTS

The following table summarizes some of Greenblat's findings. The investigator collapsed the data for the years subsequent to the first year of marriage. The reason the sample size is lower for the category Subsequent rates is because five of the subjects were in their first year of marriage. The article mentions that no differences in reports of first-year marital coital rates were found as a function of how long the person had been married. In other words, it does not appear that people inflate or deflate their estimates of first-year rates as time passes.

Rates	n	Range	Mean	s
First-year	48	2–45	13.81	8.44
Subsequent	43	2–20	7.52	4.86

As you examine the means, you will note the drop in coital frequency, per month, between the first and subsequent years of marriage: 13.81 to 7.52. But look at the ranges. Clearly there is a great deal of variability in monthly rates of intercourse. At least one person reported a first-year monthly rate of 2, and at least one person reported a first-year monthly coital rate of 45! The range is also high for subsequent rates. The standard deviations similarly reflect a great deal of variability among the data. A standard deviation that is larger than half the size of the mean indicates a lot of variation among the scores.

Let's establish 95 percent confidence intervals for first-year and subsequent-year rates.

First-year Rate

$$LL = 13.81 - 2.00(8.44/\sqrt{48})$$
$$= \mathbf{11.37}$$
$$UL = 13.81 + 2.00(8.44/\sqrt{48})$$
$$= \mathbf{16.25}$$

Conclusion: You can be 95 percent confident that the interval **11.37–16.25** contains the population mean rate of monthly intercourse for couples in their first year of marriage.

Subsequent Rate

$$LL = 7.52 - 2.02(4.86/\sqrt{43})$$
$$= \mathbf{6.03}$$
$$UL = 7.52 + 2.02(4.86/\sqrt{43})$$
$$= \mathbf{9.01}$$

Conclusion: You can be 95 percent confident that the interval **6.03–9.01** contains the population mean rate of monthly intercourse for couples in their second to sixth year of marriage.

Using Confidence Intervals Instead of the Single-Sample t Test

You will be using a worked example from Chapter 7 to compare the confidence interval and t test approaches to hypothesis testing. First consider the t test approach.

■   QUESTION   *A local newspaper reports that the average high school student drinks a six-pack of beer a week. The high school principal would like to know if her students are drinking that much beer. With confidentiality assured, 15 students are randomly selected and asked about their drinking habits. The mean number of beers consumed per week is found to be 4.2, and the sample standard deviation is 1.5. Test the hypothesis that the news report is accurate for the students at this high school.*

SOLUTION

Step 1.   Identify the null and alternative hypotheses.

$$H_0: \quad \mu = 6$$

$$H_1: \quad \mu \neq 6$$

Step 2.   Set alpha. Alpha is set at .05.

Step 3.   Compute t_{obt}.

$$t_{obt} = \frac{\overline{X} - \mu}{s_{\overline{x}}}$$

$$s_{\overline{x}} = \frac{s}{\sqrt{n}}$$

$$= \frac{4.2 - 6.0}{1.5/\sqrt{15}}$$

$$= \frac{-1.8}{.39}$$

$$t_{obt} = \mathbf{-4.62}$$

Step 4.   Using the t table, find the two-tailed critical value for $df = 14$ and $\alpha = .05$ (Appendix Table B.2). The critical value is 2.145.

Step 5.   Compare the absolute value of the t_{obt} of -4.62 to the critical value of 2.145. Since t_{obt} is larger than t_{crit}, the null hypothesis is rejected, and the alternative hypothesis, $\mu \neq 6$, is retained.

Step 6.   Interpret the findings. The amount of beer consumed per week among this school's students is significantly less than the amount stated in the newspaper, $t(14) = -4.62, p < .05$.

The steps for approaching the same problem using a confidence interval are given in the following.

Step 1. Identify the null and alternative hypotheses.

$$H_0: \quad \mu = 6$$
$$H_1: \quad \mu \neq 6$$

Step 2. Set alpha. Let's set alpha at .05. The alpha level selected will indicate whether you are going to use a 90 percent, 95 percent, or 99 percent confidence interval. If you select $\alpha = .10$ (you probably should not), then a 90 percent confidence interval will be computed. An $\alpha = .05$ corresponds to a 95 percent confidence interval, and an $\alpha = .01$ corresponds to a 99 percent confidence interval.

Step 3. Using the t table, find the cutoff values beyond which lie 2.5 percent in the right tail of the t distribution and 2.5 percent in the left tail of the distribution. The task is accomplished in the same way that you found t_{crit} for the t test. With $df = 14$ and $\alpha = .05$ (two-tailed test), the cutoff points are ± 2.145.

Step 4. Compute the confidence interval. Since $\alpha = .05$, the formula for the 95 percent confidence interval is used:

$$LL = \overline{X} - t_{05}s_{\overline{x}}$$
$$UL = \overline{X} + t_{05}s_{\overline{x}}$$

$$LL = 4.20 - 2.145(1.50/\sqrt{15}) = \mathbf{3.36}$$
$$UL = 4.20 + 2.145(1.50/\sqrt{15}) = \mathbf{5.04}$$

Step 5. Decide whether to reject the null hypothesis. The null hypothesis states that the population mean is 6. The confidence interval of 3.36–5.04 marks the two points of the sampling distribution beyond which lie 5 percent of the distribution of sample means (2.5 percent in each tail). The hypothesized population mean of 6 falls *outside* of the 95 percent confidence interval. Since it is very unlikely that a confidence interval of 3.36–5.04 would be found when the true population mean is 6, you conclude that the population mean is not 6; in other words you reject H_0: $\mu = 6$ at $p < .05$.

Step 6. Interpret the findings: The amount of beer consumed per week among this school's students is significantly less than the amount stated in the newspaper. The added benefit of using a confidence interval to test the null hypothesis is that the principal can answer another question: How much do the students drink? She can be 95 percent confident that the mean number of beers consumed per week among the *population* of students at her school is somewhere between 3.36–5.04. ■

Using Confidence Intervals Instead of the Independent-Samples *t* Test

The conceptual basis for hypothesis testing using a confidence interval in place of an independent-samples *t* test is the same as using a confidence interval in lieu of a single-sample *t* test. A confidence interval is established and a value specified by the null hypothesis is checked to see if it falls outside the interval; if so, H_0 is rejected. However, unlike the use of a confidence interval when one sample is used, the confidence interval for independent sampling states an interval for the *difference between means*. Thus, if H_0 is rejected, you can be 95 percent confident that the interval contains the true difference between population means. The following procedural steps for a confidence interval are used to test the null hypothesis regarding the equivalence of population means.

Step 1.   State the null and alternative hypotheses. The null hypothesis for an independent-samples *t* test is $H_0: \mu_1 = \mu_2$, or $H_0: \mu_1 - \mu_2 = 0$. The latter expression of the null hypothesis is more useful when using a confidence interval. The alternative hypothesis can be expressed as $H_1: \mu_1 - \mu_2 \neq 0$. After establishing the confidence interval, you will be looking to see if the interval contains the number 0.

Step 2.   Set alpha, and thereby specify the appropriate confidence interval (90 percent, 95 percent, or 99 percent). The formulas for the confidence intervals appropriate to the independent-sampling situation acknowledge the characteristics of the sampling distribution of differences between means. The sampling distribution of $\overline{X}_1 - \overline{X}_2$ transforms to a *t* distribution with a mean of 0, a standard error of $s_{\overline{x}_1 - \overline{x}_2}$, and degrees of freedom equal to $n_1 + n_2 - 2$. Formula 10.7 defines the confidence interval for independent samples.

The Confidence Interval for Independent Samples

$$LL = (\overline{X}_1 - \overline{X}_2) - t_\alpha(s_{\overline{x}_1 - \overline{x}_2})$$

$$UL = (\overline{X}_1 - \overline{X}_2) + t_\alpha(s_{\overline{x}_1 - \overline{x}_2}) \quad \textit{(Formula 10.7)}$$

The value t_α is found by entering the *t* table with the stated alpha level and $df = n_1 + n_2 - 2$.

Step 3.   Compute the confidence interval and test the null hypothesis. Since the null hypothesis is $\mu_1 - \mu_2 = 0$, H_0 is rejected if 0 is outside the confidence interval.

Step 4.   Interpret the findings.

Box 10.2 compares an independent-samples *t* test to a confidence interval in testing a scientific hypothesis about the relation between premarital cohabitation and the age at which people marry.

BOX 10.2

Premarital Cohabitation: A New American Institution

In the 1950s, it was unusual for a couple to live together before marriage. In fact, those few unmarried couples who did live together faced social ostracism. During the 60s, we witnessed profound sociological changes in American society. Among these changes was a shift in the mores governing sexual behavior, and as a consequence, the number of couples living together before marriage increased. In 1970, 13 percent of newlyweds had lived with their spouses before marriage. By 1980, premarital cohabitation had increased to 53 percent. (U.S. Bureau of the Census, 1983). In just 20 years, the practice of living together before marriage changed from a social stigma to a new American institution. Such a rapid change in our behavior is of interest to sociologists. An increase in premarital cohabitation may reflect fundamental changes in our values and attitudes about the ritual of courtship and marriage. Demographers have wondered if premarital cohabitation has affected the age at which couples marry. A study by Gwartney-Gibbs (1986) may provide an answer to this question.

DATA COLLECTION

Gwartney-Gibbs examined all the 1980 marriage applications in Lane County, Oregon. If a couple listed the same home address, they were assumed to be living together. If different addresses were offered, it was assumed that the couple was not cohabitating. Therefore, it was possible to tabulate the ages of males and females by whether or not they were living together.

RESULTS

The investigator reported the average ages of cohabitating and noncohabitating males and females, accompanied by 95 percent confidence intervals. The following table includes mean ages, standard deviations, sample sizes, and confidence intervals for each category. The standard deviations were based on sample data; therefore they are estimates of the population standard deviations. However, even though $s_{\bar{x}}$ is used as an estimate of $\sigma_{\bar{x}}$, since the sample sizes are so large,

the constant 1.96 is used to establish 95 percent confidence intervals. It would be a good exercise for you to go through the steps of computing the confidence intervals for each sample. For example, the confidence interval for the cohabitating females was computed as $22.8 \pm 1.96(4.6/\sqrt{806})$.

Subjects	Cohabitants	Noncohabitants
	$n = 806$	$n = 877$
Males	$\overline{X} = 25.00$	$\overline{X} = 23.60$
	$s = 4.50$	$s = 5.50$
	$UL = 25.31$	$UL = 23.97$
	$LL = 24.69$	$LL = 23.23$
Females	$\overline{X} = 22.80$	$\overline{X} = 21.70$
	$s = 4.60$	$s = 4.40$
	$UL = 23.11$	$UL = 21.99$
	$LL = 22.49$	$LL = 21.41$

At this point, no hypothesis has been tested. The investigator could obtain the population mean for the age at which males and females marry. Two single-sample t tests could be performed to see if cohabitating males and females have means that are significantly different from their respective, hypothesized population means. However, we ask a different question: Is there a significant difference between the mean age at which cohabitating males and noncohabitating males marry?

THE t-TEST APPROACH

Step 1. State the null and alternative hypotheses.

$$H_0: \quad \mu_1 - \mu_2 = 0$$

$$H_1: \quad \mu_1 - \mu_2 \neq 0$$

Step 2. Set alpha. Use $\alpha = .05$.

Step 3. Identify t_{crit}. With the df so large $(806 + 877 - 2 = 1681)$, use $t_{crit} = 1.96$.

Step 4. Compute t_{obt} for an independent-samples t test.

$$t_{obt} = \frac{\overline{X}_1 - \overline{X}_2}{s_{\overline{x}_1 - \overline{x}_2}}$$

$$s_{\overline{x}_1 - \overline{x}_2} = \sqrt{\frac{s_1^2(n_1 - 1) + s_2^2(n_2 - 1)}{n_1 + n_2 - 2}\left(\frac{1}{n_1} + \frac{1}{n_2}\right)}$$

First compute the denominator of the t test.

$$s_{\overline{x}_1 - \overline{x}_2} =$$

$$= \sqrt{\frac{(4.5)^2(806 - 1) + (5.5)^2(877 - 1)}{806 + 877 - 2}\left(\frac{1}{806} + \frac{1}{877}\right)}$$

$$= \sqrt{\frac{20.25(805) + 30.25(876)}{1681}(.002)}$$

$$= \sqrt{25.46(.002)}$$

$$= \sqrt{.05}$$

$$s_{\overline{x}_1 - \overline{x}_2} = .22$$

$$t_{obt} = \frac{25 - 23.60}{.22}$$

$$= \frac{1.40}{.22}$$

$$t_{obt} = 6.36$$

Step 5. Make a decision about the null hypothesis. Since $t_{obt} > t_{crit}$ (6.36 > 1.96), reject H_0 and conclude $H_1: \mu_1 - \mu_2 \neq 0$.

Step 6. Interpret the findings. Males who cohabitate before marriage marry at a later age than males who do not cohabitate before marriage. One plausible interpretation of these findings is that cohabitation causes a delay in marriage. However, other explanations are also possible. For example, it might be that the cohabitating people are simply people who would have delayed marriage even if they had not lived with someone.

THE CONFIDENCE INTERVAL APPROACH TO TESTING THE NULL HYPOTHESIS

Step 1. State the null hypothesis and alternative hypotheses.

$$H_0: \quad \mu_1 - \mu_2 = 0$$
$$H_1: \quad \mu_1 - \mu_2 \neq 0$$

Step 2. Set alpha. Set $\alpha = .05$, which establishes a 95 percent confidence interval.

Step 3. Compute the confidence interval and test the null hypothesis. Use Formula 10.7.

$$LL = (\overline{X}_1 - \overline{X}_2) - t_\alpha(s_{\overline{x}_1 - \overline{x}_2})$$
$$UL = (\overline{X}_1 - \overline{X}_2) + t_\alpha(s_{\overline{x}_1 - \overline{x}_2})$$

Use the same values for the confidence interval as those that were used when conducting the t test.

$$LL = (25 - 23.60) - 1.96(.22) = \mathbf{.97}$$
$$UL = (25 - 23.60) + 1.96(.22) = \mathbf{1.83}$$

The value stated in the null hypothesis is 0, which falls outside of the confidence interval. Therefore H_0 is rejected in favor of H_1.

Step 4. Interpret the findings. The interpretation of the findings is the same as the interpretation used for the t test. However, because you used a confidence interval to test the hypothesis, you can make a statement about the range of values within which the *difference between the population means* is likely to be found. Cohabitating males are likely to delay marriage from .97 to 1.83 years longer than males who do not cohabitate.

Using Confidence Intervals Instead of the Dependent-Samples t Test

The use of a confidence interval to test the null hypothesis that is based on related samples follows the same logic as discussed in the independent-sampling context. The upper and lower limits of the interval that brackets the difference between two population means is computed by using Formula 10.8. The null hypothesis is rejected if the value stated in H_0 falls outside of the confidence interval.

The Confidence Interval for Dependent Samples

$$LL = (\overline{X} - \overline{Y}) - t_\alpha(s_{\overline{D}})$$

$$UL = (\overline{X} - \overline{Y}) + t_\alpha(s_{\overline{D}}) \quad \textit{(Formula 10.8)}$$

Confidence Intervals and Type I and II Errors

Confidence intervals are probabilistic in nature. You can never be sure if an interval contains the population mean or the difference between two population means. When using a confidence interval for hypothesis testing, the endeavor is still probabilistic. Since you are making a statement about whether to reject the null hypothesis, a decision error can be made. If the null hypothesis really is true, and a 95 percent confidence interval is used, there is a .05 probability that the interval will not contain the true population parameter (whether the parameter is a mean or mean difference). In this instance, a Type I error is made since a true null hypothesis will be mistakenly rejected. For example, the null hypothesis might state H_0: $\mu_1 - \mu_2 = 0$. Based on sample data, you compute an interval of .32–.67. Of course, you would reject the null hypothesis because 0 falls outside of the interval. If, in actuality, there is no difference between μ_1 and μ_2, a Type I error is committed.

Type II errors also occur when using confidence intervals for hypothesis testing. Using independent or dependent sampling, if your confidence limits are, say, $-.27$ and .56, the null hypothesis will not be rejected since 0 falls within the interval. If there really is a difference between the population means, you have retained a false null hypothesis and a Type II error has been committed.

SUMMARY

The field of inferential statistics includes estimation and hypothesis testing. Parameter estimation uses data from a sample to infer the value of a population parameter. There are two kinds of estimation: point estimation and interval estimation. Point estimation entails estimating a parameter as a single value. Interval estimation establishes a range of values within which the parameter is expected to lie.

When a sampling distribution is theoretically established with an n of sufficient size, the sampling distribution will assume the shape of the standard normal curve. As a consequence, the z table can be used to solve problems about the percentage of *means* that fall within a given area under the normal curve. Confidence intervals state a span between two means within which you can be highly confident that the true population mean lies. A 95 percent confidence interval marks, for instance, the upper and lower cutoffs between which 95 percent of the sampling distribution is found. Since you must use a sample mean to estimate the mean of the sampling distribution, any confidence interval that you establish may or may not contain the true population mean. Thus, confidence intervals are probabilistic in nature. Moreover, a probability of .90, .95, or .99 is attached to the interval. For example, a confidence level of 95 percent means that if an infinite number of samples are taken, and confidence intervals are established from each sample, 95 percent of the intervals would contain the true population mean.

When establishing a confidence interval when σ is unknown, the sample standard deviation is used to compute an estimate of the standard error of the sampling distribution. If the sample size is sufficiently large (around 30), the constants 1.65, 1.96, and 2.58 can be used for the 90 percent, 95 percent, and 99 percent confidence intervals, respectively, even though σ is unknown. As the sample size decreases, and $s_{\bar{x}}$ is used to estimate $\mu_{\bar{x}}$, the t distribution is used to establish cutoffs within which the desired percentage of means lie.

Confidence intervals can be used to test null hypotheses. If the value stated in the null hypothesis falls outside of the interval, the null hypothesis is rejected. When confidence intervals are used in place of an independent- or dependent-samples t test, the interval is the difference between population means.

KEY FORMULAS FOR CHAPTER 10

The 90 Percent Confidence Interval When σ is Known

$$LL = \overline{X} - 1.65\sigma_{\bar{x}}$$

$$UL = \overline{X} + 1.65\sigma_{\bar{x}} \qquad \text{(Formula 10.1)}$$

The 95 Percent Confidence Interval When σ is Known

$$LL = \overline{X} - 1.96\sigma_{\bar{x}}$$

$$UL = \overline{X} + 1.96\sigma_{\bar{x}} \qquad \text{(Formula 10.2)}$$

The 99 Percent Confidence Interval When σ is Known

$$LL = \overline{X} - 2.58\sigma_{\bar{x}}$$

$$UL = \overline{X} + 2.58\sigma_{\bar{x}} \qquad \text{(Formula 10.3)}$$

The 90 Percent Confidence Interval When σ is Unknown

$$LL = \overline{X} - t_{.10}s_{\overline{x}}$$

$$UL = \overline{X} + t_{.10}s_{\overline{x}}$$ (Formula 10.4)

The 95 Percent Confidence Interval When σ is Unknown

$$LL = \overline{X} - t_{.05}s_{\overline{x}}$$

$$UL = \overline{X} + t_{.05}s_{\overline{x}}$$ (Formula 10.5)

The 99 Percent Confidence Interval When σ is Unknown

$$LL = \overline{X} - t_{.01}s_{\overline{x}}$$

$$UL = \overline{X} + t_{.01}s_{\overline{x}}$$ (Formula 10.6)

The Confidence Interval for Independent Samples

$$LL = (\overline{X}_1 - \overline{X}_2) - t_\alpha(s_{\overline{x}_1 - \overline{x}_2})$$

$$UL = (\overline{X}_1 - \overline{X}_2) + t_\alpha(s_{\overline{x}_1 + \overline{x}_2})$$ (Formula 10.7)

The Confidence Interval for Dependent Samples

$$LL = (\overline{X} - \overline{Y}) - t_\alpha(s_{\overline{D}})$$

$$UL = (\overline{X} - \overline{Y}) + t_\alpha(s_{\overline{D}})$$ (Formula 10.8)

WORK PROBLEMS

1. What is meant when you say that there is a .95 probability that a confidence interval contains the mean of a population?

2. The following table presents sample sizes used to identify values of t when establishing confidence intervals. In each case, what t values should you use (assume a single sample)?

Sample	n	Confidence Interval
a	6	90%
b	8	95%
c	13	99%
d	13	90%
e	7	95%
f	16	90%
g	20	99%

3. Suppose you establish a 95 percent confidence interval for a sample with a given n and s. You then establish another 95 percent confidence interval with the same size n but use a larger value for s. What implications does this have for your confidence that the interval includes the population mean?

4. A manufacturer of light bulbs would like to estimate the amount of time the newest light bulbs will burn. A random sample of 100 bulbs is selected and the mean burn time is found to be 600 hr, with a standard deviation of 90. What are the 90 percent, 95 percent, and 99 percent confidence intervals? (Since the sample size is so large, use the z cutoffs from the standard normal curve.)

5. Using the data from Problem 4, suppose the sample size is 40. Compute the 90 percent, 95 percent and 99 percent confidence intervals. How has the reduction in sample size changed the width of the intervals? (Use the same cutoffs as you did in Problem 4.)

6. Using the following data, establish 90 percent confidence intervals. What effect do s and n have on the width of the intervals?

Sample	$\overline{X}$	s	n
a	25	2	50
b	25	2	100
c	25	8	50

7. The president of a bank would like to estimate the average amount of money in all the savings accounts. A sample of 80 accounts is randomly selected with $\overline{X} = \$3500$, $s = \$900$. Establish a 95 percent confidence interval. How would you explain to the president what the interval means? (Use z scores to establish the interval.)

The next three problems were given as research examples at the beginning of the chapter. Compute the 95 percent confidence interval, using the summary statistics provided in each problem.

8. The director of the Department of Mental Health has received conflicting reports about the frequency of patient assaults on inpatient units. He would like an idea of the mean number of assaults in a 1-month period. A random sample of 18 inpatient units is taken. The average number of assaults is found to be 24.50, per inpatient unit, with a standard deviation of 2.61.

9. A drug manufacturer is researching a new medication for high blood pressure. Early reports suggest that there are many negative side effects to the drug. The question is, what is the average number of drug side-effects? A random sample of 13 patients taking the drug is selected and the mean number of side effects is found to be 4.2, with a standard deviation of .86.

10. A tire company is interested in knowing the average number of highway miles its tires can tolerate before the treads wear out. A random sample of 60 tires is selected and each is placed on a highway simulator wheel. The mean for the sample is found to be 56,000 miles, with a standard deviation of 4300 miles.

11. What is wrong with the following statement, and how would you change it to be accurate? "I have established a 99 percent confidence interval, and therefore, there is a .99 probability that the population mean is the same as the sample mean."

In Chapters 7–9, the following seven problems were used to conduct various *t* tests. Should you wish to compare your conclusion regarding the null hypothesis when using a *t* test versus a confidence interval, the relevant chapter and problem number have been provided with each question.

12. Robbins (1988) found that males overestimate their life span. The life expectancy for males is 72.4 years. Nine male subjects are randomly selected and asked how long they believe they will live. Use a confidence interval to test the hypothesis that males' subjective life expectancy is significantly different from the life expectancy of the male population (Chapter 7, Problem 10).

Subjective Life Expectancy for Males (Years)

77	74	80	72	82	76	78	75	79

13. An anthropologist hypothesizes that physical stress in childhood increases height (see Landauer and Whiting, 1964). The researchers locate a tribe of people in which physical stress is a byproduct of frequent tribal rituals (piercing and molding body parts, exposure to extreme temperatures, etc.). The mean height of the people in the region who do not use physically stressful rituals with their young is used as the population mean. The following raw data are for adult men and women of the tribe in question. The population mean height for men is 65 in. and 59 in. for women. Use confidence intervals to test the hypothesis (for men and women) that early physical stress alters adult stature. Also, state the null and alternative hypotheses (Chapter 7, Problem 11).

Men	Women
67	59
69	63
72	65
70	60
70	59
72	62
64	61
70	66

14. Simon (1989) found that a sample of 54 males and 84 females (mean age of each group = 22 years) reported losing their virginity at the age of 16.1 years and 16.5 years, respectively. However, males reported having had sex with 14.6 ($s_1 = 29.2$) different partners, while females reported having had sex with 5.6 ($s_2 = 5.4$) different partners. Use a confidence interval to test if there is a significant difference between males and females in the number of past sexual partners. Set alpha at .05, and state the null and alternative hypotheses (Chapter 8, Problem 13).

15. Narcissism is characterized by a feeling of being special, self-centeredness, and a sense of entitlement. When comparing college students who were first-borns with students who were born later, Jourbert (1989) found that first-borns were more narcissistic than those subjects who were born later in the family. The effect was the same for males and females. The following hypothetical summary

data are presented for males and females. Use confidence intervals to test for a difference between first-borns and later-borns, for males and females. Set alpha at .05 (Chapter 8, Problem 12).

Males

First-Borns: $\overline{X}_1$:23, s_1:7.84, n_1:10
Later-Borns: $\overline{X}_2$:16, s_2:6.43, n_2:15

Females

First-Borns: $\overline{X}_1$:17, s_1:6.52, n_1:19
Later-Borns: $\overline{X}_2$:12, s_2:6.57, n_2:28

16. Addison (1989) found that people perceive bearded men differently from nonbearded men. Compared to nonbearded men, fellows with beards are rated as more masculine, more aggressive, stronger, and more dominant. However, they are not viewed as more intelligent. The researcher used a repeated-measures design in which one group of subjects rated pictures of bearded and nonbearded men. The summary statistics that follow are based on the raw data from Chapter 9, Problem 1. A score can range from 1–feminine to 10–masculine. Bearded: $\overline{X}$ = 7.62, Nonbearded: $\overline{Y}$ = 5.62, n_p = 8, s_D = 2.07. Set alpha at .05 and use a confidence interval to test the difference between bearded and nonbearded men. Interpret the findings.

17. An industrial psychologist working for a marketing firm wants to know which of two cheeses are preferred by college students. Subjects taste a piece of Gouda cheese and then Swiss cheese. Taste ratings are obtained after each test and can range from 1—lousy to 7—fantastic. Using the following summary statistics, establish a 95 percent confidence interval to test the hypothesis that there is no difference in taste preference for the two cheeses. Gouda cheese: $\overline{X}$ = 7.0, Swiss cheese: $\overline{Y}$ = 5.6, s_D = 2.51, n_p = 5 (Chapter 9, Problem 3).

Work Problems for the Computer

If your software program does not compute confidence intervals, you will have to conduct the proper *t* test and use the appropriate values for the confidence interval.

18. A study referenced in the *Chronicle of Higher Education* (1990) showed that students write papers of higher quality when they use an IBM-compatible computer instead of a Macintosh computer. One explanation of the findings is that the Macintosh is so user-friendly that students tend to write very casually. The following hypothetical data are based on a repeated-measures design. Each subject writes a paper using an IBM-compatible computer and a Macintosh computer. The interpretation of the confidence interval is consistent with the findings of the original study. Each raw score in the table represents a composite index of the length of the paper and its quality. Higher numbers reflect greater quantity and quality. Set alpha at .05. Interpret the findings in terms of the test of the null hypothesis and interpret the interval as saying something about the

difference between population means. If you saved this data set, there is no need to type the numbers in again (Chapter 9, Problem 9).

IBM-Compatible	Macintosh
95	80
88	70
99	88
79	54
80	80
77	87
92	75
55	34
79	72
65	70
29	32
88	66
42	42
55	39
71	65
97	84
75	72
45	65
84	77
73	56

19. Assume that the foregoing study is conducted with independent samples. Use a 95 percent confidence interval to test H_0: $\mu_1 - \mu_2 = 0$.

20. Provide a 90 percent interval estimate of the population mean for paper quality using the IBM-compatible computer. Provide a 99 percent confidence interval for the population mean for paper quality using the Macintosh.

Power Analysis and Hypothesis Testing

11.1 DECISION MAKING WHILE HYPOTHESIS TESTING

In the experimental context, the purpose of hypothesis testing is to determine if there is a treatment effect. The researcher attempts to reject the null hypothesis, which always states that there is no effect due to treatment. Hypothesis testing is a decision-making process; there is always the possibility of making an error. A Type I error is made when a true null hypothesis is rejected—that is—the investigator states that there is a treatment effect when, in fact, there is not. The probability of making a Type I error is controlled directly when setting alpha. A Type II error is committed when a false null hypothesis is retained. In other words, there is a treatment effect, but the researcher concludes that no effect exists. Analyzing the probability of making Type I and Type II errors focuses attention on the *mistakes* that can be made. In this section, the topic of hypothesis testing is approached from another angle. Instead of asking questions about the probability of making an error, the issue addressed is the probability of arriving at a *correct decision*. More specifically, if there is a treatment effect, what is the probability that your test will detect the effect? The **power** of a statistical test is the probability that the test will correctly lead to a decision to reject a false null hypothesis.

In terms of probability, there is not a complementary relation between Type I and Type II errors. If the probability of a Type I error is .05, it does *not* mean that the probability of a Type II error is .95. Yes, there is a trade-off, but the trade-off does not translate directly into probability values. However, complementary probabilities do exist in the decision-making process, as indicated in Table 11.1. If the probability of making a Type I error is .05, the probability of *not rejecting* a true null hypothesis is .95. In other words, if there is a 5 percent chance of saying that there is a treatment effect when, in fact, there is no treatment effect, it stands to reason that there is a 95 percent chance of saying that there is no treatment effect when there really isn't an effect.

The probability of committing a Type II error is symbolized by β (beta). If the probability of making a Type II error is β, then the probability of *correctly rejecting* a false null hypothesis is $1 - \beta$. In other words, if there is a 20 percent

TABLE   11.1   **The Four Outcomes When Retaining or Rejecting a True or False Null Hypothesis.**

		TRUE STATE OF AFFAIRS	
		H_0 *is True*	H_0 *is False*
	Retain H_0	Correct $1 - \alpha$ (95%)	Type II error β (20%)
YOUR DECISION			
	Reject H_0	Type I error α (5%)	Correct $1 - \beta$ (Power)(80%)
		100%	100%

chance of failing to find a true treatment effect, there must be an 80 percent chance of correctly identifying a treatment effect. *The probability of correctly detecting a treatment effect is the power of the statistical test.* Hence, power equals $1 - \beta$.

11.2 WHY STUDY POWER?

Understanding the concept of power will increase your "research IQ." For example, you have probably adopted the attitude that large samples are preferred over small samples. There is nothing wrong with this way of thinking. Large samples give us better estimates of population parameters and make it easier to correctly reject the null hypothesis—that is—to detect a treatment effect when there is one. However, consider this situation. A friend is going to conduct a study that evaluates the effectiveness of a treatment for depression. The patient population has a mean depression score that is two standard deviations above the mean of a nondepressed population. The goal of the treatment is to lower the average depression score to the normal range. Your friend asks you, "How many subjects should I use?" If you blindly follow the rule that big samples are better than small samples, you might answer, "Include as many patients as you can." Suppose he replies, "Well, I have lots of money and lots of patients (and patience); I can run 500 subjects. With 500 subjects I am almost certain to detect a treatment effect if there is one." The reasoning is sound. Indeed, with so many subjects, it might be possible to reject the null hypothesis, correctly I might add, when the treatment program reduces depression scores by just a couple of points.[1] So now you have a treatment that, statistically speaking, significantly reduces depression to a level that is still way above what is psychologically normal. Why would you be interested in detecting such a small treatment effect? Let's assume that the size of the treatment effect that you want to detect is more on the order of 20 points on the depression inventory. You don't need 500 subjects to detect such a large treatment effect. Understanding the concept of power and the procedures of power analysis can lead you to intelligently advise your friend as to how many subjects need to be used to detect a treatment effect of a given size. After a power analysis, you might state, "If you use 40 patients, there is an 80 percent chance that you will be able to detect a treatment effect size of 20 points. Reduce your sample size; save your money and your time."

Here's another example of how an understanding of power can raise your research IQ. Another friend of yours is distraught over the failure of her study to show a statistically significant result. She had tested the hypothesis that viewing aggressive pornography would lead to negative attitudes toward women (which, by the way, is the case; Donnerstein, 1980; Malamuth, Heim, and Feshback, 1980).

---

[1] Cohen (1990) makes the point nicely, "... The null hypothesis, taken literally (and that's the only way you can take it in formal hypothesis testing), is *always* false in the real world ... If it is false, even to a tiny degree, it must be the case that a large enough sample will produce a significant result and lead to its rejection. So if the null hypothesis is always false, what's the big deal about rejecting it?" (p. 1308).

You examine the details of her research method, including her sample size, and because of your grasp of power, you are able to tell her, "Given the way you conducted your study, there was very little chance of rejecting the null hypothesis unless the effect of viewing aggressive pornography is extremely strong. It would be theoretically interesting, if not pragmatically important, to be able to identify even a small treatment effect. Don't give up on the hypothesis; here's how you can modify your study. . . . " A power analysis is valuable in planning a study as well as evaluating a study post hoc. But clearly, much more is gained by considering the issue of power before a study is conducted. It is hard to justify the time, expense, and hopes that go into running a study if the study has such little power that it is doomed to fail from the beginning. There are several factors that influence the probability of correctly rejecting the null hypothesis; some of these factors are under the experimenter's control, and some are not. The size of the treatment effect, which influences power, is discussed in the following section.

11.3   THE SIZE OF THE TREATMENT EFFECT AND POWER

The power of a statistical test, in part, depends on the magnitude of the treatment effect. Suppose you want to evaluate the effectiveness of a study program designed to increase scores on the SAT. Suppose the national mean for the SAT is 500. You want to know whether your sample of students, after participating in the program, is taken from a population with a mean of 500. The null and alternative hypotheses are stated as:

$$H_0: \quad \mu = 500$$

$$H_1: \quad \mu \neq 500$$

Although the alternative hypothesis is stated specifically, $\mu \neq 500$, it is a rather broad statement. You may reject H_0 and accept H_1 when μ is 550 and, under certain circumstances, you may reject H_0 and accept H_1 when μ is 501. Therefore, with H_0 stated as $\mu = 500$, the null hypothesis can be a little bit incorrect or very incorrect. Stated differently, the size of a treatment effect exists on a continuum from small to large. When conducting a significance test, it is easier to detect a large effect than a small effect. For example, if the population means differ by 50 points, a hypothesis test is more likely to identify that difference rather than if the population means differ by 10 points.[2] In other words, the power of the test will be influenced by the size of the treatment effect. It follows, then, that the probability value of power is not fixed; it changes as a function of the true difference between the population means.

---

[2] Recall that the size of the numerator in the t test is a function of treatment effect and sampling error. As the treatment effect becomes larger, t_{obt} becomes larger. The larger t_{obt}, the more likely it exceeds t_{crit}.

The null hypothesis can be false to varying degrees. The extent to which H_0 is false is the size of the treatment effect *in the population*. When determining the power of a statistical test, the size of the treatment effect must be *specifically stated*. The size of the treatment effect is stated as the number of standard deviations the population mean, hypothesized in the null hypothesis, is from the true population mean. Since you do not know the true population mean, questions of power take the form of "what if" questions: "What if the true population mean is .25 standard deviations from the hypothesized population mean, then what is the probability of detecting that difference?" or "What if the true population mean is .89 standard deviations from the hypothesized population mean, then what is the probability of detecting that difference?" Obviously, you want to maximize your chances of discovering a treatment effect in the population if one exists.

A hypothetical study is presented to further clarify the concept of power and illustrate its calculation. The manner in which you go about computing power will vary, depending on the experimental design and type of statistical analysis used. The illustrative worked example involves a one-tailed, single-sample z test.

Worked Example

A private company would like to offer a college-entrance preparation course that will help students increase their SAT-V (Verbal) scores. Before marketing the program, the company decides to evaluate the program's effectiveness. The president of the company comes to you with the following problem: "Our company is planning to evaluate the effectiveness of a course that we have developed. This course is designed to increase the SAT-V test scores of students, and, as you may know, the national average of the SAT-V is 500, with a standard deviation of 100. We plan to sample 36 graduates of our program and determine their mean SAT-V. We are not particularly interested in discovering if our program increases scores by an average of 5 or 10 points. However, we would like to be fairly certain that our study will detect a 25-point difference between the means of the populations. Given the information I have provided, what is the probability that we will detect an effect size of 25 points?"

The president has given you all the information that you need to answer the question. As you work toward the solution, examine the problem from the perspective of the sampling distributions implied by the problem. Figure 11.1 depicts two sampling distributions. Figure 11.1(a) represents the case when H_0 is true; the distribution in Figure 11.1(b) represents the case when H_0 is false, *and* when H_0 is false by 25 *raw points*. Since you are conducting a one-tailed test, the critical value when $\alpha = .05$ is $+1.65$. Figure 11.1(a) is the null distribution because it depicts the sampling distribution when H_0 is true. Figure 11.1(b) is the alternative distribution because it illustrates the sampling distribution when the null hypothesis is incorrect by 25 raw points.

The first step in computing power is to identify the sample mean that corresponds to the critical value, $+1.65$. This is the sample mean that is 1.65 standard

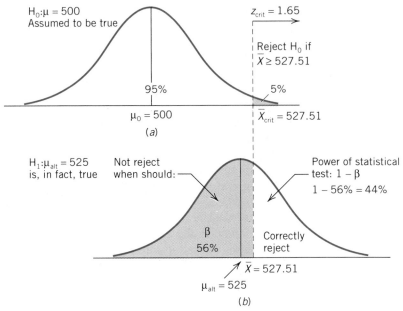

Figure 11.1 Sampling distributions of means. (*a*) Under H$_0$: $\mu = 500$. (*b*) Under H$_1$: $\mu = 525$.

errors above the mean of the null sampling distribution. Since the cutoff is $+1.65$, the formula used to identify the sample mean that is 1.65 standard errors above the mean of the null hypothesis is:

$$\overline{X} = \mu + (z_{\text{crit}})\sigma_{\overline{x}}$$
$$\overline{X} = 500 + (1.65)(100/\sqrt{36})$$
$$= 500 + (1.65)(16.67)$$
$$= 527.51$$

All sample means larger than 527.51 fall in the rejection region. Note that you are using the null distribution to define the rejection region since it is the null hypothesis that is directly tested. And if the null hypothesis is true, 5 percent of the means of the sampling distribution fall above the mean of 527.51.

Now look at the alternative distribution in Figure 11.1(*b*). Even though the true population mean is 525, obtaining a sample mean of 525 would not place you in the rejection region of the sampling distribution under the null hypothesis. You still need a sample mean greater than 527.51 to reject the null hypothesis. Now, *if* the true population mean is 525, and since you need a sample mean greater than 527.51, what is the probability of randomly selecting a mean from the *alternative sampling distribution* that falls above 527.51? It's another z-score problem. A new symbol is specified here, μ_{alt}, to indicate that you are using the mean of the alternative sampling distribution. First, using the population mean of the alternative sampling distribution, transform 527.51 to a z value.

$$z = \frac{\overline{X} - \mu_{alt}}{\sigma_{\overline{x}}}$$

$$z = \frac{527.51 - 525}{16.67}$$

$$z = .15$$

The number .15 is the number of standard error units 527.51 is above the mean of the alternative distribution, 525. Next, using the third column of the z table (Table B.1 in the Appendix), look up a z of .15. You find that the probability of randomly selecting a sample mean above *the critical mean of the alternative distribution* is .44. [See the unshaded area of the alternative distribution in Figure 11.1(*b*).] Thus, the power of the test is .44. Forty-four percent of the sample means of the *alternative distribution* fall above the critical sample mean of 527.51. In other words, the probability of rejecting the null hypothesis when the true mean of the population is 525 is .44.

   With the power analysis completed, you are now in a position to advise the president of the company that is offering the SAT-V study program. Do you think the study should be conducted as proposed? There is only a 44 percent chance of detecting the treatment effect of interest. In fact, there is a higher probability of making a Type II error (.56) than there is of correctly rejecting the null hypothesis (.44)! At this point two questions can be raised. First, what can the company do to increase the power of the test? Second, how much power is enough? The best answer to the first question is to increase the sample size (see Section 11.7). The answer to the second question, "What is an acceptable level of power?" can be answered by convention. Power in the range of .70–.90 is considered acceptable, with .80 the conventional probability value. When a statistical test has a .80 prob-ability of correctly rejecting the null hypothesis, there is a .20 probability of making a Type II error. You will note that a probability of .20 is four times greater than the conventional .05 probability of making a Type I error. Researchers are *usually* comfortable with that kind of trade-off. It reflects a conservative approach to hypothesis testing; saying that there is a treatment effect when there is no effect is considered more serious than failing to identify an effect when in fact there is one. However, each test of a hypothesis requires an investigator to consider what the acceptable probabilities are for different types of errors. The nature of the consequences for each type of error will guide the decision-making process.

11.4   USING THE POWER TABLE

The preceding section discussed how to compute the power of a one-tailed, single-sample z test. The problem required knowing the sample size, the population standard deviation, the mean hypothesized under the null hypothesis, and a mean specified under the alternative hypothesis. There is a shortcut method, which can be used to arrive at the power of a significance test. A brief calculation using the Power table in Appendix B.3 can be used to determine power. Let's use the data from the worked example to illustrate this method for determining the power of a statistical test.

To use the Power table in Appendix B.3, two new terms must be introduced: δ (delta), and γ (gamma), the symbol for effect size.

Formula for Delta

$$\delta = \gamma \sqrt{n} \quad \textit{(Formula 11.1)}$$

Note that δ combines the population effect size and the sample size into a single index. Delta will be used to enter the Power table in Appendix B.3. Note in Formula 11.2 that γ, which is the symbol for the effect size, indicates the specified number of standard deviations between the population mean hypothesized in the null hypothesis and the population mean specified when the null hypothesis is false (the true population mean). Keep in mind that the true population mean is not discovered; it is specified. A power analysis does not identify the difference between population means and it does not test to see if there is a difference between population means. The power analysis gives the probability of detecting a specified difference between population means (assuming that that difference exists). Here's how the short method works.

Formula for Gamma

$$\gamma = \frac{\mu_{alt} - \mu_0}{\sigma} \qquad \textit{(Formula 11.2)}$$

where,

μ_{alt} = the mean of the alternative (treated) population
μ_0 = the population mean when the null hypothesis is true
σ = the population standard deviation; if σ is unavailable, you will use s

---

Step 1. Specify an effect size, γ (gamma). Using the data from the worked example:

$$\gamma = \frac{525 - 500}{100}$$

$$= \frac{25}{100}$$

$$\gamma = .25$$

The number .25 is the number of standard deviation units the treated population mean is from the mean of the population stated in the null hypothesis.

Step 2. Compute delta using Formula 11.1.

$$\delta = \gamma\sqrt{n}$$
$$= .25\sqrt{36}$$
$$= 1.50$$

Step 3. Determine the power by using the Power table (Appendix B.3). In the worked example, use a one-tailed test, with $\alpha = .05$. With δ computed as 1.50, find δ in the first column of the table and move to the column for $\alpha = .05$, one-tailed test. The power of the test is .44, the value found in the original worked example.

11.5 THE BIGGER THE TREATMENT EFFECT THE GREATER THE POWER

Suppose the treatment effect that you want to detect is 50 raw-score units from the population mean of 500. The power question now becomes, "What is the power of my test to detect a population difference of 50 raw-score units?" Use the data and sample size of the worked example.

$$\gamma = \frac{\mu_{alt} - \mu_0}{\sigma}$$
$$= \frac{550 - 500}{100}$$
$$\gamma = .50$$
$$\delta = .50\sqrt{36}$$
$$\delta = 3.00$$

Now enter the Power table with $\delta = 3.00$, for a one-tailed test when $\alpha = .05$. The power of the test jumps to .91. If the population mean under the alternative hypothesis is 550, you now have a 91 percent chance of detecting the treatment effect. Recalculate δ when $\mu_{alt} = 505$. The power of the test drops to .12. Now there is a paltry 12 percent chance of detecting a false null hypothesis when the true population mean is 505.

This exercise demonstrates how the effect size in the population influences the power of a statistical test. As the effect size increases, so too does the power of the statistical test. Keep in mind that effect size refers to the difference between *population* means. The actual obtained sample mean has nothing to do with the power analysis. In addition, the power analysis has nothing to do with what you *hope* to be the effect size. The power analysis essentially says, "Given the effect size, alpha, and the sample size, here is the probability that the null hypothesis will be correctly rejected."

11.6 DETERMINING THE EFFECT SIZE: THE ACHILLES HEEL OF THE POWER ANALYSIS

Using the 1960 volume of the *Journal of Abnormal and Social Psychology,* Cohen (1962) conducted an interesting study. Although the authors of the articles in that volume did not use power analyses, Cohen computed the power of the statistical tests used in each of the studies. According to Cohen's (1962) early guidelines, a small effect size is about .20; a medium effect size is around .50; and a large effect size is around .80. Assuming that the researchers would want to detect a medium treatment-effect size, the average power of the tests in that volume was .46. This means that, on the average, there was only a 46 percent chance of detecting a medium effect size! Cohen's admonition to use power analyses is widely known among researchers (Cohen, 1977; Sedlmeier and Gigerenzer, 1989). Yet, 24 years later, a study similar to Cohen's (1962), using the 1984 volume of the *Journal of Abnormal Psychology,* found that the average statistical power for detecting a medium effect size was .37 (Sedlmeier and Gigerenzer, 1989; Rossi, Rossi, and Cottrill, 1990).[The conventional standard for what defines a small, medium, and large effect size has been lowered by Cohen (1977; 1988). Small, medium, and large effect sizes are regarded now as .10, .25, and .40, respectively.] Despite the urging of statisticians, power analyses have not become standard practice among researchers. Why not?

You can directly control the alpha level, and, within reason, you can select the sample size. The problem arises when you have to specify the size of the treatment effect. The difficulty inherent in postulating the effect size might be one reason why researchers do not routinely perform a power analysis before conducting a study (for additional, historical reasons, see Sedlmeier and Gigerenzer, 1989). However, you are not rendered helpless when having to state an effect size. There are two good sources of information for making a reasonable statement about effect size.

First, most studies have a heritage. Although you may be the first person to conduct your exact study, others have been working in the area, studying the same phenomenon. By familiarizing yourself with the effect size other researchers have detected, you can make an estimate of the effect size that applies to your experiment. Second, you may be able to conduct a pilot study. A pilot study is a trial run of the study you wish to conduct. It is conducted with a sample smaller than you will ultimately use and provides an opportunity to adjust experimental procedures. By examining the data of the pilot study, you can get a feel for the strength of your independent variable, as well as the amount of variability in the data.

For example, as a graduate student, I was involved in a research project to examine self-control techniques that could be taught to people to help them tolerate pain. We ran a pilot study and discovered that there is a tremendous difference among people in their ability (willingness) to tolerate a painful stimulus. Our sample data allowed us a peek at the amount of variability there is in the population when it comes to pain tolerance. Variability reduces the power of a test. Examine Formula 11.2, the formula for gamma. Note that the effect size in the population is influenced by the variability of the population—in other words—the greater the variability, the smaller the γ.

$$\gamma = \frac{\mu_{\text{alt}} - \mu_0}{\sigma}$$

Because the variability in our sample data was so large, we could see that we were in an area of small effects. Consider the formula for δ (Formula 11.1):

$$\delta = \gamma \sqrt{n}$$

You know that a larger delta is associated with greater power. If gamma is small, how can you increase delta? Increase the sample size. Thus, from the results of a pilot study, we were able to make a good guess as to the size of the treatment effect in the population and clearly see that we needed to use a fairly large sample size to detect the treatment effect.

11.7 DETERMINING SAMPLE SIZE FOR A SINGLE-SAMPLE TEST

In this section, how to explicitly arrive at a sample size that will allow a researcher to detect a given size treatment effect is discussed. Sometimes you will not have any reliable information to help you specify a treatment effect. In this situation, you can still perform a power analysis. All you need to do is ask yourself, "What size treatment effect do I *want* to detect?" The likelihood of detecting a given size treatment effect can be altered by changing the sample size. The question then becomes, "How many subjects do I need to detect a treatment effect of a specified size?"

To determine the sample size required to detect a specified treatment effect, you will need to state, beforehand, α, γ, and the desired power. Alpha is usually set at .10, .05, or .01, with .05 being the most common value for alpha. Desired power can be set at any value from just above 0 to just below 1. However, setting power low, for instance .20, is saying that you will accept a 20 percent chance of detecting a treatment effect. With the odds so low of correctly rejecting the null hypothesis, the study is a waste of time. Why not set the desired power at .99? The problem here is similar to the trade-off between Type I and Type II errors. In trying to minimize a Type I error, you could set alpha at .0001, but the probability of a Type II error would become unacceptably large. Likewise, if you insist that the power of your statistical test be .99, you will pay a big price in the vast number of subjects required. The conventional compromise is to set power at .80. Let's return to the worked problem in which you are a consultant to a company that wants to market a course for improving SAT-V scores. Recall that the population mean is 500 with a standard deviation of 100; the company wants to detect an average increase in SAT-V scores of 25 points (525). The company proposed to use 36 subjects. You found that if only 36 subjects are used, there is only a 44 percent chance of detecting a treatment effect. Since 44 percent is unacceptably low, you now must advise the company how many subjects should be used to detect a 25-point difference.

Formula for Determining Sample Size for a Single-Sample *t* Test

$$n = \left(\frac{\delta}{\gamma}\right)^2 \qquad \text{(Formula 11.3)}$$

Remember that γ is not the number of points between 500 and 525, rather, γ is the number of standard deviations 525 is from 500. Gamma was calculated as .25: $(525 - 500)/100 = .25$. Now you need delta, δ, to find n in Formula 11.3. Enter the Power table in Appendix B.4, for $\alpha = .05$, *one-tailed test*. This Power table is used to find delta for a given alpha level and desired power. Since your desired power is .80, look down the left column and find .80. The column immediately to the right is for a one-tailed test, when $\alpha = .05$. Delta is 2.49. You now have all the values to use the formula for determining the sample size.

$$n = \left(\frac{\delta}{\gamma}\right)^2$$

$$n = \left(\frac{2.49}{.25}\right)^2$$

$$n = 99$$

To detect a 25-point difference in SAT-V scores, the study must include 99 subjects.

■   **QUESTION**   *Suppose you wanted to be almost certain of detecting an effect size of .25, so power is set at .99. How many subjects would you now need?*

SOLUTION   Using the Power table in Appendix B.4 to find δ for a power of .99, δ is found to equal 3.97.

$$n = \left(\frac{3.97}{.25}\right)^2$$

$$n = 252$$

There is the trade-off. Increasing the probability of detecting a 25-point difference between the populations from .80 to .99 requires using 153 more subjects. If subjects are easy to come by and the cost of gathering data is low, the investigator may want to use a level of power greater than the conventional index.   ■

11.8   FAILING TO REJECT THE NULL HYPOTHESIS: CAN A POWER ANALYSIS HELP?

Hypothesis testing is a probabilistic endeavor. Whether you are referring to a Type I error, a Type II error, or power, there is always some probability associated with every aspect of hypothesis testing. Moreover, there is no way to prove the null hypothesis. If you do not identify a treatment effect, you say that you have "failed to reject" the null hypothesis; you do not conclude that you have proved the null hypothesis true. Strictly speaking, this is correct.

Researchers are usually in the position of wanting to reject the null hypothesis. Rejecting the null hypothesis usually means that a treatment effect has been identified, which is something to report to other researchers. But what do you say if you fail to find a treatment effect? Studies that fail to reject the null hypothesis are often assigned to the circular file (the wastepaper basket). A researcher will attempt to learn from a failed study, either by redesigning the study, or moving on to another hypothesis. A power analysis can help. First, if the researcher neglected to conduct a power analysis until after the study failed, he or she might have discovered that power was so low that there was not a fair chance to detect a treatment effect of an acceptable size. The study can be run again with more subjects. But what if the researcher conducts a power analysis *before* the study, conducts the study so that the power of identifying a *small* treatment effect is, say, .80, and then fails to reject the null hypothesis? Is this a potentially important finding? It could be. Although the researcher could not conclude that the null hypothesis is true, with sufficient power, it could be asserted that if there is a difference in population means, that difference is very small, and perhaps not worthy of additional research.

Consider a different example. There are times when failing to reject the null hypothesis has important theoretical and/or practical significance. Suppose a researcher wants to see if there is a decrement in intellectual performance as a result of administering antipsychotic medication to schizophrenics. One sample of patients receives the drug, and another sample of patients with schizophrenia receives a placebo. The patients are tested some time in the future, and the two groups do *not* differ in intellectual performance. This is a useful finding, but *only if the analysis has sufficient power to detect a small difference.* Box 11.1 presents two studies in which the interpretation of a retained null hypothesis is at issue.

This chapter provides you with but a brief introduction to the topic of power. Power analyses can be conducted in many more test situations than are covered in this textbook. The interested reader is referred to more advanced texts (Cohen, 1988; Hays, 1988; Keppel, 1982).

BOX
11.1

Psychopathy and Frontal Lobe Damage

Psychopathy (currently referred to as Antisocial Personality Disorder) is a diagnostic label applied to people who exhibit a reckless disregard for the rights of others, an inability to maintain relationships, irresponsibility, lying, lack of remorse for transgressions, interpersonal manipulations, and an inability to sustain employment. Some clinicians have noted a behavioral similarity between psychopaths and individuals who have frontal lobe damage (Elliott, 1978; Schalling, 1978).

A study by Gorenstein (1982) seems to support the notion that psychopathic behavior is, in part, due to cognitive deficits associated with the frontal lobe of the cortex. (One function of the frontal lobe is to inhibit impulsivity.) Gorenstein administered a number of problem-solving tasks to a group of psychopaths and two control groups. These tasks have previously shown sensitivity in identifying frontal lobe damage. Gorenstein found a significant difference between the means of the psychopathy and control groups, with the psychopaths showing poorer performance.

Robert Hare, a well-known researcher in the area of psychopathy, has taken issue with the findings of Gorenstein. Hare raised two important issues (Hare, 1984). First, he questioned the adequacy of Gorenstein's diagnostic methods for classifying individuals as psychopaths. Second, Hare pointed to a confounding variable: there were a disproportionate number of individuals with substance abuse problems in the psychopathy group (85 percent). Using a superior research design, Hare administered the same problem-solving tasks to three groups of subjects classified as high, medium, and low on measures of psychopathy. Hare failed to reject the null hypothesis for any of the problem-solving measures. In other words, there were no significant differences between the groups. Hare concluded that ". . . there is little support for the position that psychopaths have specific cognitive deficits in the processes associated with frontal lobe functioning" (p. 139).

Note that Hare is making an interpretation of the null hypothesis, which is a risky proposition since the null hypothesis cannot be proven true. However,

let us see if a power analysis can justify Hare's "assertion of the null hypothesis."

POWER ANALYSIS

The power of a statistical test is influenced by several factors, including alpha, sample size, and the effect size (i.e., the difference between population means). One difficulty in conducting a power analysis is the specification of effect size. Recall that Cohen (1988) offered revised guidelines for interpreting effect sizes: .10 (small), .25 (medium), and .40 (large). The larger the effect size in the population, the more powerful the statistical test.

Suppose you postulate a medium effect size (using current standards) and ask the following question: "What is the probability that Hare's analysis would detect an effect size of .25?" Using the alpha level and sample size stated in the article, power was determined to be .299.[3] In other words, Hare had only a 30 percent chance of detecting a medium effect size. Accordingly, there was a 70 percent chance of making a Type II error, failing to reject a false null hypothesis. When you consider that power should be approximately 80 percent, Hare's significance test has very little power. He would have had to include 150 subjects in the study to have had an 80 percent chance of detecting a medium effect size. He used 46 subjects.

Interpreting a failure to reject the null hypothesis as saying something important about the phenomenon under study, when there is only a 30 percent chance of rejecting the null hypothesis, is difficult to justify. However, in conducting the power analysis, I selected an effect size of .25. Statisticians recommend a useful strategy for specifying effect size: Find other studies in

---

[3] I performed the power analyses using Borenstein and Cohen's software package (1988), *Statistical Power Analysis: A Computer Program.* Obtained means and standard deviations for the Wisconsin Card Sorting Test were taken from the Gorenstein (1982) and Hare (1984) articles. A power analysis using the other "significant" dependent variables in the Gorenstein study would not alter the present findings.

the same area and estimate the effect size from their sample data. Since Hare's study was based on the findings of Gorenstein, there is information available to estimate the effect size in the population.

Based on the group means, standard deviations, and the number of subjects per group reported in Gorenstein's article, the estimated effect size was found to be .56, much larger than .25. Now, what implications does this have for the power of Hare's statistical analysis? Even with 46 subjects, the probability of detecting an effect size of .56 is .93! With a 93 percent chance of correctly rejecting the null hypothesis, and only a 7 percent chance of failing to reject a false null hypothesis (Type II error), there is a much stronger justification for interpreting the importance of failing to reject the null hypothesis.

Returning to the original intent of the research, what does all this mean about psychopathy and frontal lobe damage? Can a researcher conclude that psychopaths do not have frontal lobe damage? In other words, is the null hypothesis true? There is no way of knowing. What *can* be asserted is that it is highly unlikely that there is a *large* difference between psychopaths and normal people in frontal lobe damage, at least as measured by the tests used in this research. On the other hand, since Hare's statistical power was inadequate for detecting a medium effect size, a researcher cannot conclude that there is not a moderate difference between the groups in cognitive functioning.

The plausibility of "asserting the null hypothesis" lies on a continuum. It is impossible to prove that there is no effect in the population. However, as the power of a statistical test to detect smaller and smaller effect sizes increases, an investigator can persuasively argue, "If there is an effect, it is probably quite small, and most likely trivial."

SUMMARY

The probability of correctly rejecting the null hypothesis is the power of a statistical test. The power of a statistical test is greatest when the magnitude of the treatment effect is large. Increasing the sample size in a study will also increase the power of a statistical test. The conventional figure for the desired power of a statistical test is .80, meaning there is an 80 percent chance of detecting a treatment effect (if one exists). There is a complementary relation between power and a Type II error in that power equals $1 - \beta$.

Some of the factors that influence power are alpha, the effect size in the population (γ), the variability of scores in the population, and the sample size. Effect size, or gamma, is the number of standard deviations between μ_{alt} and μ_0. Small, medium, and large effect sizes are roughly .10, .25, and .40, respectively. Increasing the sample size is one way in which a small effect size can be detected. If an investigator wants to advance a substantive interpretation about the importance of failing to reject a null hypothesis, it is essential that there has been sufficient power to detect a meaningful effect size.

KEY FORMULAS FOR CHAPTER 11

Formula for Delta

$$\delta = \gamma \sqrt{n}$$

(Formula 11.1)

Formula for Gamma

$$\gamma = \frac{\mu_{alt} - \mu_0}{\sigma}$$ *(Formula 11.2)*

Formula for Determining Sample Size for a Single-Sample Test

$$N = \left(\frac{\delta}{\gamma}\right)^2$$ *(Formula 11.3)*

WORK PROBLEMS

1. Compute effect sizes for each of the following problems.

   a. $\mu_0 = 300$, $\mu_{alt} = 345$, $\sigma = 70$
   b. $\mu_0 = 300$, $\mu_{alt} = 345$, $\sigma = 20$
   c. $\mu_0 = 300$, $\mu_{alt} = 310$, $\sigma = 20$
   d. $\mu_0 = 300$, $\mu_{alt} = 310$, $\sigma = 50$

2. Using the numbers in Problem 1, how many subjects would be needed to detect each treatment effect in the population? (Assume $\alpha = .05$, two-tailed test, and desired power is .80.)

3. A researcher conducts several studies and performs single-sample t tests with each set of the following summary data. For each case, compute the power of the statistical test. Use s as an estimate of σ. (Assume $\alpha = .05$, two-tailed test, and round off delta to the nearest first decimal place.)

   a. $\mu_0 = 130$, $\mu_{alt} = 120$, $s = 15$, $n = 10$
   b. $\mu_0 = 130$, $\mu_{alt} = 120$, $s = 15$, $n = 40$
   c. $\mu_0 = 50$, $\mu_{alt} = 52$, $s = 10$, $n = 15$
   d. $\mu_0 = 50$, $\mu_{alt} = 52$, $s = 10$, $n = 100$
   e. $\mu_0 = 25$, $\mu_{alt} = 30$, $s = 7$, $n = 30$

4. What does effect size mean in relation to power?

5. Formulate a scientific hypothesis in which support for the null hypothesis would have theoretical or practical significance. How would you discuss concepts of power so that a failure to reject the null hypothesis would impress a journal editor?

One-Way Analysis
of Variance

12.1   THE RESEARCH CONTEXT

An independent-samples *t* test can be used to test for a statistically significant difference between two means. The *t* test is ideal for studies that require a comparison between two groups. However, it is frequently the case that a researcher will use more than two groups in a study. Comparing three education programs, contrasting the effectiveness of two psychotherapy groups and a control group, and evaluating the effects of three kinds of persuasive messages on attitude change are all examples that require an analysis of more than two group means. Indeed, any study that has more than two groups lends itself to the use of an **analysis of variance (ANOVA).** One statistical approach to compare the means of a study with three or more groups is to conduct *t* tests on all possible two-group (pairwise) comparisons. For example, in a study with three groups, you could calculate *t* values for Group 1 versus Group 2, Group 1 versus Group 3, and Group 2 versus Group 3. However, conducting multiple *t* tests raises a serious statistical problem.

Multiple *t* Tests and the Type I Error

A Type I error is committed when a true null hypothesis is mistakenly rejected. The probability of making a Type I error is determined directly when setting the alpha level. Thus, when the alpha level is set at .05, and a *t* test is conducted, the probability of mistakenly rejecting a true null hypothesis is .05, *for that one t test.* Over a *series* of *t* tests, however, the probability of making a Type I error is inflated. For example, if you performed three *t* tests, the probability of a Type I error is closer to .14. If ten *t* tests were conducted, the probability of a Type I error would be an astonishing .40. Over a series of *t* tests the error rate inflates by $1 - (1 - \alpha)^c$, where *c* is the number of independent comparisons.

This alpha inflation is eliminated by using ANOVA since only one test is performed: the *F* test. The *F* test, named after its originator, Sir Ronald Fisher, provides a comparison of all the population means (see Spotlight 12.1). A significant *F* value means that at least two of the sample means come from different populations. The problem is that a significant overall *F* test does not tell you which means are significantly different from one another. To make *pairwise* comparisons among all the means, special analyses are used that control the Type I error rate. One such analysis is presented at the end of this chapter.

 A **one-way ANOVA** is used in designs having one independent variable of three or more levels. If the design has two levels of one independent variable— that is—two groups, an ANOVA can be used instead of a simple *t* test. Both tests will lead to the same conclusion, however. If your design has two independent variables, a two-way ANOVA is used. (The two-way ANOVA is discussed in Chapter 13.) By its name, analysis of variance, it may seem that the ANOVA is a test of variances. However, the analysis contrasts *means* by examining the sources of variation in the data. The ANOVA allows the researcher to conclude whether the group means come from identical or different populations. How this is accomplished will become clear as the discussion progresses.

Sir Ronald Fisher

Ronald Fisher (1890–1962) was born in England. He is considered a child prodigy. His daughter and biographer offers the following story.

At about age three when he had been set up in his high chair for breakfast, he asked: "What is a half of a half?" His nurse answered that it was a quarter. After a pause, he asked, "And what's a half of a quarter?" She told him that it was an eighth. There was a longer pause before he asked again, "What's a half of an eighth, Nurse?" When she had given her reply there was a long silence. Finally, Ronnie looked up, a plump pink and white baby face framed with waving red-gold hair, and said slowly, "Then, I suppose that a half of a sixteenth must be a thirty-toof." (Box, 1978, pp. 12–13).

Fisher's early mathematical ability flourished and led to the development of the most popular significance test in experimentation: the analysis of variance (ANOVA).

Fisher received his training in mathematics at Cambridge, and subsequently taught math in public schools. His daughter points out that he was a lousy teacher and hated the noble profession. In 1917 he married Ruth Guinness, the cousin of the well-known Irish brewery operators. (You may recall that Gossett developed the *t* test while employed by Guinness.) When he quit teaching, Fisher was offered two jobs. One was an offer from Karl Pearson, who Fisher disliked

because Pearson, as the editor of *Biometrica,* kept rejecting Fisher's articles. The other offer was from the Rothamsted Experimental Station, the oldest agricultural research station in the world. It was here that Fisher made many of his most brilliant statistical and research design contributions.

One of the problems in agricultural experimentation was how to determine the effects of a multitude of variables on plant yield; factors for consideration were soil, fertilizer, weeds, seeds, and weather. Fisher devised several experimental designs suited to answer these questions. Some research-design terminology dates from this period, for example, the *split-plot* design. The nature of the experimental questions led Fisher to develop the factorial design and the analysis of variance. To appreciate the context within which Fisher was working, it is interesting to note that the article that presented the ANOVA is titled "Studies in Crop Variation. II. The Manurial Response of Different Potato Varieties" (Fisher and MacKenzie, 1923).

Fisher's contributions covered a broad range. He is responsible for many of the common terms in statistics: *variance, randomization,* and *statistic*—the latter term to refer to a quantity based on sample data. Fisher also worked out many sampling distributions that allow for hypothesis testing, and was an influential figure in establishing the 5 percent level of significance as the conventional cutoff for rejecting the null hypothesis.

12.2 THE CONCEPTUAL BASIS OF ANOVA: SOURCES OF VARIATION

Between-Group Variation

If you conduct a study with two or more groups, the resulting group means will almost never be identical. This is true whether or not there is an experimental effect. Your task is to decide if the independent variable has influenced the group means. Your decision will be based on the outcome of a significance test. When the group means are similar, there is little variation between the means. When the means are very different, there is a greater degree of variation between the means. The difference between the means is called **between-group variation.** The question is: what could account for the differences among group means? There are three possible explanations for between-group variation.

1. ***Treatment Effect.***   The effect is due to treatment—that is—the effect is caused by the independent variable. This source of variation is what researchers attempt to maximize.

2. ***Individual Differences.***   Each research participant comes to the experiment with a unique constellation of personality traits, called *subject variables* (see Chapter 1). Since each subject is unique, he or she will inevitably respond differently to the task used to assess the influence of the independent variable. Even though subjects are randomly assigned to treatment conditions, it is possible for group means to differ because of individual differences. For example, consider a study comparing three teaching techniques. If, by chance, brighter students are assigned to one treatment condition, this treatment group may show superior performance—not because of the teaching technique (the independent variable) employed—but because of unequally distributed individual differences.

3. ***Experimental Error.***   There are several potential sources of experimental error. Measuring instruments might be unreliable. For example, polygraph recordings can be influenced by power surges. Some subjects might be distracted while listening to experimental instructions or when completing a task. The experimenter might deliver instructions inconsistently to subjects. In short, any uncontrolled aspect of the experiment could account for the variation among group means. These uncontrolled aspects of the experiment intrude *unsystematically.* (Do not confuse experimental error with confounding. Confounds *systematically* vary among the groups and provide unintended, yet plausible explanations for differences among group means. Because experimental error influences data in an unsystematic manner, confounding is not at issue.)

 Individual differences and experimental error are considered **random factors.** They are called random because they are not intentionally and systematically manipulated by the experimenter, yet they may intrude and produce differences between means. In summary, any one, or combination, of the foregoing reasons could explain the variation among means. The other source of variation in an experiment is the variation within each group.

Within-Group Variation

 Between-group variation considers the variation between means. **Within-group variation** refers to the variation among scores *within* a group. Irrespective of whether there is a treatment effect, would you expect every person within a given group to obtain the exact same score? They won't, for the following two reasons.

1. ***Individual Differences.*** The variation among means could be due to individual differences. However, when considering the variation of *scores within a group,* individual differences always produce variability. Once again, let's the teaching technique example. With respect to *between-group variation,* an individual difference variable (IQ) could be unequally distributed *across* groups and could present a confound that accounts for differences among means. With respect to *within-group variation,* the focus shifts to just one given group (it doesn't matter which one). Students in the group will vary in IQ. Some measure of the effectiveness of the teaching technique will be administered. Whether the technique improves learning, there will be *within-group variation* among the scores of the dependent variable because there are differences among the students in IQ. Each group in the study will show within-group variability. In considering the study as a whole, the overall amount of within-group variability is based on a combination of the within-group variation in each of the groups.

2. ***Experimental Error.*** The variation among scores within a group could also be due to experimental error. The errors are the same as those that occur in between-group variation. Since individual differences and experimental error are random factors, the only source of variation within groups is due to random factors. The treatment administered to each group does not contribute to within-group variability since each subject in a group is exposed to the same treatment.[1] The analysis of variance is a statistical technique that analyzes the sources of variability in the experiment. The sources of variation are depicted in the diagram of Figure 12.1.

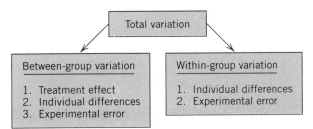

Figure 12.1 The ANOVA partitions the sources of variation in an experiment into between-group variation and within-group variation.

---

[1] ANOVA assumes that the effect of a treatment is to add a constant to, or subtract a constant from, each score within a group.

Sources of Variation When the Null Hypothesis is Correct and Incorrect

 The amount of variation due to treatment is called **treatment variance.** The variation due to random factors (individual differences and experimental error) is called **error variance.**

Suppose H_0 is true (there is *no* treatment effect). In this instance, any difference between the means is completely due to the random variation of scores within the groups. Since group means will never be identical—even when H_0 is correct—the question becomes, "How different do the means have to be to conclude that there is an effect due to treatment?" To reject the null hypothesis, the between-group variation has to be sufficiently greater that the overall within-group variation in the experiment. The F test is the ratio between these two measures of variation.

$$F = \frac{\text{treatment variance} + \text{error variance}}{\text{error variance}}$$

Stated differently,

$$F = \frac{\text{between-group variance}}{\text{within-group variance}}$$

In the absence of a treatment effect, the between-group variance will be nothing but error variance. Hence, when H_0 is correct, the F ratio will be close to

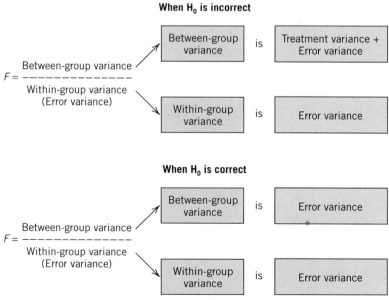

Figure 12.2 Sources of variance when the null hypothesis is correct and incorrect.

1 (error variance divided by error variance). As the influence of treatment becomes stronger, the F ratio becomes larger. The larger the value of F, the more likely it is statistically significant.

Between-group variation refers to the difference among group means. When H_0 is correct, any differences between groups are due entirely to error variance. When H_0 is false, the difference between means is due to error variance plus the treatment effect. As the amount of between-group variation due to treatment increases, the numerator of the F ratio obviously becomes larger. If the effect of treatment is sufficiently great, then the F ratio will achieve significance. Figure 12.2 summarizes the sources of variance when H_0 is correct and incorrect.

Assumptions of the Analysis of Variance

Following is a list of assumptions underlying the ANOVA. Note that the assumptions are the same as those for the independent-samples t test.

1. ***Normally distributed population distributions.***   This assumption states that each sample is drawn from a population that is normally distributed.

2. ***Homogeneity of variances.***   The variances of each population distribution are the same, thus: $\sigma_1^2 = \sigma_2^2 = \sigma_3^2 \cdots = \sigma_k^2$, where k is the last group. Since the F test is *robust*, it is not essential that the first two assumptions be met, particularly if each sample contains the same number of subjects. However, gross violations of these assumptions will adversely affect the validity of the F test. These violations would require the use of a type of analysis that does not require assumptions about the shape of the population distributions (see Chapter 18).

3. ***Independent observations.***   It must be the case that each *observation* within a group be independent of all other observations. One example of how this assumption could be violated is when studying social interactions. Suppose you want to measure hostile remarks between two subjects placed under stress. When the first subject says something hostile, the likelihood of the second subject responding with hostility is increased. The hostility scores of each subject are linked; in other words, the scores are *not independent.* If you include the data from both subjects in your stress condition, the independence assumption is violated. The fact that the F test is robust is of no help when this assumption is violated.

The Null and Alternative Hypotheses

The ANOVA provides a direct test of the null hypothesis, which is always:

$$H_0: \quad \mu_1 = \mu_2 = \mu_3 = \mu_k$$

A significant difference between any two means will yield a significant F test. The alternative hypothesis is always:

$$H_1: \text{ at least two of the means are different}$$

Note that H_1 is not $\mu_1 \neq \mu_2 \neq \mu_3 \neq \mu_k$. This erroneous statement of the alternative hypothesis would indicate that all the means are significantly different from one another. However, a significant F ratio can be obtained when just two of the means are significantly different.

Mean Square Within: One Estimate of σ^2

Recall the two population assumptions underlying the analysis of variance: the populations from which the samples are drawn are normal and the populations have the same variances. Since you have already learned the logic of hypothesis testing in previous chapters, you know that when testing a null hypothesis you proceed as if the null hypothesis is true. Although all the mathematics takes place at the level of samples, the real question is, do the samples come from one population or several populations? If you find a significant difference among the sample means, then you conclude that the samples were drawn from different populations. If there is no significant difference between means, then you conclude that the samples were drawn from the same population.

Whether you are conducting a single-sample t test, an independent-samples t test, or a dependent-samples t test, there is *always* an estimate made of the population variance. To decide if a difference between means is unlikely, you need an estimate of how variable the distribution is from which you are sampling. The analysis of variance is no different in this regard, so you need an estimate of σ^2.

In a study with three groups, there are three estimates of σ^2: s_1^2, s_2^2, and s_3^2. Which one should be used? Rather than rely on any one of the estimates, why not use all of them? The best estimate of σ^2 is made by pooling the variances of the samples. The term that is used for the pooled variance is the **Mean Square Within (MS_W)**. You have encountered this concept before. You may recall from the discussion of the independent-samples t test that the denominator of the t test is the pooled variance, which is a weighted average of the variances of two samples. The MS_W term merely extends the pooled variance to more than two groups.

Pooled Variance Formula for MS_W

$$MS_W = \frac{s_1^2(n_1 - 1) + s_2^2(n_2 - 1) + \cdots + s_k^2(n_k - 1)}{(n_1 - 1) + (n_2 - 1) + \cdots + (n_k - 1)}$$ *(Formula 12.1)*

Since MS_W is a combination of sample variances, the degrees of freedom associated with MS_W is also the addition of each of their respective degrees of freedom.

$$df_W = (n_1 - 1) + (n_2 - 1) + (n_k - 1) = N - k$$

where,
$N =$ total number of subjects
$k =$ number of groups or designation for last group

The MS_W is a good estimate of σ^2 (error variance). Most importantly, it is a good estimate of σ^2 when H_0 is correct and when H_0 is incorrect. The MS_W is based on the pooled average of the within-group variances. In the absence of a treatment effect, the sample variances are all taken from the same population. When there is a treatment effect, you are, in fact, sampling from different populations. In either case, MS_W is a good estimate of σ^2 because the ANOVA assumes: $\sigma_1^2 = \sigma_2^2 = \sigma_k^2$.

Mean Square Between: Another Estimate of σ^2

The numerator of the F ratio is the average variation among the group means, the **Mean Square Between** (Groups), MS_{BG}. When H_0 is true, the only source of variation among the group means is random factors (error variance). When there is a treatment effect, the variation among group means is due to the treatment effect *plus* error variance. When H_0 is true, the average variation among the means is nothing but error variance. Thus, when H_0 is true, MS_{BG} and MS_W are both estimating the same value, σ^2. However, unlike MS_W, MS_{BG} is not always a good estimate of σ^2. At this point, what is needed is a measure of the amount of variation among the means.

You have learned of a measure that serves as an index of the amount of variation among means. A sampling distribution of means has a standard deviation, the standard error of the mean ($\sigma_{\bar{x}}$). In fact, the relation between the population standard deviation and the standard error of the mean is $\sigma_{\bar{x}} = \sigma/\sqrt{n}$. Since variances, not standard deviations, are used in ANOVA, both sides of the equation are squared to obtain:

$$\sigma_{\bar{x}}^2 = \frac{\sigma^2}{n}$$

Multiplying each side of the equation by n gives:

$$n\sigma_{\bar{x}}^2 = \sigma^2$$

When using sample means to estimate σ^2, simply treat the sample means as raw scores, apply your favorite formula for calculating the *variance* (not standard deviation), and multiply the result by n ($n =$ the number of subjects in any group, assuming equal numbers of subjects). The between-groups *estimate* of σ^2 is given by Formula 12.2.

> **Between-Group Variance (MS_{BG}) as an Estimate of σ^2**
>
> $$ns_{\overline{x}}^2 = \sigma^2 \qquad \textit{(Formula 12.2)}$$

This is the measure of between-group variance. Table 12.1 presents an example of how to calculate the between-group variance using this method. The means are borrowed from Table 12.2. Note that the three means are treated not only as raw scores but as a *sample* of scores that *estimate* σ^2. Hence, a sample formula for s^2 is used. As you examine the computational flow of the problem, keep in mind that the n in the $s_{\overline{x}}^2$ formula refers to the number of groups, which you are treating as if they are individual scores. (Since you are computing the variance of *means*, the symbol $s_{\overline{x}}^2$ is used instead of s^2.) The n in the formula for between-group

TABLE 12.1 **Between-Group Variation—The Variance of the Sample Means Multiplied by Sample Size**[a]

$$\overline{X}_1 = 4.75$$
$$\overline{X}_2 = 8.75$$
$$\overline{X}_3 = 2.25$$
$$n = 3 \text{ (number of groups)}$$
$$\Sigma X^2 = 104.19$$
$$\Sigma X = 15.75$$

$$s_{\overline{x}}^2 = \frac{\Sigma X^2 - [(\Sigma X)^2/n]}{n-1}$$

$$s_{\overline{x}}^2 = \frac{104.19 - [(15.75)^2/3]}{3-1}$$

$$= \frac{104.19 - [248.06/3]}{2}$$

$$= \frac{104.19 - 82.69}{2}$$

$$= \frac{21.50}{2}$$

$$s_{\overline{x}}^2 = 10.75$$

Between-group variance $= ns_{\overline{x}}^2$

$$ns_{\overline{x}}^2 = (4)(10.75)$$
$$= \mathbf{43}$$

[a] The n in the formula for $s_{\overline{x}}^2$ is the number of group means; the n in the formula $ns_{\overline{x}}^2$ is the number of subjects in one group, assuming equal numbers of subjects per group.

variance, $ns_{\bar{x}}^2$, refers to the number of subjects in *each* of the samples ($n_1 = n_2 = n_3 = 4$), not the total number of subjects across all groups.

Putting It All Together

MS_W is a good estimate of σ^2—whether H_0 is correct or incorrect. If H_0 is correct, then you are sampling from one population; thus, you have several estimates of the variance of that one population. If H_0 is incorrect, then you are sampling from more than one population. One of the assumptions of ANOVA is that, when sampling from more than one population (as is the case when H_0 is incorrect), the variances of the populations are the same—that is, $\sigma_1^2 = \sigma_2^2 = \sigma_k^2$. Since $\sigma_1^2 = \sigma_2^2 = \sigma_k^2$, whether there is one or several populations is not important since the same value is being estimated by the sample variances.

The situation is different with respect to the variance of the group means (between-group variance). This variance, which conceptually is like the standard

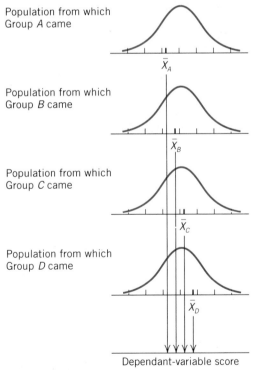

Population from which
Group *A* came

$\bar{X}_A$

Population from which
Group *B* came

$\bar{X}_B$

Population from which
Group *C* came

$\bar{X}_C$

Population from which
Group *D* came

$\bar{X}_D$

Dependant-variable score

Figure 12.3   When H_0 is true, the sample means are drawn from identical populations, which, in effect, is the same as saying "drawn from one population." Here you would expect the sample means to show little variation.

error of the mean, is a good estimate of σ^2 only when it is based on a sampling distribution established by taking repeated samples from *one* population. Here is the beauty of the analysis of variance. When H_0 is correct—that is—all the sample means in the experiment come from the same population, $ns_{\bar{x}}^2$ (between-group variance, MS_{BG}) is a good estimate of σ^2. If $ns_{\bar{x}}^2$ is a good estimate of σ^2, then it should be very close to the value of MS_W. If these two estimates of σ^2 are similar, the F ratio will be close to 1. However, if the sample means come from different populations, $ns_{\bar{x}}^2$ will be a poor estimate of σ^2, although MS_W remains a good estimate. When $ns_{\bar{x}}^2$ is a poor estimate of σ^2 it will *overestimate* σ^2. The greater the differences among the sample means, the larger the overestimate of σ^2. Since $ns_{\bar{x}}^2$ is the measure of between-group variance, it is placed in the numerator of the F ratio. The result is an F ratio that becomes larger as the value of $ns_{\bar{x}}^2$ increases.

A point that has been stressed throughout this text, which cannot be over-emphasized, is that hypothesis testing uses samples to draw conclusions about populations. You fly blind, in a sense, because you *never* know the true nature of the populations. Tests of significance involve logic and mathematics as aids to allow the researcher to infer the characteristics of populations; yet all inferences involve a degree of uncertainty. Figures 12.3 and 12.4 illustrate the inferential situation in which a researcher is involved when using samples to make statements

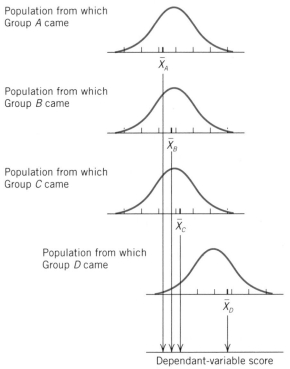

Figure 12.4 When H_0 is false, at least one sample is drawn from a population that is different from the rest.

about populations. In Figure 12.3, a study with four groups is illustrated under the condition that the null hypothesis is true. When the null hypothesis is true, the four populations that are sampled are identical—that is—they have the same means and variances. Sampling from four identical populations is like sampling from one population. The four arrows at the bottom of Figure 12.3 reflect the sample means. Note that they are close together; they show little variability. This is just what you would expect when taking random samples from four identical populations (or four samples from the same population). In Figure 12.4, the sample means depicted by the arrows at the bottom of the diagram are more variable. Why? Because the population from which the fourth sample was drawn has a mean that is greater than that of the other three populations.

12.3   COMPUTING THE *F* RATIO IN ANOVA

Both MS_{BG} and MS_W are measures of variation. They are appropriately termed *Mean* Square Between and *Mean* Square Within because they reflect the average (mean) amount of variation. MS_{BG} is the average variation of the group means around the grand mean. The **grand mean** is the mean of all the scores in the experiment, irrespective of individual groups. MS_W is the average amount of variation of the individual scores with respect to the group from which the scores are taken.

MS_{BG} and the Sum of Squares Between (SS_{BG})

The definitional and computational formulas used to compute MS_{BG} and MS_W are presented in this section. Immediately following the presentation of formulas, a hypothetical data set will be used to illustrate the steps for computing MS_{BG}, MS_W, and the *F* ratio.

MS_{BG} is a ratio of SS_{BG} divided by the degrees of freedom for SS_{BG}. (Degrees of freedom is discussed later.) Formula 12.3 is the definitional formula for SS_{BG}.

Definitional Formula for SS_{BG}

$$SS_{BG} = \Sigma n_k (\overline{X}_k - \overline{X}_G)^2 \qquad \textit{(Formula 12.3)}$$

where,
n_k = the number of subjects in group k
$\overline{X}_k$ = the mean of group k
$\overline{X}_G$ = grand mean

This formula shows that SS_{BG} is the variation of group means about the grand mean. To use this formula in computing SS_{BG}, you would subtract the grand mean from the mean of group 1, square the value, and multiply by the number of subjects in that group. Perform the same set of operations for each of the group means in the experiment. Finally, sum all the values.

Formula 12.4 is the computational formula for calculating SS_{BG}.

Computational Formula for SS_{BG}

$$SS_{BG} = \frac{(\Sigma X_1)^2}{n_1} + \frac{(\Sigma X_2)^2}{n_2} + \cdots + \frac{(\Sigma X_k)^2}{n_k} - \left[\frac{(\Sigma X)^2}{N} \right] \quad \textit{(Formula 12.4)}$$

where,

ΣX_1 = the sum of scores in group 1

ΣX_2 = the sum of scores in the second group, and so on

ΣX_k = the sum of scores in the last group; if the experiment has four groups then ΣX_k is the sum of scores in group 4

ΣX = sum of all the scores in the study

n_1 = the number of subjects in group 1

n_k = the number of subjects in the last group

N = total number of subjects in the study

MS_W and the Sum of Squares Within (SS_w)

MS_W is a ratio of SS_W divided by the degrees of freedom associated with SS_W. The definitional formula for SS_W (Formula 12.5) reminds us that within-group error variance is the amount of deviation of individual scores about the mean of the group from which the scores are taken.

Definitional Formula for SS_w

$$SS_W = \Sigma(X_1 - \overline{X}_1)^2 + \Sigma(X_2 - \overline{X}_2)^2 + \cdots + \Sigma(X_k - \overline{X}_k)^2 \quad \textit{(Formula 12.5)}$$

where,

$\overline{X}_1$ = the mean of group 1; $\overline{X}_2$ is the mean of group 2

$\overline{X}_k$ = the mean of the last group

X_1 = each score in group 1

X_2 = each score in group 2

X_k = each score in the last group

If using the definitional formula for computing SS_W, subtract the mean of group 1 from the first score in that group and square the value. Repeat the operation for each raw score in group 1. Next, sum all these squared deviation scores. Do the same for each group in the study, remembering to use the relevant group mean. The sums of the squared deviations for each group are then summed. The computational formula is given in Formula 12.6.

Computational Formula for SS_W

$$SS_W = \Sigma X^2 - \left[\frac{(\Sigma X_1)^2}{n_1} + \frac{(\Sigma X_2)^2}{n_2} + \cdots + \frac{(\Sigma X_k)^2}{n_k} \right] \qquad \text{(Formula 12.6)}$$

where,

ΣX^2 = sum of *all* squared scores
$(\Sigma X_1)^2$ = the sum of the scores in group 1, quantity squared
$(\Sigma X_2)^2$ = the sum of the scores in group 2, quantity squared
$(\Sigma X_k)^2$ = the sum of the scores in the last group, quantity squared
n_1 = number of subjects in group 1
n_k = number of subjects in the last group

The Total Sum of Squares (SS_T)

SS_T is not used when computing the *F* ratio. The Total Sum of Squares equals the Sum of Squares Between plus the Sum of Squares Within:

$$SS_T = SS_{BG} + SS_W$$

Independently computing SS_T allows you to make sure that your SS_{BG} and SS_W calculations are accurate. The definitional formula for SS_T reveals the fact that the total variation in scores is the difference between each score in the study and the grand mean, squared and summed.

Definitional Formula for SS_T

$$SS_T = \Sigma(X - \overline{X}_G)^2 \qquad \text{(Formula 12.7)}$$

where,

X = each score in the study
$\overline{X}_G$ = grand mean

When using the definitional formula, simply subtract the grand mean from each score, squaring each difference as you go. Finally, sum all the squared values.

Formula 12.8 is the computational formula for SS_T.

Computational Formula for SS_T

$$SS_T = \Sigma X^2 - \frac{(\Sigma X)^2}{N}$$ *(Formula 12.8)*

where,

ΣX^2 = the sum of *all* squared scores
$(\Sigma X)^2$ = the sum of *all* scores, quantity squared
N = the total number of subjects

Degrees of Freedom

To arrive at the F ratio, SS_{BG} and SS_W must be divided by their appropriate degrees of freedom to compute MS_{BG} and MS_W. Dividing by df makes a Sum of Squares an average Sum of Squares, which is what Mean Squares is. The degrees of freedom for the between-groups term (df_{BG}) is:

$$df_{BG} = k - 1$$

where,

k = the number of groups

The degrees of freedom used for the within-groups term, df_W, is:

$$df_W = (n_1 - 1) + (n_2 - 1) + \cdots + (n_k - 1) = N - k$$

The degrees of freedom for SS_T is $N - 1$. Although SS_T is not divided by its degrees of freedom (df_T), calculating df_T can serve as a computational check since

$$df_T = df_{BG} + df_W$$

Computing MS_{BG} and MS_W is accomplished in the following manner.

Calculating MS_{BG} and MS_W

$$MS_{BG} = \frac{SS_{BG}}{df_{BG}}$$

$$MS_W = \frac{SS_W}{df_W}$$

and, of course,

$$F = \frac{MS_{BG}}{MS_W}$$

Illustrating the Computational Steps with Raw Data

Table 12.2 presents the raw scores and summary statistics for a hypothetical study with three groups. These data will be used to illustrate the computational steps required to arrive at the *F* ratio. The calculations can be tedious but you have had extensive practice in performing the arithmetic operations needed to compute *F*.

Step 1.   Compute SS_{BG} using Formula 12.4.

Computational Formula for SS_{BG}

$$SS_{BG} = \frac{(\Sigma X_1)^2}{n_1} + \frac{(\Sigma X_2)^2}{n_2} + \cdots + \frac{(\Sigma X_k)^2}{n_k} - \left[\frac{(\Sigma X)^2}{N}\right]$$

$$SS_{BG} = \frac{(19)^2}{4} + \frac{(35)^2}{4} + \frac{(9)^2}{4} - \left[\frac{(19 + 35 + 9)^2}{12}\right]$$

$$= 416.75 - 330.75$$

$$SS_{BG} = 86$$

Step 2.   Compute df_{BG}: $df_{BG} = k - 1 = 3 - 1 = 2$.
Step 3.   Calculate MS_{BG}.[2]

$$MS_{BG} = \frac{SS_{BG}}{df_{BG}}$$

$$= \frac{86}{2}$$

$$MS_{BG} = 43$$

TABLE   12.2   **Hypothetical Raw Data and Summary Statistics for a Study with Three Groups**

Group 1		Group 2		Group 3	
S_1	4	S_5	8	S_9	3
S_2	5	S_6	8	S_{10}	2
S_3	4	S_7	9	S_{11}	1
S_4	6	S_8	10	S_{12}	3
$\overline{X}_1 = 4.75$		$\overline{X}_2 = 8.75$		$\overline{X}_3 = 2.25$	
$\Sigma X_1 = 19$		$\Sigma X_2 = 35$		$\Sigma X_3 = 9$	
$\Sigma X_1^2 = 93$		$\Sigma X_2^2 = 309$		$\Sigma X_3^2 = 23$	
$n_1 = 4$		$n_2 = 4$		$n_3 = 4$	

[2] Refer to Table 12.1. Note that the value computed for MS_{BG} is the same as the value arrived at by using $ns_{\overline{x}}^2$.

Step 4.   Compute SS_W using Formula 12.6.

Computational Formula for SS_W

$$SS_W = \Sigma X^2 - \left[\frac{(\Sigma X_1)^2}{n_1} + \frac{(\Sigma X_2)^2}{n_2} + \cdots + \frac{(\Sigma X_k)^2}{n_k} \right]$$

$$SS_W = (4)^2 + (5)^2 + (4)^2 + \cdots + (2)^2$$

$$+ (1)^2 + (3)^2 - \left[\frac{(19)^2}{4} + \frac{(35)^2}{4} + \frac{(9)^2}{4} \right]$$

$$= 425 - 416.75$$

$$SS_W = 8.25$$

Step 5.   Compute df_W: $df_W = N - k = 12 - 3 = 9$.
Step 6.   Compute MS_W.

$$MS_W = \frac{SS_W}{df_W} = \frac{8.25}{9}$$

$$MS_W = .92$$

Step 7. (Optional)   Compute SS_T using Formula 12.8.

Computational Formula for SS_T

$$SS_T = \Sigma X^2 - \frac{(\Sigma X)^2}{N}$$

$$SS_T = (4)^2 + (5)^2 + (4)^2 + \cdots + (2)^2 + (1)^2 + (3)^2 - \left[\frac{(63)^2}{12} \right]$$

$$= 425 - 330.75$$

$$SS_T = 94.25$$

If the calculations are correct then SS_T should equal $SS_{BG} + SS_W$:

$$SS_T = SS_{BG} + SS_W$$

$$94.25 = 86 + 8.25$$

Even though SS_T is not used to calculate F, you are strongly urged to use SS_T as a computational check. The vast number of calculations required almost guarantees that you will make at least one undetected error. (After arriving at SS_T, I discovered that I had made four undetected errors in calculating SS_{BG} and SS_W!)

Step 8.   Compute the F ratio.

$$F = \frac{MS_{BG}}{MS_W}$$

$$F = \frac{43}{.92}$$

$$F = \mathbf{46.74}$$

12.4 TESTING FOR STATISTICAL SIGNIFICANCE

The *F* Distributions

The shape of each distribution in a family of sampling distributions is affected by the sample size used in repeated sampling. For this reason, when testing the significance of t_{obt} you find the critical value by using the appropriate degrees of freedom. Likewise, when testing the significance of the *F* statistic, the sampling distribution of relevance is an **F distribution** based on the same degrees of freedom associated with the numerator and denominator of the *F* ratio.

As is the case with all sampling distributions, an *F* distribution is theoretical in that you never go through the arduous task of establishing the sampling distribution. Since the *F* statistic is a ratio of variances, it should make sense to you that the sampling distributions of *F* are based on ratios of variances.

Recall that the *F* ratio is:

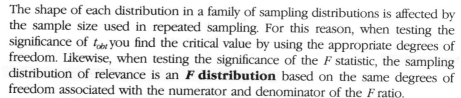

When the null hypothesis is true, there is no treatment effect—that is—there is no treatment variance in the numerator of the *F* ratio. Thus, when H_0 is true:

$$F = \frac{MS_{BG}}{MS_W} = \frac{\text{error variance}}{\text{error variance}}$$

The sampling distributions of *F* ratios are established under the assumption that the null hypothesis is true, $\mu_1 = \mu_2 = \mu_3 = \mu_k$. Here is how you would go about constructing one sampling distribution of *F* ratios. Imagine that you conduct an experiment with four groups, six subjects in each group ($df_{BG} = 3$, $df_W = 20$), and the null hypothesis is true. MS_{BG} is obtained by computing the variance of the four group means. MS_W is obtained by computing the pooled, within-group variance. The *F* ratio is then calculated. Since the null hypothesis is true—no treatment variance—MS_{BG} and MS_W both reflect nothing but error variance. Since both values are estimates of the same thing, they should be equal, and the *F* ratio will be 1. Constructing the sampling distribution proceeds by conducting the same experiment, still with H_0 true, and computing another *F* ratio. The process continues an infinite number of times. The resulting F distribution (sampling distribution) is a frequency distribution of F ratios, for $df_{BG} = 3$ and $df_W = 20$.

Given the foregoing method for generating a sampling distribution of F ratios, what must be true about an F distribution?

1. Since variability can never be indexed by a negative number, all F values must be positive.
2. The smallest value that F can obtain is 0.
3. Since H_0 is true, MS_{BG} and MS_W independently estimate the same value; therefore most F ratios cluster around 1.
4. Even when H_0 is true, due to sampling error, F ratios can be very large.
5. F distributions are positively skewed.

When testing the significance of an obtained F value, a sampling distribution is available that matches the degrees of freedom appropriate to the number of groups (numerator) and the number of subjects (denominator) in the study. The exact shape of an F distribution will depend on the number of groups and sample sizes used to calculate the F ratios. Figure 12.5 shows two F distributions that are based on different degrees of freedom. Note that as the degrees of freedom change, and thus the shape of the F distribution changes, the critical values beyond which lie 5 percent and 1 percent of the F ratios shift accordingly.

As you examine Figure 12.5, bear in mind that the F distributions are distributions obtained when H_0 is true. Note that the number of F ratios comprising the F distribution become fewer and fewer as the value of F increases. When deciding whether to reject H_0, you have one F ratio available. If the F ratio obtained from your study falls in the right tail of the distribution, say, beyond the point that marks the upper 5 percent of the distribution, you have a decision to make. Either

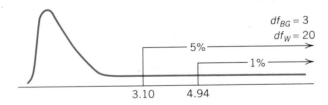

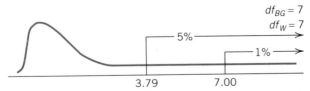

Figure 12.5 Two F distribution for $df_{BG} = 3$ and $df_W = 20$, and $df_{BG} = 7$ and $df_W = 7$.

the null hypothesis is true and sampling error has given rise to an unlikely large F ratio, or the null hypothesis is false and MS_{BG} is influenced by a treatment effect. Here the logic of significance testing directs you to reject the null hypothesis.

Using the *F* Table

The F table in Appendix B.5 is used to determine if an F ratio is statistically significant. The following is a portion of the table. The F table provides critical values for alphas of .05 and .01. The boldface values in the body of the table are used when testing at the 1 percent level of significance. The critical values in lightface type are the cutoffs beyond which lie 5 percent of the F ratios.

.05 (roman) and .01 (boldface) α *levels for the F distribution*

		Degrees of Freedom (Numerator)		
		$\cdots 3$	4	$5 \cdots$
	$\vdots$			
	19	3.13	2.90	2.74
		5.01	**4.50**	**4.17**
Degrees of	20	3.10	2.87	2.71
Freedom (Denominator)		**4.94**	**4.43**	**4.10**
	21	3.07	2.84	2.68
		4.87	**4.37**	**4.04**
	$\vdots$			

Locating the relevant critical value is accomplished by entering the table with the degrees of freedom from the numerator of the F ratio, df_{BG}, and the degrees of freedom from the denominator of the F ratio, df_W. The degrees of freedom for MS_{BG} is found in the row at the top of the table and the degrees of freedom for MS_W is found in the left column of the table. When testing the significance of an F ratio where $df_{BG} = 4$ and $df_W = 20$, the critical values for the 5 percent and 1 percent levels of significance are 2.87 and 4.43, respectively.

Let's test the significance of the F ratio found in the worked example using an alpha of .05. The obtained F was 46.74. The $df_{BG} = 2$ $(k - 1)$ and $df_W = 9$ $(N - k)$. Referring to the F table in Appendix B.5, the critical value is thus 4.26. Since the obtained F value is larger than the critical value of 4.26, you reject the null hypothesis that $\mu_1 = \mu_2 = \mu_3$.

12.5   THE ANOVA SUMMARY TABLE

Table 12.3 is one customary way to summarize the results of an ANOVA. The values in the table are taken from the worked example. Some source tables substitute the word Treatment for Between groups and Error for Within groups. The ANOVA table supplies the most relevant information used in calculating the F ratio.

TABLE 12.3 **An ANOVA Summary Table**[a]

Source of Variation	SS	df	MS	F	p
Between groups	86	2	43	46.74	< .05
Within groups (error)	8.25	9	.92		
Total	94.25	11			

[a] See text for computations.

12.6 REPORTING THE RESULTS OF THE ANOVA

Every journal has a standard format for reporting the results of a statistical test in the text of an article. Most psychology journals rely on the format offered by the American Psychological Association (APA, 1984). When reporting a significant F, you must include the df_{BG}, df_W, the F value and the level of significance. For instance, "The effect of the drug was most pronounced when administered in the morning instead of the evening, $F(3, 69) = 9.59$, $p < .05$."

Box 12.1 presents a study on the topic of people's loyalty to a group. The experiment has three groups, yet the researchers did not use an ANOVA. This raises an important statistical issue that is discussed in Box 12.1.

BOX 12.1

Initiation Rites and Club Loyalty

Many clubs require an initiation. The rites of passage may range from simply learning a password and a secret handshake to initiations that are life threatening. The more dramatic displays of fraternity hazing have been banned by universities amid reports of fatalities. The Marine Corps is infamous for its treatment of young men and women during basic training. Yet it is a common observation that clubs that require severe initiations have a great deal of group cohesion and many members that remain loyal for a lifetime. One explanation for this observation is that clubs that require severe initiations attract a certain type of person who is prone to develop strong loyalties. However, might there be something about the kind of initiation experienced by club members and their subsequent feelings about the group? This is the question asked by

Aronson and Mills (1959). Due to a self-selection factor that invariably operates in club membership, only a randomized, controlled experiment could discover if there is a causal relationship between severity of initiation and attitudes of the initiate toward the club.

One theory that can account for this initiation-induced loyalty phenomenon is *cognitive dissonance* (Festinger, 1957). According to this theory, we are strongly inclined to maintain consistency between our attitudes and behavior. When an attitude that we hold is inconsistent with our behavior, a state of dissonance arises, creating an unpleasant psychological state. A reduction in dissonance can be accomplished by altering our behavior, or more commonly, by changing our attitude so that consonance is achieved. How does this relate to initiations and club loyalty? No matter how attractive a group is to someone, there are always some negative aspects of the group. After going through an unpleasant initiation, a state of dissonance arises. It's as if the person asks, "How could I have gone through all this when there are things about this group that I do not like?" To resolve the dissonance, the person can either view the initiation as not that bad, or disregard the negative aspects of the group and magnify the positive characteristics of the group. The more unpleasant the initiation, the more difficult it is to view the initiation as not that bad. The only avenue left to achieve consonance is to see the group as more positive. The more severe the initiation, the more positive the person will tend to see the group. In other words, the greater the dissonance, the larger the shift in how one perceives the group. Aronson and Mills tested this theory in the following manner.

Sixty-three female undergraduates volunteered to join a discussion group, ostensibly so that the researchers could study the dynamics of group interaction. The subjects were told that they would have to be screened before being allowed to join the group, and since the discussion topic was to be sexual behavior, it was important that they be able to discuss the topic freely. The "screening" constituted the experimental manipulation. In the Severe condition, subjects were required to read aloud a number of obscene words related to sex and body parts (e.g., fuck, cock, screw, etc.) (We can speculate that this task was much more stressful for subjects in 1959 than would be the case today.) Moreover, the participants were told that the experimenter was rating them on how embarrassed they appeared while reading the words, and that the ratings would be used to determine if they would be admitted to group membership. Subjects in the Mild condition read words that were related to sex but were not obscene (e.g., virgin, prostitute, and petting). Those subjects assigned to the Control condition were not required to read any words; their admission to the group was based only on their willingness to discuss the topic of sex. Of course, irrespective of performance, all subjects were admitted to the "club."

The subjects were told that their participation would begin at the next meeting. However, in order for the subjects to "become familiar with the group discussion" they were allowed to listen, via intercom, to a discussion among other initiates. Subjects actually heard a tape recording of three women discussing the sexual practices of lower animals. The discussion was dull, trite, and filled with contradictions. Depending on the condition to which the subject was assigned, dissonance had been created. After going through the initiation they would become a member of a club that would include rather unimpressive people who discussed a potentially interesting topic in a boring manner.

After listening to the discussion, subjects completed a questionnaire, which asked them to rate the discussion and the participants along a number of dimensions (e.g., dull-interesting, intelligent-unintelligent). The sum of the ratings served as the dependent variable. One dependent variable was the ratings of the *discussion;* a second dependent variable was the ratings of the *participants.* The authors predicted that the more severe the initiation, the more positive would be subjects' ratings of the discussion *and* the three group members heard on the tape. To test their hypothesis, they performed multiple *t* tests, making all possible comparisons among group means, for each dependent variable.

With respect to the ratings of the discussion, subjects in the Severe condition offered more positive ratings of the discussion than those subjects in the Mild and Control conditions. No significant differences were found between the Mild and Control groups. Thus, it would appear that people who experience a severe initiation reduce dissonance by increasing their positive evaluations of the discussion among the members of the group.

The second dependent variable was especially important because it reflected the subjects' favorable regard toward the other members of the group. Did the experimental manipulation influence the subjects' liking for the other participants in the group discussion? According to the *t* tests, the answer was a qualified yes. The difference between the Severe and Control conditions was statistically significant. However, there were no differences between the Severe and Mild conditions, nor the Mild and Control conditions. Based on all of these analyses, the authors concluded, "The results clearly substantiate the hypothesis: persons who undergo a severe initiation to attain membership in a group increase their liking for the group" (p. 181).

You have learned that multiple *t* tests should not be conducted in the absence of a significant *F* ratio. Aronson and Mills (1959) neglected to perform the requisite *F* tests on the dependent variables. Instead they proceeded straight to the multiple comparisons. What would have happened if the *F* tests were conducted? Since the authors reported means and standard deviations, I used Formulas 12.1 and 12.2 to compute an F ratio for each dependent variable. The F test for the Discussion ratings was significant, $F(2, 60) = 6.54$, $p < .05$. For this variable, the authors were warranted in conducting the t tests. However, the F test performed on the ratings of the participants was nonsignificant, $F(2, 60) = 2.81$. Thus, for this dependent variable, the authors should *not* have performed t tests when mak-

ing all possible comparisons among the means of the groups.

The findings of this study are not as "clean" as they originally appeared. The reanalysis suggests a more limited conclusion than the one made by the authors. A researcher would now conclude that a severe initiation increases liking for the *opinions* of the group but not necessarily the *members* of the group.

12.7   AN EXAMPLE OF ANOVA WITH UNEQUAL NUMBERS OF SUBJECTS

When conducting an experiment it is always desirable to use the same number of subjects in each experimental condition. The best reason for this practice is that it makes any violation of the population assumptions underlying the test less serious. However, sometimes subjects drop out of the study and replacing them is difficult or impossible. The same formulas that were used in the worked example, in which the number of subjects in each group were equal, can be used when there are an unequal number of subjects in the groups. This is possible since the formulas used sample sizes as weights when multiplying variances.

Consider the following hypothetical study. A child psychologist is interested in evaluating the effectiveness of two treatments for children who are afraid of the dark. One treatment, Emotive Imagery, teaches the children to imagine that they are brave superheroes, like Wonder Woman or Superman, on a mission to save a friend. A second treatment, Relaxation, involves training other fearful children to breathe slowly and deeply when they are in the dark. A third condition serves as a control condition and these children are simply asked to remain in the dark as long as they can. The dependent variable is the number of seconds elapsed before the child turns on the light. Table 12.4 presents raw data, summary statistics, the calculation of the F ratio, and the ANOVA summary table.

12.8   STRENGTH OF ASSOCIATION

The F test provides information about a significant difference between at least two means of a study. A significant F ratio indicates that the observed differences between means are unlikely to occur by chance. Stated differently, the sample means are unlikely to have come from the same population.

The critical value used when testing the significance of an F ratio depends on df_{BG} and df_W. The power of the F test (the likelihood of rejecting the null hypothesis) is partly due to the sample size used in the study. A look at the F table reveals that as your sample size increases, the critical F value *decreases*. In other words, it is increasingly easier to find a significant difference among means as the number of subjects in the study increases. What you should be most interested

TABLE 12.4 An ANOVA with Unequal Numbers of Subjects[a]

Emotive Imagery	Relaxation Training	Control
40	33	23
45	39	32
45	51	33
53	40	29
49	42	40
	40	25
		28
$\overline{X}_1 = 46.40$	$\overline{X}_2 = 40.83$	$\overline{X}_3 = 30.00$

$\Sigma X_1 = 232$	$n_1 = 5$	$df_{BG} = k - 1 = 2$
$\Sigma X_2 = 245$	$n_2 = 6$	$df_W = N - k = 15$
$\Sigma X_3 = 210$	$n_3 = 7$	$df_T = N - 1 = 17$
$\Sigma X_G = 687$	$N = 18$	
$\Sigma X^2 = 27527$		

$$SS_{BG} = \frac{(232)^2}{5} + \frac{(245)^2}{6} + \frac{(210)^2}{7} - \left[\frac{(687)^2}{18}\right] = 848.47$$

$$MS_{BG} = \frac{SS_{BG}}{df_{BG}} = \frac{848.47}{2} = 424.24$$

$$SS_W = 27527 - \left[\frac{(232)^2}{5} + \frac{(245)^2}{6} + \frac{(210)^2}{7}\right] = 458.03$$

$$MS_W = \frac{SS_W}{df_W} = \frac{458.03}{15} = 30.54$$

$$SS_T = 27527 - \frac{(687)^2}{18} = 1306.50$$

$$F = \frac{MS_{BG}}{MS_W} = \frac{424.24}{30.54} = \mathbf{13.89}$$

$$F_{df} = 2,15$$

$$\alpha = .05$$

$$F_{crit} = 3.68$$

$$H_0: \quad \mu_1 = \mu_2 = \mu_3$$

Since **13.89** > 3.68, reject the null hypothesis.

Source of Variation	SS	df	MS	F	p
Between groups	848.47	2	424.24	13.89	< .05
Within groups (error)	458.03	15	30.54		
Total	1306.50	17			

[a] The dependent variable is the number of seconds until the child turns on the light. The variation among means is sufficiently large to reject the null hypothesis. Therefore you conclude that the treatment approaches are differentially effective in altering children's fear of the dark.

in is not how statistically significant the F ratio is, but rather how strongly the treatment conditions have affected the subjects' performance on the dependent variable. If in one study the F value was found to be significant at the 1 percent level, and in another study the F was discovered to be significant at the 5 percent level, it would be a mistake to assume that the magnitude of the treatment effect was stronger in the first study. Statisticians have developed several measures of the *strength of relationship* between the independent variable and the variation of scores on the dependent variable (see Keppel, 1982, pp. 89–95). The statistic offered here is an index of the estimated magnitude of the treatment effect in the population, **omega-squared (ω^2)**. Omega-squared is easy to calculate, requiring only values from the ANOVA summary table.

Formula for Omega-Squared, ω^2

$$\omega^2 = \frac{SS_{BG} - (k-1)MS_W}{SS_T + MS_W} \quad \textbf{\textit{(Formula 12.9)}}$$

Using the values from Table 12.2, what is ω^2?

$$\omega^2 = \frac{86 - 2(.92)}{94.25 + .92}$$

$$= \frac{84.16}{95.17}$$

$$\omega^2 = \mathbf{.88}$$

The interpretation of $\omega^2 = .88$ is that 88 percent of the variation in scores is accounted for by the levels of the independent variable. The total amount of variation in the data is due to treatment effect plus random factors. Omega-squared estimates the amount of variation due to treatment. When ω^2 is less than 100 percent, the difference between ω^2 and 100 percent is the amount of variation due to random factors. Thus, if $\omega^2 = 88$ percent, then 12 percent of the variation in scores is due to random factors. Logically, ω^2 can range from 0–100 percent. Is 88 percent a large treatment effect? Yes, very large! In fact, it would be highly unlikely that such an effect size would be shown in the real world of behavioral science research. Cohen (1977) suggests a rough guide for interpreting the size of ω^2. A large effect is when ω^2 is greater than 15 percent, a medium effect is when ω^2 is around 6 percent, and a small effect size is when ω^2 is equal to 1 percent. Clearly, at least in behavioral research, scientists deal with independent variables that have a relatively weak influence on behavior. It is a rather humbling experience to obtain a "highly significant" F ratio, only to see that the effect size is 3 percent.

In a recently published study, an F value of 1.23 was found to be statistically significant beyond the 2 percent level of significance (Hupka and Eshett, 1988).

An *F* of 1.23 is usually nonsignificant, but the degrees of freedom were 192 and 13440. Using the formula for ω^2, we find that the effect size is .003 percent![3] It is hoped that reporting ω^2, or other available indices of effect size, will become a common practice in psychology journals.

12.9 LOCATING THE SOURCE OF SIGNIFICANCE: THE PROTECTED *t* TEST

After obtaining a significant *F* ratio, the researcher knows that at least two of the means come from different populations. But that is all that is known. It is hard to imagine a situation in which a researcher would not want to discover which means are different from one another; however, the matter is a bit more complicated. An investigator may wish to make all possible comparisons among the means, which is the most typical course of action. In a study with three groups, three comparisons would be required, with four groups, six comparisons would be made. The number of all possible comparisons is $k(k-1)/2$. Although some comparisons may have important theoretical implications, other comparisons between means may be of no interest to the investigator. Deciding to make all possible comparisons among means *after* observing the sample data is called **post hoc** or **posteriori tests.** When a researcher decides to test a specific set of null hypotheses before collecting the data, the analyses are called **a priori tests** or planned comparisons. A priori tests often involve only a subset of all possible comparisons among sample means. Whether a priori or post hoc tests are performed is determined by the nature of the hypotheses in the study. In addition, controlling the probability of a Type I error is still an issue, even when making comparisons after obtaining a significant *F* value. The topic of **multiple comparisons** is complex and the investigator has many statistical issues and options to consider. For example, some post hoc tests are only allowed if there is a significant *F* test. The post hoc test presented at the end of this section is a case in point. Other post hoc tests can be used without even performing an *F* test (e.g., Tukey's HSD). When reading journal articles, be alert to some of the common procedures for multiple comparisons: Scheffé, Newman-Keuls, Duncan, and Bonferroni corrected *t* tests. Of course, you will be able to identify that a multiple comparisons test is used by its context. Even a cursory coverage of this area is beyond the scope of this book; the interested reader is referred to Kirk (1982). This text presents the **Fisher LSD (Least Significant Difference)** test, also called the **protected *t* test.** Carmer and Swanson (1973) have shown that, when compared to other tests of multiple comparisons, Fisher's LSD test performs well under many circumstances. However, Hochberg and Tamhane (1987) advise against using this test when making all possible comparisons with more than three sample means. Under these conditions alpha begins to inflate beyond the 5 percent level.

---

[3] I would like to thank Professor Hupka for making the summary statistics available that allowed for the computation of ω^2.

To use the protected t test, it is essential that the ANOVA yield a significant F ratio. With this requirement, the probability of a Type I error is much less than if the ANOVA were bypassed and multiple t tests performed. Formula 12.10 is the formula for the protected t test.

$$
\boxed{
\begin{array}{c}
\textbf{Formula for Fisher's LSD Test} \\[2mm]
t = \dfrac{\overline{X}_i - \overline{X}_j}{\sqrt{MS_W\left(\dfrac{1}{n_i} + \dfrac{1}{n_j}\right)}} \qquad \textit{(Formula 12.10)}
\end{array}
}
$$

The formula for the protected t test is different from what you have encountered when conducting independent- or dependent-samples t tests. Even though only two means are contrasted in Formula 12.10, the pooled variance used is MS_W and is based on the variance estimates from *all* the groups in the study. The result is a more stable estimate of the population variance. The protected t test consequently has more power than an independent-samples t test when multiple comparisons are performed.

If your study has three groups and you wish to make all possible comparisons, you will have to perform three protected t tests (Group 1 versus Group 2; Group 1 versus Group 3; Group 2 versus Group 3). The means in the numerator will change with each test, n_i and n_j may change, depending on sample sizes, but MS_W is taken from the ANOVA, and remains *the same* for each analysis. The critical

TABLE 12.5 Protected t Tests Following a Significant ANOVA[a]

Emotive Imagery	Relaxation Training	Control
$\overline{X}_1 = 46.40$	$\overline{X}_2 = 40.83$	$\overline{X}_3 = 30.00$
$n_1 = 5$	$n_2 = 6$	$n_3 = 7$

$MS_w = 30.54$ (taken from the ANOVA)

$$\overline{X}_1 \text{ versus } \overline{X}_2 = \frac{46.40 - 40.83}{\sqrt{30.54(1/5 + 1/6)}} = \frac{5.57}{3.36} = \textbf{1.66} \ (n.s.)$$

$$\overline{X}_1 \text{ versus } \overline{X}_3 = \frac{46.40 - 30.00}{\sqrt{30.54(1/5 + 1/7)}} = \frac{16.40}{3.22} = \textbf{5.09} \ (p < .05)$$

$$\overline{X}_2 \text{ versus } \overline{X}_3 = \frac{40.83 - 30.00}{\sqrt{30.54(1/6 + 1/7)}} = \frac{10.83}{3.13} = \textbf{3.46} \ (p < .05)$$

df for t's = $df_W = N - k = 18 - 3 = 15$
  $\alpha = .05$
$t_{\text{crit}} = 2.13$

[a] The t tests are based on the ANOVA in Table 12.4.

value is based on $N - k$ degrees of freedom and is found in the *t* table, *not* the *F* table. Using the data from Table 12.4, Table 12.5 provides an example of how protected *t* tests are conducted. Each comparison uses an alpha level of .05.

The results of the protected *t* tests show that both Emotive Imagery and Relaxation are more effective than the control condition in reducing children's fear of the dark, $t(15) = 5.09$, $p < .05$; $t(15) = 3.46$, $p < .05$, respectively. No significant difference between the treatment conditions was found, $t(15) = 1.66$, $p > .05$. The three *t* test comparisons have allowed you to locate the source of significance detected by the *F* test.

SUMMARY

A one-way ANOVA can be used when a study has two or more levels of one independent variable. When conducting an ANOVA it is assumed that the *k* populations are normally distributed with equal variances. Minor violations of these assumptions are not serious since the *F* test is robust. However, it is essential that each subject's score on the dependent variable be independent of every other subject's score.

The variation among scores within each group is due to random factors: individual differences and experimental error. The influence of random factors creates error variance, also called within-group variance. Between-group variance is caused by error variance and the effect of the treatment variable (if any). For the *F* test to achieve significance, the between-group variance has to be sufficiently greater than the within-group variance.

The *F* ratio is MS_{BG}/MS_W. Both MS_{BG} and MS_W are estimates of the population variance. The MS_W is a good estimate of σ^2, irrespective of whether H_0 is correct. The MS_{BG} is only a good estimate of σ^2 when H_0 is correct. When H_0 is incorrect, MS_{BG} overestimates σ^2 and the *F* ratio becomes increasingly larger than 1. For a given MS_W, as the effect due to treatment becomes greater, the *F* ratio becomes larger.

The sampling distribution (*F* distribution) that is used to test the significance of the *F* ratio is determined by the df_{BG} $(k - 1)$ and df_W $(N - k)$. Although the shape of the *F* distribution will vary depending on sample sizes, the *F* distribution is always positively skewed.

The size of the *F* ratio is not an indication of the magnitude of the treatment effect. To assess the strength of association between the independent variable and the variation of scores on the dependent variable, ω^2 is used. To locate the source of a significant *F* test, Fisher's LSD can be used to make pairwise comparisons between means.

KEY FORMULAS FOR CHAPTER 12

Pooled Variance Formula for MS_w

$$MS_W = \frac{s_1^2(n_1 - 1) + s_2^2(n_2 - 1) + \cdots + s_k^2(n_k - 1)}{(n_1 - 1) + (n_2 - 1) + \cdots + (n_k - 1)} \qquad \text{(Formula 12.1)}$$

Between-Group Variance (MS_{BG}) as an Estimate of σ^2

$$ns_{\bar{x}}^2 = \sigma^2 \qquad \text{(Formula 12.2)}$$

Definitional Formula for SS_{BG}

$$SS_{BG} = \Sigma n_k(\bar{X}_k - \bar{X}_G)^2 \qquad \text{(Formula 12.3)}$$

Computational Formula for SS_{BG}

$$SS_{BG} = \frac{(\Sigma X_1)^2}{n_1} + \frac{(\Sigma X_2)^2}{n_2} + \cdots + \frac{(\Sigma X_k)^2}{n_k} - \left[\frac{(\Sigma X)^2}{N}\right] \qquad \text{(Formula 12.4)}$$

Definitional Formula for SS_W

$$SS_W = \Sigma(X_1 - \bar{X}_1)^2 + \Sigma(X_2 - \bar{X}_2)^2 + \cdots + \Sigma(X_k - \bar{X}_k)^2 \qquad \text{(Formula 12.5)}$$

Computational Formula for SS_W

$$SS_W = \Sigma X^2 - \left[\frac{(\Sigma X_1)^2}{n_1} + \frac{(\Sigma X_2)^2}{n_2} + \cdots + \frac{(\Sigma X_k)^2}{n_k}\right] \qquad \text{(Formula 12.6)}$$

Definitional Formula for SS_T

$$SS_T = \Sigma(X - \bar{X}_G)^2 \qquad \text{(Formula 12.7)}$$

Computational Formula for SS_T

$$SS_T = \Sigma X^2 - \frac{(\Sigma X)^2}{N} \qquad \text{(Formula 12.8)}$$

$$SS_T = SS_{BG} + SS_W$$

Formula for Omega-Squared, ω^2

$$\omega^2 = \frac{SS_{BG} - (k-1)MS_W}{SS_T + MS_W} \qquad \text{(Formula 12.9)}$$

Formula for Fisher's LSD Test

$$t = \frac{\bar{X}_i - \bar{X}_j}{\sqrt{MS_W\left(\frac{1}{n_i} + \frac{1}{n_j}\right)}} \qquad \text{(Formula 12.10)}$$

WORK PROBLEMS

1. A sports psychologist would like to compare the effects of different exercise programs on cardiovascular fitness. The measure of fitness is the resting heart rate of subjects after they complete the program, with lower heart rates in-

dicating greater physical fitness. Twelve college students are randomly assigned to three groups (four subjects per group). Subjects in the Aerobic condition walk a treadmill for 30 minutes, three times a week. Subjects in the Circuit condition perform exercises on weight machines for 30 minutes, with a 10-second rest between exercises. In the Control condition, subjects are asked to simply maintain their usual amount of exercise. The resting heart rates of all subjects are taken after 10 weeks. Data from this hypothetical study are presented in the following table.

Aerobic	Circuit	Control
65	74	74
62	65	78
56	62	86
60	72	75

a. State the null and alternative hypotheses.
   Calculate the following values.
b. SS_{BG} e. df_W h. SS_T
c. SS_W f. MS_{BG} i. df_T
d. df_{BG} g. MS_W j. F ratio
k. What is F_{crit} for the 5 percent level of significance?
l. Should you retain or reject H_0?
m. Make an ANOVA summary table.
n. Provide a nonstatistical interpretation of the results.
o. Calculate omega-squared and interpret.
p. Conduct protected t tests if appropriate and interpret.
q. Does this F test allow for a causal interpretation?

2. A political scientist hypothesizes that persons from the midwest part of the United States are more conservative in their political views than individuals from either coast of the country. Five subjects between the ages of 21 and 60 are randomly selected from the western, midwestern, and eastern parts of the nation ($N = 15$). A questionnaire measuring conservatism is administered, with higher scores reflecting greater conservatism. The data are presented in the following table.

West	Midwest	East
3	9	4
6	15	9
2	9	1
4	4	2
3	6	3

a. State the null and alternative hypotheses.
   Calculate the following values.
b. SS_{BG} e. df_W h. SS_T
c. SS_W f. MS_{BG} i. df_T
d. df_{BG} g. MS_W j. F ratio

    k. What is F_{crit} for the 5 percent level of significance?
    l. Should you retain or reject H_0?
    m. Make an ANOVA summary table.
    n. Provide a nonstatistical interpretation of the results.
    o. Calculate omega-squared and interpret.
    p. Conduct protected t tests if appropriate and interpret.
    q. Does this F test allow for a causal interpretation?

3. A clinical psychologist is interested in evaluating treatments for panic attacks. The number of reported panic attacks during the 6-month program of treatment is used as the dependent variable. Fifteen clients suffering from panic disorder are randomly assigned to three conditions (five subjects per group). In the Breathing condition, clients are taught how to breathe slowly and deeply at the first sign of an attack. Clients in the Medication condition are administered 1 mg of Xanax, three times a day. Clients in the Control condition are not provided with any treatment. The data are presented in the following table.

Breathing	Medication	Control
16	12	9
22	15	12
15	13	16
9	18	18
13	12	10

    a. State the null and alternative hypotheses.
      Calculate the following values.
    b. SS_{BG} e. df_W h. SS_T
    c. SS_W f. MS_{BG} i. df_T
    d. df_{BG} g. MS_W j. F ratio
    k. What is F_{crit} for the 5 percent level of significance?
    l. Should you retain or reject H_0?
    m. Make an ANOVA summary table.
    n. Provide a nonstatistical interpretation of the results.
    o. Calculate omega-squared and interpret.
    p. Conduct protected t tests if appropriate and interpret.
    q. Does this F test allow for a causal interpretation?

4. State the sources of variance of the numerator of the F ratio when H_0 is correct and when H_0 is incorrect.

5. Why is an F distribution always positively skewed?

6. True or False. In a study that has two levels of one independent variable, it is better to conduct an F test rather than a t test because the F test is more powerful.

7. What are the three sources of variation that can account for mean differences?

8. What are the two sources of variation that can account for within-group variability?

9. Why do most F ratios in the F distribution cluster around 1?

Work Problems for the Computer

10. A clinical psychologist hypothesizes that tension produced by frustration can be relieved if the person is allowed to respond aggressively. However, it is unknown what form the aggression must take in order for tension reduction to occur. All subjects in the experiment are asked to complete an intellectually demanding task. While working on the task, the experimenter keeps interrupting the subject, correcting mistakes, offering advice, and slowing the progress of the subject. After this phase of the experiment, the independent variable is defined by the opportunity afforded the subject to express aggression. In the Overt Aggression condition, subjects become a "teacher" and are required to administer a loud, noxious noise when a confederate-learner makes a mistake on a memory task. In the Verbal Aggression condition, subjects are asked to write an evaluation of the experimenter, which will be made available to the experimenter's supervisor. In the Fantasy Aggression condition, subjects are administered the Thematic Apperception Test. This test is comprised of several pictures depicting, for the most part, interpersonal scenes. The subject is asked to make up a story for each card, thus allowing for the expression of aggressive fantasies. The dependent variable is the change in systolic blood pressure from just after the frustration induction experience to just after the opportunity for subjects to express aggression.

Use $\alpha = .05$ to test the null hypothesis. Conduct all possible post hoc comparisons if the *F* test is significant. You can either use Fisher's LSD or the method of pairwise comparisons offered in your statistical package.

OPPORTUNITY FOR AGGRESSION		
Overt	*Verbal*	*Fantasy*
−10	−2	0
−5	+2	−4
−8	0	0
−3	−1	+5
−11	−5	0
+3	+1	−2
−15	−9	0
+3	−1	−2
+4	0	−6
−12	−3	−2
−3	−5	−4
+6	−1	0

11. Researchers have noted that chronic severe muscle-contraction headaches respond quite well to antidepressant medication, as well as biofeedback for relaxing the muscles of the forehead (Bourianoff and Stubis, 1988). A health psychologist is interested in making a direct comparison between these two modes of treatment. Forty-five headache sufferers are randomly assigned to three conditions: Medication, Biofeedback, and No Treatment control. Treatment lasts for 5 months, during which time the number of weekly headaches is recorded. Conduct an *F* test ($\alpha = .05$) and post hoc comparisons to determine the relative effects of these three treatment conditions. The raw scores

are the average number of headaches per week, over the 5-month period of treatment.

Medication	Biofeedback	Control
2	4	5
1	2	7
2	3	8
6	5	10
7	4	8
8	2	2
6	7	8
3	4	8
2	0	2
0	3	5
1	0	1
2	5	6
0	1	2
4	2	1
5	3	8

Two-Way Analysis of Variance

13.1   THE RESEARCH CONTEXT

Factorial Designs

In previous chapters, experimental designs were presented with only one independent variable. However, we do not live in a "one-variable world." Our behavior is constantly affected by the combined influence of two or more sets of conditions. For this reason, the majority of experimental designs used in behavioral research are constructed in a manner that allows the researcher to evaluate the **interaction** among independent variables, and how this interaction produces behavioral effects (Edgington, 1974). **Factorial designs** are a blend of two or more single-variable designs. In using a factorial design, an investigator can ascertain information about the effect of each independent variable, thus saving the time, expense, and effort required to conduct separate, single-variable experiments. Most importantly, by combining independent variables, information can be gained about the combined effect of the independent variables on the dependent variable. When factorial designs are used, there is always a prediction made regarding an interaction. The researcher believes that the effect of one independent variable will be altered, depending on the value of the second independent variable. An example serves to illustrate this point.

If you saw someone in trouble would you come to his or her aid? As you think about this question you may answer, "it depends." It may depend on how many people are present, how dangerous the situation is, or it may even depend on what the person in trouble looks like (Latane and Darley, 1970). "It depends" qualifies your answer, which, in effect, says your action is determined by the joint presence of certain conditions. For instance, you may only help *if* it's not too dangerous *and* you are the only person around to offer assistance. In the language of factorial designs, this is an interaction effect since your behavior depends on the joint occurrence of two or more variables.

Examples of Factorial Designs and Cell Notations

Three examples of factorial designs are provided. A system of notation is used to identify each **cell** of the design, which is called an *AB* matrix. Each cell corresponds to a treatment condition, and each treatment condition is one group of subjects. Each independent variable is referred to as a **factor** (thus the name factorial design). When there are two independent variables, one variable is designated Factor *A* and the other Factor *B*. A cell designation of A_1B_3 refers to the group of subjects who are in the first level of Factor *A* and the third level of Factor *B*. In Example 1 below, A_1B_3 refers to the subjects who have an anxiety disorder with panic attacks (first level of Factor *A*) and receive Tofranil (third level of Factor *B*). By convention, when the design is depicted with two rows and three columns, it is referred to as a 2 × 3 (pronounced "2 by 3") factorial design. If one of the independent variables has more levels than the other independent variable, the variable with more levels is usually placed at the top of the figure, thus creating more columns than rows. For instance, a 2 × 4 factorial design would be stated as such, instead of referred to as a 4 × 2 factorial design. In addition, either independent variable can be designated Factor *A*.[1]

▶   EXAMPLE 1   A psychiatrist is interested in comparing the effectiveness of three different psychopharmacological treatments for anxiety with two types of

---

[1] Some statistical software programs will ask you to enter the data for A_1B_1, A_2B_1, and so on. Make sure that there is agreement between you and the program as to which variable is designated Factor *A* and which is Factor *B*.

patients, those with and without panic attacks. Factor *A* is *type of patient,* Factor *B* is *treatment,* and the dependent variable is the subjects self-reports of anxiety. This design is a 2 × 3 factorial design.

	Factor B		
	Valium	*Xanax*	*Tofranil*
Anxiety with Panic	A_1B_1	A_1B_2	A_1B_3
Anxiety without Panic	A_2B_1	A_2B_2	A_2B_3

Factor A (labels the rows)

◀

▶ **EXAMPLE 2** A social psychologist hypothesizes that two advertising techniques will be differentially effective, depending on the product. Factor *A* is the advertising technique, Factor *B* is the product, and the dependent variable is the subjects' attitudes toward the product. This design is a 2 × 2 factorial design.

	Factor B	
	Autos	*Stereos*
Image Appeal	A_1B_1	A_1B_2
Technical Information	A_2B_1	A_2B_2

Factor A (labels the rows)

◀

▶ **EXAMPLE 3** A psychologist hypothesizes that aggression is more likely when a person is physiologically aroused *and* is exposed to aggressive cues. Factor *A* is arousal, Factor *B* is the presence or absence of aggressive cues, and the dependent variable is aggression.

	Factor B: (Aggressive Cues)	
	Present	*Absent*
Aroused	A_1B_1	A_1B_2
Not Aroused	A_2B_2	A_2B_2

Factor A (labels the rows)

◀

Main Effects and Interactions

To illustrate how two single-independent variable experiments can be combined in one factorial design, consider two hypothetical studies on memory.

In Experiment 1, a psychologist hypothesizes that memory will be better if a person is in a good mood when attempting to *recall* a list of words. On the first day of the study, all participants are given a list of words to memorize. A test for recall is conducted on the second day, with half of the subjects tested immediately after reading a mood-elevating passage. The other half of the subjects are tested after reading a depressing passage. Accordingly, those subjects who just finished the mood-elevating passage should remember more words than the subjects who just finished the depressing passage (see Experiment 1, Table 13.1).

In Experiment 2, a researcher hypothesizes that memory will be best if an individual is in a good mood while *memorizing* a list of words. Thus, the mood manipulation—reading a happy or depressing passage—is accomplished on the first day, just prior to having the subjects memorize the word list. On the second day all subjects are asked to recall as much of the list as they can. This experiment is also depicted in Table 13.1

Now suppose a psychologist develops a state-dependent theory of memory in which it is predicted that memory will be facilitated when a person recalls a list of words while in the same emotional state that existed when the list was memorized. Neither one of the experiments in Table 13.1 can test this hypothesis since the prediction requires experimentally manipulating mood state during memorization *and* inducing a mood state during recall. However, by combining the two studies, you can obtain all the information gathered from each single-variable experiment, as well as the interactive effects of the two independent variables. A treatment difference between the levels of one independent variable is called a **main effect.** If the independent variables combine to produce an effect, there is an **interaction** between Factor *A* and *B*.

The two independent variables are Mood During Recall and Mood During Memorization. Each independent variable, or factor, has two levels: Happy and Sad. The formal name of this design is a *Completely Randomized 2 × 2 Factorial Design*. It is completely randomized in that subjects are randomly assigned to the four treatment conditions. It is a factorial design because there is more than one independent variable. And it is a 2 × 2 because there are two levels of each factor

---

TABLE   13.1   **Two Separate Between-Group Designs, Each with One Independent Variable**[a]

Experiment 1: Mood State During Recall

Day 1	*Day 2*
Both groups memorize list	Group 1: Recall While Happy
	Group 2: Recall While Sad

Experiment 2: Mood State During Memorization

Day 1	*Day 2*
Group 1: Memorize While Happy	Both groups recall list
Group 2: Memorize While Sad	

[a] In Experiment 1, the independent variable is "mood during recall." In Experiment 2, the independent variable is "mood during memorization." In both experiments the dependent variable is the number of words recalled correctly.

(Happy/Sad During Memorization and Happy/Sad During Recall). Table 13.2 illustrates this 2 × 2 factorial design.

Using Diagrams and Graphs to Examine Main Effects and Interactions

How to *speculate* about the presence of both main effects and an interaction by viewing diagrams and graphs is addressed in this section. You must conduct statistical analyses to discover if there really are main effects and an interaction. Not only is it helpful to graph group means before performing a statistical analysis, but researchers often display graphs as a visual accompaniment to the verbal summary of the results of the study.

Throughout this section, we will stay with the 2 × 2 memory experiment. Group means will be altered in each successive example so that you can learn what the diagrams and graphs look like as the experimental results change. A word of caution: if you read the text without referring to the relevant diagrams and graphs, you will get lost. You need to bounce back and forth between the illustrations and the text to understand the discussion.

In Table 13.2, the numbers within each cell are group means representing the number of words recalled. The means in the margins (called marginal means) are averaged across rows and columns. Let's first consider each independent variable separately. When addressing only Factor B, the question is, "What is the effect of mood state during recall on the number of words remembered?" The average of cells 1 and 3 versus the average of cells 2 and 4 reveals no difference in the marginal means—both are 15 ($\overline{X}_{B_1} = 15$ and $\overline{X}_{B_2} = 15$). Comparing the levels within one independent variable allows you to determine if there is a main effect for that factor. Since, in this example, there is no main effect for Factor B, you would conclude that the mood state present *during recall* has no effect on the number of words remembered.

The same logic is applied when considering Factor A. Now the question is, "What is the effect of mood state during memorization on later recall?" Examine the marginal row means. The average of cells 1 and 2 versus 3 and 4 are identical

TABLE 13.2 **A 2 × 2 Factorial Design with a Significant Interaction and No Significant Main Effects**[a]

		Factor B: Mood During Recall		
		Happy	*Sad*	
Factor A: Mood During Memorization	*Happy*	(1) 20	(2) 10	$\overline{X}_{A_1} = 15$
	Sad	(3) 10	(4) 20	$\overline{X}_{A_2} = 15$
		$\overline{X}_{B_1} = 15$	$\overline{X}_{B_2} = 15$	

[a] The numbers in parentheses are group designations, also called cell numbers.

($\overline{X}_{A_1} = 15$ and $\overline{X}_{A_2} = 15$). There is no main effect for Factor *A*. Therefore, you would conclude that recall is unaffected by the mood state present *during memorization*. Bear in mind that these data are hypothetical. The marginal means in Table 13.2 have purposely been presented as identical to simplify the example. With real data, the marginal means are rarely identical, even when there is no main effect. Nevertheless, if each independent variable were examined in separate, single-variable studies, each study would be a wash-out. However, by using a factorial design, a third question is possible: "Does the mood state during memorization interact with the mood state during recall?" Although there are no main effects in this study, it would appear that there is an interaction. By examining the pattern of means within the cells, you may conclude that recall is facilitated when there is a congruence between mood during memorization and mood during recall. It doesn't seem to matter what the moods are as long as they are similar.[2] These results would thus lend support to the proposed state-dependent theory of memory.

When speculating on an interaction, in addition to examining the cell (group) means, a graph of the means proves helpful. Figure 13.1 is a graph of the means presented in Table 13.2.

When graphing means from a factorial design, the levels of one independent variable are indicated on the horizontal axis. In Figure 13.1, Mood During Recall has been placed on the horizontal axis. The dependent variable is represented as

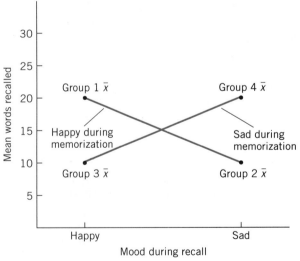

Figure 13.1 A graph of the group means in Table 13.2. There is an interaction but no main effects.

---

[2] Since this example uses a 2 × 2 design, the interaction is examined by taking the average of the diagonals. Thus the average of cells 1 and 4 is 20 and the average of cells 2 and 3 is 10. The difference between the marginal means of 10 and 20 (not depicted) likely indicates an interaction effect. This method *only* applies to a 2 × 2 factorial design since any other factorial design (e.g., a 2 × 3) will not have diagonals.

means on the vertical axis. The second independent variable is placed within the graph. In the example, the second independent variable is Mood During Memorization. Students often have trouble transferring the means from a table onto a graph. In a 2 × 2 factorial design, there will be two lines. If Factor *B* is put on the horizontal axis, then the two lines correspond to the two *levels* of Factor *A*. Do not make the mistake of thinking that each line depicts each independent variable.[3]

In Figure 13.1, the line drawn from the upper left to the lower right of the graph represents the Happy Mood During Memorization level of Factor *A*. The line connects the means of two groups: Happy During Memorization/Happy During Recall (Group 1) and Happy During Memorization/Sad During Recall (Group 2). Examine the means in Table 13.2 and the graph in Figure 13.1 so that you understand how the means are plotted and the lines are drawn. Which points on the graph correspond to which group means is indicated. This information is an aid to you and is not included when graphing.

Table 13.2 illustrates data in which there are no main effects but there is an interaction. On a graph, *an interaction is revealed when the lines are not parallel.* Figure 13.1 reveals the interaction; the lines are not only nonparallel, they cross. The lines, however, do not have to cross when there is an interaction, they just have to be nonparallel. It is unclear how nonparallel the lines need to be in order to say there is an interaction. Yet, the more they depart from being parallel, the more likely it is that there is an interaction. Only by performing a statistical test could you, in fact, tell if there is an interaction.

Thus far, data have been used in which there is an interaction but no main effects. We will now use the same experiment, adjust the cell means, and illustrate various combinations of main effects and interactions.

The data in Table 13.3 show a main effect for Factor *B* but no main effect for Factor *A* and no interaction. Although the marginal means for Factor *A* are not identical, this does not necessarily indicate a main effect. However, since the means are so close, it is safe to say there is no significant effect here. Factor *B* is another matter. The marginal means of 29 and 11 are strikingly different and, thus, a main effect likely exists.

The interpretation of the experimental results depicted in Table 13.3 is as follows. The number of words remembered is greatest when participants are happy during the recall task (main effect for Factor *B*). It makes no difference what mood subjects are in when they memorize the word list (no main effect for Factor *A*). Further, whether the mood states during memorization and recall are congruent or incongruent is of no consequence (no interaction effect).

Figure 13.2 graphically displays the means in Table 13.3. Notice that the lines are parallel, reflecting the absence of an interaction. When examining a graph for a main effect, look to see if one of the lines is higher than the other; if so, then there may be a main effect. In identifying a main effect, to what extent does one line have to be higher than the other? Only a statistical analysis can identify the

---

[3] Another common mistake among students is thinking that the number of cells equals the number of independent variables. Keep in mind that independent variables *always* have levels.

TABLE 13.3 A 2 × 2 Factorial Design with One Main Effect (Factor *B*) and No Interaction

	Factor B: Mood During Recall		
	Happy	*Sad*	
Happy	(1) 30	(2) 12	$\overline{X}_{A_1} = 21$
Sad	(3) 28	(4) 10	$\overline{X}_{A_2} = 19$
	$\overline{X}_{B_1} = 29$	$\overline{X}_{B_2} = 11$	

Factor A: Mood During Memorization

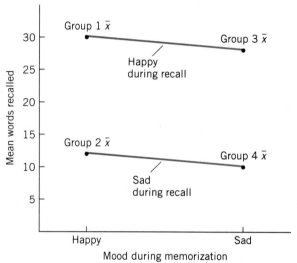

Figure 13.2 A graph of the means in Table 13.3. There is one main effect but no interaction.

presence of a main effect.[4] In Figure 13.2, Mood During Memorization is placed on the horizontal axis; therefore, two lines are drawn, which indicate the two levels of Mood During Recall. Why the switch from Figure 13.1 to Figure 13.2? By changing the variable on the horizontal axis, the main effect is shown more clearly. Figure 13.3 also illustrates a graph using the means in Table 13.3. This time, however, the *X* axis is Mood During Recall. The lines are still parallel, indicating the absence of an interaction. The Happy During Memorization line is only slightly higher than the line drawn for Sad During Memorization. Displaying the graph in this manner

[4] Strictly speaking, since statistical significance tests are probabilistic, there is no way to ever know with certainty whether there is a main effect or an interaction.

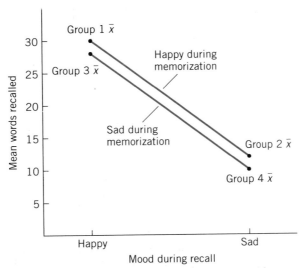

Figure 13.3 Group means from Table 13.3 are graphed. There is a main effect for Mood During Recall. However, by placing Mood During Recall on the X axis, the main effect is more difficult to identify. Figure 13.2 is a more useful display of the main effect presented in Table 13.3.

obscures the main effect for Factor *B* (Mood During Recall), and is therefore not very helpful.

After the data are analyzed, you will know which factors (if any) show a main effect, and the graph can be drawn accordingly. When computing a two-way ANOVA by hand, it's a good idea to draw the graph both ways beforehand—with Factor *A* on the *X* axis, and then with Factor *B* on the *X* axis. This will enable you to know ahead of time what the results of the ANOVA are likely to reveal. The guiding principle in graphing is to draw your figure so that it can be easily interpreted at a glance. If there is a main effect, put the factor on the horizontal axis, which clearly illustrates that one line is higher than the other.

At this point you should be able to place means in the cells of a diagram that illustrate a main effect for Factor *A*. Table 13.4 is one way to illustrate a main effect for Mood During Memorization.

The pattern of means in Table 13.4 shows that recall is facilitated when subjects are happy while memorizing the list of words (main effect for Factor *A*). Irrespective of the level of Factor *A*, recall is not affected by the mood state present during recall (no main effect for Factor *B*). Finally, the manner in which mood states combine during memorization and during recall has no influence on the number of words recalled (no interaction).

In Figure 13.4, the lines are nearly parallel: no interaction. The main effect for Mood During Memorization is revealed by the different heights of the lines. The Happy During Memorization line is highest, which reflects the greater recall of information among the two Happy During Memorization groups in comparison to the two Sad During Memorization groups.

TABLE 13.4   A 2 × 2 Factorial Design with One Main Effect (Factor *A*) and No Interaction

		Factor B: Mood During Recall		
		Happy	*Sad*	
Factor A: Mood During Memorization	*Happy*	(1) 30	(2) 28	$\overline{X}_{A_1} = 29$
	Sad	(3) 20	(4) 20	$\overline{X}_{A_2} = 20$
		$\overline{X}_{B_1} = 25$	$\overline{X}_{B_2} = 24$	

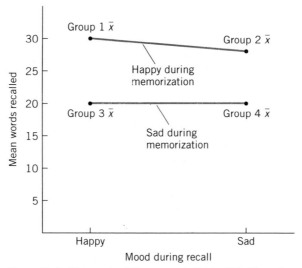

Figure 13.4 The graph of the means in Table 13.4. There is a main effect for Factor *A* but no interaction.

Illustrated thus far have been cases in which there is an interaction with no main effects; there has been a main effect for Factor *B* but neither a main effect for Factor *A* nor an interaction; and there has been a main effect for Factor *A* with no main effect for Factor *B* and no interaction. Table 13.5 shows a main effect for Factor *A*, as well as an interaction, but no main effect for Factor *B*.

Table 13.5 shows that mood state during recall has no independent influence on the number of words recalled (no main effect for Factor *B*.) However, the main effect revealed for Factor *A* indicates that recall is enhanced when words are memorized while in a happy mood. Now examine Figure 13.5. One line is higher than the other, revealing the main effect for Mood During Memorization. Because

TABLE 13.5 **A 2 × 2 Factorial Design with One Main Effect (Factor A) as well as an Interaction**

		Factor B: Mood During Recall		
		Happy	*Sad*	
Factor A: Mood During	*Happy*	(1) 40	(2) 28	$\overline{X}_{A_1} = 34$
Memorization	*Sad*	(3) 20	(4) 26	$\overline{X}_{A_2} = 23$
		$\overline{X}_{B_1} = 30$	$\overline{X}_{B_2} = 27$	

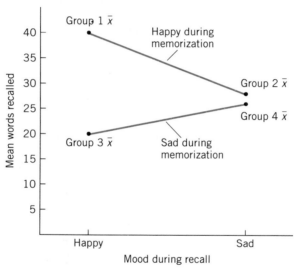

Figure 13.5 The graph of the means from Table 13.5. There is a main effect for Factor A and an interaction.

the lines are not parallel, an interaction is indicated. The interaction would be interpreted as follows: recall is, on the average, greatest when the mood states between memorization and recall are the same. However, the presence of an interaction and a main effect increases the complexity of the interpretation of the results.

Refer to Table 13.5. Notice the marginal means for Mood During Memorization (34 versus 23). That is the main effect. However, the mean in cell 1 (40) is pulling up the marginal mean of 34. The interaction may be *carrying* the main effect. It is the Happy/Happy condition that shows the greatest influence on recall. The congruence between Sad/Sad (cell 4) does not show a similar influence on recall

($\overline{X}_4 = 26$). Thus, not only does the Happy/Happy condition contribute to a main effect for Factor A, it also accounts for the interaction (the Sad/Sad condition does not seem to bolster the conclusion that mood congruence is always important). In this instance, you must be very specific (and cautious) in drawing conclusions about the relation between mood and recall. The results of a statistical analysis might very well lead to the conclusion that recall is facilitated *only* when subjects are happy during memorization and happy during recall.

Whenever there is a main effect and an interaction, *always* interpret the interaction first; be cautious in your interpretation of the main effect.

Some methodologists take the extreme position that main effects should not be interpreted when an interaction is found. An apparent contradiction exists because a main effect is an unqualified effect, whereas an interaction indicates that the action of one independent variable is moderated by the influence of the other independent variable. A reasonable approach to this interpretive dilemma is to statistically test the difference between all possible pairs of means, and judge the meaning of the differences in the context of theory.

Our illustrations of some of the outcomes of a 2×2 factorial design have not exhausted all the possible outcomes that can occur. The entire set of potential outcomes is:

1. A Factor A main effect, no Factor B main effect, and no interaction.
2. A Factor B main effect, no Factor A main effect, and no interaction.
3. Main effects for Factors A and B, no interaction.
4. A main effect for Factor A, no main effect for Factor B, but an interaction.
5. A main effect for Factor B, no main effect for Factor A, but an interaction.
6. Main effects for both factors and an interaction.
7. No main effects for either factor but an interaction.
8. No main effects and no interaction.

A main effect addresses the differences among levels of an independent variable. The number of independent variables is the same as the number of potential main effects. An interaction is the combined influence of two or more independent variables. A significant interaction means that the influence of an independent variable is affected by the value of a second independent variable.

Factorial Designs with More Than Two Independent Variables

When three independent variables are combined in a factorial design, the number of possible outcomes is increased. Not only are there potential main effects for each independent variable, but more than one interaction can occur. When there are three independent variables, the investigator will test for four interactions: $A \times B$, $A \times C$, $B \times C$, and $A \times B \times C$. The latter interaction is called a three-way interaction. It is possible to design experiments with four- and five-way interactions. However, a significant four- or five-way interaction is often very difficult to interpret; for this reason, researchers tend to avoid overly complex factorial designs.

13.2   THE LOGIC OF THE TWO-WAY ANOVA

The Null and Alternative Hypotheses

There are three separate null hypotheses when conducting a two-way ANOVA. Thus, three F ratios are calculated and tested for statistical significance.

Main Effect for Factor A

The independent variable that is designated as Factor A has two or more levels. The null hypothesis is that there are no differences in the population means of the *levels* of Factor A. Symbolically,

$$H_0: \quad \mu_{A_1} = \mu_{A_2} = \mu_{A_k}$$

The subscript k refers to the last level of Factor A. The alternative hypothesis is that at least one of the levels of the Factor A population means is different from one of the other levels of Factor A. Thus,

$$H_1: \quad H_0 \text{ is false}$$

Main Effect for Factor B

The independent variable that is designated as Factor B has two or more levels. The null hypothesis is that there are no differences in the population means of the *levels* of Factor B. Symbolically,

$$H_0: \quad \mu_{B_1} = \mu_{B_2} = \mu_{B_k}$$

Now the subscript k refers to the last level of Factor B. The alternative hypothesis is that at least one of the levels of the Factor B population means is different from one of the other levels of Factor B. Thus,

$$H_1: \quad H_0 \text{ is false}$$

The $A \times B$ Interaction

The null hypothesis for the interaction is that there is no interaction. That is, the effect of Factor A is independent of the effect of Factor B.

Assumptions of the Two-Way ANOVA

The assumptions for the two-way ANOVA are the same as those for the one-way ANOVA:

1. The population distributions are normal.
2. The variances of the populations are the same (homogeneity of variances).
3. Observations are independent of one another.

The F test is robust and thus can be performed when the first two assumptions are not *strictly* met. However, gross violations of these assumptions require the use of statistical tests (nonparametric tests), which do not require the populations to be normally distributed with equal variances. As with a one-way ANOVA, the assumption that scores are independent of one another must not be violated.

Partitioning Variability

The structure of the two-way ANOVA depicted in Figure 13.6 is an extension of the one-way ANOVA. In fact, the first stage of the structure for a two-way ANOVA is identical to the one-way ANOVA: total variance is due to between-group variance plus within-group variance. The second stage of the model is a further partitioning of the between-group variance into the variance due to Factor A, the variance due to Factor B, and the variance due to the interaction. The second stage of the model yields the F ratios that are tested for significance. An explanation of each source of variability is provided in the following sections.

Between-Group Variability

Between-group variability refers to the variability among *all* the means in the study.[5] In the one-way ANOVA, between-group variability goes into the numerator of the F ratio. This is not the case with the two-way ANOVA. Rather, it is the three components of between-group variance that are used for the three F ratios: variability due to Factors A and B, and the interaction.

Factor A Variability

Factor A variance refers to the difference among the means of the levels of Factor A. These mean differences, if indeed there are any, are due to Factor A treatment plus error.

Factor B Variability

Factor B variability refers to the difference among means of the levels of Factor B. Any difference among the means of Factor B is due to Factor B treatment plus error.

Interaction Variability

The variability of the interaction is due to the combined influence of Factors A and B, plus error.

Within-Group Variability

Within-group variance is the average of the variances of each group. Within-group variance is also called *error variance* or simply, *error*. The variability within each group is due to two sets of factors: individual differences and experimental error.

---

[5] You might want to refer to Chapter 12 to review the concepts of between-group and within-group variability, error variance, random factors, experimental error, and individual differences.

Recall that individual differences refers to the influence of subject variables on the dependent variable. Experimental error is the variability among scores due to such things as measurement error and lapses in attention among the experimenter and subjects. Individual differences and experimental error are random factors. Random factors are sources of error and are independent of any effects due to treatment.

The Conceptual Form of the Three *F* Ratios

The two-way ANOVA yields an *F* ratio for Factor *A*, an *F* ratio for Factor *B*, and an *F* ratio for the interaction. The conceptual basis of these *F* ratios should have a familiar look.

$$F_A = \frac{\text{Treatment } A \text{ effect} + \text{error variance}}{\text{error variance}}$$

$$F_B = \frac{\text{Treatment } B \text{ effect} + \text{error variance}}{\text{error variance}}$$

$$F_{A \times B} = \frac{\text{Treatment } A \times B \text{ effect} + \text{error variance}}{\text{error variance}}$$

As with the one-way ANOVA, the effect due to treatment is placed in the numerator. If there is no treatment effect, or, in other words, if H_0 is true, the *F* ratio is nothing but error variance divided by error variance. Thus, when the null hypothesis is correct, the *F* ratio will be close to 1. As the effect due to treatment increases, the *F* ratio will become increasingly greater than 1. At some point, the *F* ratio will become large enough to exceed the critical *F* value, and will be designated statistically significant.

We now turn to the computational steps and formulas used to calculate the three *F* ratios of the two-way ANOVA.[6]

13.3   DEFINITIONAL AND COMPUTATIONAL FORMULAS FOR THE TWO-WAY ANOVA

Summary of the Computational Steps

The two-way ANOVA involves the computation of the following values.

1. SS_T
2. SS_{BG}
3. SS_W

---

[6] Many students who avoid learning to use statistical software to analyze data are led to reconsider their avoidance after computing a two-way ANOVA by hand.

4. SS_A
5. SS_B
6. $SS_{A \times B}$
7. df for each SS
8. MS_A
9. MS_B
10. $MS_{A \times B}$
11. F_A
12. F_B
13. $F_{A \times B}$

Formulas for the Sums of Squares

The Total Sum of Squares, SS_T

The definitional formula for SS_T is the sum of the squared deviations of all the scores from the grand mean $\overline{X}_G$. The grand mean is the mean of *all* the scores in the study.

Definitional Formula for SS_T

$$SS_T = \Sigma(X - \overline{X}_G)^2 \quad \textit{(Formula 13.1)}$$

The definitional and computational formulas for SS_T are identical to those used in conducting a one-way ANOVA. The SS_T computes the sum of squares for the *entire* set of scores, N.

Computational Formula for SS_T

$$SS_T = \Sigma X^2 - \frac{(\Sigma X)^2}{N} \quad \textit{(Formula 13.2)}$$

The Sum of Squares Between-Groups, SS_{BG}

The definitional formula for SS_{BG} reminds the researcher that the overall between-group variability is the amount of variation obtained by the sum of the squared differences between each group's mean and the grand mean.

Definitional Formula for SS_{BG}

$$SS_{BG} = \Sigma n_k (\overline{X}_k - \overline{X}_G)^2 \quad \textit{(Formula 13.3)}$$

This formula is identical to the formula for SS_{BG} used in the one-way ANOVA. However, with the two-way ANOVA, remember that the SS_{BG} is not used in an F ratio. The SS_{BG} is used as a computational check. The computational formula for SS_{BG} is the same for the one-way ANOVA and the two-way ANOVA.

Computational Formula for SS_{BG}

$$SS_{BG} = \frac{(\Sigma X_{A_1B_1})^2}{n_{A_1B_1}} + \frac{(\Sigma X_{A_1B_2})^2}{n_{A_1B_2}} + \cdots + \frac{(\Sigma X_k)^2}{n_k} - \left(\frac{(\Sigma X)^2}{N} \right) \quad \textit{(Formula 13.4)}$$

where,

$(\Sigma X_{A_1B_1})^2, (\Sigma X_{A_1B_2})^2 =$ the sum of the scores in Group 1, quantity squared; the sum of the scores in Group 2, quantity squared, etc.

$(\Sigma X_k)^2 =$ the sum of the scores in the last Group, quantity squared

$(\Sigma X)^2 =$ the sum of all the scores in the study, quantity squared

$n_{A_1B_1}, n_{A_1B_2}, n_K =$ the number of subjects in Groups 1, 2, and the last group, respectively

$N =$ the total number of subjects

The Sum of Squares Within-Groups, SS_W

The SS_W is found by calculating the sum of squares within each cell (group) and adding them together. The definitional formula reflects the fact that within-group variability is derived from the deviation of single scores about the mean of the group from which the scores are taken. This formula has the same form as SS_W used in the one-way ANOVA. The subscripts of X identify specific cells.

Definitional Formula for SS_W

$$SS_W = \Sigma (X_{A_1B_1} - \overline{X}_{A_1B_1})^2 + \Sigma (X_{A_1B_2} - \overline{X}_{A_1B_2})^2$$
$$+ \Sigma (X_{A_2B_1} - \overline{X}_{A_2B_1})^2 + \cdots + \Sigma (X_k - \overline{X}_k)^2 \quad \textit{(Formula 13.5)}$$

> ### Computational Formula for SS_W
>
> $$SS_W = \Sigma X^2 - \left[\frac{(\Sigma X_{A_1B_1})^2}{n_{A_1B_1}} + \frac{(\Sigma X_{A_1B_2})^2}{n_{A_1B_2}} + \cdots + \frac{(\Sigma X_k)^2}{n_k} \right] \quad \textit{(Formula 13.6)}$$

Computational Check

Formulas have been presented for SS_T, SS_{BG}, and SS_W. In the first stage of the two-way ANOVA, total variability is partitioned into between-group and within-group variability (see Figure 13.6). Thus,

$$SS_T = SS_{BG} + SS_W$$

The second stage of the two-way ANOVA partitions the sum of squares between-groups into the sum of squares for Factor A, SS_A, the sum of squares for Factor B, SS_B, and the sum of squares for the interaction, $SS_{A \times B}$.

The Sum of Squares for Factor A, SS_A

You are used to working with deviations of raw scores about group means (SS_W) and the deviations of group means about the grand mean (SS_{BG}). When calculating the sum of squares for a factor, the means of the *levels* of the factor are used, not individual cell means. The definitional formula for SS_A reveals that SS_A is the deviations of the means of each level about the grand mean.

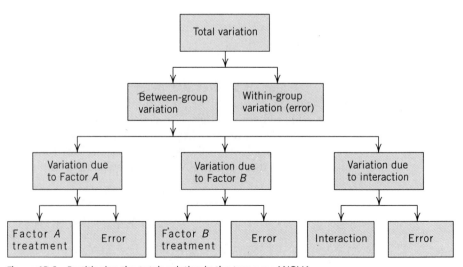

Figure 13.6   Partitioning the total variation in the two-way ANOVA.

Definitional Formula for SS_A

$$SS_A = n_{A_1}(\overline{X}_{A_1} - \overline{X}_G)^2 + n_{A_2}(\overline{X}_{A_2} - \overline{X}_G)^2$$
$$+ n_{\text{last }A\text{ level}}(\overline{X}_{\text{last }A\text{ level}} - \overline{X}_G)^2 \quad \textit{(Formula 13.7)}$$

where

$n_{A_1}, n_{A_2}, n_{\text{last }A\text{ level}}$ = the number of subjects in Factor A levels 1, 2, and the last level, respectively

$\overline{X}_{A_1}, \overline{X}_{A_2}, \overline{X}_{\text{last }A\text{ level}}$ = the Factor A means for levels 1, 2, and the last level, respectively; also called *marginal means of each level*

Computational Formula for SS_A

$$SS_A = \frac{(\Sigma X_{A_1})^2}{n_{A_1}} + \frac{(\Sigma X_{A_2})^2}{n_{A_2}} + \frac{(\Sigma X_{\text{last }A\text{ level}})^2}{n_{\text{last }A\text{ level}}} - \left[\frac{(\Sigma X)^2}{N}\right] \quad \textit{(Formula 13.8)}$$

The computational formula requires you to sum scores *across* the cells of each level of Factor A. Hence, ΣX_{A_1} is the sum of the scores in cell A_1B_1 plus the sum of the scores in cell A_1B_2, plus the sum of scores in A_1B_k. The ΣX_{A_2} is the sum of scores in cell A_2B_1 plus A_2B_2, plus A_2B_k. The terms n_{A_1}, n_{A_2}, and $n_{\text{last }A\text{ level}}$ refer to the number of scores in each level of Factor A.

The Sum of Squares for Factor B, SS_B

Everything said about Factor A applies to Factor B. Just keep in mind that the action now occurs with the *levels* of Factor B. Remember to attend to the subscripts.

Definitional Formula for SS_B

$$SS_B = n_{B_1}(\overline{X}_{B_1} - \overline{X}_G)^2 + n_{B_2}(\overline{X}_{B_2} - \overline{X}_G)^2$$
$$+ n_{\text{last }B\text{ level}}(\overline{X}_{\text{last }B\text{ level}} - \overline{X}_G)^2 \quad \textit{(Formula 13.9)}$$

Computational Formula for SS_B

$$SS_B = \frac{(\Sigma X_{B_1})^2}{n_{B_1}} + \frac{\Sigma X_{B_2})^2}{n_{B_2}} + \frac{(\Sigma X_{\text{last }B\text{ level}})^2}{n_{\text{last }B\text{ level}}} - \left[\frac{(\Sigma X)^2}{N}\right] \quad \textit{(Formula 13.10)}$$

The Interaction Sum of Squares, $SS_{A \times B}$

The sum of squares for the interaction, $SS_{A \times B}$, involves subtracting various marginal means from cell means, adding the grand mean, and multiplying everything by the number of subjects in one group. Giving a detailed verbal description of the formula runs the risk of creating more confusion than clarity. So without further comment, Formula 13.11 is used to compute $SS_{A \times B}$.

Formula for $SS_{A \times B}$

$$
\begin{aligned}
SS_{A \times B} = n_k \big[& (\overline{X}_{A_1 B_1} - \overline{X}_{A_1} - \overline{X}_{B_1} + \overline{X}_G)^2 \\
+ & (\overline{X}_{A_2 B_1} - \overline{X}_{A_2} - \overline{X}_{B_1} + \overline{X}_G)^2 \\
+ & (\overline{X}_{A_1 B_2} - \overline{X}_{A_1} - \overline{X}_{B_2} + \overline{X}_G)^2 \\
+ & (\overline{X}_{A_2 B_2} - \overline{X}_{A_2} - \overline{X}_{B_2} + \overline{X}_G)^2 \big]
\end{aligned}
\qquad \text{(Formula 13.11)}
$$

This formula can only be used when each group has the same number of subjects. The value n_k is the number of subjects in *one* group, not the total number of subjects in the study. It is assumed that $n_1 = n_2 = n_3 = n_k$. Note that multiplying by n_k is the last step in the formula. It is *not* the case that each separate term of the equation is multiplied by n_k.

Computational Checks

In the second stage of the two-way ANOVA, the SS_{BG} is partitioned into SS_A, SS_B, and $SS_{A \times B}$ (see Figure 13.6). Thus,

$$
SS_{BG} = SS_A + SS_B + SS_{A \times B}
$$

Even though SS_{BG} is not used in an F ratio, its calculation is justified because it serves as a computational check for SS_A, SS_B, and $SS_{A \times B}$.

The $SS_{A \times B}$ term can be computed by,

$$
SS_{A \times B} = SS_{BG} - SS_A - SS_B
$$

However, it is recommended that $SS_{A \times B}$ be computed separately, using Formula 13.11, and then a computational check performed.

Unequal Numbers of Subjects

Researchers strive to include the same number of subjects in each experimental condition. Statisticians have noted that the F test is more robust under minor violations of the population assumptions (i.e., normality and equivalent variances) when there are the same number of subjects in each group. Most importantly, unequal sample sizes present serious difficulties when they occur in the context

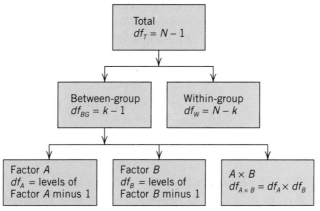

Figure 13.7 Partitioning the degrees of freedom in the two-way ANOVA.

of a factorial design. For a discussion of the conceptual issues and computational adjustments related to factorial designs with unequal sample sizes, refer to Keppel (1982, Chapter 15).

Partitioning Degrees of Freedom

Each *SS* in the analysis of variance has a corresponding degrees of freedom. Partitioning the degrees of freedom follows the same logic as partitioning variability. Figure 13.7 shows the degrees of freedom partitioned. Table 13.6 lists the various

TABLE 13.6 **The Degrees of Freedom and Their Computation**

Source	Degrees of Freedom	Symbol
Total	$N - 1$	df_T
Within-groups	$N - k$	df_W
Between-groups	$k - 1$	df_{BG}
Factor A	Levels of Factor A minus 1	df_A
Factor B	Levels of Factor B minus 1	df_B
Interaction	$df_A \times df_B$	$df_{A \times B}$

degrees of freedom and their computation. Note that,

$$df_{BG} = df_A + df_B + df_{A \times B} \quad \text{and} \quad df_T = df_{BG} + df_W$$

thus,

$$df_T = df_A + df_B + df_{A \times B} + df_W$$

Calculating Mean Squares and *F* Ratios

The last step in the analysis of variance is to calculate the Mean Squares and the *F* ratios for Factor *A*, Factor *B*, and the interaction. As in the one-way ANOVA, a Mean Square is a sample variance and has the general form:

$$MS = \frac{SS}{df}$$

The *MS* for the factors, interaction, and error term are:

$$MS_A = \frac{SS_A}{df_A}$$

$$MS_B = \frac{SS_B}{df_B}$$

$$MS_{A \times B} = \frac{SS_{A \times B}}{df_{A \times B}}$$

$$MS_W = \frac{SS_W}{df_W}$$

When calculating the *F* ratios, the denominator of each *F* is MS_W. Thus,

$$F_A = \frac{MS_A}{MS_W}$$

$$F_B = \frac{MS_B}{MS_W}$$

$$F_{A \times B} = \frac{MS_{A \times B}}{MS_W}$$

Worked Problem

To provide an experimental context for the calculations of the two-way ANOVA, the following hypothetical experiment will be used. Table 13.7 presents the design. A clinical psychologist is interested in the relative effectiveness of two popular

TABLE 13.7 The 2 × 2 Factorial Design of the Worked Problem, Including Cell Notations

		Factor B		
		Behavioral Therapy	Psychoanalysis	
Factor A	Anxiety	A_1B_1	A_1B_2	A_1
	Depression	A_2B_1	A_2B_2	A_2
		B_1	B_2	

forms of therapy: behavioral therapy and psychoanalysis. However, let's assume that there is some reason to believe that behavioral therapy may be more effective with anxiety problems and psychoanalysis may be a more effective treatment for depression. In other words, an interaction is predicted. Factor A is the type of clinical problem, and has two levels: anxiety and depression. Note that the Factor A independent variable is not experimentally manipulated. This independent variable is formed on the basis of a subject variable. If it turns out that there is a significant main effect for this factor, no cause-effect statement can be advanced. This is not the case for Factor B. Factor B also has two levels: behavioral therapy and psychoanalysis. Since this independent variable is *created* and manipulated by the experimenter, a mean difference between the levels of this factor can be interpreted as being caused by the treatments. Since Factor A and Factor B each have two levels, this is an example of a 2 × 2 factorial design. The dependent variable is improvement ratings offered by an independent observer, with higher numbers indicating greater improvement. Table 13.8 contains the raw data for each group in the study. Table 13.9 shows the summary statistics of the raw data. Figure

TABLE 13.8 The Raw Data for the Worked Problem

		Factor B	
		Behavioral Therapy	Psychoanalysis
Factor A	Anxiety	8 6 6 9 8	3 4 1 6 2
	Depression	4 7 4 5 5	8 9 7 7 8

TABLE 13.9 Summary Statistics for the Raw Data of Table 13.8

		Factor B		
		Behavioral Therapy	*Psychoanalysis*	
Factor A	*Anxiety*	$\overline{X}_{A_1B_1} = 7.40$ $\Sigma X^2_{A_1B_1} = 281$ $\Sigma X_{A_1B_1} = 37$ $n_{A_1B_1} = 5$	$\overline{X}_{A_1B_2} = 3.20$ $\Sigma X^2_{A_1B_2} = 66$ $\Sigma X_{A_1B_2} = 16$ $n_{A_1B_1} = 5$	$\overline{X}_{A_1} = 5.30$
	Depression	$\overline{X}_{A_2B_1} = 5.00$ $\Sigma X^2_{A_2B_1} = 131$ $\Sigma X_{A_2B_1} = 25$ $n_{A_2B_1} = 5$	$\overline{X}_{A_2B_2} = 7.80$ $\Sigma X^2_{A_2B_2} = 307$ $\Sigma X_{A_2B_2} = 39$ $n_{A_2B_2} = 5$	$\overline{X}_{A_2} = 6.40$
		$\overline{X}_{B_1} = 6.20$	$\overline{X}_{B_2} = 5.50$	$\overline{X}_G = 5.85$

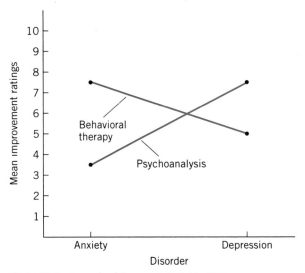

Figure 13.8 A graph of the means in Table 13.9.

13.8 is a graph of the means. By examining the graph, you should be able to predict how the analysis will turn out.

Calculating the Sums of Squares

Step 1. Find the total sum of squares, SS_T.

$$SS_T = \Sigma X^2 - \frac{(\Sigma X)^2}{N} \qquad \textit{(Formula 13.2)}$$

$$SS_T = 785 - \frac{(117)^2}{20}$$

$$= \mathbf{100.55}$$

(ΣX^2 can be found by summing all the squared scores in the study or by summing the squared scores for each group.

Step 2. Find the sum of squares between-groups, SS_{BG}.

$$SS_{BG} = \frac{(\Sigma X_{A_1B_1})^2}{n_{A_1B_1}} + \frac{(\Sigma X_{A_1B_2})^2}{n_{A_1B_2}} + \cdots + \frac{(\Sigma X_k)^2}{n_k} - \left[\frac{(\Sigma X)^2}{N}\right]$$ *(Formula 13.4)*

$$SS_{BG} = \frac{(37)^2}{5} + \frac{(16)^2}{5} + \frac{(25)^2}{5} + \frac{(39)^2}{5} - \left[\frac{(117)^2}{20}\right]$$

$$= 754.20 - 684.45$$

$$= \mathbf{69.75}$$

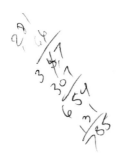

Step 3. Find sum of squares within-groups, SS_W.

$$SS_W = \Sigma X^2 - \left[\frac{(\Sigma X_{A_1B_1})^2}{n_{A_1B_1}} + \frac{(\Sigma X_{A_1B_2})^2}{n_{A_1B_2}} + \cdots + \frac{(\Sigma X_k)^2}{n_k}\right]$$ *(Formula 13.6)*

$$SS_W = 785 - \left[\frac{(37)^2}{5} + \frac{(16)^2}{5} + \frac{(25)^2}{5} + \frac{(39)^2}{5}\right]$$

$$= 785 - 754.20$$

$$= \mathbf{30.80}$$

Step 4. Perform a computational check for SS_T.
In the first stage of the ANOVA, total variability is partitioned into between-group and within-group variability. Thus,

$$SS_T = SS_{BG} + SS_W$$

Using the obtained sums of squares values,

$$100.55 = 69.75 + 30.80$$

The second stage of the two-way ANOVA partitions the sum of squares between-groups into the sum of squares for Factor A, SS_A, the sum of squares for Factor B, SS_B, and the sum of squares for the interaction, $SS_{A \times B}$.

Step 5. Find the sum of squares for Factor A, SS_A.

$$SS_A = \frac{(\Sigma X_{A_1})^2}{n_{A_1}} + \frac{(\Sigma X_{A_2})^2}{n_{A_2}} + \frac{(\Sigma X_{\text{last } A \text{ level}})^2}{n_{\text{last } A \text{ level}}} - \left[\frac{(\Sigma X)^2}{N}\right]$$ *(Formula 13.8)*

$$SS_A = \frac{(53)^2}{10} + \frac{(64)^2}{10} - \left[\frac{(117)^2}{20}\right]$$

$$= 690.50 - 684.45$$

$$= \mathbf{6.05}$$

Refer to Table 13.9 and note that $\Sigma X_{A_1} = \Sigma X_{A_1B_1} + \Sigma X_{A_1B_2} = 37 + 16 = 53$. Likewise, $\Sigma X_{A_2} = \Sigma X_{A_2B_1} + \Sigma X_{A_2B_2} = 25 + 39 = 64$.

Step 6. Find the sum of squares for Factor B, SS_B.

$$SS_B = \frac{(\Sigma X_{B_1})^2}{n_{B_1}} + \frac{(\Sigma X_{B_2})^2}{n_{B_2}} + \frac{(\Sigma X_{\text{last } B \text{ level}})^2}{n_{\text{last } B \text{ level}}} - \left[\frac{(\Sigma X)^2}{N}\right] \qquad \textit{(Formula 13.10)}$$

$$SS_B = \frac{(62)^2}{10} + \frac{(55)^2}{10} - \left[\frac{(117)^2}{20}\right]$$

$$= 686.90 + 684.45$$

$$= \mathbf{2.45}$$

Step 7. Find the interaction sum of squares, $SS_{A \times B}$.

$$SS_{A \times B} = n_k \, [(\overline{X}_{A_1B_1} - \overline{X}_{A_1} - \overline{X}_{B_1} + \overline{X}_G)^2$$
$$+ \, (\overline{X}_{A_2B_1} - \overline{X}_{A_2} - \overline{X}_{B_1} + \overline{X}_G)^2$$
$$+ \, (\overline{X}_{A_1B_2} - \overline{X}_{A_1} - \overline{X}_{B_2} + \overline{X}_G)^2$$
$$+ \, (\overline{X}_{A_2B_2} - \overline{X}_{A_2} - \overline{X}_{B_2} + \overline{X}_G)^2] \qquad \textit{(Formula 13.11)}$$

$$SS_{A \times B} = 5[(7.40 - 5.30 - 6.20 + 5.85)^2$$
$$+ \, (5.00 - 6.40 - 6.20 + 5.85)^2$$
$$+ \, (3.20 - 5.30 - 5.50 + 5.85)^2$$
$$+ \, (7.80 - 6.40 - 5.50 + 5.85)^2]$$

$$= \mathbf{61.25}$$

Step 8. Perform a computational check for SS_{BG}.
In the second stage of the two-way ANOVA, the SS_{BG} is partitioned into SS_A, SS_B, and $SS_{A \times B}$ (see Figure 13.b). Thus,

$$SS_{BG} = SS_A + SS_B + SS_{A \times B}$$

A check of the calculations shows,

$$69.75 = 6.05 + 2.45 + 61.25$$

Step 9. Compute MS_W using SS_W and df_W. The df_W = the total number of subjects minus the number of groups ($df_W = N - k = 20 - 4 = 16$).

$$MS_W = \frac{SS_W}{df_W} = \frac{30.80}{16} = \mathbf{1.93}$$

Step 10. Compute MS_A using SS_A and df_A. The df_A = the number of levels of Factor A minus 1 ($2 - 1 = 1$).

$$MS_A = \frac{SS_A}{df_A} = \frac{6.05}{1} = \textbf{6.05}$$

Step 11.   Compute F_A.

$$F_A = \frac{MS_A}{MS_W} = \frac{6.05}{1.93} = \textbf{3.13}$$

Step 12.   Compute MS_B using SS_B and df_B. The df_B = the number of levels of Factor B minus 1 $(2 - 1 = 1)$.

$$MS_B = \frac{SS_B}{df_B} = \frac{2.45}{1} = \textbf{2.45}$$

Step 13.   Compute F_B.

$$F_B = \frac{MS_B}{MS_W} = \frac{2.45}{1.93} = \textbf{1.27}$$

Step 14.   Compute $MS_{A \times B}$ using $SS_{A \times B}$ and $df_{A \times B}$. The $df_{A \times B} = df_A \times df_B$ $(1 \times 1 = 1)$.

$$MS_{A \times B} = \frac{SS_{A \times B}}{df_{A \times B}} = \frac{61.25}{1} = \textbf{61.25}$$

Step 15.   Compute $F_{A \times B}$.

$$F_{A \times B} = \frac{MS_{A \times B}}{MS_W} = \frac{61.25}{1.93} = \textbf{31.74}$$

The remaining steps involve testing the significance of the three F ratios.

13.4   TESTING THE STATISTICAL SIGNIFICANCE OF THE F RATIOS

To determine if the F ratios are statistically significant, the obtained F's are compared to the appropriate F_{crit} values found in Appendix B.5. This is the same table used to test the F ratio in a one-way ANOVA. Each F ratio has degrees of freedom for the numerator and the denominator (refer to Table 13.6).

The degrees of freedom for F_A is df_A, df_W, which is 1 and 16.
The degrees of freedom for F_B is df_B, df_W, which is 1 and 16.
The degrees of freedom for $F_{A \times B}$ is $df_{A \times B}$, df_W, which is 1 and 16.

The reason df is the same for each F ratio is because a 2×2 design is being used. A design in which the number of levels of Factor A do not equal the number of levels of Factor B will yield a different df for each F ratio.

Since df is the same for each F ratio, there is only one F_{crit} value with which every F ratio is compared. According to the F table, F_{crit} is 4.49 at the 5 percent level of significance, and 8.53 at the 1 percent level of significance. Let's use the critical value for $\alpha = .05$.

Since F_A (3.13) is smaller than F_{crit} when alpha is .05 (4.49), you retain the null hypothesis for Factor A. The same conclusion is reached for Factor B because $F_B = 1.27$ and $1.27 < 4.49$. However, $F_{A \times B} = 31.74$ and is larger than F_{crit} (4.49). Thus, you would reject the null hypothesis that there is no interaction.

Interpreting the Findings

What do these findings mean about the therapy study? First, because there is no significant main effect for Factor B, in general, behavioral therapy is neither more nor less effective than psychoanalysis. The phrase "in general" only applies to the types of disorders examined in this study. It is possible that one form of therapy is more effective than the other when applied to different disorders. Because Factor A is nonsignificant, a researcher cannot conclude that people with an anxiety disorder do better or worse in therapy than people with a depressive disorder. Again, this statement only holds in the context of the two therapies employed in this study.

Interpreting the interaction is straightforward. Examining the group means indicates that psychoanalysis is a superior treatment for people suffering from depression. The treatment of choice for people troubled by anxiety is behavioral therapy. Discovering a significant interaction always leads to a qualified conclusion about the effect of an independent variable.

The ANOVA Summary Table

The results of the foregoing analysis are summarized in Table 13.10. The form of the ANOVA summary table is the same for a one-way and two-way ANOVA. However,

TABLE 13.10   The ANOVA Summary Table Based on the Analysis of the Data in Table 13.8

Source	SS	df	MS	F	p
Factor A (disorder)	6.05	1	6.05	3.13	n.s.
Factor B (treatment)	2.45	1	2.45	1.27	n.s.
$A \times B$	61.25	1	61.25	31.74	$p < .05$
Within-groups	30.80	16	1.93		
Total	100.55	19			

the summary table for a two-way ANOVA includes the *F* test for the interaction. As you examine the values in the table, verify that SS_T equals the sum of all the sum of squares and that df_T equals the sum of all the *df*'s.

Box 13.1 presents a study on aggression. The researchers used a factorial design to examine the independent and combined effects of arousal and the presence of aggressive cues on aggression.

BOX 13.1

Do Firearms Create Aggression?

All of us have displayed aggressive behavior, at times to our benefit, and at times, perhaps, to our embarrassment. Psychologists disagree on the roots of aggression. Freud believed that everyone is born with an aggressive instinct. Social learning theorists believe that aggression is learned. Because aggression can have such a profound effect on the course of our lives, ranging from verbal abuse between spouses to wars among nations, the factors that influence aggression have received a great deal of attention from psychologists. Leonard Berkowitz has conducted research on aggression for over 30 years. Common sense tells us that we are more likely to act aggressively when we are angry. Berkowitz took this observation one step further by hypothesizing that, once angry, people will behave even more aggressively if there are aggressive cues present. An aggressive cue is anything that we associate in our minds with aggression. A gun is one of the best examples of an aggressive cue. To test this hypothesis that aggressive cues augment aggression, Berkowitz conducted the following study (Berkowitz and LePage, 1967).

OVERVIEW OF THE DESIGN

The design was a 2 × 3 factorial. One independent variable manipulated subjects' anger; the two levels of this variable were low anger and high anger (Factor *A*). The second independent variable manipulated the presence of aggressive cues; this factor (Factor *B*) had three levels: presence of aggressive cues associated with someone in the study, presence of aggressive cues not associated with someone in the study, and the absence of aggressive cues. The design is illustrated in Table 1.

EXPERIMENTAL PROCEDURE

Male undergraduates served as participants in this study. They believed the purpose of the research was to examine physiological reactions to stress. Each subject would have to solve a problem, with the foreknowledge that his partner would evaluate the adequacy of his solution. The partner was actually a confederate— someone the subject thought was another subject but who was working for the experimenter. The subject was asked to list ideas that a publicity agent could use to increase the popularity of a professional singer. The confederate evaluated the subject's ideas by delivering electric shocks. The number of electric shocks administered to the subject served as the Anger manipulation. In the Low-anger condition, the subject received only one shock, which meant that the subject's ideas were deemed good by the confederate. In the High-anger condition, the subject received seven shocks, which meant that his ideas were poor. Then the situation was reversed so that the subject had an opportunity to evaluate the confederate's ideas by administering anywhere from one to ten shocks to the confederate. If we consider only this aspect of the experiment, we have a nonfactorial design. We could address the question of whether angered subjects are more aggressive than unangered subjects. The means of the two groups could be analyzed with a *t* test. Now let's consider the second independent variable.

When it came time for the subject to evaluate the confederate's answers, the experimental instructions and the table upon which rested the shock apparatus were rearranged. In the Associated Weapons condition, a 12-gauge shotgun and a .38-caliber

TABLE 1   Mean Number of Shocks Delivered to the Confederate

| | | Factor B: Aggressive Cues (Weapons) | | |
		Associated	Unassociated	None
Factor A: Anger	One Shock (Low)	2.60	2.20	3.07
	Seven Shocks (High)	6.07	5.67	4.67

TABLE 2   The ANOVA Summary Table

Source	SS	df	MS	F	p
Anger (A)	182.04	1	182.04	104.62	<.01
Weapons Associated (B)	3.80	2	1.90	1.09	n.s.
A × B	17.46	2	8.73	5.02	<.01
Within-groups	146.16	84	1.74		
Total	349.46	89			

handgun were placed in full view of the subject, next to the shock apparatus. These subjects were told that the guns were to be used by the "confederate" in another experiment.[8] In the Unassociated Weapons condition, the subjects were told that the guns "belonged to someone else who must have been doing an experiment in here." The Associated/Unassociated manipulation was included in the design to test the hypothesis "that aggressive stimuli, which also were associated with the anger instigator, would evoke the strongest aggressive reaction from the subjects." The third level of this independent variable, No Aggressive Cues, had the subjects use the shock apparatus in the absence of the guns. Again, the dependent variable was the number of shocks the subjects delivered to the confederate. Factor A allowed Berkowitz and LePage to examine the effect of anger on aggression. Factor B allowed them to see if there are differences in aggression due to aggressive cues. Because this is a factorial design, the researchers could look for an interaction. The interaction of interest was, "Will the most aggression be observed among subjects who are angered *and* exposed to aggressive cues?" Table 1

shows the mean number of shocks delivered by the subjects to the confederate. Table 2 presents the ANOVA summary table.

Examine Tables 1 and 2 and interpret the findings (you may want to compute all the marginal means to help you see the main effect). By examining the rows of Table 1 and noting the significant main effect for anger (shocks received), it is clear that the number of shocks delivered by the subjects in these two conditions is affected by how many shocks they received from the confederate. More aggression was displayed by those subjects who had just received a high number of shocks. What about the main effect for Factor B? The nonsignificant F ratio in Table 2 means that the manipulation of aggressive cues alone has no effect on aggression. In other words, simply viewing guns does not induce aggression.

The significant interaction tells us that aggression is also affected by the *combined* influence of anger and aggressive cues. Exactly how these variables combine to influence aggression cannot be determined by the two-way ANOVA. Post hoc tests are required to identify which groups differ among each other. After conducting post hoc tests, the authors were able to conclude that, while anger increases aggression, the presence of aggressive cues during an episode of anger further increases a person's level of aggression.

---

[8] Understandably, the data from 20 percent of the subjects in this condition had to be discarded because they didn't believe the experimenter.

13.5   STRENGTH OF ASSOCIATION

The F tests in the two-way ANOVA allow you to test the null hypothesis for each independent variable and the interaction. However, the F values do not provide information about the *strength* of each effect. Chapter 12 used omega-squared (ω^2) to determine the amount of variability in the scores due to the independent variable. With a two-way ANOVA, ω^2 can be computed for the effect of Factor A, Factor B, and the interaction. Of course, the issue of effect size only arises when an F ratio is statistically significant. The formulas for calculating ω^2 are slightly different for each factor and the interaction.

Omega-Squared for Factor A

$$\omega_A^2 = \frac{SS_A - (df_A)MS_W}{SS_T + MS_W} \quad \textit{(Formula 13.12)}$$

Omega-Squared for Factor B

$$\omega_B^2 = \frac{SS_B - (df_B)MS_W}{SS_T + MS_W} \quad \textit{(Formula 13.13)}$$

Omega-Squared for the Interaction

$$\omega_{A \times B}^2 = \frac{SS_{A \times B} - (df_{A \times B})MS_W}{SS_T + MS_W} \quad \textit{(Formula 13.14)}$$

Since, in the worked problem, only the interaction was significant, you would only calculate $\omega_{A \times B}^2$.

$$\omega_{A \times B}^2 = \frac{61.25 - (1)\,1.93}{100.55 + 1.93} = \mathbf{.58}$$

An effect size of .58 is large. Recall that an effect size of 15 percent is considered large (Cohen, 1977). The interaction in the study accounts for 58 percent of the variance in the dependent variable.

13.6   MULTIPLE COMPARISONS

Multiple comparisons are conducted to locate the source of a significant F ratio. If you were to conduct a study with only two groups, perform a t test, and find it significant, would you need to follow with a post hoc test? No, because with only two groups, a significant t ends the story. Likewise, in a 2 × 2 factorial design, a significant main effect tells you that there is a significant difference between the two levels of the independent variable. However, a significant interaction means that at least two cell means differ significantly. Post hoc tests allow you to make pairwise comparisons between any two group means. The pattern of significant and nonsignificant pairwise comparisons is interpreted by the researcher to gain a complete understanding of how the independent variables are affecting the behavior of the subjects.

To illustrate the use of a post hoc test, another hypothetical study is provided. The multiple comparison procedure that is used is the same one presented in Chapter 12: Fisher's LSD or protected t test. This test can only be conducted following a significant F ratio. Conducting the test only after obtaining a significant F ratio protects the investigator from an increased probability of making a Type I error. A Type I error is committed when you reject a true null hypothesis.

The formula for Fisher's LSD is:

$$t = \frac{\overline{X}_i - \overline{X}_j}{\sqrt{MS_W \left(\dfrac{1}{n_i} + \dfrac{1}{n_j} \right)}}$$

If you are testing the difference between two levels of one independent variable, $\overline{X}_i$ and $\overline{X}_j$ refer to the means of the two levels. Similarly, n_i and n_j refer to the number of subjects in each level. If you are making a comparison between two cells, $\overline{X}_i$ and $\overline{X}_j$ refer to the two cell means and n_i and n_j are the number of subjects in each cell. MS_W is taken from the denominator of the F ratios and is the same value in each protected t test.

Our hypothetical study for demonstrating the use of protected t tests is an extension of the previous study, which involves the effectiveness of two therapy techniques for the treatment of anxiety and depression. By adding a control group, the design becomes a 2 × 3 factorial design. Table 13.11 illustrates the design.

We will forego the computational steps of this study and proceed directly to the results of the analysis of variance. Table 13.12 presents the cell and marginal means, as well as the sample sizes. Table 13.13 presents the ANOVA summary table.

The results of the ANOVA show a significant main effect for Factor B, mode of therapy. The Factor A main effect, clinical disorder, and the interaction are not statistically significant. Therefore, the issue of locating the source of significance

TABLE   13.11   A 2 × 3 Factorial Design

		Factor B		
		Behavioral Therapy	Psychoanalysis	Control
Factor A	Anxiety	A_1B_1	A_1B_2	A_1B_3
	Depression	A_2B_1	A_2B_2	A_2B_3

TABLE   13.12   The Sample Sizes, Cell, and Marginal Means for a Hypothetical Therapy Study

		Factor B			
		Behavioral Therapy	Psychoanalysis	Control	
	Anxiety	$\overline{X}_{A_1B_1} = 5.80$ $n_{A_1B_1} = 10$	$\overline{X}_{A_1B_2} = 7.70$ $n_{A_1B_2} = 10$	$\overline{X}_{A_1B_3} = 4.60$ $n_{A_1B_3} = 10$	$\overline{X}_{A_1} = 6.03$
Factor A	Depression	$\overline{X}_{A_2B_1} = 5.50$ $n_{A_2B_1} = 10$	$\overline{X}_{A_2B_2} = 7.80$ $n_{A_2B_2} = 10$	$\overline{X}_{A_2B_3} = 2.80$ $n_{A_2B_3} = 10$	$\overline{X}_{A_2} = 5.37$
		$\overline{X}_{B_1} = 5.65$	$\overline{X}_{B_2} = 7.75$	$\overline{X}_{B_3} = 3.70$	

only arises for Factor B. Fisher's LSD test relies on the t distribution. The null hypothesis for each comparison is that $\overline{X}_i$ and $\overline{X}_j$ come from the same population. The critical value is the same for each pairwise comparison and is found in the t table (Appendix B.2). The critical value is found by entering the column for a two-tailed test at the desired alpha level, and entering the row corresponding to the degrees of freedom. Let's set alpha at .05. The degrees of freedom is df_W or $N - k$. From the ANOVA summary table, df_W is 54. The critical value is thus approximately 2.01. Each protected t value is compared to this critical value of 2.01.

Behavioral Therapy versus Control

$$t = \frac{\overline{X}_i - \overline{X}_j}{\sqrt{MS_W \left(\dfrac{1}{n_i} + \dfrac{1}{n_j} \right)}}$$

$$t = \frac{5.65 - 3.70}{\sqrt{3.37 \left(\dfrac{1}{20} + \dfrac{1}{20} \right)}}$$

$$= \frac{1.95}{.58}$$

$$t = \mathbf{3.36}$$

TABLE   13.13   The ANOVA Summary Table Based on the Data in Table 13.12

Source	SS	df	MS	F	p
Factor A (disorder)	6.67	1	6.67	1.98	n.s.
Factor B (treatment)	164.10	2	82.05	24.35	$p < .01$
$A \times B$	10.03	2	5.01	1.49	n.s.
Within-groups	181.80	54	3.37		
Total	362.60	59			

Since the t obtained value of 3.36 is larger than the critical value of 2.01, reject the null hypothesis. You would conclude that behavioral therapy leads to greater improvement than the procedures defining the control condition.

Psychoanalysis versus Control

$$t = \frac{\overline{X}_i - \overline{X}_j}{\sqrt{MS_W \left(\dfrac{1}{n_i} + \dfrac{1}{n_j} \right)}}$$

$$t = \frac{7.75 - 3.70}{\sqrt{3.37 \left(\dfrac{1}{20} + \dfrac{1}{20} \right)}}$$

$$= \frac{4.05}{.58}$$

$$t = \mathbf{6.98}$$

The obtained t value of 6.98 is greater than the critical value of 2.01, and the null hypothesis is rejected. Psychoanalysis proved to be a more effective treatment than the control condition. At this point you can conclude that at least two treatments exist for anxiety and depression, which can help those who suffer from these emotional problems. The next comparison addresses the question of whether one form of therapy is superior to the other.

Behavioral Therapy versus Psychoanalysis

$$t = \frac{\overline{X}_i - \overline{X}_j}{\sqrt{MS_W \left(\dfrac{1}{n_i} + \dfrac{1}{n_j} \right)}}$$

$$t = \frac{5.65 - 7.75}{\sqrt{3.37 \left(\dfrac{1}{20} + \dfrac{1}{20} \right)}}$$

$$= \frac{-2.10}{.58}$$

$$t = \mathbf{-3.62}$$

The absolute value of the obtained t value, 3.62, is larger than the critical value of 2.01. The null hypothesis is rejected and you would conclude that psychoanalysis is more effective with these types of problems than is behavioral therapy.

13.7 INTERPRETING THE FACTORS IN A TWO-WAY ANOVA

Factorial designs frequently use a subject variable as one of the independent variables. Personality type, sex, age, and psychodiagnosis are examples of subject variables that might be used as one factor in a two-way ANOVA design. It is important to remember that when a subject variable is an independent variable, no cause-effect statement can be made regarding the relation between this independent variable and the dependent variable. This aspect of the design is correlational because subjects are selected based on their standing on the subject variable. In other words, the subject variable is not manipulated by the experimenter. The fact that subjects are randomly sampled from a population does not alter this fact.

In the foregoing study, one factor used diagnosis as an independent variable: anxiety versus depression. The experimenter did not randomly assign subjects and then create the anxiety or depression. Subjects were selected into the study because they were already either anxious or depressed. If the experimenter had used an experimental operation to induce anxiety or depression, then anxiety and depression would not be subject variables.

Suppose one factor is a subject variable and the second factor is manipulated by the experimenter. The second factor can be interpreted in the language of cause-effect. Now suppose that there is an interaction between a subject variable and an experimental variable. Can you make a cause-effect statement, or is the interaction correlational in nature? The interpretation lies somewhere in the middle. For example, suppose you find that Type A people are more conforming than Type B people, but only when there is a clear payoff for conforming. When there is no identifiable payoff, Type A's are less conforming than Type B people. The payoff versus no payoff is experimentally manipulated; Type A and B subjects are randomly assigned to conditions, the conditions are manipulated by the experimenter, and they *cause* a differential behavioral effect among Type A and B subjects. However, how do you answer the question, "What is it about Type A and Type B subjects that caused them to respond differently?" Now you are asked to make a causal statement with respect to the aspect of the design that is correlational. You can only speculate about the answer. Because this independent variable is a subject variable, there is an unknown number of other subject variables that are correlated with this personality type (competitiveness, hostility, time urgency, and dominance, to name a few). There is simply no way to nail down the causal connection.

A researcher must always determine the methodological status of each independent variable in a factorial design. There are even two-way factorial designs in which both independent variables are subject variables. In this instance, the entire study is correlational. The causal interpretation of research results resides in the *design* of the study, not the type of statistical analysis used to analyze the data.

SUMMARY

A factorial design combines at least two independent variables. This arrangement allows an investigator to examine the effect of each independent variable separately (called main effects) and the joint effect of the independent variables (called the interaction). Each independent variable in a factorial design has at least two levels. A two-way factorial design, with two levels of each independent variable is a 2 × 2 design. If one of the variables has three levels and the other has two levels, it is a 2 × 3 factorial design. A cell mean is the mean of the scores for a single group. A marginal mean is the mean of one level of an independent variable (factor).

When conducting a two-way ANOVA there are three separate null hypotheses. Three F ratios are thus calculated and tested for statistical significance. The null hypothesis for Factor A is that there are no differences in the population means of the levels of Factor A. The null hypothesis for Factor B is that there are no differences in the population means of the levels of Factor B. The null hypothesis for the interaction is that there is no interaction.

The structure of the two-way ANOVA is an extension of the one-way ANOVA. In fact, the first stage of the structure for a two-way ANOVA is identical to the one-way ANOVA: total variance is due to between-group variance plus within-group variance. The second stage of the model is a further partitioning of the between-group variance into the variance due to Factor A, the variance due to Factor B, and the variance due to the interaction. The second stage of the model yields the F ratios that are tested for significance: F_A, F_B, and $F_{A \times B}$.

The F tests in the two-way ANOVA allow you to test the null hypothesis for each independent variable and the interaction. However, the F values do not provide information about the *strength* of each effect. Omega-squared is a statistic that states the percentage of variance in the dependent variable due to Factor A, Factor B, and the interaction.

If the factorial design has an independent variable with more than two levels, a significant main effect for that factor does not tell you which levels of the factor are significantly different from one another. In addition, the two-way ANOVA does not analyze differences between specific groups. Post hoc comparisons are used to locate the source of significance. This chapter presented one such test, Fisher's LSD, also called the protected t test.

The assumptions of the two-way ANOVA are the same as the assumptions of the one-way ANOVA. Scores in the populations should be normally distributed and have equal variances. The F test is robust with respect to these assumptions. The third assumption is that the observations should be independent of one another.

Finally, when interpreting the results of a two-way ANOVA, consider whether a subject variable is used as an independent variable. Subject variables maintain the status of correlated variables. Manipulated variables with random assignment allow causal statements.

KEY FORMULAS FOR CHAPTER 13

Definitional Formula for SS_T

$$SS_T = \Sigma(X - \overline{X}_G)^2$$ *(Formula 13.1)*

Computational Formula for SS_T

$$SS_T = \Sigma X^2 - \frac{(\Sigma X)^2}{N}$$

(Formula 13.2)

Definitional Formula for SS_{BG}

$$SS_{BG} = \Sigma n_k(\overline{X}_k - \overline{X}_G)^2$$

(Formula 13.3)

Computational Formula for SS_{BG}

$$SS_{BG} = \frac{(\Sigma X_{A_1B_1})^2}{n_{A_1B_1}} + \frac{(\Sigma X_{A_1B_2})^2}{n_{A_1B_2}} + \cdots + \frac{(\Sigma X_k)^2}{n_k} - \left[\frac{(\Sigma X)^2}{N}\right]$$

(Formula 13.4)

Definitional Formula for SS_W

$$SS_W = \Sigma(X_{A_1B_1} - \overline{X}_{A_1B_1})^2 + \Sigma(X_{A_1B_2} - \overline{X}_{A_1B_2})^2 \\ + \Sigma(X_{A_2B_1} - \overline{X}_{A_2B_1})^2 + \cdots + \Sigma(X_k - \overline{X}_k)^2$$

(Formula (13.5))

Computational Formula for SS_W

$$SS_W = \Sigma X^2 - \left[\frac{(\Sigma X_{A_1B_1})^2}{n_{A_1B_1}} + \frac{(\Sigma X_{A_1B_2})^2}{n_{A_2B_2}} + \cdots + \frac{(\Sigma X_k)^2}{n_k}\right]$$

(Formula 13.6)

Definitional Formula for SS_A

$$SS_A = n_{A_1}(\overline{X}_{A_1} - \overline{X}_G)^2 + n_{A_2}(\overline{X}_{A_2} - \overline{X}_G)^2 \\ + n_{\text{last } A \text{ level}}(\overline{X}_{\text{last } A \text{ level}} - \overline{X}_G)^2$$

(Formula 13.7)

Computational Formula for SS_A

$$SS_A = \frac{(\Sigma X_{A_1})^2}{n_{A_1}} + \frac{(\Sigma X_{A_2})^2}{n_{A_2}} + \frac{(\Sigma X_{\text{last } A \text{ level}})^2}{n_{\text{last } A \text{ level}}} - \left[\frac{(\Sigma X)^2}{N}\right]$$

(Formula 13.8)

Definitional Formula for SS_B

$$SS_B = n_{B_1}(\overline{X}_{B_1} - \overline{X}_G)^2 + n_{B_2}(\overline{X}_{B_2} - \overline{X}_G)^2 \\ + n_{\text{last } B \text{ level}}(\overline{X}_{\text{last } B \text{ level}} - \overline{X}_G)^2$$

(Formula 13.9)

Computational Formula for SS_B

$$SS_B = \frac{(\Sigma X_{B_1})^2}{n_{B_1}} + \frac{(\Sigma X_{B_2})^2}{n_{B_2}} + \frac{(\Sigma X_{\text{last } B \text{ level}})^2}{n_{\text{last } B \text{ level}}} - \left[\frac{(\Sigma X)^2}{N}\right]$$

(Formula 13.10)

Formula for $SS_{A \times B}$

$$SS_{A \times B} = n_k[(\overline{X}_{A_1B_1} - \overline{X}_{A_1} - \overline{X}_{B_1} + \overline{X}_G)^2 \\ + (\overline{X}_{A_2B_1} - \overline{X}_{A_2} - \overline{X}_{B_1} + \overline{X}_G)^2 \\ + (\overline{X}_{A_1B_2} - \overline{X}_{A_1} - \overline{X}_{B_2} + \overline{X}_G)^2 \\ + (\overline{X}_{A_2B_2} - \overline{X}_{A_2} - \overline{X}_{B_2} + \overline{X}_G)^2]$$

(Formula 13.11)

Omega-Squared for Factor A

$$\omega_A^2 = \frac{SS_A - (df_A)MS_W}{SS_T + MS_W}$$

(Formula 13.12)

Omega-Squared for Factor B

$$\omega_B^2 = \frac{SS_B - (df_B)MS_W}{SS_T + MS_W}$$

(Formula 13.13)

Omega-Squared for the Interaction

$$\omega_{A \times B}^2 = \frac{SS_{A \times B} - (df_{A \times B})MS_W}{SS_T + MS_W}$$

(Formula 13.14)

Work Problem

1. Specify the first and second partitioned stages of the two-way ANOVA.
2. What are the null and alternative hypotheses for:
   a. Factor A b. Factor B c. Interaction
3. Complete these ANOVA summary tables. Test for significance at the 5 percent level.

a.

Source	SS	df	MS	F	p
Factor A	147.00	2	73.50		
Factor B	27.44	2	13.72		
$A \times B$	12.22	4	3.06		
Within-groups	95.33	45	2.12		
Total	281.99	53			

b.

Source	SS	df	MS	F	p
Factor A	3.36		3.36		
Factor B	66.67	2			
$A \times B$	56.89				
Within-groups					
Total	238.75	35			

c.

Source	SS	df	MS	F	p
Factor A		1	.45		
Factor B	6.05				
$A \times B$	84.05	1			
Within-groups		16	1.28		
Total					

4. Draw a graph for each of the following data sets. Place Factor B on the X axis, and the means on the Y axis. The two lines on the graphs correspond to the levels of Factor A. For each graph, indicate if you think there is an $A \times B$ interaction.

a.

Factor B

35	5	A_1
55	25	A_2

Factor A

B_1 B_2

b.

Factor B

30	30	A_1
10	50	A_2

Factor A

B_1 B_2

c.

Factor B

25	10	A_1
10	30	A_2

Factor A

B_1 B_2

5. An experimental psychologist is interested in how performance is affected by reinforcement and amount of food deprivation. Performance is measured by the time, in seconds, it takes a rat to run down an alley to a food box. Twenty rats are randomly assigned to four treatment conditions: High Incentive–High Deprivation, High Incentive–Low Deprivation, Low Incentive–High Deprivation, and Low Incentive–Low Deprivation. Deprivation level is manipulated by maintaining one group of rats at 85 percent of their normal weight and a second group at 95 percent of their normal weight. Incentive is manipulated by the size of the reward at the end of the alley. In the Low-Incentive condition, a 45-mg food pellet is waiting. In the High-Incentive condition, a 260-mg food pellet is waiting. The raw data for this hypothetical experiment are presented in the following 2 × 2 matrix. Set alpha at .05 and perform a two-way ANOVA.
   a. Summarize the results in an ANOVA table.
   b. Provide a graph with Incentive on the X axis.
   c. Calculate omega-squared for the significant effect.
   d. What do these results tell us about the effect of incentive and deprivation on performance?

Factor B: Deprivation (Body Weight)

		85% (High)	95% (Low)
Factor A: (Incentive)	45 mg (Low)	7 8 6 7 7	10 7 6 8 6
	260 mg (High)	5 4 4 5 6	9 9 6 7 7

6. An educational psychologist is interested in the effect of delayed feedback on learning, and if delayed feedback operates differently as a function of educational level. All subjects, comprised of freshmen and seniors, are administered a 15-question test; after answering the questions, the subjects are given the correct answers at various intervals, depending on which experimental condition they are assigned. All subjects are given the same test four days later. The dependent variable is how many questions they answer correctly. Set alpha at .05. For the following data set,
   a. Provide an ANOVA summary table.
   b. Graph the results with delayed feedback on the X axis.
   c. Conduct protected t tests if appropriate.
   d. Interpret the findings
   e. Calculate omega-squared for any significant effect.

		Factor B		
		No Delay	2-Hr Delay	1-Day Delay
Factor A	Freshmen	15 12 13 10 11	7 9 5 8 8	4 6 7 7 7
	Seniors	13 15 13 10 10	6 5 6 9 6	8 5 5 6 7

7. A clinical psychologist is interested in the effects of cognitive therapy alone, medication alone, and the combined effects of therapy and medication for depression. The following table provides the summary statistics for each cell, the marginal means, and the grand mean.
   a. Summarize the results in an ANOVA table.

b. If the person could not afford therapy, is there reason to recommend medication alone?

c. If the person could not tolerate medication, is there reason to recommend therapy alone?

d. Is cognitive therapy alone more effective than medication alone? (*Hint:* Fisher's LSD).

e. Is cognitive therapy plus medication more effective than cognitive therapy alone? (*Hint:* Fisher's LSD)

f. Is cognitive therapy plus medication more effective than medication alone?

Factor B: Medication

		Yes	No	
Factor A: Cognitive Therapy	Yes	$\overline{X}_{A_1B_1} = 8.6$ $\Sigma X_{A_1B_1} = 43$ $\Sigma X^2_{A_1B_1} = 375$ $n_{A_1B_1} = 5$	$\overline{X}_{A_1B_2} = 5.2$ $\Sigma X_{A_1B_2} = 26$ $\Sigma X^2_{A_1B_2} = 138$ $n_{A_1B_2} = 5$	$\overline{X}_{A_1} = 6.9$
	No	$\overline{X}_{A_2B_1} = 3.8$ $\Sigma X_{A_2B_1} = 19$ $\Sigma X^2_{A_2B_1} = 75$ $n_{A_2B_1} = 5$	$\overline{X}_{A_2B_2} = 2.2$ $\Sigma X_{A_2B_2} = 11$ $\Sigma X^2_{A_2B_2} = 27$ $n_{A_2B_2} = 5$	$\overline{X}_{A_2} = 3.0$
		$\overline{X}_{B_1} = 6.2$	$\overline{X}_{B_2} = 3.7$	$\overline{X}_G = 4.95$

8. Romano and Bordiere (1989) conducted a study to determine if the physical attractiveness of a professor influences students' perceptions of how much they think they will learn from the professor. The design was a 2 × 2 factorial with one factor physical attractiveness of the professor (Attractive/Unattractive), and the other factor sex of the student (Male/Female). Students provided ratings on a 9-point scale, which reflected how much they thought they would learn, with higher numbers reflecting more learning. Slides of professors were use to obtain the ratings. The following data set is hypothetical, but is constructed so that you arrive at the same results as the investigators.

a. Provide an ANOVA summary table.

b. Interpret the findings.

Factor B: Professor

		Attractive	Unattractive
	Male	8 6 6 7 5	4 5 7 4 6
Factor A	Female	9 7 5 7 7	3 7 4 4 4

9. A psychologist is interested in whether Black defendants draw stiffer sentences than white defendants, whether Black judges give stiffer sentences than white judges, and if there is an interaction between the race of the judge and the race of the defendant when it comes to sentencing. A hypothetical data set was constructed. The first table shows the group means and the second table is a partial ANOVA table. Set alpha at .05. (Higher means reflect stiffer sentences.)
   a. Complete the ANOVA summary table.
   b. Interpret the findings.

		Factor B: Defendant	
		Black	*White*
Factor A: Judge	*Black*	27.33	20.00
	White	29.50	23.67

Source	SS	df	MS	F	p
Factor *A* (race of judge)	51.04	1			
Factor *B* (race of defendant)	260.04	1			
A × *B*	3.38	1			
Within-groups					
Total	1396.63	23			

10. The Type A personality is defined in part by a sense of time urgency and a hard-driving, competitive approach in achievement situations. The Type B individual takes a more relaxed approach to achievement-oriented tasks. The Type X personality is a mixture of Type A and Type B characteristics. An organizational psychologist is interested in whether there is an interaction between personality type and an incentive program on sales production. Factor *B* is personality type, Factor *A* is the manner in which the salesperson is paid—by salary or commission. The first table presents the cell means and sample sizes. The second table is a partial ANOVA table. Set alpha at .05.
    a. Complete the ANOVA table.
    b. Conduct protected *t* tests to locate the sources of significance.
    c. Interpret the findings.

		Factor B		
		Type A	*Type B*	*Type X*
Factor A	*Salary*	17.33 $n = 6$	14.83 $n = 6$	12.17 $n = 6$
	Commission	25.0 $n = 6$	17.17 $n = 6$	17.0 $n = 6$

Source	SS	df	MS	F	p
Factor A (incentive)					
Factor B (personality)	288.17	2			
$A \times B$	42.72	2			
Within-groups	731.83	30			
Total	1282.75	35			

11. Define a main effect.

12. Define an interaction.

13. In a t test, are you testing for a main effect or an interaction?

14. In a one-way ANOVA, are you testing for a main effect or an interaction?

15. Why should you use caution when interpreting a main effect when there is an interaction?

16. Suppose a constant were added to each score in a 2×3 factorial design. What effect would this have on the main effects and interaction? How would MS_W be affected?

Work Problems for the Computer

17. A psychologist is interested in the following research questions:
    a. Can cognitive strategies increase the delay of gratification among children?
    b. Is there a difference between girls and boys in delay of gratification?
    c. Is there an interaction between sex and the effectiveness of cognitive strategies?

    The experimental task required the subject to sit facing a bowl of marshmallows on a table. He or she was told, "You can eat as many of the marshmallows as you want, but I would like you to try and wait until I return. If you can't wait, that's OK, but please try. To help you not eat any marshmallows I am going to give you something to think about." In the Cognitive Transformation condition, subjects were taught to imagine that the marshmallows were white, fluffy clouds. In the Self-talk condition, subjects were told to repeat to themselves," Don't eat the marshmallows." In the Control condition, subjects were not provided with any cognitive technique. The experimenter left the room and observed the subject through a one-way mirror, recording the number of seconds elapsed before the child ate a marshmallow. Use $\alpha = .05$ to test for main effects and an interaction. Provide an ANOVA summary table and interpret the findings.

		Cognitive Strategy: Factor B								
		Transformation			*Self-Talk*			*Control*		
	Boys	15	12	13	14	10	15	30	12	17
		15	15	30	16	17	28	19	22	25
		10	19	32	11	22	32	14	43	32
		20	25	29	19	18	29	10	18	39
		30	35	19	29	47	25	25	45	16
		75	60	25	74	55	18	70	50	20
		40	50		45	60		40	62	
Sex: Factor A										
	Girls	65	89	61	72	90	65	85	80	60
		45	22	49	35	18	49	25	30	59
		50	78	35	60	75	39	60	70	25
		53	74	74	43	74	72	70	90	75
		75	99	77	75	89	60	67	80	80
		64	77	82	68	85	80	63	82	75
		55	43		50	48		50	42	

18. An experimental psychologist hypothesizes that a High-drive state will increase errors on a mental arithmetic task in comparison to a Low-drive state. Drive state is experimentally manipulated by telling half the subjects that performance on the task is related to intelligence (High-drive state). Subjects in the Low-drive condition are told that their answers to the problems are to be used as normative data for a future study. The researcher also hypothesizes that drive state will interact with the difficulty of the task. More specifically, subjects experiencing high drive will not perform as well when the task is difficult rather than easy. Subjects in the Difficult condition receive more complicated problems than those subjects in the Easy condition. The researcher is predicting a main effect for drive, and an interaction between task difficulty and level of drive state. The dependent variable is the number of errors made over a long series of mental arithmetic problems. Perform a two-way ANOVA on the following data, with alpha set at .05. You will find that there are main effects for both factors, in addition to a significant interaction. Answer the following questions.

   a. What accounts for the interaction?

   b. How should the main effects be interpreted in view of the significant interaction?

Task Difficulty: Factor B

		Easy			Difficult		
		18	12	15	28	20	19
		10	16	18	30	15	15
	High drive	19	15	20	35	30	27
		15	12	17	37	37	29
		20	22	17	25	29	30
Drive State:							
Factor A		16	14	15	15	17	18
		12	29	20	20	25	16
	Low drive	10	27	20	10	16	25
		22	30	25	18	13	11
		20	16	19	19	12	16

Repeated-Measures Analysis of Variance

14.1 THE RESEARCH CONTEXT

Repeated-Measures Designs

In a between-groups design, each subject receives one and only one treatment. This is true whether the design has one or more independent variables. The effect of the independent variable is evaluated by comparing the average performance of each of the groups. In a **repeated-measures design** (also called a **within-subjects design**), every subject is exposed to *each* of the treatment conditions.[1] Since you can obtain information about the effect of each treatment condition by using the same group of subjects, this type of design requires fewer subjects than a between-groups design, and as a result, is more efficient. Chapter 9 used the dependent-samples *t* test as the analysis of choice in a repeated-measures design with two experimental conditions. In this chapter, the number of conditions is greater than two. The appropriate statistical analysis is called a repeated-measures ANOVA.

The main advantage of a repeated-measures design is that there is greater control over subject variables. Chapter 1 explained that subject variables are fixed attributes of a person—that is—fixed at the time the subject enters the experiment. Intelligence, sex, psychiatric diagnosis, and personality traits are examples of subject variables. When using a between-groups design, subject variables can present a problem. Suppose a researcher is interested in a teaching technique to enhance learning. If, by chance, the experimental group has more intelligent people, the superior performance of this group may be due to intelligence rather than the new teaching technique. In this instance, "intelligence" is confounded with "treatment." How is this problem circumvented when using a repeated-measures design? By using the *same* subjects in every treatment condition, it is *impossible* for one treatment condition to have more or less of a subject variable than another treatment condition.

Suppose you are interested in testing the effectiveness of three different studying strategies on examination performance. In a between-groups design you would randomly assign, for instance, 60 subjects to the three training programs (20 subjects per group). In a within-subjects design you would take 20 subjects and run them through each program (see Table 14.1). Your measure of performance, which is the dependent variable, would be taken after completing each program. Not only does a repeated-measures design eliminate any systematic bias due to subject variables, the design is more economical than a between-groups design.

One problem that can arise when using a within-subjects design has to do with the order in which treatments are presented. Assume that Treatment III proves to be the most effective approach. If all the subjects received this program *after* being exposed to the other two training programs, you would not know if this result was due to the strategy taught in Treatment III or the fact that this strategy was taught after Treatments I and II. In other words, the *position* of Treatment III

---

[1] The terms repeated-measures and within-subjects will be used interchangeably.

TABLE 14.1 A Within-Subjects Design: 20 Subjects are Exposed to Each Treatment Condition

Treatment I	Treatment II	Treatment III
Subject 1	Subject 1	Subject 1
Subject 2	Subject 2	Subject 2
Subject 3	Subject 3	Subject 3
⋮	⋮	⋮
Subject 20	Subject 20	Subject 20

(as well as Treatment II) is confounded with the treatment strategy. Since the effect of a treatment condition as it follows some other treatment is usually not of interest, **order effects** present problems for the repeated-measures design. An order effect is a confounding variable because the order in which the treatment occurs may account for the results—instead of, or in addition to, the treatment itself.

There are several types of order effects. Given that measurements of the dependent variable are taken after each treatment, performance may improve due to *practice.* On the other hand, if all the treatment conditions are presented in one session, participants may become *fatigued* and show a performance deterioration. Additionally, subsequent treatments may be influenced by a *carryover* effect. In the strategies for studying example, it would be impossible to have subjects forget what they learned in the prior training programs. Thus, the effects of Treatment III are actually the effects of Treatment III *after* learning the strategies of the first two treatments. In other words, what is learned in Treatments I and II carries over to the subjects' performance in Treatment III.

 To reduce order effects, investigators use a research design strategy called counterbalancing. **Counterbalancing** involves the presentation of experimental conditions in a different order for different subjects. Treatment I would be presented first for some subjects, second for some subjects, and third for other subjects. The same would hold true for Treatments II and III. Order effects would be eliminated in that they are spread equally across conditions. Therefore, they would be eliminated as confounding variables—that is—as alternative explanations of the results of the study.[2]

Not all research questions lend themselves to a within-subjects design. For instance, it is very unusual to find a psychotherapy study that uses a repeated-measures design. However, drug treatments are often investigated with a repeated-measures design. Since drugs typically do not affect behavior through learning, different drugs can be administered in a repeated-measures design. Investigators control for carryover effects by allowing the first drug to clear the patient's system before beginning the second drug trial. In general, however, any treatment that produces relatively permanent changes in the measured variable is best evaluated in a between-groups design.

---

[2] Whenever a repeated-measures design is used in this chapter, assume that the experimental conditions are counterbalanced.

Examples of Repeated-Measures Designs

▶ **EXAMPLE 1**   An experimental psychologist is interested in whether a subject's level of physiological arousal influences olfactory sensitivity (Halpin, 1978). Subjects are asked to detect the presence of a solution of 1-propanol in distilled water. The ability to detect increasingly weak solutions is the measure of olfactory sensitivity. The independent variable is arousal. Three levels of arousal are used: low, medium, and high. Low arousal is induced by having subjects relax, medium arousal is induced by having subjects listen to an annoying sound, and high arousal is created by threatening the subjects with an electric shock. What makes this a repeated-measures design is that the same sample of subjects is exposed to each arousal condition. Olfactory sensitivity is assessed after each experimental manipulation (i.e., arousal manipulation).   ◀

▶ **EXAMPLE 2**   A psychologist in marketing wants to see if people can tell the difference in the smoothness of the ride among three cars. One sample of subjects is blindfolded and given a ride in a Lincoln Continental, a Cadillac Fleetwood, and a Rolls Royce. Ratings of smoothness are obtained after each ride.   ◀

▶ **EXAMPLE 3**   A cognitive psychologist is interested in the effects of caffeine on memory. The same sample of subjects is asked to memorize and recall nonsense syllables under three levels of caffeine intake.   ◀

The type of repeated-measures design and analysis discussed in this chapter is limited to the case in which *one* independent variable is used. However, factorial designs that have a repeated-measures factor are common in the behavioral sciences. For instance, any study that has one factor that is treatment, and a second factor that is a pretest/post-test qualifies as a repeated-measures factorial design. Most advanced statistics textbooks cover factorial designs in which one independent variable is represented by a pretest/post-test (Keppel, 1982; Kirk, 1982).

Since you have likely read the previous two chapters on ANOVA, you will find the logic of the repeated-measures ANOVA familiar.

14.2   THE LOGIC OF THE REPEATED-MEASURES ANOVA

The Null Hypothesis

When conducting a repeated-measures ANOVA there is one F ratio which is the F ratio that tests for a significant difference among the levels of the independent variable. Therefore, there is only one null hypothesis:

$$H_0: \quad \mu_1 = \mu_2 = \mu_3 = \mu_k$$

The alternative hypothesis is that at least two of the group means come from different populations:

$$H_1: \quad \text{the null hypothesis is false}$$

Partitioning Variability

The basic structure of the F ratio in the repeated-measures ANOVA is the same as F ratios computed in other designs.

$$F = \frac{\text{between-group variance}}{\text{within-group variance}}$$

In the context of a repeated-measures design, "between-group" refers to the difference between treatment conditions. There is only one sample of subjects; they form different groups only in the sense that they are exposed to different treatment conditions.

In the repeated-measures ANOVA, total variability is partitioned into between-group variability and within-group variability. The analysis proceeds in two stages, not unlike the two-way ANOVA. Figure 14.1 illustrates the sources of variability in the repeated-measures ANOVA.

Between-Group Variability

In the one-way ANOVA, between-group variability is due to three factors: the effect due to treatment, the effect due to individual differences, and variation accounted for by experimental error. Individual differences and experimental error are included in the term error or error variance. The critical difference in the repeated-measures ANOVA is that the effect due to individual differences is absent from between-group variation. Any difference among the treatment means cannot be

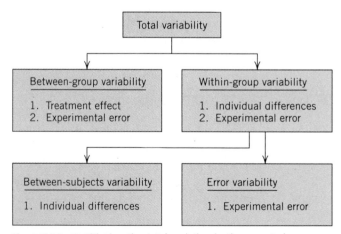

Figure 14.1   Partitioning the total variation in the repeated-measures ANOVA.

due to individual differences because the same subjects are participating in each condition. Therefore, subject variables are held constant over experimental conditions. Thus,

between-group variance = treatment effect + experimental error

Within-Group Variability

In a one-way ANOVA, the variability within a treatment condition is due to two factors: individual differences and experimental error. This is also true in a repeated-measures ANOVA. However, the repeated-measures ANOVA allows for the partitioning of the within-group variability into variance due to individual differences and variation due to experimental error. Because the effects due to individual differences and experimental error can be separated, the variability due to individual differences can be removed. Thus, the denominator of the F ratio only includes experimental error. Therefore,

$$F = \frac{\text{between-group variance}}{\text{within-group variance}}$$

$$= \frac{\text{treatment effect} + \text{experimental error}}{\text{experimental error}}$$

Since the effect due to individual differences can be removed from the denominator, the size of the denominator decreases. As the denominator becomes smaller, the F ratio becomes larger. As the F ratio increases, it is easier to reject the null hypothesis. As a consequence, the repeated-measures ANOVA has greater power than the between-groups ANOVA.

Refer to Figure 14.1. Note that in the second stage of the model, within-group variability has been partitioned. A new term has been introduced: *between-subjects variability*. Do not confuse this with between-group variability. Between-group variation is the variation among group means and is due to treatment effect plus error. Between-subjects variability is the variation in scores due only to individual differences. Also, since the denominator of any F ratio is referred to as error, in the repeated-measures ANOVA the term error refers to the variability *only* due to experimental error.

Does Removing the Effect Due to Individual Differences Really Matter?

In a one-way ANOVA, the effect due to individual differences shows up in the numerator and the denominator. The numerator also includes the treatment effect and, if large enough, will yield an F ratio that is statistically significant. But if the variation due to individual differences is removed from both the numerator and the denominator, what is gained? A simple illustration answers this question. Suppose two experiments are contrasted, one using a between-groups design and another using a repeated-measures design. Further, let's arbitrarily assign units of variation to each component of the F ratio.

treatment effect = 100 units

individual differences = 1400 units

experimental error = 3 units

F Ratio for Between-Groups Design

$$F = \frac{\text{treatment} + \text{individual differences} + \text{experimental error}}{\text{individual differences} + \text{experimental error}}$$

$$= \frac{100 + 1400 + 3}{1400 + 3}$$

$$F = 1.07$$

Now what happens to the F ratio if the variation due to individual differences is removed?

F Ratio for Repeated-Measures Design

$$F = \frac{\text{treatment} + \text{experimental error}}{\text{experimental error}}$$

$$= \frac{100 + 3}{3}$$

$$F = 34.33$$

The result is dramatic. However, removing the variability due to individual differences does not always make such a big difference. It depends on the size of the effect that is due to individual differences. If subject variables account for a small amount of the variation in scores, there is only a small increase in the size of the F ratio. However, since there is *always* variation due to individual differences, the F ratio is always going to be larger with a repeated-measures ANOVA, all things being equal. Since larger F ratios are, obviously, more likely to lead you to reject the null hypothesis, a repeated-measures ANOVA has more *power* than an ANOVA conducted in a between-groups design. If you have a choice between a repeated-meaures design and a design that uses independent groups, use the repeated-measures design.

14.3   THE FORMULAS FOR THE REPEATED-MEASURES ANOVA

The formulas for the repeated-measures ANOVA are presented first, followed by a worked problem, which illustrates the computational steps in the repeated-measures ANOVA.

The Sums of Squares

The Total Sum of Squares, SS_T

The repeated-measures ANOVA begins with the calculation of SS_T. Since the sums of squares, which you will be computing later, should add up to the SS_T, arriving at SS_T allows for a computational check. Moreover, SS_T is stated in the ANOVA summary table. The SS_T measures the total variability among all the scores in the study. Formula 14.1 is identical to the formula for the SS_T in the one-way and two-way ANOVA.

Formula for SS_T

$$SS_T = \Sigma X^2 - \frac{(\Sigma X)^2}{N}$$

(Formula 14.1)

where,

ΣX^2 = the sum of all the squared scores
$(\Sigma X)^2$ = the sum of all the scores, quantity squared
N = the total number of scores, *not* the total number of subjects

---

The Sum of Squares Between-Groups, SS_{BG}

In the first stage of the partitioning of the total variability, the total variation among all the scores is partitioned into between-group variability and within-group variability (refer to Figure 14.1).

Formula for SS_{BG}

$$SS_{BG} = \frac{(\Sigma X_1)^2}{n_1} + \frac{(\Sigma X_2)^2}{n_2} + \cdots + \frac{(\Sigma X_k)^2}{n_k} - \left[\frac{(\Sigma X)^2}{N}\right]$$

(Formula 14.2)

where,

$(\Sigma X_1)^2, (\Sigma X_2)^2, (\Sigma X_k)^2$ = the sum of the scores in the first experimental condition, the second experimental condition, and so on, quantity squared; here you are summing the scores in each column

n_1, n_2, n_k = the number of scores in the first experimental condition, the second experimental condition, and so on; i.e., the number of scores in each column (see Table 14.1)

The Sum of Squares Within-Groups, SS_W

You are about to complete the first stage of the partitioning of the total variability. The SS_T is partitioned into the SS_{BG} and the SS_W. You have already computed SS_T and SS_{BG}. Next comes the computation of SS_W. Recall that the SS_W refers to variability within the treatment conditions.

> **Formula for SS_W**
>
> $$SS_W = \Sigma X^2 - \left[\frac{(\Sigma X_1)^2}{n_1} + \frac{(\Sigma X_2)^2}{n_2} + \cdots + \frac{(\Sigma X_k)^2}{n_k} \right]$$
>
> *(Formula 14.3)*

Computational Check

Since SS_T is partitioned into SS_{BG} and SS_W, it must be the case that:

$$SS_T = SS_{BG} + SS_W$$

The Sum of Squares Between-Subjects, SS_{BS}

The first stage of the partitioning of the total variation has been completed. What remains is to further partition the within-group variability, SS_W. The SS_W is partitioned into SS_{BS} and SS_{error}. Instead of summing scores within columns, you sum scores within rows. Note that a new symbol, P, is introduced.

> **Formula for SS_{BS}**
>
> $$SS_{BS} = \frac{(\Sigma P_1)^2}{k} + \frac{(\Sigma P_2)^2}{k} + \cdots + \frac{(\Sigma P_{\text{last person}})^2}{k} - \left[\frac{(\Sigma X)^2}{N} \right]$$
>
> *(Formula 14.4)*
>
> *where,*
>
> $(\Sigma P_1)^2$, $(\Sigma P_2)^2$, $(\Sigma P_{\text{last person}})^2$ = each *person's* score in every experimental condition is summed; all the first person's scores are summed, all the second person's scores are summed, and so on, until the last person's scores are summed; each quantity is squared
>
> $(\Sigma X)^2$ = the sum of all the scores in the study, quantity squared.
>
> k = the number of experimental conditions

The Sum of Squares Error, SS_{error}

Recall that within-group variability is partitioned into between-subjects variation (individual differences) and variation due to error (experimental error). Thus,

$$SS_W = SS_{BS} + SS_{error}$$

The SS_{error} is found by subtraction.[3] Rearranging the foregoing equation gives:

$$SS_{error} = SS_W - SS_{BS}$$

Partitioning the Degrees of Freedom

Partitioning the total degrees of freedom follows the same form as partitioning the total variation of scores. Figure 14.2 illustrates this fact. Table 14.2 lists the various degrees of freedom and their computation.

The Mean Squares and *F* Ratio

The last step in the repeated-measures ANOVA is to calculate the various Mean Squares used in the *F* ratio. Since the type of repeated-measures ANOVA in this

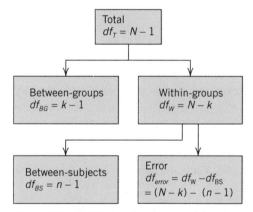

Figure 14.2 Partitioning the degrees of freedom in the repeated-measures ANOVA.

TABLE 14.2 **The Degrees of Freedom for a Repeated-Measures ANOVA**

Source	Computation	Degrees of Freedom
Total	$N-1$	df_T
Between-groups	$k-1$	df_{BG}
Within-groups	$N-k$	df_W
Between-subjects	$n-1$	df_{BS}
Error	$(N-k)-(n-1)$	$df_{error} = df_W - df_{BS}$

[3] In some textbooks, SS_{error} is referred to as SS_{res} (residual sum of squares). Another designation for SS_{error} is $SS_{A \times B}$.

chapter has only one independent variable, there is only one F ratio:

$$F = \frac{MS_{BG}}{MS_{error}}$$

where,

$$MS_{BG} = SS_{BG}/df_{BG}$$
$$MS_{error} = SS_{error}/df_{error}$$

Be reminded that the denominator of the F ratio in the repeated-measures ANOVA is MS_{error} rather than MS_W. With the effect of individual differences removed, using MS_{error} preserves the basic structure of the F ratio:

$$F = \frac{\text{treatment} + \text{experimental error}}{\text{experimental error}}$$

Worked Problem

Clinical psychologists have noted that anxious people sometimes have difficulty concentrating. Suppose a researcher is interested in the effects of a drug, which is administered at different dosages, on cognitive performance. Ten anxious subjects are selected and exposed to four treatment conditions. In one treatment condition, the subjects are administered 2.5 mg of Valium. A second and third condition involve the administration of 5 mg and 10 mg of Valium. The fourth condition serves as a control; here the subjects receive a placebo. Subjects are asked to solve a series of mental arithmetic problems, with the dependent variable being the number of errors committed. The treatment conditions are presented one week apart to assure that the drug has cleared from the subjects' systems before the effect of a new dosage is assessed. In addition, the order in which the treatments are delivered is counterbalanced among the subjects to remove order as a confounding variable. Table 14.3 presents the design of this experiment. In the body

TABLE 14.3   The Repeated-Measures Design for the Hypothetical Worked Problem

Subjects	Placebo (1)	2.5 mg (2)	5 mg (3)	10 mg (4)
S_1	X_{11}	X_{12}	X_{13}	X_{14}
S_2	X_{21}	X_{22}	X_{23}	X_{24}
S_3	X_{31}	X_{32}	X_{33}	X_{34}
S_4	X_{41}	X_{42}	X_{43}	X_{44}
S_5	X_{51}	X_{52}	X_{53}	X_{54}
S_6	X_{61}	X_{62}	X_{63}	X_{64}
S_7	X_{71}	X_{72}	X_{73}	X_{74}
S_8	X_{81}	X_{82}	X_{83}	X_{84}
S_9	X_{91}	X_{92}	X_{93}	X_{94}
S_{10}	X_{101}	X_{102}	X_{103}	X_{104}

of the table, each X symbolizes a score. The first subscript of X identifies the subject, the second subscript identifies the experimental condition. Thus, X_{23} refers to the obtained score for subject number 2 under experimental condition number 3. Note that although the total number of subjects is 10, the total number of scores is 40. This point will become important when you analyze degrees of freedom. The data for this study are presented in Table 14.4.

Summary of the Computational Steps
Compute:

1. SS_T
2. SS_{BG}
3. SS_W
4. SS_{BS}
5. SS_{error}
6. Compute the df for each of the foregoing SS
7. MS_{BG}
8. MS_{error}
9. F ratio

Calculating the Sums of Squares
Step 1. Compute the total sum of squares, SS_T.

$$SS_T = \Sigma X^2 - \frac{(\Sigma X)^2}{N}$$

TABLE 14.4 Raw Data for the Worked Problem

Subjects	Placebo	2.5 mg	5 mg	10 mg	
S_1	14	5	9	15	$\Sigma P_1 = 43^a$
S_2	12	3	6	11	$\Sigma P_2 = 32$
S_3	10	2	7	9	$\Sigma P_3 = 28$
S_4	7	4	5	7	$\Sigma P_4 = 23$
S_5	9	4	6	8	$\Sigma P_5 = 27$
S_6	9	1	3	7	$\Sigma P_6 = 20$
S_7	10	3	4	9	$\Sigma P_7 = 26$
S_8	5	0	0	13	$\Sigma P_8 = 18$
S_9	6	4	4	6	$\Sigma P_9 = 20$
S_{10}	8	6	6	7	$\Sigma P_{10} = 27$
	$\Sigma_1 = 90$	$\Sigma X_2 = 32$	$\Sigma X_3 = 50$	$\Sigma X_4 = 92$	$\Sigma X = 264$
	$\overline{X_1} = 9.0$	$\overline{X_2} = 3.2$	$\overline{X_3} = 5.0$	$\overline{X_4} = 9.2$	

^{a} P (person) is the symbol used for a subject in a repeated-measures design.

Thus,

$$SS_T = 2236 - \frac{(264)^2}{40}$$

$$= 2236 - 1742.40$$

$$SS_T = \mathbf{493.60}$$

Step 2. Compute the sum of squares between-groups, SS_{BG}.

$$SS_{BG} = \frac{(\Sigma X_1)^2}{n_1} + \frac{(\Sigma X_2)^2}{n_2} + \cdots + \frac{(\Sigma X_k)^2}{n_k} - \left[\frac{(\Sigma X)^2}{N} \right]$$

Placing the numbers in the formula,

$$SS_{BG} = \frac{(90)^2}{10} + \frac{(32)^2}{10} + \frac{(50)^2}{10} + \frac{(92)^2}{10} - \left[\frac{(264)^2}{40} \right]$$

$$= 810 + 102.40 + 250 + 846.40 - 1742.40$$

$$= 2008.80 - 1742.40$$

$$SS_{BG} = \mathbf{266.40}$$

Step 3. Compute the sum of squares within-groups, SS_W.
You are about to complete the first stage of the partitioning of the total variability. The SS_T is partitioned into the SS_{BG} and the SS_W. SS_T and SS_{BG} have been computed. Next comes the calculation of SS_W. Recall that the SS_W refers to variability within the treatment conditions.
The formula for SS_W is:

$$SS_W = \Sigma X^2 - \left[\frac{(\Sigma X_1)^2}{n_1} + \frac{(\Sigma X_2)^2}{n_2} + \cdots + \frac{(\Sigma X_k)^2}{n_k} \right]$$

For the worked problem,

$$SS_W = 2236 - \left[\frac{(90)^2}{10} + \frac{(32)^2}{10} + \frac{(50)^2}{10} + \frac{(92)^2}{10} \right]$$

$$= 2236 - 810 + 102.40 + 250 + 846.40$$

$$= 2236 - 2008.80$$

$$SS_W = \mathbf{227.20}$$

Step 4. Perform a computational check.
Since SS_T is partitioned into SS_{BG} and SS_W,

$$SS_T = SS_{BG} + SS_W$$

Therefore,

$$493.60 = 266.40 + 227.20$$

Step 5.   Compute the sum of squares between-subjects, SS_{BS}.

$$SS_{BS} = \frac{(\Sigma P_1)^2}{k} + \frac{(\Sigma P_2)^2}{k} + \cdots + \frac{(\Sigma P_{\text{last person}})^2}{k} - \left[\frac{(\Sigma X)^2}{N}\right]$$

$$SS_{BS} = \frac{(43)^2}{4} + \frac{(32)^2}{4} + \frac{(28)^2}{4} + \frac{(23)^2}{4} + \frac{(27)^2}{4}$$

$$+ \frac{(20)^2}{4} + \frac{(26)^2}{4} + \frac{(18)^2}{4} + \frac{(20)^2}{4} + \frac{(27)^2}{4} - \left[\frac{(264)^2}{40}\right]$$

$$= 1861 - 1742.40$$

$$SS_{BS} = \mathbf{118.60}$$

Step 6.   Compute the sum of squares error, SS_{error}.
Within-group variability is partitioned into between-subjects variation (individual differences) and variation due to error (experimental error). Therefore,

$$SS_W = SS_{BS} + SS_{\text{error}}$$

As noted previously, the SS_{error} is found by subtraction. Rearranging the terms,

$$SS_{\text{error}} = SS_W - SS_{BS}$$

From the data,

$$SS_{\text{error}} = 227.20 - 118.60 = \mathbf{108.60}$$

You have now completed stage two of the partitioning of the total variation of scores. Here is a summary of the calculations.

$$SS_T = \mathbf{493.60}$$

$$SS_{BG} = \mathbf{266.40}$$

$$SS_W = \mathbf{227.20}$$

$$SS_{BS} = \mathbf{118.60}$$

$$SS_{\text{error}} = \mathbf{108.60}$$

To arrive at the F ratio, you need to compute MS_{BG} and MS_{error}.

Step 7. Compute MS_{BG}. The $df_{BG} = k - 1 = 4 - 1 = 3$.

$$MS_{BG} = \frac{SS_{BG}}{df_{BG}} = \frac{266.40}{3} = \mathbf{88.80}$$

Step 8. Compute MS_{error}. The $df_{error} = df_W - df_{BS} = 36 - 9 = 27$

$$MS_{error} = \frac{SS_{error}}{df_{error}} = \frac{108.60}{27} = \mathbf{4.02}$$

Step 9. Compute the F ratio. The F ratio is:

$$F = \frac{MS_{BG}}{MS_{error}} = \frac{88.80}{4.02} = \mathbf{22.09}$$

The remaining steps of the repeated-measures ANOVA test the significance of the F ratio.

14.4 TESTING THE STATISTICAL SIGNIFICANCE OF THE *F* RATIO

The null hypothesis for the worked problem is $H_0: \mu_1 = \mu_2 = \mu_3 = \mu_4$. The alternative hypothesis is that H_0 is false. If the null hypothesis is rejected, you would conclude that at least two of the sample means come from different populations. To reject the null hypothesis, the obtained F ratio must be larger than the critical value of F, which is found in the F table in Appendix B.5. The degrees of freedom for F is the degrees of freedom associated with the numerator and denominator of the F ratio, df_{BG} and df_{error}, respectively. The degrees of freedom for this study is $df_{BG} = 3$ and $df_{error} = 27$. Entering the F table, the critical value at the 5 percent level of significance is 2.96. The critical value at the 1 percent level of significance is 4.60. The obtained F value is 22.09. Whether you had set alpha at .05 or .01, the null hypothesis is rejected.

14.5 INTERPRETING THE FINDINGS

What does the significant F ratio mean about the study? The independent variable has four levels: placebo, 2.5 mg, 5 mg, and 10 mg of Valium. A statistically significant F test means that at least two of the group means differ on the dependent variable. Therefore, the number of errors committed during the mental arithmetic test is affected by dosage level. At this point you have the same dilemma as when you find a significant F ratio in a one-way ANOVA. There is no way to know the source of the significance—that is—which groups differ from one another. To locate the source of significance, pairwise comparisons among the means are required. This topic will be discussed shortly. We turn now to the form of the summary table in the repeated-measures ANOVA.

14.6 THE ANOVA SUMMARY TABLE

The general form of the ANOVA table for a repeated-measures ANOVA is shown in Table 14.5. The presentation of the findings is shown in Table 14.6.

TABLE 14.5 General Form of the Summary Table for a Repeated-Measures ANOVA

Source	SS	df	MS	F	p
Between-groups	SS_{BG}	df_{BG}	MS_{BG}	F	
Within-groups	SS_W	df_W			
Between-subjects	SS_{BS}	df_{BS}			
Error	SS_{error}	df_{error}	MS_{error}		
Total	SS_T	df_T			

TABLE 14.6 The ANOVA Summary Table for the Hypothetical Study

Source	SS	df	MS	F	p
Between-groups (dose level)	266.40	3	88.80	22.09	$p < .01$
Within-groups	227.20	36			
Between-subjects	118.60	9			
Error	108.60	27	4.02		
Total	493.60	39			

14.7 MULTIPLE COMPARISONS

A significant F ratio in a repeated-measures design that has more than two levels of the independent variable requires post hoc comparisons to locate the source of the significance. To remain consistent with the preceding two chapters, Fisher's LSD, or protected t test is used. The formula for the protected t test always has the error term from the ANOVA in its denominator. In the one-way and two-way ANOVA, the denominator of the F ratios is MS_W. Thus the denominator of the protected t tests include MS_W. In a repeated-measures ANOVA the denominator is MS_{error}, not MS_W. Thus, protected t tests following a repeated-measures ANOVA have MS_{error} in their denominator.

Fisher's LSD for Repeated-Measures ANOVA

$$t = \frac{\overline{X}_i - \overline{X}_j}{\sqrt{MS_{error}\left(\dfrac{1}{n_i} + \dfrac{1}{n_j}\right)}}$$

(Formula 14.5)

where,

$\overline{X}_i, n_i$ = the mean and number of scores of one experimental condition
$\overline{X}_j, n_j$ = the mean and number of scores of some other experimental condition

The critical value is found in the t table in Appendix B.2. The df used to find the critical value is taken from the MS_{error} term ($df_{error} = df_W - df_{BS}$).

In the worked problem, there are four levels to the independent variable. To make all possible pairwise comparisons requires six t tests. Only one comparison is made to illustrate how the formula works. You are invited to make the remaining comparisons.[4]

Placebo versus 5 mg

$$t = \frac{\overline{X}_i - \overline{X}_j}{\sqrt{MS_{error}\left(\dfrac{1}{n_i} + \dfrac{1}{n_j}\right)}}$$

$$t = \frac{9 - 5}{\sqrt{4.02\left(\dfrac{1}{10} + \dfrac{1}{10}\right)}}$$

$$= \frac{4}{\sqrt{.804}}$$

$$= \frac{4}{.90}$$

$$t = 4.44$$

The df_{error} is found by subtracting the df_{BS} from df_W: $(N - k) - (n - 1)$, or $(40 - 4) - (10 - 1) = 36 - 9 = 27$. The critical value in the t table that corresponds to a df of 27 is 2.05. Since the obtained value of 4.44 is greater than the

---

[4] The protected t test is presented in this worked problem to maintain consistency with Chapters 12 and 13. However, when using Fisher's LSD for more than three pairwise comparisons, the probability of a Type I error increases.

BOX
14.1
The Inverted U Relation Between Arousal and Task Performance

Most students in an introductory psychology class learn of the inverted **U** relation between arousal and task performance. Optimal performance in problem solving is observed during a moderate level of arousal, with poorer performance found during low and high levels of arousal (Obrist, 1962). The inverted **U** relationship is called a *curvilinear* relationship because a graph of the relationship describes a curved line. Another example of a curvilinear relationship would be if the line were not drawn as an inverted **U**, but rather, simply as a **U**. Almost every book that covers either introductory psychology, research methods, or statistics uses the arousal-performance phenomenon as an example of a curvilinear relation between two variables. Ask any psychology professor for an example of a curvilinear relationship and you will likely be given a description of the arousal-performance phenomenon. Why is this example so often used? Because it is difficult to think of another curvilinear relationship in psychology.

Halpin (1978) wondered if perhaps increasing levels of physiological arousal would produce a curvilinear relationship with olfactory sensitivity. In other words, are people better able to detect a smell under a moderate level of arousal than under a low or high level of physiological arousal? To answer this question, Halpin used a repeated-measures design.

EXPERIMENTAL PROCEDURE

Thirty-six college students were exposed to each of three experimental conditions: low, medium, and high arousal. Arousal was manipulated in the following manner. In the Low-arousal condition, subjects listened to a relaxation tape. In the Medium-arousal condition, subjects were exposed to loud, continuous white noise (white noise sounds like static). In the High-arousal condition, subjects heard intermittent bursts of loud, white noise, and were led to expect periodic electric shocks.

During each experimental condition, subjects were presented with an odorant of 1-propanol in dis-

tilled water. Several presentations of the odorant were administered in each experimental condition. With each successive presentation, the strength of the solution was increased. The subjects were asked to indicate at what point they could smell the substance. Thus, for each subject, under each experimental condition, an olfactory sensitivity threshold was identified and served as the dependent variable. If a curvilinear relation holds for arousal and olfactory sensitivity, then the lowest thresholds should be observed when subjects are experiencing a medium level of arousal. Higher and similar thresholds should be found during low and high levels of arousal.

The dependent variable was the percentage of concentration of 1-propanol present when the subjects signaled that they detected a smell. The following table presents the mean thresholds, in precentage of concentration, for each of the experimental conditions. The standard deviations are also shown. You may want to draw a graph of the relation between arousal and olfactory sensitivity to depict the curvilinear relationship. The author conducted a repeated-measures ANOVA and a significant difference among the conditions was found, $F(2, 70) = 8.80$, $p < .005$. To locate the source of significance, multiple comparisons were conducted among the three means. The mean for the Medium-arousal condition was significantly different from the means of both the Low- and High-arousal conditions. No difference between the Low- and High-arousal conditions was found. Thus, Halpin has extended the generality of the arousal-performance, curvilinear phenomenon. He has extended it to another response domain, namely, olfactory perception.

	Arousal		
	Low	*Medium*	*High*
$\overline{X}$	.66	.21	.60
s	.008	.01	.07

critical value of 2.05, reject the null hypothesis that these two means come from the same population.

You would interpret this statistically significant difference by saying that the mental concentration of anxious subjects is significantly improved when the subjects are administered 5 mg of Valium instead of a pill that they *think* will help their concentration.

Box 14.1 presents a study that examines the influence of physiological arousal on olfactory sensitivity. The investigator uses a repeated-measures design by exposing the same group of subjects to three arousal conditions.

14.8 STRENGTH OF ASSOCIATION

In the chapters covering one-way and two-way ANOVA, it was emphasized that the size of the F ratio does not indicate the degree to which the levels of the independent variable influence the dependent variable. The strength of association between the independent and dependent variables, also called effect size, can be determined with the statistic omega-squared, ω^2.

Omega-Squared for Repeated-Measures ANOVA

$$\omega^2 = \frac{SS_{BG} - (k-1)MS_{error}}{SS_T + MS_{error}} \quad \textit{(Formula 14.6)}$$

Using the data from the hypothetical worked problem,

$$\omega^2 = \frac{266.40 - (4-1)4.02}{493.60 + 4.02}$$

$$= \frac{254.34}{497.62}$$

$$\omega^2 = \mathbf{.51}$$

Since $\omega^2 = .51$, 51 percent of the variance in the measure of concentration is due to dosage level. An effect size of .51 is considered very large. Recall Cohen's guidelines (Cohen, 1977). A "large" effect is when ω^2 is greater than 15 percent, a "medium" effect is when ω^2 is around 6 percent, and a "small" effect size is when ω^2 is about 1 percent.

14.9 ASSUMPTIONS OF THE REPEATED-MEASURES ANOVA

The assumptions for the repeated-measures ANOVA are the same as those for the two-way ANOVA and the one-way ANOVA, with the exception of the fourth assumption.

1. The population distributions are normal.
2. The variances of the populations are the same.
3. The observations within treatment conditions are independent of one another.
4. The variances of difference scores are homogeneous.

The F test in the repeated-measures ANOVA is robust. Violations of the first two assumptions are not serious, especially if the number of observations in each condition are the same. The fact that the F test is robust is of no help if the third assumption is violated; the behavior of a subject in a given condition should be independent of the behavior of other subjects in the same condition. This assumption is easy to meet. The fourth assumption requires some explanation.

Since each subject provides a score within each level of the independent variable, it is possible to arrange the data as pairs of scores for any two treatments. In a study with four treatment conditions, there would be six pairs of scores (treatments 1 and 2; 1 and 3; 1 and 4; 2 and 3; 2 and 4; 3 and 4). By subtracting the two scores for each of the subjects, the variance can be calculated on the difference scores. With four treatment conditions, you would calculate six variances. It is assumed that these variances are equal in the population. It is possible to test this assumption and make corrections in the ANOVA if this assumption is violated (see Keppel, 1982).

SUMMARY

In a repeated-measures design, also called a within-subjects design, every subject is exposed to each of the treatment conditions. Since you can obtain information about the effect of each treatment condition by using the same group of subjects, this type of design requires fewer subjects than a between-subjects design, and as a result, is more efficient. In addition, a repeated-measures design eliminates individual differences as a potential explanation for the results of the study, because the same sample of subjects is run in each experimental condition. However, not all research questions lend themselves to a within-subjects design.

When conducting a repeated-measures ANOVA, there is one F ratio, which is the F ratio that tests for a significant difference among the levels of the independent variable. Therefore, there is only one null hypothesis:

$$H_0: \quad \mu_1 = \mu_2 = \mu_3 = \mu_K$$

The alternative hypothesis is that at least two of the group means come from different populations.

$$H_1: \quad \text{the null hypothesis is false}$$

The total variation of scores is partitioned into between-group variability and within-group variability. The F ratio in the repeated-measures ANOVA has the following structure:

$$F = \frac{\text{between-group variance}}{\text{within-group variance}}$$

Between-group variance is due to treatment effect and experimental error. Within-group variance is partitioned into variability due to individual differences and variability due to experimental error, with the variability due to individual differences removed. The F ratio thus has the form:

$$F = \frac{\text{treatment effect} + \text{experimental error}}{\text{experimental error}}$$

A significant F ratio requires post hoc tests where pairwise comparisons among the means are made to locate the source of statistical significance. Fisher's LSD procedure was discussed and illustrated. Further, a significant F ratio does not provide direct information about the strength of association between the independent and dependent variables. Omega-squared is a statistic that measures effect size.

The assumptions of the repeated-measures ANOVA are:

1. The population distributions are normal.
2. The variances of the populations are the same.
3. The observations within treatment conditions are independent of one another.
4. The variances of difference scores are homogeneous.

KEY FORMULAS FOR CHAPTER 14

Formula for SS_T

$$SS_T = \Sigma X^2 - \frac{(\Sigma X)^2}{N} \qquad \text{(Formula 14.1)}$$

Formula for SS_{BG}

$$SS_{BG} = \frac{(\Sigma X_1)^2}{n_1} + \frac{(\Sigma X_2)^2}{n_2} + \cdots + \frac{(\Sigma X_k)^2}{n_k} - \left[\frac{(\Sigma X)^2}{N}\right] \qquad \text{(Formula 14.2)}$$

Formula for SS_W

$$SS_W = \Sigma X^2 - \left[\frac{(\Sigma X_1)^2}{n_1} + \frac{(\Sigma X_2)^2}{n_2} + \cdots + \frac{(\Sigma X_k)^2}{n_k}\right] \qquad \text{(Formula 14.3)}$$

Formula for SS_{BS}

$$SS_{BS} = \frac{(\Sigma P_1)^2}{k} + \frac{(\Sigma P_2)^2}{k} + \cdots + \frac{(\Sigma P_{\text{last person}})^2}{k} - \left[\frac{(\Sigma X)^2}{N}\right]$$

(Formula 14.4)

Fisher's LSD for Repeated-Measures ANOVA

$$t = \frac{\overline{X}_i - \overline{X}_j}{\sqrt{MS_{error}\left(\frac{1}{n_i} + \frac{1}{n_j}\right)}}$$

(Formula 14.5)

Omega-Squared for Repeated Measures ANOVA

$$\omega^2 = \frac{SS_{BG} - (k-1)MS_{error}}{SS_T + MS_{error}}$$

(Formula 14.6)

WORK PROBLEMS

1. What is the difference between a repeated-measures design and a between-groups design?
2. In a repeated-measures design, what accounts for between-group variation and what accounts for within-group variation?
3. How does the error term differ between an independent-groups design and a within-groups design?
4. How is it that individual differences are controlled in a repeated-measures design?
5. If you conduct a repeated-measures study with five treatment conditions and 20 subjects, what would be the *df* for the *F* ratio?
6. Fill in the missing values in the following ANOVA summary table. The study has three experimental conditions; five subjects are run under each condition.

Source	SS	df	MS	F	p
Between-groups				11.51	
Within-groups	20				
Between-subjects					
Error			2.30		
Total					

7. An educational psychologist is interested in comparing three visual scanning techniques on reading speed. The reading speeds of six subjects are recorded after training in each technique. Conduct a repeated-measures ANOVA on the following data. Set alpha at .05.
   a. Provide a summary table.

b. Conduct all possible protected t tests.

c. What percent of the variance of reading scores is accounted for by the scanning technique?

Technique A	Technique B	Technique C
450	250	500
426	300	456
399	170	300
400	227	310
420	225	250
350	270	350

8. A study is conducted to examine sales performance as a function of incentive program. Over a 1-month period, three incentive programs are used at a local car dealership. The number of cars sold by each salesman, under each incentive program, is presented in the following table. Set alpha at .05.
   a. Provide a summary table.
   b. Conduct all possible protected t tests.
   c. What percent of the variance of car sales is accounted for by the incentive program?

Incentive A	Incentive B	Incentive C
8	7	4
6	6	4
9	5	3
7	4	3
7	5	5

9. A psychologist is interested in the effects of subliminal messages on problem solving. Simple arithmetic problems are presented on a computer screen; the subjects are told to work as quickly as possible. In the Positive condition, the phrase "Good Work" is flashed just below recognition threshold, every 30 seconds. In the Negative condition, the phrase "Don't Fail" is flashed. In the control condition, no subliminal phrase is projected. The number of problems correctly solved is presented in the following table. Set alpha at .05.
   a. Provide an ANOVA summary table.
   b. Conduct protected t tests.
   c. What is omega-squared?
   d. Interpret the findings.

Positive	Negative	Control
45	20	30
56	18	29
59	10	24
48	15	25

10. A wine manufacturer would like to know which of three hors d'oeuvres goes best with their white chardonnay. Subjects are asked to take a bite of an hors d'oeuvre, sip the wine, and provide a taste rating from 1–atrocious to 10–

fantastic. Taste ratings are provided in the following table. Test at the 5 percent level of significance.

a. Provide an ANOVA summary table.
b. Conduct protected t tests.
c. Interpret the findings.
d. What would you advise the manufacturer about how to advertise the hors d'oeuvre they should recommend be served with their chardonnay?

Feta Cheese	Caviar	Popcorn
1	1	3
1	2	4
2	2	6
2	3	5
1	3	6

11. A psychologist is interested in the effects of distraction on pain tolerance. Three different slide shows, varying in distraction, are projected on a screen while subjects have their hands immersed in ice cold water. A 20-minute interval is used between experimental conditions to allow subjects to recover from the preceding hand immersion. The number of seconds subjects kept their hands in the water is presented in the following table. Set alpha at .05.

a. Provide a summary table.
b. Conduct all possible protected t tests.
c. What percent of the variance of pain tolerance scores is accounted for by distraction levels?
d. Interpret the findings.

	Distraction	
Low	Medium	High
56	32	120
76	65	90
60	55	69
72	70	100
50	57	111

Work Problems for the Computer

12. Dion, Berscheid, and Walster (1972) examined the stereotypes we hold about attractive people. Subjects looked at three types of photographs: one of a physically attractive person, one of a person of average attractiveness, and a photograph of an unattractive person. Subjects supplied ratings along various dimensions, including occupational success, marital and parental competence, happiness, and their social desirability as a person. Even though the photographs were of people unknown to the subjects, attractive people were viewed as superior to unattractive people, whether the target person was male or female. The following data set is hypothetical, providing scores for the social desirability of the person's personality. Higher scores reflect greater social desirability. The scores have been generated so that the results of your analysis

will be consistent with those of the authors. Set alpha at .05 and test the null hypothesis that there is no difference in ratings among the three conditions.

TARGET PERSON

Unattractive	Average	Attractive
35	60	65
39	59	74
45	59	47
50	45	65
30	58	72
37	56	74
50	59	69
44	63	55
59	60	49
65	49	57
51	58	65
49	48	62
47	47	67
53	48	66
36	43	59
39	57	70

13. A social psychologist is interested in sex-typing stereotypes among females. Fifteen females read three descriptions of a male and provide ratings on how likely the target person is to achieve success in the corporate world (1–very unlikely to 10–very likely). In the Masculine condition, a male is described as possessing the traditional characteristics of masculinity (e.g., values rationality over intuition, more task-oriented than relationship-oriented). In the Feminine condition, subjects read a description of a male in which traditional feminine characteristics are attributed to the target person (e.g., values intuition over rationality, more relationship-oriented than task-oriented). In the Androgenous condition, the target person is described as possessing a balance of feminine and masculine traits. Set alpha at .05 and conduct a repeated-measures ANOVA. Perform *pairwise* comparisons if warranted.

Masculine	Feminine	Androgenous
10	7	8
9	4	7
7	3	4
8	6	5
6	3	6
9	2	4
10	6	7
5	10	7
3	5	10
4	4	4
8	3	6
7	2	3
2	8	6
9	3	5
7	1	3

Linear Correlation

15.1   THE RESEARCH CONTEXT

This chapter discusses correlational analysis. A **correlation coefficient** is an index of the strength of association between two variables. A correlation coefficient can range from -1 to $+1$. The larger the absolute value of the correlation, the stronger the association between two variables. Indexing the strength of association between two variables has a very broad and useful function in science. In this chapter, the focus is on the use of correlations in the behavioral sciences, especially psychology. Bear in mind, however, that correlations can be computed to answer questions from many different fields including: economics (is there a relation between gross national product and the value of the dollar?); meteorology (is there a correlation between rainfall and number of trees per acre of land?); and medical epidemiology (is there a relation between the size of the local deer population and the incidence of Lyme disease?).

In psychology, the variables to which a correlational analysis is applied are often measures of two attributes or an attribute and overt behavior. Two scores are obtained from each subject. Together, the two scores define a *pair* of scores. The distribution of pairs of scores is called a **bivariate distribution** (*bi* meaning two, *variate* meaning variable). IQ and academic performance, anxiety and fine-motor movements, depression and self-reinforcement are all examples in which correlations have been found. This chapter addresses the application of a correlational analysis to data that are continuous (ratio or interval) measures. Chapter 18 discusses the application of a correlational analysis when one or both variables are ordinal (rankings).

The statistical methods for calculating the correlation were invented by Sir Francis Galton (1822–1911); the precise formula comes from Karl Pearson (1857–1936), and is called the Pearson product-moment correlation coefficient. The correlation based on a sample is symbolized r; the population coefficient is symbolized ρ (*rho*).

The correlation coefficient is an index that reflects the degree to which two variables are associated. However, it cannot be inferred from this association that a causal relation in either direction exists between the two variables. For example, psychologists know that depressed persons are less likely to reward themselves for achieving a goal. However, this could be because they are less likely to reward themselves because they are depressed, minimizing rewards leads to depression, or some third variable is responsible for both depression and a low rate of self-reward. The methodological context within which the correlation between two variables is found determines the most reasonable interpretation of the correlation.[1]

The Distinction Between a Correlational Design and the Correlation Coefficient

You probably have heard the phrase "correlation does not imply causation." This phrase can be misleading if you don't keep in mind the difference between how data are collected and the statistical analysis used to treat the data. If you conduct a study in which some procedural variables are held constant, and others are purposely allowed to vary, the study is called an experiment. Under these conditions you may be warranted in making causal statements about the relationship between independent and dependent variables. If you conduct a study and do not exert control over the phenomenon under investigation, then you are using a correlational design. To illustrate the difference between a correlational design and an experiment, consider the following example.

Some people believe that a person's mood is affected by the temperature outside. Suppose you tested this hypothesis by recording the daily temperature

---

[1] If you were not assigned Chapter 1, you may want to read now the couple of pages under the subheading "Causality and Correlation." If you have already read Chapter 1, it wouldn't hurt to reread that section to refresh your memory.

and obtaining mood ratings every day from several people. After analyzing the data, you discover that more positive mood ratings are associated with warmer temperatures. Is there a causal connection? Well, obviously mood didn't affect the weather, so it must be that the changes in temperature directly caused the changes in mood. Maybe. However, because you used a correlational design, no causal conclusion can be made. It could be that when it is cold, people don't socialize as often; thus their mood is depressed due to the loss of social contact. In other words, a third variable (socializing) may account for the observed relation between temperature and mood.

If you wanted to determine if there is a direct, causal relation between temperature and mood, you would have to find a way to manipulate systematically the temperature, and then examine its effect on mood. Perhaps you could alter the temperature in a room, holding all other conditions constant, and then see if the relation between temperature and mood holds. Now you are conducting an experiment that may allow a causal statement.

It is the research methodology that determines how you interpret a correlation. The phrase "correlation does not imply causation" is more accurately stated as "an association between two variables in a *correlational design* does not imply causation."

Suppose you want to test the hypothesis that Type A (coronary-prone) individuals finish their exams faster than Type B (noncoronary-prone) individuals. Based on a standard assessment technique, you classify everyone in class as either a Type A or B. Without the students' knowledge, you time how long it takes each student to complete his or her exam. You then analyze the data by conducting a t test between the time-to-completion means of the two groups. Even though you have used a t test, an analysis that is usually associated with an experiment, can you make a causal statement? No, because you have not manipulated any variables. Whenever the independent variable is a subject variable (e.g., personality trait, sex, psychiatric diagnosis), irrespective of the type of data analysis, the design is correlational (see Chapter 1 for a discussion of subject variables).

When using a correlational design it is common to calculate a correlation coefficient (r). When conducting an experiment, a t test or F test is frequently used to determine if there is a statistically significant difference among group means. Here is where confusion can occur, which invalidates the statement "correlation does not imply causation." Suppose your interest is to find out if the use of practice imagery can improve bowling scores. You randomly assign subjects to either the Experimental condition, where the subjects learn to practice visualizing themselves bowling with perfect form, or a Control condition, where subjects do not receive instructions about the visualization technique. The dependent variable is bowling scores. You could analyze the difference between the mean bowling scores of the two groups using a t test. However, a type of correlational analysis could be used that identifies the strength of association between bowling scores and the group to which subjects were assigned (called a point-biserial correlation). Assuming there is a high correlation between bowling scores and whether the subjects received training, could you state that the visualization technique led to an increase in bowling performance? Yes, because you manipulated the independent variable. In this context, you would be justified in saying, "correlation

Karl Pearson was born in London in 1857, two years before Darwin published *Origin of Species,* a work that would shape Pearson's entire academic life. If Pearson was not the father of modern statistics, there are but a few who could lay claim to the distinction. Pearson completed the work on correlation that Galton had started, arriving at the coefficient that bears his name (the Pearson product-moment correlation). He subsequently devised formulas for computing correlations for variables that are noncontinuous (see Chapter 18). Pearson is responsible for many of the concepts and statistical terms that were introduced earlier in this book: histogram, mode, and standard deviation. He also invented the chi-square test (see Chapter 17).

It appears that Karl Pearson was a scientist from the beginning. His earliest memory was sitting in a high chair, sucking his thumb when someone urged him to stop, so his thumb would not wither away. Upon examining both thumbs he thought, "I can't see that the thumb I suck is any smaller than the other; I wonder if she could be lying to me" (Walker, 1968, p. 497).

Pearson's abiding belief in the importance of observation, if not his rejection of authority, guided his lifelong pursuit: the development of mathematical tools that could be used to test the theory of evolution. Over his lifetime he published more than 500 works. When asked how he found the time to publish so much, he offered, "You Americans would not understand, but I never answer a telephone or attend a committee meeting" (Stouffer, 1958, p. 25). Were Pearson alive today, he would no doubt find his American colleagues kindred souls!

After earning a degree in mathematics at King's College, Cambridge, Pearson studied law, and subsequently established a private practice for three years. In 1884 he abandoned law, became a professor of mathematics at University College London, and began his illustrious career. The first major influence on Pearson's thinking was a book published by Sir Francis Galton, *Natural Inheritance.* Although Pearson was never a formal student of Galton's, he became his disciple and defender. Pearson was looking for a model of semi-determinism as an alternative to what he believed was the biological sciences' rigid adherence to causality. He found this semideterminism in the concept of the correlation. For Pearson, the correlation represented a fundamental paradigm shift, which, he believed, would revolutionize the biological, as well as the social sciences. Researchers could use the correlation as an important index of the "degree of relatedness" between two variables without having the strict determinist's burden of claiming causality. In 1896 Pearson introduced the formula that we now use to compute the correlation between two continuous measures. [As an historical aside, the Pearson formula was actually first published a year earlier by Yule (1895), a student of Pearson's who gave his mentor full credit for the formula.]

Pearson was (as are we all) a product of his times. Darwin's ideas about the fundamental principles that guide evolution—namely heredity, variation, and natural selection—influenced the thinking of many scholars. Galton had introduced the term eugenics and started the eugenics movement, which was dedicated to improving the human race through selective breeding. It was a period in history in which many scientists believed that nature (heredity) was far more important in determining personal qualities than nurture (environment). Indeed, Pearson developed formulas for correlation coefficients appropriate for noncontinuous measures in his attempt to show that " . . . the degree of resemblance of the physical and mental characteristics in children is one and the same" (Pearson, 1903, p. 203). Pearson took the eugenics movement beyond what Galton had intended, and most certainly, beyond what Darwin ever meant to imply. Pearson was a Social Darwinist, an imperialist, nationalist, and a racist (Grosskurth, 1980). For instance, he believed that war was necessary to eliminate "inferior stock." And he opposed legislation to aid the oppressed. According to Pearson, "No degenerate and feeble stock will ever be converted into healthy and sound stock by the accumulated effects of education, good laws, and sanitary surroundings" (Semmel, 1958). The eugenics movement died in England and the United States when Hitler adopted a policy of involuntary sterilization in the 1930s.

    Pearson died in 1936, just before the outbreak of World War II. We have fortunately inherited only the best of Karl Pearson: his insistence on the importance of quantifying social phenomena and numerous correlational techniques to achieve the goal. His vision to accomplish a paradigm shift in the social sciences has led to many innovative, multivariate methods that bridge the gap between experimental and correlational designs.

does imply causation." The basis for making causal statements *never* resides with the type of analysis, but rather with the manner in which the data are collected.[2] Cronbach (1967, p. 27) offers a nice metaphorical distinction between the experimental and correlation approaches, ". . . the experimentalist [is] an expert puppeteer, able to keep untangled the strands to half-a-dozen independent variables. The correlational psychologist is a mere observer of a play where Nature pulls a thousand strings."

    To learn something of the man who has contributed so much to correlational analyses, please read the Spotlight Box 15.1 on Karl Pearson.

15.2 THE CORRELATION COEFFICIENT AND SCATTER DIAGRAMS

This section addresses the statistical aspects of correlation and hypothesis testing. The correlation coefficient is represented by a number that ranges from -1 to $+1$. The higher the coefficient's absolute value, the stronger the association between the two variables. An r of $-.80$ reflects a strength of association as strong as an r of $+.80$. A correlation of 0 means that the two variables are unrelated. If higher values of one variable are associated with higher values of the other variable (as with IQ and academic performance), then the correlation is *positive*. If higher values of one variable are associated with lower values of the second variable, then the correlation is *negative*. For instance, the number of years people spend in school and the number of children they subsequently have is negatively correlated. That is, the more educated the people, the fewer children they have.

    Chapter 2 showed a few ways in which a distribution of scores can be displayed. For instance, polygons and histograms are common ways of displaying data from a univariate distribution. When a bivariate distribution is plotted on a graph it is called a **scatter diagram** (or **scatter plot**). Consider a study in which a child psychologist is interested in developing a measure of aggression. A rating scale is given to each of the ten children in a third-grade class; they are asked to rate how aggressive their peers are (on a scale from 1–not aggressive at all to 10–extremely aggressive). To ascertain if the perceptions of aggression measured

---

[2] For an introductory, yet in-depth treatment of the use of correlational techniques as applied to experimental designs, refer to Keppel and Zedeck (1989).

by the rating scale correspond to observed aggression, the psychologist conducts behavioral observations of interactions among the children during recess. In Table 15.1, the X column lists the average peer ratings gathered for each of the ten children in the class. The Y column lists the number of observed instances of aggression, over three days, for each child. The designation of the X and Y variables is arbitrary. The X scores for all the children constitute one univariate distribution, and the Y scores constitute another univariate distribution. Since two scores are recorded for each child (peer ratings and behavioral observations), the ten pairs of scores define one bivariate distribution.

The bivariate distribution can be represented visually by plotting each subject's X and Y score on a graph. For this data set, there are ten points; each point corresponds to a subject's X and Y score. Figure 15.1 is the scatter plot of the data in Table 15.1.

Here is how you draw a scatter plot. Place the X variable on the horizontal axis and the Y variable on the vertical axis. To plot Subject 1's point, follow the X axis to the number 8. Imagine a line drawn vertically, parallel to the Y axis. Now locate the subject's Y score along the Y axis. The Y score for Subject 1 is 14. Imagine drawing a horizontal line, parallel to the X axis. Where the two imaginary lines intersect is where you plot the subject's point. As you examine Figure 15.1, make sure that all the pairs of scores in Table 15.1 have been accurately plotted.

Interpreting the Scatter Diagram

The scatter plot provides a wealth of information about the relationship between two variables. Figure 15.2 shows the scatter diagrams for several correlations. The magnitude of the correlation can be estimated by looking at the general shape formed by the points. The magnitude of the correlation is estimated by examining the width of the oval: the more narrow the oval, the higher the correlation. Compare the correlation of $+.70$ in Figure 15.2(a) with the $+.40$ correlation in Figure 15.2(c). As the correlation approaches 0, the shape of the plot becomes more circular. If the points have no trend and are best contained within a circle, the

TABLE   15.1   Hypothetical Data Depicting Peer Ratings of Aggression (X) and Observed Aggression (Y)

	Peer Ratings of Aggression: X	Observed Aggression: Y
S_1	8	14
S_2	10	12
S_3	4	9
S_4	1	4
S_5	5	11
S_6	6	10
S_7	3	1
S_8	9	12
S_9	7	10
S_{10}	2	4

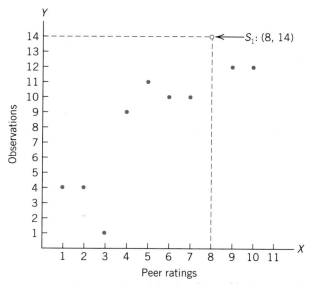

Figure 15.1 The scatter plot of the data from Table 15.1.

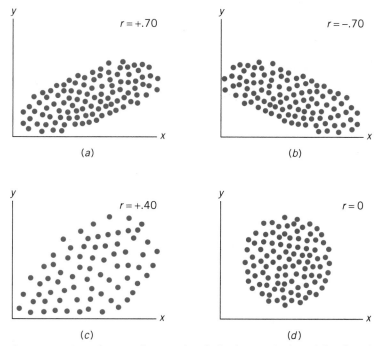

Figure 15.2 Several scatter diagrams that depict the magnitude and direction of the correlation.

correlation is 0—that is—the variables are unrelated. Figure 15.2(*d*) illustrates a plot of unrelated variables.

Not only does the scatter plot indicate the strength of association between *X* and *Y*, it also reveals the direction of the correlation. If the oval containing the majority of the points slopes from the lower left to the upper right, the correlation is positive. As the *X* scores tend to have higher values, the *Y* scores are apt to be larger [see Figure 15.2(*a*) and (*c*)]. If the plot slopes from the upper left to the lower right, then the correlation is negative. Thus, as the value of the *X* score increases, the value of the *Y* score decreases. The scatter plots of two correlations with the same magnitude, but with different signs, are shown in Figures 15.2(*a*) and (*b*).

Linear and Nonlinear Correlations

The scatter diagram provides a graphic representation of the relation between the distributions of both variables. Viewing the plot's approximate shape allows you to make a crude estimation of the strength of association of the variables. However, a researcher would *never* report a correlation merely based on looking at the shape and direction of the oval. So why use it? In the examples of correlations provided thus far, the higher values of one variable are associated with higher values of the second variable (positive correlation); or the higher values of one variable are associated with lower values of the second variable (negative correlation). Whether the correlation is positive or negative, the scatter plots illustrated in Figure 15.2(*a–c*) show linear relationships between *X* and *Y*. When *X* and *Y* have a **linear relation,** the correlation is called a linear correlation. In a linear relation, each time the value of one variable increases, the value of the other variable shows a constant change. On the other hand, what if you observed that lower scores on *X* were associated with lower scores on *Y*, medium *X* scores were associated with medium *Y* scores, *but* higher *X* scores were found to be associated with *lower Y* scores? (See Figure 15.3.) If you were shown a scatter plot of the left half of this bivariate distribution, you would estimate a positive correlation. However, you would assume a negative correlation between *X* and *Y* if only the right portion of the distribution were illustrated. Figure 15.3 depicts the overall relation between arousal and task performance. In this example the oval curve is like an arch, or inverted **U.** The variables are obviously associated (notice the narrowness of the arch). This is a **curvilinear relationship.** How would you interpret the curvilinear relation between arousal and performance, depicted in Figure 15.3? Given a certain level of task difficulty, performance is optimal when the person performing a task is experiencing a moderate level of arousal. A low or high level of arousal is associated with poor performance.

The formulas for calculating a linear correlation are different from those used to calculate a curvilinear correlation. In fact, if a linear formula were applied to the data of Figure 15.3, the correlation would be 0, suggesting *no* association between performance and arousal. In actuality, there is a strong correlation between the variables. However, looking at the scatter diagram would immediately reveal

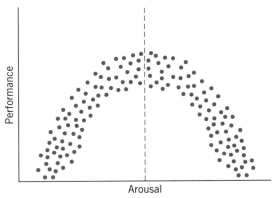

Figure 15.3 A plot of a curvilinear relation between X and Y. As arousal increases, performance improves until arousal becomes too high, then performance declines.

the true nature of the relationship. Indeed, you should *always* inspect the scatter plot of your data *before* you interpret the correlation coefficient. If the plot shows an arch, the formula for linear correlation should not be used. This chapter only addresses linear correlation since it is the most common type of correlated relationship (and the easiest to compute).

Now that you are familiar with how to plot a bivariate distribution and how to interpret the scatter diagram, we turn to the statistical basis and computational methods of the correlation coefficient.

The *z*-Score Formula for the Correlation Coefficient

The *z*-score formula for the following correlation is not the preferred method for computing the correlation. It is much too tedious. However, an examination of the *z*-score formula is a very good way to introduce the statistical conceptualization of the correlation coefficient.

Recall that a z score locates a raw score in a univariate distribution. A z score is the number of standard deviations a raw score is from the mean of the distribution. All raw scores above the mean transform to positive z scores; all raw scores below the mean transform to negative z scores. Table 15.2 presents the X and Y scores for five subjects, as well as each score's z score. In a bivariate distribution, it is important to note that when transforming a raw score of variable X to a z score (z_x), the mean and standard deviation of variable X is used in the z-score formula. In Table 15.2, the mean and standard deviation for the X scores is 17 and 2.83, respectively. The same point holds for the Y scores: the transformation to z scores (z_y) uses the mean and standard deviation of the Y distribution.

The *z*-score formula for the correlation coefficient of a *population* is given in Formula 15.1.

> ### The *z*-Score Formula for the Population Correlation
>
> $$\rho = \frac{\Sigma(z_x z_y)}{N_p}$$
>
> *(Formula 15.1)*
>
> *where,*
>
> ρ = rho, the symbol for the population correlation
> $\Sigma(z_x z_y)$ = sum of the cross products of z scores
> N_p = number of *pairs* of scores

TABLE 15.2 Computing the Population Correlation with the *z*-Score Formula

Subject	X	μ	$z_x = (X - \mu_x)/\sigma_x$	Y	μ	$z_y = (Y - \mu_y)/\sigma_y$	$z_x z_y$
S_1	13	17	−1.41	23	30	−1.52	+2.14
S_2	15	17	−.71	28	30	−.43	+.31
S_3	17	17	0	30	30	0	0
S_4	21	17	+1.41	32	30	+.43	+.61
S_5	19	17	+.71	37	30	+1.52	+1.08
							$\Sigma z_x z_y = +4.14$

Summary Values
$\mu_x = 17;\ \sigma_x = 2.83;\ \mu_y = 30;\ \sigma_y = 4.60;\ N_p = 5$

$$\rho = \frac{\Sigma(z_x z_y)}{N_p}$$

$$= \frac{+4.14}{5}$$

$$\rho = +.83$$

The term $z_x z_y$ is called a cross product. A cross product is a given subject's z_x score multiplied by the corresponding z_y score. In Table 15.2, the cross product for subject 1 is $(-1.41)(-1.52) = +2.14$. The numerator of the *z*-score formula is the sum of all individual cross products.

There are two important points to make about the *z*-score formula for the correlation. First, under what condition would the *z*-score formula yield a positive correlation? Remember that a positive correlation results when higher scores on one variable are associated with higher scores on the second variable. In terms of *z* scores, subjects who score relatively high on the *X* variable will receive z_x scores that are positive. If they also tend to score high on the *Y* variable, their z_y scores will also be positive. This will produce a lot of positive cross products. Furthermore, those subjects with *X* and *Y* scores below the means of the *X* and *Y* distributions will have negative z_x and negative z_y scores. Two negative *z* scores multiplied together produce a positive cross product. Refer to Table 15.2. The correlation between X and Y is positive ($+.83$). As you inspect the z_x and z_y columns note that negative z scores on X are associated with negative z scores on Y, and positive z scores on X are associated with positive z scores on Y. Although, in this example, every cross product is positive, it is not necessary for *all* cross products to be positive for the correlation to be positive. As long as the sum of the cross products is positive, the correlation will be positive.

Given this explanation of how a positive correlation can arise, it should be easy to determine how a negative correlation can occur. A negative correlation occurs when the higher scores on one variable are associated with lower scores on the second variable. In terms of z scores, positive z scores would tend to be associated with negative z scores. This would yield many cross products with a negative sign. The sum of these cross products would be negative.[3]

The second important point about the z-score formula has to do with the magnitude of the correlation. A z score not only specifies whether a raw score is above or below the mean, it also states how far the score is from the mean (in standard deviations). Refer to Table 15.2. Think about the relative rankings of the subjects' z_x and z_y scores. Notice that Subject 1 has the lowest X score in the X distribution, and thus the largest, negative z_x score. Subject 1 also has the lowest Y score in the Y distribution, and accordingly, the largest, negative z_y score in the distribution. Subject 1 ranks at the bottom of each distribution. Note that Subject 2 ranks second from the bottom of each distribution. Subject 3 ranks at the middle of each distribution. However, Subject 4 ranks the highest in the X distribution, but the second highest in the Y distribution. Subject 5 ranks the second highest in the X distribution, but the highest in the Y distribution. Considering the entire bivariate distribution in Table 15.2, the rankings of the z_x scores are very similar to the way in which their corresponding z_y scores are ordered. When the rankings of the X scores have a high degree of correspondence to the rankings of the Y scores, the correlation will be large. The bivariate distribution in Table 15.2 shows a good deal of correspondence; thus the correlation is high: $+.83$. If the correlation were high and negative, there would still be a good deal of correspondence among the ranks of X and Y. However, high rankings on X would be associated with low rankings of Y.[4]

The Computational Formula for the Correlation Coefficient

The z-score formula is instructive because it provides a way to conceptualize the statistical basis of the correlation coefficient. However, since each raw score has to be transformed to a z score, using the z-score formula to calculate the correlation

---

[3] I do not want to give the impression that it is the *number* of positive cross products or the *number* of negative cross products that determine the sign of the sum of the cross products. Although this will often be the case, summing a few very large positive cross products with many small, negative cross products *could* yield a positive correlation.

[4] Using the notion of corresponding ranks is presented as a *conceptual guide*. When the X and Y variables are measured on an interval or ratio scale, the z-score formula actually takes the spacing of the X scores into consideration, and how that spacing corresponds to the spacing of the Y scores.

is an arduous task. Formula 15.2 is much easier to use when working with raw scores. It is the *computational formula* for computing the correlation. In addition, the symbol r indicates that the correlation is based on a sample and is used to estimate the population correlation.

Computational Formula for Pearson's r

$$r_{\text{obt}} = \frac{n_p(\Sigma XY) - (\Sigma X)(\Sigma Y)}{\sqrt{[n_p(\Sigma X^2) - (\Sigma X)^2][n_p(\Sigma Y^2) - (\Sigma Y)^2]}} \quad \textit{(Formula 15.2)}$$

where,

$\Sigma X^2 =$ the sum of all the squared X scores

$\Sigma Y^2 =$ the sum of all the squared Y scores

$XY =$ the cross product of an X and Y score

$\Sigma XY =$ the sum of the cross products; don't try to obtain ΣXY by multiplying $(\Sigma X)(\Sigma Y)$; you'll obtain the wrong answer.

$(\Sigma X)^2 =$ the sum of all the X scores, quantity squared

$(\Sigma Y)^2 =$ the sum of all the Y scores, quantity squared

$n_p =$ number of *pairs* of observations

At first glance, this appears to be an imposing formula. If you accidentally turned to this page the first day of class, you might have thought, "I'll never be able to do this stuff." However, you are already familiar with all these terms. Even the notion of cross products is not new; you just encountered it with the z-score formula for correlation. If you obtain the incorrect answer when using the computational formula, it is because you either made a simple arithmetic error, or you don't understand the correct sequence of the arithmetic operations. If you carefully follow the next worked problem, you should have no trouble using the computational formula.

■ QUESTION *An investigator wants to know the correlation between subjective ratings of discomfort and how long subjects maintain their hands in ice water. The X variable in the following table is the amount of discomfort; higher scores indicate greater discomfort. The Y variable is the number of minutes subjects kept their hands in the water. What is the correlation between discomfort ratings and duration of hand immersion for this sample of subjects?*

SOLUTION

X	Y	X^2	Y^2	XY
3	2	9	4	6
5	3	25	9	15
4	4	16	16	16
7	5	49	25	35
10	6	100	36	60
$\Sigma X = 29$	$\Sigma Y = 20$	$\Sigma X^2 = 199$	$\Sigma Y^2 = 90$	$\Sigma XY = 132$	■

Steps When Using the Computational Formula

After you compute the summary statistics shown at the bottom of each column, proceed as follows.

Step 1. In the numerator, multiply *only* (ΣXY) by n_p. Do *not* multiply the entire numerator by n_p.

Step 2. Multiply (ΣY) by (ΣX).

Step 3. Subtract the obtained value in Step 2 from the value obtained in Step 1. That finishes the numerator. The sign of the numerator will determine the sign of the correlation.

Step 4. In the denominator, first multiply only (ΣX^2) by n_p. Do *not* multiply the entire quantity in the first set of brackets by n_p.

Step 5. Subtract $(\Sigma X)^2$ from the value obtained in Step 4.

Step 6. Move to the second set of brackets and repeat Steps 4 and 5 for the Y variable.

Step 7. Multiply the obtained value from the first set of brackets by the value in the second set of brackets.

Step 8. Take the square root of the number arrived at in Step 7.

Step 9. Divide the numerator by the denominator.

Step 10. Reinforce yourself!

$$r_{obt} = \frac{n_p(\Sigma XY) - (\Sigma X)(\Sigma Y)}{\sqrt{[n_p(\Sigma X^2) - (\Sigma X)^2][n_p(\Sigma Y^2) - (\Sigma Y)^2]}}$$

Step 3

$$r_{obt} = \frac{\overbrace{5(132)}^{\text{Step 1}} - \overbrace{(29)(20)}^{\text{Step 2}}}{\sqrt{[\underbrace{5(199) - (29)^2}_{\text{Step 4}}][\underbrace{(5(90) - (20)^2}_{\text{Step 6}}]}}$$

Step 5   **Step 6**

$$= \frac{660 - 580}{\sqrt{[995 - 841][450 - 400]}}$$

Step 7

$$= \frac{80}{\sqrt{(154)(50)}}$$

$$= \frac{80}{\sqrt{7700}} \quad \textbf{(Step 8)}$$

$$= \frac{80}{87.75} \quad \textbf{(Step 9)}$$

$$r_{obt} = +.91 \quad \textbf{(Step 10)}$$

The Coefficient of Determination, r^2

If you have already covered the chapter on one-way ANOVA, you will recall the statistic, ω^2, omega-squared. Omega-squared is an index of effect size; it reflects the amount of variation in the scores of the dependent variable, which are accounted for by the levels of the independent variable. The **coefficient of determination,** calculated by r^2, accomplishes for the correlation coefficient what ω^2 accomplishes after an F test has been performed. r^2 is a measure of the amount of variation of the Y variable, which is accounted for by variation in the X variable. r^2 is a bidirectional concept. Therefore, r^2 also can be stated as the *amount* of the X variable, which is accounted for by variation in the Y variable. In other words, the amount of the change in one variable is attributable to changes in the other variable, called shared variance.

Shared variance is usually stated as a percentage. If the correlation between two measures is .80, then the amount of shared variance is $.80^2 \times 100 = 64$ percent. What is the coefficient of determination when the correlation is $-.30$? Square the correlation and multiply by 100 to arrive at 9 percent. Researchers will use different phrases when referring to shared variance:

1. Sixteen percent of the variance of Y scores is *explained* by the variation of X scores.
2. Nine percent of X *is due to Y.*
3. Twenty-five percent of the variance of Y is *accounted for* by X.

Keep in mind that shared variance is a bidirectional notion. Whether you state it from the perspective of X or Y makes no difference. In addition, don't be confused by the terms "explained" or "accounted for." Strictly speaking, the coefficient of determination does not *explain* or *account for* anything. In other words, the coefficient of determination does not tell you *why* there is a relation between two variables.

The coefficient of determination is a concept more difficult to understand than the correlation coefficient. However, many behavioral scientists believe that r^2 is a more useful index of the relation between X and Y than is the correlation coefficient.

The key concept in understanding the coefficient of determination is **common variance** (or **shared variance**). Suppose you administer two *different* tests of anxiety to a group of individuals. From previous research that employed either Test 1 alone or Test 2 alone, you know that more anxious people score higher than less anxious people, whether they are given Test 1 or Test 2. Now you give *both* tests to the *same* group of people. Since both scales are measuring anxiety, would you expect the correlation between them to be $+1$? If not, why not; they are both measuring the same thing. In fact, the correlation will *not* be perfect.

Subjects' scores on either test of anxiety are affected by more than just their level of anxiety. The total score of *any* test is based on more than what the test is designed to measure. In the example, in addition to tapping anxiety, a person's score could be affected by fatigue, misunderstanding the instructions, distractions during the testing, or perhaps the tests use different ways of wording the questions. Moreover, one of the tests may ask more questions aimed at the physical experience of anxiety (e.g., "How often do you feel your heart pounding?") whereas the other test may ask more questions aimed at the cognitive aspect of anxiety (e.g., "How often do you find yourself worrying more than other people?"). Two scales that you think should measure the same trait may be tapping different aspects of the trait. Nonetheless, if the scales are correlated, to some extent they are measuring the same thing. It is the task of the researcher to determine specifically what that *thing* is. Whatever it is that the tests are both measuring about anxiety is what the two scales share in common. In Figure 15.4, the shaded, overlapping area is what the two tests have in common. It is the *shared variance* or *common variance* of the tests. Note how the amount of shared variance (shaded area) is larger as the correlation—and thus r^2—increases in magnitude. The nonoverlapping areas define the extent of *uncommon variance* or *unshared variance*. Differences in the way questions are worded, distractions in the room, fatigue, and so on are all factors that account for the size of the unshaded area.

Since the concept of r^2 is so important, and because it can be difficult to grasp, let us consider another, more detailed example. The Wechsler Intelligence Scale for Children (WISC-R) includes dozens of questions and tasks that are used to assess various aspects of intelligence. The Block Design task requires the child to look at a picture of a design (e.g., a diamond). Several wooden blocks, some white, some red, some half white, and some half red are given to the child who must arrange the blocks to reproduce the design in the picture. The Object Assembly task presents the pieces of a puzzle; the child must fit them together to form the correct figure (e.g., a horse). Some of the abilities that would lead a child to do well on Block Design would also lead to good performance on the Object Assembly task. These abilities are what the tests share in common. These abilities make up the shared variance of the tasks. Table 15.3 lists some of these common sources of variance. However, each test is influenced by unique factors or sources of variance. Table 15.3 also lists some of these unshared sources of variance. Suppose that the correlation between performance on Block Design and Object Assembly is +.70. Refer to Figure 15.4, the middle illustration. If the correlation is +.70, r^2 is approximately 50 percent. The overlapping segment of the ovals—the shaded area—is what the tasks share in common. In other words, they are

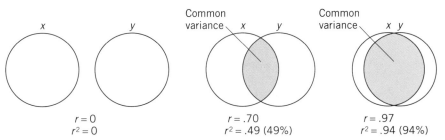

Figure 15.4   The shaded, overlapping areas depict shared variance. As r increases so does r^2.

TABLE   15.3   **Some Shared and Unshared Abilities Between the Block Design and Object Assembly Tasks of the WISC-R**[a, b]

BLOCK DESIGN AND OBJECT ASSEMBLY	
Shared Abilities	*Abilities Not Shared*
(Common Variance; Shared Variance; Variance Accounted for)	*(Uncommon Variance; Unshared Variance; Variance not Accounted for)*
Visual-motor coordination	Analysis of whole into component parts (BD)
Spatial relations	Reproduction of models (BD)
Perceptual organization	Ability to benefit from sensory-motor feedback (OA)
Working under time pressure	

[a] See Kaufmann, 1979.
[b] Those abilities in common will contribute to shared variance, r^2. (BD = Block Design; OA = Object Assembly)

the common abilities that influence the performance on each task. The nonoverlapping segments of the ovals make up the proportion of variance unique to each test. These are the abilities that are measured by one test but not the other.

Comparing r and r^2

You can compare two correlation coefficients to see that one is larger than the other. If you compare an r of $+.50$ to an r of $+.25$, *mathematically speaking,* one is twice the size of the other. However, the *worth* of the correlations is captured by r^2 not r. Thus, correlations should be compared in terms of their shared variance, r^2.

$$(.50)^2 \times 100 = 25\%$$

$$(.25)^2 \times 100 = 6.25\%$$

$$\frac{25\%}{6.25\%} = 4$$

In terms of r^2, a correlation of .50 is actually four times as large as a correlation of .25. The coefficient of determination, r^2, is not *directly* related to r. In fact, as Table 15.4 illustrates, you have to go all the way up to an r of .70 to find shared variance equal to 50 percent. To give an account of shared variance from 50 percent to 100 percent requires correlations from .70 to 1. Another way to clarify that there is not a direct relation between changes in r and changes in r^2 is to compare two sets of adjacent correlations. In Table 15.4, the adjacent correlations of .20 and .30 translate to a 5 percent increment in the amount of variance accounted for. Yet, the difference between correlations of .80 and .90 translate into a difference of 17 percent of the variance accounted for. In other words, the difference between a correlation of .20 and .30 is not worth as much as the difference between correlations of .80 and .90.

TABLE   15.4   The Relationship Between r and r^{2a}

	r	r^2		
	.00	.00		
Small r's	.10	.01		
	.20	.04	4%	Difference of 5%
	.30	.09	9%	
Moderate r's	.40	.16		
	.50	.25		
	.60	.36		
Large r's	.70	.49		
	.80	.64	64%	Difference of 17%
	.90	.81	81%	
	1.00	1.00		

[a] Correlations of small, moderate, and large are indicated on the left.

15.3   TESTING THE SIGNIFICANCE OF THE PEARSON r

The Null and Alternative Hypotheses

The statistic, r, is based on a bivariate sample of scores. It is an estimate of ρ. The statistic, r, can be used to make a number of inferences about ρ. For example, confidence intervals for ρ can be established; two r's can be compared to see if they have been drawn from populations having different ρ's; a given r can be tested to see if it is different from a specified value of ρ (e.g., $+.50$); and r can be tested to determine if the population correlation is different from 0. This section only addresses the most common form of hypothesis testing: is ρ different from 0? When asking the question, "Is the population correlation different from 0?", the null and alternative hypotheses are stated as,

$$H_0: \quad \rho = 0$$
$$H_1: \quad \rho \neq 0$$

Sampling Distributions

Whenever testing the statistical significance of a value, be it a mean, the difference between two means, the variance, or a correlation, a sampling distribution is required. A **sampling distribution** is a theoretical distribution made up of the statistic that is being tested. If you are testing to see whether a sample mean differs from a specified population mean, then the appropriate sampling distribution is made up of means. If you are testing the difference between two sample means, then the relevant sampling distribution is a distribution of differences between means. Although a sampling distribution is never actually constructed, the characteristics of the appropriate sampling distribution are known, provided certain assumptions are met.

A statistical test of significance asks the question, "What is the probability that I would obtain this sample statistic by chance when the null hypothesis is true?" If the probability is low (e.g., less than five times out of 100), then the null hypothesis is rejected; therefore, you conclude that there is a statistically significant finding. Given this line of reasoning, testing the null hypothesis that $\rho = 0$ involves computing r from a sample, and determining how unlikely it is that the obtained r would occur if the population correlation was 0.

The appropriate statistical model for testing the significance of an r is the t distribution.[5] The t distributions are transformations of sampling distributions of correlations of differing sample sizes. However, you do not need to compute a t ratio to test the significance of r. A direct method for testing the null hypothesis is to use a table of critical r's (see Appendix B.6). This table is derived from the sampling distributions of t; it allows you to make a direct comparison between the size of the sample correlation and the critical value of r in the table. The following worked problem illustrates how to use the table of critical values to test the null hypothesis that there is no correlation between X and Y in the population.

■   QUESTION   *An educational psychologist hypothesizes a relation between trait anxiety and GPA. A sample of 20 students is randomly selected; the correlation between anxiety and GPA is found to be* $-.50$. *Is* ρ *different from 0?*

SOLUTION

Step 1.   State the null and alternative hypotheses. In this case, H_0: $\rho = 0$ and H_1: $\rho \neq 0$.

Step 2.   Establish an alpha level. Use $\alpha = .05$.

Step 3.   Compute r_{obt}. It is given as $-.50$.

Step 4.   Locate r_{crit} in Appendix B.6, using $df = n_p - 2 = 18$, two-tailed test. The critical value equals .444.

Step 5.   Compare the absolute value of r_{obt} to r_{crit}. If the sample correlation is equal to or *larger* than r_{crit}, reject the null hypothesis. Since $|-.50| > .444$, reject H_0: $\rho = 0$ in favor of H_1: $\rho \neq 0$.

Step 6.   Interpret the findings. "There is a significant negative correlation between trait anxiety and GPA, $r(18) = -.50$, $p < .05$. Students who are anxious tend to have lower GPAs."

Note that you cannot make a causal statement that trait anxiety *leads* to lower grades. It could be the case that having lower grades leads to a chronic feeling of anxiety. And then there is always the possibility of a third, unmeasured variable, which accounts for the correlation between trait anxiety and GPA.   ■

The following worked problem shows the steps involved in testing H_0: $\rho = 0$. It begins with raw data and finishes with a test of the null hypothesis. Follow the

---

[5] The sampling distribution of t values is based on the formula, $t = r\sqrt{n_p - 2}/\sqrt{1 - r^2}$ with $df = n_p - 2$.

steps of the problem to be sure you understand the procedural flow in computing r_{obt} and testing H_0: $\rho = 0$.

■   QUESTION   *A clinical psychologist hypothesizes a correlation between a personality dimension, extroversion/introversion, and depression. Two questionnaires are administered. One measures the personality trait, with higher scores indicating more extroversion and lower scores tending toward introversion. The other measures depression, with higher scores reflecting greater depression. Lower scores on the depression inventory are not indicative of depression. Conduct a nondirectional test of r using the .05 level of significance.*

Extroversion/Introversion: X	Depression: Y
16	22
14	18
15	20
6	9
3	10
5	3
10	10
2	4
13	15

SOLUTION

Step 1. State the null and alternative hypotheses. In this case, H_0: $\rho = 0$ and H_1: $\rho \neq 0$.

Step 2. Establish an alpha level. Use $\alpha = .05$.

Step 3. Compute r_{obt}.

$$r_{obt} = \frac{n_p(\Sigma XY) - (\Sigma X)(\Sigma Y)}{\sqrt{[n_p(\Sigma X^2) - (\Sigma X)^2][n_p(\Sigma Y^2) - (\Sigma Y)^2]}}$$

$$= \frac{9(1306) - (84)(111)}{\sqrt{[9(1020) - (84)^2][9(1739) - (111)^2]}}$$

$$= \frac{2430}{\sqrt{(2124)(3330)}}$$

$$= \frac{2430}{\sqrt{7072920}}$$

$$= \frac{2430}{2659.50}$$

$$r_{obt} = \mathbf{+.91}$$

Step 4. Locate r_{crit} in Appendix B.6, using $df = n_p - 2$ $(9 - 2 = 7)$, two-tailed test. The critical value equals .666.

Step 5.   Compare the absolute value of r_{obt} to r_{crit}. If the sample correlation is *larger* than r_{crit}, reject the null hypothesis. Since $.91 > .67$, reject $H_0: \rho = 0$ in favor of $H_1: \rho \neq 0$.

Step 6.   Interpret the findings. "There is a significant correlation between extroversion and depression, $r(7) = +.91$, $p < .05$. Those people who are depressed are more likely to be extroverts; those people who are not depressed are more likely to be introverts." ■

General Considerations in Testing $H_0: \rho = 0$

Hypothesis testing is an inferential procedure. In the context of correlational analyses, a decision is made as to whether the population correlation differs from 0 (the null hypothesis). As with any test of a null hypothesis, two types of decision errors can be made. A Type I error is committed if a researcher concludes that the population correlation is *not* 0, when, in fact, it is 0 (a true null hypothesis is rejected). A Type II error is made when a researcher concludes that the population correlation is not different from 0, when, in fact, it is different from 0 (a false null hypothesis is not rejected).

The power of a statistical test is the probability that the test will correctly reject the null hypothesis. In the context of correlation, power is the sensitivity of the statistical test to detect a nonzero population correlation. For a given sample size, as ρ departs from 0, it is easier to reject correctly the null hypothesis (detect a nonzero ρ). Moreover, increasing the sample size will make it easier to detect a nonzero population correlation. Indeed, with very large samples, extremely small population correlations can be detected. Whether a researcher would want to detect such small correlations is questionable.

Statistical Significance and r^2

Refer to Appendix B.6, which gives the critical values for a direct test of r. Look at any column. Notice that r_{crit} becomes *smaller* as the sample size becomes *larger*. This means that an r_{obt} of a given magnitude may be statistically significant for one sample size, but the same correlation may be nonsignificant if it is based on a smaller sample size. Although the table of critical correlations only provides for df up to 100, all computer programs test for the significance of a correlation for any sample size. With very large samples, it is possible for a correlation to achieve statistical significance even though the magnitude of the correlation is very small. Under these circumstances, it is especially important that you keep the proportion of shared variance, r^2, in mind. A correlation that is *statistically* significant may not be *theoretically* and/or practically significant. A striking example of how small correlations can achieve statistical significance comes from a study on antismoking attitudes and general prejudice among West Germans (Grossarth-Maticek, Eysenck, and Vetter, 1988).

Table 15.5 lists the types of general prejudice, the correlation with antismoking attitudes, r^2, and the level of significance attained by each correlation. The correlation between anti-Semitism and antismoking prejudice is .06, signifi-

TABLE   15.5   Correlations Between Political Prejudice
and Anti-Smoking Attitudes

Prejudice	r	p	r²	Percent Shared Variance
Anti-Semitic	.06	.001	.0036	.36%
Anti-Arab	.05	.001	.0025	.25%
Racist	.11	.001	.0121	1.21%
Anti-American	.05	.001	.0025	.25%

cant at the .001 level. The r^2 is .0036; thus, .36 percent of the variance in anti-smoking attitudes is accounted for by variation in the anti-Semitic scores.

How could such small correlations be so highly significant? The sample size was 5977! With such a large sample, the statistical test of the null hypothesis was very powerful. Obtaining data from 5977 subjects is a time-consuming and expensive undertaking. You might ask the question, "Given the effort and expense, how important is it to be able to detect correlations that are so small they are trivial?" You should not be impressed by the *level of attained significance;* always look at the magnitude of the correlation and then square it.

Box 15.1 addresses the development of aggressive behavior in children and illustrates the use and interpretation of correlation coefficients.

BOX 15.1

Maternal Cognitions and Aggressive Children

Over the past several decades, studies have revealed that aggression is a relatively stable, self-perpetuating behavior (Huesmann and Eron, 1984; Olweus, 1979). Aggressive behavior in children is of significant concern to psychologists because it is predictive of later behavior, including the number and seriousness of criminal convictions (Huesmann and Eron, 1984), substance abuse, unemployment, divorce, and psychiatric illness (Caspi, Elder, and Bem, 1987).

The processes that perpetuate aggression are still unknown. While genetic, physiological, and other constitutional factors most likely contribute to the stability of aggression, research suggests that, in most cases, environmental conditions are probably the most important source of influence. Factors from each of the major systems in which young children interact (e.g., school, family, peers, media, etc.) have been implicated

as influencing the development and maintenance of aggression (Slaby and Roedell, 1982).

Miller (1990) was interested in the relation between one aspect of family life and children's aggression. She hypothesized that maternal cognitions would be correlated with children's aggression. More specifically, Miller expected to find a correlation between how dissatisfied mothers are with their children and the aggressiveness of their children. Although Miller measured numerous maternal attitudes and behaviors to test competing models of aggression, we will consider only a couple of simple correlations for the purposes of illustrating the concepts discussed in this chapter.[7]

[7] Miller's hypotheses and statistical analyses were much more complex than I am presenting here. The interested reader is referred to Miller (1990).

To assess child aggression, a peer-nomination measure was used; each child's aggression score was derived from the reports of a sample of his/her classmates. The children were asked to name as many other children in the class as they wished who behaved in a certain way (e.g., "Who pushes or shoves children?"). The aggression score for a given child was the percentage of times he or she was nominated by classmates on ten aggression items.

A second variable of interest was mothers' dissatisfaction with their child. A mother who scored high on the dissatisfaction questionnaire was one who complained that her child "is too forgetful," "doesn't follow directions," and "wastes too much time." The following table presents the correlations between maternal dissatisfaction and child aggression for boys and girls.

Correlations Between Maternal Dissatisfaction and Child Aggression

Boys (n = 54)		Girls (n = 45)	
r	p	r	p
.33	< .01	.31	< .05

A positive correlation means that the more the mother is dissatisfied with her child, the more aggressive is the child. Alternatively stated, the more aggressive children have mothers who were more dissatisfied with them. The correlations for both boys and girls are statistically significant, boys: $r(54) = .33$, $p < .01$; girls: $r(45) = .31$, $p < .05$.

Considering these two correlations, an issue arises—one that frequently arises when doing correlational research. Is there a causal connection between the variables? Given only the information that I have presented from Miller's study, there is no way to know if a child's aggression is influenced by maternal dissatisfaction, or if maternal dissatisfaction is influenced by the child's aggression. Furthermore, it is possible that some third variable accounts for the relation between maternal dissatisfaction and aggression. Perhaps the level of aggression *among the mothers* directly influences their dissatisfaction with their children *and* directly affects the level of aggression among their children.

15.4 FACTORS THAT CAN CREATE MISLEADING CORRELATION COEFFICIENTS

The definition of a correlation coefficient can be deceptively simple: it is an index of the strength of association between two variables. However, there are several factors that can affect the size of the correlation; these factors can hide the real nature of the relationship between the variables being correlated. This section addresses some of the issues that arise when interpreting correlations.

Restricted Range

One problem that can arise when calculating correlations has to do with the range of each measure. Each measure will have a potential range of scores and an obtained range of scores. For instance, a scale that measures kindness might range from 20 to 60. If, for example, due to sampling error, the range of scores obtained from a group of subjects ranges from 39 to 60, the entire range of test scores is not reflected in the sample. The range of scores is restricted. If you correlate the kindness scale with some other measure, a problem arises. *Restricted ranges have a tendency to reduce the correlation.*

In Figure 15.5, the correlation, based on the entire plot, is quite high, about +.80. Now look at just the plot within the inset in the upper right corner. Those scores are restricted to the upper ranges of *X* and *Y.* The plot in the inset reflects a very low correlation, perhaps 0.

The problem of restricted ranges can arise when examining the relation between Graduate Record Examination (GRE) scores and the GPAs obtained by students at the end of the first year of graduate school. Admissions committees obviously do not admit students to graduate school at random. They favor students who have performed very well on the GREs (in addition to other criteria). As a result, the group of successful applicants will not show much variability on GREs, at least not as much variability as the scores of all students applying to the program. Likewise, students' GPAs at the end of the first year tend to be restricted to the upper grades. What would happen if you computed a correlation between GRE scores and the GPA obtained at the end of the first year of graduate school? The correlation would be spuriously (artificially) low.[6] Failing to consider the effect of range restrictions, a researcher could erroneously conclude that GRE scores have no relation to subsequent GPA; therefore, they should not be used as one criterion of admission. Since admissions committees purposely restrict the range of GREs,

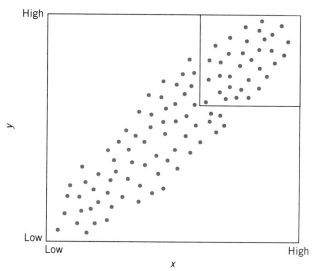

Figure 15.5   The true strength of association between *X* and *Y* is underestimated when the range of scores is restricted.

---

[6] According to the Educational Testing Service, the correlation between the GRE Quantitative test and first-year graduate GPA among engineering students is .02; among psychology students, it is .23. You can only speculate as to the difference between the correlations. It may be because engineering admissions committees accept students within a smaller range of GRE-Q scores compared to psychology admissions committees. (I would like to thank an anonymous reviewer for calling these correlations to my attention.)

no one is surprised that the correlation between GREs and GPA is low. The restricted range issue becomes a problem when the investigator fails to realize that one or both variables are restricted in range. Since you will always know the potential range of each variable, it is helpful to "eyeball" the data to see if you have scores spread over the possible values of the X and Y distributions.

A Nonlinear Relation Between X and Y

The formula for the Pearson correlation discussed in this chapter is only appropriate when there is a linear relation between X and Y. The use of the Pearson formula becomes less appropriate as the relation between X and Y increasingly departs from linearity. When this occurs, the Pearson r will underestimate the correlation between X and Y. Other correlational techniques can be used to capture the strength of association between X and Y when there is a nonlinear relation. Figure 15.3 was an example in which there was a curvilinear relation between arousal and task performance. It was pointed out that using the Pearson formula would yield a spuriously low correlation, when, in fact, the association between the two variables was high. You need to protect yourself from misapplying the Pearson formula; fortunately, to do so is not difficult. Simply examine the scatter plot. If the oval you draw does not arch, then you are safe in using the Pearson formula. Figure 15.6 illustrates some nonlinear relations between X and Y. Note that nonlinearity is a matter of degree. Nonlinearity is not confined to a plot that takes the shape of a U or inverted U. Nonlinearity is reflected by any plot that shows a curve. The Pearson formula for r presented in this chapter would not be used with bivariate distributions that have any of the shapes shown in Figure 15.6.

The X and Y Distributions are Skewed

When the X and Y distributions are skewed in opposite directions, there is a limit to how high the correlation can be. Under normal circumstances, you might view a correlation of .50 as moderate. However, if the distributions are oppositely skewed,

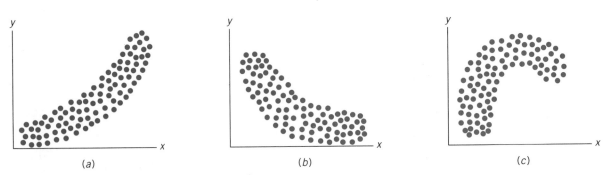

Figure 15.6   Some nonlinear relations between X and Y.

it is conceivable for the highest possible correlation to be .60. Now an r of .50 is very high, given that limit. Consider the following two frequency distributions.

Score on X:	0	1	2	3	4	5	6	7	8	9	10
Frequency:	25	14	13	14	12	11	6	4	2	3	1

Score on Y:	0	1	2	3	4	5	6	7	8	9	10
Frequency:	0	1	3	2	2	5	3	10	15	20	44

The X distribution is positively skewed and the Y distribution is negatively skewed. To understand how this *bivariate* distribution has a ceiling on the size of the correlation that is mathematically possible, it is helpful to think in terms of the z-score formula for correlation:

$$\rho = \frac{\Sigma(z_x z_y)}{N_p}$$

With relatively few scores *above* the mean of the positively skewed X distribution, and so few scores *below* the mean of the negatively skewed Y distribution, it is impossible for every positive z_x score to be associated with a positive z_y score. For this reason, the correlation could never be $+1$ or -1. In fact, unless the X and Y distributions have identical shapes, the extreme values of $+1$ and -1 are impossible to attain. The recommended approach to this problem is to examine first the univariate curve of each distribution (not the scatter plot). If a problem with skewness exists, there are several types of transformations that can be applied to the raw data, which normalize the shape of the distribution. A discussion of these transformations is beyond the scope of an introductory-level textbook, but most advanced texts provide a useful treatment of the subject (see Kirk, 1982).

The Use of Extreme Groups

A common type of correlational design, particularly in the field of personality research, is to compare extreme groups with respect to some variable. For example, suppose you are interested in comparing Type A and Type B individuals with respect to interpersonal dominance. You administer a questionnaire that provides a continuous measure of the degree to which an individual exhibits the characteristics of the Type A personality. You later select those individuals who scored in the top 10 percent (Type A's) and the bottom 10 percent (Type B's). Now you administer your dominance questionnaire to the members of the extreme groups, and correlate the Type A/B scores with dominance.

This methodological approach will typically yield a correlation between X and Y that is larger than if extreme groups were not used. If, instead of selecting those subjects with high and low scores, you included *all* the subjects that had been administered the Type A questionnaire, the correlation would have been comparatively lower. The reason for this phenomenon is that the association

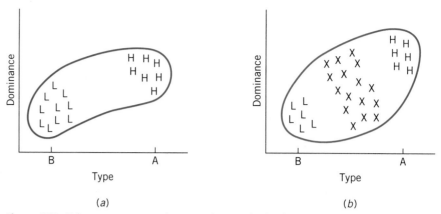

Figure 15.7 Using extreme groups increases the magnitude of the correlation between X and Y. (a) The oval surrounding the scatter plot is relatively more narrow than the scatter plot surrounding the data points in (b).

between X and Y is usually not as strong in the midrange of the distributions. Figure 15.7 depicts this point.

Figure 15.7(a) shows that the oval is fairly narrow when using only extreme groups, which reflects an r of about $+.80$. When the entire range of the Type A/B scores is used, the oval is more circular, which accommodates the spread of scores from the midrange [Figure 15.7(b)]. Because the use of extreme groups can inflate the correlation, some statisticians warn against this type of methodology. However, the theory that you use may only be relevant to extreme groups. Prudence dictates that you exercise caution when interpreting a correlation based on groups that are selected because their subjects score in the extreme ends of the distribution.

The Effect of an Extreme Score

A data point that stands off by itself, be it abnormally low or high, is called an outlier. An outlier can create a spuriously low or high correlation. This problem arises when the sample size is small. A simple example illustrates this point. The only difference between Distribution A and Distribution B is that the Y score of the last subject has been tripled in Distribution B.

Distribution A		Distribution B	
X	Y	X	Y
2	4	2	4
3	4	3	4
5	6	5	6
9	8	9	8
3	3	3	9

The r between X and Y from Distribution A is $+.94$. By creating an outlier, the r drops to $+.49$.

Wainer and Thissen (1976) presented a bivariate distribution of heights and weights. The correlation for 25 subjects was computed as $+.83$. However, they showed that if a transcription error was made, and the height and weight values for one subject were switched, the correlation changed to $-.26$!

Outliers present a dilemma for researchers. There is a strict rule in research that investigators should not simply discard data because it is inconsistent with their expectation of what the data should look like. It is a good rule because it guards against biasing the outcome of a study to fit preconceived notions. Without the rule, there is no point in doing research in the first place.

The conventional approach to the extreme score problem is to analyze the data with and without the outlier, noting the difference it makes in the type of conclusion you would draw from the results. Sometimes an outlier will have but a small effect on the analysis, particularly when the sample size is sufficiently large (yet another argument for large samples). If the outlier does make a difference, the researcher may be justified in basing conclusions on the analysis conducted *without* the outlier. Since that one subject's score is so aberrant, the researcher might suspect that the score is unreliable. Perhaps the subject's score was a function of fatigue or inattention. It could have arisen by any number of reasons, which have nothing to do with the true nature of the relationship between the variables being studied. An attempt to try to account for the unusual score (perhaps interviewing the subject) may lead to an interesting hypothesis that could be pursued in a subsequent study. A note of caution is in order. Outliers should be examined irrespective of the obtained correlation. Discarding an outlier *only* when it affects the correlation in a way that disconfirms your experimental hypothesis biases your findings. Thus, to be fair, you should attend to outliers irrespective of the magnitude of the correlation.

The correlation coefficient is one of the most useful indices for assessing the degree to which two variables are related. However, since there are numerous factors that affect the interpretation of the correlation, it is imperative that you "dig into the data." Keep in mind r^2 when r is statistically significant. Moreover, pay close attention to the scatter plot to check for linearity, the distributions of X and Y (for skewness), restricted ranges, the use of extreme groups, and the presence of outliers.

SUMMARY

A correlation is an index of the strength of association between two variables. The distribution of pairs of scores is called a bivariate distribution. The correlation based on a sample is symbolized r; the population coefficient is symbolized ρ. However, it cannot be inferred from a correlation that a causal relation in either direction exists between the two variables.

If you conduct a study in which some procedural variables are held constant and others are purposely allowed to vary, the study is called an experiment. If you conduct a study and do not exert control over the variables under investigation, then you are using a correlational design. The basis for making causal statements never resides with the type of analysis, but rather with the manner in which the data are collected.

A correlation coefficient is represented by a number that ranges from $+1$ to -1. The higher the coefficient's absolute value, the stronger the association between the two variables. An r of $+.60$ reflects a strength of association as strong as an r of $-.60$. If higher values of one variable are associated with higher values of the other variable, then the correlation is positive. If higher values of one variable are associated with lower values of the second variable, then the correlation is negative.

When a bivariate distribution is plotted on a graph, it is called a scatter diagram or scatter plot. The scatter plot provides a great deal of information about the relationship between two variables. The magnitude of the correlation can be estimated by looking at the general shape formed by the points. The size of the correlation is estimated by examining the width of the oval: the more narrow the oval, the higher the correlation. If the points have no trend and are best contained within a circle, the correlation is zero—that is—the variables are unrelated.

Not only does the scatter plot indicate the strength of association between X and Y, it also reveals the direction of the correlation. If the oval that contains the majority of the points slopes from the lower left to the upper right, the correlation is positive. If the plot slopes from the upper left to the lower right, then the correlation is negative.

The scatter plot can also reveal when the oval arches or forms a **U** or inverted **U**. Plots shaped like this reveal a nonlinear relation between X and Y. The formulas for calculating a linear correlation are different from those used to calculate a correlation based on a curvilinear relationship.

Raw scores above the mean of a distribution transform to positive z scores, and raw scores below the mean transform to negative z scores. If X and Y are positively correlated, then positive z scores of variable X will occur more often with the positive z scores of variable Y; the negative z scores of the X distribution will occur more often with the negative z scores of the Y distribution. If X and Y are negatively correlated, then the positive z scores of X will occur more often with the negative z scores of Y. This is the underlying logic of the z-score formula for the correlation coefficient.

The coefficient of determination, r^2, is a measure of the amount of variation of the Y variable, which is accounted for by variation in the X variable. Conversely, the amount of the change in the X variable attributable to changes in the Y variable. Shared variance is usually stated as a percentage. If the correlation between two measures is .60, then the amount of variance held in common is $.60^2 \times 100 = 36$ percent. Shared variance is a nondirectional notion. Whether you state it from the perspective of X or Y makes no difference.

You can compare two correlation coefficients and see that one is larger than the other. However, you cannot say that an r of $+.80$ is twice as large as an r of $+.40$, or that .50 is half the size of a perfect correlation. Correlations should be compared in terms of their shared variance, r^2.

The test of significance for r asks the question, "Is the magnitude of r sufficiently large to conclude that ρ is not 0?" For any test of significance, a theoretical sampling distribution is needed. The correct sampling distribution for testing the significance of r is a t statistic, based on a transformation of r's. The transformation has the effect of normalizing the sampling distribution of correlations.

When testing the significance of a correlation, the most common null and alternative hypotheses are: H_0: $\rho = 0$; H_1: $\rho \neq 0$.

There are several factors that can affect the size of the correlation; these factors can hide the real nature of the relationship between the variables being correlated.

When the distribution of X and/or Y is restricted, then the correlation is likely to be spuriously low. Furthermore, the use of the Pearson formula is inappropriate if the relation between X and Y departs from linearity. In this instance, the Pearson r will underestimate the relation between X and Y. Other correlational techniques can be used to capture the strength of association between X and Y when there is a nonlinear relation between the variables.

When the X and Y distributions are skewed in opposite directions, there is a limit to how high the correlation can be. Several mathematical transformations can be considered to change the shape of either the X and/or Y distributions.

A common type of correlational design is to compare extreme groups with respect to some variable. This methodological approach typically yields a correlation between X and Y that is larger than if extreme groups were not used. However, exercise caution when interpreting the correlation obtained from a design that uses extreme groups.

A data point that stands off by itself, be it abnormally low or high, is called an outlier. An outlier can create a misleading r. This problem arises when the sample size is small.

KEY FORMULAS FOR CHAPTER 15

z-Score Formula for the Population Correlation

$$\rho = \frac{\Sigma(z_x z_y)}{N_p}$$

(Formula 15.1)

Computational Formula for Pearson's r

$$r_{\text{obt}} = \frac{n_p(\Sigma XY) - (\Sigma X)(\Sigma Y)}{\sqrt{[n_p(\Sigma X^2) - (\Sigma X)^2][n_p(\Sigma Y^2) - (\Sigma Y)^2]}}$$

(Formula 15.2)

WORK PROBLEMS

1. What is the distinction between a correlational and experimental design? Why does an experimental design offer the potential for making causal statements about the relation between two variables?

2. Provide examples of variables that are positively correlated and variables that are negatively correlated.

3. What information can be gleaned by examining a scatter plot?

4. Given the following population of z scores, what is the correlation between X and Y?

z_x	z_y
−.32	−.56
−.10	0
.42	−.12
0	.68

5. Estimate the r for each of these scatter plots.

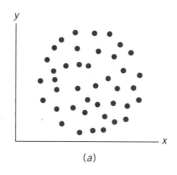

(a)

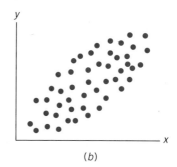

(b)

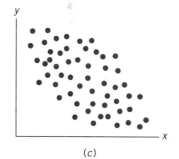

(c)

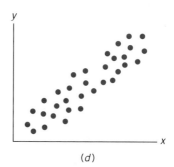

(d)

6. For the following correlations and df, what are the critical r's when using a 5 percent and a 1 percent level of significance. In each case, would you accept or reject the null hypothesis at the 5 percent level? At the 1 percent level?

a. $r = .67$, $df = 24$
b. $r = .39$, $df = 24$
c. $r = .89$, $df = 12$
d. $r = .74$, $df = 18$
e. $r = .45$, $df = 29$
f. $r = .95$, $df = 7$
g. $r = .62$, $df = 13$
h. $r = .24$, $df = 100$

7. For the following data set:

a. Calculate r and conduct a two-tailed test of significance with an alpha of .05.

b. Specify the null and alternative hypotheses.

    c. What is r_{crit}?

    d. Accept or reject the null hypothesis?

    e. What percent of the variance of Y is accounted for by the variance of X?

X	Y
6	4
7	5
7	6
4	6

8. For the following data set:

    a. Calculate r and conduct a two-tailed test of significance with an alpha of .05.

    b. Specify the null and alternative hypotheses.

    c. What is r_{crit}?

    d. Accept or reject the null hypothesis?

    e. What percent of the variance of Y is accounted for by the variance of X?

X	Y
6	3
9	7
7	6
10	9

9. For the following data set:

    a. Calculate r and conduct a two-tailed test of significance with an alpha of .05.

    b. Specify the null and alternative hypotheses.

    c. What is r_{crit}?

    d. Accept or reject the null hypothesis?

    e. What percent of the variance of Y is accounted for by the variance of X?

X	Y
10	12
9	6
11	10
13	13

10. For the following data set:

    a. Calculate r and conduct a two-tailed test of significance with an alpha of .05.

    b. Specify the null and alternative hypotheses.

    c. What is r_{crit}?

    d. Accept or reject the null hypothesis?

    e. What percent of the variance of Y is accounted for by the variance of X?

X	Y
1	3
2	4
4	5
6	5
7	7

11. Provide an example of a correlational design in which X is a personality variable and Y is a measure of observed behavior.

12. Answer these questions for the following data set.
    a. Calculate r. Conduct a nondirectional test at the .05 level of significance.
    b. Specify the null and alternative hypotheses.
    c. What is r_{crit}?
    d. Accept or reject the null hypothesis?
    e. What percent of the variance of X scores is explained by the variance of Y scores?

X	Y
1	8
3	7
3	6
5	5
6	4

13. Draw the scatter plots for the data of Problems 7, 8, 9 and 12.

14. For a group of 75 subjects, $\Sigma(z_x z_y)$ is 64. What is ρ?

15. In what way does the range of scores sampled influence the size of the correlation?

16. In what way does the use of extreme groups affect the correlation?

17. If you use the Pearson r to calculate the correlation when the relation between X and Y is nonlinear, what is the effect on r?

18. A sports psychologist is interested in the relation between how many weeks someone has been exercising and his or her resting heart rate. Using the following data, answer these questions.
    a. What is r?
    b. What are the null and alternative hypotheses?
    c. What is r_{crit} for a nondirectional test at the 5 percent level of significance?
    d. What percent of the variance of resting heart-rate scores is accounted for by the number of weeks of exercise?
    e. Should you accept or reject the null hypothesis?

Weeks of Exercise	Resting Heart Rate
2	82
4	78
8	72
14	66
10	66
9	70
9	69

19. A school psychologist hypothesizes a relation between IQ and number of siblings. Please answer the following questions.
    a. What is r?
    b. What are the null and alternative hypotheses?
    c. What is r_{crit} for a nondirectional test at the 5 percent level of significance?

d. What percent of the variance of IQ scores is accounted for by the number of siblings?

e. Should you accept or reject the null hypothesis?

Number of Siblings	IQ
8	123
3	100
1	90
4	111
2	102
0	95

20. A psychologist is interested in the strength of association between age and performance on a certain task requiring motor skills. Plot the scatter diagram of the following data and decide on the most reasonable course of action for testing the hypothesis.

Age in Years	Number of Errors
6	23
7	19
8	17
9	16
10	16
11	18
12	18
13	19
14	20
15	22

Work Problems for the Computer

21. Baron, Logan, and Kao (1990) studied the relation between student dentists' perceptions of their patients' discomfort and the patients' perceptions of their own discomfort. Discomfort was defined as a combination of anxiety, pain, and distress (with low numbers indicating low discomfort). Discomfort ratings were obtained under two conditions: during drilling and during the rubber-dam placement. (The rubber dam is a thin rubber sheath attached to a metal frame. It fits around the tooth, which isolates it and prevents debris from being swallowed. Placement of the rubber dam requires more of the dentist's attention than does a simple filling.) Correlations between dental students' ratings and patients' ratings were computed under these two conditions. The correlation between ratings during drilling was significant, $r(41) = +.52$, $p < .05$. The correlation between students' and patients' ratings during the rubber-dam procedure was also significant, but considerably smaller, $r(41) = +.23$, $p < .05$. The authors speculate that the ability of dentists to detect distress depends on what they are doing: " ... dentists' ability to monitor patient discomfort might be impaired during particularly challenging segments of the treatment procedure. The assumption here is that being sensitive to stress requires substantial attentional capacity" (p. 151).

The following data set is hypothetical. The numbers are selected so that your correlations will lead to conclusions that are consistent with the authors'. Be sure to examine the scatter plots of the data.

Discomfort Ratings During Drilling

Dental Students	Patients
8	6
6	9
3	1
1	4
5	5
4	6
8	8
7	6
9	6
2	3
1	1
6	8
4	6
3	3
9	7
7	8
6	9
2	8
5	7
6	6
3	2
1	1
5	7
6	9
8	8
9	6

Discomfort Ratings During Rubber Dam

Dental Students	Patients
8	6
6	9
3	1
1	4
5	5
4	6
8	8
7	6
9	6
2	3
1	1
6	8
4	6
3	3
9	7
7	8
6	9
2	8

Discomfort Ratings During Rubber Dam

Dental Students	Patients
5	7
6	6
3	2
1	1
5	7
6	9
8	1
9	4

22. Carrie (1981) investigated the relation between women's symptomatic reports during pregnancy and menstruation, and the association of these reports with the general tendency to report psychological and physical symptoms. Among her findings was the fact that there is a significant correlation between the number of symptoms experienced during menstruation and the number of symptoms reported during pregnancy. The following raw data are hypothetical, yet will give a correlation consistent with the level of significance found in the study by Carrie.

Hypothetical Questionnaire Scores

Last Menstruation Symptoms	Last Pregnancy Symptoms
93	87
75	64
34	78
23	55
76	43
34	45
21	20
34	54
60	60
45	82
67	67
50	48
89	72
61	68
56	45
82	75
45	34
53	55
71	50
59	90
90	56
43	62
49	32

Linear Regression

16.1   THE RESEARCH CONTEXT

 Regression is a set of statistical procedures that allows a researcher to use information about one variable to predict the value of a second variable. There are many occasions when behavioral scientists would like to make predictions; of course, the more accurate the predictions, the better. Graduate admissions committees, for instance, would like to select students who will do well in graduate school. If a measure such as Graduate Record Examination scores is found to correlate with future grade point averages, then an individual's GRE scores can be used to predict that person's subsequent GPA. If a researcher finds a correlation between the number of times prisoners get into fights while in prison and the number of domestic quarrels after release, a parole board may be able to predict the level of post-release, familial fighting. Any time two variables are correlated, one variable can be used to predict the value of a second variable. A study by Zullow and Seligman (1990) showed that the outcome of presidential elections could be predicted by examining the content of campaign speeches. They found that the more a candidate dwells on negative events, the less likely he is to win the election. They conclude that the American voter "places a high premium on the appearance of hope."

In addition to using regression for practical problems, researchers often use regression strategies to make behavioral predictions in order to build and test theories. For example, Zullow and Seligman's study not only has obvious practical implications for speech writers, their data are also of theoretical interest to behavioral scientists. Indeed, Zullow and Seligman derived their research hypothesis about election outcomes from work in the area of depression! They noted that people who tend to dwell on negative events are more subject to depression (Zullow, 1984). They found depressed people to be relatively passive, to convey a sense of hopelessness and to be more disliked by others. Zullow and Seligman predicted that voters would react to a candidate who dwells on negative events in a manner similar to the way people respond to those who are depressed— that is—with rejection.[1]

16.2   OVERVIEW OF REGRESSION

Regression is a set of procedures that can be used to make predictions about one variable based on knowledge of another variable. The actual prediction is accomplished through the use of a **regression equation.** For linear regression to be of use to an investigator, the two variables *must* be linearly related (correlated). This precondition makes perfect sense. If high school GPA is uncorrelated with college GPA, then there is no way to use high school GPA to predict subsequent GPA. Not only must two variables be correlated, but to use linear regression, the relation between the variables must be linear. In a linear relation, each time the value of one variable increases, the value of the other variable shows a constant change. If the change in the second variable is not constant, the relation between X and Y is nonlinear, which will be reflected in the scatter plot. Chapter 15 presented numerous scatter plots in which the oval surrounding the majority of data points was curved, thus indicating a nonlinear relation between X and Y. The Pearson formula for the correlation is not used when there is a nonlinear relation between X and Y; likewise, the regression methods presented in this chapter cannot be used when X and Y are related in a nonlinear fashion. Inspecting the scatter plot is very helpful when deciding whether linearity exists.

---

[1] Technically speaking, Zullow and Seligman (1990) did not analyze their data using simple regression. However, their data set lends itself to the use of regression.

This chapter considers the use of simple regression in which information about only one variable (called the predictor or independent variable) is used to predict a second variable (called either the predicted, criterion, or dependent variable). The terms independent and dependent variable have a slightly different meaning in the context of regression. In regression, the independent variable is *not* manipulated by the experimenter in order to observe its effect on the dependent variable.[2] With respect to the dependent variable, the value of Y that is predicted for a given X *depends* on the value of X.

Regression analyses are bidirectional. For instance, if there is a correlation between stubbornness and empathy, regression can be used to predict a person's level of empathy based on knowing his or her level of stubbornness. Conversely, a person's stubbornness can be predicted based on knowing his or her empathy score. In either case, that which is predicted is the dependent variable.

The word prediction connotes a temporality, which is potentially misleading in a discussion of regression. You might conclude that a current independent variable is used to predict a future dependent variable. No futurity is implied with regression. Using the variables stubbornness and empathy has no implied futurity. In fact, you could use SAT scores to predict IQ scores even though IQ has preceded SAT performance.

 In simple regression only one predictor variable is used. **Multiple regression** employs more than one predictor. Multiple regression is used more often in the social sciences because combining two or more variables often leads to more accurate predictions of a dependent variable. For example, multiple regression was used in a study that found that panic attacks can be predicted by combining information about a person's fear of losing control, use of medication, whether the person is in psychotherapy, *and* the person's general level of anxiety (Maller, 1988). Although multiple regression is beyond the scope of this text, it is merely an extension of the concepts that are discussed in this chapter.

Using Correlated Information to Make Predictions

If you were asked to predict the height of a randomly selected American male, you could make the prediction by stating the mean height for all American males. Imagine this process was repeated over and over again. Suppose the mean height for American males is 5 ft 10 in. Each time you are asked to predict the height of a randomly selected male, you would state the height as 5 ft 10 in. Sometimes you would be correct, but most of the time you would be incorrect. Moreover, when incorrect, you could be a little bit incorrect (the selected person might be 5 ft 9 in.) or very incorrect (the person might be 6 ft 7 in.). Ultimately, predicting the

---

[2] The use of regression techniques is not confined to correlational designs. The interested reader is referred to advanced statistics textbooks (e.g., Hays, 1988) for a discussion of regression analysis in the context of true experiments.

mean height for all males is not very accurate, but at least it is unbiased. That is, after you have made a large number of predictions, and you have examined your overall accuracy, you will find that you have overpredicted to the same extent that you have underpredicted.

Now the game changes. You are told that there is a correlation between the heights of fathers and sons. Furthermore, you are given a table that states the mean height of sons for fathers of a specific height. Let's say that for fathers who are 5 ft 5 in., the mean height of their sons is 5 ft 7 in. For fathers who are 6 ft 6 in., the mean height of their sons is 6 ft 3 in. Now someone says, "I have selected a male. The height of his father is 5 ft 5 in. How tall do you think the son is?" Now you have correlated information available to aid in prediction. Instead of predicting the mean height of all males, you should predict 5 ft 7 in., the mean height of all males that have fathers who are 5 ft 5 in. Every time you have to make a prediction, you obtain the height of the father and use the table to predict the average height of sons who have fathers of the given height.

By using correlated information in prediction, you will still make errors (unbiased, I might add), but the overall error will be smaller than if you ignore the correlated information. If this strategy seems obvious to you, then you already have an intuitive understanding of what regression is about. Although regression does not entail using a table to make predictions, an equation accomplishes the same thing. Some score (e.g., height of father) is entered into the regression equation and the predicted score (e.g., height of son) is computed.

Regression as a Two-Step Process

The regression procedure involves two steps. The first step is to identify two variables that are correlated. To do this, you first need a sample in which measures of two variables are provided for every subject. If your ultimate goal is to predict GPAs from performance on the GREs, a large sample of subjects is required to obtain both GRE scores and subsequent GPAs. If these variables are indeed correlated, a **regression equation** can be established for later use. The second step in regression involves the application of the regression equation to data from subjects *not* included in the original sample. In this step you only have the value of the X variable available, which is the predictor variable. Thus, the correlation between GREs and GPAs may be established with a large, random sample of students over a two-year period; the X variable (GREs) is measured one year and the Y variable (GPAs) is measured the following year. A regression equation is established, which is used to predict the GPAs of new applicants. A prediction is made for *each* applicant based only on that person's GRE score. The regression equation initially emerges from group data; it is later applied on an individual basis.

16.3 ESTABLISHING THE REGRESSION LINE

 In linear regression, the regression equation is used to plot a straight prediction line, which goes through the middle of the scatter plot. This is called the **regression line.** The term middle, however, has a precise meaning, which will be explained shortly. Formula 16.1 is the formula for a straight line.

> **Straight Line Formula**
>
> $Y = a + bX$ *(Formula 16.1)*

 In this formula, a is the Y **intercept**—that point at which the line crosses the ordinate (i.e., the Y axis) when X is 0. The other constant, b, defines the angle, or slope, of the line.[3] Figure 16.1 shows a scatter plot with several straight lines drawn through the plot. Since each line has a different angle and a different point at which it crosses the Y axis, the constants a and b are different for each line. Yet each line is described by the general equation for a straight line.

The regression equation chooses among an infinite number of straight lines that could be drawn through the scatter plot. A criterion has to be established, which must be met when estimating a and b; then formulas have to be developed for a and b that meet the criterion. The Least Squares Method is used to determine where the regression line will be drawn through the scatter plot. Before discussing the criterion that is met by the Least Squares Method, it is important that you understand how to interpret a regression line.

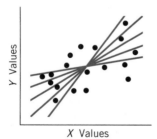

Figure 16.1 Several straight lines drawn through a scatter plot. The regression equation establishes which of a potentially infinite number of lines is the best one to predict a Y score given an X score.

---

[3] Algebra texts usually use different symbols in the formula for a straight line, e.g., $Y = mX + b$, where m is the slope of the line and b is the intercept.

Reading the Regression Line: All Predicted Y's are on the Regression Line

In regression, an X score is used to predict the value of a Y score. Provided there is a correlation between X and Y (which is the only time you would use regression), there is a different Y predicted for each value of X. Every predicted Y (symbolized Y_p) lies on the regression line.[4] To find Y_p for a given X, find the X value on the horizontal axis (abscissa) and draw a line parallel to the vertical axis (ordinate). When that line meets the regression line, another line is drawn at a right angle (parallel to the X axis) until it meets the vertical (Y) axis. The value at which this line intersects the Y axis is Y_p. In Figure 16.2, a Y of 6 would be predicted for anyone who obtained an X of 4.

Reading the Regression Line: The Slope of the Regression Line

 The slope of the regression line (or any straight line) is referred to as the "rise over the run." The **slope** indicates how many units the line rises on the Y axis for every one unit you move to the right on the X axis. For instance, if $b = .93$, the regression line ascends .93 Y units with each successive unit of X. Suppose for the relation between height (the Y variable in in.) and weight (the X variable in lbs), a regression line has a slope of $+2$. An increase of 1 lb corresponds to an increase of 2 in. In addition, a positive slope corresponds to a positive correlation,

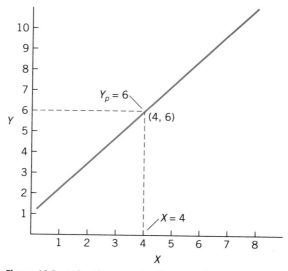

Figure 16.2   Using the regression line to predict Y given $X = 4$.

---

[4] Some textbooks use the symbol Y' ("Y prime") instead of Y_p. I will use Y_p to prompt you to think "predicted Y."

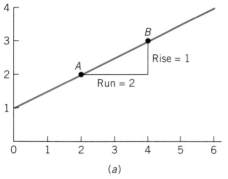
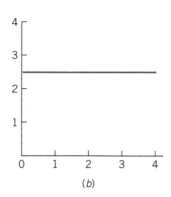
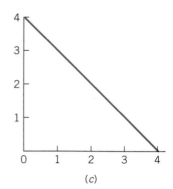

(a)   (b)   (c)

Figure 16.3   The straight lines with different slopes.

and a negative slope corresponds to a negative correlation. The larger the value of b, the steeper the slope of the regression line. Figure 16.3 illustrates lines with three different slopes. In Figure 16.3(a), the line "rises" one unit on the Y axis for every "run" of two units on the X axis. How many units would the line ascend for one unit on the X axis? The answer is .50; therefore, the slope of this line is .50. In Figure 16.3(b), the slope of the line neither ascends nor descends. A line that is parallel to the X axis has a slope of 0. In Figure 16.3(c), the line descends one unit for every one unit of increase on the X axis. The slope is -1.

The Least Squares Criterion

 The criterion that is used to select the best straight line that could be drawn through the scatter plot is called the **Least Squares Criterion.** This criterion assures that the regression line is chosen so that the amount of prediction error is as small as possible.

If the relation between X and Y is perfect ($r = \pm 1$), then all data points will lie along a straight line. The regression line will have all the points of the scatter plot on it. Since a correlation of ± 1 is extremely rare, there typically is a spread of points surrounding the line; every point not on the line defines an amount of error. An error is the difference between the actual Y score obtained by an individual and Y_p, the score predicted for that person.

Figure 16.4 shows a hypothetical regression line for the relationship between GRE scores and subsequent GPA. For purposes of visual clarity, the swarm of data points surrounding the regression line is not depicted. Rick received a GRE score of 650. His next year's GPA is predicted to be 3.62. If his GPA is actually 3.00, you have missed by .62 points. Carol also scored 650 on her GREs. Thus the same GPA (3.62) was predicted. She later achieved a 4.00 GPA. Therefore you have erred by .38 points.

Of all the straight lines that could be drawn through the scatter plot, you want the line that is positioned so that the amount of error is at a minimum.

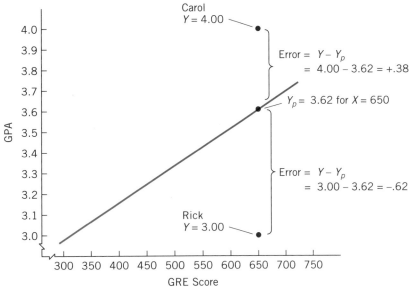

Figure 16.4 An error is the deviation of an actual Y from the predicted Y (Y_p).

Moreover, if you have to settle for less than perfect prediction (and you always must), the next best thing is that your predictions be unbiased, which means you overpredict to the same extent that you underpredict. Every data point not on the regression line has a margin of error associated with it, defined as $Y - Y_p$ (symbolized as e; $Y - Y_p = e$), the difference between the actual Y score and the predicted Y. Sometimes $Y - Y_p$ will be positive and sometimes it will be negative, depending on whether Y falls above or below the regression line. An unbiased regression line will perfectly balance the positive and negative values, such that $\Sigma(Y - Y_p) = 0$. However, to use $\Sigma(Y - Y_p)$ as the Least Squares Criterion would be misleading because it suggests an overall summed error of zero. This problem is akin to what you encountered when establishing a measure of deviation (error) in a univariate distribution. When developing the formula for standard deviation, it was noted that $\Sigma(X - \overline{X}) = 0$. The solution was to square each deviation score in order to remove the negative signs. The same solution is applied when determining the regression line. What you want is a line that is positioned so that when all of the errors are squared and summed, the resultant value is as small as possible. The Least Squares Criterion requires that the regression line be fitted to the scatter plot in such a way that the sum of the squared errors (Σe^2) is minimized.

 The way in which the criterion is met mathematically is called the **Least Squares Method.**

In Figure 16.5(b), a regression line has been fitted to the scatter plot depicted in Figure 16.5(a). Each point not on the line is an error. No other line drawn through the plot will yield a smaller value for Σe^2.

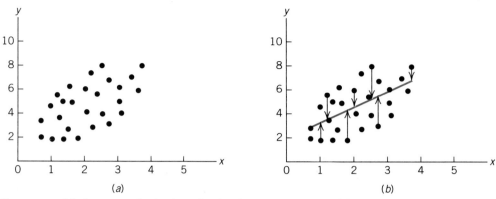

Figure 16.5 (a) The scatter plot has been fitted with a regression line in (b). The line is drawn so that Σe^2 is minimized.

Establishing the Regression Equation

Linear regression produces a straight line drawn through the middle of a scatter plot. The general form of the equation for a straight line is: $Y = a + bX$. Once the Least Squares Criterion has been specified (i.e., Σe^2 is at a minimum), formulas for a and b can be derived so that the criterion is met (see Draper and Smith, 1968).

Estimate for the Intercept

$$a = \overline{Y} - b\overline{X} \quad \text{(Formula 16.2)}$$

where,

$a = Y$ intercept
$b = $ slope of the regression line

To arrive at the regression equation, we first substitute the formula for a into the general equation for a straight line.

$$Y = a + bX$$

By substitution

Regression Equation: Interim Step 1

$$Y_p = \overline{Y} - b\overline{X} + bX \quad \text{(Formula 16.3)}$$

Rearranging the terms yields Formula 16.4.

Regression Equation: Interim Step 2

$$Y_p = \overline{Y} + bX - b\overline{X} \quad \textit{(Formula 16.4)}$$

Since both X and $\overline{X}$ are multiplied by b, b can be factored out to form Formula 16.5.

Linear Regression Equation

$$Y_p = \overline{Y} + b(X - \overline{X}) \quad \textit{(Formula 16.5)}$$

Formula 16.5 is the general linear regression equation for predicting Y given X (also called Y on X).[5] This equation, as well as others presented later, are for predicting Y on X. The addendum to this chapter presents formulas for predicting X on Y. Formula 16.6 is the computational formula for the slope, given the Least Squares Criterion.

Computational Formula for the Slope

$$b = \frac{n_p(\Sigma XY) - (\Sigma X)(\Sigma Y)}{[n_p(\Sigma X^2)] - (\Sigma X)^2} \quad \textit{(Formula 16.6)}$$

Although it is possible to find Y_p for a given X using a graph with the regression line, this strategy is less precise than plugging the X value into the regression equation and performing the simple arithmetic.

■   QUESTION   *Use the following data to find Y_p for $X = 9$ and plot the regression line.*

X	X²	Y	Y²	XY
9	81	11	121	99
6	36	8	64	48
5	25	6	36	30
7	49	9	81	63
4	16	7	49	28

---

[5] There are numerous equivalent formulas for the regression equation. Some textbooks use $Y_p = a + bX$, and provide formulas for b and a. In my opinion, the easiest one to work with is the regression equation used in this text.

SOLUTION

$\overline{X} = 6.20; \overline{Y} = 8.20; \Sigma X^2 = 207; \Sigma X = 31; \Sigma Y = 41; \Sigma XY = 268; n_p = 5$

$$b = \frac{n_p(\Sigma XY) - (\Sigma X)(\Sigma Y)}{[n_p(\Sigma X^2)] - (\Sigma X)^2}$$

$$b = \frac{5(268) - (31)(41)}{[5(207)] - (31)^2}$$

$$= \frac{1340 - 1271}{1035 - 961}$$

$$= \frac{69}{74}$$

$$b = +.93$$

$$Y_p = \overline{Y} + b(X - \overline{X})$$

$$Y_p = 8.20 + .93(X - 6.20)$$

$Y_p = 8.20 + .93(X - 6.20)$ is the regression equation for Y on X. Any X value can be placed in the equation to yield the Y_p for that given X. The question asks the Y value predicted for an X value of 9.

$$Y_p = 8.20 + .93(9 - 6.20)$$

$$= 8.20 + (.93)(2.80)$$

$$= 8.20 + 2.60$$

$$Y_p = \mathbf{10.80} \qquad \blacksquare$$

Plotting the Regression Line

To plot the regression line, two points are required. Simply solve the regression equation for any two values of X. If you make $X = 0$, the Y_p will fall on the Y axis. The point at which the regression line crosses the Y axis, when $X = 0$, is called the Y intercept. There is nothing particularly special about the intercept. In fact, it is difficult to think of a situation in which a researcher would be interested in Y_p when $X = 0$. It is rare in psychology for 0 to have any "psychological meaning." However, for purposes of plotting the line, it is perfectly acceptable to find one point by setting $X = 0$.

Let's select X's of 4 and 8 to establish two coordinates for drawing the regression line.

$$Y_p = 8.20 + .93(4 - 6.20)$$

$$= 8.20 + (.93)(-2.20)$$

$$= 8.20 - 2.05$$

$$Y_p = 6.15$$

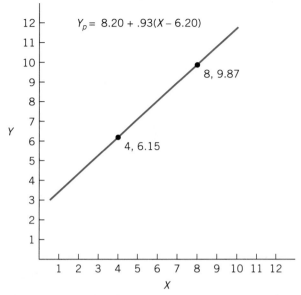

Figure 16.6 Drawing the regression line using two points:
(4, 6.15) and (8, 9.87).

A Y of 6.15 is predicted for every person who has an X score of 4. What is Y_p
when $X = 8$?

$$Y_p = 8.20 + .93(8 - 6.20)$$
$$= 8.20 + .93(1.80)$$
$$= 8.20 + 1.67$$
$$Y_p = 9.87$$

The two coordinates are $X = 4$, $Y_p = 6.15$, and $X = 8$, $Y_p = 9.87$. Figure 16.6 shows
the regression line for Y on X.

More About the Slope
Formula 16.6 is used to compute the slope from raw data. Formula 16.7 can be
used if r (the correlation), s_y (the standard deviation of Y), and s_x (the standard
deviation of X) are provided. Since the correlation is used in Formula 16.7 to
compute b, this formula is referred to as the correlation formula for the slope.

Correlation Formula for the Slope

$$b = r\left(\frac{s_y}{s_x}\right) \quad \textit{(Formula 16.7)}$$

■   QUESTION   *What is the slope and Y_p when $r = 0$?*

SOLUTION

$$b = 0\left(\frac{s_y}{s_x}\right) = 0$$

It does not matter what values s_y and s_x take, when $r = 0$, $b = 0$. A slope of zero means that the regression line neither goes up nor down as the value of X changes. In Figure 16.7, the scatter plot shows a regression line when $b = 0$. When $r = 0$, b will always $= 0$ and Y_p is always $\overline{Y}$:

$$Y_p = \overline{Y} + 0(X - \overline{X})$$
$$Y_p = \overline{Y}$$

Hence, when $r = 0$ you must predict the mean of the Y distribution for every X score. In Figure 16.7, note that the regression line is parallel to the X axis and intersects the Y axis at $\overline{Y}$. Recall the discussion in which the task was to predict the height of an American male. In the absence of information about a correlated variable (heights of fathers), the unbiased strategy of always stating the mean height of all American males was used. Stating the mean height of all American males is stating the mean of the Y distribution.

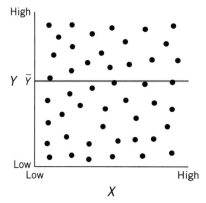

Figure 16.7   When $r = 0$, the slope of the regression line is zero ($b = 0$). The regression line will intersect the Y axis at $\overline{Y}$. Thus, when $r = 0$, irrespective of the value of X, $\overline{Y}$ is predicted.

■

How Accurate is the Regression Equation?
Regression equations look very scientific. There is a tendency to equate scientific with accurate. However, regression equations are tools, and just as some tools work better than others, some regression equations perform better than others.

A regression equation is only as good as its accuracy; the measure of accuracy is embodied in the concept of prediction error. In regression, the index of prediction error is called the **standard error of the estimate,** which is symbolized, s_e.[6] An understanding of the conceptual basis of the standard error of the estimate first requires a discussion of conditional distributions.

Conditional Distributions

A bivariate distribution is based on two related univariate distributions. One univariate distribution is comprised of all of the observations of X and the other univariate distribution is all of the Y scores. They have a correlated relationship; together, the distribution of the pairs of scores comprises one bivariate distribution.

Imagine you have conducted a study and recorded each subject's X and Y scores on a chip and then deposited all the chips in a box. Someone asks to see all of the chips that have an X score of 5. Do you think every single Y score written on those chips will be the same? Unless the correlation between X and Y is $+1$ or -1, there will be an array of Y values associated with an X of 5. In other words, for that given X, there exists a corresponding distribution of Y scores. The spread of Y scores for a given X is called a **conditional distribution.** Every X score has a conditional distribution of Y scores (i.e., each conditional distribution of Y scores is *conditional* on the value of X). Each conditional distribution has all the characteristics of any distribution of scores—mean, median, standard deviation, range, and so forth.

Figure 16.8 represents a few conditional distributions for different values of X. The figure is idealized in that each conditional distribution assumes a normal

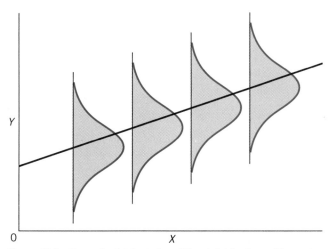

Figure 16.8 Normally distributed conditional distributions of four values of X.

---

[6] Another common symbol for the standard error of the estimate is $s_{y.x}$. I have chosen to use the less common symbol, s_e, so that the subscript reminds you that s_e is an index of error.

shape. (This figure is also a bit misleading since the page forces us to illustrate on two dimensions. In actuality, the distributions extend out from the page.) With very large samples, normally distributed conditional distributions are usually the case. Later a discussion of the implications for prediction when this condition is not met will be presented.

In the absence of correlated information, repeatedly predicting the mean of a univariate distribution will minimize prediction errors. If information regarding a correlated variable is present, then a researcher's strategy changes. Assuming normally distributed conditional distributions in regression, a mean is still the best prediction. Now, however, it is the mean of each conditional distribution that is used. Each X score has an associated Y distribution of scores. When asked the question, "What would you predict for this X?", the regression equation answers, "The mean of the conditional distribution of Y scores associated with that X." The regression line connects all the means of the conditional distributions (see Figure 16.8). Because the regression line connects the means of each conditional distribution, a regression line can be referred to as the "line of moving means."

Francis Galton has the distinction of originating the concept of regression. Spotlight Box 16.1 presents the man and the context of his discoveries.

Formulas for the Standard Error of the Estimate[7]

The regression line connects the means of all of the conditional distributions; Y_p is the mean of the conditional distribution associated with a given X value. If a conditional distribution has little variability, most of the Y scores bunch around the mean of the distribution. As a result, less error in prediction is made relative to prediction wherein the conditional distribution is highly variable. It would make sense that an overall measure of prediction error would be based on the amount of variability of the conditional distributions. Therefore, it should come as no surprise that the definitional formula for the estimated standard error of the estimate looks very much like a standard deviation formula. Formula 16.8 is based on the average of the squared errors for all possible predicted Y scores.

Definitional Formula for s_e

$$s_e = \sqrt{\frac{\Sigma(Y - Y_p)^2}{(n-2)}} \quad \text{(Formula 16.8)}$$

The measure of error for a given X is the standard deviation of the Y scores about Y_p. If the amount of variability of Y scores differed for each value of X, then a researcher would be in the awkward position of having a different s_e for each X. With two assumptions, s_e can be used as an index of prediction error for any value

Francis Galton (1822–1911) is credited with developing the concepts of correlation and regression, although his young contemporary, Karl Pearson, was responsible for many of the mathematical underpinnings of correlation. Galton led a full and varied life. Born to a wealthy English family, he was afforded the luxury of indulging his scientific curiosities. In the mid-1800s, European explorers were mapping the interior of Africa. Perhaps inspired by the travels of his prodigious cousin, Charles Darwin, Galton departed for Africa at the age of 28. His maps of unknown regions of Africa were published, for which he received a Gold Medal from the Geographical Society. For the next few years, Galton dabbled in geography and meteorology. He coined the term *anticyclone*, invented three-dimensional weather maps, and even invented spectacles that could be used to read underwater (they did not sell well).

Galton was no intellectual lightweight. Terman, the psychologist responsible for the Stanford–Binet Intelligence Test, estimated Galton's IQ at 200, one of the highest IQs ever known. From an early age, Galton was obsessed with counting things. Once, when attending a lecture, he counted the number of fidgets per minute of members of the audience, and looked for variation as a function of audience attentiveness versus boredom. His observations were published in *Nature* (Galton, 1885). While his portrait was being painted, he counted the number of brush strokes in an hour. Multiplying by the number of hours it took to paint his portrait, he estimated the total number of strokes at 20,000. (Contemporary clinicians might wonder whether Galton was an obsessive-compulsive fellow!)

Without question, the greatest influence on Galton's work was Darwin's *Origin of Species*, published in 1859. The mature years of Galton's career were devoted almost entirely to the quantification of heredity. It was this context that led to the development of correlation and regression. He established the Anthropometric Laboratory and collected thousands of observations on physical and mental attributes, many from parents and their offspring. Indeed, Galton is viewed as the father of *biometrics,* the quantitative aspect of biology, as well as the father of mental testing. Galton's book, *Hereditary Genius* (1869), put forth the belief that intelligence is inherited. At that time, the evidence for inherited intelligence was based primarily on studies that counted the number of eminent people who also had prominent relatives, an admittedly weak methodology by today's standards; Galton realized this. In trying to find a quantitative method for showing a link between cross-generational abilities, he invented the correlation. Galton's discovery of *regression* was based on data he had collected on the heights of parents and their children. He had drawn a graph with the average of the parents' heights on one axis and the height of their child on the other axis. However, he was unable to arrive at a suitable method for statistically relating the two distributions. Galton wrote in his autobiography of the moment in which he was struck by the solution to his problem.

> But I could not see my way to express the results of the complete table in a single formula. At length, one morning, while waiting at a roadside station near Ramsgate for a train, and poring over the diagram in my notebook, it struck me that the lines of equal frequency ran in concentric ellipses (Galton, 1908, p. 302).

The insight that "struck" Galton was the *bivariate normal surface*—that is—the infinite series of conditional distributions depicted in the text of this chapter. Galton's discovery of correlation and regression has revolutionized the fields of biology and the social sciences.

Galton's abiding belief in the inheritance of physical, mental, and, in fact, moral attributes led him to begin a movement to better the human race through selective breeding, which he called *eugenics*. Eugenics was an unfortunate, indeed irrational, spin-off of Darwin's theory of evolution. It held great appeal for many of the brightest scientists and writers of the era. Karl Pearson, Sir Ronald Fisher (the originator of the analysis of variance and many experimental designs), George Bernard Shaw, Havelock Ellis, and George Orwell were some of the ardent supporters of the eugenics movement—a striking example of the lack of correlation between intelligence and political beliefs!

Nonetheless, "Galton's Utopian ideal of a society built on eugenics may have been doomed to failure, but the techniques he invented for investigating the factual basis of that cause have led to a revolution in the fields of psychology, education, and medicine" (Tankard, 1984, p. 56).

of X. The first assumption is that each conditional distribution is normally distributed. The second assumption is that the standard deviation is the same for each conditional distribution, called the assumption of **homoscedasticity** (*homo* meaning same, *scedastic* meaning scatter). Formula 16.8 is the definitional formula for the overall amount of prediction error, irrespective of the value of X and the predicted Y score.

The definitional formula for s_e emphasizes the fact that the standard error of the estimate is a standard deviation. The definitional formula is computationally prohibitive since every X score would have to be entered into the regression equation, and then $\Sigma(Y - Y_p)^2$ would have to be computed for all obtained Y values. When working from raw data, however, the following computational formula can be used.

Computational Formula for s_e

$$s_e = \sqrt{\left[\frac{1}{n_p(n_p-2)}\right]\left[(n_p\Sigma Y^2 - (\Sigma Y)^2) - \left(\frac{[n_p\Sigma XY - (\Sigma X)(\Sigma Y)]^2}{n_p\Sigma X^2 - (\Sigma X)^2}\right)\right]}$$

(Formula 16.9)

How Does the Size of the Correlation Affect Prediction Error?

An equivalent formula for estimating the standard error of the estimate is presented, which allows a researcher to examine the relation between r and s_e. Formula 16.10 is the correlation formula for the estimated standard error of the estimate. It can be used for computational purposes if s_y and r are provided.

Correlation Formula for s_e

$$s_e = s_y\sqrt{(1 - r^2)} \quad \textit{(Formula 16.10)}[8]$$

Suppose the correlation between X and Y is perfect. Substituting r in the formula with either $+1$ or -1 yields $s_e = 0$. Hence, a perfect correlation means no prediction error—that is—perfect prediction.

Interpreting the Standard Error of the Estimate

With a normal distribution, 68 percent of the scores fall within ± 1 standard deviation of the mean. In regression, Y_p is the mean of a conditional distribution; 68 percent of the actual Y scores fall within ± 1 standard error of the estimate

---

[8] This formula should technically include a term that takes the sample size into consideration. Under the radical sign, $(1 - r^2)$ is multiplied by $n_p/(n_p - 2)$. However, for sample sizes around 30, the effect of this term on s_e becomes negligible. For expository purposes, it has been left out of Formula 16.10.

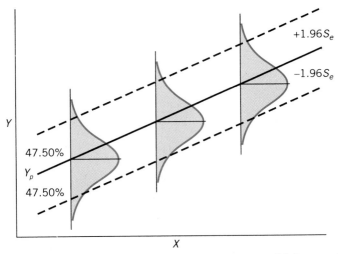

Figure 16.9 Ninety-five percent of the actual Y scores fall between $Y_p \pm 1.96s_e$.

from the mean (Y_p) of the conditional distribution. For a given X score, 95 percent of the actual Y scores fall between $Y_p \pm 1.96s_e$ (Glass and Stanley, 1970; Shavelson, 1988; Wiggins, 1973). Figure 16.9 shows conditional distributions for three values of X. The dotted lines mark the cutoffs between which 95 percent of the actual Y scores lie, for each value of X.

Suppose you are interested in predicting the GPAs of first-year graduate students from Quantitative GRE (GRE-Q) scores. Assume that $s_e = .25$; the regression equation predicts a GPA of 3.50 for everyone with a GRE-Q of 650. Although you predict a GPA of 3.50 for every student with a GRE-Q of 650, there will be error since the correlation between GRE-Q and GPA is not perfect. You can estimate that 68 percent of the students with a GRE-Q of 650 will achieve a GPA between 3.75 and 3.25 ($Y_p \pm s_e = 3.50 \pm .25$). You can also estimate that 95 percent of the students with a GRE-Q of 650 will achieve a GPA between 3.99 and 3.01 $[Y_p \pm 1.96s_e = 3.50 \pm 1.96(.25)]$.

16.4 PUTTING IT ALL TOGETHER: A WORKED PROBLEM

A clinical psychologist is interested in the relation between marital satisfaction among couples and the subsequent marital satisfaction reported by their children. A large sample of couples had been studied 15 years earlier; their scores from a Marital Satisfaction Questionnaire (MSQ) are still available. The investigator obtains the data from all couples who had a 15-year-old child at the time of the original study. A random sample of seven couples is drawn, their MSQ scores are recorded, and their children, now 30 years of age, are located. All seven children are now married and the MSQ is administered to each of them. The investigator is interested

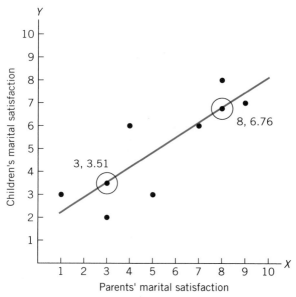

Figure 16.10 The scatter plot and regression line for the data on marital satisfaction.

in the correlation between parents' and children's level of marital satisfaction. She would also like a regression equation that can be used to predict the future marital satisfaction of children, knowing only the level of satisfaction reported by their parents. The following table and step list show the calculation of the correlation, regression equation, and the standard error of the estimate. Figure 16.10 shows the scatter plot of the pairs of scores. Marital satisfaction scores can range from 0–very dissatisfied to 10–very satisfied. An interpretation of the findings is also provided.

MARITAL SATISFACTION	
Parents: X	*Children: Y*
1	3
3	2
7	6
9	7
8	8
4	6
5	3
$\overline{X} = 5.29$	$\overline{Y} = 5.00$
$n_p = 7$	
$\Sigma X = 37$	$\Sigma Y = 35$
$\Sigma X^2 = 245$	$\Sigma Y^2 = 207$
$s_x = 2.87$	$s_y = 2.31$
$\Sigma XY = 217$	

Step 1. Construct a scatter diagram to see if there is a linear relation between X and Y. Figure 16.10 indicates that the relation is linear; there is no curve to the swarm of data points. (The regression line is drawn later.) Moreover, the scatter plot reveals a positive correlation between X and Y because the swarm of points ascends from the lower left to the upper right of the graph.

Step 2. Compute the correlation between X and Y. Mathematically speaking, it is not necessary to compute the correlation in order to establish the regression equation. However, the correlation is always of substantive interest; in addition, regression is useless if there is no correlation between the variables. The correlation coefficient is computed using the Pearson raw-score formula, and is found to be large, $+.80$.

$$r = \frac{n_p(\Sigma XY) - (\Sigma X)(\Sigma Y)}{\sqrt{[n_p(\Sigma X^2) - (\Sigma X)^2][n_p(\Sigma Y^2) - (\Sigma Y)^2]}}$$

$$r = \frac{7(217) - (37)(35)}{\sqrt{[7(245) - (37)^2][7(207) - (35)^2]}}$$

$$= \frac{1519 - 1295}{\sqrt{(1715 - 1369)(1449 - 1225)}}$$

$$= \frac{224}{\sqrt{(346)(224)}}$$

$$= \frac{224}{278.40}$$

$$r = +.80$$

Step 3. Compute the slope. Formula 16.6 is used when working from raw data. Since r has been computed, and s_x and s_y are provided, Formula 16.7 would be the formula of choice. Nonetheless, the raw-score formula is used for illustrative purposes.

$$b = \frac{n_p(\Sigma XY) - (\Sigma X)(\Sigma Y)}{[n_p(\Sigma X^2)] - (\Sigma X)^2}$$

$$= \frac{7(217) - (37)(35)}{[7(245)] - (37)^2}$$

$$= \frac{1519 - 1295}{1715 - 1369}$$

$$= \frac{224}{346}$$

$$b = +.65$$

Step 4. The necessary values for establishing the regression equation are now available. Use the regression equation to plot the regression line.

Pick any two values of X, compute Y_p for each value, plot each Y_p, and draw a straight line. I have chosen X values of 3 and 8. Figure 16.10 shows the regression line.

$$Y_p = \overline{Y} + b(X - \overline{X})$$

$$Y_p = 5.00 + .65(X - 5.29)$$

$$Y_{p \text{ for } X = 3} = 5.00 + .65(3 - 5.29) = \mathbf{3.51}$$

$$Y_{p \text{ for } X = 8} = 5.00 + .65(8 - 5.29) = \mathbf{6.76}$$

Plot points at coordinates 3, 3.51 and 8, 6.76.

Step 5. Compute the standard error of the estimate. Formula 16.9 would be the easiest to use because r and s_y are known. However, the raw-score formula will be used to illustrate its computational steps.

$$s_e = \sqrt{\left[\frac{1}{n_p(n_p-2)}\right]\left[(n_p \Sigma Y^2 - (\Sigma Y)^2) - \left(\frac{[n_p \Sigma XY - (\Sigma X)(\Sigma Y)]^2}{n_p \Sigma X^2 - (\Sigma X)^2}\right)\right]}$$

$$s_e = \sqrt{\left[\frac{1}{7(7-2)}\right]\left[(7(207) - (35)^2) - \left(\frac{[7(217) - (37)(35)]^2}{7(245) - (37)^2}\right)\right]}$$

$$= \sqrt{[.029]\left[(1449 - 1225) - \left(\frac{[1519 - 1295]^2}{1715 - 1369}\right)\right]}$$

$$= \sqrt{[.029]\left[(224) - \left(\frac{(224)^2}{346}\right)\right]}$$

$$= \sqrt{(.029)(224 - 145.02)}$$

$$= \sqrt{(.029)(78.98)}$$

$$= \sqrt{2.29}$$

$$s_e = \mathbf{1.51}$$

The index of prediction error is $s_e = 1.51$. Suppose, for a specific 15-year-old adolescent, you want to predict his level of marital satisfaction when he is 30 years old. You administer the MSQ to his parents, find that their score is 7, and using the regression equation, find $Y_p = 5.00 + .65(7 - 5.29) = 6.11$. Therefore, you would predict that he will report a level of marital satisfaction of 6.11 when he is 30 years old. But what about the accuracy of your prediction? You can state that approximately 68 percent of all 15-year-old children who have parents who scored a 7 on the MSQ will report, 15 years later, marital satisfaction scores between 4.60–7.62 (6.11 ± 1.51).

By now you might have wondered why a prediction equation is called a regression equation. Galton coined the term for good reason. Box 16.1 details the origin of the term regression and the fact that the term reflects a fundamental aspect of prediction.

BOX
16.1

Why is a Prediction Equation Called a Regression Equation?

When I was in grade school, I had a teacher who wanted to reward effort. She gave a test at the beginning of the term (pretest) and another test at the end of the term (post-test). She subtracted each student's pretest score from his or her post-test score to arrive at a difference score $(Y - X = D)$. A positive D score indicated improvement, a 0 showed no improvement, and a negative D score meant that the student had done worse on the second test. She then used the D score as a measure of effort, and assigned her grades accordingly; those students with positive D scores received the highest grades, and those students with negative D scores received the lower grades. Her intent was laudatory. She wanted to make her grading fair by not disadvantaging the students who performed poorly on the pretest. She wanted to impress on us the importance of always "trying really hard," irrespective of how good our scores were. As she reminded us, "No matter how good you are, there is always room for improvement." Although I did quite well on the pretest, I recall that I did not do as well on the post-test, and received a rather mediocre grade. Years later, after learning something about regression analysis, I can say, "I was robbed!" (Not that I harbor any deep-seated resentment, however.) The teacher had failed to understand a fundamental concept of regression, called *regression to the mean*. Without intending to, she had doomed most of the students who did well on the pretest. By the same token, she had practically assured that the students who scored low on the pretest would eventually receive high grades. Regression to the mean is a built-in characteristic of using one variable to predict a second variable, *when the correlation between the variables is less than perfect.*

Galton was the first to discover this phenomenon and referred to it as "regression to mediocrity." In his work on heredity, he gathered measures of fathers' and sons' heights. He found that fathers' and sons' heights were positively correlated (although not perfectly). Tall fathers tended to have tall sons and short fathers tended to have short sons. However, tall fathers tended to have sons who were not as tall as the fathers, and short fathers tended to have sons who were not as short as their fathers. In general, the heights of sons tended to "regress" toward the mean height of all sons. This is the meaning of regression to the mean. A statistical way of stating the regression effect is as follows. Suppose you examine just those fathers who have heights that are two standard deviations above the mean height of all fathers. You will find that their sons will not, on the average, be two standard deviations above the mean of the height of all sons. The sons of these tall fathers will tend to be above the mean of all sons, but not two standard deviations above the mean. The same logic holds for short fathers and their sons. The regression effect is found in situations that have nothing to do with heredity.

Whenever two variables are imperfectly correlated (i.e., less than ± 1), regression to the mean occurs. This fact has a very important implication for designing studies. Suppose you want to show the advantages of a study program for poor students. You administer some test of ability, take the lowest 10 percent of the group, and put them into the study. After 6 months in the program, you administer the same ability test and conduct a dependent-samples t test, comparing the pretest and post-test means. You will most likely find a significant improvement in ability. Should you conclude the study program was effective? Not according to the foregoing discussion of the regression effect. Those students who scored low on the pretest will tend to score higher on the post-test. The change may have absolutely nothing to do with the educational program. (A control group of low-ability students who did not receive the program would not eliminate the regression effect, but would allow the investigator to examine how much improvement was due to regression to the mean.)

So, if you ever have a teacher who hands out grades based on improvement, kindly explain the concept of regression to the mean.

16.5   THE COEFFICIENT OF DETERMINATION
IN THE CONTEXT OF PREDICTION

The concept of r^2 was discussed in Chapter 15. r^2 reflects the amount of shared variance between X and Y—that is—the amount of variance in the Y scores accounted for by the variance in X scores. Now that you have learned some of the intricacies of regression, r^2 can be presented from the perspective of prediction. Indeed, the coefficients of determination is easier to understand when viewed with respect to prediction.

From the discussion of the standard error of the estimate, you know that as the correlation increases, the amount of prediction error decreases. The correlation formula for the standard error of the estimate (Formula 16.10), was stated as:

$$s_e = s_y \sqrt{1 - r^2}$$

The percentage of prediction error can range from 100 percent to 0 percent. When $r = 0$, there is no improvement (reduction in error) over the value of s_y ($s_e = s_y \sqrt{1 - 0^2} = s_y$). In this case, prediction error is at a maximum: 100 percent. What happens when $r = .50$, and thus the coefficient of determination is $r^2 = .25$?

$$s_e = s_y \sqrt{1 - (.50)^2}$$
$$= s_y \sqrt{1 - .25}$$
$$= s_y \sqrt{.75}$$
$$= s_y(.87)$$

Prediction error is now 87 percent of the value of s_y. If prediction error is 100 percent when $s_e = s_y$, then when $r = .50$, prediction error decreases by 13 percent (100 percent $-$ 87 percent). You might ask, "decreases prediction error relative to what?" It is relative to predicting merely the mean of the Y distribution. Some correlations and their corresponding reductions in prediction error follow.

r	Reduction in Prediction Error
1.00	100%
.75	34%
.50	13%
.25	3%
.00	0%

Whenever correlated information is available, you should use it to improve prediction. However, as can be seen in the preceding table, substantial reductions in prediction error are only achieved with large correlations. Also note that the relative reduction in prediction error "gains speed" as the size of the correlation increases. While there is only a 10 percent improvement in error between correlations of .25 and .50, there is a 21 percent improvement in error rate between the correlations of .50 and .75.

16.6   THE PITFALLS OF LINEAR REGRESSION

Chapter 15 discussed several factors that lead to misinterpretation of a correlation. Since regression is intimately connected with correlation, it is no surprise that the same conditions that create misleading correlations will adversely affect the usefulness of regression analysis. This section discusses some factors that can undermine the accuracy of the prediction equation.[9]

Restricted Range

Figure 16.11 reveals a linear relation between X and Y. What if the sampled values of X are confined to the area between the vertical lines? The scatter plot between the lines fails to capture the true relation between X and Y. The problem of range restriction can arise when using GRE scores to predict GPA in graduate school. The GREs that are available are the GREs of the students who have been accepted to a graduate program. The distribution of GRE scores does not reflect the full range of GRE scores; there is an overabundance of scores above the population mean. Not only will the correlation between GRE and GPA underestimate the strength of the relation between the variables, the accuracy of the regression equation will diminish.

Examining the scatter plot will be of no help in deciding if there is a range restriction for X and/or Y. You will need to know the range of possible values for

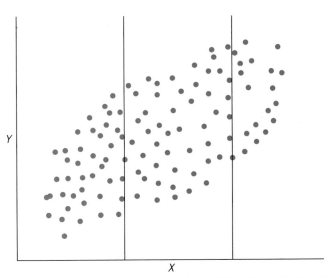

Figure 16.11   A linear relation may be impossible to detect if either X or Y has a restricted range of scores.

---

[9] For a more detailed discussion of these factors, refer to Chapter 15, Section 15.4.

each variable, and then separately examine the X and Y sample distributions to see if these scores are an accurate representation of the population from which they are drawn.

Extreme Scores

An extreme score can create the impression that there is a linear relation between X and Y. Figure 16.12 shows a scatter plot in which there is one outlier in the upper right corner of the plot. Were it not for this extreme point, the regression line would be parallel to the X axis, indicating no relation between X and Y. However, the extreme point could lift the regression line so that its slope is nonzero. Here, the regression equation would be used for prediction when, in fact, there is no relation between X and Y. Large sample sizes will overwhelm an outlier and mitigate its distorting effect. Examining the scatter plot will reveal the presence of an extreme score.

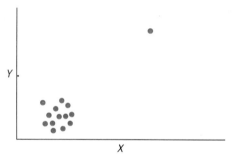

Figure 16.12 Even though the majority of scores fail to reveal a relation between X and Y, the extreme score in the upper right can create the impression of a linear relation between X and Y.

Overgeneralization

It is a mistake to apply a regression equation to populations that are different from the population used to establish the regression equation. Recall the hypothetical study in which parents' marital satisfaction was used to predict the level of marital satisfaction among their children, 15 years later. All the children in the sample were 15 years old when values of the predictor variable (parents' MSQ score) were obtained. The regression equation can properly be used today to predict the future marital satisfaction of any 15-year-old adolescent. However, you cannot use the equation to predict the future marital satisfaction of 2-year-old children or 20-year-old children. There is no evidence that there is a correlation between parents' marital satisfaction and the future marital satisfaction of children who are not 15 years old when the parents are questioned. To apply the regression equation to a different population is to overgeneralize the results obtained from one sample.

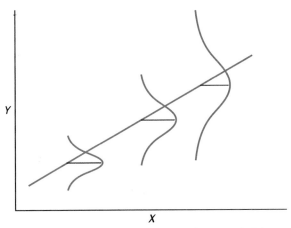

Figure 16.13   Conditional distributions with progressively larger standard deviations as the value of X increases—which is a violation of homoscedasticity.

Violating Homoscedasticity

 What happens to prediction error when the standard deviations of the conditional distributions are dissimilar (called **heteroscedasticity**)? Figure 16.13 shows a heteroscedastic plot for Y on X. There is a positive, linear relationship between the variables, but the amount of prediction error increases as the value of X increases. The standard error of the estimate would be different for every value of X. Since the magnitude of prediction error will be greater when predicting a Y score with a more variable conditional distribution, prediction in this case would be worse for higher values of X in comparison to lower values of X. Thus, you would not be justified in assuming that 68 percent of the actual Y scores for a given X score lie between $Y_p \pm 1s_e$.

Be careful that you do not get lost in the mechanics of calculating regression equations. Regression is a tool that can lead to very misleading decisions if careful attention is not paid to invalidating conditions.

SUMMARY

Linear regression is a statistical method that is used to predict the value of one variable when information about another, correlated variable is available. Regression proceeds in two steps. First, a prediction equation is established from a random sample of subjects. Second, the prediction equation is then applied in individual cases when the value of only one variable is known.

The regression equation defines a line along which each predicted Y for any given X lies. The slope is the angle of the regression line. It reflects the "rise over the run." The slope states the number of units Y changes as X changes by one unit. A positive slope indicates a positive correlation whereas a negative slope is indicative of a negative correlation. A slope of zero is a straight line parallel with the X axis, intersecting the Y axis at the mean of the Y distribution.

A correlation of zero will yield a slope of zero, and thus will not ascend or descend with increasing values of X. Since a slope of zero will intersect the Y axis at $\overline{Y}$, a correlation of zero means that $\overline{Y}$ should always be predicted in the absence of correlated information. However, prediction is rarely of practical significance without the presence of a correlated relation between two variables.

A single error in prediction is the difference between the actual score obtained by an individual and the score predicted for that person. Summing all the errors will equal zero, indicating an unbiased prediction equation. The Least Squares Method is used to determine where the regression line will be drawn through the scatter plot. This method is based on the Least Squares Criterion, which states that the regression line is drawn so that the sum of the squared errors, Σe^2, is at a minimum.

Each X score is associated with an array or distribution of Y scores. These are called conditional distributions, which are assumed to be normal with similar standard deviations (the assumption of homoscedasticity). For any given X score, it is the mean of that score's conditional distribution that is predicted.

The standard error of the estimate is an index of prediction accuracy. Sixty-eight percent of the actual Y scores fall within $\pm 1 s_e$ of any Y_p. When the correlation is ± 1, prediction error is zero. This reflects the fact that when $r = \pm 1$, *all* points lie on the regression line, and there is no array of Y scores associated with any X score.

The viability of a regression analysis is based on several factors. A regression equation should only be used with individuals who are represented in the sample from which the regression equation was established. In addition, range restrictions of X and/or Y as well as extreme scores will invalidate regression analyses.

KEY FORMULAS FOR CHAPTER 16

Straight Line Formula

$$Y = a + bX \qquad \text{(Formula 16.1)}$$

Estimate for the Intercept

$$a = \overline{Y} - b\overline{X} \qquad \text{(Formula 16.2)}$$

Regression Equation: Interim Step 1

$$Y_p = \overline{Y} - b\overline{X} + bX \qquad \text{(Formula 16.3)}$$

Regression Equation: Interim Step 2

$$Y_p = \overline{Y} + bX - b\overline{X} \qquad \text{(Formula 16.4)}$$

Linear Regression Equation

$$Y_p = \overline{Y} + b(X - \overline{X})$$ *(Formula 16.5)*

Computational Formula for the Slope

$$b = \frac{n_p(\Sigma XY) - (\Sigma X)(\Sigma Y)}{[n_p(\Sigma X^2)] - (\Sigma X)^2}$$ *(Formula 16.6)*

Correlation Formula for the Slope

$$b = r\left(\frac{s_y}{s_x}\right)$$ *(Formula 16.7)*

Definitional Formula for s_e

$$s_e = \sqrt{\frac{\Sigma(Y - Y_p)^2}{n - 2}}$$ *(Formula 16.8)*

Computational Formula for s_e

$$s_e = \sqrt{\left[\frac{1}{n_p(n_p - 2)}\right]\left[(n_p\Sigma Y^2 - (\Sigma Y)^2) - \left(\frac{[n_p\Sigma XY - (\Sigma X)(\Sigma Y)]^2}{n_p\Sigma X^2 - (\Sigma X)^2}\right)\right]}$$

(Formula 16.9)

Correlation Formula for s_e

$$s_e = s_y\sqrt{(1 - r^2)}$$ *(Formula 16.10)*

ADDENDUM

The following formulas predict X on Y.

Regression Equation

$$X_p = \overline{X} + b(Y - \overline{Y})$$

Formulas for the Slope

$$b = \frac{n_p(\Sigma XY) - (\Sigma X)(\Sigma Y)}{n_p(\Sigma Y^2) - (\Sigma Y)^2}$$

$$b = r\left(\frac{s_x}{s_y}\right)$$

Formulas for the Estimated Standard Error of the Estimate

Correlation Formula for s_e

$$s_e = s_x\sqrt{(1 - r^2)}$$

Computational Formula for s_e

$$s_e = \sqrt{\left[\frac{1}{n_p(n_p - 2)}\right]\left[(n_p\Sigma X^2 - (\Sigma X)^2) - \left(\frac{[n_p\Sigma XY - (\Sigma X)(\Sigma Y)]^2}{n_p\Sigma Y^2 - (\Sigma Y)^2}\right)\right]}$$

WORK PROBLEMS

1. What are the two important uses of regression analysis?
2. What does it mean that the regression line is based on the Least Squares Method?
3. Why can't $\Sigma(Y - Y_p)$ be used as the basis for measuring error?
4. If $r = 0$, what must b equal?
5. Describe in what way r is related to prediction error.
6. When using the standard error of the estimate as a measure of prediction error, why is the assumption of homoscedasticity important?
7. Why must a researcher be careful when using a prediction equation with an individual who has characteristics unlike the people who were included in the original sample from which the regression equation was derived?
8. In a study on pain tolerance, a researcher is interested in predicting the amount of time that subjects are able to keep their hands in ice cold water. Based on previous research, the researcher knows that Vitamin E intake over the past 12 hours is correlated with tolerating a painful stimulus, at least when the stimulus is freezing water. The following table lists the pairs of scores for the study sample.

Vitamin E: (X)	Tolerance Times (in seconds): (Y)
5	23
9	32
22	65
12	40
16	42

   a. What is b?
   b. What is the Y intercept?
   c. What is s_e?
   d. What tolerance time would you predict for someone who has taken 16 units of Vitamin E the morning of the study?

9. A sociologist is interested in predicting yearly income (Y) based on prior education level (X), with education level defined as the number of years of formal schooling. The following data were collected from six individuals.

Education: (X)	Income X 1000: (Y)
10	15
14	29
9	14
14	37
12	20
13	23

a. What is b?

b. What is the Y intercept?

c. What is s_e?

d. What income would you predict for someone with ten years of education?

10. An admissions committee needs to predict whether a particular student will be able to make passing grades during the first year of graduate school. In order to make it past the first year, the student will have to achieve a 3.00 GPA in the first semester of graduate school. The admissions committee has data from past years on the relation between undergraduate GPA and the subsequent first-year graduate school GPA. Those data are as follows.

Undergraduate GPA: (X)	Graduate School GPA: (Y)
3.50	3.33
3.98	3.63
3.10	3.40
2.90	3.41
3.40	3.40

a. What is b?

b. Should you admit a student with a 3.00 GPA?

c. Of the incoming students with a GPA of 3.67, what are the graduate-school grade point averages between which 68 percent of those students who have the GPA of 3.67 would be included?

Work Problems for the Computer

11. (Based on Problem 21, Chapter 15.) Compute the regression equation and s_e for both conditions. If, during drilling, the dentist rates the patient's discomfort as 7, what would you predict is the patient's discomfort rating? Answer the same question for the Rubber-dam condition, and report the standard error of the estimate.

12. (Based on Problem 22, Chapter 15.) For a woman who reports 54 menstrual symptoms, how many symptoms will she report during pregnancy? Identify two values of pregnancy symptoms, between which 68 percent of the women who report 54 menstrual symptoms lie.

INFERENTIAL STATISTICS: NONPARAMETRIC TESTS

The Chi-Square Test

17.1 THE RESEARCH CONTEXT

Statistical methods that test inferences about population parameters have been discussed in previous chapters. Both *t* tests and *F* tests use interval or ratio scales of measurement in which numbers are added, squared, divided, and subtracted. Interval and ratio scales are used with continuous measures and represent *how much* of something (see Chapter 2). However, not all research questions can be answered by using continuous measures; instead of asking "how much," many research questions ask "how many." The following research situations are examples in which the data are in the form of a **frequency count.**

1. A developmental psychologist hypothesizes that fear of strangers occurs more often at a certain age. A random sample of children, ages 2–6, is taken. For each age category, the number of children who are afraid of strangers is counted. The dependent variable is *not* how afraid the children are, but rather how many children are afraid. Each child is categorized based on the presence or absence of fear.

2. A political scientist hypothesizes that students become more liberal over their four years of undergraduate education. A random sample of freshmen and seniors is obtained, and the number of students reporting liberal and conservative views is tabulated for each class. Once again, the dependent variable is *not* how liberal or conservative the student is. Each student is classified as *either* liberal *or* conservative.

3. A health psychologist hypothesizes that the percentage of urban dwellers who exhibit the Type A personality is 75 percent, and 30 percent of rural residents are Type A. A random sample of urban and rural residents is assessed for Type A characteristics. A frequency count of the number (percentage) of Type A's in each environmental setting is tabulated.

4. A social psychologist is interested in the relation between obedience and whether a person has served in the armed forces. A random sample is obtained of former service personnel and individuals who never served in the military. An experimental task is administered that allows the researcher to assess *whether* the subject will follow an unpleasant order. The data are collected in the form of a frequency count of the number of subjects who obey or disobey the order.

5. A clinical psychologist hypothesizes that schizophrenics who are prescribed medication after being discharged from the hospital are less likely to be rehospitalized, compared to schizophrenic patients who are not maintained on medication. A year after discharge, the number of medicated and nonmedicated patients who were and were not rehospitalized is counted.

In each of the preceding research contexts, the data are in the form of a frequency count, which is tabulated for each category. In addition, note that the frequency-count data have a discontinuous, either/or quality. For example, either the subject obeys or does not obey; either the child is or is not afraid of strangers; either the student is liberal or conservative; and so on. Recall from Chapter 2 that variables having an either/or quality are measured on a nominal scale. Because nominal data are arranged by categories, nominal data are also called **categorical data.**

A statistical test that analyzes categorical data is the **chi-square test** (pronounced "*kigh*" square, symbolized χ^2). One important difference between the chi-square test and the t test (and the F test) is that the chi-square test makes no assumptions about population parameters or population characteristics for its use. For this reason, the chi-square test is one example of a **nonparametric test.** Tests that *do* make assumptions about population parameters are known as **parametric tests.** For example, the F test assumes that the population distributions are normally distributed and have equal variances. If these assumptions are grossly violated, interpretations of the test results can be misleading. Nonparametric tests do not make assumptions about the shape of population distributions; for this reason, they are also called **distribution-free** tests. There are times when an investigator uses a scale of measurement that would naturally lead to a parametric test of significance. However, if the assumptions of the test are not met, the data can be transformed and analyzed using a nonparametric test. The decision to switch from a parametric to a nonparametric test is not taken lightly. Nonparametric tests are generally not as powerful as parametric tests—that is—it is more difficult to reject a false null hypothesis when using a nonparametric test. When given the choice to conduct either a parametric or a nonparametric test, *always* select the parametric alternative. Of course, if the data are based on a nominal scale, there is no alternative; a nonparametric test must be used. A more detailed discussion of parametric versus nonparametric tests is provided in Chapter 18. The following sections present the chi-square test as it is applied in two different situations: testing for goodness-of-fit and testing for independence.

17.2   THE CHI-SQUARE TEST FOR ONE-WAY DESIGNS: THE GOODNESS-OF-FIT TEST

The goodness-of-fit test is the categorical counterpart of a one-way ANOVA that uses two or more groups. An ANOVA is used when an interval or ratio scale is used to collect data; the chi-square test is used when a nominal scale is used to collect data. Chapter 2 defined a frequency distribution as the number of observations for each score in a distribution. When using nominal data, the frequency distribution is the number of observations per category. The chi-square test uses the frequency distribution of a sample to make an inference about the frequency distribution of a population. The **goodness-of-fit test** uses the chi-square test to analyze how well the sample data "fit" (correspond) with the hypothesized frequency distribution. When the chi-square statistic is used to test the goodness-of-fit of your data, you must first state a null hypothesis that indicates what the population data would look like if there is *no* effect. The frequencies of the distribution specified by the null hypothesis are called **expected frequencies,** symbolized f_e. The frequencies of the distribution obtained from the sample are called **observed frequencies,** symbolized f_o.

The Null and Alternative Hypotheses for the Chi-Square Test for Goodness-of-Fit

The goodness-of-fit test requires you to specify the population frequency distribution that will be used as the null hypothesis. Frequencies are typically presented as percentages. How do you arrive at the null hypothesis—that is—what frequencies should be specified for each category? Hypothesized population frequencies can be determined either rationally or empirically. First consider the rational approach. Suppose you would like to find out if people prefer Coke or Pepsi. You conduct a blind taste test with 100 subjects. If there is no preference among the participants for Coke or Pepsi, what percentage of people would you expect to pick Coke, and what percentage would you expect to choose Pepsi? On the average, 50 percent of the subjects will select Coke and 50 percent will choose Pepsi. Thus, the null hypothesis can be represented as follows:

	Coke	Pepsi
H_0:	50%	50%

Now suppose you add a third drink, say, Orange Crush. What would be the expected frequency distribution for the null hypothesis? The answer:

	Coke	Pepsi	Orange Crush
H_0:	33%	33%	33%

If you add a fourth beverage, the expected frequencies would be 25 percent for each category. The null hypothesis states that the expected frequencies are equally distributed across the categories. The alternative hypothesis states that the population frequencies are not distributed equally across the categories.

Another example of the rational approach to specifying the null hypothesis is when the distribution of expected frequencies is predicted by a theory. A genetic theory of ulcer susceptibility might predict the percentage of rats that will develop ulcers under stress. The theory might hypothesize that after four generations of inbreeding, 40 percent of the offspring of rats will show stomach ulcers under stress. The null hypothesis would thus be:

	Ulcers	
	Yes	No
H_0:	40%	60%

The alternative hypothesis states that the population distribution of frequencies is not distributed in the expected manner.

The empirical approach to specifying expected frequencies requires existing data, although not necessarily data that you have collected. For example, suppose the percentage of people who voted Democratic in the last gubernatorial election was 60 percent, whereas 30 percent voted Republican, and 10 percent of the population voted Other. Since the last election, however, a popular Republican president campaigned for the present Republican gubernatorial candidate. Before the election, several thousand voters are polled to determine if the percentage of people in the Democrat, Republican, and Other categories has changed. Thus, using the data from the last election, the null hypothesis would be stated as:

	Democrat	Republican	Other
H_0:	60%	30%	10%

The alternative hypothesis states that the relative frequency of voters across the categories differs from the last election.

Computing the Chi-Square Statistic for the Goodness-of-Fit Test

The purpose of the goodness-of-fit test is to determine if the observed frequencies, obtained from a sample of subjects, differ from the expected frequencies. It is *highly* unlikely that the observed and expected frequencies will be identical, even when H_0 is true. The chi-square test allows an investigator to determine the probability that the difference between expected and observed frequencies is due to chance. The next section discusses how to decide whether to reject the null hypothesis. First, however, the mechanics of computing the chi-square statistic for a one-way design are presented.

Two students are discussing the reasons why their peers choose a particular undergraduate major. The psychology student makes the somewhat provocative statement that business majors select their program of study because they are most interested in making money. The other student, a business major, insists that money is one motive, but not the most important reason for entering the business world. She proposes that they conduct a study in which business majors are asked to respond to one statement: "Making money is the most important reason for majoring in business." Subjects are told to Agree, Disagree, or say they are Undecided. The null hypothesis states that the percentage of responses in each category is the same.

Agree	Disagree	Undecided
33%	33%	33%

Although the null hypothesis typically is stated in terms of percentages, the chi-square test is not performed using percentages. Specifying the exact expected frequencies in each category requires knowledge of the total number of subjects in the study. Assume that 90 subjects participate in the study. To determine the exact (expected) frequency for a given cell (category), f_e, each percentage (or proportion) is multiplied by n, the number of subjects.

$$33\% \text{ of } 90 = .33(90) = 30 \text{ Agree responses}$$

$$33\% \text{ of } 90 = .33(90) = 30 \text{ Disagree responses}$$

$$33\% \text{ of } 90 = .33(90) = 30 \text{ Undecided responses}$$

Instead of converting percentages to frequencies, the f_e for each category can be found by dividing the number of subjects (observations) by the number of categories: $N/C = 90/3 = 30$. The expected frequencies for each cell are the same because the null hypothesis states that the percentages in each cell will be the same. However, there will be times when the null hypothesis will state different percentages for each cell; therefore, the expected frequencies can differ from cell to cell.

The next step in computing the χ^2 statistic is to find the observed frequencies, f_o. This is accomplished by simply counting the number of subjects in the sample who agreed, disagreed and were undecided. With expected and observed frequencies calculated, Formula 17.1 is used to compute χ^2.

Formula for χ^2

$$\chi^2 = \sum \frac{(f_o - f_e)^2}{f_e} \quad \text{(Formula 17.1)}$$

Assume the data show observed frequencies in each category as indicated in the following.

Agree	Disagree	Undecided
$f_e = 30$	$f_e = 30$	$f_e = 30$
$f_o = 60$	$f_o = 20$	$f_o = 10$

In using Formula 17.1, arithmetic operations are performed for each cell:

$$\frac{(f_o - f_e)^2}{f_e}$$

After you obtain this value for each cell, the $\sum$, in Formula 17.1 directs you to sum all the values in each category.

Computational Steps

Step 1. For the first category, subtract the expected (hypothesized) frequency from the observed frequency (the data), $f_o - f_e$.

Step 2. Square the difference $(f_o - f_e)^2$. This removes any negative signs.

Step 3. Divide the number found in Step 2 by the f_e specified for that cell $(f_o - f_e)^2/f_e$.

Step 4. Repeat the first three steps for each cell.

Step 5. Sum all the quantities from all the categories.

$$\chi^2 = \sum \frac{(f_o - f_e)^2}{f_e}$$

$$\begin{array}{ccc} \textit{Agree} & \textit{Disagree} & \textit{Undecided} \\ \dfrac{(60-30)^2}{30} + & \dfrac{(20-30)^2}{30} + & \dfrac{(10-30)^2}{30} \end{array}$$

$$= \frac{900}{30} + \frac{100}{30} + \frac{400}{30}$$

$$= 30 + 3.33 + 13.33$$

$$\chi^2 = \mathbf{46.66}$$

Deciding Whether to Reject the Null Hypothesis

This section teaches you the steps involved in deciding whether to reject the null hypothesis. The next section addresses the characteristics of the sampling distribution of the χ^2 statistic, which will give you a deeper understanding of hypothesis testing when using the chi-square analysis.

In viewing the formula for χ^2, it is clear that χ^2 will become larger as the difference between the expected and observed frequencies increases.

$$\chi^2 = \sum \frac{(f_o - f_e)^2}{f_e}$$

A close fit between the expected frequency distribution and the observed frequency distribution will lead to a relatively small χ^2.

Similar to other statistical tests, the larger the χ^2 statistic, the more likely it is to be statistically significant. In addition, the χ^2 statistic is compared to a critical value, χ^2_{crit}, to determine whether to reject the null hypothesis. If χ^2_{obt} is greater than χ^2_{crit}, the null hypothesis is rejected. You conclude that the difference between the expected and observed frequency distributions is probably not due to chance.

The critical value for χ^2 is found by using Appendix B.8, a portion of which is shown in Table 17.1.

TABLE   17.1   **A Portion of the Table of Critical Values for the Chi-Square Distribution**

	PROPORTION OF CRITICAL REGION				
	Alpha Level				
df	*.10*	*.05*	*.02*	*.01*	*.001*
1	2.71	3.84	5.41	6.64	10.83
2	4.60	5.99	7.82	9.21	13.82
3	6.25	7.82	9.84	11.34	16.27
4	7.78	9.49	11.67	13.28	18.46
5	9.24	11.07	13.39	15.09	20.52
6	10.64	12.59	15.03	16.81	22.46

The degrees of freedom for the goodness-of-fit test is the number of columns in the design minus one. In the undergraduate major example, the number of columns (categories) is equal to 3. Thus, $df = C - 1 = 3 - 1 = 2$. What would be the critical value for χ^2 if alpha is set at .05? Referring to Table 17.1, the answer is 5.99. Since the obtained $\chi^2 = 46.66$, and $46.66 > 5.99$, you reject the null hypothesis.

By inspecting the observed frequencies in the cells, you would interpret the significant χ^2 as an indication that business students believe that making money is the most important reason for majoring in business, $\chi^2(2, n = 90) = 46.66$, $p < .05$.

Consider another worked problem using the goodness-of-fit test where the expected cell frequencies are not all the same.

■ QUESTION *A professor states that she grades papers using the following categories: excellent, above average, average, and below average. Further, she maintains that she is quite generous in her grading, and offers the following distribution of percentages as an estimate of the manner in which her grades are distributed.*

Excellent	Above Average	Average	Below Average
25%	35%	25%	15%

A group of students suspect that the professor may indeed be generous—but only in her perception of herself as an easy grader. All of the students who had previously taken her course in the last three years are available, and amazingly, they still have their papers. A random sample of 100 former students is taken and the actual distribution of evaluations is recorded.

Excellent	Above Average	Average	Below Average
25%	35%	25%	15%
$f_o = 20$	$f_o = 25$	$f_o = 30$	$f_o = 25$

Note that since the sample size is 100, the observed frequencies sum to 100. Is there reason to conclude that the professor is perhaps mistaken in her claim?

SOLUTION Before the formula for χ^2 can be used, the cell percentages need to be converted to expected frequencies.

$$25\% = (.25)\,100 = 25 \text{ expected Excellents}$$
$$35\% = (.35)\,100 = 35 \text{ expected Above Averages}$$
$$25\% = (.25)\,100 = 25 \text{ expected Averages}$$
$$15\% = (.15)\,100 = 15 \text{ expected Below Averages}$$

Placing the expected and observed frequencies in a table shows:

Excellent	Above Average	Average	Below Average
$f_e = 25$	$f_e = 35$	$f_e = 25$	$f_e = 15$
$f_o = 20$	$f_o = 25$	$f_o = 30$	$f_o = 25$

Computing χ^2,

$$\chi^2 = \sum \frac{(f_o - f_e)^2}{f_e}$$

$$\frac{(20-25)^2}{25} + \frac{(25-35)^2}{35} + \frac{(30-25)^2}{25} + \frac{(25-15)^2}{15}$$

$$= \frac{25}{25} + \frac{100}{35} + \frac{25}{25} + \frac{100}{15}$$

$$= 1 + 2.86 + 1 + 6.67$$

$$\chi^2 = \mathbf{11.53}$$

$$df = C - 1 = 4 - 1 = 3$$

$$\alpha = .05, \text{ therefore } \chi^2_{\text{crit}} = 7.82$$

Since 11.53 > 7.82, H_0 is rejected.

As a consequence of rejecting the null hypothesis, you can conclude that the observed frequency distribution differs significantly from the expected frequency distribution stated by the professor. By examining the observed frequencies in the cells, note that the excellent category has the fewest number of students. Indeed, the sample shows that most of the students received an average on their papers. This is contrary to the professor's assertion that she is an easy grader. The mere fact that the χ^2 statistic is statistically significant does not automatically mean that the professor is mistaken. Suppose that the observed frequency of the excellent category was found to be 70, with the remaining 30 frequency counts spread across the other categories. The χ^2 statistic would have been statistically significant, but the fact that the excellent category had such a high count would, in fact, strengthen the professor's claim. After obtaining a significant χ^2, you have to examine the pattern of observed frequencies to interpret the meaning of the *statistically significant* finding.   ∎

17.3   THE CHI-SQUARE DISTRIBUTION AND DEGREES OF FREEDOM

The chi-square statistic indicates how well the hypothesized expected frequencies correspond to the observed frequencies. The closer the fit, the smaller the value of χ^2. The test statistic for the chi-square distribution is χ^2, which is the basis for the sampling distribution, just as the t statistic and F ratio are the bases of the t and F distributions.

✓   The **chi-square distribution** is a theoretical distribution formed by taking an infinite number of samples in which the chi-square statistic is computed for each sample. The relative frequency of each value of chi-square is plotted to show the chi-square distribution. A separate chi-square distribution is created for each df (in this case, $C - 1$), thus establishing a family of chi-square distributions. The shape of each distribution is defined by the number of categories used to compute χ^2.

Note that the degrees of freedom for a χ^2 test is not based on the number of subjects in the study. Instead, the degrees of freedom for χ^2 is determined by the number of categories. Suppose you conducted a study with four categories and 150 subjects. If the first three categories contained a total of 100 subjects, the number of subjects in the fourth category would be automatically determined (50). In other words, the frequency count of three of the four categories is free to vary. Once the count of three categories is specified, the count in the fourth category is strictly determined. Thus, in the simple one-way design, $df = C - 1$.

Characteristics of Chi-Square Distributions and Rejecting the Null Hypothesis

Rejecting the Null Hypothesis

The null hypothesis for the χ^2 test is specified by the expected frequencies in each cell of the design. The χ^2 test measures the degree to which the observed frequencies correspond to the expected frequencies. If the null hypothesis is true, then the observed frequencies for each cell will be very close to the expected frequencies, and the value of χ^2 will be small. If the null hypothesis is false, the expected and observed frequencies will, to a sufficient degree, depart from one another. Even if the null hypothesis is true, you would not expect the observed frequencies to match perfectly the expected frequencies due to sampling error. As the expected and observed frequencies become increasingly discrepant, χ^2 becomes larger. How large does χ^2 have to be in order to reject the null hypothesis? If the χ^2 computed on the sample data is unlikely to occur when the null hypothesis is true, then you conclude that the null hypothesis is false. The meaning of "unlikely" is defined by the level of alpha. If $\alpha = .05$, the null hypothesis is rejected if the probability of obtaining a χ^2 statistic of a given size is less than .05, *when the null hypothesis is true.* Thus, each chi-square distribution can be marked with a critical value to identify the percentage of χ^2 values that lie, for instance, in the upper 10 percent, 5 percent, or 1 percent of the sampling distribution.

Figure 17.1 shows chi-square distributions for 1, 5, and 8 degrees of freedom. The rejection region for each of the distributions when $\alpha = .05$ is also shown in Figure 17.1. An obtained value of χ^2 that falls in the rejection region would naturally lead you to reject the null hypothesis. Note, however, that as the degrees of freedom increase, a larger χ^2_{obt} is required to reject the null hypothesis. Take another look at the formula for χ^2.

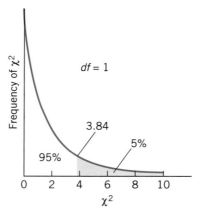

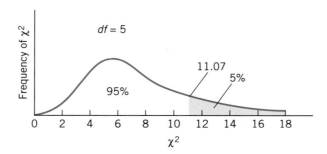

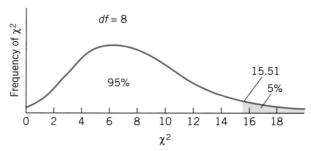

Figure 17.1 Chi-square distributions for degrees of freedom of 1, 5, and 8.

$$\chi^2 = \sum \frac{(f_o - f_e)^2}{f_e}$$

Assume that the null hypothesis is true and, therefore, any discrepancies between f_o and f_e are due to sampling error. Remember that the formula for χ^2 requires that you sum all the categories in the design. What happens as the number of categories increases? Even if the value of $(f_o - f_e)$ for each cell is quite small, summing a large number of cells will lead to a large χ^2, even when the null hypothesis is true.

Therefore, for a given level of alpha, as the number of categories increases, a larger χ^2_{obt} is necessary to reject the null hypothesis.

Finally, the null hypothesis is stated by the expected frequencies. The alternative hypothesis states that the expected frequencies are not arranged as hypothesized. The statistical test is, therefore, nondirectional.

Characteristics of the Chi-Square Distribution
The characteristics of the chi-square distribution are as follows:

1. Since the numerator of the χ^2 statistic is squared, all values of χ^2 are positive.
2. Chi-square distributions are unimodal and typically, positively skewed. However, as the *df* increases, the chi-square distribution approximates the shape of a normal distribution.
3. As the *df* increases, the critical value of χ^2, beyond which the rejection region lies, becomes relatively larger.

17.4 TWO-WAY DESIGNS: THE CHI-SQUARE TEST FOR INDEPENDENCE

The chi-square test can also be used to determine if there is a relationship between two variables. The type of design with two independent variables is a two-way design. Similar to the goodness-of-fit test, the basic data used are a frequency count of observations. Some examples of research questions in which the chi-square test is applied with two variables are as follows.

1. A clinical psychologist hypothesizes that birth complications are associated with a subsequent diagnosis of schizophrenia. Three comparison groups are included in the study: a group of schizophrenic patients, a group of depressed patients, and a group of normal subjects. Each subject in the study is categorized on *two* variables: diagnosis and history of birth complications. This design is represented in the following, which is called a **contingency table** (also called a **frequency** or **cross-tabulation table**). Since there are two rows and three columns, the table is called a 2 × 3 contingency table.

	Schizophrenic	Depressed	Normal
Birth Complications	20	6	8
No Birth Complications	8	20	22

The numbers in the cells refer to the number of subjects that meet the classification criteria for both variables. Thus, 20 schizophrenics were found to have had birth complications, 20 depressed patients did not have birth complications, 8 normal subjects had birth complications, and so on.

2. A social psychologist hypothesizes that males are more likely than females to help someone in an emergency and that helping will also be affected by the presence or absence of bystanders. This two-way design, without obtained frequencies, is represented in the following 2 × 2 contingency table.

| | **Bystanders** | |
	Present	*Absent*
Males		
Females		

3. A psychologist hypothesizes that Type A, coronary-prone individuals are tougher negotiators than Type B, noncoronary-prone people. A sample of college students is classified as Type A, Type B, and Type X (an even mixture of the two personality types). An experimental task that requires negotiating a conflict is presented to each subject. The outcome is either win or lose. The design is represented as a 2 × 3 contingency table.

	Type A	*Type B*	*Type X*
Win			
Lose			

The Null Hypothesis and the Concept of Independence

The null hypothesis, H_0, for the chi-square test applied to the two-way design states that the two variables are independent. The alternative hypothesis, H_1, states that the two variables are not independent—that is—they are related. Figure 17.2 shows bar graphs of the hypothetical data from the schizophrenia and birth complications example. The illustration on the left shows the relative number of schizophrenics, depressed, and normal subjects who had complications associated with their births. Compare this graph with the one adjacent, which depicts the relative number of subjects among the diagnostic categories who do *not* have a history of birth complications. Just by "eyeballing" the two graphs (birth complications versus no birth complications), you can see that there are many more birth complications among schizophrenics than depressed subjects and normal subjects. The pattern of data is different in the birth complications category compared to the pattern of data in the no birth complications category. This indicates that the manner in which the data are distributed for one variable *depends* on the level of the second variable.[1] In this example, the two variables are not independent.

---

[1] The word "depends" has no implication here for a causal relation among the variables.

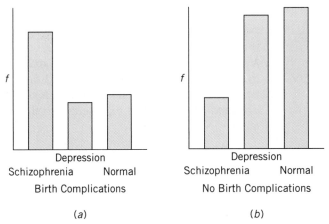

Figure 17.2 Each bar reflects the number of people given one of the three diagnoses. The pattern of bars in (*a*) is different from the pattern of bars in (*b*). This indicates that the distribution of various diagnosis *depends* on the presence or absence of a history of birth complications. Viewed together, these graphs reflect on association between diagnostic category and birth complications, with schizophrenics showing a greater frequency of birth complications.

Now consider Figure 17.3. Hypothetical data have been used to reflect independence between the diagnostic category and birth complications category. The graph on the left is now quite similar to the graph on the right in the pattern of the bars representing relative frequency. In other words, the likelihood of someone being classified a schizophrenic, depressed, or normal, is in no way related to the presence or absence of birth complications. Stated differently, the frequency distribution for one variable has the same pattern for each level of the second variable. The chi-square test for independence checks to see if the frequency distribution for one classification variable is different, depending on the level of the second classification variable. If the distributions are different, then the null hypothesis that the variables are independent is rejected.

Computing χ^2 for a Two-Way Design

Whether you are conducting a goodness-of-fit test or are testing the independence of two variables, the formula for χ^2 is the same:

$$\chi^2 = \sum \frac{(f_o - f_e)^2}{f_e}$$

Moreover, observed frequencies are still obtained from sample data. Specifying the expected frequencies under the null hypothesis is not, however, as straightforward as it was with the goodness-of-fit test.

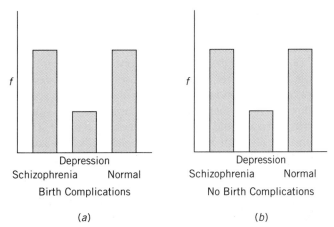

Figure 17.3 Unlike Figure 17.2, the relative occurrence of different diagnosis is similar in (*a*) and (*b*). This reflects the fact that birth complications and diagnostic category are independent—that is—unrelated.

Computing Expected Frequencies in the Two-Way Design

Computing f_e for each cell is a matter of simple arithmetic. Let's use the schizophrenia and birth complications study, with new frequency counts, as a worked example to illustrate the calculation of expected frequencies. Table 17.2 presents the observed and expected frequencies for each cell of the 2×3 matrix.

The numbers along the margins of the matrix are the number of subjects for each row and column. The total number of subjects is 84. To be sure that you understand what marginal frequencies are, use Table 17.2 to answer the following questions. In the total sample of 84 subjects, how many subjects had birth complications? The answer is 34. How many subjects in the total sample have a diagnosis of schizophrenia? The asnwer is 28. How many subjects have no psychiatric diagnosis? The answer is 30.

TABLE 17.2 Observed, Expected, and Marginal Frequencies for a Worked Problem[a]

	Schizophrenic	*Depressed*	*Normal*	
Birth Complications	$f_o = 20$ $f_e = 11.33$	$f_o = 6$ $f_e = 10.52$	$f_o = 8$ $f_e = 12.14$	**34**
No Birth Complications	$f_o = 8$ $f_e = 16.67$	$f_o = 20$ $f_e = 15.48$	$f_o = 22$ $f_e = 17.86$	**50**
	28	**26**	**30**	**84**

[a] See text for details.

Table 17.2 also shows the expected frequencies for each cell of the matrix, as well as the marginal frequencies for the rows and columns. The following explains how the expected frequency is calculated for the uppermost left cell, which is the cell that corresponds to schizophrenic *and* birth complications. In computing the expected frequency for this cell, you only need to consider the Birth Complication row and the Schizophrenic column. If you were to take a subject at random from the total number of subjects in the study, what is the probability that that subject would have had a complicated birth? Since there is a total of 84 subjects and 34 of them had birth complications, the answer is **34/84 = .4048**. Now consider just the Schizophrenic column. What is the probability that a subject selected at random from the entire study sample would have a diagnosis of schizophrenia? Since there are 28 schizophrenics in the total sample of 84 subjects, the answer is **28/84 = .3333**. Hence, the probability of someone in the study having had birth complications is .4048, and the probability of someone in the study with a diagnosis of schizophrenia is .3333. To find the probability of someone being diagnosed as schizophrenic *and* having had birth complications, multiply (.4048)(.3333) to arrive at **.1349**. The expected frequency for this cell is the number of people you would expect to find in this cell if the null hypothesis is true: **.1349 (84) = 11.33**.

This method of computing expected frequencies has been presented so that you can follow the logic of expected frequencies. There is a shortcut method, which you can use that will allow you to compute the expected frequency for each cell.[2]

Formula for Computing f_e

$$f_e = \frac{f_c f_r}{N}$$

(Formula 17.2)

where,

f_c = the frequency total for the relevant *column*
f_r = the frequency total for the relevant *row*
N = the total number of subjects

---

[2] Statisticians have raised concerns over those chi-square distributions based on one degree of freedom. When $df = 1$, and expected frequencies are less than 5, the chi-square test will not hold the probability of a Type I error (rejecting a true null hypothesis) at, say .05, even when alpha is set at .05. The solution has been to apply the Yates' correction formula when at least one expected frequency is small. The Yates' correction reduces the size of χ^2, and thus compensates for the alpha inflation believed to exist with small expected frequencies. Recent research, however, has led to the conclusion that the Yates' correction procedure is unnecessarily conservative and that the chi-square test gives accurate probabilities, even when expected frequencies are less than 5 (Camilli and Hopkins, 1978; Jaccard and Becker, 1988; see also Bradley, Bradley, McGrath, and Cutcomb, 1979, for the same conclusion when $df > 1$). Based on these findings, many textbooks on statistics, including this one, are no longer recommending a correction procedure be used when expected frequencies are small (e.g., Jaccard and Becker, 1990; Runyon and Haber, 1988; Spatz and Johnston, 1989; however, see Siegel and Castellan, 1988).

Formula 17.2 is now used to compute the expected frequencies for each of the cells represented in Table 17.2.

Schizophrenic and Birth Complications
$$f_e = \frac{(28)(34)}{84} = 11.33$$

Depressed and Birth Complications
$$f_e = \frac{(26)(34)}{84} = 10.52$$

Normal and Birth Complications
$$f_e = \frac{(30)(34)}{84} = 12.14$$

Schizophrenic and No Birth Complications
$$f_e = \frac{(28)(50)}{84} = 16.67$$

Depressed and No Birth Complications
$$f_e = \frac{(26)(50)}{84} = 15.48$$

Normal and No Birth Complications
$$f_e = \frac{(30)(50)}{84} = 17.86$$

Computing χ^2 and Testing for Significance

The task of computing χ^2 is easier if you work from a frequency summary table. In Table 17.3, the observed and expected frequencies are ordered in the first two columns. The next two columns are interim calculations necessary for computing χ^2. The value of χ^2 computes to 16.77.

The degrees of freedom associated with a two-way design is $df = (R-1)(C-1)$, which is the number of rows minus one multiplied by the number of columns minus one. For the foregoing example, $df = (2-1)(3-1) = 2$.

The critical value for the chi-square test is found in Appendix B.8. If alpha is set at .05, the critical value associated with $df = 2$ is 5.99. Since 16.77 is larger than 5.99, the null hypothesis is rejected. Thus, psychiatric diagnosis and birth complications are not independent of one another. The finding can be interpreted as, "The frequency of birth complications among those individuals diagnosed as schizophrenic is greater than would be expected by chance, $\chi^2(2, n = 84) = 16.77, p < .05$."

The steps involved in conducting a chi-square analysis for a two-way design are:

Step 1. Specify the null and alternative hypotheses. H_0 is a statement that the two variables are unrelated. H_1 states that the two variables are not independent.

Step 2. Specify alpha—typically .05 or .01.

Step 3. Use Formula 17.2, $f_e = f_c f_r / N$, to compute all expected cell frequencies.

Step 4. Place the observed and expected frequencies in a frequency summary table and perform the computational steps for χ^2.

Step 5. Compute df by $(R-1)(C-1)$.

Step 6. Find χ^2_{crit} in Table B.8 of the Appendix and decide whether to reject the null hypothesis.

Step 7. Interpret the findings.

TABLE 17.3   Computing χ^2

f_o	f_e	$(f_o - f_e)$	$(f_o - f_e)^2$	$(f_o - f_e)^2/f_e$
20	11.33	8.67	75.17	6.63
6	10.52	−4.52	20.43	1.94
8	12.14	−4.14	17.14	1.41
8	16.67	−8.67	75.17	4.51
20	15.48	4.52	20.43	1.32
22	17.86	4.14	17.14	.96
				$\chi^2 = \mathbf{16.77}$

$$\chi^2 = \sum \frac{(f_o - f_e)^2}{f_e} = \mathbf{16.77}$$

17.5   THE CHI-SQUARE TEST FOR A 2 × 2 CONTINGENCY TABLE

We have just completed an example of how to compute χ^2 for a 2 × 3 contingency table. If the two-way design is in the form of a 2 × 2 table, there is a shortcut method, which can be used that does not involve computing expected frequencies for each cell. Formula 17.3 requires you to place the letters A, B, C, and D in the cells as indicated in the following. In this case, only the observed cell frequencies are needed to compute χ^2.

A	B	$A + B$
C	D	$C + D$
$A + C$	$B + D$	N

Chi-Square Formula for a 2 × 2 Contingency Table

$$\chi^2 = \frac{N(AD - BC)^2}{(A + B)(C + D)(A + C)(B + D)} \qquad \text{(Formula 17.3)}$$

where,

A, B, C, D = the observed frequencies, f_o, in each cell
$AD = f_o$ for cell A × f_o for cell D
$BC = f_o$ for cell B × f_o for cell C
N = total number of subjects

Box 17.1 applies Formula 17.3. A study is presented that hypothesizes an attractive woman is more likely to be helped than an unattractive woman.

BOX 17.1

What is Beautiful is Good

Social psychologists have discovered that attractive people are the recipients of a positive social stereotype, which can be summarized as, "What is Beautiful is Good." Compared to physically unattractive people, those who are good-looking are assumed to be more successful, mentally healthier, smarter, and happier (Dion, Bercheid, and Walster, 1972). The research in this area is based almost exclusively on paper-and-pencil ratings of pictures of attractive and unattractive "target" persons. Benson, Karabenick, and Lerner (1976) wondered if people's *overt behavior* would be influenced by the attractiveness of another person. More specifically, they hypothesized that males would be more likely to help an attractive female in comparison to an unattractive female.

METHOD

The study took place at an airport. The experimenters placed a completed graduate-school application on a shelf in a telephone booth. Attached to the application was a picture of the applicant. In the Attractive condition, the picture was of a female that had been rated by judges to be extremely attractive. In the Unattractive condition, the picture affixed to the application was of a female rated as extremely unattractive. An addressed, stamped envelope accompanied the application, with a clearly displayed note from the applicant: "Dear Dad, Have a nice trip. Please remember to mail this application before you leave Detroit on your (*time of departure*) flight to New York. Love, Linda." The time of departure was constantly altered to indicate that the flight had already left.

The experimenter surreptitiously observed the subject enter the telephone booth and categorized him as either Helpful or Nonhelpful, based on the following criteria. First, only subjects who looked at the application were included in the study. A helpful response consisted of either mailing the application in a nearby mailbox or turning the application over to an employee at the airport. If the experimenter lost sight of the subject, a helpful response could be determined by whether the application arrived at the experimenter's psychology department. A response was considered nonhelpful if the subject, after looking at the application, either left it in the telephone booth, destroyed it, or left with the application but never mailed it.

The design of this study conforms to a 2 × 2 contingency table with one factor Attractive/Unattractive and the other factor Helpful/Nonhelpful. The dependent variable is in the form of a frequency count; therefore, a chi-square test is appropriate. Observed frequencies for each cell are shown in the following table, and Formula 17.3 is used to analyze the data.

	Attractive	Unattractive	
Helpful	A 55	B 35	$A + B$ $55 + 35 = 90$
Non helpful	C 55	D 71	$C + D$ $55 + 71 = 126$
	$A + C$ $55 + 55 = 110$	$B + D$ $35 + 71 = 106$	$N = 216$

$$\chi^2 = \frac{N(AD - BC)^2}{(A + B)(C + D)(A + C)(B + D)}$$

$$\chi^2 = \frac{216[(55)(71) - (35)(55)]^2}{(55 + 35)(55 + 71)(55 + 55)(35 + 71)}$$

$$= \frac{216(3905 - 1925)^2}{(90)(126)(110)(106)}$$

$$= \frac{216(3,920,400)}{132,224,400}$$

$$= \frac{846,806,400}{132,224,400}$$

$$\chi^2_{obt} = 6.40$$

With $\alpha = .05$ and $df = 1$, the critical value of χ^2 is 3.84. The obtained value of χ^2 exceeds the critical value ($6.40 > 3.84$); thus the null hypothesis that states there is no association between helping and the attractiveness of the target person is rejected.

And how are the findings interpreted? Men are more likely to help an unknown female when she is attractive rather than unattractive, $\chi^2(1, n = 216) = 6.40, p < .05$.

17.6 WHICH CELLS ARE MAJOR CONTRIBUTORS TO A SIGNIFICANT CHI-SQUARE TEST?

In the chapters covering the analysis of variance, you learned that a significant F ratio could be followed by pairwise, post hoc comparisons. The purpose of post hoc analyses is to locate the source of a significant F ratio. Within the context of the chi-square analysis, a post hoc analysis answers the question, "Which cells are major contributors to a significant chi-square test?" Unlike post hoc comparisons that are used with parametric data, this analysis does *not* contrast two cells to see if they differ from one another. Rather, each cell is analyzed separately to determine which cells make a *major* contribution to the significant chi-square test. This involves an analysis of the standardized residuals (Haberman, 1973). Formula 17.4 is thus applied to each cell of the matrix.

Formula for the Standardized Residual

$$R = \frac{f_o - f_e}{\sqrt{f_e}} \quad \textit{(Formula 17.4)}$$

If the absolute value of the standardized residual for a category *exceeds* 2.00, then it is concluded that that cell makes a major contribution to the significant chi-square test. Formula 17.4 is only used after the null hypothesis is rejected. Table 17.4 presents the standardized residuals for each category of the schizophrenia and birth complications study. Although the sign of R is ignored when comparing R to 2.00, the sign of R *is* used to interpret the findings. If R is greater than 2.00 and positive, it means that the number of observations in that cell is more than would be expected by chance. If R is greater than 2.00 and negative in value, it means that the number of observations in the cell is lower than would be expected by chance. In Table 17.4, note that two cells have R values greater than 2.00. Cell 1, Schizophrenic/Birth Complications, has a positive R (2.57), which exceeds 2.00. This means that there are *more* schizophrenics *with* a history of birth complications than would be expected by chance. Cell 4, No Birth Complications/Schizophrenic, has a negative R (-2.13), which exceeds 2.00. This means that there are *fewer* schizophrenics *without* a history of birth complications than would be expected by chance. Since none of the other cells yield an R that exceeds 2.00, they do not offer a major contribution to the significant chi-square test.

TABLE 17.4 The Standardized Residuals for Each Category of the Hypothetical Study on Schizophrenia and Birth Complications (BC)[a]

Cell	f_o	f_e	$\sqrt{f_e}$	R
Cell 1	20	11.33	3.37	2.57
Cell 2	6	10.52	3.24	-1.40
Cell 3	8	12.14	3.48	-1.19
Cell 4	8	16.67	4.08	-2.13
Cell 5	20	15.48	3.93	1.15
Cell 6	22	17.86	4.23	.98

[a] Cell 1: Schizophrenic/BC; Cell 2: Depressed/BC; Cell 3: Normal/BC; Cell 4; Schizophrenic/No BC; Cell 5: Depressed/No BC; Cell 6: Normal/No BC. Cells with $R > 2.00$ make a major contribution to the significant chi-square test.

The use of standardized residuals is a useful post hoc technique, which allows you to make a more specific interpretation of an overall significant χ^2.

17.7 USING THE CHI-SQUARE TEST WITH QUANTITATIVE VARIABLES

Although the chi-square test is usually performed when variables are discrete (e.g., male versus female, returned a favor versus did not return a favor, married versus single), it is possible to use the test with a quantitative variable that is treated as a categorical variable. For example, subjects may be administered a scale measuring dominance. The scores may range from 0–30, but the subjects can be classified as either High Dominance or Low Dominance. In fact, the chi-square test can be used when two variables are continuous. A researcher, for instance, may hypothesize a relationship between need for achievement and yearly income. In Table 17.5, subjects are assigned to one of three categories of need for achievement and one of four categories of yearly income.

If there is some reason to suspect that the variable underlying the continuous measure is *not*, in fact, continuous (interval or ratio), forming discrete categories and using the chi-square test is a good idea. However, if it can be assumed that the underlying dimension is continuous, the use of a parametric text provides more power. For example, the data in Table 17.5 could be analyzed by using the Pearson formula for continuous measures—that is—a correlation would be obtained between need for achievement scores and yearly income.

TABLE 17.5 **A 3 × 4 Contingency Table[a]**

NEED FOR ACHIEVEMENT	ANNUAL INCOME ($1000)			
	< 20	21–40	41–60	> 60
> 40	19	24	37	65
21–40	25	20	33	42
< 20	56	32	20	10

[a] Two quantitative variables are presented as discrete variables. Scores on a measure of need for achievement are collapsed to form Low, Medium, and High categories. Income is represented as four discrete categories. Cell values are observed frequency counts.

17.8 ASSUMPTIONS OF THE CHI-SQUARE TEST

One of the advantages of the chi-square test is that there are very few assumptions that need to be met to conduct the test.

1. As with any test of significance, the sample should be representative of the population to which you want to generalize your findings.

2. The data should be in the form of a frequency count. The chi-square analysis does not analyze differences between means.

3. Each observation must be *independent* of every other observation. This assumption requires that a single subject be represented only once, and in only one cell.

SUMMARY

The chi-square test is used to analyze nominal data, which is in the form of a frequency count. Tests that make inferences about population parameters are called parametric tests. The chi-square test does not use means or standard deviations to infer population parameters; therefore, it is called a nonparametric test. A chi-square analysis tests the correspondence between a hypothesized distribution of frequency counts and an observed distribution of frequency counts. The null hypothesis states that there is no difference between expected and observed frequency distributions. The alternative hypothesis is a statement that the expected and observed distributions are sufficiently different such that the difference is unlikely due to sampling error.

The goodness-of-fit test is analogous to a one-way ANOVA with two or more groups (categories). A two-way design that uses categorical data is called a contingency table. In a two-way design, the chi-square analysis tests whether two variables are unrelated. The null hypothesis states that there is no relation between two variables; the alternative hypothesis states that the variables are related—that is—not independent.

The assumptions of the chi-square test are that the data are in the form of a frequency count, the sample is representative of the population of interest, and each observation is independent of every other observation—that is—a single subject is represented in only one cell.

KEY FORMULAS FOR CHAPTER 17

Formula for χ^2

$$\chi^2 = \sum \frac{(f_o - f_e)^2}{f_e}$$

(Formula 17.1)

Formula for Computing f_e

$$f_e = \frac{f_c f_r}{N}$$

(Formula 17.2)

Chi-Square Formula for a 2 × 2 Contingency Table

$$\chi^2 = \frac{N(AD - BC)^2}{(A + B)(C + D)(A + C)(B + D)}$$

(Formula 17.3)

Formula for the Standardized Residual

$$R = \frac{f_o - f_e}{\sqrt{f_e}}$$

(Formula 17.4)

WORK PROBLEMS

1. Three different drug treatments are used to control hypertension. At the end of treatment, the investigator classifies patients as having either a favorable or unfavorable response to the medication. Set alpha at .05 and conduct a chi-square test. Use the R statistic to determine which cells make a contribution to the significant χ^2. Interpret the findings.

| | TREATMENT | | | |
RESPONSE	*I*	*II*	*III*	
Favorable	70	160	168	398
Unfavorable	30	40	32	102
	100	200	200	500

2. Freud postulated that women have an unconscious envy of the male penis. Johnson (1966) tested the penis-envy hypothesis in the following manner. Male and female students were loaned No. 2 pencils with which to take a multiple-choice exam. A box labeled "pencils" was positioned next to a table upon which students were to place their answer sheets. The investigator counted the number of males and females who returned the pencils. The hypothesis was that females would be more likely to keep the phallic-like object. The data were consistent with the hypothesis. The following hypothetical data are consistent with the findings of Johnson. Conduct a chi-square test. (Can you think of an interpretation of the data that has nothing to do with penis envy?)

	Kept Pencil	Returned Pencil
Males	15	40
Females	38	17

3. Specify the correct *df* for each of these designs.
   a. 2 × 2   b. 3 × 4   c. 4 × 5   d. 1 × 3

4. You find yourself in a discussion with a friend about the ways in which police decide to pull people over for traffic violations. You maintain that police are more likely to pull someone over if there is some evidence that the driver has beliefs that are offensive to the officer. You and your friend enlist the aid of 50 drivers. Twenty-five of them are asked to place the following sticker on their car bumper: Stop Police Brutality! The other 25 drivers are given a sticker that reads Smile! Assume that there is, in fact, no difference in the way in which

the participants of the two groups drive. Over the next 6 months, the number of times the police stop the drivers of each group is recorded. Drivers displaying the brutality sticker are stopped 18 times; drivers displaying the smile sticker are stopped only 5 times. No driver is stopped more than once.

a. State the null and alternative hypotheses.

b. Specify f_o for each cell.

c. Compute χ^2 and test for significance. Set $\alpha = .05$.

d. Interpret the findings.

5. For each matrix, fill in the missing observed and marginal frequencies. Next, compute the f_e for each cell.

a.

30	?	?	20	120
?	?	40	?	100
?	80	60	40	N = ?

b.

7	?	14
?	?	?
?	18	30

6. Assume that all marginal frequencies are given for a 3 × 4 design. What are the fewest number of cells that must have frequencies specified in order to determine the rest of the cell frequencies?

7. Without knowing the number of rows and columns in a two-way design, what are the fewest number of cells that must have cell frequencies given in order to determine the frequencies of the remaining cells?

8. Frank and Lester (1988) have found that young adults, ages 15–24 years old, more often commit suicide on a Sunday. The following hypothetical data are consistent with their findings. Conduct a chi-square test on these data.

Sun.	Mon.	Tues.	Wed.	Thurs.	Fri.	Sat.
56	29	17	22	25	15	33

9. Mothers frequently report that they had more difficulty delivering their first child in comparison to subsequent children. Kaitz, Roken, and Eidelman (1988) tested this common belief by obtaining data from primiparous (first-time mothers) and multiparous (more than one past delivery) mothers. Primiparous ($n = 49$) and multiparous ($n = 75$) mothers were asked to rate their labor as Easy, Medium, or Difficult. The following data are adapted from their study. Conduct a chi-square analysis and test the hypothesis that there is a difference between primiparous and multiparous mothers in the amount of discomfort

experienced during delivery. Set alpha at .05. In addition, using R, identify those cells that make a major contribution to the significant χ^2.

	Easy	Medium	Difficult
Primiparous Mothers	2	20	27
Multiparous Mothers	19	46	10

10. Kaitz, Roken, and Eidelman (1988) tested the hypothesis that primiparous mothers are less successful at recognizing their newborn babies in comparison to multiparous mothers. After less than 5 hr of exposure to their newborns, both primiparous and multiparous mothers were presented with seven photographs of babies, one of which was their own child. The investigators found that 30 percent (8/27) of the primiparous mothers and 79 percent (34/43) of multiparous mothers accurately identified their babies. The authors attribute this difference to a "short-lived impairment of perceptual/cognitive skills associated with their more stressful childbearing experience." Conduct a chi-square analysis on the preceding data.

11. You have learned that the df for a goodness-of-fit test is $C - 1$, and $(R - 1)(C - 1)$ for a two-way design. As the number of categories or cells of a design increases, χ^2_{crit} increases. Look at the formula for χ^2 and explain why it makes sense for χ^2_{crit} to increase as the number of categories increases.

12. During the 1950s, Samuel Steward left his position as a university professor and became a tattoo artist in Chicago. Alfred Kinsey, the noted sex researcher, asked Steward to keep a diary of his experiences, and to pay special attention to the possible sexual motivations that may underlie a person's decision to get tattooed. Steward (1990) has reported the following data:
    a. The boys who came back and said (either with questioning or without) that after their tattoo they went out and had sex with a girl **1724**
    b. Boys who got into a fight following a tattoo **635**
    c. Boys who said that they got drunk afterwards (over 800 in question a. also said this) **1031**
    d. Number of boys admitting they masturbated while admiring their new tattoo **879**

    Does this data set lend itself to a chi-square test? What assumption of the chi-square test is violated by the manner in which the data are reported? (Ignore the fact that the subjects are not a random sample of all those who received a tattoo.)

13. Is a younger mother more likely to give birth to a physically immature baby? In this study, younger mothers (under 20 years of age) are compared to older mothers (30–35 years of age). An immature baby is defined as having a birth weight equal to or less than 2500 grams. Every baby is assigned to a category based on the age of his or her mother and whether he or she is below or above the weight cutoff defining physical immaturity. Set alpha at .05 and

perform a chi-square analysis on the following hypothetical data. Interpret the findings.

AGE	BIRTH WEIGHT		
	≤ 2500 grams	> 2500 grams	
Under 20	45	20	65
30–35	10	39	49
	55	59	114

Work Problems for the Computer

14. A researcher is interested in the association between diabetes and prolonged healing of wounds. The research question is, "Do diabetics show prolonged healing?" Conduct a chi-square analysis on the following data. Set alpha at .05.

Patient	HEALING		
	Normal	Prolonged	
Diabetic	125	329	454
Nondiabetic	245	111	356
	370	440	810

15. A dermatologist is interested in comparing four different treatments for dandruff. After 6 weeks of treatment, a colleague judges each patient as either improved or not improved. Is there any reason to conclude that the treatments have a differential effect on dandruff? Set alpha at .05 and conduct a chi-square analysis.

Preparation	No Improvement	Satisfactory Improvement	
A	22	24	46
B	19	17	36
C	23	28	51
D	17	22	39
	81	91	172

Other Nonparametric Tests

18.1   THE RESEARCH CONTEXT

 Popular significance tests, such as the *t* test or the ANOVA, are known as **parametric tests** because they test hypotheses about population parameters. In addition, these tests rest on certain assumptions: scores in the populations are normally distributed, population distributions have equal variances, and the tests are applied to either interval or ratio scales of measurement. Although the *t* test and the ANOVA are robust tests (i.e., they can be used even when, for example, the populations are not normally distributed), gross violations of the population assumptions can invalidate parametric tests. In addition, some research questions do not lend themselves to the use of interval or ratio scales; therefore, a parametric test may not be applicable. In Chapter 17, for example, the chi-square test was presented as a test performed on frequency counts.

Statisticians have developed numerous hypothesis tests that do not necessarily involve inferences about population parameters; these tests are called nonparametric tests. These tests can be used when assumptions about population characteristics are violated and when the scale of measurement is a frequency count or ordinal (rankings).

Most of the parametric tests discussed so far in this text have a nonparametric alternative. Only four nonparametric tests will be covered in this chapter.[1] The *Spearman rank* correlation coefficient is used to measure the strength of association between two variables when both variables are measured on an ordinal scale. The *point-biserial* correlation coefficient is used to measure the strength of association between a variable measured with an interval or ratio scale (a continuous measure) and a nominal variable (a noncontinuous measure). The *Mann-Whitney U test* is the nonparametric alternative to an independent-groups *t* test. It is performed using ranked data. The *Wilcoxon signed-ranks test* is the nonparametric counterpart to the dependent-measures *t* test. It too is performed using ordinal data. As each test is discussed, appropriate research examples for the test are given. In addition, the method of calculation and procedures for testing the null hypothesis are presented.

18.2   THE USE OF RANKED DATA IN RESEARCH

There are two avenues that lead to the use of a nonparametric test on ranked data. In one instance, the researcher collects data in the form of ranks. For example, an investigator might ask if there is a relation between popularity and intelligence of children. The data are collected by asking a teacher to *rank* students from most to least popular *and* from most to least intelligent. Using another example, suppose a researcher wants to know if there is a relation between tennis players' national rankings and the heights of the players. All the players would be ranked according to height, and then the two ranked variables would be correlated. In many situations, the use of an ordinal scale has advantages. Recall from Chapter 2 that one of the assumptions of an interval scale is that numerically equal distances on the scale represent equal distances on the dimension underlying the scale. Imagine how you would go about rating the talent of several football teams. If you use an interval scale, it would be difficult to convince someone that the rating distance between any two adjacent teams is the same. For example, the difference between the best team and the second best team may be closer than the difference between the

---

[1] For a detailed treatment of nonparametric tests, see Siegel and Castellan, 1988, and Marascuilo and McSweeney, 1977.

tenth- and eleventh-place teams. Using an ordinal scale circumvents this problem because rankings only make claim to the relative position among various ranks.

There is a second instance in which a researcher may use ordinal data. Data may be collected using an interval or ratio scale. If the data lead the researcher to suspect that the assumptions for a parametric test are violated, the scores are converted to ranks. To accomplish the conversion to ranks, you simply order the original scores in ascending or descending order and assigns ranks accordingly. The original scores are discarded and an appropriate analysis is performed on ranks.

A correlational technique that can be used when both the X and Y variables are in the form of ranks is now presented.

18.3   THE SPEARMAN RANK CORRELATION COEFFICIENT

Chapter 15 explained that the Pearson formula is used to compute a correlation, which is a statistic that indexes the degree to which two variables are associated. One assumption underlying the use of the Pearson formula is that X and Y have a linear relation. By viewing the scatter plot of X and Y you may discover that X and Y are not linearly related. When the scatter plot of a bivariate distribution reveals a nonlinear relation, each person's score on the X and Y variable can be converted to ranks. In doing so, scores on an interval or ratio scale are changed to scores on an ordinal scale. By using this procedure, the resultant scatter plot based on a plot of the ranks will usually show a linear relation between X and Y. This transformation allows you to use the Pearson computational formula on ranked data. However, the Spearman rank correlation formula, presented later, is preferred for its computational ease.

Suppose a researcher hypothesizes a relationship between Need for Approval and Ingratiating Behaviors. In Table 18.1, the score columns are the continuous

TABLE   18.1   Converting Continuous Measures to Ranks

Subject	Need for Approval		Ingratiation	
	Score	Rank	Score	Rank
S_1	8	1	11	1.5
S_2	7	2.5	11	1.5
S_3	7	2.5	10	3
S_4	6	4	9	4
S_5	5	5	8	5
S_6	4	6	7	6
S_7	3	7	6	7
S_8	2	8	2	8

measures for the two variables. The rank columns show each score's rank in the distribution. The analysis is unaffected by whether a rank of 1 is assigned to the highest or lowest score. In this example, a rank of 1 is assigned to the highest score, a rank of 2 to the next highest score, and so on. Subject 1 scored an 8 on need for approval, which was the highest score, and so a rank of 1 has been assigned to that subject's score. Subject 7 scored a 6 on the measure of Ingratiation, and since a 6 is seven scores from the *top of the distribution,* a rank of 7 has been assigned.

Figure 18.1(*a*) is the scatter plot for the continuous measures of Need for Approval and Ingratiation. Since the correlation is extremely high, the points of the scatter plot look almost like a line. Observe how the line is curved (nonlinear) when the variables are plotted as continuous measures. After converting to ranks, the line becomes straight, forming a linear relation between X and Y [Figure 18.1(*b*)]. The bivariate distribution of ranks now lends itself nicely to the use of the Pearson formula. If the relation between X and Y is markedly curvilinear, for instance, a **U** or inverted **U,** conversion to ranks will not work. Nonetheless, if ranking the scores straightens out the plot, you have a choice of correlation formulas. You can use the Pearson formula presented in Chapter 15, or you can use a formula that is easier to work with: the **Spearman rank correlation,** symbolized as r_s. (Spearman symbolized his coefficient ρ_s. However, since ρ has come to symbolize a population correlation, modern usage favors r_s for the Spearman rank correlation.) The Spearman formula is basically a computationally simplified Pearson formula applied to rankings. The Spearman rank correlation is not a new type of correlation. Accordingly, the essential features of the correlation coefficient still apply:

1. The correlation can assume any value between -1 and $+1$.
2. The sign of the correlation reflects the direction of the correlation.
3. r_s^2 reflects the amount of shared variance between X and Y.
4. When testing the statistical significance of r_s, the null hypothesis is *usually* $\rho_s = 0$.
5. Tests of significance can be directional or nondirectional.

Spearman Rank Correlation

$$r_s = 1 - \frac{6 \, \Sigma D^2}{n_p(n_p^2 - 1)}$$ *(Formula 18.1)*

where,

D^2 = the squared difference between a pair of ranks

n_p = the number of *pairs*

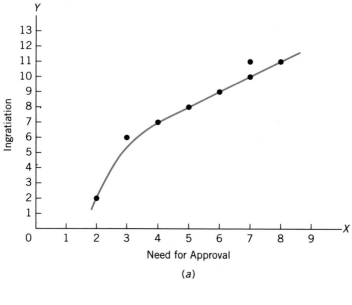

(a)

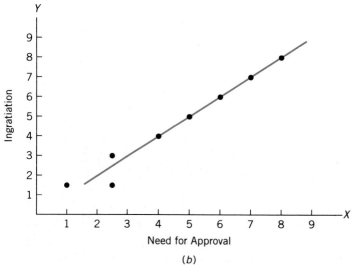

(b)

Figure 18.1 Observe how the nonlinear scatter plot in (a) becomes linear when the continuous measures have been changed to ranks in (b).

■   QUESTION   *Applying Formula 18.1 to the ranked data in Table 18.1, what is the correlation between Need for Approval and ingratiation?*

SOLUTION

Need for Approval		Ingratiation		
Subject	*Rank*	*Rank*	*D*	*D²*
S_1	1	1.5	−.5	.25
S_2	2.5	1.5	1	1
S_3	2.5	3	−.5	.25
S_4	4	4	0	0
S_5	5	5	0	0
S_6	6	6	0	0
S_7	7	7	0	0
S_8	8	8	0	0
			$\Sigma D = 0$	$\Sigma D^2 = 1.5$

$$\Sigma D^2 = 1.5$$

$$n_p = 8$$

$$r_s = 1 - \frac{6\,\Sigma D^2}{n_p(n_p^2 - 1)}$$

$$r_s = 1 - \frac{6(1.5)}{8(8^2 - 1)}$$

$$= 1 - \frac{9}{8(63)}$$

$$= 1 - .018$$

$$r_s = \mathbf{+.98}$$

■

Tied Ranks

When converting continuous measures to ranks, you frequently will encounter two or more subjects that have identical X scores or identical Y scores. When the ranks of two scores are tied, take the average of the two contiguous ranks. For example, in Table 18.1, Subjects 2 and 3 both scored a 7 on Need for Approval, which happens to be the second highest score, but you cannot simply assign a rank of 2 to both subjects. The customary method takes the average of the ranks 2 and 3 and assigns a 2.5 to each subject. The next highest score in the distribution will be assigned a rank of 4 (*not* 3). You should try to avoid tied ranks because ties have the effect of inflating the correlation. But if there are not too many ties and not too many long ties (three- or more-way ties), then the overestimation will be acceptably small (approximately .02; Welkowitz, Ewen, and Cohen, 1988). There may be no way to avoid tied ranks when you are converting continuous measures; the scores determine the ranks and you have no control over the scores. Of course, in those studies in which the investigator collects the data in the form of ranks, ties can be avoided. The following section presents an example in which data are ranked from the beginning of data collection.

The Planned Use of Ranks

Imagine the following hypothetical theory and study. A social psychologist believes that, in the course of a year, children in a classroom will form a dominance hierarchy, similar to the dominance hierarchies observed with chickens and baboons. Furthermore, the psychologist believes that the hierarchy is formed based on popularity, with the most popular child ascending to the top of the hierarchy and the least popular child stuck at the bottom of the hierarchy.

As a measure of popularity, the classroom teacher is asked to rank all of the children from the most to least popular. To measure dominance, the children are given the opportunity to play a new video game, but they must come to an agreement about which of them will go first, which will go second, and so on. The order in which the children play the game is taken as the dominance hierarchy. Table 18.2 presents the rankings for every child on both variables. A rank of 1 on Dominance is assigned to the most dominant child, a rank of 10 is assigned to the least dominant child. A rank of 1 is assigned to the most popular child; the child who receives a rank of 10 is considered the least popular.

TABLE 18.2 Using the Spearman Rank Formula to Compute the Correlation Between Dominance and Popularity

Child	Dominance	Popularity	D	D²
Laurie	1	1	0	0
Rick	7	8	−1	1
Jennifer	6	9	−3	9
Pamela	8	5	3	9
Clyde	3	2	1	1
Weegee	4	3	1	1
Jim	5	4	1	1
Shawn	10	6	4	16
Victoria	9	7	2	4
Gus	2	10	−8	64
			$\Sigma D = 0$	$\Sigma D^2 = 106$

$$r_s = 1 - \frac{6\,\Sigma D^2}{n_p(n_p^2 - 1)}$$

$$r_s = 1 - \frac{6(106)}{10(100 - 1)}$$

$$= 1 - \frac{636}{990}$$

$$= 1 - .642$$

$$r_s = +.36$$

Follow each step of the calculations of r_s in Table 18.2. The obtained r_s of +.36 is consistent with the hypothesis that the more popular the child, the more likely he or she will assume a dominant position in the class. Whether the relationship between popularity and dominance would hold using other measures of these variables—as well as another sample of children—would need to be tested in future research. However, before making any conclusions about this correlation, a test for statistical significance would need to be conducted, which is covered in a later section.

Another Example Using Planned Ranks

Another occasion in which subjects are ranked from the beginning of the study is when two judges provide rankings on *one* variable. For instance, two psychiatrists might rank hospitalized patients along the dimension of how disturbed the patients appear, with a rank of 1 given to the most disturbed person, a rank of 2 assigned to the next most disturbed person, and so on. Two gym teachers could rank students on athletic ability, with a 1 assigned to the student who is viewed as the best athlete, a 2 given to the next best athlete, and so on.

You may become confused when interpreting r_s when two judges provide rankings on one variable. The correlation reflects the *strength of association of the rankings of the two judges.* Alternatively stated, the correlation indicates the degree to which the judges agree as to how the subjects should be ranked on the variable of interest. If the correlation is high, you can be confident that the judges are consistent in ranking the subjects. If the correlation is low, you can infer that the judges are using different criteria when making their rankings; or perhaps, they are using the same criteria but they don't have access to the same information (e.g., maybe they have observed the subjects in different settings).

Here is an example of how *not* to interpret r_s when two judges provide rankings on one variable. Suppose two school psychologists rank a group of children from the most to the least friendly. The r_s turns out to be +.54. Do *not* conclude that there is a correlation between children's friendliness and the judges' rankings. The correct interpretation should be that the judges agree as to how the children would be ranked with respect to friendliness. The fact that the correlation is +.54 means that they show only a moderate degree of agreement. You should expect r_s to be high when two judges rank subjects on one variable. If the correlation drops below +.80, you should begin to wonder about the judging process.

Table 18.3 provides a hypothetical example of two judges ranking bodybuilders competing for the title of Mr. Too Wonderful. The obtained r_s of +.98 indicates that the judges are in strong agreement as to how the bodybuilders should be ranked.

Some Problems with Using Ranks

Converting continuous measures to ranks (i.e., changing an interval or ratio scale to an ordinal scale) is a procedure that is imposed on a researcher because the scatter plot reveals an unacceptable degree of nonlinearity. However, sometimes,

TABLE   18.3   **Using the Spearman Rank Formula to Correlate Rankings of Two Judges**

Bodybuilder	Judge 1	Judge 2	D	D²
Haney	1	1	0	0
Gaspari	2	2	0	0
Quinn	10	9	1	1
Robinson	6	7	−1	1
Paris	8	8	0	0
DeMay	4	4	0	0
Strydom	7	6	1	1
Christian	3	3	0	0
Kawak	9	10	−1	1
Grimm	5	5	0	0
			$\Sigma D = 0$	$\Sigma D^2 = 4$

$$r_s = 1 - \frac{6\,\Sigma D^2}{n_p(n_p^2 - 1)}$$

$$= 1 - \frac{6(4)}{10(100 - 1)}$$

$$= 1 - \frac{24}{990}$$

$$= 1 - .024$$

$$r_s = +.98$$

from the beginning of a study, an investigator will choose to use rankings. This practice is often due to the absence of a suitable continuous measure. There is a bias among behavioral scientists against using ranks; ranks are less sensitive measures than interval or ratio scales. The reason for the insensitivity is because the distance between, for instance, a rank of 2 and 3 may be very different from the distance between a rank of 7 and 8. In addition, a high rank may not necessarily correspond to a large amount of the variable being ranked. For example, you might rank five comedians on how funny they are to you. In your estimation, the comedian receiving the highest rank is funnier than the other four, but you may think none of them are very funny. The same point can be made about the lowest rank: the lowest-ranked comedian may be very funny but not as funny as the others.

Another disadvantage in using ranked data is that the statistical test for the correlation is not as powerful compared to a significance test performed on a correlation based on continuous measures. In other words, the test on ranks is less sensitive in detecting if the population correlation is different from 0. If you ever have the choice between using an interval scale or an ordinal scale, don't opt for rankings.

Testing the Statistical Significance of Spearman's r_s

When testing the statistical significance of r_s, use Table B.7 in the Appendix. This table specifies the critical values for testing the significance of Spearman's r_s. Note that the critical value is found by entering the left column using the *number of pairs* of scores (not $n_p - 2$). You can conduct a directional or nondirectional test of significance by using the appropriate column in Table B.7. The null hypothesis states that the population correlation, ρ_s, is 0. A significant r_s means that you reject the null hypothesis and retain the alternative hypothesis that $\rho_s \neq 0$. To reject the null hypothesis, the absolute value of the obtained r_s must equal or exceed the critical value found in Table B.7.

So that you can work through the steps of testing for significance, let's use the correlation obtained between dominance and popularity in Table 18.2. The r_s was found to be $+.36$. Setting alpha at .05, the critical value for a nondirectional test, with the number of pairs of scores 10, is about .65. The absolute value of the obtained value of $+.36$ does *not* exceed .65. Therefore, you should *not* reject the null hypothesis that the population correlation is 0. This means that there is no evidence that popularity and dominance are related. Keep in mind that testing for significance is an inferential process that you engage in when you want to make statements about the characteristics of populations. To test the significance of the correlation found between judges' rankings of bodybuilders would have little meaning.

18.4 THE POINT-BISERIAL CORRELATION COEFFICIENT

  The **point-biserial correlation** analysis is used when one variable is continuous and the second variable is dichotomous. Examples of dichotomous variables are male/female, married/single, Protestant/Jewish, and American/Asian. To use the point-biserial formula, the **dichotomous variable** must be *genuinely dichotomous*. Administering a personality questionnaire and designating highs and lows does *not* fit the definition of a truly dichotomous variable because the dichotomous designations are imposed on an underlying continuous measure. To compute the point-biserial correlation coefficient, each subject is assigned either a 0 or a 1, depending on which in two categories the subject belongs. Assigning numbers to

 dichotomous groups is called **dummy coding.** For example, if one variable is gender, all males are assigned a 0 and all females are assigned a 1. You could assign 3s and 4s if you like, but researchers use either 0s and 1s or 1s and 2s. The term *biserial* reflects the fact that there are two series of persons being observed on Y: those who are assigned a 0 on X and those assigned a 1 on X.

Suppose a researcher wants to examine the relation between gender and assertiveness, with assertiveness assessed using an interval scale. One series of subjects, males, receives a 0, and the other series, females, receives a 1. The X variable is gender. The Y variable is the continuous measure—assertiveness. The point-biserial correlation would thus be a measure of the strength of association between gender and assertiveness.

Point-Biserial Correlation

$$r_{pb} = \frac{\overline{Y}_1 - \overline{Y}_0}{s_y} \sqrt{\frac{n_1 n_0}{n(n-1)}}$$

(Formula 18.2)

where,

$\overline{Y}_1$ = the mean of the continuous measure for just those subjects assigned a 1

$\overline{Y}_0$ = the mean of the continuous measure for just those subjects assigned a 0

s_y = the standard deviation of *all* the scores on the continuous measure, i.e., irrespective of group designation

n_1 = the number of subjects assigned a 1 for the X variable

n_0 = the number of subjects assigned a 0 for the X variable

$n = n_1 + n_0$; total number of subjects

■ QUESTION *A clinical psychologist is interested in the relation between gender and the fear of making a long-term commitment to a member of the opposite sex. A continuous measure of fear of commitment is administered to males and females. Using the data presented in Table 18.4, compute the point-biserial correlation coefficient.*

SOLUTION In Table 18.4, the numbers in the Male and Female columns are scores on the Y, continuous measure. Note how the X, dichotomous variable (male/female), has been dummy-coded as male = 0 and female = 1.

Interpreting the Point-Biserial Correlation Coefficient

Students sometimes have difficulty interpreting the meaning of a point-biserial correlation coefficient, especially the direction of the correlation. As you examine the male and female columns in Table 18.4, remember that the scores across from one another are *not pairs* of scores. If the data were presented as pairs of scores, there would be two columns, one column of 0s and 1s, and one column with each subject's score on the continuous measure. Organized as pairs of scores, the data

TABLE   18.4   **Calculating the Point-Biserial Correlation Coefficient Between Sex and Fear of Commitment**

Male: (0)		Female: (1)	
S_1	22	S_8	13
S_2	14	S_9	16
S_3	20	S_{10}	11
S_4	8	S_{11}	12
S_5	11	S_{12}	4
S_6	9	S_{13}	3
S_7	9	S_{14}	6

$$r_{pb} = \frac{\overline{Y}_1 - \overline{Y}_0}{s_y} \sqrt{\frac{n_1 n_0}{n(n-1)}}$$

$\overline{Y}_0$ (mean of males) $= 13.29$

$\overline{Y}_1$ (mean of females) $= 9.29$

$s_y = 5.51$

n_0 (number of males) $= 7$

n_1 (number of females) $= 7$

n (total number of subjects) $= 14$

$$r_{pb} = \frac{9.29 - 13.29}{5.51} \sqrt{\frac{(7)(7)}{14(14-1)}}$$

$$= \frac{-4.00}{5.51} \sqrt{\frac{49}{182}}$$

$$= -.73\sqrt{.269}$$

$$= -.73\,(.52)$$

$$r_{pb} = \mathbf{-.38}$$

in Table 18.4 would look like this:

S	X	Y
S_1	0	22
S_2	0	14
S_3	0	20
⋮	⋮	⋮
S_8	1	13
S_9	1	16
S_{10}	1	11
⋮	⋮	⋮
S_{14}	1	6

You could, in fact, compute the correlation between a dichotomous and continuous measure using the Pearson raw score formula presented in Chapter 15; the answer would be the same. Indeed, just as the Spearman rank formula is a simplified application of the Pearson formula applied to ranks, the point-biserial formula is basically the Pearson formula applied when one variable is dichotomous.[2]

When interpreting the direction of the correlation, pay attention to which group members received the lower of the two dummy codes and which received the higher of the two codes. Recall that a positive correlation means that lower numbers on the X variable are associated with lower numbers of the Y variable, and, of course, higher numbers of the X variable are associated with higher numbers of the Y variable. The reverse is true for a negative correlation: lower numbers on one variable are associated with higher numbers on the second variable. For the worked problem in Table 18.4, a negative correlation was obtained; males were assigned the lower number (0) and females the higher number (1). A negative correlation means that *higher* numbers on the continuous measure are associated with the *lower* dummy code. Thus, the negative correlation means that higher fear of commitment scores are associated with males. Had the dummy codes been reversed and females assigned a 0 and males a 1, the correlation would have been $+.38$ instead of $-.38$. However, the interpretation of the correlation would have remained the same. An example of how you might verbally communicate the meaning of the obtained correlation is, "There is a .38 correlation between gender and fear of commitment, with males showing greater fear." Simply stating that there is a $+.38$ or $-.38$ correlation between gender and fear of commitment would confuse readers since they wouldn't necessarily know how you assigned the dummy codes. Also, another incorrect way of interpreting the correlation is to say, "There is a negative correlation of .38 between males and fear of commitment." Remember, the X variable is *gender*—that is—males *and* females, not males alone and not females alone.

Testing the Statistical Significance of the Point-Biserial Correlation Coefficient

The point-biserial correlation coefficient is tested for statistical significance using the same table of critical values as the Pearson r (Table B.6 in the Appendix). The degrees of freedom is $n-2$, where n is the total number of subjects. If the absolute value of the r_{pb} is equal to or exceeds the critical value, then the null hypothesis is rejected and the obtained correlation is significant. The null hypothesis states that the population correlation is zero. Test the correlation of $-.38$, which was obtained between gender and fear of commitment, using a nondirectional test with an alpha level of .05. Entering the appropriate column in Table B.6, note that the critical value for 12 df (14−2) is .532. Since the absolute value of $-.38$ fails to exceed .532, do *not* reject the null hypothesis. In other words, there is no evidence that there is a relation between gender and fear of commitment.

---

[2] As an exercise, use the Pearson raw score formula with the data in Table 18.4. The X variable is comprised of 0s and 1s assigned according to the gender of the subject. The Y variable is the scores for fear of commitment.

■ QUESTION *A psychologist hypothesizes an association between marital sta-tus and need for achievement. A questionnaire measuring need for achievement is administered to married and single people. Higher scores indicate a greater need for achievement. As you examine the following data set, notice that there are more single than married people in the sample. This is perfectly all right (within reason), since the point-biserial formula takes into account unequal numbers of subjects in each group. Married individuals are assigned a 0 and single individuals are assigned a 1. Test the significance of the correlation at the .05 level of significance and interpret the correlation.*

Marital Status	Need for Achievement
0	3
0	7
1	12
1	16
1	24
0	11
1	15
0	10
0	11
1	18
1	22
0	9
1	19
1	17

SOLUTION

$$r_{pb} = \frac{\overline{Y}_1 - \overline{Y}_0}{s_y} \sqrt{\frac{n_1 n_0}{n(n-1)}}$$

$\overline{Y}_0$ (mean of married subjects) = 8.5

$\overline{Y}_1$ (mean of single subjects) = 17.9

$s_y = 5.89$

$n_0 = 6$

$n_1 = 8$

$n = 14$

$$r_{pb} = \frac{17.9 - 8.5}{5.89} \sqrt{\frac{(8)(6)}{14(14-1)}}$$

$$= \frac{+9.4}{5.89} \sqrt{\frac{48}{182}}$$

$$= +1.60\sqrt{.264}$$

$$= +1.60(.51)$$

$$r_{pb} = \mathbf{+.82}$$

To test the significance of this correlation, turn to Table B.6 in the Appendix and find the critical value for an alpha of .05, with 12 *df.* The critical value is .532. The obtained correlation of .82 exceeds the tabled value; thus you reject the null hypothesis that the population correlation is zero. Since the correlation is positive, single individuals were assigned the higher dummy code, and higher scores on the continuous measure mean a greater need for achievement, interpret the correlation as follows: "There is a significant correlation between marital status and need for achievement, with single individuals showing a higher need for achievement, $r_{pb}(12) = +.82, p < .05$." ■

18.5   THE MANN-WHITNEY *U* TEST

The **Mann-Whitney *U* test** is the nonparametric alternative to the independent-groups *t* test. Any research design that has two independent groups of subjects is a candidate for the use of a Mann-Whitney *U* test. The decision to use a *t* test or the Mann-Whitney *U* test is based on whether you believe that you have met the assumptions for a *t* test. If there is reason to suspect that the population distributions depart radically from normality or that the variances of the populations are unequal, the Mann-Whitney *U* test is preferred to the *t* test. Therefore, the most common pathway to the Mann-Whitney *U* test is to collect data using an interval or ratio scale of measurement, discover that the assumptions for a *t* test have been violated, *convert the raw scores to ranks,* and perform the Mann-Whitney *U* test on the ranked data.

The Rationale Underlying the Mann-Whitney *U* Test

The experimental situation appropriate for the use of the Mann-Whitney *U* test is one in which there are two independent groups of subjects, with each subject providing one score. Once the decision is made to use the Mann-Whitney test, the scores from *both* groups are combined, forming one large group. The entire set of scores is listed from lowest to highest. Each score is then assigned its corresponding rank: the lowest is ranked 1, the next lowest is ranked 2, and so on.[3] Next, the subjects' ranks are placed back into the original two groups of the design.

Now, suppose that there is a treatment effect. How do you think the ranks would be distributed across the two treatment groups? You will find that one group will have many more ranks at the lower end of the scale in comparison to the second group. What if there is no treatment effect? Observe that the ranks look like they have been randomly distributed across conditions. Figure 18.2(*a*) illustrates a distribution of ranks when there is a treatment effect. Note that Con-

---

[3] When discussing the Spearman rank correlation, the highest score in the distribution was given a rank of 1. Now the lowest score is given a rank of 1. This is not meant to confuse you. Remember, any analysis using ranks will be unaffected by your chosen rule for ranking. The reason I'm reversing the rank assignments is so that you become accustomed to both methods of assigning ranks.

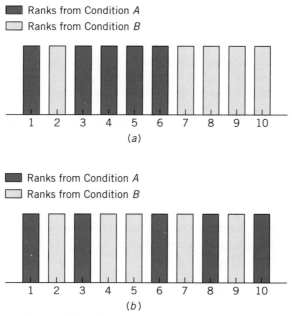

Figure 18.2 (*a*) More ranks of Condition *A* are shown at the lower end of the scale and more ranks from Condition *B* are at the higher end of the scale, which indicates the presence of a treatment effect. (*b*) The ranks of Conditions *A* and *B* fail to show a systematic grouping in either end of the scale. When there is no treatment effect, the ranks of Conditions *A* and *B* are intermixed and evenly distributed over the scale.

dition A has many more lower ranks than Condition B. The ranks are not evenly distributed between the two groups. Figure 18.2(*b*) illustrates a case in which there is no treatment effect. The ranks from one group do not systematically fall in either end of the scale. The ranks appear to be randomly distributed between the groups. The Mann-Whitney test helps us decide if the arrangement of ranks between the groups is likely due to chance. The hypothesis testing aspect of the Mann-Whitney *U* test will be discussed in later sections.

Calculating the Mann-Whitney *U* without a Formula

Worked Example

As a means for demonstrating how to calculate the Mann-Whitney *U*, let's evaluate a hypothetical program for increasing vocabulary. Ten subjects are randomly assigned to the experimental and control conditions (five subjects in each group). After two days of training, subjects are tested on the number of words they can define.

> **Step 1.** The vocabulary scores for each subject are listed according to experimental condition.

Condition A (*treatment*): 75, 4, 32, 140, 20
Condition B (*control*): 33, 49, 90, 100, 9

Step 2. Arrange all the scores from lowest to highest and rank them. Although the scores are combined into one list, you need to keep track of which score comes from which condition.

Score: 4, 9, 20, 32, 33, 49, 75, 90, 100, 140
Rank: 1, 2, 3, 4, 5, 6, 7, 8, 9, 10
Condition: A, B, A, A, B, B, A, B, B, A

Step 3. Now work only with the ranks and their respective group assignments. For each subject (rank) from Condition A, count the number of subjects (ranks) from Condition B that are *above* that rank. The number of ranks above a given rank will be referred to as points (Gravetter and Wallnau, 1988).

Rank: 1, 2, 3, 4, 5, 6, 7, 8, 9, 10
Condition: A, B, A, A, B, B, A, B, B, A
Points for
Condition A: 5   4 4   2   0

Step 4. Add all the points for Condition A: $5 + 4 + 4 + 2 + 0 = 15$. Fifteen is the U value for Condition A, symbolized U_A.

Step 5. Steps 3 and 4 are repeated for the ranks of Condition B.

Rank: 1, 2, 3, 4, 5, 6, 7, 8, 9, 10
Condition: A, B, A, A, B, B, A, B, B, A
Points for
Condition B: 4   2 2   1 1

$$U_B = 4 + 2 + 2 + 1 + 1 = 10$$

Step 6. Determine the Mann-Whitney U. The Mann-Whitney U value is the *smaller* of U_A and U_B—in this case—10. As a computational check, the number of subjects in Condition A, n_A, multiplied by the number of subjects in Condition B, n_B, should equal $U_A + U_B$. Thus, $U_A + U_B = 15 + 10 = n_A n_B = 5(5) = 25$.

Calculating the Mann-Whitney *U* with Formulas

The Mann-Whitney U value can be found without counting points, using formulas to determine U_A and U_B. With this method, all subjects are rank-ordered in the manner described in the preceding step list. For the subjects in Condition A, ΣR_A

is computed, the sum of the *ranks* (not the sum of points) is then computed for the subjects in Condition B, ΣR_B. The following presents formulas for U_A and U_B. Remember that n_A and n_B refer to the number of subjects in Conditions A and B, respectively.

Formula for Computing U_A

$$U_A = n_A n_B + \frac{n_A(n_A + 1)}{2} - \Sigma R_A$$

(Formula 18.3)

Formula for Computing U_B

$$U_B = n_A n_B + \frac{n_B(n_B + 1)}{2} - \Sigma R_B$$

(Formula 18.4)

Let's use the last worked problem to illustrate how these formulas are applied.

$$\text{Rank:} \quad 1, 2, 3, 4, 5, 6, 7, 8, 9, 10$$
$$\text{Condition:} \quad \text{A, B, A, A, B, B A, B, B, A}$$

$$\Sigma R_A = 1 + 3 + 4 + 7 + 10 = 25$$
$$n_A = 5$$
$$n_B = 5$$

$$U_A = n_A n_B + \frac{n_A(n_A + 1)}{2} - \Sigma R_A$$

$$U_A = 5(5) + \frac{5(5 + 1)}{2} - 25$$

$$= 25 + \frac{5(6)}{2} - 25$$

$$= 25 + 15 - 25$$

$$U_A = 15$$

Note that U_A is 15, the same value computed using the points method. Now use Formula 18.4 to determine U_B.

$$U_B = n_A n_B + \frac{n_B(n_B + 1)}{2} - \Sigma R_B$$

$$\Sigma R_B = 2 + 5 + 6 + 8 + 9 = 30$$

$$n_B = 5$$

$$U_B = 25 + \frac{5(6)}{2} - 30$$

$$= 25 + 15 - 30$$

$$U_B = \mathbf{10}$$

Again, note that the value of $U_B = 10$ is the same whether the point or formula method is used. The Mann-Whitney U is the smaller of U_A and U_B: $U = 10$.

Hypothesis Testing and the Mann-Whitney U

The Null and Alternative Hypotheses
If the null hypothesis is true, the two samples are taken from a single population. Under this condition, the distribution of ranks for Conditions A and B should not show a systematic difference. As noted previously, and illustrated in Figure 18.2, the ranks of both conditions will be *highly* intermixed when the null hypothesis is true. However, hypothesis testing is probabilistic and, therefore, it is possible for the distribution of ranks to show a systematic ordering—even when the null hypothesis is true. As with other significance tests, when using the Mann-Whitney U test, sampling error can lead you to commit a Type I error by erroneously rejecting the null hypothesis. The null hypothesis is a statement about the equivalence of population distributions:

H_0: The population distribution of A is the same as the population distribution of B.

The alternative hypothesis is a statement about the nonequivalence of the population distributions:

H_1: The population distribution of A is not the same as the population distribution of B.

Finding the Critical Value for U
The sampling distribution of U is based on the number of subjects in each group, n_A and n_B. Table B.9 a and b in the Appendix contains the critical values for various alpha levels and all combinations of n_A and n_B, provided the largest sample size of either group does not exceed 20 (more on this point later). Critical values are provided in lightface and boldface for directional and nondirectional tests, respectively. A dash mark in the table indicates that no decision is possible at the stated level of significance and values of n_A and n_B. For two-tailed tests, Table B.9

part *a* is used when alpha is set at .02 or .01. Table B.9 part *b* is consulted when conducting a two-tailed test and alpha is set at .10 or .05.

■   QUESTION   *What is the critical value for a two-tailed test when* $\alpha = .05$, $n_A = 9$, *and* $n_B = 12$?

SOLUTION   26.   ■

Comparing *U* to U_{crit}
In all other significance tests discussed up to this point, the null hypothesis is rejected when the obtained statistic *equals or exceeds* the critical value. The Mann-Whitney *U* test is different. To reject the null hypothesis, *U* must be *equal to or smaller than the critical value*. Consider the following example in which the distributions of Conditions A and B depart maximally.

Rank:	1, 2, 3, 4, 5, 6, 7, 8, 9, 10, 11
Condition:	A, A, A, A, A, B, B, B, B, B, B
Points:	6, 6, 6, 6, 6, 0, 0, 0, 0, 0, 0

Recalling that *U* is the smaller value of U_A and U_B, since U_B is 0, $U = 0$. Hence, the strongest evidence for rejecting the null hypothesis is when $U = 0$. The smaller the value of *U*, the more likely it is to be statistically significant.
　　Let's test *U* obtained from the vocabulary study. The critical value for $n_A = 5$, $n_B = 5$, $\alpha = .05$, two-tailed test is 2. The *U* value is 10. Since 10 is not smaller than 2, the null hypothesis is *not* rejected. You would thus conclude that the program for increasing vocabulary is no more effective than receiving no training.

Hypothesis Testing with a Large Sample Size

You will note that the Mann-Whitney *U* table does not provide critical values when either n_A or n_B is greater than 20. When either sample size exceeds 20, the sampling distribution of *U* approximates a normal distribution. In this instance, the standard normal curve can be used to identify critical values. These values have become familiar to you: 1.96 and 2.58 for a nondirectional test when alpha is .05 or .01, respectively. When using a large sample size, the *U* value is transformed to a *z* value, z_U, which is compared to the desired critical value of *z*. The old rule of comparison now applies. If $|z_U| > z_{crit}$, then the null hypothesis is rejected. Formula 18.5 is used to transform *U* to z_U.

The *U* to z_U Transformation Formula

$$z_U = \frac{U - (n_A n_B / 2)}{\sqrt{\dfrac{n_A n_B (n_A + n_B + 1)}{12}}} \quad \text{(Formula 18.5)}$$

Formula 18.5 would not be applied to the data from the vocabulary study because neither group has more than 20 subjects, but for the sake of illustration, we will use those data to illustrate the workings of the transformation formula.

$$z_U = \frac{10 - 5(5)/2}{\sqrt{\dfrac{5(5)(5 + 5 + 1)}{12}}}$$

$$= \frac{-2.5}{\sqrt{275/12}}$$

$$z_U = -.52$$

The z_{crit} value for $\alpha = .05$, two-tailed test, is 1.96. The $|z_U|$ of $-.52$ does not exceed 1.96. Therefore, the null hypothesis is not rejected.

Ranking Tied Scores

When using the Mann-Whitney U test, resolving tied ranks is handled in the same manner as the Spearman rank correlation analysis. Briefly, tied ranks are resolved by taking the average of the ranks. Each tied score is assigned the same averaged rank.

Several tied ranks within a condition do not present a problem for the Mann-Whitney U test. However, when a rank from Condition A is tied with a rank from Condition B, and the number of ties is large, the Mann-Whitney U test becomes excessively conservative. A correction factor can be applied in these instances, but the procedure is rather complex. The interested reader is referred to Kirk (1984) or Siegel and Castellan (1988).

18.6 THE WILCOXON SIGNED-RANKS TEST

The **Wilcoxon signed-ranks test** is the nonparametric alternative to the paired-observations t test. The research design is a repeated-measures design in which one group of subjects receives two treatments. The treatments can be two experimental conditions, an experimental and control condition, or a pretest and post-test. The Wilcoxon signed-ranks test assumes that the dependent variable is a continuous measure, even though the analysis is performed on ranks. No assumptions are made regarding equal variances and normally distributed scores in the population. The null hypothesis states that there is no treatment effect.

Calculating the Wilcoxon *T*

The Wilcoxon signed-ranks test is performed on the rankings of *difference scores*. In a repeated-measures design, a difference score is a single subject's score in Condition B, subtracted from his or her score in Condition A. The difference scores are ranked, from smallest to largest, based on the *absolute value* of the scores.

Thus, a score of -72 is ranked higher than a score of 2. Next, the ranks of the positive-difference scores are placed in one group and the ranks of the negative-difference scores are placed in a second group. The ranks of the positive-difference scores are summed, ΣR_{pos}, and the ranks of the negative-difference scores are summed, ΣR_{neg}. Of the values of ΣR_{pos} and ΣR_{neg}, the one that is smaller is the Wilcoxon statistic, T. The T value is compared to a critical value found in Table B.10 in the Appendix to test the null hypothesis. The steps for calculating T are shown in the following worked example.

Worked Example

A cognitive psychologist would like to compare two techniques for enhancing the recollection of nonsense syllables. In Condition A, subjects are told to study a list of syllables by repeating them over and over (Repetition). In Condition B, the same subjects are told to examine a different list of nonsense syllables, and to try and associate them with a common word (Association). Half of the subjects receive the Repetition method first; the remaining half of the subjects receive the Association method first. The dependent variable is the number of nonsense syllables correctly recalled. Assume that there is some reason to suspect that the population assumptions for a paired-observations t test have been violated and that the Wilcoxon signed-ranks test is the analysis of choice.

NUMBER CORRECT

Condition

Subject	A	B	Difference	Rank
S_1	32	27	$+5$	6
S_2	40	44	-4	-5
S_3	12	12	0	1.5
S_4	2	16	-14	-10
S_5	56	53	$+3$	4
S_6	16	6	$+10$	8
S_7	29	22	$+7$	7
S_8	49	20	$+29$	11
S_9	20	21	-1	-3
S_{10}	15	15	0	-1.5
S_{11}	13	2	$+11$	9

Step 1. Arrange the data in a table and compute a difference score for each subject.

Step 2. Arrange the difference scores from smallest to largest and rank these scores based on their absolute values. Handle tied ranks in the usual manner—take the average of the ranks. Notice that ranks associated with negative-difference scores have a negative sign in front of them. This is simply to remind you which ranks are assigned to the positive group and which ranks are assigned to the negative group.

Step 3. Group all the ranks associated with a positive-difference score. Form a second group of ranks that correspond to negative-difference scores. If there is a tie between two subjects with *difference scores of* 0, assign one rank to the first group, the other rank to the second group. Note that two subjects received a difference score of 0, and both were assigned a rank of 1.5; one is placed in group one, the other in group two. If there is an odd number of ties, discard one of them and divide the remaining tied ranks equally among the groups. *This method only applies to ties based on difference scores of* 0. If two positive-difference scores are the same, their ranks are averaged, and both ranks are assigned to the positive group. The same rule holds for ties based on negative-difference scores.

Step 4.   Sum the ranks of each group. When adding, *do not consider ranks with negative signs as negative numbers.* Again, the negative signs before ranks are only to aid you in arranging the ranks into their appropriate groups.

$$\Sigma R_{pos}: \quad 1.5 + 4 + 6 + 7 + 8 + 9 + 11 = 46.5$$
$$\Sigma R_{neg}: \quad 1.5 + 3 + 5 + 10 = 19.5$$

Step 5.   The value T is the smaller of ΣR_{pos} and ΣR_{neg}. Thus, $T = \mathbf{19.5}$.

Hypothesis Testing and the Wilcoxon Signed-Ranks Test

The Null and Alternative Hypotheses
Similar to the Mann-Whitney U test, the null and alternative hypotheses for the Wilcoxon signed-ranks test are statements regarding the equivalence and non-equivalence of the population distributions.

H_0:   The population distribution of A is the same as the population distribution of B.

The alternative hypothesis is a statement about the nonequivalence of the population distributions:

H_1:   The population distribution of A is not the same as the population distribution of B.

Finding the Critical Value for T and Deciding Whether to Reject the Null Hypothesis
The critical values for the T statistic are found in Table B.10 of the Appendix. T_{crit} is found by locating the number in the left column that corresponds to the number of subjects in the study. Move to the column that specifies the desired alpha level. The null hypothesis is rejected if T is less than or equal to T_{crit}.

For the worked example, it was found that $T = 19.5$. Since there were eleven subjects in the study, the critical value, assuming $\alpha = .05$, is 10. The obtained value of T is *greater* than T_{crit}: $19.5 > 10$. Therefore, do not reject the null hypothesis. In conclusion, there is no evidence for the differential effectiveness of the Repetition versus the Association techniques.

The Wilcoxon Signed-Ranks Test with Large Samples

Table B.10 in the Appendix provides critical values for the Wilcoxon T statistic for sample sizes up to 50. When a sample size is greater than 50, T is transformed to a z value. The z_{obt} is compared to a critical value of z found using the z table (Table B.1 the Appendix). You have made extensive use of the z table throughout this text. Recall that when the z table is used to determine critical values, the z_{crit} that corresponds to $\alpha = .05$ is 1.96, when $\alpha = .01$, $z_{crit} = 2.58$, and when $\alpha = .10$, $z_{crit} = 1.645$, for two-tailed tests. The Wilcoxon T statistic is transformed to a z value by Formula 18.6.

Formula for the Wilcoxon Signed-Ranks Test for Large Sample Sizes

$$z_{obt} = \frac{T - [n(n + 1)/4]}{\sqrt{\dfrac{n(n + 1)(2n + 1)}{24}}}$$ (Formula 18.6)

where,

$n = $ the number of subjects in the analysis

When using Formula 18.6, all subjects that have a difference score that is 0 are excluded from the analysis. This practice will not affect z_{crit} but n will equal *the number of subjects that are used in the analysis.* When performing a nondirectional test of the null hypothesis, if the absolute value of z_{obt} is greater than z_{crit}, H_0 is rejected.

So that you can examine the computational steps involved in Formula 18.6, assume that T equals 17 and $n = 60$.

$$z_{obt} = \frac{17 - [60(60 + 1)/4]}{\sqrt{\dfrac{60(60 + 1)(2 \times 60 + 1)}{24}}}$$

$$= \frac{17 - 3660/4}{\sqrt{(3660)(121)/24}}$$

$$= \frac{-898}{\sqrt{442860/24}}$$

$$= \frac{-898}{\sqrt{18452.50}}$$

$$= \frac{-898}{135.84}$$

$$z_{obt} = \mathbf{-6.61}$$

If alpha is set at .05, the critical value for z is 1.96. The obtained value of z is −6.61 and its absolute value exceeds the critical value of 1.96. As a consequence, the null hypothesis is rejected.

Box 18.1 reports an interesting study that examines how infants' attention to an adult's speech is influenced by how closely the adult's lip movements correspond to their spoken words. The author uses a repeated-measures design and applies the Wilcoxon signed-ranks test to the ranked data.

BOX 18.1

Do Infants Notice the Difference Between Lip Movements and Speech Sounds?

I have a friend who is slowly losing her hearing. She has noticed that she increasingly relies on observing the lip movements of a speaker to help her process auditory information. All of us have experienced a similar phenomenon. Think back to the last time you had a conversation with someone in a very noisy environment. Didn't you pay particular attention to the lip movements of the person to whom you were listening? Even under normal listening conditions, we do use lip movements in processing speech. So automatic is this process that we are scarcely aware of it. We need only watch a Japanese karate movie to realize how much we take the congruence between lip movements and speech for granted.

Developmental psychologists have found that our awareness of the synchrony between speech sounds and lip movements is evident by the age of 6 months. Developmental psychologists are frequently interested in the earliest age a behavioral skill emerges. Dodd (1979) conducted a study to see if 10- to 16-week-old babies are able to tell the difference between a speaker who shows synchronous speech and lip movements and a speaker who shows a lack of congruence between speech and lip movements.

STUDY METHOD

Infants were placed in a soundproof room with a window through which they could see an adult speaking to them through a microphone. In the Synchrony condition, the sound of the adult's voice was direct, a perfect congruence between lip movements and auditory sound. In the Asynchrony condition, the same

infants viewed an adult speaking to them with a 400-millisecond delay between lip movements and speech sounds. The question was, "Are infants this young able to tell the difference between synchronous and asynchronous speech?" If infants are unable to tell the difference, irrespective of experimental condition, they should attend to the speaker approximately the same amount of time. On the other hand, if these infants are able to discriminate between the two conditions, it should be reflected in the amount of time they spend looking at the adult in each condition. Since the point of the study was to see if the infants could make the discrimination, no prediction was made regarding which condition would lead to a greater amount of attentional deployment. In fact, you could speculate that the children would spend more time attending to the synchronous adult because it is a familiar experience. Equally plausible, however, is the hypothesis that children would attend more to the asynchronous adult due to novelty. Clearly, this repeated-measures design requires a nondirectional hypothesis test.

The dependent variable was the percentage of time the child spent looking at the speaker.

DATA ANALYSIS AND RESULTS

Although the percentage of time looking at the speaker is a reasonable way of measuring attention, Dodd was not so confident in treating her dependent variable as an interval or ratio scale of measurement. She was uncertain, for example, about whether the difference between attending 20 percent and 30 percent of the time reflects the same amount of difference as attend-

PERCENTAGE OF TIME ATTENDING

Subject	Asynchrony	Synchrony	Difference	Rank
S_1	50.4	20.3	30.1	10
S_2	87.0	17.0	70.0	12
S_3	25.1	6.5	18.6	6
S_4	28.5	25.0	3.5	3
S_5	26.9	5.4	21.5	8
S_6	36.6	29.2	7.4	5
S_7	1.0	2.9	-1.9	-1
S_8	43.8	6.6	37.2	11
S_9	44.2	15.8	28.4	9
S_{10}	10.4	8.3	2.1	2
S_{11}	29.9	34.0	-4.1	-4
S_{12}	27.7	8.0	19.7	7

$$\Sigma R_{pos} = 10 + 12 + 6 + 3 + 8 + 5 + 11 + 9 + 2 + 7 = 73$$

$$\Sigma R_{neg} = 1 + 4 = 5$$

$$\alpha = .05$$

$$T_{crit} = 13$$

$$T = \mathbf{5}$$

ing 80 percent and 90 percent of the time. Because Dodd had more confidence that the *rankings* of the differences in looking indicate an *order* of difference in attending, she decided to use a Wilcoxon signed-ranks test instead of a paired-observations *t* test.

Since the *T* of 5 is *less than* the T_{crit} of 13, the null hypothesis is rejected. You would, therefore, conclude that infants 10–16 weeks old are able to tell the difference between speech and lip movements that are congruent as opposed to incongruent.

18.7   USING NONPARAMETRIC TESTS

In comparison to parametric tests, nonparametric tests have certain advantages. Nonparametric tests can, and should be used when population assumptions for a parametric test are grossly violated. In addition, nonparametric tests require only that data be scaled according to ranks. Nonetheless, despite these advantages, nonparametric tests are not nearly as popular as parametric tests. Why?

First, nonparametric tests are not as powerful as parametric tests. The probability of detecting a treatment effect is lower than when using a parametric test. And, it follows that there is a greater probability of making a Type II error when using a nonparametric test.[4]

---

[4] Zimmerman and Zumbo (1989) have shown that independent and paired-observations *t* tests *applied to ranks* are equivalent to the use of a Mann-Whitney *U* or Wilcoxon signed-ranks test. Under these conditions, the probabilities of Type I and Type II errors are the same whether we use a parametric or nonparametric test. However, this is not to say that a nonparametric test with *ordinal* data is equivalent to a parametric test applied to *interval* data.

Second, when using complex factorial designs, there is no nonparametric test that yields as much information as a two- or three-way ANOVA.

Third, two-sample parametric tests analyze population differences between means. Two population distributions can vary in a number of ways: central tendency, variability, skewness, and so on. To test the null hypothesis that $\mu_1 = \mu_2$ requires that other aspects of the population distributions be similar. Since nonparametric procedures do not require such assumptions, they are less specific in what they tell us.

Fourth, statisticians remind us that parametric tests are relatively robust with respect to the violation of population assumptions. Researchers are told that they should become suspicious of the use of parametric analyses when there are gross violations of population assumptions: population distributions that depart radically from normality and violations of homogeneity of variances. But how "gross" do the violations have to be to justify using the less powerful nonparametric tests? There are no clear-cut rules for when to transform the continuous-measure dependent variable to ranks. Given this unclarity about exactly when to use a nonparametric test, researchers tend to lean heavily toward the application of parametric analyses. Of course, when data are collected using an ordinal scale, a nonparametric test is routinely performed.

SUMMARY

Statisticians have developed an array of nonparametric tests that have become useful additions to parametric significance tests. This chapter addressed four nonparametric tests.

The Spearman rank correlation is a simplified Pearson formula applied to ordinal data. This analysis can be used when the scatter diagram of X and Y shows a nonlinear relation. Converting scores to ranks often "straightens out" the scatter plot, thus allowing for the use of the Spearman rank correlation analysis. The Spearman rank analysis can also be used when data are collected using an ordinal scale, one example being the application of r_s to judges' rankings of some variable.

The point-biserial correlation is used when one variable is genuinely dichotomous and the second variable is continuous. Examples of dichotomous variables are gender, religion, and marital status. The null hypothesis for both the Spearman and point-biserial correlation analyses is typically $\rho = 0$.

The Mann-Whitney U test is the nonparametric alternative to the independent-groups t test. When the population assumptions for using a t test are violated, the Mann-Whitney U test can be applied to data transformed to ranks. The null hypothesis states that the population distributions are the same. The alternative hypothesis states that the population distributions are not the same. When the null hypothesis is true, the rankings of the treatment groups are randomly distributed across the ordinal scale. When the null hypothesis is false, one of the treatment groups will show a preponderance of lower ranks. Of course, with any hypothesis test, due to sampling error, it is possible to observe a systematic difference between samples, even though the null hypothesis is true. In this instance, a Type I error will be committed.

The Wilcoxon signed-ranks test is the nonparametric alternative to the paired-observations t test. The Wilcoxon test is performed on the ranks of difference scores. Similar to the Mann-Whitney U test, the null hypothesis states that the population distribution of ranks is the same for both treatment conditions.

Although nonparametric tests have their place in inferential statistics, the decision to use a nonparametric test is not lightly made. Nonparametric tests are not as powerful as parametric tests. They should only be used when data are collected using a nominal or ordinal scale, or when the population assumptions for using a parametric test are violated.

KEY FORMULAS FOR CHAPTER 18

Spearman Rank Correlation

$$r_s = 1 - \frac{6 \, \Sigma D^2}{n_p(n_p^2 - 1)}$$

(Formula 18.1)

Point-Biserial Correlation

$$r_{pb} = \frac{\overline{Y}_1 - \overline{Y}_0}{s_y} \sqrt{\frac{n_1 n_0}{n(n-1)}}$$

(Formula 18.2)

Formula for Computing U_A

$$U_A = n_A n_B + \frac{n_A(n_A + 1)}{2} - \Sigma R_A$$

(Formula 18.3)

Formula for Computing U_B

$$U_B = n_A n_B + \frac{n_B(n_B + 1)}{2} - \Sigma R_B$$

(Formula 18.4)

The U to z_U Transformation Formula

$$z_U = \frac{U - (n_A n_B/2)}{\sqrt{\dfrac{n_A n_B(n_A + n_B + 1)}{12}}}$$

(Formula 18.5)

Formula for the Wilcoxon Signed-Ranks Test for Large Sample Sizes

$$z_{\text{obt}} = \frac{T - [n(n+1)/4]}{\sqrt{\dfrac{n(n+1)(2n+1)}{24}}}$$

(Formula 18.6)

WORK PROBLEMS

1. The following represents a bivariate distribution, using continuous measures. Convert these scores to ranks. Assign a rank of 1 to the lowest score.

X	Y
3	7
2	2
4	4
9	12
8	8
4	2

2. For the data presented in Problem 1, assume that X represents an experimental group and Y represents a control group. You plan to conduct a Mann-Whitney U test. Convert the scores to ranks.

3. For the data in Problem 1, assume that a repeated-measures design is used. You plan to conduct a Wilcoxon signed-ranks test. Convert each subject's scores to a rank.

4. A researcher is interested in seeing if there is a relationship between Need for Affiliation and Fear of Criticism. Questionnaires that measure each trait are administered to eight subjects. For the following data set:
   a. Draw the scatter plot of the continuous measures.
   b. Convert the scores to ranks.
   c. Draw the scatter plot based on ranks.
   d. Compute the Spearman rank correlation.
   e. State the null and alternative hypotheses.
   f. Test for significance at the 5 percent level.

	Need for Affiliation		Fear of Criticism	
Subject	Score	Rank	Score	Rank
S_1	16		40	
S_2	14		35	
S_3	14		30	
S_4	12		18	
S_5	10		14	
S_6	8		13	
S_7	9		12	
S_8	4		4	

5. A social psychologist hypothesizes a relationship between physical attractiveness and popularity. Ten high-school students are ranked on each variable. For the following ranks:
   a. Compute the Spearman rank correlation.
   b. State the null and alternative hypotheses.
   c. Test for significance at the 5 percent level.
   d. Interpret the findings.

Subject	Physical Attractiveness Rank	Popularity Rank
S_1	1	1
S_2	2	3
S_3	5	2
S_4	3	4
S_5	4	5
S_6	7	7
S_7	9	6
S_8	6	8
S_9	8	9
S_{10}	10	10

6. A sociologist is interested in the relation between political affiliation and attitudes toward military intervention in Central America. The measure of attitudes is continuous, with 1 meaning "no intervention" and 10 meaning "aggressive intervention."
   a. Compute r_{pb}.
   b. State the null and alternative hypotheses.
   c. Test for significance at the 5 percent level.
   d. Interpret the correlation.
   e. State how much of the variance in attitudes is due to political affiliation.

Democrat	Republican
1	10
4	7
7	8
3	6
2	9
1	5
1	10

7. A teacher has developed a mathematical ability test and believes that the answer to one question is correlated with the total score on the test. The teacher assigns a 0 if the answer is correct and a 1 if the answer is incorrect.
   a. Calculate r_{pb}.
   b. State the null and alternative hypotheses.
   c. Test for significance at the 5 percent level.
   d. Interpret the correlation.

Subject	Question	Test Score
1	0	36
2	0	39
3	1	16
4	1	14
5	0	22
6	1	26
7	1	9
8	1	7
9	0	30
10	1	11

8. In a dog show, rankings are based on body shape and posture. For the following results:
    a. Compute r_s.
    b. State the null and alternative hypotheses.
    c. Test for significance at the 5 percent level.
    d. Interpret the findings.

Dog	Posture	Body Shape
1	1	2
2	2	1
3	3	3
4	7	5.5
5	9	7
6	4	9
7	5	5.5
8	6	8
9	8	4

9. Twelve medical students are ranked on their clinical and written examination performance over the past year.
    a. Calculate the Spearman rank correlation.
    b. State the null and alternative hypotheses.
    c. Test for significance at the 5 percent level.
    d. Interpret the findings.

Student	Clinical	Written
1	4	2
2	12	10
3	1	1
4	7	5
5	8	8
6	2	3
7	11	9
8	3	4
9	9	7
10	6	6
11	5	11
12	10	12

10. A child psychologist hypothesizes a relationship between when a child first walks (months) and whether the child has an older sibling. For the following data set:
    a. Calculate r_{pb}.
    b. State the null and alternative hypotheses.
    c. Test for significance at the 5 percent level.
    d. Interpret the correlation.

Older Sibling (0)	No Older Sibling (1)
10.9	11.6
11.2	13.7
11.4	15.2
12.4	10.9
10.3	16.0
10.0	15.8
12.0	12.8
11.9	10.8
13.2	14.7
11.4	15.0

11. A psychologist hypothesizes a relationship between gender and attitudes toward legalized abortion. The range of values measuring attitudes is from 1−strongly opposed to 10−strongly in favor. Males = 0, females = 1.
    a. Compute the appropriate correlation coefficient.
    b. State the null and alternative hypotheses.
    c. Test for significance at the 5 percent level.
    d. Interpret the correlation.

Subject	Gender	Attitudes about Abortion
1	0	3
2	0	6
3	1	9
4	0	4
5	1	1
6	1	10
7	1	8
8	0	3
9	1	5
10	0	9

12. Eight students are ranked by a faculty member based on their performance in statistics class. A year later, the same students are ranked on the quality of their senior thesis.
    a. Compute r_s.
    b. State the null and alternative hypotheses.
    c. Test for significance at the 5 percent level.
    d. State the amount of variance in the quality of the papers due to performance in the statistics class.

Statistics	Senior Thesis
1	1
3	2
5	4
8	8
6	6
7	3
2	7
4	5

13. A clinical psychology program has two training tracks: behavioral therapy and psychoanalysis. First-year graduate students are randomly assigned to these tracks. A professor wonders if there is a difference between the tracks in how well students learn basic interviewing skills. After one year of training, the professor ranks *all* the students as to how well they demonstrate fundamental interviewing techniques. For the following data set, perform the appropriate nonparametric test. Higher ranks indicate better interviewing skills.
    a. State the null and alternative hypotheses.
    b. Compute the appropriate test statistic.
    c. Test for significance.
    d. Interpret the findings.

Behavioral Therapy	Psychoanalysis
12	10
9	2
11	3
8	1
4	5
7	6

14. When conducting a Mann-Whitney U Test when one of the sample sizes is greater than 20, what should you do, and why?

15. Suppose you are about to perform a Wilcoxon signed-ranks test, and you notice that three subjects out of twenty have a difference score of 0. What should you do when it comes time to separate positive and negative ranks?

16. Assume that you are about to perform a Mann-Whitney U test. You look at the ordering of ranks among the two groups and observe that the rankings indicate that "the null hypothesis is as wrong as it can be." What number will the smaller ΣR be? What will U equal?

17. Perform a Mann-Whitney U test on the following ranked data. Even though sample sizes are small, use the z_U formula. Let $\alpha = .05$.

R_A	R_B
1	2
3	6
4	7
5	8
9	10

18. A high-school counselor wonders if the type of music played during lunch hour influences the speed with which students eat. In one condition, soft, New Age music is piped through the sound system. In a second condition, Rap music is played. Assume that relevant aspects of the setting are controlled (e.g., menu, portions, seating arrangements, etc.). Six students are observed for 5 minutes, and the dependent variable is the average number of bites per minute. Since this is a repeated-measures design, half of the subjects listen to the New Age music first and half of the subjects listen to the Rap music first. The

dependent variable is measured during each experimental condition. Perform a Wilcoxon signed-ranks test on the following data. Set alpha at .05.

MUSIC	
New Age	Rap
2	6
1	6
3	2
4	8
3	6
1	5

19. Assume that the data from Problem 18 are obtained using an independent-groups design. Perform a Mann-Whitney U test, with $\alpha = .05$.

20. For each of the following situations, specify which statistic you would compute.
   a. Design: independent groups
      Data: ordinal
   b. Design: repeated measures
      Data: ordinal
   c. Design: correlational
      Data: nonlinear relation between X and Y
   d. Design: correlational
      Data: X is nominal, Y is continuous
   e. Design: correlational
      Data: X and Y are ordinal

21. Perform a Wilcoxon signed-ranks test using the formula for large samples. $T = 14$ and $n = 55$. Set alpha at .05 and test H_0.

Work Problems for the Computer

22. A cardiologist is testing the effectiveness of propranolol versus a diuretic for lowering systolic blood pressure. Seven subjects are started on propranolol and eight subjects are started on a diuretic. After 90 days, all subjects switch to the other drug. The systolic blood pressure readings for each subject are provided in the following. (This data set could be analyzed with a dependent-samples t test. However, for the sake of practice, use a nonparametric test.)
   a. State the null and alternative hypotheses.
   b. Compute the appropriate nonparametric test statistic.
   c. What is the critical value for $\alpha = .05$?
   d. Interpret the findings.

Subject	Propranolol	Diuretic
S_1	127	140
S_2	116	130
S_3	120	150
S_4	132	132
S_5	110	111

(continued)

Subject	Propranolol	Diuretic
S_6	125	120
S_7	131	138
S_8	129	148
S_9	134	149
S_{10}	119	118
S_{11}	116	149
S_{12}	119	121
S_{13}	116	124
S_{14}	144	152
S_{15}	115	126

23. Using the data from Problem 22, assume that the design is an independent-groups design. Perform a Mann-Whitney U test on the data. Set alpha at .05.

APPENDIX

A

Some Basic Concepts of Probability

A.1 THE LANGUAGE OF PROBABILITY

 The **probability** of an event occurring can range from 0 to 1. Zero probability means that the event cannot occur, whereas a probability of 1 means that the event is certain to occur. Since probability is essentially a proportion, there is no such thing as a negative probability. There are several ways that a researcher can phrase a probability statement. Suppose you want to state the probability that one toss of a coin will yield a head. The probability of heads can be stated as 1/2, .50 (1 ÷ 2), or 50/50. Statisticians typically use the decimal designation for probabilities (e.g., .50). Statisticians also state probabilities in terms of percentages. For example, "There is a 5 percent chance of selecting a score greater than 23 from this distribution" (5 chances out of 100). No matter which way probability is stated, the likelihood of an event occurring lies on a continuum from virtual certainty that the event will *not* occur to virtual certainty that the event *will* occur.

A.2 SAMPLING WITH AND WITHOUT REPLACEMENT

Sampling with replacement is a method of sampling wherein a member of a population is randomly selected and then returned to the population before the next member is selected. This is not a difficult concept. Suppose you want to know the probability of selecting a red card from a deck of playing cards. Since half of the cards are red and half of the cards are black, the probability of selecting a red card at random is .50. If you return the selected card to the deck, the probability of selecting another red card is still .50. However, suppose you do not return the card to the deck and ask, "Now what is the probability of selecting a red card at random?" Since there are now more black cards than red cards in the deck, the probability of selecting a red card is *not* .50 (it's a bit less). In the latter example, you have sampled without replacement. Sampling without replacement is a method of sampling in which a member of a population is not returned to the population before selecting another member of the population.

Sampling with or without replacement has obvious implications for the probability of occurrence of subsequent events. The distinction between sampling with replacement versus sampling without replacement is also important to mathematical statisticians interested in hypothesis testing. The mathematical foundation of statistical tests is based on the assumption of sampling with replacement.

Later in this appendix, worked examples will show how the two methods of sampling influence the solution of probability problems.

A.3 A PRIORI AND A POSTERIORI APPROACHES TO PROBABILITY

 The **a priori** or **classical approach** to probability is based on logic alone. There is no need to collect data when using the a priori approach.

A Priori Probability

$$p(A) = \frac{\text{number of events classifiable as } A}{\text{total number of possible events}} \quad \textit{(Formula A.1)}$$

The symbol $p(A)$ is read as, "the probability of A occurring" or "the probability of the occurrence of A." The entire equation can be read as, "The probability of A occurring is equal to the number of events classifiable as A, divided by the total number of possible events."

A.4   AN EXAMPLE OF THE A PRIORI APPROACH TO PROBABILITY

What is the probability of randomly selecting a face card from a deck of playing cards? First, how many events (cards) are classifiable as A? There are 12 face cards in a deck of cards. Next, what is the total number of possible events? The total number of cards in a deck is 52. Thus,

$$p(A) = \frac{\text{number of cards classifiable as face cards}}{\text{total number of cards in the deck}} = \frac{12}{52} = .23$$

The probability of randomly selecting a face card from a playing deck is .23. Now how would you approach this problem within the a posteriori framework?

A.5   AN EXAMPLE USING THE A POSTERIORI APPROACH TO PROBABILITY

 The a **posteriori approach** to probability is an empirical approach to probability because it requires the collection of data. Using the preceding example, how would you determine the probability of selecting a face card? The formula for the a posteriori probability is given in Formula A.2.

A Posteriori Probability

$$p(A) = \frac{\text{number of times } A \text{ has occurred}}{\text{total number of occurrences}} \quad \textit{(Formula A.2)}$$

Formula A.2 clearly mandates the collection of data. Therefore, you would have to randomly select a card, return it to the deck, select another card, return it to the deck, and continue this process many times. Suppose you do this 10,000 times and find that a face card has occurred 2500 times. Using Formula A.2,

$$p(A) = \frac{\text{number of times a face card occurred}}{\text{total number of occurrences}} = \frac{2500}{10000} = .25$$

Note that the probability of a face card occurring is .25—close—but not identical to the .23 probability determined by the a priori method. If you had taken an infinite number of occurrences (samples), the a posteriori approach would have yielded a probability of .23.

For the foregoing problem of determining the probability of selecting a face card, nothing is gained by using the a posteriori approach because reason alone (the a priori method) could solve the problem. However, in actual research, the a priori approach is often inappropriate because, without collecting data, you do not know the number of events classifiable as A (the numerator of the a priori formula). For example, suppose you would like to know the probability that someone will be hospitalized with a diagnosis of depression. There is no way to use logic alone to determine the answer. You would have to take a random sample (preferably a large one) of all hospitalized patients and observe the proportion of patients who received a diagnosis of depression. You could then make a statement about the probability that a hospitalized patient receives a diagnosis of depression.

Since the purpose of this appendix is to provide a brief introduction to some basic concepts of probability, considering only the a priori approach to probability will suffice.

A.6 USING THE ADDITION RULE WHEN EVENTS ARE MUTUALLY EXCLUSIVE

 The **addition rule** is used to determine the probability of occurrence of one of many possible events. It is typically applied when the question has the word "or" in it. For example, "What is the probability of rolling a die and obtaining a 4 *or* a 6?; What is the probability of drawing a club *or* a heart from a deck of cards?" Here, the addition rule is illustrated only in the context of mutually exclusive events.

 Mutually exclusive events occur when one event precludes the occurrence of another event. For example, when you role a die once, it is impossible to obtain a 4 and a 6—one precludes the other. When you select a card from the deck, it cannot have more than one suit. The formula for the addition rule when two events are mutually exclusive follows.

> ### Addition-Rule Formula for Two Mutually Exclusive Events
>
> $$p(A \text{ or } B) = p(A) + p(B) \qquad \textit{(Formula A.3)}$$

Formula A.3 is read as, "The probability of occurrence of event *A* or event *B* equals the probability of occurrence of event *A* *plus* the probability of occurrence of event *B*."

■ QUESTION *Assume that you role one die. What is the probability of coming up with a 2 or a 5?*

SOLUTION
Step 1. First determine the $p(A)$. Let's call rolling a 2 event *A*.

$$p(A) = \frac{\text{number of events classifiable as 2}}{\text{total number of sides on the die}} = \frac{1}{6} = .1666$$

The probability of rolling a 2 is .1666.

Step 2. Determine the probability of event *B* occurring.

$$p(B) = \frac{\text{number of events classifiable as 5}}{\text{total number of sides on the die}} = \frac{1}{6} = .1666$$

The probability of rolling a 5 is .1666.

Step 3. Use the addition rule to determine the probability of rolling a 2 or a 5.

$$p(A \text{ or } B) = p(A) + p(B)$$
$$p(A \text{ or } B) = .1666 + .1666 = .33$$

The probability of rolling a 2 or a 5 on a single toss of the die is .33. ■

A.7 THE ADDITION RULE FOR MORE THAN TWO MUTUALLY EXCLUSIVE EVENTS

The addition rule is generalizable to situations where you want to determine the probability of occurrence of one of several events. The general equation for the addition rule with more than two mutually exclusive events follows.

General Equation for the Addition Rule When There are More than Two Mutually Exclusive Events

$$p(A \text{ or } B \text{ or } C \text{ or } \cdots Z) = p(A) + p(B) + p(C) + \cdots + p(Z)$$

(Formula A.4)

where,
$p(Z)$ = the probability of occurrence of the last event

Formula A.4 is merely an extension of the addition-rule formula for two mutually exclusive events. As a consequence, the computational steps follow the same format as outlined in the preceding worked example.

■   QUESTION   *What is the probability of randomly selecting a 3, 7, or 9 from a deck of cards?*

SOLUTION
Step 1.   First determine the $p(A)$.

$$p(A) = \frac{\text{number of cards classifiable as 3}}{\text{total number of cards in the deck}} = \frac{4}{52} = .0769$$

The probability of randomly selecting a 3 from the deck is .0769.
Step 2.   Determine the probability of event B occurring.

$$p(B) = \frac{\text{number of cards classifiable as 7}}{\text{total number of cards in the deck}} = \frac{4}{52} = .0769$$

The probability of randomly selecting a 7 from the deck is .0769.
Step 3.   Determine the probability of occurrence of event C.

$$p(C) = \frac{\text{number of cards classifiable as 9}}{\text{total number of cards in the deck}} = \frac{4}{52} = .0769$$

The probability of randomly selecting a 9 from the deck is .0769.
Step 4.   Use the addition rule to sum the separate probabilities.

$$p(A \text{ or } B \text{ or } C) = p(A) + p(B) + p(C)$$
$$p(A \text{ or } B \text{ or } C) = .0769 + .0769 + .0769 = .23$$

Hence, the probability of selecting a 3, 7, or 9, on a single draw, is .23.   ■

A.8   THE MULTIPLICATION RULE WHEN EVENTS ARE MUTUALLY EXCLUSIVE

   The addition rule is used when you want to determine the probability of one *or* more events occurring. The **multiplication rule** is used when a problem is framed as the probability of event A *and* event B occurring. Of course, the multiplication rule can be extended to problems that address more than two events, just as the addition rule can be used when there are more than two events considered. We consider the multiplication rule under two conditions: when the events are independent and when the events are dependent.

A.9   THE MULTIPLICATION RULE WITH INDEPENDENT EVENTS

Two events are considered independent if the probability of one event has no effect on the probability of occurrence of a second event. The formula for the multiplication rule with mutually exclusive independent events follows.

Multiplication Rule for Two Independent Events

$$p(A \text{ and } B) = p(A)p(B) \quad \textit{(Formula A.5)}$$

Formula A.5 is read, "The probability of events A and B occurring is equal to the probability of event A occurring multiplied by the probability of event B occurring." Formula A.5 is used when the problem involves sampling with replacement.

■   QUESTION   *What is the probability of randomly selecting a 4 and an 8 on two successive draws from a deck of cards? Since sampling with replacement is used, one card is randomly drawn from the deck, then put back into the deck, and then a second card is randomly selected.*

SOLUTION
Step 1.   First determine the $p(A)$.

$$p(A) = \frac{\text{number of cards classifiable as 4}}{\text{total number of cards in the deck}} = \frac{4}{52} = .0769$$

The probability of randomly selecting a 4 is .0769.

Step 2.   Determine the probability of event B occurring. Note that $p(B)$ is unaffected by the probability of occurrence of event A. This is because the first card is put back into the deck; therefore, the second draw is basically like starting all over again.

$$p(B) = \frac{\text{number of cards classifiable as 8}}{\text{total number of cards in the deck}} = \frac{4}{52} = .0769$$

The probability of randomly selecting a 8 is .0769.

Step 3.   The multiplication rule is now applied.

$$p(A \text{ and } B) = p(A)p(B)$$

$$p(A \text{ and } B) = .0769(.0769) = .0059$$

The probability of obtaining a 4 on the first draw and an 8 on the second draw is .0059. Stated differently, only 59 times out of 10,000 would these two events occur together.   ■

Formula A.5 can be extended to any number of independent events. If you wanted to know the probability of drawing an ace, a 2, and a 6 on three successive draws, you would merely multiply the three probabilities of occurrence.

A.10   THE MULTIPLICATION RULE WITH DEPENDENT EVENTS

Dependent events occur when the probability of occurrence of the second event is affected by the occurrence of the first event. Sampling without replacement would lead you to use the formula for the multiplication rule with dependent events.

Multiplication Rule for Two Dependent Events

$$p(A \text{ and } B) = p(A)p(B|A)$$

(Formula A.6)

The symbol $p(B|A)$ is read, "The probability of event B given the occurrence of event A." [The $p(B)$ is *not* divided by $p(A)$]. The symbol $p(B|A)$ is also referred to as a **conditional probability** since $p(B)$ is conditional on the occurrence of A. A worked problem clarifies the use of Formula A.6.

■   QUESTION   *What is the probability of randomly drawing two 10s from a deck of cards? In this problem, the first card is not returned to the deck (sampling without replacement).*

SOLUTION
Step 1.   Determine the probability of occurrence of event A.

$$p(A) = \frac{\text{number of cards classifiable as 10}}{\text{total number of cards in the deck}} = \frac{4}{52} = .0769$$

Step 2.   Determine $p(B|A)$. The probability of event B occurring, given that event A has occurred is translated as, "The probability of obtaining a 10 on the second draw (event B), given that one 10 has already been drawn (event A)." It is critical that you keep in mind that dependent events occur in sampling without replacement. Since the first 10 has not been returned to the deck, the number of cards now classifiable as 10 is reduced by one. There are only three 10s left in the deck. In addition, the number of cards left in the deck also has been reduced by one. Hence,

$$p(B|A) = \frac{3}{51} = .0588$$

Step 3.   With $p(A)$ and $p(B|A)$ now determined, the solution is at hand. Applying Formula A.6,

$$p(A \text{ and } B) = p(A)p(B|A)$$

$$p(A \text{ and } B) = .0769(.0588) = .0045$$

The probability of randomly selecting two 10s in a row, using sampling without replacement, is .0045.   ■

The preceding problem should make it clear what is meant by dependent events. By sampling without replacement, the number of cards in the numerator and the number of cards in the denominator change for the second draw. Thus, the probability of drawing the second 10 is dependent on the fact that a 10 was drawn first and *not* replaced.

This appendix includes only a cursory treatment of the branch of statistics known as probability. Indeed the focus has been confined to the addition and multiplication rules of probability. If you are interested in additional reading on the topic, a very entertaining book has been written by Huff and Geis (1959), *How To Take A Chance.* Another entertaining look at probability is found in John Paulos' (1988) recent book, *Innumeracy: Mathematical Illiteracy And Its Consequences.* More extensive treatments of the subject can be found in several extant textbooks on statistics.

SUMMARY

Probability is a proportion that ranges from 0 to 1. A probability of 0 means that an event is certain to not occur; a probability of 1 means that an event is certain to occur. A distinction is made between sampling with or without replacement. Sampling with replacement is a method of sampling whereby a member of a population is randomly selected and then returned to the population before the next member is selected. Sampling without replacement is a method of sampling in which a member of a population is not returned to the population before selecting another member of the population. These two forms of sampling have implications for the probability of occurrence of successive events.

The a priori approach to probability is based solely on reason; no data need be collected. On the other hand, the a posteriori approach requires that data be collected. The latter approach is an empirical approach to probability. Mutually exclusive events are events that cannot occur together. Independent events means that the probability of one event is not affected by the occurrence of another event. Dependent events means that the probability of one event *is* influenced by the occurrence of another event. In sampling with replacement, successive events are independent. In sampling without replacement, successive events are influenced by the occurrence of previous events; therefore, subsequent events are dependent on the occurrence of prior events.

The addition rule is used to determine the probability of occurrence of one of many possible events. The multiplication rule is used to determine the probability of one event *and* another event.

KEY FORMULAS FOR APPENDIX A

A Priori Probability

$$p(A) = \frac{\text{number of events classifiable as } A}{\text{total number of possible events}}$$

(Formula A.1)

A Posteriori Probability

$$p(A) = \frac{\text{number of times } A \text{ has occurred}}{\text{total number of occurrences}}$$

(Formula A.2)

Addition-Rule Formula for Two Mutually Exclusive Events

$$p(A \text{ or } B) = p(A) + p(B)$$

(Formula A.3)

General Equation for the Addition Rule When There Are More than Two Mutually Exclusive Events

$$p(A \text{ or } B \text{ or } C \text{ or } \cdots Z) = p(A) + p(B) + p(C) + \cdots + p(Z)$$

(Formula A.4)

Multiplication Rule for Two Independent Events

$$p(A \text{ and } B) = p(A)p(B)$$

(Formula A.5)

Multiplication Rule for Two Dependent Events

$$p(A \text{ and } B) = p(A)p(B|A)$$

(Formula A.6)

WORK PROBLEMS

1. Which of the following events are mutually exclusive?
   a. Drawing a 5 and a 2 from a deck of cards on successive draws. Would your answer depend on whether sampling was with or without replacement?
   b. Making one toss of a die and obtaining either an even number or a 2.
   c. Drawing a 5 and a 2 on a single draw from a deck of cards.
   d. A person has black hair and blue eyes.
   e. Obtaining a 1 and a 6 when rolling two dice at once.
   f. Being a dog and a cat.
2. Suppose there is a bin with 40 red marbles and 60 white marbles. In each of the following problems, selections are made blindly and the marbles are randomly distributed throughout the bin.

    a. What is the probability of picking a red marble?

    b. What is the probability of drawing a white marble?

    c. What is the probability of drawing either a red or a white marble?

    d. What is the probability of picking two red marbles in a row, with the first marble replaced?

    e. What is the probability of drawing two white marbles in a row, with the first marble replaced?

    f. What is the probability of selecting a white marble, given that a red marble has already been picked and not returned to the bin?

    g. What is the probability of selecting two red marbles in a row if the first red marble is not put back into the bin?

3. For each of the following situations, specify whether the events are independent or dependent.

    a. The weekly state lottery is conducted by drawing six numbers from a bin that has 54 balls, each with a number. Is the successive selection of balls during the drawing an instance of independent or dependent events?

    b. The six balls selected one week and the six balls selected the next week.

    c. Drawing two 5s from a deck of cards without replacing the first card.

    d. Drawing a 3 from a deck of cards, replacing it, and then drawing a 6.

Statistical Tables

TABLE   B.1   z Table[a]

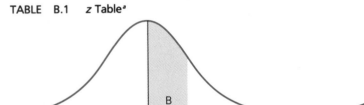

(A)	(B) Area Between Mean and z	(C) Area Beyond z	(A)	(B) Area Between Mean and z	(C) Area Beyond z	(A)	(B) Area Between Mean and z	(C) Area Beyond z
z			z			z		
.00	.0000	.5000	.10	.0398	.4602	.20	.0793	.4207
.01	.0040	.4960	.11	.0438	.4562	.21	.0832	.4168
.02	.0080	.4920	.12	.0478	.4522	.22	.0871	.4129
.03	.0120	.4880	.13	.0517	.4483	.23	.0910	.4090
.04	.0160	.4840	.14	.0557	.4443	.24	.0948	.4052
.05	.0199	.4801	.15	.0596	.4404	.25	.0987	.4013
.06	.0239	.4761	.16	.0636	.4364	.26	.1026	.3974
.07	.0279	.4721	.17	.0675	.4325	.27	.1064	.3936
.08	.0319	.4681	.18	.0714	.4286	.28	.1103	.3897
.09	.0359	.4641	.19	.0753	.4247	.29	.1141	.3859

Table   B.1   (continued)

(A) z	(B) Area Between Mean and z	(C) Area Beyond z	(A) z	(B) Area Between Mean and z	(C) Area Beyond z	(A) z	(B) Area Between Mean and z	(C) Area Beyond z
.30	.1179	.3821	.70	.2580	.2420	1.10	.3643	.1357
.31	.1217	.3783	.71	.2611	.2389	1.11	.3665	.1335
.32	.1255	.3745	.72	.2642	.2358	1.12	.3686	.1314
.33	.1293	.3707	.73	.2673	.2327	1.13	.3708	.1292
.34	.1331	.3669	.74	.2704	.2296	1.14	.3729	.1271
.35	.1368	.3632	.75	.2734	.2266	1.15	.3749	.1251
.36	.1406	.3594	.76	.2764	.2236	1.16	.3770	.1230
.37	.1443	.3557	.77	.2794	.2206	1.17	.3790	.1210
.38	.1480	.3520	.78	.2823	.2177	1.18	.3810	.1190
.39	.1517	.3483	.79	.2852	.2148	1.19	.3830	.1170
.40	.1554	.3446	.80	.2881	.2119	1.20	.3849	.1151
.41	.1591	.3409	.81	.2910	.2090	1.21	.3869	.1131
.42	.1628	.3372	.82	.2939	.2061	1.22	.3888	.1112
.43	.1664	.3336	.83	.2967	.2033	1.23	.3907	.1093
.44	.1700	.3300	.84	.2995	.2005	1.24	.3925	.1075
.45	.1736	.3264	.85	.3023	.1977	1.25	.3944	.1056
.46	.1772	.3228	.86	.3051	.1949	1.26	.3962	.1038
.47	.1808	.3192	.87	.3078	.1922	1.27	.3980	.1020
.48	.1844	.3156	.88	.3106	.1894	1.28	.3997	.1003
.49	.1879	.3121	.89	.3133	.1867	1.29	.4015	.0985
.50	.1915	.3085	.90	.3159	.1841	1.30	.4032	.0968
.51	.1950	.3050	.91	.3186	.1814	1.31	.4049	.0951
.52	.1985	.3015	.92	.3212	.1788	1.32	.4066	.0934
.53	.2019	.2981	.93	.3238	.1762	1.33	.4082	.0918
.54	.2054	.2946	.94	.3264	.1736	1.34	.4099	.0901
.55	.2088	.2912	.95	.3289	.1711	1.35	.4115	.0885
.56	.2123	.2877	.96	.3315	.1685	1.36	.4131	.0869
.57	.2157	.2843	.97	.3340	.1660	1.37	.4147	.0853
.58	.2190	.2810	.98	.3365	.1635	1.38	.4162	.0838
.59	.2224	.2776	.99	.3389	.1611	1.39	.4177	.0823
.60	.2257	.2743	1.00	.3413	.1587	1.40	.4192	.0808
.61	.2291	.2709	1.01	.3438	.1562	1.41	.4207	.0793
.62	.2324	.2676	1.02	.3461	.1539	1.42	.4222	.0778
.63	.2357	.2643	1.03	.3485	.1515	1.43	.4236	.0764
.64	.2389	.2611	1.04	.3508	.1492	1.44	.4251	.0749
.65	.2422	.2578	1.05	.3531	.1469	1.45	.4265	.0735
.66	.2454	.2546	1.06	.3554	.1446	1.46	.4279	.0721
.67	.2486	.2514	1.07	.3577	.1423	1.47	.4292	.0708
.68	.2517	.2483	1.08	.3599	.1401	1.48	.4306	.0694
.69	.2549	.2451	1.09	.3621	.1379	1.49	.4319	.0681

continued

Table B.1 (continued)

(A) z	(B) Area Between Mean and z	(C) Area Beyond z	(A) z	(B) Area Between Mean and z	(C) Area Beyond z	(A) z	(B) Area Between Mean and z	(C) Area Beyond z
1.50	.4332	.0668	1.90	.4713	.0287	2.30	.4893	.0107
1.51	.4345	.0655	1.91	.4719	.0281	2.31	.4896	.0104
1.52	.4357	.0643	1.92	.4726	.0274	2.32	.4898	.0102
1.53	.4370	.0630	1.93	.4732	.0268	2.33	.4901	.0099
1.54	.4382	.0618	1.94	.4738	.0262	2.34	.4904	.0096
1.55	.4394	.0606	1.95	.4744	.0256	2.35	.4906	.0094
1.56	.4406	.0594	1.96	.4750	.0250	2.36	.4909	.0091
1.57	.4418	.0582	1.97	.4756	.0244	2.37	.4911	.0089
1.58	.4429	.0571	1.98	.4761	.0239	2.38	.4913	.0087
1.59	.4441	.0559	1.99	.4767	.0233	2.39	.4916	.0084
1.60	.4452	.0548	2.00	.4772	.0228	2.40	.4918	.0082
1.61	.4463	.0537	2.01	.4778	.0222	2.41	.4920	.0080
1.62	.4474	.0526	2.02	.4783	.0217	2.42	.4922	.0078
1.63	.4484	.0516	2.03	.4788	.0212	2.43	.4925	.0075
1.64	.4495	.0505	2.04	.4793	.0207	2.44	.4927	.0073
1.65	.4505	.0495	2.05	.4798	.0202	2.45	.4929	.0071
1.66	.4515	.0485	2.06	.4803	.0197	2.46	.4931	.0069
1.67	.4525	.0475	2.07	.4808	.0192	2.47	.4932	.0068
1.68	.4535	.0465	2.08	.4812	.0188	2.48	.4934	.0066
1.69	.4545	.0455	2.09	.4817	.0183	2.49	.4936	.0064
1.70	.4554	.0446	2.10	.4821	.0179	2.50	.4938	.0062
1.71	.4564	.0436	2.11	.4826	.0174	2.51	.4940	.0060
1.72	.4573	.0427	2.12	.4830	.0170	2.52	.4941	.0059
1.73	.4582	.0418	2.13	.4834	.0166	2.53	.4943	.0057
1.74	.4591	.0409	2.14	.4838	.0162	2.54	.4945	.0055
1.75	.4599	.0401	2.15	.4842	.0158	2.55	.4946	.0054
1.76	.4608	.0392	2.16	.4846	.0154	2.56	.4948	.0052
1.77	.4616	.0384	2.17	.4850	.0150	2.57	.4949	.0051
1.78	.4625	.0375	2.18	.4854	.0146	2.58	.4951	.0049
1.79	.4633	.0367	2.19	.4857	.0143	2.59	.4952	.0048
1.80	.4641	.0359	2.20	.4861	.0139	2.60	.4953	.0047
1.81	.4649	.0351	2.21	.4864	.0136	2.61	.4955	.0045
1.82	.4656	.0344	2.22	.4868	.0132	2.62	.4956	.0044
1.83	.4664	.0336	2.23	.4871	.0129	2.63	.4957	.0043
1.84	.4671	.0329	2.24	.4875	.0125	2.64	.4959	.0041
1.85	.4678	.0322	2.25	.4878	.0122	2.65	.4960	.0040
1.86	.4686	.0314	2.26	.4881	.0119	2.66	.4961	.0039
1.87	.4693	.0307	2.27	.4884	.0116	2.67	.4962	.0038
1.88	.4699	.0301	2.28	.4887	.0113	2.68	.4963	.0037
1.89	.4706	.0294	2.29	.4890	.0110	2.69	.4964	.0036

Table   B.1   (continued)

(A) z	(B) Area Between Mean and z	(C) Area Beyond z	(A) z	(B) Area Between Mean and z	(C) Area Beyond z	(A) z	(B) Area Between Mean and z	(C) Area Beyond z
2.70	.4965	.0035	2.92	.4982	.0018	3.13	.4991	.0009
2.71	.4966	.0034	2.93	.4983	.0017	3.14	.4992	.0008
2.72	.4967	.0033	2.94	.4984	.0016	3.15	.4992	.0008
2.73	.4968	.0032	2.95	.4984	.0016	3.16	.4992	.0008
2.74	.4969	.0031	2.96	.4985	.0015	3.17	.4992	.0008
2.75	.4970	.0030	2.97	.4985	.0015	3.18	.4993	.0007
2.76	.4971	.0029	2.98	.4986	.0014	3.19	.4993	.0007
2.77	.4972	.0028	2.99	.4986	.0014	3.20	.4993	.0007
2.78	.4973	.0027	3.00	.4987	.0013	3.21	.4993	.0007
2.79	.4974	.0026	3.01	.4987	.0013	3.22	.4994	.0006
2.80	.4974	.0026	3.02	.4987	.0013	3.23	.4994	.0006
2.81	.4975	.0025	3.03	.4988	.0012	3.24	.4994	.0006
2.82	.4976	.0024	3.04	.4988	.0012	3.30	.4995	.0005
2.83	.4977	.0023	3.05	.4989	.0011	3.40	.4997	.0003
2.84	.4977	.0023	3.06	.4989	.0011	3.50	.4998	.0002
2.85	.4978	.0022	3.07	.4989	.0011	3.60	.4998	.0002
2.86	.4979	.0021	3.08	.4990	.0010	3.70	.4999	.0001
2.87	.4979	.0021	3.09	.4990	.0010	3.80	.49993	.00007
2.88	.4980	.0020	3.10	.4990	.0010	3.90	.49995	.00005
2.89	.4981	.0019	3.11	.4991	.0009	4.00	.49997	.00003
2.90	.4981	.0019	3.12	.4991	.0009			
2.91	.4982	.0018						

[a] Column A lists the z-score values. Column B provides the proportion of area between the mean and the z-score value. Column C provides the proportion of area beyond the z score.

Note: Because the normal distribution is symmetrical, areas for negative z scores are the same as those for positive z scores.

TABLE   B.2   *t* Table[a]

df	α Levels for Two-Tailed Test					
	.20	.10	.05	.02	.01	.001
	α Levels for One-Tailed Test					
	.10	.05	.025	.01	.005	.0005
1	3.078	6.314	12.706	31.821	63.657	636.619
2	1.886	2.920	4.303	6.965	9.925	31.598
3	1.638	2.353	3.182	4.541	5.841	12.924
4	1.533	2.132	2.776	3.747	4.604	8.610
5	1.476	2.015	2.571	3.365	4.032	6.869
6	1.440	1.943	2.447	3.143	3.707	5.959
7	1.415	1.895	2.365	2.998	3.499	5.408
8	1.397	1.860	2.306	2.896	3.355	5.041
9	1.383	1.833	2.262	2.821	3.250	4.781
10	1.372	1.812	2.228	2.764	3.169	4.587
11	1.363	1.796	2.201	2.718	3.106	4.437
12	1.356	1.782	2.179	2.681	3.055	4.318
13	1.350	1.771	2.160	2.650	3.012	4.221
14	1.345	1.761	2.145	2.624	2.977	4.140
15	1.341	1.753	2.131	2.602	2.947	4.073
16	1.337	1.746	2.120	2.583	2.921	4.015
17	1.333	1.740	2.110	2.567	2.898	3.965
18	1.330	1.734	2.101	2.552	2.878	3.922
19	1.328	1.729	2.093	2.539	2.861	3.883
20	1.325	1.725	2.086	2.528	2.845	3.850
21	1.323	1.721	2.080	2.518	2.831	3.819
22	1.321	1.717	2.074	2.508	2.819	3.792
23	1.319	1.714	2.069	2.500	2.807	3.767
24	1.318	1.711	2.064	2.492	2.797	3.745
25	1.316	1.708	2.060	2.485	2.787	3.725
26	1.315	1.706	2.056	2.479	2.779	3.707
27	1.314	1.703	2.052	2.473	2.771	3.690
28	1.313	1.701	2.048	2.467	2.763	3.674
29	1.311	1.699	2.045	2.462	2.756	3.659
30	1.310	1.697	2.042	2.457	2.750	3.646
40	1.303	1.684	2.021	2.423	2.704	3.551
60	1.296	1.671	2.000	2.390	2.660	3.460
120	1.289	1.658	1.980	2.358	2.617	3.373
∞	1.282	1.645	1.960	2.326	2.576	3.291

[a] To be significant the *t* obtained from the data must be equal to or larger than the value shown in the table.

Source: Table III of Fisher and Yates': *Statistical Tables for Biological, Agricultural and Medical Research,* published by Longman Group UK, London (previously published by Oliver & Boyd Ltd, Edinburgh), and by permission of the authors and publishers.

TABLE   B.3   **Power Table (Finding Power)**

	One-tailed Test (α)					One-tailed Test (α)			
	.05	.025	.01	.005		.05	.025	.01	.005
	Two-tailed Test (α)					Two-tailed Test (α)			
δ	.10	.05	.02	.01	δ	.10	.05	.02	.01
.0	.10*	.05*	.02	.01	2.5	.80	.71	.57	.47
.1	.10*	.05*	.02	.01	2.6	.83	.74	.61	.51
.2	.11*	.05	.02	.01	2.7	.85	.77	.65	.55
.3	.12*	.06	.03	.01	2.8	.88	.80	.68	.59
.4	.13*	.07	.03	.01	2.9	.90	.83	.72	.63
.5	.14	.08	.03	.02	3.0	.91	.85	.75	.66
.6	.16	.09	.04	.02	3.1	.93	.87	.78	.70
.7	.18	.11	.05	.03	3.2	.94	.89	.81	.73
.8	.21	.13	.06	.04	3.3	.96	.91	.83	.77
.9	.23	.15	.08	.05	3.4	.96	.93	.86	.80
1.0	.26	.17	.09	.06	3.5	.97	.94	.88	.82
1.1	.30	.20	.11	.07	3.6	.97	.95	.90	.85
1.2	.33	.22	.13	.08	3.7	.98	.96	.92	.87
1.3	.37	.26	.15	.10	3.8	.98	.97	.93	.89
1.4	.40	.29	.18	.12	3.9	.99	.97	.94	.91
1.5	.44	.32	.20	.14	4.0	.99	.98	.95	.92
1.6	.48	.36	.23	.16	4.1	.99	.98	.96	.94
1.7	.52	.40	.27	.19	4.2	.99	.99	.97	.95
1.8	.56	.44	.30	.22	4.3	**	.99	.98	.96
1.9	.60	.48	.33	.25	4.4		.99	.98	.97
2.0	.64	.52	.37	.28	4.5		.99	.99	.97
2.1	.68	.56	.41	.32	4.6		**	.99	.98
2.2	.71	.59	.45	.35	4.7			.99	.98
2.3	.74	.63	.49	.39	4.8			.99	.99
2.4	.77	.67	.53	.43	4.9			.99	.99
					5.0			**	.99
					5.1				.99
					5.2				**

* Values inaccurate for *one-tailed* test by more than .01.

** The power at and below this point is greater than .995.

TABLE B.4 Power Table (Finding Delta)

Power	One-tailed Test (α)			
	.05	.025	.01	.005
	Two-tailed Test (α)			
	.10	.05	.02	.01
.25	.97	1.29	1.65	1.90
.50	1.64	1.96	2.33	2.58
.60	1.90	2.21	2.58	2.83
.67	2.08	2.39	2.76	3.01
.70	2.17	2.48	2.85	3.10
.75	2.32	2.63	3.00	3.25
.80	2.49	2.80	3.17	3.42
.85	2.68	3.00	3.36	3.61
.90	2.93	3.24	3.61	3.86
.95	3.29	3.60	3.97	4.22
.99	3.97	4.29	4.65	4.90
.999	4.37	5.05	5.42	5.67

Tables B.3 and B.4 from INTRODUCTORY STATISTICS
FOR THE BEHAVIORAL SCIENCES, Third Edition by J.
Welkowitz, R. Ewen and J. Cohen, copyright © 1982 by
Harcourt Brace Jovanovich, Inc., reprinted by permission
of the publisher.

TABLE B.5 F Table[a]

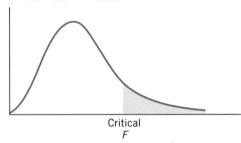

Critical
F

Within

Degrees of Freedom: Denominator	Degrees of Freedom: Numerator *Between*															
	1	2	3	4	5	6	7	8	9	10	11	12	14	16	20
1	161	200	216	225	230	234	237	239	241	242	243	244	245	246	248
	4052	4999	5403	5625	5764	5859	5928	5981	6022	6056	6082	6106	6142	6169	6208
2	18.51	19.00	19.16	19.25	19.30	19.33	19.36	19.37	19.38	19.39	19.40	19.41	19.42	19.43	19.44
	98.49	99.00	99.17	99.25	99.30	99.33	99.34	99.36	99.38	99.40	99.41	99.42	99.43	99.44	99.45
3	10.13	9.55	9.28	9.12	9.01	8.94	8.88	8.84	8.81	8.78	8.76	8.74	8.71	8.69	8.66
	34.12	30.82	29.46	28.71	28.24	27.91	27.67	27.49	27.34	27.23	27.13	27.05	26.92	26.83	26.69
4	7.71	6.94	6.59	6.39	6.26	6.16	6.09	6.04	6.00	5.96	5.93	5.91	5.87	5.84	5.80
	21.20	18.00	16.69	15.98	15.52	15.21	14.98	14.80	14.66	14.54	14.45	14.37	14.24	14.15	14.02

Bdw [handwritten note]

| Degrees of Freedom: Denominator | \multicolumn{14}{c}{Degrees of Freedom: Numerator} |
	1	2	3	4	5	6	7	8	9	10	11	12	14	16	20
Within 5	6.61	5.79	5.41	5.19	5.05	4.95	4.88	4.82	4.78	4.74	4.70	4.68	4.64	4.60	4.56
	16.26	13.27	12.06	11.39	10.97	10.67	10.45	10.27	10.15	10.05	9.96	9.89	9.77	9.68	9.55
6	5.99	5.14	4.76	4.53	4.39	4.28	4.21	4.15	4.10	4.06	4.03	4.00	3.96	3.92	3.87
	13.74	10.92	9.78	9.15	8.75	8.47	8.26	8.10	7.98	7.87	7.79	7.72	7.60	7.52	7.39
7	5.59	4.47	4.35	4.12	3.97	3.87	3.79	3.73	3.68	3.63	3.60	3.57	3.52	3.49	3.44
	12.25	9.55	8.45	7.85	7.46	7.19	7.00	6.84	6.71	6.62	6.54	6.47	6.35	6.27	6.15
8	5.32	4.46	4.07	3.84	3.69	3.58	3.50	3.44	3.39	3.34	3.31	3.28	3.23	3.20	3.15
	11.26	8.65	7.59	7.01	6.63	6.37	6.19	6.03	5.91	5.82	5.74	5.67	5.56	5.48	5.36
9	5.12	4.26	3.86	3.63	3.48	3.37	3.29	3.23	3.18	3.13	3.10	3.07	3.02	2.98	2.93
	10.56	8.02	6.99	6.42	6.06	5.80	5.62	5.47	5.35	5.26	5.18	5.11	5.00	4.92	4.80
10	4.96	4.10	3.71	3.48	3.33	3.22	3.14	3.07	3.02	2.97	2.94	2.91	2.86	2.82	2.77
	10.04	7.56	6.55	5.99	5.64	5.39	5.21	5.06	4.95	4.85	4.78	4.71	4.60	4.52	4.41
11	4.84	3.98	3.59	3.36	3.20	3.09	3.01	2.95	2.90	2.86	2.82	2.79	2.74	2.70	2.65
	9.65	7.20	6.22	5.67	5.32	5.07	4.88	4.74	4.63	4.54	4.46	4.40	4.29	4.21	4.10
12	4.75	3.88	3.49	3.26	3.11	3.00	2.92	2.85	2.80	2.76	2.72	2.69	2.64	2.60	2.54
	9.33	6.93	5.95	5.41	5.06	4.82	4.65	4.50	4.39	4.30	4.22	4.16	4.05	3.98	3.86
13	4.67	3.80	3.41	3.18	3.02	2.92	2.84	2.77	2.72	2.67	2.63	2.60	2.55	2.51	2.46
	9.07	6.70	5.74	5.20	4.86	4.62	4.44	4.30	4.19	4.10	4.02	3.96	3.85	3.78	3.67
14	4.60	3.74	3.34	3.11	2.96	2.85	2.77	2.70	2.65	2.60	2.56	2.53	2.48	2.44	2.39
	8.86	6.51	5.56	5.03	4.69	4.46	4.28	4.14	4.03	3.94	3.86	3.80	3.70	3.62	3.51
15	4.54	3.68	3.29	3.06	2.90	2.79	2.70	2.64	2.59	2.55	2.51	2.48	2.43	2.39	2.33
	8.68	6.36	5.42	4.89	4.56	4.32	4.14	4.00	3.89	3.80	3.73	3.67	3.56	3.48	3.36
16	4.49	3.63	3.24	3.01	2.85	2.74	2.66	2.59	2.54	2.49	2.45	2.42	2.37	2.33	2.28
	8.53	6.23	5.29	4.77	4.44	4.20	4.03	3.89	3.78	3.69	3.61	3.55	3.45	3.37	3.25
17	4.45	3.59	3.20	2.96	2.81	2.70	2.62	2.55	2.50	2.45	2.41	2.38	2.33	2.29	2.23
	8.40	6.11	5.18	4.67	4.34	4.10	3.93	3.79	3.68	3.59	3.52	3.45	3.35	3.27	3.16
18	4.41	3.55	3.16	2.93	2.77	2.66	2.58	2.51	2.46	2.41	2.37	2.34	2.29	2.25	2.19
	8.28	6.01	5.09	4.58	4.25	4.01	3.85	3.71	3.60	3.51	3.44	3.37	3.27	3.19	3.07
19	4.38	3.52	3.13	2.90	2.74	2.63	2.55	2.48	2.43	2.38	2.34	2.31	2.26	2.21	2.15
	8.18	5.93	5.01	4.50	4.17	3.94	3.77	3.63	3.52	3.43	3.36	3.30	3.19	3.12	3.00
20	4.35	3.49	3.10	2.87	2.71	2.60	2.52	2.45	2.40	2.35	2.31	2.28	2.23	2.18	2.12
	8.10	5.85	4.94	4.43	4.10	3.87	3.71	3.56	3.45	3.37	3.30	3.23	3.13	3.05	2.94
21	4.32	3.47	3.07	2.84	2.68	2.57	2.49	2.42	2.37	2.32	2.28	2.25	2.20	2.15	2.09
	8.02	5.78	4.87	4.37	4.04	3.81	3.65	3.51	3.40	3.31	3.24	3.17	3.07	2.99	2.88
22	4.30	3.44	3.05	2.82	2.66	2.55	2.47	2.40	2.35	2.30	2.26	2.23	2.18	2.13	2.07
	7.94	5.72	4.82	4.31	3.99	3.76	3.59	3.45	3.35	3.26	3.18	3.12	3.02	2.94	2.83
23	4.28	3.42	3.03	2.80	2.64	2.53	2.45	2.38	2.32	2.28	2.24	2.20	2.14	2.10	2.04
	7.88	5.66	4.76	4.26	3.94	3.71	3.54	3.41	3.30	3.21	3.14	3.07	2.97	2.89	2.78
24	4.26	3.40	3.01	2.78	2.62	2.51	2.43	2.36	2.30	2.26	2.22	2.18	2.13	2.09	2.02
	7.82	5.61	4.72	4.22	3.90	3.67	3.50	3.36	3.25	3.17	3.09	3.03	2.93	2.85	2.74
25	4.24	3.38	2.99	2.76	2.60	2.49	2.41	2.34	2.28	2.24	2.20	2.16	2.11	2.06	2.00
	7.77	5.57	4.68	4.18	3.86	3.63	3.46	3.32	3.21	3.13	3.05	2.99	2.89	2.81	2.70
26	4.22	3.37	2.98	2.74	2.59	2.47	2.39	2.32	2.27	2.22	2.18	2.15	2.10	2.05	1.99
	7.72	5.53	4.64	4.14	3.82	3.59	3.42	3.29	3.17	3.09	3.02	2.96	2.86	2.77	2.66
27	4.21	3.35	2.96	2.73	2.57	2.46	2.37	2.30	2.25	2.20	2.16	2.13	2.08	2.03	1.97
	7.68	5.49	4.60	4.11	3.79	3.56	3.39	3.26	3.14	3.06	2.98	2.93	2.83	2.74	2.63
28	4.20	3.34	2.95	2.71	2.56	2.44	2.36	2.29	2.24	2.19	2.15	2.12	2.06	2.02	1.96
	7.64	5.45	4.57	4.07	3.76	3.53	3.36	3.23	3.11	3.03	2.95	2.90	2.80	2.71	2.60
29	4.18	3.33	2.93	2.70	2.54	2.43	2.35	2.28	2.22	2.18	2.14	2.10	2.05	2.00	1.94
	7.60	5.42	4.54	4.04	3.73	3.50	3.33	3.20	3.08	3.00	2.92	2.87	2.77	2.68	2.57

continued

Table B.5   (continued)

Degrees of Freedom: Denominator	Degrees of Freedom: Numerator														
	1	2	3	4	5	6	7	8	9	10	11	12	14	16	20
30	4.17	3.32	2.92	2.69	2.53	2.42	2.34	2.27	2.21	2.16	2.12	2.09	2.04	1.99	1.93
	7.56	**5.39**	**4.51**	**4.02**	**3.70**	**3.47**	**3.30**	**3.17**	**3.06**	**2.98**	**2.90**	**2.84**	**2.74**	**2.66**	**2.55**
32	4.15	3.30	2.90	2.67	2.51	2.40	2.32	2.25	2.19	2.14	2.10	2.07	2.02	1.97	1.91
	7.50	**5.34**	**4.46**	**3.97**	**3.66**	**3.42**	**3.25**	**3.12**	**3.01**	**2.94**	**2.86**	**2.80**	**2.70**	**2.62**	**2.51**
34	4.13	3.28	2.88	2.65	2.49	2.38	2.30	2.23	2.17	2.12	2.08	2.05	2.00	1.95	1.89
	7.44	**5.29**	**4.42**	**3.93**	**3.61**	**3.38**	**3.21**	**3.08**	**2.97**	**2.89**	**2.82**	**2.76**	**2.66**	**2.58**	**2.47**
36	4.11	3.26	2.86	2.63	2.48	2.36	2.28	2.21	2.15	2.10	2.06	2.03	1.98	1.93	1.87
	7.39	**5.25**	**4.38**	**3.89**	**3.58**	**3.35**	**3.18**	**3.04**	**2.94**	**2.86**	**2.78**	**2.72**	**2.62**	**2.54**	**2.43**
38	4.10	3.25	2.85	2.62	2.46	2.35	2.26	2.19	2.14	2.09	2.05	2.02	1.96	1.92	1.85
	7.35	**5.21**	**4.34**	**3.86**	**3.54**	**3.32**	**3.15**	**3.02**	**2.91**	**2.82**	**2.75**	**2.69**	**2.59**	**2.51**	**2.40**
40	4.08	3.23	2.84	2.61	2.45	2.34	2.25	2.18	2.12	2.07	2.04	2.00	1.95	1.90	1.84
	7.31	**5.18**	**4.31**	**3.83**	**3.51**	**3.29**	**3.12**	**2.99**	**2.88**	**2.80**	**2.73**	**2.66**	**2.56**	**2.49**	**2.37**
42	4.07	3.22	2.83	2.59	2.44	2.32	2.24	2.17	2.11	2.06	2.02	1.99	1.94	1.89	1.82
	7.27	**5.15**	**4.29**	**3.80**	**3.49**	**3.26**	**3.10**	**2.96**	**2.86**	**2.77**	**2.70**	**2.64**	**2.54**	**2.46**	**2.35**
44	4.06	3.21	2.82	2.58	2.43	2.31	2.23	2.16	2.10	2.05	2.01	1.98	1.92	1.88	1.81
	7.24	**5.12**	**4.26**	**3.78**	**3.46**	**3.24**	**3.07**	**2.94**	**2.84**	**2.75**	**2.68**	**2.62**	**2.52**	**2.44**	**2.32**
46	4.05	3.20	2.81	2.57	2.42	2.30	2.22	2.14	2.09	2.04	2.00	1.97	1.91	1.87	1.80
	7.21	**5.10**	**4.24**	**3.76**	**3.44**	**3.22**	**3.05**	**2.92**	**2.82**	**2.73**	**2.66**	**2.60**	**2.50**	**2.42**	**2.30**
48	4.04	3.19	2.80	2.56	2.41	2.30	2.21	2.14	2.08	2.03	1.99	1.96	1.90	1.86	1.79
	7.19	**5.08**	**4.22**	**3.74**	**3.42**	**3.20**	**3.04**	**2.90**	**2.80**	**2.71**	**2.64**	**2.58**	**2.48**	**2.40**	**2.28**
50	4.03	3.18	2.79	2.56	2.40	2.29	2.20	2.13	2.07	2.02	1.98	1.95	1.90	1.85	1.78
	7.17	**5.06**	**4.20**	**3.72**	**3.41**	**3.18**	**3.02**	**2.88**	**2.78**	**2.70**	**2.62**	**2.56**	**2.46**	**2.39**	**2.26**
55	4.02	3.17	2.78	2.54	2.38	2.27	2.18	2.11	2.05	2.00	1.97	1.93	1.88	1.83	1.76
	7.12	**5.01**	**4.16**	**3.68**	**3.37**	**3.15**	**2.98**	**2.85**	**2.75**	**2.66**	**2.59**	**2.53**	**2.43**	**2.35**	**2.23**
60	4.00	3.15	2.76	2.52	2.37	2.25	2.17	2.10	2.04	1.99	1.95	1.92	1.86	1.81	1.75
	7.08	**4.98**	**4.13**	**3.65**	**3.34**	**3.12**	**2.95**	**2.82**	**2.72**	**2.63**	**2.56**	**2.50**	**2.40**	**2.32**	**2.20**
65	3.99	3.14	2.75	2.51	2.36	2.24	2.15	2.08	2.02	1.98	1.94	1.90	1.85	1.80	1.73
	7.04	**4.95**	**4.10**	**3.62**	**3.31**	**3.09**	**2.93**	**2.79**	**2.70**	**2.61**	**2.54**	**2.47**	**2.37**	**2.30**	**2.18**
70	3.98	3.13	2.74	2.50	2.35	2.23	2.14	2.07	2.01	1.97	1.93	1.89	1.84	1.79	1.72
	7.01	**4.92**	**4.08**	**3.60**	**3.29**	**3.07**	**2.91**	**2.77**	**2.67**	**2.59**	**2.51**	**2.45**	**2.35**	**2.28**	**2.15**
80	3.96	3.11	2.72	2.48	2.33	2.21	2.12	2.05	1.99	1.95	1.91	1.88	1.82	1.77	1.70
	6.96	**4.88**	**4.04**	**3.56**	**3.25**	**3.04**	**2.87**	**2.74**	**2.64**	**2.55**	**2.48**	**2.41**	**2.32**	**2.24**	**2.11**
100	3.94	3.09	2.70	2.46	2.30	2.19	2.10	2.03	1.97	1.92	1.88	1.85	1.79	1.75	1.68
	6.90	**4.82**	**3.98**	**3.51**	**3.20**	**2.99**	**2.82**	**2.69**	**2.59**	**2.51**	**2.43**	**2.36**	**2.26**	**2.19**	**2.06**
125	3.92	3.07	2.68	2.44	2.29	2.17	2.08	2.01	1.95	1.90	1.86	1.83	1.77	1.72	1.65
	6.84	**4.78**	**3.94**	**3.47**	**3.17**	**2.95**	**2.79**	**2.65**	**2.56**	**2.47**	**2.40**	**2.33**	**2.23**	**2.15**	**2.03**
150	3.91	3.06	2.67	2.43	2.27	2.16	2.07	2.00	1.94	1.89	1.85	1.82	1.76	1.71	1.64
	6.81	**4.75**	**3.91**	**3.44**	**3.14**	**2.92**	**2.76**	**2.62**	**2.53**	**2.44**	**2.37**	**2.30**	**2.20**	**2.12**	**2.00**
200	3.89	3.04	2.65	2.41	2.26	2.14	2.05	1.98	1.92	1.87	1.83	1.80	1.74	1.69	1.62
	6.76	**4.71**	**3.88**	**3.41**	**3.11**	**2.90**	**2.73**	**2.60**	**2.50**	**2.41**	**2.34**	**2.28**	**2.17**	**2.09**	**1.97**
400	3.86	3.02	2.62	2.39	2.23	2.12	2.03	1.96	1.90	1.85	1.81	1.78	1.72	1.67	1.60
	6.70	**4.66**	**3.83**	**3.36**	**3.06**	**2.85**	**2.69**	**2.55**	**2.46**	**2.37**	**2.29**	**2.23**	**2.12**	**2.04**	**1.92**
1000	3.85	3.00	2.61	2.38	2.22	2.10	2.02	1.95	1.89	1.84	1.80	1.76	1.70	1.65	1.58
	6.66	**4.62**	**3.80**	**3.34**	**3.04**	**2.82**	**2.66**	**2.53**	**2.43**	**2.34**	**2.26**	**2.20**	**2.09**	**2.01**	**1.89**
∞	3.84	2.99	2.60	2.37	2.21	2.09	2.01	1.94	1.88	1.83	1.79	1.75	1.69	1.64	1.57
	6.64	**4.60**	**3.78**	**3.32**	**3.02**	**2.80**	**2.64**	**2.51**	**2.41**	**2.32**	**2.24**	**2.18**	**2.07**	**1.99**	**1.87**

[a] Table entries in lightface type are critical values for the .05 level of significance. Boldface type values are for the .01 level of significance.

Source: Reproduced by permission from Statistical Methods, 8th ed., by G. W. Snedecor and W. G. Cochran. © 1956 by The Iowa State University Press.

TABLE B.6 Pearson *r* Table[a]

(df = N − 2)	α Levels for Two-Tailed Test				
	.10	.05	.02	.01	.001
	α Levels for One-Tailed Test				
	.05	.025	.01	.005	.0005
1	.98769	.99692	.999507	.999877	.9999988
2	.90000	.95000	.98000	.990000	.99900
3	.8054	.8783	.93433	.95873	.99116
4	.7293	.8114	.8822	.91720	.97406
5	.6694	.7545	.8329	.8745	.95074
6	.6215	.7067	.7887	.8343	.92493
7	.5822	.6664	.7498	.7977	.8982
8	.5494	.6319	.7155	.7646	.8721
9	.5214	.6021	.6851	.7348	.8371
10	.4973	.5760	.6581	.7079	.8233
11	.4762	.5529	.6339	.6835	.8010
12	.4575	.5324	.6120	.6614	.7800
13	.4409	.5139	.5923	.6411	.7603
14	.4259	.4973	.5742	.6226	.7420
15	.4124	.4821	.5577	.6055	.7246
16	.4000	.4683	.5425	.5897	.7084
17	.3887	.4555	.5285	.5751	.6932
18	.3783	.4438	.5155	.5614	.6787
19	.3687	.4329	.5034	.5487	.6652
20	.3598	.4227	.4921	.5368	.6524
25	.3233	.3809	.4451	.4869	.5974
30	.2960	.3494	.4093	.4487	.5541
35	.2746	.3246	.3810	.4182	.5189
40	.2573	.3044	.3578	.3932	.4896
45	.2428	.2875	.3384	.3721	.4648
50	.2306	.2732	.3218	.3541	.4433
60	.2108	.2500	.2948	.3248	.4078
70	.1954	.2319	.2737	.3017	.3799
80	.1829	.2172	.2565	.2830	.3568
90	.1726	.2050	.2422	.2673	.3375
100	.1638	.1946	.2301	.2540	.3211

[a] To be significant the *r* obtained from the data must be equal to or larger than the value shown in the table.

Source: Table VII of Fisher and Yates': *Statistical Tables for Biological, Agricultural and Medical Research* published by Longman Group UK, London (previously published by Oliver and Boyd Ltd., Edinburgh) and by permission of the authors and publishers.

TABLE B.7   Spearman r_s Table

	Level of Significance for a One-Tailed Test			
	.05	.025	.01	.005
Number of pairs, n_p	Level of Significance for a Two-Tailed Test			
	.10	.05	.02	.01
5	.900	1.000	1.000	
6	.829	.886	.943	1.000
7	.714	.786	.893	.929
8	.643	.738	.833	.881
9	.600	.700	.783	.833
10	.564	.648	.745	.794
11	.536	.618	.709	.755
12	.503	.587	.671	.727
13	.484	.560	.648	.703
14	.464	.538	.622	.675
15	.443	.521	.604	.654
16	.429	.503	.582	.635
17	.414	.485	.566	.615
18	.401	.472	.550	.600
19	.391	.460	.535	.584
20	.380	.447	.520	.570
21	.370	.435	.508	.556
22	.361	.425	.496	.544
23	.353	.415	.486	.532
24	.344	.406	.476	.521
25	.337	.398	.466	.511
26	.331	.390	.457	.501
27	.324	.382	.448	.491
28	.317	.375	.440	.483
29	.312	.368	.433	.475
30	.306	.362	.425	.467
32	.296	.350	.412	.452
34	.287	.340	.399	.439
36	.279	.330	.388	.427
38	.271	.321	.378	.415
40	.264	.313	.368	.405
42	.257	.305	.359	.395
44	.251	.298	.351	.386
46	.246	.291	.343	.378
48	.240	.285	.336	.370
50	.235	.279	.329	.363
52	.231	.274	.323	.356
54	.226	.268	.317	.349
56	.222	.264	.311	.343
58	.218	.259	.306	.337
60	.214	.255	.300	.331
70	.198	.235	.278	.307
80	.185	.220	.260	.287
90	.174	.207	.245	.271
100	.165	.197	.233	.257

If obtained value of r_s is equal to or greater than tabled value for the appropriate alpha, reject H_0. Glasser, G. J., and Winter, R. F. "Critical Values of the Coefficient of Rank Correlation for Testing the Hypothesis of Independence," *Biometrika*, 48, 444 (1961). Reprinted by permission of the Biometrika Trustees.

TABLE   B.8   **Chi-Square Table**[a]

df	α Levels				
	.10	.05	.02	.01	.001
1	2.71	3.84	5.41	6.64	10.83
2	4.60	5.99	7.82	9.21	13.82
3	6.25	7.82	9.84	11.34	16.27
4	7.78	9.49	11.67	13.28	18.46
5	9.24	11.07	13.39	15.09	20.52
6	10.64	12.59	15.03	16.81	22.46
7	12.02	14.07	16.62	18.48	24.32
8	13.36	15.51	18.17	20.09	26.12
9	14.68	16.92	19.68	21.67	27.88
10	15.99	18.31	21.16	23.21	29.59
11	17.28	19.68	22.62	24.72	31.26
12	18.55	21.03	24.05	26.22	32.91
13	19.81	22.36	25.47	27.69	34.53
14	21.06	23.68	26.87	29.14	36.12
15	22.31	25.00	28.26	30.58	37.70
16	23.54	26.30	29.63	32.00	39.25
17	24.77	27.59	31.00	33.41	40.79
18	25.99	28.87	32.35	34.80	42.31
19	27.20	30.14	33.69	36.19	43.82
20	28.41	31.41	35.02	37.57	45.32
21	29.62	32.67	36.34	38.93	46.80
22	30.81	33.92	37.66	40.29	48.27
23	32.01	35.17	38.97	41.64	49.73
24	33.20	36.42	40.27	42.98	51.18
25	34.38	37.65	41.57	44.31	52.62
26	35.56	38.88	42.86	45.64	54.05
27	36.74	40.11	44.14	46.96	55.48
28	37.92	41.34	45.42	48.28	56.89
29	39.09	42.56	46.69	49.59	58.30
30	40.26	43.77	47.96	50.89	59.70

[a] To be significant the χ^2 obtained from the data must be equal to or larger than the value shown in the table.

Source: Table IV of Fisher and Yates': *Statistical Tables for Biological, Agricultural and Medical Research,* published by Longman Group UK, London (previously published by Oliver and Boyd Ltd., Edinburgh), and by permission of the authors and publishers.

TABLE B.9a Mann-Whitney U table, critical values for a one-tailed test at $\alpha = .01$ (roman type) and $\alpha = .005$ (boldface type) and for a two-tailed test at $\alpha = .02$ (roman type) and $\alpha = .01$ (boldface type)[a]

n_B \ n_A	1	2	3	4	5	6	7	8	9	10	11	12	13	14	15	16	17	18	19	20
1	—[b]	—	—	—	—	—	—	—	—	—	—	—	—	—	—	—	—	—	—	—
2	—	—	—	—	—	—	—	—	—	—	—	—	0	0	0	0	0	0	1	1
	—	—	—	—	—	—	—	—	—	—	—	—	—	—	—	—	—	—	0	0
3	—	—	—	—	—	—	0	0	1	1	1	2	2	2	3	3	4	4	4	5
							—	—	0	0	0	1	1	1	2	2	2	2	3	3
4	—	—	—	—	0	1	1	2	3	3	4	5	5	6	7	7	8	9	9	10
				—	—	0	0	1	1	2	2	3	3	4	5	5	6	6	7	8
5	—	—	—	0	1	2	3	4	5	6	7	8	9	10	11	12	13	14	15	16
				—	0	1	1	2	3	4	5	6	7	7	8	9	10	11	12	13
6	—	—	—	1	2	3	4	6	7	8	9	11	12	13	15	16	18	19	20	22
				0	1	2	3	4	5	6	7	9	10	11	12	13	15	16	17	18
7	—	—	0	1	3	4	6	7	9	11	12	14	16	17	19	21	23	24	26	28
			—	0	1	3	4	6	7	9	10	12	13	15	16	18	19	21	22	24
8	—	—	0	2	4	6	7	9	11	13	15	17	20	22	24	26	28	30	32	34
			—	1	2	4	6	7	9	11	13	15	17	18	20	22	24	26	28	30
9	—	—	1	3	5	7	9	11	14	16	18	21	23	26	28	31	33	36	38	40
			0	1	3	5	7	9	11	13	16	18	20	22	24	27	29	31	33	36
10	—	—	1	3	6	8	11	13	16	19	22	24	27	30	33	36	38	41	44	47
			0	2	4	6	9	11	13	16	18	21	24	26	29	31	34	37	39	42
11	—	—	1	4	7	9	12	15	18	22	25	28	31	34	37	41	44	47	50	53
			0	2	5	7	10	13	16	18	21	24	27	30	33	36	39	42	45	48
12	—	—	2	5	8	11	14	17	21	24	28	31	35	38	42	46	49	53	56	60
			1	3	6	9	12	15	18	21	24	27	31	34	37	41	44	47	51	54
13	—	0	2	5	9	12	16	20	23	27	31	35	39	43	47	51	55	59	63	67
		—	1	3	7	10	13	17	20	24	27	31	34	38	42	45	49	53	56	60
14	—	0	2	6	10	13	17	22	26	30	34	38	43	47	51	56	60	65	69	73
		—	1	4	7	11	15	18	22	26	30	34	38	42	46	50	54	58	63	67
15	—	0	3	7	11	15	19	24	28	33	37	42	47	51	56	61	66	70	75	80
		—	2	5	8	12	16	20	24	29	33	37	42	46	51	55	60	64	69	73
16	—	0	3	7	12	16	21	26	31	36	41	46	51	56	61	66	71	76	82	87
		—	2	5	9	13	18	22	27	31	36	41	45	50	55	60	65	70	74	79
17	—	0	4	8	13	18	23	28	33	38	44	49	55	60	66	71	77	82	88	93
		—	2	6	10	15	19	24	29	34	39	44	49	54	60	65	70	75	81	86
18	—	0	4	9	14	19	24	30	36	41	47	53	59	65	70	76	82	88	94	100
		—	2	6	11	16	21	26	31	37	42	47	53	58	64	70	75	81	87	92
19	—	1	4	9	15	20	26	32	38	44	50	56	63	69	75	82	88	94	101	107
		0	3	7	12	17	22	28	33	39	45	51	56	63	69	74	81	87	93	99
20	—	1	5	10	16	22	28	34	40	47	53	60	67	73	80	87	93	100	107	114
		0	3	8	13	18	24	30	36	42	48	54	60	67	73	79	86	92	99	105

[a] To be significant for any given n_A and n_B, the obtained U must be *equal to* or *less than* the value shown in the table.

[b] Dashes in the body of the table indicate that no decision is possible at the stated level of significance.

Source: Table B.9a and B.9b are from *Statistics: An Introduction*, 3rd. ed., R. Kirk © 1990 Holt, Rinehart and Winston, Inc., reprinted by permission of the publisher.

TABLE B.9*b*   Mann-Whitney *U* table, critical values for a one-tailed test at $\alpha = .05$ (roman type) and $\alpha = .025$ (boldface type) and for a two-tailed test at $\alpha = .10$ (roman type) and $\alpha = .05$ (boldface type)

n_B \ n_A	1	2	3	4	5	6	7	8	9	10	11	12	13	14	15	16	17	18	19	20
1	—	—	—	—	—	—	—	—	—	—	—	—	—	—	—	—	—	—	0	0
	—	—	—	—	—	—	—	—	—	—	—	—	—	—	—	—	—	—	—	—
2	—	—	—	—	0	0	0	1	1	1	1	2	2	2	3	3	3	4	4	4
	—	—	—	—	—	—	—	**0**	**0**	**0**	**0**	**1**	**1**	**1**	**1**	**1**	**2**	**2**	**2**	**2**
3	—	—	0	0	1	2	2	3	3	4	5	5	6	7	7	8	9	9	10	11
	—	—	—	—	**0**	**1**	**1**	**2**	**2**	**3**	**3**	**4**	**4**	**5**	**5**	**6**	**6**	**7**	**7**	**8**
4	—	—	0	1	2	3	4	5	6	7	8	9	10	11	12	14	15	16	17	18
	—	—	—	**0**	**1**	**2**	**3**	**4**	**4**	**5**	**6**	**7**	**8**	**9**	**10**	**11**	**11**	**12**	**13**	**13**
5	—	0	1	2	4	5	6	8	9	11	12	13	15	16	18	19	20	22	23	25
	—	—	**0**	**1**	**2**	**3**	**5**	**6**	**7**	**8**	**9**	**11**	**12**	**13**	**14**	**15**	**17**	**18**	**19**	**20**
6	—	0	2	3	5	7	8	10	12	14	16	17	19	21	23	25	26	28	30	32
	—	—	**1**	**2**	**3**	**5**	**6**	**8**	**10**	**11**	**13**	**14**	**16**	**17**	**19**	**21**	**22**	**24**	**25**	**27**
7	—	0	2	4	6	8	11	13	15	17	19	21	24	26	28	30	33	35	37	39
	—	—	**1**	**3**	**5**	**6**	**8**	**10**	**12**	**14**	**16**	**18**	**20**	**22**	**24**	**26**	**28**	**30**	**32**	**34**
8	—	1	3	5	8	10	13	15	18	20	23	26	28	31	33	36	39	41	44	47
	—	**0**	**2**	**4**	**6**	**8**	**10**	**13**	**15**	**17**	**19**	**22**	**24**	**26**	**29**	**31**	**34**	**36**	**38**	**41**
9	—	1	3	6	9	12	15	18	21	24	27	30	33	36	39	42	45	48	51	54
	—	**0**	**2**	**4**	**7**	**10**	**12**	**15**	**17**	**20**	**23**	**26**	**28**	**31**	**34**	**37**	**39**	**42**	**45**	**48**
10	—	1	4	7	11	14	17	20	24	27	31	34	37	41	44	48	51	55	58	62
	—	**0**	**3**	**5**	**8**	**11**	**14**	**17**	**20**	**23**	**26**	**29**	**33**	**36**	**39**	**42**	**45**	**48**	**52**	**55**
11	—	1	5	8	12	16	19	23	27	31	34	38	42	46	50	54	57	61	65	69
	—	**0**	**3**	**6**	**9**	**13**	**16**	**19**	**23**	**26**	**30**	**33**	**37**	**40**	**44**	**47**	**51**	**55**	**58**	**62**
12	—	2	5	9	13	17	21	26	30	34	38	42	47	51	55	60	64	68	72	77
	—	**1**	**4**	**7**	**11**	**14**	**18**	**22**	**26**	**29**	**33**	**37**	**41**	**45**	**49**	**53**	**57**	**61**	**65**	**69**
13	—	2	6	10	15	19	24	28	33	37	42	47	51	56	61	65	70	75	80	84
	—	**1**	**4**	**8**	**12**	**16**	**20**	**24**	**28**	**33**	**37**	**41**	**45**	**50**	**54**	**59**	**63**	**67**	**72**	**76**
14	—	2	7	11	16	21	26	31	36	41	46	51	56	61	66	71	77	82	87	92
	—	**1**	**5**	**9**	**13**	**17**	**22**	**26**	**31**	**36**	**40**	**45**	**50**	**55**	**59**	**64**	**67**	**74**	**78**	**83**
15	—	3	7	12	18	23	28	33	39	44	50	55	61	66	72	77	83	88	94	100
	—	**1**	**5**	**10**	**14**	**19**	**24**	**29**	**34**	**39**	**44**	**49**	**54**	**59**	**64**	**70**	**75**	**80**	**85**	**90**
16	—	3	8	14	19	25	30	36	42	48	54	60	65	71	77	83	89	95	101	107
	—	**1**	**6**	**11**	**15**	**21**	**26**	**31**	**37**	**42**	**47**	**53**	**59**	**64**	**70**	**75**	**81**	**86**	**92**	**98**
17	—	3	9	15	20	26	33	39	45	51	57	64	70	77	83	89	96	102	109	115
	—	**2**	**6**	**11**	**17**	**22**	**28**	**34**	**39**	**45**	**51**	**57**	**63**	**67**	**75**	**81**	**87**	**93**	**99**	**105**
18	—	4	9	16	22	28	35	41	48	55	61	68	75	82	88	95	102	109	116	123
	—	**2**	**7**	**12**	**18**	**24**	**30**	**36**	**42**	**48**	**55**	**61**	**67**	**74**	**80**	**86**	**93**	**99**	**106**	**112**
19	0	4	10	17	23	30	37	44	51	58	65	72	80	87	94	101	109	116	123	130
	—	**2**	**7**	**13**	**19**	**25**	**32**	**38**	**45**	**52**	**58**	**65**	**72**	**78**	**85**	**92**	**99**	**106**	**113**	**119**
20	0	4	11	18	25	32	39	47	54	62	69	77	84	92	100	107	115	123	130	138
	—	**2**	**8**	**13**	**20**	**27**	**34**	**41**	**48**	**55**	**62**	**69**	**76**	**83**	**90**	**98**	**105**	**112**	**119**	**127**

TABLE B.10 Wilcoxon Signed-Ranks Table[a]

n	Level of Significance for a One-tailed Test				n	Level of Significance for a One-tailed Test			
	.05	.025	.01	.005		.05	.025	.01	.005
	Level of Significance for a Two-tailed Test					Level of Significance for a Two-tailed Test			
	.10	.05	.02	.01		.10	.05	.02	.01
5	0	—	—	—	28	130	116	101	91
6	2	0	—	—	29	140	126	110	100
7	3	2	0	—	30	151	137	120	109
8	5	3	1	0	31	163	147	130	118
9	8	5	3	1	32	175	159	140	128
10	10	8	5	3	33	187	170	151	138
11	13	10	7	5	34	200	182	162	148
12	17	13	9	7	35	213	195	173	159
13	21	17	12	9	36	227	208	185	171
14	25	21	15	12	37	241	221	198	182
15	30	25	19	15	38	256	235	211	194
16	35	29	23	19	39	271	249	224	207
17	41	34	27	23	40	286	264	238	220
18	47	40	32	27	41	302	279	252	233
19	53	46	37	32	42	319	294	266	247
20	60	52	43	37	43	336	310	281	261
21	67	58	49	42	44	353	327	296	276
22	75	65	55	48	45	371	343	312	291
23	83	73	62	54	46	389	361	328	307
24	91	81	69	61	47	407	378	345	322
25	100	89	76	68	48	426	396	362	339
26	110	98	84	75	49	446	415	379	355
27	119	107	92	83	50	466	434	397	373

[a] The obtained T is significant at a given level if it is *equal to* or *less than* the value shown in the table.

Source: Statistics: An Introduction, 3rd. ed., R. Kirk, © 1990 Holt, Rinehart and Winston, Inc., reprinted by permission of the publisher.

Answers to Problems

Chapter 1

1. Independent variable: Vitamin E or amount of Vitamin E. Dependent variable: Time subjects spend riding the bicycle. There is one level of the independent variable.

2. Independent variable: Educational programs. Dependent variable: There are two dependent variables—comprehension and reading speed.

3. Independent variable: Choice or attitude change technique. Dependent variable: Amount of attitude change.

4. Independent variable: Amount of natural light. Dependent variable: Number of widgets made.

5. The letter on the can is confounded with beer. Coors always has the letter M and Old Style always has the letter Z. Is it the taste that subjects are responding to or are they simply showing a preference for the letter M?

6. The abnormal behavior of the mice might be due to the loud blast of noise.

7. The presence of the radar units could have caused motorists to drive more carefully. Without using the radar, it is possible that just reducing the speed limit (even if motorists obey the new speed limit) would not have an effect on traffic accidents.

8. This is a tough one. However, it is possible that giving the patients a *choice* is what is important. Perhaps patients feel that they have more control over the pain when given a choice of method of pain control. Note that after the study is completed, the dentist no longer allows patients to choose the method. All are given earphones. (This problem is a good example of the importance of knowing the research literature in the area being studied. It is well known among pain researchers that subjects' beliefs that they have control over pain reduces pain.) Another problem with this study is that subjects are not randomly

assigned to the two pain control conditions. It is possible that those subjects who select the earphones are different in some way from those subjects who select novocaine. Perhaps the earphone subjects are less anxious about having work done on their teeth, and therefore report less pain.

9. Yes. It is possible that hearing a fast heart rate causes subjects' actual heart rates to rise and hearing a low heart rate causes subjects' heart rates to lower. The experimental effect might, therefore, be due to the difference between groups in actual heart rate. Thus, the variable "belief" may be confounded with true level of heart rate. The researcher should record all subjects' heart rates to make sure that there is no difference in actual heart rates between the groups.

10. Since subjects were not randomly assigned to the typed versus handwritten conditions, it is possible that higher grades are associated with typed papers because the better students use typewriters.

11. a. *Experiment:* First select a method for inducing pain. Next, randomly assign subjects to at least two levels of pain induction that differ in intensity. For the dependent variable, select a known method for measuring anxiety; perhaps a self-report anxiety questionnaire and/or psychophysiological recordings. (As a check on the experimental manipulation, it would be a good idea to ask for pain ratings from the subjects to document that the groups differ in their perception of how painful the stimulus is.)
   Correlational Design: Have one group of subjects experience a painful stimulus. Do not manipulate the level of pain. Measure each subject's pain perception and anxiety level.

   b. *Experiment:* Randomly assign subjects to a high frequency of exercise condition and a low frequency of exercise condition. After a predetermined length of time, say, 3 months, obtain a measure of resting heart rate. It would be a good idea to document that the two groups do not differ in resting heart rate before the exercise program begins. In addition, you can use more than two experimental conditions. You could also have a group that is not asked to exercise. (Of course, you would have to document that this group actually exercises less than the low-frequency group.)
   Correlational Design: Randomly select a group of subjects. Find out how much each subject exercises and measure each subject's resting heart rate. Note that subjects are not randomly assigned to different exercise conditions.

   c. *Experiment:* Need for achievement is a personality (subject) variable. There is no way to manipulate it and use it as an independent variable in an experiment. However, it would be possible to see if the number of hours worked per week leads to changes in need for achievement. Here you would randomly assign subjects to different experimental conditions that differ in the amount of hours subjects are required to work. At the end of some predetermined amount of time, the groups are compared on a measure of need for achievement.
   Correlational Design: Take a random sample of subjects and have them record the number of hours they work per week, over a 1-month period. Also measure each subject's need for achievement.

d. *Experiment:* Preschool children would be randomly assigned to attend or not attend day care. Measure all children's level of social skills when they are in first grade.

Correlational Design: Take a random sample of children, making sure that the sample includes some children who will attend preschool and some children who will not attend preschool. Measure their social skills in first grade. Another approach is to take a random sample of first-grade students, measure social skills, and identify which students attended preschool and which students did not.

Chapter 2

1. a. Ratio.
   b. Nominal.
   c. Ordinal.
   d. Ratio.
   e. Ratio. (If you had trouble with this one, ask yourself if a 0 heart rate has meaning. It certainly does, especially for the person with such a heart rate! Also, a rate of 80 beats per minute is twice as much as 40 beats per minute, another defining feature of a ratio scale.)
   f. Interval. (Assume that need for approval has no meaningful zero point. This is usually the case for most self-report measures of personality traits.)
   g. Ratio.
   h. Nominal.
   i. Nominal.
   j. Nominal.
   k. Ordinal.

2.

	Width	*LL*	*Midpoint*	*UL*
a.	3	.5	2	3.5
b.	6	4.5	7.5	10.5
c.	5	−8.5	−6	−3.5
d.	5	−2.5	0	2.5
e.	3	1.000	2.5	4.000
f.	26	24.5	37.5	50.5

3 and 4 a. Only the top and bottom four numbers of the distribution are provided here and in *b*.

LL	*X*	*UL*	*f*	*cf*
97.5	98	98.5	1	36
96.5	97	97.5	0	35
95.5	96	96.5	0	35
94.5	95	95.5	0	35
⋮	⋮	⋮	⋮	⋮
43.5	44	44.5	0	3
42.5	43	43.5	2	3
41.5	42	42.5	0	1
40.5	41	41.5	1	1

3 and 4 b.

LL	X	UL	f	cf
95.5	96–98	98.5	1	36
92.5	93–95	95.5	0	35
89.5	90–92	92.5	3	35
86.5	87–89	89.5	3	32
⋮	⋮	⋮	⋮	⋮
47.5	48–50	50.5	1	5
44.5	45–47	47.5	1	4
41.5	42–44	44.5	2	3
38.5	39–41	41.5	1	1

$i = 3$

3 and 4 c.

LL	X	UL	f	cf
89.5	90–99	99.5	4	36
79.5	80–89	89.5	11	32
69.5	70–79	79.5	9	21
59.5	60–69	69.5	5	12
49.5	50–59	59.5	2	7
39.5	40–49	49.5	5	5

3 and 4 d.

LL	X	UL	f	cf
79.5	80–99	99.5	15	36
59.5	60–79	79.5	14	21
39.5	40–59	59.5	7	7

5. Refer to graph.

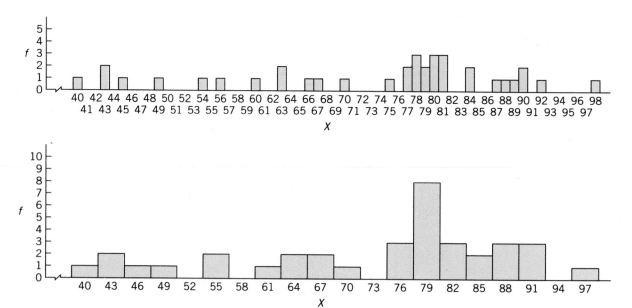

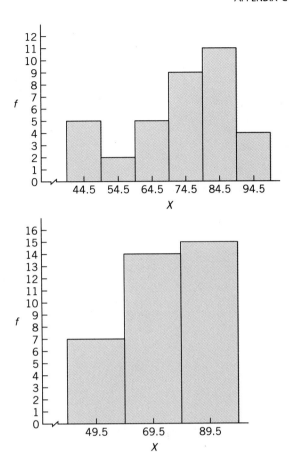

6. Refer to graph.

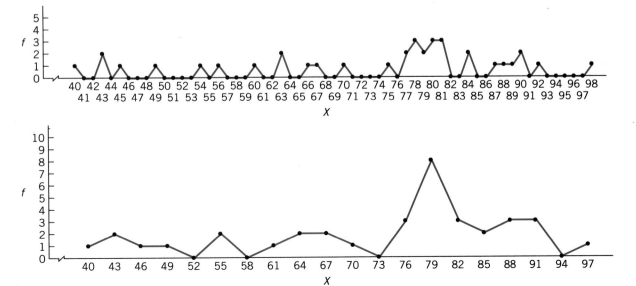

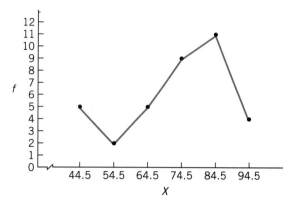

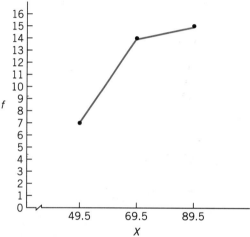

7. Graphs not provided.

Chapter 3

1. It must be symmetrical.

2. a. $\overline{X} = 6$ Median = 6   Mode = 8
   b. $\overline{X} = 4.86$ Median = 4   Mode = 4
   c. $\overline{X} = 8.71$ Median = 9   Mode = 10
   d. $\overline{X} = 3.86$ Median = 4   Mode = 1 and 4

3. a. *Distribution A $\Sigma(X - \overline{X})$*   *Distribution B $\Sigma(X - \overline{X})$*

$X - \overline{X}$	x	$X - \overline{X}$	x
$3 - 6$	-3	$2 - 4.86$	-2.86
$3 - 6$	-3	$4 - 4.86$	$-.86$
$4 - 6$	-2	$4 - 4.86$	$-.86$
$5 - 6$	-1	$4 - 4.86$	$-.86$
$6 - 6$	0	$6 - 4.86$	$+1.14$
$8 - 6$	$+2$	$7 - 4.86$	$+2.14$
$8 - 6$	$+2$	$7 - 4.86$	$+2.14$
$8 - 6$	$+2$		
$9 - 6$	$+3$		

Distribution A: $\Sigma x = 0$

Distribution B: $\Sigma x = -.02$ (will be 0 without rounding error)

b. *Distribution A $\Sigma(X - Median)$*   *Distribution B $\Sigma(X - Median)$*

$X - Median$	$X - Median$
$3 - 6 = -3$	$2 - 4 = -2$
$3 - 6 = -3$	$4 - 4 = 0$
$4 - 6 = -2$	$4 - 4 = 0$
$5 - 6 = -1$	$4 - 4 = 0$
$6 - 6 = 0$	$6 - 4 = +2$
$8 - 6 = +2$	$7 - 4 = +3$
$8 - 6 = +2$	$7 - 4 = +3$
$8 - 6 = +2$	$\Sigma(X - Median) = +6$
$9 - 6 = +3$	

$\Sigma(X - Median) = 0$

c. *Distribution A $\Sigma(X - Mode)$*   *Distribution B $\Sigma(X - Mode)$*

$X - Mode$	$X - Mode$
$3 - 8 = -5$	$2 - 4 = -2$
$3 - 8 = -5$	$4 - 4 = 0$
$4 - 8 = -4$	$4 - 4 = 0$
$5 - 8 = -3$	$4 - 4 = 0$
$6 - 8 = -2$	$6 - 4 = +2$
$8 - 8 = 0$	$7 - 4 = +3$
$8 - 8 = 0$	$7 - 4 = +3$
$8 - 8 = 0$	$\Sigma(X - Mode) = +6$
$9 - 8 = +1$	

$\Sigma(X - Mode) = -18$

The preceding exercise illustrates that $\Sigma(X - \overline{X})$ equals 0. The sum of X minus the median or mode will only equal 0 if these values are the same as the mean, which is the case in a normal distribution. Neither distribution A nor B are normal. The fact that $\Sigma(X - Median) = 0$ for distribution A is coincidental.

4. a. $\overline{X} = 8.65$.
   b. Mode = 9.
5. a. $\overline{X} = 17.93$
   b. Mode = 15 and 16
6. Median = $6.5 + .5 = 7$
7. Median = $5.5 + [(30/2 - 4)/11 \cdot 5] = 10.50$
8. Median = $21.5 + [(16/2 - 4)/6 \cdot 3] = 23.50$
9. a. Positively skewed.
   b. Negatively skewed.
   c. Symmetrical, unimodal.
   d. Symmetrical, bimodal.
   e. Negatively skewed.
   f. Positively skewed.
10. $\overline{X} = \dfrac{552 + 551 + 448}{107} = 14.50$
11. a. $\overline{X} = 104.80$
    b. Median = 101
12. $\overline{X} = 109.73$; median = 100.50; mode = 100

The following histogram reveals a positively skewed distribution, which is consistent with the fact that the mean is greater than the median. (Note: Some computer printouts represent histograms as bar graphs in that adjacent bars do not share a common border, which is the case here.)

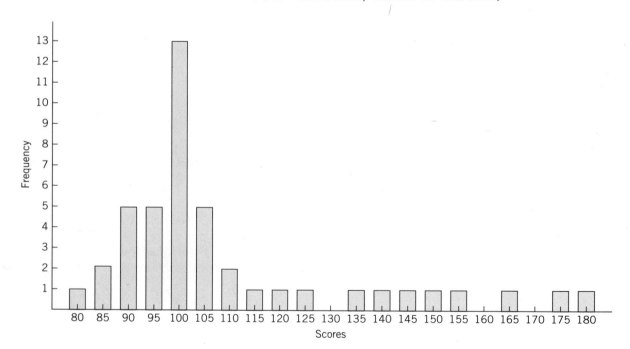

13. $\mu = 28.12$; median $= 32$; mode $= 35$

The histogram shows this distribution to be negatively skewed, consistent with the fact that the mean is smaller than the median.

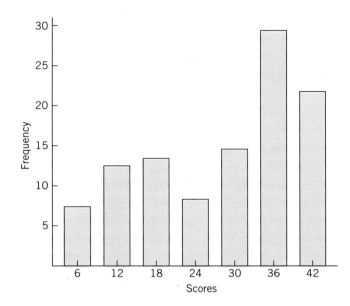

Chapter 4

1. Cannot say which would have the *larger* variance, but $n = 60$ would likely give a more accurate estimate of the population variance. A sample size of 60 would likely have the larger range.

2. You cannot estimate the variance based on the size of $\overline{X}$.

3. a. $\overline{X} = 103.50$
   b. $s = 5.24$

4. a. Range $= 8 - 1 = 7$
   b. $s^2 = 4.27$
   c. $s = 2.07$

5. a. IQR $= 111 - 81 = 30$
   b. SIQR $= (111 - 81)/2 = 15$

6. a. σ
   b. s
   c. σ
   d. s

7. $\sigma = 4.83$ and $\sigma^2 = 23.35$

8. $s_A^2 = 7.125$ $s_B^2 = 5.90$

9. No.

10. Affected by extreme scores.

11. The standard deviation is the easiest to interpret because it is in the original units of the measured variable.

12. $\sigma = 2.66$

13. $\overline{X} = 14.50$ $s^2 = 1.60$

14.

	Experimental (Biofeedback)	Control
a.	Pre: $s = 12.95$	Pre: $s = 9.11$
b.	Post: $s = 10.89$	Post: $s = 11.19$

15.

	Technique A	Technique B
a.	$\overline{X}_{PRE} = 3.50$	$\overline{X}_{PRE} = 3.50$
b.	$s^2_{PRE} = 1.67$	$s^2_{PRE} = .67$
c.	$s_{PRE} = 1.29$	$s_{PRE} = .82$
d.	$\overline{X}_{POST} = 5.50$	$\overline{X}_{POST} = 3.50$
e.	$s^2_{POST} = 1.67$	$s^2_{POST} = 1.67$
f.	$s_{POST} = 1.29$	$s_{POST} = 1.29$

16.

$X + 10$	$X - 10$	$X(10)$	$X/10$
$\mu = 60$	$\mu = 40$	$\mu = 500$	$\mu = 5$
$\sigma^2 = 25$	$\sigma^2 = 25$	$\sigma^2 = 2500$	$\sigma^2 = .25$

17. $\overline{X} = 7.07$ $s^2 = 17.61$ $s = 4.20$ Range $= 14$

18. $\overline{X} = 96.52$ $s^2 = 138.56$ $s = 11.77$ Range $= 39$

19. $\overline{X} = 965.24$ $s^2 = 13856.20$ $s = 117.71$ Range $= 390$

Chapter 5

1. a. $PR = \dfrac{23 + .5(12)}{49} \cdot 100 = .59(100) = 59$

   b. $PR = \dfrac{42 + .5(4)}{49} \cdot 100 = .90(100) = 90$

   c. $PR = \dfrac{13 + .5(10)}{49} \cdot 100 = .37(100) = 37$

   d. $PR = \dfrac{6 + .5(7)}{49} \cdot 100 = .19(100) = 19$

2. $\mu = 7.67$ $\sigma = 2.56$

X	z	T
4	-1.43	$-1.43(10) + 50 = 36$
5	-1.04	$-1.04(10) + 50 = 40$
7	-0.26	$-0.26(10) + 50 = 47$
9	$+0.52$	$+0.52(10) + 50 = 55$
10	$+0.91$	$+0.91(10) + 50 = 59$
11	$+1.30$	$+1.30(10) + 50 = 63$

3. $z = \dfrac{11 - 14}{4} = \dfrac{-3}{4} = -.75$

4. $X = 25 + .36(3) = 25 + 1.08 = 26.08$

5. $z = \dfrac{140 - 130}{13} = \dfrac{10}{13} = .77$ **Answer: .22**

6. $z = \dfrac{27 - 34}{3} = -2.33$ **Answer: .99%**

7. $.025 + .025 = 2.5\% + 2.5\% = 5\%$

8. $.45 + .45 = 45\% + 45\% = 90\%$

9. a. $z = -.20$
   b. $z = -.30$
   c. $z = +.47$
   d. $z = +1.48$
   e. $z = -1.20$
   f. $z = +.54$
   g. $z = +.09$
   h. $z = -.19$
   i. $z = +.80$

10. $.3849 + .2123 = .5972$

11. $.3051 + .1141 = .4192$

12. $.1587 + .1587 = .3174 = 31.74\%$

13. $(z\text{'s} = \pm 1)$ *Answer: .6826*

14. $z\text{'s} = \pm 1.28$ (from table)
      $X = 70 \pm 1.28(7) = 61$ and 79
   $> 79 =$ best students and < 61 worst students

15. $\mu = 5.67$ $\sigma = 2.36$

X	z	T
2	−1.56	$-1.56(10) + 50 = 34$
4	−0.71	$-0.71(10) + 50 = 43$
5	−0.28	$-0.28(10) + 50 = 47$
6	+0.14	$+0.14(10) + 50 = 51$
8	+0.99	$+0.99(10) + 50 = 60$
9	+1.41	$+1.41(10) + 50 = 64$

16. z scores are used to find the percentage of scores **below** the raw scores.
   a. $z = -1.25$ PR $= 10.56$
   b. $z = +2.25$ PR $= 98.78$
   c. $z = 0$ PR $= 50$
   d. $z = +.50$ PR $= 69.15$
   e. $z = -.25$ PR $= 40.13$

17. a. $z = 1.645$ (from table) $X = 78 + 1.645(7) = 90$ (rounded)
   b. $z = .84$ (from table) $X = 78 + .84(7) = 84$ (rounded)
   c. $z = -.52$ (from table) $X = 78 + (-.52)(7) = 74$ (rounded)
   d. $z = -.13$ (from table) $X = 78 + (-.13)(7) = 77$ (rounded)

18. a. 11.51%
    b. 50% + 14.06% = 64.06%
    c. 28.77%
    d. 21.48%
    e. 13.57%
    f. 50% + 33.65% = 83.65%
    g. 44.83%

19. a. $z = \dfrac{38 - 56}{5} = -3.6$ **Answer: .02%** (She's easy!)

    b. $z = \pm.39$
       $X\text{'s} = 56 \pm (.39)(5) = 54.05$ and 57.95
       C category is 54 to 58.

    c. $z = 1.28$
        $X = 56 + 1.28(5) = 62.4$
        The A category is 62 and up.

20. a. $z = .84$ (from table).
    b. No; you need a mean and standard deviation.

21. $PR = \dfrac{42 + (.5)16}{76} \cdot 100 = 66$

22. $X_{.40} = 13.5 + \dfrac{(126)(.40) - 46}{27} \cdot 4 = 14$ (rounded)

    $X_{.50} = 13.5 + \dfrac{(126)(.50) - 46}{27} \cdot 4 = 16$ (rounded)

    $X_{.65} = 17.5 + \dfrac{(126)(.65) - 73}{23} \cdot 4 = 19$ (rounded)

    $X_{.90} = 25.5 + \dfrac{(126)(.90) - 109}{13} \cdot 4 = 27$ (rounded)

23. $X_{.25} = 15$; $X_{.50}$ (median) $= 20$; $X_{.75} = 25.25$

24. Should be $\mu = 0$ and $\sigma = 1.0$; minor discrepancies due to rounding.

25. *Population:* $\mu = 20.28$; $\sigma^2 = 43.51$; $\sigma = 6.60$
    Sample: $\overline{X} = 20.28$; $s^2 = 44.08$; $s = 6.64$

Chapter 6

1. Choose a population of scores. Decide on a sample size, n. Take a random sample of size n. Compute the mean and replace the scores back into the population. Repeat the sampling procedure until all possible samples have been drawn. Plot the relative frequency distribution of the means.

2. The variability of the sampling distribution is determined by the population standard deviation and the size of the samples drawn. The relation is $\sigma_{\overline{X}} = \sigma/\sqrt{n}$.

3. Point estimation estimates a parameter as a single value. Interval estimation establishes a range of values within which the population parameter is expected to lie.

4. Estimation is an inferential procedure that uses data from a sample to infer the value of a population parameter. Hypothesis testing is a set of inferential procedures that uses data from samples to establish the credibility of a hypothesis about population parameters.

5. The standard error of the mean decreases as the sample size (n) increases. This is because a larger sample is less likely to include extreme scores that would combine to produce an extreme mean.

6. Case I research uses one sample to test a hypothesis about the mean of a population. Case II research uses two samples to test a hypothesis about the difference between two population means. Case I and II research are experimental research methods that attempt to identify causal relations among variables. The correlational method does not attempt to exert an influence on a measured response. It cannot identify causal relations among variables; instead, it is aimed at identifying the strength of association between variables.

7. A scientific hypothesis is a formal statement or expectation about the outcome of a study, often specifying the relation between an independent and dependent variable. A statistical hypothesis is a numerical statement about the outcome of a study. The null and alternative hypotheses are statistical hypotheses.

8. The null hypothesis states there is no effect of the independent variable on the dependent variable (no relation between variables). The alternative hypothesis states there is an experimental effect (a relation between variables).

9. Your example of Case I research should specify an exact numerical value for the null hypothesis. The alternative hypothesis is that the population mean does not equal *that* numerical value.

10. $\mu_{\bar{X}} = 100$; $\sigma_{\bar{X}} = 10/\sqrt{9} = 3.33$. Its shape is normal because it comes from a normally distributed population.

11. Since I do not know what scores you randomly selected, there is no way to give you sample means. However, for n's of 5, 10, 15, and 20, the standard errors are 4.80, 3.40, 2.77, 2.40, respectively. As the sample size increases, the standard error decreases.

Chapter 7

1. Depending on the particular sample drawn, you might show a treatment effect by chance—due to extreme scores being included in the sample but not because of an experimental treatment. We cannot know for sure that an effect was not due to chance since we are always dealing with probabilities. However, we can control the level of certainty with which we can claim to have an experimental effect by the level at which we set alpha.

2. No answer offered.

3. a. H_0: $\mu = 8$; H_1: $\mu \neq 8$
   b. H_0: $\mu = 12$; H_1: $\mu \neq 12$
   c. H_0: $\mu = 20$; H_1: $\mu \neq 20$

4. You should use the t distribution when the population standard deviation is unknown.

5. The relative consequences of a Type I versus a Type II error.

6. a. Use the z distribution since σ is known.
   b. $H_0: \mu = 60$; $H_1: \mu \neq 60$
   c. $z_{crit} = 1.96$
   d. $z_{obt} = \dfrac{65 - 60}{5/\sqrt{50}} = \dfrac{65 - 60}{5/7.07} = 7.04$
   e. Reject the null hypothesis.
   f. Yes. Typing speed is significantly enhanced when using the manufacturer's PC.

7. a. Use the z distribution since σ is known.
   b. $H_0: \mu = 100$; $H_1: \mu \neq 100$
   c. $z_{crit} = 1.96$
   d. $z_{obt} = \dfrac{110 - 100}{15/\sqrt{100}} = 6.67$
   e. Reject the null hypothesis.
   f. Yes. Children of parents with a college education have IQ's that are significantly higher than the average IQ.

8. a. Use the t distribution since σ is unknown.
   b. $H_0: \mu = 90$; $H_1: \mu \neq 90$
   c. $t_{crit} = 2.021$ $(df = 39)$
   d. $t_{obt} = \dfrac{110 - 90}{30/\sqrt{40}} = 4.21$
   e. Reject the null hypothesis.
   f. Administration of this hormone produces Golden Retrievers that are significantly heavier than the average weight of Retrievers.

9. The random selection of subjects may result in sampling error. The procedures of hypothesis testing help determine the likelihood that sampling error accounts for the experimental results.

10. a. Use the t distribution since σ is unknown.
    b. $H_0: \mu = 72.40$; $H_1: \mu \neq 72.40$
    c. $t_{crit} = 2.306$ $(df = 8)$
    d. $t_{obt} = \dfrac{77 - 72.4}{3.1/\sqrt{9}} = 4.47$
    e. Reject the null hypothesis.
    f. Males overestimate their life expectancy.

11. a.–d. $t_{crit} = 2.365$ $(df = 7)$. The mean height for physically stressed males $(\overline{X} = 69.25)$ is significantly greater than the average height for males, $t(7) = 4.52$, $p < .05$. Females who have been physically stressed $(\overline{X} = 61.88)$ also are significantly taller than the average female, $t(7) = 3.08$, $p < .05$.

12. $t_{obt} = \dfrac{20 - 16}{2.8/\sqrt{8}} = 4.04$

$t_{crit} = 2.365 \quad (df = 7)$

The mean number of publications among the faculty members of this sociology department is significantly higher than the national average, $t(7) = 4.04$, $p < .05$.

13. Students who participated in the program now smoke significantly fewer cigarettes ($\overline{X} = 10.34$) than the average number of cigarettes consumed by students who smoke, $t(49) = -4.17$, $p < .05$.

14. There is no evidence that the average number of days to process a claim is different from 15, $t(39) = -.83$, n.s.

15. The addition of extra trains during rush hour significantly reduced the amount of time the train is late, $t(29) = -5.18$, $p < .05$. (If you used 6.40 as the population standard deviation, $z_{obt} = -7.84$, and the same interpretation of the results holds.)

Chapter 8

1. a. $H_0: \mu_1 = \mu_2; H_1: \mu_1 \neq \mu_2$
   b. $t_{crit} = 2.228 \quad (df = 10)$

   c.

No Siblings	Siblings
$\overline{X}_1 = 7.33$	$\overline{X}_2 = 3.17$
$s_1 = 2.16$	$s_2 = 2.14$
$n_1 = 6$	$n_2 = 6$

   Using the computational formula,

   $$t_{obt} = \dfrac{7.33 - 3.17}{\sqrt{\{[(346 - (44)^2/6) + (83 - (19)^2/6)]/(6 + 6 - 2)\}(1/6 + 1/6)}}$$

   $t_{obt} = 3.33$

   d. Reject the null hypothesis. Two-year-olds with siblings have significantly less fear than two-year-olds with no siblings, $t(10) = 3.33, p < .05$.

2. a. $H_0: \mu_1 = \mu_2; H_1: \mu_1 \neq \mu_2$
   b. $t_{crit} = 2.101 \quad (df = 18)$
   c. $t_{obt} = \dfrac{4.2 - 2.2}{\sqrt{[(.5(9) + .7(9))/(10 + 10 - 2)](1/10 + 1/10)}}$

   $t_{obt} = 5.71$

   d. Reject the null hypothesis. Among males, a high level of anxiety leads to greater attraction toward females than a low level of anxiety, $t(18) = 5.71$, $p < .05$.

3. a. $t_{obt} = \dfrac{4.2 - 2.2}{\sqrt{[(5.2(9) + 5.4(9))/(10 + 10 - 2)](1/10 + 1/10)}}$

    $t_{obt} = 1.94$

    b. With $t_{crit} = 2.101$, the t_{obt} of 1.94 does not lead to rejection of the null hypothesis.

    c. Increasing the variability of scores has increased the size of the denominator of the t ratio and reduced the size of t_{obt}.

4. a. $t_{obt} = \dfrac{4.2 - 2.2}{\sqrt{[(5.2(29) + 5.4(29))/(30 + 30 - 2)](1/30 + 1/30)}}$

    $t_{obt} = 3.51$

    b. See Problem 2d for interpretation of results.

    c. Increasing the sample size increases t_{obt} by decreasing the size of the denominator.

5. The standard deviation of the sampling distribution of differences between the means is the standard error of the difference.

6. As the sample size increases, df increases, and t_{crit} decreases. As the sample size increases, the t distribution approaches the standard normal curve. As the tails of the t distribution are lowered, the likelihood of extreme t values decreases. As a consequence, you do not have to go as far from the mean of the t distribution to mark the cutoffs beyond which 2.5 percent of the distribution lie.

7. Increasing the sample size will decrease the size of the denominator of the t ratio and result in a larger t_{obt}. This increases the chances of rejecting the null hypothesis.

8. a. H_0: $\mu_1 = \mu_2$; H_1: $\mu_1 \neq \mu_2$

    b. $t_{crit} = 2.306$ (with $df = 8$)

    c.

Males	Females
$\overline{X}_1 = 15.60$	$\overline{X}_2 = 9.0$
$s_1 = 4.16$	$s_2 = 3.61$
$n_1 = 5$	$n_2 = 5$

    Using the computational formula,

    $$t_{obt} = \dfrac{15.6 - 9.0}{\sqrt{\{[(1286 - 1216.8) + (457 - 405)]/(5 + 5 - 2)\}(1/5 + 1/5)}}$$

    $t_{obt} = 2.68$

    d. Male college students report significantly more anger reactions than female college students, $t(8) = 2.68, p < .05$.

9. a. H_0: $\mu_1 = \mu_2$; H_1: $\mu_1 \neq \mu_2$

    b. $t_{crit} = 2.228$ ($df = 10$)

c.
Teachers	Principals
$\overline{X} = 41.33$	$\overline{X}_2 = 32.50$
$s_1 = 5.43$	$s_2 = 6.19$
$n_1 = 6$	$n_2 = 6$

Using the computational formula,

$$t_{obt} = \frac{41.33 - 32.50}{\sqrt{\{[(10398 - 10250.67) + (6529 - 6337.50)]/(6 + 6 - 2)\}(1/6 + 1/6)}}$$

$$t_{obt} = 2.60$$

d. Teachers experience significantly more burnout than principals, $t(10) = 2.60$, $p < .05$

10. a. $H_0: \mu_1 = \mu_2$; $H_1: \mu_1 \neq \mu_2$
b. $t_{crit} = 2.306$ (with $df = 8$)

c.
Lonely	Not Lonely
$\overline{X} = 5.00$	$\overline{X}_2 = 7.40$
$s_1 = 1.58$	$s_2 = 1.52$
$n_1 = 5$	$n_2 = 5$

Using the computational formula,

$$t_{obt} = \frac{5 - 7.4}{\sqrt{\{[(135 - 125) + (283 - 273.8)]/(5 + 5 - 2)\}(1/5 + 1/5)}}$$

$$t_{obt} = -2.45$$

d. Reject the null hypothesis. Note that the absolute value of t_{obt} is larger than the critical value of 2.306. Conclusion: Lonely males are rated as significantly less attractive than males who are not lonely, $t(8) = -2.45$, $p < .05$.

11. a. $H_0: \mu_1 = \mu_2$; $H_1: \mu_1 \neq \mu_2$
b. $t_{crit} = 2.228$ ($df = 10$)

c.
Buffalo Creek	Kopperston
$\overline{X}_1 = 43.83$	$\overline{X}_2 = 37.50$
$s_1 = 4.67$	$s_2 = 1.87$
$n_1 = 6$	$n_2 = 6$

Using the computational formula,

$$t_{obt} = \frac{43.83 - 37.50}{\sqrt{\{[(11637 - 11528.17) + (8455 - 8437.50)]/(6 + 6 - 2)\}(1/6 + 1/6)}}$$

$$t_{obt} = 3.06$$

d. Residents of Buffalo Creek experience significantly higher trait anxiety than residents of Kopperston, $t(10) = 3.06$, $p < .05$. Recall that one of the assumptions of the t test is that the population variances are equal. In this case, $s_1^2 = 21.81$ and $s_2^2 = 3.50$. You might wonder if perhaps the assumption of homogeneity of variances is violated here. Methods for testing whether two variances are significantly different are discussed in more advanced statistics books.

12. a. *Males:*

$$t_{obt} = \frac{23 - 16}{\sqrt{[(61.47(9) + 41.34(14))/(10 + 15 - 2)](1/10 + 1/15)}}$$

$t_{obt} = 2.42$

$t_{crit} = 2.069$ (with $df = 23$)

First-born males are significantly more narcissistic than later-born males, $t(23) = 2.42$, $p < .05$.

b. *Females:*

$$t_{obt} = \frac{17 - 12}{\sqrt{[(42.51(18) + 43.16(27))/(19 + 28 - 2)](1/19 + 1/28)}}$$

$t_{obt} = 2.55$

$t_{crit} = $ approximately 2.00

First-born females are significantly more narcissistic than later-born females, $t(45) = 2.55$, $p < .05$.

13. $t_{obt} = \dfrac{14.6 - 5.6}{\sqrt{[(852.64(53) + 29.16(83))/(54 + 84 - 2)](1/54 + 1/84)}}$

$t_{obt} = 2.78$

$t_{crit} = $ approximately 1.98

Males report having had significantly more sexual partners than females report, $t(136) = 2.78$, $p < .05$. (Note: The same point can be made here as in Problem 11: the homogeneity of variances assumption of the t test is likely violated. Violating this assumption, however, becomes less serious when the sample size is as large as it is in this problem. Nonetheless, what to do when this assumption is violated goes beyond the scope of this text. One solution is to use a type of significance test that is discussed in Chapter 18.)

14. a. $H_0: \mu_1 = \mu_2$; $H_1: \mu_1 \neq \mu_2$

b. $t_{obt} = \dfrac{17.0 - 13.5}{2.0} = 1.75$

c. $t_{crit} = $ approximately 2.00

d. There is no significant difference in children's time spent with peers based on their ability to start conversations, $t(58) = 1.75$, n.s.

15. a. H_0: $\mu_1 > \mu_2$; H_1: $\mu_1 \leq \mu_2$ (where 1 is the experimental group and 2 is the control group).

    b. (Same as Problem 14b) $t_{obt} = 1.75$

    c. t_{crit} = approximately 1.671. Now, using a one-tailed test, the null hypothesis would be rejected. *Conclusion:* Children who receive training in starting conversations spend more time interacting with peers than children who do not receive training, $t(58) = 1.75$, $p < .05$.

    d. No. There is no compelling reason for using a one-tailed test. Indeed, a finding in the opposite direction—that children who receive training engage in *less* peer interaction—would certainly be theoretically, if not practically important to know.

16. No answer is provided here.

17. $t(48) = 1.85$, n.s.; t_{crit} = approximately 2.01 for a two-tailed test and 1.67 for a one-tailed test. Thus, the null hypothesis would be rejected only if a one-tailed test were used.

18. Subjects in the low-arousal condition show significantly greater approach behavior than subjects in the high-arousal condition, $t(58) = 2.77$, $p < .05$.

Chapter 9

1. a. H_0: $\mu_x = \mu_y$; H_1: $\mu_x \neq \mu_y$

   b. $t_{crit} == 2.365$

   c. $\overline{X} = 7.625$; $\overline{Y} = 5.625$; $\Sigma D = 16$; $\Sigma D^2 = 62$

   $$t_{obt} = \frac{7.625 - 5.625}{.73} = \frac{2.0}{.73} = 2.74$$

   d. Reject the null hypothesis and conclude a significant difference in perceptions of bearded and nonbearded men, $t(7) = 2.74$, $p < .05$. Bearded men are perceived as significantly more masculine than nonbearded men.

2. a. H_0: $\mu_x = \mu_y$; H_1: $\mu_x \neq \mu_y$

   b. $t_{crit} = 2.571$

   c. $\overline{X} = 5.0$; $\overline{Y} = 2.83$; $\Sigma D = 13$; $\Sigma D^2 = 35$

   $$t_{obt} = \frac{5.0 - 2.83}{.48} = \frac{2.17}{.48} = 4.52$$

   d. Reject the null hypothesis and conclude a significant difference in preference for products advertised with sexual symbolism versus nonsexual symbolism. People are significantly more willing to buy liquor products advertised with sexual symbolism, $t(5) = 4.52$, $p < .05$.

3. a. H_0: $\mu_x = \mu_y$; H_1: $\mu_x \neq \mu_y$

   b. $t_{crit} = 2.776$

   c. $\overline{X} = 7.0$; $\overline{Y} = 5.60$; $\Sigma D = 7$; $\Sigma D^2 = 35$

   $$t_{obt} = \frac{7.0 - 5.60}{1.12} = \frac{1.40}{1.12} = 1.25$$

d. Retain the null hypothesis and conclude that there is no significant difference in preference for Gouda or Swiss cheese, $t(4) = 1.25$, n.s.

4. The dependent-samples t test increases the power of an experiment—that is—the probability of correctly rejecting a false null hypothesis, by statistically removing variability due to individual differences.

5. a. $H_0: \mu_x \le \mu_y$; $H_1: \mu_x > \mu_y$ $(X = \text{Pre}; Y = \text{Post})$
   b. $t_{crit} = 2.353$
   c. $\overline{X} = 92.50$; $\overline{Y} = 45.0$; $\Sigma D = 190$; $\Sigma D^2 = 12{,}500$

$$t_{obt} = \frac{92.50 - 45.0}{17.015} = 2.79$$

   d. Reject the null hypothesis and conclude that there is a significant difference in time to sleep. Administering the drug leads to falling asleep in significantly less time, $t(3) = 2.79$, $p < .05$.

6. a. $t_{crit} = 1.729$
   b. $t_{crit} = 1.746$
   c. $t_{crit} = 2.33$
   d. $t_{crit} = 1.895$
   e. $t_{crit} = \text{approx. } 2.58$
   f. $t_{crit} = 2.896$
   g. $t_{crit} = 2.132$
   h. $t_{crit} = 1.86$

7. Use independent-samples t test.
   a. $H_0: \mu_1 = \mu_2$; $H_1: \mu_1 \ne \mu_2$
   b. $\overline{X}_1 = 5.375$; $\overline{X}_2 = 3.0$; $s_1^2 = 3.41$; $s_2^2 = 5.14$; $n_1 = 8$; $n_2 = 8$

$$t_{obt} = \frac{5.375 - 3.0}{\sqrt{\{[(3.41)(7) + (5.14)(7)]/(8 + 8 - 2)\}(1/8 + 1/8)}}$$

$$t_{obt} = 2.31$$

   c. $df = 14$; $\alpha = .05$; $t_{crit} = 2.145$
   d. Reject the null hypothesis and conclude that there is a significant difference between means. The anabolic steroid leads to a significantly greater weight gain than the growth stimulant, $t(14) = 2.31$, $p < .05$.

8. a. $H_0: \mu_x = \mu_y$; $H_1: \mu_x \ne \mu_y$
   b. $\overline{X} = 5.375$; $\overline{Y} = 3.0$; $\Sigma D = 19$; $\Sigma D^2 = 87$

$$t_{obt} = \frac{5.375 - 3.0}{.87} = \frac{2.375}{.87} = 2.73$$

   c. $df = 7$; $\alpha = .05$, $t_{crit} = 2.365$
   d. The anabolic steroid leads to a significantly greater weight gain than the growth stimulant, $t(7) = 2.73$, $p < .05$.

9. Students write papers of higher quality when using the IBM-compatible computer instead of the Macintosh, $t(19) = 3.05$, $p < .05$.

10. There is no evidence that vision is differentially affected by lens color, $t(15) = .17$, n.s.

11. When subjects use a soft mattress, they experience significantly more pain than when they sleep on a firm mattress, $t(11) = -5.52$, $p < .05$.

Chapter 10

1. A .95 probability that the true population mean is contained within the confidence interval means that we have used cutoffs between which 95 percent of the sampling distribution lie, and that 95 out of 100 samples would contain the true population mean. (Technically speaking, there is no guarantee that of 100 established intervals, 95 would contain μ. With an infinite number of samples, 95 percent of the intervals *would* contain μ.)

2. a. 2.015   e. 2.447
   b. 2.365   f. 1.753
   c. 3.055   g. 2.861
   d. 1.782

3. Our confidence interval is unchanged; it remains at 95 percent. The larger value of s leads to a wider interval.

4. 90 percent confidence interval:

$$LL = 600 - 1.65\left(\frac{90}{\sqrt{100}}\right) = 600 - 14.85 = 585.15$$

$$UL = 600 + 1.65\left(\frac{90}{\sqrt{100}}\right) = 600 + 14.85 = 614.85$$

95 percent confidence interval:

$$LL = 600 - 17.64 = 582.36$$

$$UL = 600 + 17.64 = 617.64$$

99 percent confidence interval:

$$LL = 600 - 23.22 = 576.78$$

$$UL = 600 + 23.22 = 623.22$$

5. 90 percent confidence interval:

$$LL = 600 - 1.65\left(\frac{90}{\sqrt{40}}\right) = 600 - 23.50 = 576.50$$

$$UL = 600 + 1.65\left(\frac{90}{\sqrt{40}}\right) = 600 + 23.50 = 623.50$$

95 percent confidence interval:

$$LL = 600 - 27.91 = 572.09$$
$$UL = 600 + 27.91 = 627.91$$

99 percent confidence interval:

$$LL = 600 - 36.74 = 563.26$$
$$UL = 600 + 36.74 = 636.74$$

Reducing the sample size from 100 to 40 increased the width of the intervals.

6. a.
$$LL = 25 - 1.65\left(\frac{2}{\sqrt{50}}\right) = 25 - .46 = 24.54$$

$$UL = 25 + 1.65\left(\frac{2}{\sqrt{50}}\right) = 25 + .46 = 25.46$$

b.
$$LL = 25 - 1.65\left(\frac{2}{\sqrt{100}}\right) = 25 - .33 = 24.67$$

$$UL = 25 + 1.65\left(\frac{2}{\sqrt{100}}\right) = 25 + .33 = 25.33$$

c.
$$LL = 25 - 1.65\left(\frac{8}{\sqrt{50}}\right) = 25 - 1.86 = 23.14$$

$$UL = 25 + 1.65\left(\frac{8}{\sqrt{50}}\right) = 25 + 1.86 = 26.86$$

Increasing n reduces the width of the interval (if all else remains constant). Reducing s decreases the width of the interval.

7.
$$LL = 3500 - 1.96\left(\frac{900}{\sqrt{80}}\right) = 3500 - 197.31 = 3302.69$$

$$UL = 3500 + 1.96\left(\frac{900}{\sqrt{80}}\right) = 3500 + 197.31 = 3697.31$$

We can state that we are 95 percent confident that the average amount of money in all the savings accounts is between $3302.69 and $3697.31.

8.
$$LL = 24.50 - 1.31 = 23.19$$
$$UL = 24.50 + 1.31 = 25.81$$

9.
$$LL = 4.2 - .52 = 3.68$$
$$UL = 4.2 + .52 = 4.72$$

10.
$$LL = 56,000 - 1087.49 = 54,912.51$$
$$UL = 56,000 + 1087.49 = 57,087.49$$

11. The confidence interval says nothing about the probability of the population mean equaling the sample mean. The confidence interval says we are 99 percent confident that the interval contains the true population mean.

12.
$$LL = 77 - 2.306\left(\frac{3.12}{\sqrt{9}}\right) = 77 - 2.40 = 74.60$$

$$UL = 77 + 2.306\left(\frac{3.12}{\sqrt{9}}\right) = 77 + 2.40 = 79.40$$

Since 72.40 is outside the 95 percent confidence interval, reject H_0: $\mu = 72.40$ and conclude that males' subjective life expectancy is significantly different from the life expectancy of the male population.

13. *Males:* H_0: $\mu = 65$; H_1: $\mu \neq 65$

$$LL = 69.25 - 2.365\left(\frac{2.66}{\sqrt{8}}\right) = 69.25 - 2.22 = 67.03$$

$$UL = 69.25 + 2.365\left(\frac{2.66}{\sqrt{8}}\right) = 69.25 + 2.22 = 71.47$$

Since 65 is outside the 95 percent confidence interval, reject H_0 and conclude a significant difference in male height due to early physical stress.

Females: H_0: $\mu = 59$; H_1: $\mu \neq 59$

$$LL = 61.88 - 2.365\left(\frac{2.64}{\sqrt{8}}\right) = 61.88 - 2.20 = 59.68$$

$$UL = 61.88 + 2.365\left(\frac{2.64}{\sqrt{8}}\right) = 61.88 + 2.20 = 64.08$$

Since 59 is outside the 95 percent confidence interval, reject H_0 and conclude a significant difference in female height due to early physical stress.

14. H_0: $\mu_1 - \mu_2 = 0$; H_1: $\mu_1 - \mu_2 \neq 0$; $= 3.24$

$$LL = (14.60 - 5.60) - 1.96(3.24) = 9 - 6.35 = 2.65$$

$$UL = (14.60 - 5.60) + 1.96(3.24) = 9 + 6.35 = 15.35$$

Since 0 is outside the 95 percent confidence interval, reject H_0 and conclude a significant difference between males and females in number of prior sexual partners.

15. *Males:* $s_{\bar{X}_1 - \bar{X}_2} = 2.89$

$$LL = (23 - 16) - 2.069(2.89) = 7 - 5.98 = 1.02$$

$$UL = (23 - 16) + 2.069(2.89) = 7 + 5.98 = 12.98$$

Since 0 is outside the 95 percent confidence interval, reject H_0 and conclude a significant difference between first- and later-born males in narcissism.

Females: $s_{\bar{X}_1 - \bar{X}_2} = 1.96$

$$LL = (17 - 12) - 2.021(1.96) = 5 - 3.96 = 1.04$$
$$UL = (17 - 12) + 2.021(1.96) = 5 + 3.96 = 8.96$$

Since 0 is outside the 95 percent confidence interval, reject H_0 and conclude a significant difference between first- and later-born females in narcissism.

16. $$LL = (7.62 - 5.62) - 2.365(2.07/\sqrt{8}) = 2 - 1.73 = .27$$
$$UL = (7.62 - 5.62) + 2.365(2.07/\sqrt{8}) = 2 + 1.73 = 3.73$$

Since 0 is outside the 95 percent confidence interval, reject H_0 and conclude a significant difference between perceptions of bearded and nonbearded men.

17. $$LL = (7.0 - 5.60) - 2.776\left(\frac{2.51}{\sqrt{5}}\right) = 1.4 - 3.11 = -1.71$$

$$UL = (7.0 - 5.60) + 2.776\left(\frac{2.51}{\sqrt{5}}\right) = 1.4 + 3.11 = 4.51$$

Since 0 is contained within the 95 percent confidence interval, retain H_0 and conclude no significant difference in taste preference for the two cheeses.

18. $LL = 2.50$; $UL = 13.50$. Since zero falls outside of the 95 percent confidence interval, reject the null hypothesis and conclude that students who use an IBM-compatible computer write higher quality papers than those using a Macintosh computer. (After rejecting the null hypothesis, you would need to examine the means to see which treatment condition is superior.)

19. $LL = -3.80$; $UL = 19.80$. If the design were a between-groups design instead of a within-group design, the null hypothesis would *not* be rejected because the confidence interval contains the number 0. This is a useful demonstration of the fact that a within-group design has more power for rejecting the null hypothesis.

20. IBM-compatible for 90 percent confidence interval:
$LL = 65.87$; $UL = 80.93$
Macintosh for 99 percent confidence interval:
$LL = 54.35$; $UL = 76.45$

Chapter 11

1. a. $\gamma = \dfrac{345 - 300}{70} = .64$

b. $\gamma = \dfrac{345 - 300}{20} = 2.25$

c. $\gamma = \dfrac{310 - 300}{20} = .50$

d. $\gamma = \dfrac{310 - 300}{50} = .20$

2. a. $n = \left(\dfrac{2.8}{.64}\right)^2 = 19$

   b. $n = \left(\dfrac{2.8}{2.25}\right)^2 = 2$

   c. $n' = \left(\dfrac{2.8}{.50}\right)^2 = 31$

   d. $n = \left(\dfrac{2.8}{.20}\right)^2 = 196$

3. a. $\gamma = \dfrac{120 - 130}{15} = -.67$

   $\delta = -.67(\sqrt{10}) = -2.12$ Power = .56
   b. $\gamma = -.67$ $\delta = -4.24$ Power = .99
   c. $\gamma = .20$ $\delta = .77$ Power = .13
   d. $\gamma = .20$ $\delta = 2.00$ Power = .52
   e. $\gamma = .71$ $\delta = 3.89$ Power = .97

4. Effect size is the treatment effect stated in standard deviation units; it is the number of standard deviations the population mean (hypothesized in the null hypothesis) is from the true population mean (hypothesized in the alternative hypothesis).

5. It could be hypothesized that smokers experience more stress than nonsmokers. Assume that you ran an experiment using 150 subjects, one-tailed test, $\alpha = .05$, searched for a medium effect size (.25), and found no significant difference between groups. You could argue that the power of your test was .91—a 91 percent chance of correctly rejecting H_0 if it were false (given the stated effect size). You could further argue that although there might be a small difference between smokers' and nonsmokers' stress, the effect is trivial and not worth instituting a stress-reduction treatment program.

Chapter 12

1. a. H_0: $\mu_1 = \mu_2 = \mu_3$; H_1: at least two of the means are different.

Aerobics	Circuit	Control	Summary Values
$\Sigma X_1 = 243$	$\Sigma X_2 = 273$	$\Sigma X_3 = 313$	$\Sigma X = 829$
$n_1 = 4$	$n_2 = 4$	$n_3 = 4$	$\Sigma X^2 = 58115$
$\overline{X}_1 = 60.75$	$\overline{X}_2 = 68.25$	$\overline{X}_3 = 78.25$	$(\Sigma X)^2 = 687{,}241$
			$N = 12,\ k = 3$

   b. $SS_{BG} = \dfrac{(243)^2}{4} + \dfrac{(273)^2}{4} + \dfrac{(313)^2}{4} - \dfrac{(829)^2}{12}$

   $= 57886.75 - 57270.08 = \textbf{616.67}$

   c. $SS_W = 58115 - \dfrac{(243)^2}{4} + \dfrac{(273)^2}{4} + \dfrac{(313)^2}{4} = \textbf{228.25}$

d. $df_{BG} = k - 1 = 3 - 1 = 2$

e. $df_W = N - k = 12 - 3 = 9$

f. $MS_{BG} = \dfrac{616.67}{2} = \textbf{308.34}$

g. $MS_W = \dfrac{228.25}{9} = \textbf{25.36}$

h. $SS_T = 58115 - \dfrac{(829)^2}{12} = \textbf{844.92}$

i. $df_T = N - 1 = df_{BG} + df_W = 11$

j. $F = \dfrac{308.34}{25.36} = \textbf{12.16}$

k. $F_{crit}(2, 9) = 4.26$ (for $\alpha = .05$)

l. reject H_0

m.

Source of Variation	SS	df	MS	F	p
Between groups	616.67	2	308.34	12.16	<.05
Within groups (error)	228.25	9	25.36		
Total	844.92	11			

n. Among the three experimental conditions—Aerobics, Circuit, and Control—there is a significant difference in resting heart rate.

o. $\omega^2 = \dfrac{616.67 - 2(25.36)}{844.92 + 25.36} = .65$

65 percent of the variance in heart rate is accounted for by the levels of the independent variable.

p. (t_{crit} for all t's = 2.201, $df = 11$, = .05)

Aerobics versus Circuit:

$$t = \frac{68.25 - 60.75}{\sqrt{25.36 \left(\frac{1}{4} + \frac{1}{4}\right)}} = 2.11 \quad (p > .05)$$

Aerobics versus Control:

$$t = \frac{78.25 - 60.75}{3.56} = 4.92 \quad (p < .05)$$

Circuit versus Control:

$$t = \frac{78.25 - 68.25}{3.56} = 2.81 \quad (p < .05)$$

Using a 5 percent level of significance, both the Aerobic and Circuit training conditions are superior to the Control condition. There is no significant difference between Aerobic and Circuit training.

q. Yes. It is likely that Aerobics and Circuit methods of training significantly reduce resting heart rate. It would be helpful to know, however, what constitutes usual amount of exercise in the Control condition.

2. a. $H_0: \mu_1 = \mu_2 = \mu_3$; H_1: at least two of the means are different.

West	Midwest	East	Summary Values
$\Sigma X_1 = 18$	$\Sigma X_2 = 43$	$\Sigma X_3 = 19$	$\Sigma X = 80$
$n_1 = 5$	$n_2 = 5$	$n_3 = 5$	$\Sigma X^2 = 624$
$\overline{X}_1 = 3.60$	$\overline{X}_2 = 8.60$	$\overline{X}_3 = 3.80$	$(\Sigma X)^2 = 6400$
			$N = 15,\ k = 3$

b. $SS_{BG} = 506.80 - 426.67 = \mathbf{80.13}$

c. $SS_W = 624 - 506.80 = \mathbf{117.20}$

d. $df_{BG} = 3 - 1 = 2$

e. $df_W = 15 - 3 = 12$

f. $MS_{BG} = \dfrac{80.13}{2} = \mathbf{40.07}$

g. $MS_W = \dfrac{117.20}{12} = \mathbf{9.77}$

h. $SS_T = 624 - 426.67 = \mathbf{197.33}$

i. $df_T = 15 - 1 = 2 + 12 = 14$

j. $F = \dfrac{40.07}{9.77} = \mathbf{4.10}$

k. $F_{crit}(2, 12) = 3.88$ (for $\alpha = .05$)

l. reject H_0

m.

Source of Variation	SS	df	MS	F	p
Between groups	80.13	2	40.07	4.10	<.05
Within groups (error)	117.20	12	9.77		
Total	197.33	14			

n. There is a significant difference in conservatism among subjects in the West, Midwest, and East.

o. $\omega^2 = \dfrac{80.13 - 2(9.77)}{197.33 + 9.77} = .29$

29 percent of the variance in conservatism is accounted for by geographical location.

p. West versus Midwest:
(t_{crit} for all t's = 2.145 with $df = 14$, $\alpha = .05$)

$$t = \frac{8.60 - 3.60}{\sqrt{9.77\left(\frac{1}{5} + \frac{1}{5}\right)}} = 2.53 \quad (p < .05)$$

East versus Midwest:

$$t = \frac{8.60 - 3.80}{1.98} = 2.42 \quad (p < .05)$$

West versus East:

$$t = \frac{3.60 - 3.80}{1.98} = -.10 \quad (p > .05)$$

Midwesterners are significantly more conservative than either Easterners or Westerners; there is no significant difference between Easterners and Westerners.

q. No. This is a correlational design. The independent variable (geographical region) is not manipulated. Although subjects are randomly *selected* from each region, subjects are not randomly *assigned* to regions to determine the causal effect of regional residence. Therefore, the correct interpretation of these data is that there is an *association* between geographical residence and conservatism.

3. a. $H_0: \mu_1 = \mu_2 = \mu_3$; H_1: at least two of the means are different.

Breathing	Medication	Control	Summary Values
$\Sigma X_1 = 75$	$\Sigma X_2 = 70$	$\Sigma X_3 = 65$	$\Sigma X = 210$
$n_1 = 5$	$n_2 = 5$	$n_3 = 5$	$\Sigma X^2 = 3126$
$\overline{X}_1 = 15$	$\overline{X}_2 = 14$	$\overline{X}_3 = 13$	$(\Sigma X)^2 = 44{,}100$
			$N = 15, \ k = 3$

b. $SS_{BG} = 2950 - 2940 = 10$
c. $SS_W = 3126 - 2950 = 176$
d. $df_{BG} = 3 - 1 = 2$
e. $df_W = 15 - 3 = 12$
f. $MS_{BG} = \dfrac{10}{2} = 5$

g. $MS_W = \dfrac{176}{12} = 14.67$

h. $SS_T = 3126 - 2940 = 186$
i. $df_T = 15 - 1 = 2 + 12 = 14$

j. $F = \dfrac{5}{14.67} = .34$

k. $F_{crit}(2, 12) = 3.88$ (for $\alpha = .05$)
l. retain H_0

m.

Source of Variation	SS	df	MS	F	p
Between groups	10	2	5	.34	n.s.
Within groups (error)	176	12	14.67		
Total	186	14			

n. There is no significant difference among treatment conditions in the alleviation of panic attacks.

o. Since the F ratio is nonsignificant, ω^2 is superfluous.

p. Conducting post hoc comparisons is unwarranted since the F ratio is nonsignificant.

q. No. Since you cannot prove the null hypothesis, all that can be said is that these data show no effect of treatment type on panic attacks.

4. When H_0 is correct, the numerator of the F ratio is the result of only error variance (random factors). When H_0 is incorrect, the numerator includes error variance plus the effect due to treatment.

5. Since the F distribution is established with the assumption that H_0 is true, most F ratios cluster around 1, with the minimum value being 0, and all F values positive. Even with H_0 true, sampling error may sometimes lead to large F values, resulting in the distribution being positively skewed.

6. False. Both will lead to the same conclusion about the null hypothesis; power is determined by other factors.

7. Between-group variation can be the result of treatment effect, individual differences, and experimental error.

8. Individual differences and experimental error.

9. Most F ratios cluster around 1 since the F distribution is based on the assumption that H_0 is true, in which case the numerator and denominator estimate the same value.

10. There is no significant difference between groups in systolic blood pressure, $F(2, 33) = 1.30$, n.s.

11. There is a significant reduction in the number of weekly headaches as a result of treatment, $F(2, 42) = 3.22, p < .05$. (Your post hoc analyses will probably show the following results.) Both medication and biofeedback significantly reduce headaches in comparison to the control condition. There is no significant difference between the two forms of therapy, however.

Chapter 13

1. In the first stage of a two-way ANOVA, the total variance is partitioned into between-group and within-group variance. In the second stage, the between-group variance is partitioned into variance due to Factor A, variance due to Factor B, and variance due to the interaction.

2. a. H_0: $\mu_{A_1} = \mu_{A_2} = \mu_{A_k}$; there is a difference in population means of the levels of Factor A.

   H_1: H_0 is false, or at least one of the means of a level of Factor A is different from another level.

   b. H_0: $\mu_{B_1} = \mu_{B_2} = \mu_{B_k}$

   H_1: H_0 is false.

   c. H_0: There is no interaction.

   H_1: There is an interaction.

3. a. $F_A = \dfrac{73.50}{2.12} = 34.67, p < .05; F_{\text{crit}}\,(2,45) = 3.23$

   $F_B = \dfrac{13.72}{2.12} = 6.47, p < .05; F_{\text{crit}}\,(2,45) = 3.23$

   $F_{A \times B} = \dfrac{3.05}{2.12} = 1.44, \text{ns}; F_{\text{crit}}\,(4,45) = 2.61$

   b. Critical values: $F_A(1, 30) = 4.17$; $F_B(2, 30) = 3.32$; $F_{A \times B}(2, 30) = 3.32$

Source	SS	df	MS	F	p
Factor A	3.36	1	3.36	.90	n.s.
Factor B	66.67	2	33.34	8.94	<.05
$A \times B$	56.89	2	28.45	7.63	<.05
Within-groups	111.83	30	3.73		
Total	238.75	35			

   c. All critical values are based on $df = 1,16$ and equal 4.49.

Source	SS	df	MS	F	p
Factor A	.45	1	.45	.35	n.s.
Factor B	6.05	1	6.05	4.73	<.05
$A \times B$	84.05	1	84.05	65.66	<.05
Within-groups	20.48	16	1.28		
Total	111.03	19			

4. Refer to graphs.

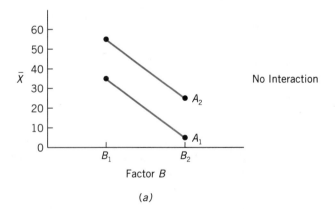

(a)

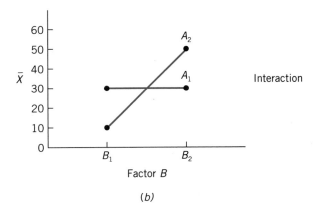

(b)

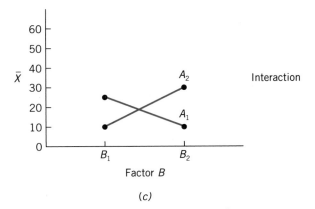

(c)

5. a.

		Factor B: Deprivation		
		High-Deprivation	Low-Deprivation	
Factor A	Low-Incentive	$\overline{X}_1 = 7.0$ $\Sigma X_1 = 35$ $\Sigma X_1^2 = 247$ $n_1 = 5$	$\overline{X}_2 = 7.4$ $\Sigma X_2 = 37$ $\Sigma X_2^2 = 285$ $n_2 = 5$	$\overline{X}_{A_1} = 7.2$
	High-Incentive	$\overline{X}_3 = 4.8$ $\Sigma X_3 = 24$ $\Sigma X_3^2 = 118$ $n_3 = 5$	$\overline{X}_4 = 7.6$ $\Sigma X_4 = 38$ $\Sigma X_4^2 = 296$ $n_4 = 5$	$\overline{X}_{A_2} = 6.2$
		$\overline{X}_{B_1} = 5.9$	$\overline{X}_{B_2} = 7.5$	

$\overline{X}_G = 6.7$; $\Sigma X = 134$; $\Sigma X^2 = 946$; $N = 20$; critical values for all F's $(1, 16) = 4.49$.

Source	SS	df	MS	F	p
Factor A	5.0	1	5.0	3.45	n.s.
Factor B	12.80	1	12.80	8.83	<.05
$A \times B$	7.20	1	7.20	4.97	<.05
Within-groups	23.20	16	1.45		
Total	48.20	19			

b.

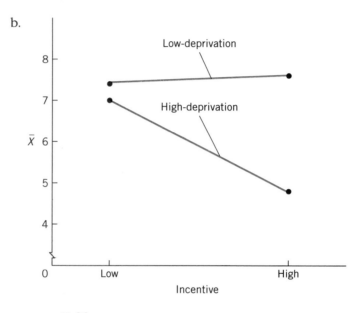

c. $\omega_B^2 = \dfrac{11.35}{49.65} = .23$ or 23%

$\omega_{A \times B}^2 = \dfrac{5.75}{49.65} = .12$ or 12%

d. Because there is no significant effect for Factor A, conclude that incentive has no effect on performance. Because Factor B is significant, conclude that deprivation has an effect on performance. However, since the interaction is also significant, conclude that deprivation has a greater effect on performance under high-incentive conditions than low-incentive conditions. Use caution in interpreting the main effect for deprivation. All the cell means are almost equivalent, except the mean for the High-Deprivation/High-Incentive condition. This is a case in which the interaction is carrying the main effect for deprivation.

6. a. Factor A level 1 is Freshmen; level 2 is Seniors; Factor B level 1 is No-Delay; level 2 is 2-Hour Delay; level 3 is 1-Day Delay.
   Freshmen/No-Delay: $\overline{X}_1 = 12.20$; $\Sigma X_1 = 61$; $\Sigma X_1^2 = 759$; $n_1 = 5$
   Freshmen/2-Hour Delay: $\overline{X}_2 = 7.40$; $\Sigma X_2 = 37$; $\Sigma X_2^2 = 283$; $n_2 = 5$
   Freshmen/1-Day Delay: $\overline{X}_3 = 6.20$; $\Sigma X_3 = 31$; $\Sigma X_3^2 = 199$; $n_3 = 5$
   Seniors/No-Delay: $\overline{X}_4 = 12.20$; $\Sigma X_4 = 61$; $\Sigma X_4^2 = 763$; $n_4 = 5$
   Seniors/2-Hour Delay: $\overline{X}_5 = 6.40$; $\Sigma X_5 = 32$; $\Sigma X_5^2 = 214$; $n_5 = 5$

Seniors/1-Day Delay: $\overline{X}_6 = 6.20$; $\Sigma X_6 = 31$; $\Sigma X_6^2 = 199$; $n_6 = 5$
Freshmen: $\overline{X}_{A_1} = 8.60$; Seniors: $\overline{X}_{A_2} = 8.27$
No-Delay: $\overline{X}_{B_1} = 12.20$; 2-Hour Delay: $\overline{X}_{B_2} = 6.90$;
1-Day Delay: $\overline{X}_{B_3} = 6.20$
$\overline{X}_G = 8.43$; $\Sigma X = 253$; $\Sigma X^2 = 2417$; $N = 30$

Source	SS	df	MS	F	p
Factor A	.84	1	.84	.31	n.s.
Factor B	215.27	2	107.64	39.43	<.05
$A \times B$	1.66	2	.83	.30	n.s.
Within-groups	65.60	24	2.73		
Total	283.37	29			

b.

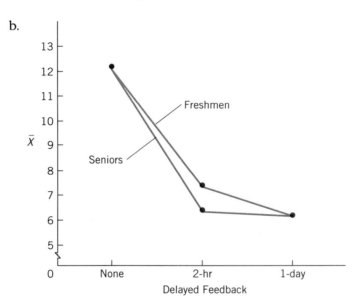

c. No-Delay versus 1-Day Delay: $t = \dfrac{6}{.74} = 8.11$, $p < .05$

No-Delay versus 2-Hour Delay: $t = \dfrac{5.3}{.74} = 7.16$, $p < .05$

2-Hour Delay versus 1-Day Delay: $t = \dfrac{.7}{.74} = .95$, n.s.

$t_{crit}(24) = 2.064$

d. No significant effect for Factor A: educational level has no effect on learning. No significant interaction between educational level and delayed feedback. Significant effect for Factor B: delayed feedback has an effect on learning, with 2-Hour and 1-Day Delay both showing lower retention than No-Delay, but no significant difference from each other.

e. $\omega_B^2 = \dfrac{209.81}{286.10} = .73$ or 73%

7. a.

Source	SS	df	MS	F	p
Factor A	76.05	1	76.05	89.47	<.05
Factor B	31.25	1	31.25	36.76	<.05
$A \times B$	4.05	1	4.05	4.76	<.05
Within-groups	13.60	16	.85		
Total	124.95	19			

b. Yes, since there is a significant main effect for medication.

c. Yes, since there is a significant main effect for cognitive therapy.

d. (t_{crit} (16) = 2.120 for each of the following comparisons).

Cognitive therapy only versus medication only:

$$t = \frac{1.40}{.58} = 2.41, p < .05, \text{Yes}$$

e. Cognitive therapy and medication versus cognitive therapy alone:

$$t = \frac{3.40}{.58} = 5.86, p < .05, \text{Yes}$$

f. Cognitive therapy and medication versus medication alone:

$$t = \frac{4.80}{.58} = 8.28, p < .05, \text{Yes}$$

8. a.

Source	SS	df	MS	F	p
Factor A	.05	1	.05	.03	n.s.
Factor B	18.05	1	18.05	9.86	<.05
$A \times B$	2.45	1	2.45	1.34	n.s.
Within-groups	29.20	16	1.83		
Total	49.75	19			

b. No significant effect for Factor A: sex of student has no effect on perception of learning. No significant interaction between sex of student and attractiveness of professor. Significant effect for Factor B: attractiveness has an effect on perception of learning, with students believing they can learn more from a physically attractive professor.

9. a.

Source	SS	df	MS	F	p
Factor A	51.04	1	51.04	.94	n.s.
Factor B	260.04	1	260.04	4.81	<.05
$A \times B$	3.38	1	3.38	.06	n.s.
Within-groups	1082.17	20	54.11		
Total	1396.63	23			

b. $\overline{X}_{B_1} = 28.42$, $\overline{X}_{B_2} = 21.84$. Since there is a significant effect for Factor B, conclude that the race of the defendant has an effect on sentencing, with Black defendants drawing stiffer sentences.

10. a.

Source	SS	df	MS	F	p
Factor A	220.03	1	220.03	9.02	<.05
Factor B	288.17	2	144.09	5.91	<.05
$A \times B$	42.72	2	21.36	.88	n.s.
Within-groups	731.83	30	24.39		
Total	1282.75	35			

b. $\overline{X}_{A_1} = 14.78$; $\overline{X}_{A_2} = 19.72$; $\overline{X}_{B_1} = 21.17$; $\overline{X}_{B_2} = 16.0$; $\overline{X}_{B_3} = 14.59$
All critical values are $t_{crit}(30) = 2.042$. Since Factor A is significant and there are only two levels of Factor A, it is not necessary to perform a t test between the two levels.

$$\text{Type A versus Type B:} \quad t = \frac{5.17}{1.98} = 2.61, p < .05$$

$$\text{Type A versus Type X:} \quad t = \frac{6.58}{1.98} = 3.32, p < .05$$

$$\text{Type B versus Type X:} \quad t = \frac{1.41}{1.98} = .71, \text{n.s.}$$

c. Since there is a significant effect for Factor A, conclude that incentive affects sales production, with commission producing more sales than salary. Since there is a significant effect for Factor B, conclude that personality type affects sales production with Type A's producing more than Type B's or Type X's, and Type B's and Type X's not differing significantly from each other. There is no interaction between incentive and type of personality on sales production.

11. A main effect is a treatment difference between the levels of one independent variable.

12. An interaction is the combined effect of independent variables on the dependent variable, such that the effect of one independent variable is different at different levels of the other independent variable(s).

13. In an independent-samples t test, you are testing for a main effect since there is only one independent variable. However, protected t tests can be used in a two-way ANOVA to elucidate the nature of an interaction effect.

14. A one-way ANOVA tests for a main effect since there is only one independent variable, although that independent variable can have more than two levels.

15. The presence of a significant interaction qualifies a straightforward interpretation of a main effect.

16. There would be no effect on the main effects, interaction, or MS_W. Adding a constant does not affect the variance; therefore it has no effect on an ANOVA.

17.

Source	SS	df	MS	F	p
Factor *A*	34,003.34	1	34,003.34	100.24	<.05
Factor *B*	31.86	2	15.93	.05	n.s.
A × *B*	23.03	2	11.52	.03	n.s.
Within-groups	38,671	114	339.22		
Total	72,729.20	119			

a.–c. There is a significant effect of sex on ability to delay gratification, with girls being able to delay longer than boys. There is no difference between cognitive strategies, and no interaction between sex and cognitive strategy.

18.

Source	SS	df	MS	F	p
Factor *A*	187.26	1	187.26	6.35	<.05
Factor *B*	224.26	1	224.26	7.61	<.05
A × *B*	693.60	1	693.60	23.53	<.05
Within-groups	1650.80	56	29.48		
Total	2755.93	59			

a. Subjects made far more errors in the Difficult High-Drive condition than the Easy High-Drive condition; the subjects in the Difficult Low-Drive condition actually made fewer errors than subjects in the Easy Low-Drive condition.

b. There is a significant effect of drive state (more errors in the High-Drive condition). There is also a significant effect of task difficulty (more errors in the Difficult condition); however, subjects' errors differ, depending on task difficulty and drive state.

Chapter 14

1. In a repeated-measures design, each subject is exposed to each treatment condition. In a between-groups design, each subject receives only one treatment.

2. In a repeated-measures design, between-groups variation is made up of treatment effect and experimental error; within-group variation consists of individual differences (between-subjects variability) and experimental error.

3. The effect due to individual differences is removed from the error term of a within-groups design.

4. By using the same subjects in every treatment condition, it is impossible for one treatment condition to have more or less of a subject variable than another treatment condition. This variance due to individual differences can then be partitioned out, providing a more powerful test.

5. $df_{BG}, df_{error} = k - 1, (N - k) - (n - 1) = 4, 76$

6.

Source	SS	df	MS	F	p
Between-groups	52.94	2	26.47	11.51	<.05
Within-groups	20	12			
Between-subjects	1.60	4			
Error	18.40	8	2.30		
Total	72.94	14			

7. a.

Source	SS	df	MS	F	p
Between-groups	89334.77	2	44,667.39	16.24	<.05
Within-groups	62,742.83	15			
Between-subjects	35,236.93	5			
Error	27,505.90	10	2750.59		
Total	152,077.61	17			

b. $t_{crit}(10) = 2.228$

Technique A versus Technique B: $t = \dfrac{407.50 - 240.33}{30.28} = 5.52, p < .05$

Technique A versus Technique C: $t = \dfrac{407.50 - 361}{30.28} = 1.54$, n.s.

Technique B versus Technique C: $t = \dfrac{240.33 - 361}{30.28} = -3.99, p < .05$

c. $\omega^2 = \dfrac{83,833.59}{154,828.20} = .54$ or 54%

8. a.

Source	SS	df	MS	F	p
Between-groups	32.53	2	16.27	14.79	<.05
Within-groups	13.20	12			
Between-subjects	4.40	4			
Error	8.80	8	1.10		
Total	45.73	14			

b. $t_{crit}(8) = 2.306$

Incentive A versus Incentive B: $t = \dfrac{7.40 - 5.40}{.66} = 3.03, p < .05$

Incentive A versus Incentive C: $t = \dfrac{7.40 - 3.80}{.66} = 5.45, p < .05$

Incentive B versus Incentive C: $t = \dfrac{5.40 - 3.80}{.66} = 2.42, p < .05$

c. $\omega^2 = \dfrac{30.33}{46.83} = .65$ or 65%

9. a.

Source	SS	df	MS	F	p
Between-groups	2754.17	2	1377.09	47.54	<.05
Within-groups	212.75	9			
Between-subjects	38.92	3			
Error	173.83	6	28.97		
Total	2966.92	11			

b. $t_{crit}(6) = 2.447$

Positive versus Negative: $t = \dfrac{52 - 15.75}{3.81} = 9.51, p < .05$

Positive versus Control: $t = \dfrac{52 - 27}{3.81} = 6.56, p < .05$

Negative versus Control: $t = \dfrac{15.75 - 27}{3.81} = -2.95, p < .05$

c. $\omega^2 = \dfrac{2696.23}{2937.95} = .92$ or 92%

d. The number of problems correctly solved is affected by the type of subliminal message. Since all pairwise comparisons are significant, conclude that positive messages lead to more correct answers than either negative or no messages, and negative messages lead to fewer correct answers than no messages.

10. a.

Source	SS	df	MS	F	p
Between-groups	31.60	2	15.80	33.62	<.05
Within-groups	10.80	12			
Between-subjects	7.06	4			
Error	3.74	8	.47		
Total	42.40	14			

b. $t_{crit}(8) = 2.306$

Feta versus Caviar: $t = \dfrac{1.40 - 2.20}{.43} = -1.86$, n.s.

Feta versus Popcorn: $t = \dfrac{1.40 - 4.80}{.43} = -7.91, p < .05$

Caviar versus Popcorn: $t = \dfrac{2.20 - 4.80}{.43} = -6.05, p < .05$

c. Taste ratings are affected by type of hors d'oeuvres. Popcorn shows better taste ratings than either feta cheese or caviar, and there is no difference between feta cheese and caviar.

d. Advertise that it goes well with popcorn.

11. a.

Source	SS	df	MS	F	p
Between-groups	5114.80	2	2557.40	9.18	<.05
Within-groups	2893.60	12			
Between-subjects	663.73	4			
Error	2229.87	8	278.73		
Total	8008.40	14			

b. $t_{crit} (8) = 2.306$

Low versus Medium: $t = \dfrac{62.80 - 55.80}{10.56} = .66$, n.s.

Low versus High: $t = \dfrac{62.80 - 98}{10.56} = -3.33, p < .05$

Medium versus High: $t = \dfrac{55.80 - 98}{10.56} = -4.00, p < .05$

c. $\omega^2 = \dfrac{4557.34}{8287.13} = .55$ or 55%

d. Pain tolerance is affected by type of distraction. High distraction allows longer tolerance than either medium or low distraction, with no difference between medium and low amounts of distraction.

12.

Source	SS	df	MS	F	p
Between-groups	2574.55	2	1287.28	15.60	<.05
Within-groups	2933.38	45			
Between-subjects	457.25	15			
Error	2476.13	30	82.54		
Total	5507.92	47			

Social desirability is affected by attractiveness. (To locate the source of the significant effect, you would perform pairwise comparisons.)

13.

Source	SS	df	MS	F	p
Between-groups	45.64	2	22.82	4.35	<.05
Within-groups	228	42			
Between-subjects	80.97	14			
Error	147.03	28	5.25		
Total	273.64	44			

Success-achievement ratings are affected by sex-type stereotypes. Your pairwise comparisons should reveal that "masculine" males are rated as having a higher likelihood of achieving success than "feminine" males.

Chapter 15

1. In a correlational design, a study is conducted without exerting control over the phenomenon under investigation. In an experimental design, some procedural variables are held constant and others are purposely allowed to vary. By manipulating an independent variable in an experimental design, you are more likely to be able to show a causal relationship in the effect of the independent variable on the dependent variable.

2. No answer provided.

3. An estimate of the magnitude of the correlation, direction of correlation (i.e., positive or negative), linearity, and presence of outliers.

4. $\rho = \dfrac{.13}{4} = .03$

5. a. $r = 0$
   b. $r = +.50$
   c. $r = -.50$
   d. $r = +.90$

6.

	r_{crit} 5%	r_{crit} 1%	r_{crit} 5%	r_{crit} 1%
a.	.388	.496	reject	reject
b.	.388	.496	reject	accept
c.	.532	.661	reject	reject
d.	.444	.561	reject	reject
e.	.355	.456	reject	accept
f.	.666	.798	reject	reject
g.	.514	.641	reject	accept
h.	.195	.254	reject	accept

(Critical values for h are approximate, based on $df = 100$)

7. a. $\Sigma X = 24$ $\Sigma Y = 21$ $\Sigma XY = 125$
   $(\Sigma X)^2 = 576$ $(\Sigma Y)^2 = 441$ $n_p = 4$
   $\Sigma X^2 = 150$ $\Sigma Y^2 = 113$

$$r_{obt} = \frac{-4}{16.25} = -.25$$

   b. $H_0: \rho = 0; H_1: \rho \neq 0$
   c. r_{crit} (2) $= .950$
   d. Do not reject the null hypothesis.
   e. $r^2 = (-.25)^2 = .0625$ or 6.25% (However, r^2 would not be reported since r is nonsignificant.)

8. a. $\Sigma X = 32$ $\Sigma Y = 25$ $\Sigma XY = 213$

    $(\Sigma X)^2 = 1024$ $(\Sigma Y)^2 = 625$ $n_p = 4$

    $\Sigma X^2 = 266$ $\Sigma Y^2 = 175$

$$r_{obt} = \frac{52}{54.78} = .95$$

   b. $H_0: \rho = 0; H_1: \rho \neq 0$
   c. $r_{crit} (2) = .950$
   d. Reject the null hypothesis when r is equal to or greater than r_{crit}.
   e. $r^2 = (.95)^2 = .90$, or 90%

9. a. $\Sigma X = 43$ $\Sigma Y = 41$ $\Sigma XY = 453$

    $(\Sigma X)^2 = 1849$ $(\Sigma Y)^2 = 1681$ $n_p = 4$

    $\Sigma X^2 = 471$ $\Sigma Y^2 = 449$

$$r_{obt} = \frac{49}{63.44} = .77$$

   b. $H_0: \rho = 0; H_1: \rho \neq 0$
   c. $r_{crit} (2) = .950$
   d. Do not reject the null hypothesis.
   e. 59.3 percent (r^2 would not be reported since r is nonsignificant.)

10. a. $\Sigma X = 20$ $\Sigma Y = 24$ $\Sigma XY = 110$

    $(\Sigma X)^2 = 400$ $(\Sigma Y)^2 = 576$ $n_p = 5$

    $\Sigma X^2 = 106$ $\Sigma Y^2 = 124$

$$r_{obt} = \frac{70}{75.63} = .93$$

   b. $H_0: \rho = 0; H_1: \rho \neq 0$
   c. $r_{crit} (3) = .878$
   d. Reject the null hypothesis.
   e. 86.5 percent

11. No answer is provided.

12. a. $\Sigma X = 18$ $\Sigma Y = 30$ $\Sigma XY = 96$

    $(\Sigma X)^2 = 324$ $(\Sigma Y)^2 = 900$ $n_p = 5$

    $\Sigma X^2 = 80$ $\Sigma Y^2 = 190$

$$r_{obt} = \frac{-60}{61.64} = -.97$$

b. $H_0: \rho = 0; H_1: \rho \neq 0$

c. $r_{crit}(3) = .878$

d. Reject the null hypothesis.

e. 94.10 precent.

13. Refer to graph.

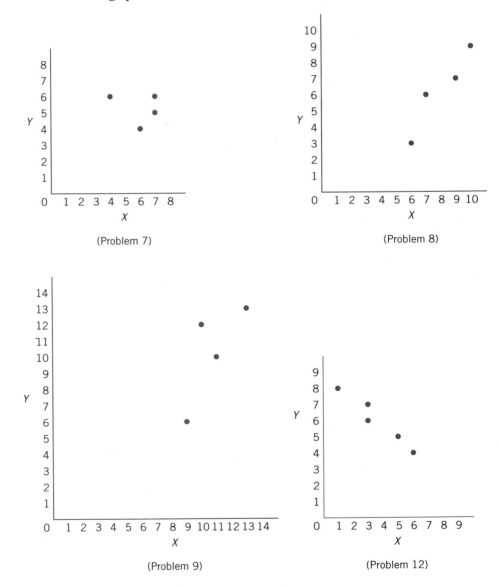

(Problem 7)

(Problem 8)

(Problem 9)

(Problem 12)

14. $\rho = \dfrac{64}{75} = .85$

15. A restricted range of scores may underestimate the size of the population correlation.

16. Use of extreme groups may increase the size of the correlation.
17. r will underestimate ρ.

18. a. $\Sigma X = 56$ $\Sigma Y = 503$ $\Sigma XY = 3887$

   $(\Sigma X)^2 = 3136$ $(\Sigma Y)^2 = 253{,}009$ $n_p = 7$

   $\Sigma X^2 = 542$ $\Sigma Y^2 = 36{,}365$

$$r_{obt} = \frac{-959}{1008.60} = -.95$$

   b. $H_0: \rho = 0; H_1: \rho \neq 0$
   c. $r_{crit}(5) = .754$
   d. 90.25 percent
   e. Reject the null hypothesis.

19. a. $\Sigma X = 18$ $\Sigma Y = 621$ $\Sigma XY = 2022$

   $(\Sigma X)^2 = 324$ $(\Sigma Y)^2 = 385{,}641$ $n_p = 6$

   $\Sigma X^2 = 94$ $\Sigma Y^2 = 64{,}979$

$$r_{obt} = \frac{954}{1007.93} = .95$$

   b. $H_0: \rho = 0; H_1: \rho \neq 0$
   c. $r_{crit}(4) = .811$
   d. 90.25 percent
   e. Reject the null hypothesis.
20. Refer to graph.

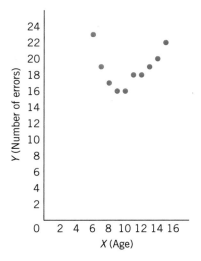

21. Drilling: $r(24) = .65, p < .05$
    Rubber Dam: $r(24) = .46, p < .05$
22. $r(21) = .413, p < .05$

Chapter 16

1. Regression analysis is important for making predictions to solve practical problems and to build and test theories.
2. The regression line is fitted to the scatter plot in such a way that the sum of the squared errors (Σe^2) is minimized.
3. $\Sigma(Y - Y_p)$ results in a summed error of 0.
4. If $r = 0$, then $b = 0$.
5. As the size of the correlation increases, prediction error decreases.
6. The assumption of homoscedasticity allows you to assume s_e is the same for every value of X. If each X were associated with conditional distributions of differing variances, there would have to be a different standard error of the estimate for each X score.
7. Overgeneralizing to populations different from the populations used to establish the regression equation may lead to predictions that are no better than chance or systematically biased.

8. $\overline{X} = 12.80$ $\overline{Y} = 40.40$
    $\Sigma X = 64$ $\Sigma Y = 202$ $\Sigma XY = 2985$
    $(\Sigma X)^2 = 4096$ $(\Sigma Y)^2 = 40,804$ $n_p = 5$
    $\Sigma X^2 = 990$ $\Sigma Y^2 = 9142$

    a. $b = \dfrac{1997}{854} = 2.34$

    b. $Y_p = 40.40 + 2.34(0 - 12.80) = 10.45$ $(14925 - 12998)^2$

    c. $s_e = \sqrt{\left[\dfrac{1}{5(3)}\right]\left[5(9142) - 40,804 - \left(\dfrac{[5(2985) - (64)(202)]^2}{5(990) - 4096}\right)\right]} = 4.07$

    d. $Y_p = 40.40 + 2.34(16 - 12.80) = 47.89$ seconds 854

9. $\overline{X} = 12$ $\overline{Y} = 23$
    $\Sigma X = 72$ $\Sigma Y = 138$ $\Sigma XY = 1739$
    $(\Sigma X)^2 = 5184$ $(\Sigma Y)^2 = 19,044$ $n_p = 6$
    $\Sigma X^2 = 886$ $\Sigma Y^2 = 3560$

    a. $b = \dfrac{10,434 - 9936}{5316 - 5184} = 3.77$

    b. $Y_p = 23 + 3.77(0 - 12) = -22.24$

c. $s_e = \sqrt{\left[\dfrac{1}{6(4)}\right]\left[6(3560) - 19{,}044) - \left(\dfrac{[6(1739) - (72)(138)]^2}{6(886) - 5184}\right)\right]} = 4.18$

d. $Y_p = 23 + 3.77(10 - 12) = 15.46\ (\$15{,}460)$

10. $\overline{X} = 3.38$ $\overline{Y} = 3.43$

   $\Sigma X = 16.88$ $\Sigma Y = 17.17$ $\Sigma XY = 58.09$

   $(\Sigma X)^2 = 284.93$ $(\Sigma Y)^2 = 294.81$ $n_p = 5$

   $\Sigma X^2 = 57.67$ $\Sigma Y^2 = 59.01$

a. $b = \dfrac{290.45 - 289.83}{288.35 - 284.93} = .18$

b. $Y_p = 3.43 + .18(3.00 - 3.38) = 3.36$
   Yes, since we would predict the student to achieve a GPA of 3.36 (3.00 minimum required).

c. $s_e = .095$
   $Y_p = 3.43 + .18(3.67 - 3.38) = 3.48$
   $3.48 \pm .095 = 3.575$ and 3.385

11. Drilling: $Y_p = 5.77 + .64(X - 5.15)$
   $s_e = 1.98$ (A small discrepancy is due to rounding error.)

$$Y_p = 5.77 + .64(7 - 5.15) = 6.95$$

Rubber Dam: $Y_p = 5.42 + .47(X - 5.15)$
   $s_e = 2.44$ (A small discrepancy is due to rounding error.)

$$Y_p = 5.42 + .47(7 - 5.15) = 6.29$$

12. $Y_p = 58.35 + .35(54 - 56.96) = 57.31$
   $s_e = 16.36$
   $Y_p = 57.31 \pm 16.36 = 73.67$ and 40.95

Chapter 17

1.

f_o	f_e	$(f_o - f_e)^2$	$(f_o - f_e)^2/f_e$	R
70	79.60	92.16	1.16	−1.08
160	159.20	.64	.004	.06
168	159.20	77.44	.49	.70
30	20.40	92.16	4.52	2.13
40	40.80	.64	.016	−.13
32	40.80	77.44	1.90	−1.38

$\chi^2 = \mathbf{8.09}$
$\chi^2_{crit} = 5.99$

There are more unfavorable responses to Treatment I than would be expected by chance, $\chi^2(2, N = 500) = 8.09$. The cell, Unfavorable Response to Treatment I, makes a significant contribution to the significant χ^2.

2. $\chi^2 = \dfrac{110(255 - 1520)^2}{(55)(55)(53)(57)} = 19.26$

$\chi^2_{crit} = 3.84 \qquad \chi^2(1, N = 110) = 19.26, p < .05$

3. a. $df = 1$
   b. $df = 6$
   c. $df = 12$
   d. $df = 2$

4. a. H_0: There is no relation between type of bumper sticker and being stopped by the police.

   H_1: The variables are related (not independent).

   b. and c.

	Stop Brutality Sticker	Smile Sticker	
Stopped	18	5	23
Not Stopped	7	20	27
	25	25	$N = 50$

f_o	f_e	$(f_o - f_e)^2$	$(f_o - f_e)^2/f_e$
18	11.50	42.25	3.67
5	11.50	42.25	3.67
7	13.50	42.25	3.13
20	13.50	42.25	3.13
			$\chi^2 = 13.60$

$\chi^2_{crit} = 3.84$

Drivers displaying Stop Brutality stickers are stopped significantly more often than drivers displaying Smile stickers, $\chi^2(1, N = 50) = 13.60, p < .05.$.

5. a. (f_o)

30	50	20	20	120
10	30	40	20	100
40	80	60	40	$N = 220$

(f_e)

21.82	43.64	32.73	21.82
18.18	36.36	27.27	18.18

b. (f_o)

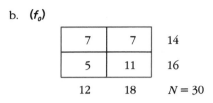

7	7	14
5	11	16
12	18	$N = 30$

(f_e)

| 5.60 | 8.40 |
| 6.40 | 9.60 |

6. 6

7. df, or $(R - 1)(C - 1)$

8.

	Sun.	Mon.	Tues.	Wed.	Thurs.	Fri.	Sat.
f_o	56	29	17	22	25	15	33
f_e	28.14	28.14	28.14	28.14	28.14	28.14	28.14

f_o	f_e	$(f_o - f_e)^2$	$(f_o - f_e)^2/f_e$
56	28.14	776.18	27.58
29	28.14	.74	.03
17	28.14	124.10	4.41
22	28.14	37.70	1.34
25	28.14	9.86	.35
15	28.14	172.66	6.14
33	28.14	23.62	.84
			$\chi^2 = 40.69$

$\chi^2_{crit} = 12.59$

$\chi^2(6, N = 197) = 40.69, p < .05$

9.

f_o	f_e	$(f_o - f_e)^2$	$(f_o - f_e)^2/f_e$	R
2	8.30	39.69	4.78	-2.18^*
20	26.08	36.97	1.42	-1.19
27	14.62	153.26	10.48	3.24^*
19	12.70	39.69	3.13	1.77
46	39.92	36.97	.93	.96
10	22.38	153.26	6.85	-2.62^*
			$\chi^2 = 27.59$	
			$\chi^2_{crit} = 5.99$	

There are fewer easy births among primiparous mothers, fewer difficult births among multiparous mothers, and more difficult births among primiparous mothers than would be expected by chance, $\chi^2(2, N = 124) = 27.59, p < .05$. Those R values with asterisks reflect cells that make a significant contribution to the χ^2 value.

10.

	Correct ID	Incorrect ID	
Primiparous	8	19	27
Multiparous	34	9	43
	42	28	N = 70

$$\chi^2 = \frac{70(72 - 646)^2}{(27)(43)(42)(28)} = 16.89$$

$$\chi^2_{crit} = 3.84; \chi^2(1, N = 70) = 16.89, p < .05$$

11. Because you are summing across all cells, χ^2 will increase as the number of categories increases. Therefore, χ^2_{crit} needs to become corresponding larger as well.

12. No. Assumptions of independence of observations is violated since some subjects are represented in more than one cell.

13. Younger mothers give birth to more physically immature and fewer physically mature babies than would be expected by chance. Older mothers give birth to more physically mature and fewer physically immature babies than would be expected by chance, $\chi^2(1, N = 114) = 26.67, p < .05$.

14. There is an association between diabetes and prolonged healing, with diabetics showing longer healing times, $\chi^2(1, N = 810) = 137.08, p < .05$.

15. There is no differential effect due to treatment, $\chi^2(1, N = 172) = .75$, n.s.

Chapter 18

1.

X	R_x	Y	R_y
3	2	7	4
2	1	2	1.5
4	3.5	4	3
9	6	12	6
8	5	8	5
4	3.5	2	1.5

2.

Score	Rank	Condition
2	2	X
2	2	Y
2	2	Y
3	4	X
4	6	X
4	6	X
4	6	Y
7	8	Y
8	9.5	X
8	9.5	Y
9	11	X
12	12	Y

3.

X	Y	D	Rank
3	7	−4	−6
2	2	0	2
4	4	0	−2
9	12	−3	−5
8	8	0	− (Discard)
4	2	2	4

4. Graphs for a. and c.

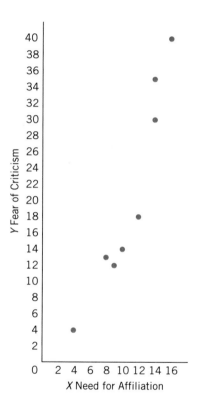

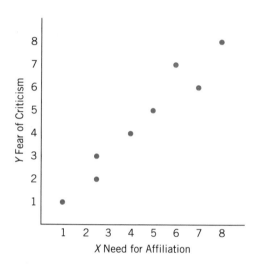

b.

Affiliation		Criticism		D	D²
Score	Rank	Score	Rank		
16	1	40	1	0	0
14	2.5	35	2	.5	.25
14	2.5	30	3	−.5	.25
12	4	18	4	0	0
10	5	14	5	0	0
8	7	13	6	1	1
9	6	12	7	−1	1
4	8	4	8	0	0
				$\Sigma D = 0$	$\Sigma D^2 = 2.5$

c. Refer to graph.

d. $r_s = 1 - \dfrac{6(2.5)}{8(8^2 - 1)} = .97$

e. $H_0: \rho_s = 0$; $H_1: \rho_s \neq 0$

f. $r_{s_{crit}} = .738$; $r_s(8) = .97, p < .05$

5.

Attractiveness	Popularity		
Rank	Rank	D	D²
1	1	0	0
2	3	−1	1
5	2	+3	9
3	4	−1	1
4	5	−1	1
7	7	0	0
9	6	+3	9
6	8	−2	4
8	9	−1	1
10	10	0	0
		$\Sigma D = 0$	$\Sigma D^2 = 26$

a. $r_s = 1 - \dfrac{6(26)}{10(10^2 - 1)} = .84$

b. $H_0: \rho_s = 0$; $H_1: \rho_s \neq 0$

c. $r_{s_{crit}} = .648$; $r_s(10) = .84, p < .05$

d. There is a significant, positive correlation between physical attractiveness and popularity, $r_s(10) = .84, p < .05$.

6.

Democrat	Republican
$\overline{Y}_1 = 2.71$	$\overline{Y}_0 = 7.86$
$n_1 = 7$	$n_0 = 7$

$s_y = 3.34$; $N = 14$

a. $r_{pb} = \dfrac{2.71 - 7.86}{3.34} \sqrt{\dfrac{(7)(7)}{(14)(13)}} = -.80$

b. $H_0: \rho = 0$; $H_1: \rho \neq 0$

c. $r_{crit} = .532$; $r_{pb}(12) = -.80, p < .05$

d. There is a negative correlation between political affiliation and attitudes toward military intervention in Central America, with Republicans favoring more aggressive intervention, $r_{pb}(12) = -.80, p < .05$.

e. $r_{pb}^2 = (-.80)^2 = .64$ or 64%

7.

Correct	Incorrect
36	16
39	14
22	26
30	9
	7
	11

$\Sigma Y_0 = 127$; $\Sigma Y_1 = 83$; $\overline{Y}_0 = 31.75$; $\overline{Y}_1 = 13.83$; $n_0 = 4$; $n_1 = 6$; $s_y = 11.40$;
$N = 10$

a. $r_{pb} = \dfrac{13.83 - 31.75}{11.40} \sqrt{\dfrac{(6)(4)}{(10)(9)}} = -.82$

b. $H_0: \rho = 0$; $H_1: \rho \neq 0$

c. $r_{crit} = .632$; $r_{pb}(8) = -.82$, $p < .05$

d. There is a negative correlation between the answer to the critical question and the total score on the test, with an incorrect answer associated with lower total test scores, $r_{pb}(8) = -.82$, $p < .05$. [Note: In interpreting this correlation, you should not be thinking, "Of course missing a question will lead to a lower overall score, this is a trivial finding." Since the difference between $\overline{Y}_0$ and $\overline{Y}_1$ is not one point, clearly something else is going on here. Most likely, those students who answer the critical question correctly are more likely to answer other questions correctly (note the much higher mean (31.75) for the correct group.)]

8. a. $r_s = 1 - \dfrac{6(53.5)}{9(9^2 - 1)} = .55$

b. $H_0: \rho_s = 0$; $H_1: \rho_s \neq 0$

c. $r_{s_{crit}} = .683$; $r_s(9) = .55$, n.s.

d. There is no evidence that posture and body shape are related, $r_s(9) = .55$, n.s.

9. a. $r_s = 1 - \dfrac{6(62)}{12(12^2 - 1)} = .78$

b. $H_0: \rho = 0$; $H_1: \rho \neq 0$

c. $r_{s_{crit}} = .591$; $r_s(12) = .78$, $p < .05$

d. There is a positive correlation between performance on clinical and written exams, $r_s(12) = .78$, $p < .05$.

10. a. $r_{pb} = \dfrac{13.65 - 11.47}{1.89} \sqrt{\dfrac{(10)(10)}{(20)(19)}} = .59$

b. $H_0: \rho = 0$; $H_1: \rho \neq 0$

c. $r_{crit} = .444$; $r_{pb}(18) = .59$, $p < .05$

d. There is a positive correlation between age a child first walks and presence or absence of an older sibling, with earlier age of walking associated with the presence of an older sibling, $r_{pb}(18) = .59$, $p < .05$.

11. a. $r_{pb} = \dfrac{6.6 - 5.0}{3.08}\sqrt{\dfrac{(5)(5)}{(10)(9)}} = .28$

   b. $H_0: \rho = 0; H_1: \rho \neq 0$

   c. $r_{crit} = .632; r_{pb}(8) = .28$, n.s.

   d. There is no evidence that gender and attitudes about abortion are related, $r_{pb}(8) = .28$, n.s.

12. a. $r_s = 1 - \dfrac{6(44)}{8(8^2 - 1)} = .48$

   b. $H_0: \rho_s = 0; H_1: \rho_s \neq 0$

   c. $r_{s_{crit}} = .738; r_s(8) = .48$, n.s.

   d. Since r_s is nonsignificant, there would be little point in reporting r_s^2.

13. a. H_0: The population distribution of A (behavioral therapy) is the same as the population distribution of B (psychoanalysis).

   H_1: The population distribution of A is not the same as the population distribution of B.

   b.   Rank: 1, 2, 3, 4, 5, 6, 7, 8, 9, 10, 11, 12

   Condition: $B, B, B, A, B, B, A, A, A, B, A, A,$

ΣR_A	ΣR_B
4	1
7	2
8	3
9	5
11	6
12	10
51	27

   $n_A = 6 \quad n_B = 6$

   $U_A = (6)(6) + \dfrac{6(6+1)}{2} - 51 = 6$

   $U_B = (6)(6) + \dfrac{6(6+1)}{2} - 27 = 30$

   $U = 6$

   c. $U_{crit} = 5$ (with $df = 6, 6$) $U = 6$, n.s.

   d. There is no evidence of a difference in interviewing skills based on training track, $U(6, 6) = 6$, n.s.

14. When using the Mann-Whitney U test when one of the samples is greater than 20, transform the U value to a z value and use critical z values as cutoffs. This can be done because a sample size greater than 20 yields a sampling distribution of U that approximates a normal distribution.

15. With three scores having difference scores of 0, discard one and assign one of the remaining two ranks to the Positive group and the other to the Negative group.

16. Both the smaller ΣR and U will equal 0.

17.   Rank: 1, 2, 3, 4, 5, 6, 7, 8, 9, 10
    Condition: A, B, A, A, A, B, B, B, A, B

ΣR_A	ΣR_B
1	2
3	6
4	7
5	8
9	10
22	33
$n_A = 5$	$n_B = 5$

$$U_A = (5)(5) + \frac{5(5+1)}{2} - 22 = 18$$

$$U_B = (5)(5) + \frac{5(5+1)}{2} - 33 = 7$$

$$U = 7$$

$$z_U = \frac{7 - (5)(5)/2}{\sqrt{[(5)(5)][(5+5+1)]/12}} = -1.15$$

$$z_{crit} = 1.96$$

Since $z_U < z_{crit}$, do not reject the null hypothesis.

18. $T_{crit} = 0$ (with $df = 6$); $T = 1$, n.s. Type of music has no effect on how fast students eat, $T(6) = 1$, n.s.

19. $U_A = (6)(6) + \dfrac{6(6+1)}{2} - 24.5 = 32.50$

    $U_B = (6)(6) + \dfrac{6(6+1)}{2} - 53.5 = 3.5$

    $U_{crit} = 5$ (with $df = 6, 6$)

    $U = 3.5, p < .05$

20. a. Mann-Whitney U test
    b. Wilcoxon signed-ranks test
    c. Spearman rank correlation coefficient
    d. Point-biserial correlation coefficient
    e. Spearman rank correlation coefficient

21. $$z_{obt} = \frac{14 - 55(55 + 1)/4}{\sqrt{[(55)(55 + 1)][(2(55) + 1)]/24}} = -6.33$$

$z_{crit} = 1.96$. Therefore reject the null hypothesis.

22. a. H_0: The population distribution of A (propranolol) is the same as the population distribution of B (diuretic).

   H_1: The population distribution of A is not the same as the population distribution of

   b. $T = 8.5$, $p < .05$

   c. $T_{crit} = 25$ (with $df = 15$)

   d. There is a significant difference in effectiveness of propranolol and diuretic for lowering systolic blood pressure, with propranolol being more effective, $T(15) = 8.5$, $p < .05$.

23. $U_{crit} = 64$ (with $df = 15, 15$)

   $U_A = 165$, $U_B = 60$

   Since $U_B < U_{crit}$, reject the null hypothesis. Propranolol is significantly more effective than a diuretic.

Appendix A

1. a. No, Regardless of whether sampling was with or without replacement.
   b. No
   c. Yes
   d. No
   e. No
   f. Yes

2. a. $\frac{40}{100} = .40$

   b. $\frac{60}{100} = .60$

   c. $.40 + .60 = 1.00$

   d. $(.40)(.40) = .16$

   e. $(.60)(.60) = .36$

   f. $\frac{60}{99} = .606$

   g. $\left(\frac{40}{100}\right)\left(\frac{39}{99}\right) = (.40)(.394) = .1576$

3. a. Dependent
   b. Independent
   c. Dependent
   d. Independent

GLOSSARY

Abscissa The horizontal (X) axis of a graph.

Addition Rule Used to determine the probability of occurrence of one or more of many possible events.

Alpha Inflation The result of conducting multiple t tests such that the probability of a Type I error increases with the number of t tests.

Alpha Level The value set by the researcher that specifies the probability of a Type I error (rejecting a true null hypothesis).

Alternative Hypothesis The opposite of the null hypothesis. The hypothesis that is automatically accepted when the null hypothesis is rejected. Accepting the alternative hypothesis means that the results of a study are probably not due to chance.

Analysis of Variance (ANOVA) A statistical test designed to determine if there is a significant difference among several sample means.

A Posteriori Approach To Probability Determining the probability of an event by dividing the number of times A has occurred by the total number of occurrences.

A Priori Approach to Probability See Classical Approach to Probability.

A Priori Tests A category of tests used to test for significant differences among means. The number of comparisons conducted is typically a subset of the total number of comparisons possible. In addition, a priori tests must be planned before examining the data.

Asymptotic When a line on a graph continually approaches but never reaches the X axis.

Bar Graph A frequency distribution for categorical (nominal) data.

Between-Group Variation The amount of variation among means in a study with two or more groups.

Between-Subjects Design See *Independent-Samples Design*.

Biased Sample A nonrandomly selected sample such that all possible samples from a population do *not* have an equal chance of being selected.

Bimodal Distribution A distribution with two modes.

Bivariate Distribution A distribution of two variables in which scores are paired. A correlation is based on a bivariate distribution.

Categorical Data Nominal data arranged by categories. For example, the number of prison inmates that fall in the category of violent. See *Nominal Scale*.

Cell That portion of a table that identifies a single group. A 2 × 2 factorial design and a 2 × 2 contingency table each have four cells.

Central Limit Theorem The mathematical theorem that states that the sampling distribution of means approaches a normal curve as the sample size increases. The mean of the sampling distribution is equal to the mean of the population. The standard deviation of the sampling distribution is equal to $\sigma/\sqrt{n}$.

Central Tendency A statistic that indicates where in the distribution scores tend to bunch. The mean, median, and mode are common measures of central tendency.

Chi-Square Distribution A theoretical sampling distribution of chi-square values. The shape of the chi-square distribution changes as a function of the degrees of freedom.

Chi-Square Test A significance test used with frequency counts.

Class Interval The difference between two consecutive lower class limits in a frequency distribution.

Classical Approach to Probability (or A Priori Approach) Determining the probability of an event by dividing the number of ways the event can occur by the total number of possible outcomes.

Coefficient of Determination A squared correlation coefficient. It indexes the amount of variation of Y scores accounted for by the variation of X scores. An estimate of common or shared variance.

Common (or Shared) Variance See *Coefficient of Determination*.

Computational (or Raw-Score) Formula A formula that uses the raw scores of the distribution. Although a computational formula obscures the conceptual basis of the formula, it is used for ease in hand calculations.

Conditional Distribution In regression, the spread of Y scores for a given X score.

Conditional Probability The probability of one event is affected by the occurrence of another event.

Confidence Interval A range of values within which a researcher can state with a certain degree of confidence that a population parameter will fall.

Confidence Limits The upper and lower values of a confidence interval.

Confounding (or Extraneous) Variable An uncontrolled variable that systematically covaries with the independent variable. A confounding variable can offer a plausible alternative explanation for the results of the study.

Contingency Table (or Frequency or Cross-Tabulation Table) A two- or more-way table that categorizes observations as frequency counts.

Continuous Variable A variable with an infinite number of values.

Control Group In experimental research, a control group is used as a comparison group to help isolate the influence of an independent variable on a dependent variable.

Correlated (Dependent) Samples A research design in which the scores of one experimental condition are not independent of scores of another experimental condition; also called a *dependent-samples design* or *repeated-measures design*. Another example of a correlated samples design is a matched-subjects design in which the selection of one sample determines who will be selected for the other sample(s).

Correlated-Samples *t* Test See *Dependent-Samples t Test*.

Correlation Coefficient An index of the degree of association between two variables. A correlation coefficient can range from − 1 to + 1. The higher the absolute value of the correlation coefficient, the stronger the relationship between the two variables.

Correlational Research Studies that do not control and manipulate variables. Correlational research examines the covariation among variables.

Counterbalancing A strategy used with repeated-measures designs in which subjects differ by the order in which experimental conditions are presented. The purpose of counterbalancing is to prevent confounding of the independent variable by distributing sequencing effects across all experimental conditions.

Critical Region The area under a curve that has the values that lead to rejection of the null hypothesis.

Critical Value The value that separates the critical region from those values of the test statistic that would not lead to rejection of the null hypothesis.

Cumulative Frequency Distribution A frequency distribution, which includes a column that indicates the total frequency of scores up to and including a given class interval.

Curvilinear Relationship A nonlinear relation between X and Y. For example, when lower scores on X are associated with lower scores on Y, medium X scores are associated with medium Y scores, but higher X scores are associated with lower Y scores.

Degrees of Freedom The number of values that are free to vary with certain restrictions placed on all values.

Dependent-Samples *t* Test A significance test used in dependent sampling in which scores are arranged in pairs.

Dependent Variable In the behavioral sciences, the dependent variable is usually a measure of behavior. It is a measured variable that is expected to be a consequence of the independent variable. In experimental research, the dependent variable is causally determined by the independent variable. In correlational research in which a regression equation is used to predict the value of one variable given the value of another variable, the dependent variable is also called the *predicted variable* or *criterion variable*.

Descriptive Statistics Techniques used to describe and summarize data in an abbreviated form.

Deviation Score (x) (or Error Score) The difference between a score and the mean of the distribution.

Dichotomous Variable A variable that takes only two, contrary values (e.g., males = 0, females = 1).

Discontinuous (or Discrete) Variable A variable that typically increments from one whole number to another whole number. These variables are characterized by gaps between numbers that cannot be filled by any number.

Distribution A list of scores arranged in order of magnitude.

Distribution-Free Test In inferential statistics, tests that do not make assumptions about characteristics of the population distribution.

Dummy Coding Assigning arbitrary numbers to designate groups of observations (e.g., males = 0 and females = 1).

Error Variance The variation among scores due to uncontrolled, random factors in the experiment; within-group variance.

Expected Frequencies The number of observations expected to occur when the null hypothesis is true.

Experimental Group A group that receives a treatment and is compared to a control group.

External Validity The extent to which experimental findings can be generalized to a population at large.

Extraneous Variable See *Confounding Variable*.

Factor An independent variable. A two-way ANOVA has two factors, or independent variables.

Factorial ANOVA The factorial ANOVA analyzes data from an experiment that has two or more independent variables.

Factorial Design An experimental design that has two or more independent variables.

F Distribution A theoretical sampling distribution of F values. The shape of the F distribution is a function of the degrees of freedom. F distributions are positively skewed, with most F values bunched around 1.

Fisher's LSD (Least Significant Difference) A multiple comparison test used to locate the source of significance following a significant F test. Also called *protected t test*.

Frequency The number of times each score occurs in a distribution.

Frequency Count Data in the form of "how many" rather than "how much." A chi-square analysis uses frequency counts.

Frequency Polygon A graph with measured scores on the X axis and frequencies on the Y axis. Each point above an X score represents the frequency of occurrence of that score.

Goodness-of-Fit Test A chi-square test that examines the degree to which observed data coincides with theoretical expectations.

Grand Mean The mean of all the scores in an experiment.

Grouped Frequency Distribution Scores that are arranged into equal-sized class intervals. The number of scores occurring in each interval is placed in a column adjacent to the appropriate class interval.

Heteroscedasticity In regression analysis, a violation of homoscedasticity wherein the variances of the conditional distributions are unequal.

Histogram A graph of vertical bars in which the height of each bar corresponds to the frequency of occurrence of a given X score.

Homogeneity of Variance Variances of equivalent values in two or more populations. Parametric significance tests assume this equivalence.

Homoscedasticity An assumption in regression analysis in which all conditional distributions have equal variances.

Hypothesis Testing A method for testing claims made about population parameters. Hypothesis tests are also called *significance tests*.

Independent Events Events that are unrelated. The occurrence of one event does not affect the occurrence of another event.

Independent-Samples Design An experimental design in which the scores of one experimental condition are unrelated to (independent of) the scores in any other experimental condition.

Independent-Samples t Test A significance test used to compare the sample means of two samples. See *Independent-Samples Design*.

Independent Variable In an experimental design, the treatment variable. In regression, the predictor variable.

Inferential Statistics The procedures using sample data to make inferences about characteristics of a population.

Interaction In a factorial design, the influence of one independent variable is affected by the level of another independent variable.

Internal Validity The degree to which an experiment can allow the investigator to make a cause-and-effect statement of the relation between the independent and dependent variable. The presence of confounding variables decreases the internal validity of an experiment.

Interquartile Range (IQR) The difference between the first and third quartiles.

Interval Estimate See *Confidence Interval*.

Interval Scale A scale of measurement in which equal differences between numbers correspond to equal differences in that which is being measured. Interval scales do not have a meaningful zero point.

Kurtosis The peakedness or flatness of a curve describing a unimodal frequency distribution.

Least Squares Criterion The criterion used in the Least Squares Method to establish a regression line. See *Least Squares Method*.

Least Squares Method The method of fitting a regression line to a scatter plot such that the sum of the squared errors are at a minimum.

Leptokurtic A symmetrical curve that is more narrow in shape relative to a normal curve. A leptokurtic curve reflects the fact that scores are closely grouped around the middle of the distribution.

Level of Significance (Alpha Level) The probability value (e.g., .05) at which the null hypothesis is rejected.

Linear Relation As the value of one variable changes, the value of a second variable changes by a constant.

Main Effect In a factorial design, a main effect is produced by the action of an independent variable separate from any other independent variable.

Mann-Whitney *U* Test A significance test that is the nonparametric counterpart to the independent-samples *t* test.

Matched Subjects Design A research design in which subjects are assigned to groups based on information about the subject (e.g., IQ, age, race, etc.). Used to control for subject variables.

Mean The sum of scores divided by the number of scores.

Mean Deviation A measure of dispersion or variability in the distribution of scores. The mean deviation is the sum of the absolute values of deviation scores divided by the number of scores.

Mean Square (MS) In ANOVA, a sum of squares divided by its degree of freedom.

Mean Square Between (MS_{BG}) The average variation among group means. As the size of the treatment effect increases, the value of MS_{BG} becomes larger.

Mean Square Within (MS_w) A weighted average of variances of two or more groups; also called the pooled variance.

Measurement The assignment of numbers to events according to a set of rules.

Measures of Central Tendency See *Central Tendency*.

Measures of Dispersion (or Variability) Numerical indices that reflect the degree to which scores of a distribution are spread out.

Median The midpoint of a distribution in which 50 percent of the scores fall below the midpoint.

Mesokurtic A curve that has a degree of peakedness that is intermediate between leptokurtic and platykurtic curves.

Mode The score in a distribution that occurs most frequently.

Multiple Comparisons Tests of differences between means performed after an ANOVA. Multiple comparisons are performed to locate the source of significance found by an *F* test.

Multiple Regression A statistical technique that uses two or more variables to predict a criterion variable.

Multiple Regression Equation A regression equation in which more than one predictor variable is used to predict a criterion variable.

Multiplication Rule Used to determine the probability of the joint occurrence of several events.

Mutually Exclusive Events The occurrence of one event precludes the occurrence of another event.

Nominal Scale A measurement scale in which data are in the form of names, labels, or categories.

Nonparametric Tests Statistical tests that do not require many of the assumptions of parametric tests.

Normal Distribution (Normal Curve) A bell-shaped curve (probability distribution). The normal curve is described algebraically in Chapter 5.

Null Hypothesis Symbolized as H_0, the null hypothesis is a statement about some population characteristic. It usually states no relationship between variables.

Observed Frequency The actual frequency count recorded in a single cell of a contingency table. The number of observations that occur in a category.

Omega-Squared (ω^2) A statistic that estimates the effect size in the population.

One-Tailed (Directional) Test of Significance A statistical test in which the rejection region lies in one tail of the sampling distribution.

One-Way ANOVA A statistical test (*F* test) used to compare several sample means to determine if one or more have come from populations with different means. Used only with research designs with one independent variable.

Operational Definition The concrete measurement of a concept.

Order Effect A statistically significant difference between treatment conditions due to the order of presentation in a repeated-measures design. Order effects should be removed by altering the order of treatments among subjects.

Ordinal Scale A scale of measurement in which data are rank ordered.

Ordinate The vertical or *Y* axis of a graph.

Paired-Observations *t* Test See *Dependent-Samples t test*.

Parameter A numerical population value. Parameters are usually inferred from sample statistics.

Parametric Tests of Significance Statistical significance tests that make assumptions about the characteristics of populations.

Percentile Rank A number assigned to a score that indicates the percentage of scores found below that score.

Platykurtic A symmetrical curve that is broader than a normal curve. This reflects the fact that the scores are spread more widely than a normal or leptokurtic curve.

Point-Biserial Correlation A correlational analysis used when one variable is continuous and the other variable is dichotomous.

Point Estimation Using a sample statistic to infer the value of a population parameter.

Pooled Variance See *Mean Square Within*.

Population The entire set of observations that have at least one trait in common.

Post Hoc (or Posteriori) Tests Significance tests used after a statistically significant F test. Post hoc tests can be chosen after the data are examined.

Power The power of a statistical test is the probability that the null hypothesis will be correctly rejected.

Probability A measure of the likelihood that an event will occur. Probability values range from 0–1, inclusive.

Protected t test See *Fisher's LSD*.

Qualitative Variable A variable defined by its characteristics. For example, an independent variable might have three levels that differ in the type of drug used for treating a disorder.

Quantitative Variable A variable defined by its amount. For example, an independent variable might have three levels that differ in drug dosage.

Quartile One-fourth of a distribution of scores.

Random Factors Unsystematic sources of variation. Individual difference variables and experimental error are random factors.

Random Sample A subset of scores taken from a population in such a way that all samples have an equal probability of being selected.

Randomization The assignment of subjects to treatment conditions so that each subject is just as likely to be assigned to one or another condition. Randomization is intended to spread subject variables equally across treatment conditions to eliminate subject variables as confounds.

Range A measure of dispersion in a distribution. The highest score of a distribution minus the lowest score.

Ratio Scale A scale of measurement that has all the characteristics of an interval scale, plus a meaningful zero point.

Raw Score A quantitative score obtained in a study. Also called an *original score*.

Real Limits The upper and lower boundaries of an interval of measurement. The upper real limit of the number is one-half the unit of measurement above the number; the lower real limit of a number is one-half the unit of measurement below the number.

Regression A set of statistical procedures that allows a researcher to use the value of one variable to predict the value of another variable.

Regression Equation (or Prediction Equation) An equation used to predict a Y value given a specific X value.

Regression Line (Linear) A straight line fitted to a scatter plot by the Least Squares Criterion. The regression line includes all predicted values of Y for all X scores.

Repeated-Measures Design (or Within Subjects Design) An experimental design in which subjects are exposed to more than one level of the independent variable.

Research Hypothesis A statement (prediction) about the expected outcome of a study.

Sample A subset of observations drawn from a population.

Sampling Distributions Theoretical distributions of a statistic based on all possible random samples taken from the same population.

Sampling Error The difference between a sample statistic and a population parameter (e.g., $\overline{X} - \mu$).

Scatter Diagram (or Scatter Plot) A graphic representation of a bivariate distribution.

Scientific Hypothesis See *Research Hypothesis*.

Semi-Interquartile Range (SIQR) The interquartile range divided by 2.

Simple Frequency Distribution Scores arranged from highest to lowest, with the frequency of occurrence of each score indicated in a column beside the scores.

Skewed Distribution An asymmetrical distribution in which scores tend to bunch at either the left or right end of the curve. Skewed distributions may be either positive or negative.

Slope The angle of a straight line.

Spearman Rank Correlation Coefficient A correlation coefficient for two sets of ranked data, symbolized r_s.

Standard Deviation A measure of dispersion or variability of a distribution of scores. The standard deviation is the square root of the variance. In a normal distribution the mean plus and minus one standard deviation marks approximately the middle 68 percent of the scores.

Standard Error of the Difference The standard deviation of a sampling distribution of differences between means.

Standard Error of the Estimate In regression, a measure of prediction error. The average standard deviation of the conditional distributions.

Standard Error of the Mean The standard deviation of the sampling distribution of means.

Standard Normal Curve A graph of the standard normal distribution.

Standard Normal Distribution A distribution of z scores with a mean of 0 and a standard deviation of 1. Derived from a raw score distribution that is normally distributed.

Standard Score A raw score expressed in standard deviation units. A z-score and a T score are examples of standard scores.

Statistic A numerical value of a sample.

Statistical Hypothesis A numerical statement of the potential outcome of a study.

Statistically Significant A conclusion that a test statistic is unlikely to have occurred by chance. In a well-controlled experiment, a statistically significant finding indicates that the independent variable has had an effect on the dependent variable.

Subject Variable A characteristic of a subject that is fixed at the time of the experiment. Subject variables are not manipulated by the experimenter. Examples of these variables are age, sex, height, weight, personality traits, and psychiatric diagnosis.

Sum of Squares (SS) The sum of the squared deviations from the mean.

t Distribution A bell-shaped distribution of t values. Also called the *Student t distribution*. The t distribution has a mean of 0.

Test Statistic In hypothesis testing, the obtained value that is compared to the critical value to determine statistical significance.

Treatment Variance In ANOVA, the amount of variance among the sample means due to the independent variable.

Truncated Range When one end of a distribution of sample scores is arbitrarily cut off. In a correlational analysis, if one variable has a truncated range, the correlation of the sample will tend to underestimate the population correlation.

T Score Transformation of a raw score in which the mean equals 50 and the standard deviation equals 10. T scores are derived by applying a constant to the z scores of the distribution.

t Test A significance test based on the t distribution.

Two-Tailed (Nondirectional) Test of Significance A statistical test in which the critical region is divided equally between the two tails of the sampling distribution.

Type I Error Rejecting a true null hypothesis.

Type II Error Retaining a false null hypothesis.

Unimodal Distribution A distribution with one mode.

Univariate Distribution A frequency distribution based on one variable.

U value The test statistic used in the Mann-Whitney U test.

Variance A measure of dispersion or variability of a distribution of scores. The variance is not stated in the original units of the measured variable, unlike the standard deviation. However, the variance is a statistic commonly used in formulas for hypothesis testing.

Weighted Mean The mean of two or more individual means in which the individual means are weighted according to their respective sample sizes.

Wilcoxon signed-ranks test A nonparametric hypothesis test used to compare two dependent samples.

Within-Group Variation The variation of scores within a group.

Within-Subjects Design See *Repeated-Measures Design*.

Y Intercept The point on the Y axis at which a straight line intersects.

z Score A transformed raw score that indicates the number of standard deviation units the raw score is from the mean of the distribution.

z Test A significance test used to decide if a sample mean comes from a population with a specified mean. This test may also be used to compare two sample means. In either case, the z test requires knowledge of the population standard deviation.

References

Addison, W. E. (1989). "Beardedness as a Factor in Perceived Masculinity." *Perceptual and Motor Skills* 68, pp. 921–922.

Amercian Psychological Association. (1983). *Publication Manual of the American Psychological Association*. 3 ed. Washington, D. C.: Author.

Aronson, E., and Mills, J. (1959). "The Effects of Severity of Initiation on Liking for the Group." *Journal of Abnormal and Social Psychology* 59, pp. 177–181.

Bakan, D. (1966). "The Test of Significance in Psychological Research." *Psychological Bulletin* 66, no. 6, pp. 423–437.

Balague-Dahlberg, G. (1986). "Transfer of Biofeedback Training of Heart Rate Decrease." Master's thesis, University of Illinois at Chicago.

Barber, T. X., and Hahn, K. W., Jr. (1962). "Physiological and Subjective Responses to Pain-Producing Stimulation under Hypnotically Suggested and Waking-Imagined Analgesia." *Journal of Abnormal and Social Psychology* 65, pp. 411–418.

Baron, R. S., Logan, H., and Kao, C. F. (1990). "Some Variables Affecting Dentists' Assessment of Patients' Distress." *Health Psychology* 9, no. 2, pp. 143–153.

Beck, A. T., Rush, A. J., Shaw, B. F., and Emery, G. (1979). *Cognitive Therapy of Depression*. New York: Guilford Press.

Benson, P. L., Karabenick, S. A., and Lerner, R. M. (1976). "Pretty Pleases: The Effects of Physical Attractiveness, Race, and Sex on Receiving Help." *Journal of Experimental Social Psychology* 12, pp. 409–415.

Berkowitz, L., and Daniels, L. (1964). "Affecting the Salience of the Social Responsibility Norm: Effect of Past Help on Response to Dependency Relationships." *Journal of Abnormal and Social Psychology* 67, pp. 275–281.

Berkowitz, L., and LePage, A. (1967). "Weapons as Aggression Eliciting Stimuli." *Journal of Personality and Social Psychology* 7, no. 2, pp. 202–207.

Biaggio, M. K. (1989). "Sex Differences in Behavioral Reactions to Provocation of Anger." *Psychological Reports* 64, pp. 23–26.

Borenstein, M., and Cohen, J. (1988). *Statistical Power Analysis: A Computer Program*. Hillsdale, NJ: Lawrence Erlbaum.

Bourianoff, G. G., and Stubis, E. S. (1988). "Stress Management with Headaches." In *Stress Management for Chronic Disease*, edited by M. L. Russell. New York: Pergamon.

Box, J. F. (1978). *R. A. Fisher: The Life of a Scientist*. New York: Wiley.

Bradley, D. R., Bradley, T. D., McGrath, S. G., and Cutcomb, S. D. (1979). "Type I Error Rate of the Chi-Square Test of Independence in R × C Tables That Have Small Expected Frequencies." *Psychological Bulletin* 86, pp. 1290–1297.

Brady, J. V. (1958). "Ulcers in Executive Monkeys." *Scientific American* 199, pp. 95–100.

Burke, R. J., and Greenglass, E. R. (1989). "It May Be Lonely at the Top but It's Less Stressful: Psychological Burnout in Public Schools." *Psychological Reports* 64, pp. 615–623.

Buttery, T. J., and White, W. F. (1978). "Student Teachers' Affective Behavior and Selected Biorhythm Patterns." *Perceptual and Motor Skills* 46, pp. 1033–1034.

Camilli, G., and Hopkins, K. D. (1978). "Applicability of Chi-Square to 2 × 2 Contingency Tables with Small Expected Cell Frequencies." *Psychological Bulletin* 85, pp. 163–167.

Campbell, D. T., and Stanley, J. (1963). "Experimental and Quasi-Experimental Designs for Research on Teaching." *Handbook of Research on Teaching*, edited by N. L. Gage. Chicago: Rand McNally, pp. 171–246.

Carlsmith, J. M., and Gross, A. E. (1969). "Some Effects of Guilt on Compliance." *Journal of Personality and Social Psychology* 11, no. 3, pp. 232–239.

Carmer, S. G., and Swanson, M. R. (1973). "An Evaluation of Ten Multiple Comparisons Procedures by Monte Carlo Methods." *Journal of the American Statistical Association* 68, pp. 66–74.

Carrie, C. M. (1981). "Reproductive Symptoms: Interrelations and Determinants." *Psychology of Women Quarterly* 6, no. 2, pp. 174–186.

Caspi, A., Elder, G. H., and Bem, D. J. (1987). "Moving Against the World: Life Course Patterns of Explosive Children." *Developmental Psychology* 23, pp. 308–313.

Chicago Tribune (1989). "Lottery." Tempo Section, Nov. 13, pp. 1.

Chronicle of Higher Education (1990). "Computer Notes." March, no. 36, p. 28.

Cochran, W. G. (1976). "Early Development of Techniques in Comparative Experimentation." In *On the History of Statistics and Probability*, edited by D. B. Owen. New York: Marcel Dekker.

Cohen, J. (1962). "The Statistical Power of Abnormal Psychological Research: A Review." *Journal of Abnormal and Social Psychology* 65, pp. 145–153.

Cohen, J. (1977). *Statistical Power Analysis for the Behavioral Sciences*. Rev. ed. New York: Academic Press.

Cohen, J. (1988). *Statistical Power Analysis for the Behavioral Sciences*. 2 ed. Hillsdale, NJ: Lawrence Erlbaum.

Cohen, J. (1990). "Things I Have Learned (So Far)." *American Psychologist* 45, no. 12, pp. 1304–1312.

Cohen, M. J., Schandler, S. L., and McArthur, D. L. (1989). "Spatial Learning of Visual Nonsense Figures during Experimental Ethanol Intoxication." *Perceptual and Motor Skills* 68, pp. 599–606.

Cowles, M., and Davis, C. (1982). "On the Origins of the .05 Level of Statistical Significance." *American Psychologist* 37, no. 5, pp. 553–558.

Cronbach, L. J. (1967). "The Two Disciplines of Scientific Psychology." In *Problems in Human Assessment*, edited by D. N. Jackson and S. Messick. New York: McGraw Hill.

Cushny, A. R., and Peebles, A. R. (1904). "The Action of Optical Isomers. II. Hyocines." *Journal of Physiology* 32, pp. 501–510.

Day, R. H., and Kasperczyk, R. T. (1984). "The Morinaga Misalignment Effect with Circular Stimulus Elements." *Bulletin of the Psychonomic Society* 22, pp. 193–196.

De Moivre, A. (1738/1959). "On the Law of Normal Probability." In *A Source Book in Mathematics*, Vol. 2, edited by D. E. Smith. New York: Dover. pp. 566–575.

Dion, K. K., Berscheid, E., and Walster, E. (1972). "What is Beautiful is Good." *Journal of Personality and Social Psychology* 24, pp. 285–290.

Dodd, B. (1979). "Lip Reading in Infants: Attention to Speech Presented In-And Out-Of Synchrony." *Cognitive Psychology* 11, pp. 478–484.

Donnerstein, E. (1980). "Aggressive-Erotica and Violence Against Women." *Journal of Personality and Social Psychology* 39, pp. 269–277.

Draper, N. R., and Smith, H. (1966). *Applied Regression Analysis*. New York: Wiley.

Dunnington, G. W. (1955). *Carl Friedrich Gauss: Titan of Science*. New York: The Free Press.

Dutton, D. G., and Aron, A. P. (1974). "Some Evidence of Heightened Sexual Attraction under Conditions of High Anxiety." *Journal of Personality and Social Psychology* 30, pp. 510–517.

Edgington, E. S. (1974). "A New Tabulation of Statistical Procedures used in APA Journals." *American Psychologist* 29, pp. 25–26.

Elliott, F. (1978). "Neurological Aspects of Antisocial Behavior." In *The Psychopath: A Comprehensive Study of Antisocial Disorders and Behaviors*, edited by W. H. Reid. New York: Bruner/Mazel, pp. 146–189.

Feldman, B. G., and Paul, N. G. (1976). "Identity of Emotional Triggers in Epilepsy." *Journal of Nervous and Mental Disease* 162, pp. 345–352.

Festinger, L. (1957). *A Theory of Cognitive Dissonance*. Stanford, CA: Stanford University Press.

Fisher, R. A. (1939). "Student." *Annals of Eugenics* 9, pp. 1–9.

Fisher, R. A., and MacKenzie, W. A. (1923). "Studies in Crop Variation. II. The Manurial Response of Different Potato Varieties." *Journal of Agricultural Science* 13, pp. 311–320.

Frank, M. L., and Lester, D. (1988). "Geophysical Variables and Behavior: II. Temporal Variation of Suicide in Teens and Young Adults." *Perceptual and Motor Skills* 67, pp. 168–170.

Frazier, K., Kurtz, P., and Bob, M. L. (1988). "Astrology and the Presidency." *Skeptical Inquirer* 10, pp. 3–16.

Galton, F. (1869). *Hereditary Genius: Its Laws and Consequences*. New York: Appleton.

Galton, F. (1885). "The Measure of Fidget." *Nature* 32, pp. 174–175.

Galton, F. (1908). *Memories of My Life*. 2d ed. London: Methuen.

Glass, G. V., and Stanley, J. C. (1970). *Statistical Methods in Education and Psychology*. Englewood Cliffs: Prentice Hall.

Goranson, R. E., and Berkowitz, L. (1966). "Reciprocity and Responsibility Reactions to Prior Help." *Journal of Personality and Social Psychology* 3, pp. 227–232.

Gorenstein, E. E. (1982). "Frontal Lobe Functions in Psychopaths." *Journal of Abnormal Psychology* 91, pp. 368–379.

Gosset, W. S. (1970). *Letters from W. S. Gosset to R. A. Fisher, 1915–1936*. Issued for private circulation. Dublin: Arthur Guinness.

Gravetter, F. J., and Wallnau, L. B. (1988). *Statistics for the Behavioral Sciences*. 2d ed. New York: West.

Greenblat, C. S. (1983). "The Salience of Sexuality in the Early Years of Marriage. *Journal of Marriage and Family* May, pp. 289–299.

Grimm, L., and Kanfer, F. H. (1976). "The Tolerance of Aversive Stimulation." *Behavior Therapy* 7, pp. 593–601.

Grossarth-Maticek, R., Eysenck, H. J., and Vetter, H. (1988). "Antismoking Attitudes and General Prejudice: An Empirical Study." *Perceptual and Motor Skills* 66, pp. 927–931.

Grosskurth, P. (1980). *Havelock Ellis: A Biography*. New York: Knopf.

Gwartney-Gibbs, P. A. (1986). "The Institutionalization of Premarital Cohabitation: Estimates from Marriage License Applications, 1970 and 1980." *Journal of Marriage and Family* 48, pp. 423–434.

Haberman, S. J. (1973). "The Analysis of Residuals in Cross-Classified Tables." *Biometrics* 29, pp. 205–220.

Halpin, B. (1978). "Effects of Arousal Level on Olfactory Sensitivity." *Perceptual and Motor Skills* 46, pp. 1095–1102.

Hare, R. D. (1984). "Performance of Psychopaths on Cognitive Tasks Related to Frontal Lobe Function." *Journal of Abnormal Psychology* 93, no. 2, pp. 133–140.

Hays, W. L. (1988). *Statistics*. New York: Holt, Rinehart and Winston.

Hochberg, Y., and Tamhane, A. C. (1987). *Multiple Comparison Procedures*. New York: Wiley.

Huesmann, L. R., and Eron, L. D. (1984). "Cognitive Processes and the Persistence of Aggressive Behavior." *Aggressive Behavior* 10, pp. 243–251.

Huff, D., and Geis, I. (1959). *How to Take a Chance*. New York: Norton.

Hupka, R. B., and Eshett, C. (1988). "Cognitive Organization of Emotion: Differences Between Labels and Descriptors of Emotion in Jealousy Situations." *Perceptual and Motor Skills* 66, pp. 935–949.

Isen, A. M. (1970). "Success, Failure, Attention, and Reaction to Others: The Warm Glow of Success." *Journal of Personality and Social Psychology* 15, pp. 294–301.

Isen, A. M., and Levin, P. F. (1972). "Effect of Feeling Good on Helping: Cookies and Kindness." *Journal of Personality and Social Psychology* 21, pp. 384–388.

Jaccard, J., and Becker, M. A. (1988). "Selecting a Statistical Test for Data Analysis: The Robustness of Commonly Used Statistical Tests." Unpublished manuscript, State University of New York at Albany, Department of Psychology.

Jaccard, J., and Becker, M. A. (1990). *Statistics for the Behavioral Sciences*. 2d ed. Belmont, CA: Wadsworth.

Johnson, G. B. (1966). "Penis-Envy? or Pencil-Needing?" *Psychological Reports* 19, p. 758.

Jourbert, C. E. (1989). "Birth Order and Narcissism." *Psychological Reports* 64, pp. 721–722.

Kaitz, M., Roken, A. M., and Eidelman, A. I. (1988). "Infants' Face-Recognition by Primiparous and Multiparous Women." *Perceptual and Motor Skills* 67, pp. 495–502.

Kanfer, F. H., and Grimm, L. G. (1978). "Freedom of Choice and Behavioral Change." *Journal of Consulting and Clinical Psychology* 46, pp. 873–878.

Kanfer, F. H., and Grimm, L. G. (1980). "Managing Clinical Change: A Process Model of Therapy." *Behavior Modification* 4, pp. 419–444.

Kaufman, A. S. (1979). *Intelligent Testing with the WISC-R*. New York: Wiley.

Keppel, G. (1982). *Design and Analysis: A Researcher's Handbook*. Englewood Cliffs, NJ: Prentice-Hall.

Keppel, G., and Zedeck, S. (1989). *Data Analysis for Research Designs: Analysis of Variance and Multiple Regression/Correlation Approaches*. New York: Freeman.

Kiess, H. O. (1989). *Statistical Concepts for the Behavioral Sciences*. Boston: Allyn and Bacon.

Kirk, R. E., ed. (1972). *Statistical Issues: A Reader for the Behavioral Sciences*. Pacific Grove, CA: Brooks/Cole.

Kirk, R. E. (1982). *Experimental Design: Procedures for the Behavioral Sciences*. 2 ed. Monterey: Brooks/Cole.

Kirk, R. E. (1984). *Introductory Statistics*. 2 ed. Pacific Grove, CA: Brooks/Cole.

Kirk, R. E. (1989). *Experimental Design: Procedures for the Behavioral Sciences*. 3 ed. Belmont, CA: Brooks/Cole.

Krauss, I. K. (1980). "Between- and Within-Group Comparisons in Aging Research." In *Aging in the 1980's: Psychological issues*, edited by L. W. Poon, Washington D.C.: American Psychological Association. pp. 542–551.

Kurtz, P., and Franknoi, A. (1985). "Scientific Tests of Astrology Do Not Support Its Claims." In *Science Confronts the Paranormal*, edited by K. Frazier. Buffalo, NY: Prometheus. pp 219–221.

Landauer, T. K., and Whiting, J. W. M. (1964). "Infantile Stimulation and Adult Stature of Human Males." *American Anthropologist* 66, pp. 1007–1028.

Latane, B., and Darley, J. (1970). *The Unresponsive Bystander: Why Doesn't He Help?* New York: Appleton-Century-Crofts.

Liberman, B. (1971). *Contemporary Problems in Statistics: A Book of Readings for the Behavioral Sciences.* London: Oxford.

Malamuth, N. M., Heim, M., and Feshback, S. (1980). "Sexual Responsiveness of College Students to Rape Depictions: Inhibitory and Disinhibitory Effects." *Journal of Personality and Social Psychology* 38, pp. 399–408.

Maller, R. G. (1988). "Anxiety Sensitivity and Panic Attacks: A Longitudinal Analysis." Doctoral dissertation, University of Illinois at Chicago.

Marascuilo, L. A., and McSweeney, M. (1977). *Nonparametric and Distribution Free Methods for the Social Sciences.* Belmont, CA: Wadsworth.

Miller, L. (1990). "Relations among Cognitions and Behaviors of Aggressive Children and Their Mothers." Doctoral dissertation, University of Illinois at Chicago.

Mitchell, M., and Jolley, J. (1988). *Research Design Explained.* New York: Holt, Rinehart and Winston.

Moss, S., and Butler, D. C. (1978). "The Scientific Credibility of ESP." *Perceptual and Motor Skills* 46, pp. 1063–1079.

Obrist, P. A. (1962). "Some Autonomic Correlates of Serial Learning." *Journal of Verbal Learning and Verbal Behavior* 1, pp. 100–104.

Olweus, D. (1979). "The Stability of Aggressive Reaction Patterns in Human Males: A Review." *Psychological Bulletin* 85, pp. 852–875.

Paulos, J. A. (1988). *Innumeracy: Mathematical Illiteracy and Its Consequences.* New York: Hill and Wang.

Pearson, K. (1896). "Mathematical Contributions to the Theory of Evolution— III. Regression, Heredity and Panmixia." *Philosophical Translations of the Royal Society of London, series A* 187, pp. 253–318.

Pearson, K. (1903). "On the Inheritance of the Mental and Moral Characters in Man, and Its Comparison with the Inheritance of the Physical Characters." *Journal of the Anthropological Institute* 33, pp. 179–237.

Porter, R. W., Brady, J. V., Conrad, D., Mason. J. W., Galambos, R., and McKrioch, D. (1958). "Some Experimental Observations on Gastrointestinal Lesions in Behaviorally Conditioned Monkeys." *Psychosomatic Medicine* 20, pp. 379–394.

Puskarich, C. A. (1988). "The Effects of Progressive Muscle Relaxation on Seizure Frequency in Adults with Epileptic Seizures." Doctoral dissertation, University of Illinois at Chicago.

Robbins, R. A. (1988). *Objective and Subjective Factors in Estimating Life Expectancy.* Unpublished manuscript, The Pennsylvania State University at Harrisburg, Division of Behavioral Science and Education.

Romano, S. T., and Bordieri, J. E. (1989). "Physical Attractiveness Stereotypes and Students' Perceptions of College Professors." *Psychological Reports* 4, pp. 1099–1102.

Rosenhan, D. L., and White, G. M. (1967). "Observation and Rehearsal as Determinants of Prosocial Behavior." *Journal of Personality and Social Psychology* 5, pp. 424–431.

Runyon, R. P., and Haber, A. (1988). *Fundamentals of Behavioral Statistics*. 6th ed. New York: Random House.

Ruth. W. J., Mosatche, H. S., and Kramer, A. (1989). "Freudian Sexual Symbolism: Theoretical Considerations and an Empirical Test in Advertising." *Psychological Reports* 64, pp. 1131–1139.

Schalling, D. (1978). "Psychopathy-Related Personality Variables and the Psychophysiology of Socialization." in *Psychopathic Behavior: Approaches to Research*, edited by R. D. Hare and D. Schalling, Chichester, England: Wiley, pp. 85–106.

Science Indicators: The 1985 Report. Washington, D.C.: Government Printing Office.

Sedlmeier, P., and Gigerenzer, G. (1989). "Do Statistical Studies of Power Have an Effect on the Power of Studies?" *Psychological Bulletin* 105, no. 2, pp. 309–316.

Semmel, B. (1958). "Karl Pearson: Socialist and Darwinist." *British Journal of Sociology* IX, no. 2, pp. 111–125.

Shavelson, R. J. (1988). *Statistical Reasoning for the Behavioral Sciences*. 2 ed. Boston: Allyn and Bacon.

Shelton, T. O., and Mahoney, M. J. (1978). ."The Content and Effect of "Psyching-up" Strategies in Weight Lifters." *Cognitive Therapy and Research* 2, pp. 275–284.

Siegal, S., and Castellan, N. J. (1988). *Nonparametric Statistics for the Behavioral Sciences*. 2 ed. New York: McGraw Hill.

Simon, A. (1989). "Promiscuity as Sex Difference." *Psychological Reports* 64, p. 802.

Simpson, T. (1755). "A Letter to the Right Honourable George Earl of Macclesfield, President of the Royal Society, on the Advantage of Taking the Mean of a Number of Observations, in Practical Astronomy." *Philosophical Translations of the Royal Society of London* 46, pp. 82–93.

Simpson-Housley, P., and DeMan, A. (1989). "Flood Experience and Posttraumatic Trait Anxiety in Appalachia." *Psychological Reports* 64, pp. 896–898.

Sines, J. O. (1959). "Selective Breeding for Development of Stomach Lesions Following Stress in the Rat." *Journal of Comparative and Physiological Psychology* 52, pp. 615–617.

Sines, J. O., Cleeland, C., and Adkins, J. (1963). "The Behavior of Normal and Stomach Lesion Susceptible Rats in Several Learning Situations." *Journal of Genetic Psychology* 102, pp. 91–94.

Slaby, R. G., and Roedell, W. C. (1982). "The Development and Regulation of Aggression in Young Children." In *Psychological Development in the Elementary Years*, edited by J. Wordell. New York: Academic Press.

Snyder, C. R. (1974). "Why Horoscopes are True: The Effects of Specificity on Acceptance of Astrological Interpretations." *Journal of Clinical Psychology* 30, pp. 577–580.

Spatz, C., and Johnston, J. O. (1989). *Basic Statistics: Tales of Distributions*. 4 ed. Pacific Grove, CA Brooks/Cole.

Sprinthall, R. C. (1990). *Basic Statistical Analysis*. 3 ed. New York: Prentice Hall.

Standage, K. (1972). "Treatment of Epilepsy by the Reciprocal Inhibition of Anxiety." *Guy's Hospital Reports* 121, pp. 217–221.

Standage, K. F., and Fenton, G. W. (1975). "Psychiatric Symptom Profile of Patients with Epilepsy: A Controlled Investigation." *Psychological Medicine* 5, pp. 152–160.

Steward, S. (1990). *Bad Boys and Tough Tattoos: A Social History of the Tattoo with Gangs, Sailors, and Street-Corner Punks, 1950–1965*. New York: Haworth.

Stouffer, S. A. (1958). "Karl Pearson—An Appreciation on the 100th Anniversary of His Birth." *Journal of the American Statistical Association* 53, pp. 23–27.

Student (1908). "The Probable Error of a Mean." *Biometrika* 6, pp. 1–25.

Symonds, C. (1970). *Some Observations on the Facilitation or Arrest of Epileptic Seizures*. London: Oxford.

Tankard, J. W. (1984). *The Statistical Pioneers*. Cambridge, MA: Schenkman.

Temkin, N. R., and Davis, G. R. (1984). "Stress as a Risk Factor for Seizures among Adults with Epilepsy." *Epilepsia* 25, pp. 450–456.

U.S. Bureau of the Census (1983). "Households, Families, Marital Status, and Living Arrangements: March 1983 (advanced report)." *Current Population Reports*, Series P-20, No. 382. Washington, D.C.: Government Printing Office.

Valins, S., and Ray, A. A. (1967). "Effects of Cognitive Desensitization on Avoidance Behavior." *Journal of Personality and Social Psychology* 7, pp. 345–350.

Wainer, H., and Thissen, D. (1976). "Estimating Coefficients in Linear Models: It Don't Make No Nevermind." *Psychological Bulletin* 83, pp. 213–217.

Walker, H. M. (1934). "Abraham De Moivre." *Scripta Mathematica* 2, pp. 316–333.

Walker, H. M. (1940). "Degrees of Freedom." *Journal of Educational Psychology* 55, pp. 253–269.

Walker, H. M. (1968). "Pearson, K." In *International Encyclopedia of the Social Sciences*, edited by D. L. Sills, Vol. II, New York: Macmillan and The Free Press. pp. 496–503.

Welkowitz, J., Ewen, R. B., and Cohen, J. (1988). *Introductory Statistics for the Behavioral Sciences*. New York: Harcourt Brace Jovanovich.

Wiggins, J. (1973). *Personality and Prediction: Principles of Personality Assessment*. Menlo Park: Addison-Wesley.

Woods, A. M., and Rusin, M. J. (1988). "Stress Management and the Elderly." In

Stress Management for Chronic Disease, edited by M. L. Russell, New York: Pergamon. pp. 49–62.

Yule, G. U. (1895). "On the Correlation of Total Pauperism with Proportion of Out-Relief. I. All Ages." *Economic Journal* 5, pp. 603–611.

Zakahi, W. R., and Duran, R. L. (1988). "Physical Attractiveness as a Contributing Factor to Loneliness: An Exploratory Study." *Psychological Reports* 63, pp. 747–751.

Zimmerman, D. W., and Zumbo, B. D. (1989). "A Note on Rank Transformations and Comparative Power of the Student *t*-Test and Wilcoxon-Mann-Whitney Test." *Perceptual and Motor Skills* 68, pp. 1139–1146.

Zullow, H. M. (1984). "The Interaction of Rumination and Explanatory Style in Depression." Master's thesis, University of Pennsylvania.

Zullow, H. M., and Seligman, M. E. P. (1990). "Pessimistic Rumination Predicts Defeat of Presidential Candidates." *Psychological Inquiry* 1, no. 1, pp. 52–61.

INDEX

LIST OF SYMBOLS "cont."

Symbols		Page Reference
s_e	standard error of the estimate	410
s^2_p	pooled variance	173
s_y	standard deviation of Y scores	466
$s_{\bar{x}}$	estimated standard error of the mean	135
$s_{\bar{x}_1 - \bar{x}_2}$	estimated standard error of the difference between sample means	173
SS	sum of squares	78
SS_{BG}	between-group sum of squares	269
SS_{error}	sum of squares error	349
SS_w	within-group sum of squares	270
SS_{BS}	between-subjects sum of squares	344
σ	population standard deviation	82
σ^2	population variance	75
$\sigma_{\bar{x}}$	standard error of the mean (population)	132
$\sigma_{\bar{x}_1 - \bar{x}_2}$	standard error of the difference between means (population)	173
T	T score; Wilcoxon T statistic	113, 476
t	t statistic	154
t_{obt}	t test	154
UL	upper limit of an interval	28
U	Mann-Whitney U statistic	470
ω^2	omega squared	282
X	a raw score from an X distribution	31
$\bar{X}$	sample mean	50
$\bar{X}_G$	grand mean; mean of several groups	269
X_H	highest score in a distribution	70
X_L	lowest score in a distribution	70
x	deviation score	50
Y^P	Y predicted	401
z	z score	103
z_{obt}	z test	143
z_U	U to z transformation for Mann-Whitney U test	475